Reading Critically, Writing Well

A READER AND GUIDE

Rise B. Axelrod
University of California, Riverside

Charles R. Cooper
University of California, San Diego

Alison M. Warriner
California State University, East Bay

 bedford/st.martin's
Macmillan Learning
Boston | New York

For Bedford/St. Martin's

Vice President, Editorial, Macmillan Learning Humanities: Edwin Hill
Editorial Director, English: Karen S. Henry
Senior Publisher for Composition, Business and Technical Writing,
   Developmental Writing: Leasa Burton
Executive Editor: John E. Sullivan III
Developmental Editor: Leah Rang
Senior Production Editor: Peter Jacoby
Production Editor: Pamela Lawson
Media Producer: Sarah O'Connor
Production Supervisors: Victoria Anzalone, Robert Cherry
Marketing Manager: Joy Fisher Williams
Copy Editor: Steve Patterson
Indexer: May Hasso
Photo Researcher: Susan Doheny
Permissions Editor: Kathleen Karcher
Senior Art Director: Anna Palchik
Text Design: Jerilyn Bockorick
Cover Design: Billy Boardman
Cover Art/Cover Photo: alisher9/Getty Images
Composition: Jouve
Printing and Binding: LSC Communications

Manufactured in the United States of America.

1   0   9   8
f   e   d   c

For information, write: Bedford/St. Martin's, 75 Arlington Street, Boston, MA 02116
   (617-399-4000)

ISBN 978-1-319-03275-3 (Student Edition)
ISBN 978-1-319-06229-3 (Instructor's Annotated Edition)

Acknowledgments

*Text acknowledgments and copyrights appear at the back of the book on pages 537–39, which
constitute an extension of the copyright page. Art acknowledgments and copyrights appear on
the same page as the art selections they cover.*

Preface

Reading Critically, Writing Well is designed for today's students, many of whom have limited close reading experience and often find dense academic texts daunting. For these students, there is a disconnect between reading and writing. Without extensive reading experience, students don't develop the sophisticated critical reading skills they need to succeed in college, and this lack of critical reading skills makes it harder for them to develop an intuitive sense of the rhetorical situation and adjust their writing accordingly. No matter their major or career track, today's college students will find practice in *Reading Critically, Writing Well* for the various kinds of writing done in college:

- Analysis of content and meaning of readings
- Analysis of the rhetorical approach
- Analysis of the kind of writing (genre)
- Writing to invent, make meaning, and reflect
- Writing in different academic genres

Hands-on activities in *Reading Critically, Writing Well* give students practice in a range of reading and writing strategies — strategies that enhance comprehension, inspire thoughtful response, stimulate critical inquiry, and foster rhetorical analysis. An ample selection of contemporary readings on a variety of subjects is sure to interest students. This new edition features an additional reading in each chapter and a streamlined activity structure to provide more and better ways for students to learn by doing.

FEATURES OF *READING CRITICALLY, WRITING WELL*

An Inspiring and Practical Introduction

Chapter 1 introduces three essential Academic Habits of Mind that students need to succeed in college:

1. Intellectual curiosity (a questioning frame of mind)
2. Critical analysis (assessing evidence accurately)

3. Rhetorical sensitivity (understanding the purposes motivating writers and readers, how they work within the constraints of genre and medium, and how they treat sources and audience with civility)

These habits of mind, so crucial for success in college, are introduced by a sequence of brief reading selections on the topic of bullying, a topic students know and care about. Each reading selection is accompanied by thought-provoking reading, writing, and discussion activities that engage students in active learning from day one.

The chapter concludes with an overview of the writing process, including a helpful reference chart leading students through key steps: generating ideas, planning, drafting, getting feedback, revising deeply, editing, and proofreading.

Accessible, Engaging Readings

Reading Critically, Writing Well includes a great variety of readings — by published as well as student authors — that give instructors flexibility in constructing a course to meet the needs and interests of their students. The eleventh edition features more readings per chapter, with a new professional reading in each readings chapter, increasing the variety, number, and type of reading selections in the book.

More than a third of the reading selections in the book — eighteen of forty-nine — are new. Selected for their writing quality and level of interest, the readings include pieces by award-winning writers such as Annie Dillard, Brent Staples, Jacqueline Woodson, and David Sedaris; social critics such as Jenée Desmond-Harris, Leslie Jamison, Shankar Vedantam, and Malcolm Gladwell; and distinguished professors and researchers such as John Tierney, Sendhil Mullainathan, Sherry Turkle, and Susan Cain. The new readings engage students with current topics close to their daily lives, such as evaluations of the popular series *Game of Thrones* and new apps for recording memories on social networks, as well as arguments about the importance of "loving what you do," the mental and economic strains of getting too little sleep or making too little money, the effect of captivity on animals, and what "natural" food really means.

The flexibility of *Reading Critically, Writing Well* makes it easy for you to create your own sequence of readings based on theme, discipline, rhetorical mode, or genre. Chapters 3–10 present eight different kinds of writing familiar to us in our roles as students, citizens, and professionals. They include four expository genres (autobiography, observation, reflection, and explanation of concepts) and four argument genres (evaluation, position paper on a controversial issue, speculation about causes or effects, and proposal to solve a problem). Because selections are introduced and followed by close reading activities or annotated questions that stimulate discussion and writing, instructors have the flexibility to create their own reading list from the book's many resources.

Hands-On Activities for Active Learning

Throughout *Reading Critically, Writing Well*, students are invited to learn by doing. Because these activities are clear and doable, they make it possible for even the most inexperienced readers to complete them and engage in a serious program of active learning.

Activities include the following:

- *Before* and *As You Read* **Questions.** These pre-reading questions preceding the reading selections excite interest and lead students to adopt a questioning attitude as they prepare to read each selection.

- *Reading for Meaning* **Prompts.** Following each reading, these prompts provide students with three different kinds of activities to help in understanding and interpreting what they are reading:

  1. **Read to Summarize** activities enhance comprehension, giving students confidence that they can get the main idea of even hard-to-understand texts.

  2. **Read to Respond** activities inspire active engagement, leading students to explore the cultural contexts of the readings as well as their own responses to the readings.

  3. **Read to Analyze Assumptions** activities lead students to think more critically about the beliefs and values implicit in the text's word choices, examples, and assertions and also to examine the bases for their own assumptions as readers.

- *Reading Like a Writer* **Activities.** Following each reading, these activities show how texts work rhetorically in different writing situations to achieve the writer's purpose by addressing audience expectations and concerns and by recognizing the constraints and possibilities of the genre and medium. Annotated and highlighted example passages analyze and explain specific features of each genre, and sentence templates show students how to generate their own sentences using the patterns they have analyzed in the readings.

- *A Special Reading Strategy* **Boxes.** These boxes demonstrate how to apply additional critical reading strategies that range from annotating, synthesizing, and comparing and contrasting to evaluating the logic of an argument and judging the writer's credibility. These strategies are explained and illustrated in Chapter 2, using an excerpt from Martin Luther King Jr.'s "Letter from Birmingham Jail," and marginal notes remind students to reference this catalog of reading strategies for additional guidance as they read and compose.

IMPROVED WRITERS' QUESTIONS IN ANNOTATED READINGS

In Chapters 3–10, the first selection in each Readings section is annotated to provide students with a model of how to read critically. This new edition of *Reading Critically, Writing Well* brings the book's unique Reading Like a Writer inquiry- and action-based questions into the margins of selections, helping students see strategies in context and ask questions about writers' rhetorical choices while they read.

FOREGROUNDED READING–WRITING CONNECTION

Reading Critically, Writing Well teaches students how to analyze texts and to apply what they have learned to their own writing. For this new edition, the "Catalog of Reading Strategies" has moved to the beginning of the book (now Chapter 2), better preparing students with the strategies they need to analyze the selections and apply the strategies to their own writing. Instructors may emphasize writing analytically about the readings or writing rhetorically in the genre they are reading, or they may have students do both kinds of writing. Students may also practice writing as they respond to questions and activities or discuss them in small groups with peers. *Reading Critically, Writing Well* provides many opportunities for a variety of writing and responding to the readings.

- **Writing Analytically.** The Reading for Meaning activities as well as the additional critical reading strategies offer numerous prompts for writing analytically about the readings. Students can begin by writing brief responses to these prompts, and later expand some of them into more fully developed essays. For example, using the Read to Summarize activity, they might compose brief summaries or "gist" statements that they could use as they develop their own analysis of the reading. The Read to Respond and Read to Analyze Assumptions prompts can generate longer essays. Similarly, Chapter 2's "Catalog of Reading Strategies" could be used to generate a variety of assignments: a comparison of different readings, a synthesis essay drawing on multiple selections, a reflective essay examining how a reading challenges the readers' beliefs or values, an evaluation of a reading's logic, an analysis of its use of figurative language, or a position essay refuting a reading's argument. There are any number of possibilities.

- **Writing Rhetorically.** Students are also given many opportunities to write in the genre they have been reading. Chapters 3–10 are framed by two guides — a Guide to Reading at the beginning of the chapter and a Guide to Writing at the end — and these chapters promote genre awareness and sensitivity to different rhetorical situations, aiding the transfer of skills from one rhetorical situation to another, so that students can learn for themselves how to approach each new writing situation. Scaffolded through example and modeling, the guides teach students to employ in their own writing the genre features and rhetorical strategies they studied in their reading. These guides provide a set of flexible activities designed to help students learn to read a specific kind of writing with a critical eye and to write with a clear purpose for their own readers.

The Guides to Writing have been designed to provide flexibility and to support a fuller, more developed composing process. Commonsensical and easy to follow, these writing guides teach students to

- assess the rhetorical situation, focusing on their purpose and audience, with special attention to the genre and medium in which they are writing;
- ask probing analytical questions;
- practice finding answers through various kinds of research, including memory search, field research, and traditional source-based research;
- assess the effectiveness of their own writing and the writing of their classmates;
- troubleshoot ways to improve their draft.

In short, the guides to writing help students make their writing thoughtful, clear, organized, and compelling—in a word, effective for the rhetorical situation.

NEW PEER REVIEW GUIDES FOR CONSTRUCTIVE FEEDBACK AND REVISION

New Peer Review Guides in Chapters 3–10 simplify self- and peer-review by helping students give constructive feedback and identify strategies typical of writing in the genre. Questions such as "How well does the thesis present the position?" are followed by prompts to identify what's working well ("Identify the thesis and point to a particularly convincing reason that supports it") and what needs improvement ("Alert the writer to reasons . . . that undermine it"). The Peer Review Guides can stand alone, but they are designed to work in tandem with the Troubleshooting Your Draft Guides that follow: the sequence presents first a guide to giving a constructive reading and review, and subsequently a guide to revising based on that feedback.

INTENSIVE COVERAGE OF FINDING, EVALUATING, AND CITING SOURCES— INCLUDING COVERAGE OF THE NEW MLA STYLE

A robust appendix features strategies for research and documentation to provide students with clear, helpful guidelines for researching and evaluating sources, integrating them into their writing and citing them correctly in MLA or

APA style. The **updated MLA section** reflects the changes in the *MLA Handbook,* Eighth Edition (2016). With eight different genres, students have an opportunity to practice the full gamut of research strategies, from memory search to the field research methods of observation and interview to library and Internet research.

IMPROVED ACTIVITIES THAT ASK STUDENTS TO REFLECT ON THEIR LEARNING

Research has shown that when students reflect on their learning, they clarify their understanding and remember what they have learned longer. Reflecting also enables students to think critically about what they have learned and how they have learned it. *Reading Critically, Writing Well* provides three opportunities in each chapter for students to reflect on their learning and also to discuss what they have learned with others: Thinking about, Writing to Learn, and Reflecting on [the Genre]. These activities are placed at important transitions in each chapter, at points when looking back at what they have learned will help students move forward more productively. In this new edition, a **streamlined design** visually connects these boxes and activities to highlight the connection between reading, writing, and reflecting.

FLEXIBILITY FOR INSTRUCTORS

With more readings in each genre chapter, instructors have a better variety of topics, disciplines, and styles to choose from to engage students and model writing in each genre. Analyze & Write activities, Writing Assignments, and activities in the Guides to Writing provide instructors with a range of prompts for homework, classwork, small group or class discussion, and writing assignments. This edition of *Reading Critically, Writing Well* also features **alternative tables of contents,** listing readings by theme and discipline to allow instructors the flexibility to chart a path through the readings to meet their course goals.

ACKNOWLEDGMENTS

We first want to thank our students and colleagues at the University of California, Riverside, and the University of California, San Diego; California State University, East Bay, and California State University, San Bernardino; and the University of Nevada, Reno, who have taught us so much about reading, writing, and teaching.

We also owe a debt of gratitude to the many reviewers who made suggestions for this revision. They include Nikki Aitken, Illinois Central College; Krysten

Anderson, Wytheville Community College; Preston Becker, Delaware Technical Community College; Kathleen Black, University of Northwestern – St. Paul; Crystal Bock Thiessen, University of Nebraska – Lincoln; Kristin C. Brunnemer, Pierce College; S. V. Buffamanti, Niagara County Community College; Tiffani Butler, Ivy Tech Community College; Sandra Cavender, Middle Tennessee State University; Lori Chastaine-Michas, Boise State University; Kathryn Comer, Barry University; Stephanie Crippen-Burns, Central Maine Community College; Rebecca Duncan, Meredith College; Justin Felix, Raritan Valley Community College; Linda Streb Gannon, College of Southern Nevada; Sondra Gates, Kirkwood Community College; Howard Hastings, University of Pittsburgh at Johnstown; Charles Henebry, Boston University; Marie Iglesias-Cardinale, Genesee Community College; Melissa Keith, Boise State University; Elizabeth Langenfeld, Crafton Hills College; Judy Lloyd, Southside Virginia Community College; Shelly McEuen, College of Southern Idaho; Robert Morris, Niagara County Community College; Ervin Nieves, The University of Iowa; Janeen Parker, Central Oregon Community College; Louise Pelletier, Western New England University; Marie Pietrzykowski, Niagara County Community College; Bret Ross, Des Moines Area Community College; Tony Russell, Central Oregon Community College; Lela-may Seely, Chaffey College; Andrew J. Stout, Pace University; Samantha Sturman, Boise State University; Marian Kay Thomas, Boise State University; Susan Wald-man, Leeward Community College; Christopher Weaver, Saddleback College; Pamela Willard, Yavapai College; Martha Wilson, Southside Virginia Community College/Governor's School of Southside Virginia; and Wei Yan, St. Louis Community College – Forest Park.

We want especially to thank our developmental editor, Leah Rang, who offered constructive criticism with cheerfulness and good humor, helping us meet impossible deadlines. We also want to thank Edwin Hill, Karen Henry, Leasa Burton, and John Sullivan for their leadership and support. We are grate-ful for Pamela Lawson's and Peter Jacoby's seamless coordination of the pro-duction process, Steve Patterson's skillful copy editing, Carolyn Hassett's and Lori Lewis's careful proofreading, Kathleen Karcher's and Susan Doheny's work on permissions and art research, and Joy Fisher Williams's help in marketing.

Rise dedicates this book to Sophie and Amalia, whose writing she very much looks forward to reading. She also thanks her husband, Steven, for his continued support and encouragement.

Alison dedicates this book to her husband, Jeremiah Hallisey, his presence a joy every day, and to Kayla, who knows why she would require dedication.

Rise B. Axelrod
Charles R. Cooper
Alison M. Warriner

GET THE MOST OUT OF YOUR COURSE WITH *READING CRITICALLY, WRITING WELL*

At Bedford, providing support to teachers and their students who choose our books and digital tools is at the center of what we do. The Bedford/ St. Martin's English Community is now our home for professional resources, including Bedford *Bits*, our popular blog site offering new ideas for the composition classroom and composition teachers. In addition, you'll find an expanding collection of resources that support your teaching. Download titles from our professional resource series to support your teaching, review projects in the pipeline, sign up for professional development webinars, start a discussion, ask a question, and follow your favorite members. Join us to connect with other instructors teaching with **Reading Critically, Writing Well** at **community.macmillan.com**. To learn more about or to order any of the following products, contact your Bedford/St. Martin's sales representative, e-mail sales support (**sales_support@bfwpub.com**), or visit the website at **macmillanlearning.com**.

Choose from Alternative Formats of *Reading Critically, Writing Well*

Bedford/St. Martin's offers affordable formats — a paperback version and an electronic version — allowing students to choose the one that works best for them. For details about popular e-book formats from our e-book partners, visit **macmillanlearning.com/ebooks**.

Select Value Packages

Add value to your text by packaging one of the following resources with *Reading Critically, Writing Well*. To learn more about package options for any of the following products, contact your Bedford/St. Martin's sales representative or visit the catalog page for *Reading Critically, Writing Well* at **macmillanlearning.com**.

LaunchPad Solo for Readers and Writers allows students to work on whatever they need help with the most. At home or in class, students learn at their own pace, with instruction tailored to each student's unique needs. *LaunchPad Solo for Readers and Writers* features:

- **Pre-built units that support a learning arc**
  Each easy-to-assign unit is comprised of a pre-test check; multimedia instruction and assessment; a post-test that assesses what students have learned about critical reading, the writing process, using sources, grammar, style, and mechanics; and help for multilingual writers.

- **A video introduction to many topics**
  Introductions offer an overview of the unit's topic, and many include a brief, accessible video to illustrate the concepts at hand.
- **Adaptive quizzing for targeted learning**
  Most units include LearningCurve, game-like adaptive quizzing that focuses on the areas in which each student needs the most help.
- **The ability to monitor student progress**
  Use our gradebook to see which students are on track and which need additional help with specific topics.

LaunchPad Solo for Readers and Writers can be **packaged at a significant discount**. *Reading Critically, Writing Well* includes reading comprehension quizzes, which are available in *LaunchPad Solo for Readers and Writers*. Order ISBN 978-1-3191-0758-1 to ensure your students can take full advantage. Visit **macmillanlearning.com/readwrite** for more information.

Writer's Help 2.0 is a powerful online writing resource that helps students find answers whether they are searching for writing advice on their own or as part of an assignment.

- **Smart search**
  Built on research with more than 1,600 student writers, the smart search in Writer's Help 2.0 provides reliable results even when students use novice terms, such as *flow* and *unstuck*.
- **Trusted content from our best-selling handbooks**
  Choose *Writer's Help 2.0, Hacker Version,* or *Writer's Help 2.0, Lunsford Version*, and ensure that students have clear advice and examples for all of their writing questions.
- **Adaptive exercises that engage students**
  Writer's Help 2.0 includes *LearningCurve*, game-like online quizzing that adapts to what students already know and helps them focus on what they need to learn.
- **Reading Comprehension Quizzes**
  Reading Critically, Writing Well includes multiple-choice quizzes, which help you quickly gauge your students' understanding of the assigned reading. These are available Writer's Help 2.0.

Student access is packaged with *Reading Critically, Writing Well* at a significant discount. Order ISBN 978-1-3191-0729-1 for *Writer's Help 2.0, Hacker Version,* or ISBN 978-1-3191-0775-8 for *Writer's Help 2.0, Lunsford Version*, to ensure your students have easy access to online writing support. Students who rent a book or buy a used book can purchase access to Writer's Help 2.0 at **macmillanlearning .com/writershelp2**.

Instructors may request free access by registering as an instructor at **macmillanlearning.com/writershelp2**.

For technical support, visit **macmillanlearning.com/getsupport**.

WriterKey, built around best practices for feedback and revision, puts student writers at the center of your course. Robust review tools allow you to quickly comment on assignments — using voice or text — and link to a flexible rubric and comment library all from one screen. Students use the same tools to reflect, ask for feedback on specific areas, and review each other's work. Powerful analytics, tied to instructor comments, show writers' strengths and areas for improvement. A side-by-side view of drafts lets students revise their work while they apply teacher and reviewer feedback. After revised drafts are submitted, instructors can compare drafts and view analytic data to see revision in action. For more, visit **ml.writerkey.com/**.

Instructor Resources

macmillanlearning.com

You have a lot to do in your course. Bedford/St. Martin's wants to make it easy for you to find the support you need — and to get it quickly.

Instructor's Manual for Reading Critically, Writing Well, **Eleventh Edition,** is available as a PDF that can be downloaded from the Bedford/St. Martin's online catalog at the URL above. Visit the instructor resources tab for *Reading Critically, Writing Well.* In addition to chapter overviews and teaching tips, the instructor's manual includes sample syllabi, classroom activities, detailed plans for every chapter of the book, and discussion of every reading.

Contents

1 ACADEMIC HABITS OF MIND: FROM READING CRITICALLY TO WRITING WELL 1

2 A CATALOG OF READING STRATEGIES 16

3 AUTOBIOGRAPHY   47

6 EXPLAINING CONCEPTS   183

7 EVALUATION   238

8 ARGUING FOR A POSITION   294

Contents by Theme

MEDIA AND CULTURE

MORAL VALUES AND PUBLIC POLICY

RACE AND CULTURE

SELF-DISCOVERY AND GROWING UP

SOCIETY AND CULTURE

SPORTS

STUDENT ESSAYS

WORK AND CLASS

Contents by Discipline

Academic Habits of Mind: From Reading Critically to Writing Well

Imagine yourself on a journey to a part of your country where you have never been. You already know the language and have some background in common with the people, but some of the traditions, customs, and laws are different from what you're accustomed to. When you arrive, you are immersed in a new job with people you haven't met before, but you are expected to know the lay of the land and the rules, including how to communicate, how to produce the products the job involves, and how to deal with difficulties.

This new place is college. Sure, you've been through high school, and you've been accepted into college, so you have what it takes to do well in your courses. But the world of college has its own special requirements and demands, and knowing what they are and how to respond to them will help you succeed.

Your professors will assume you already understand what college requires. In fact, a recent survey of college professors revealed that they expect students already to have what are often called **academic habits of mind** — ways of thinking and inquiring that people in college (and often in the world of work) use every day. As the word *habit* suggests, these skills can be acquired through practice. So what are these habits of mind? Here's a list of what we think are the most crucial habits:

- *Curiosity:* The desire to ask provocative questions, generate hypotheses, respond to others' ideas, and do research to learn more information. Academic questions — those raised in college — are in the context of disciplines (such as business, psychology, chemistry, history, or communications), and are part of an ongoing conversation among the disciplines' practitioners. Often the research of college professors is based on their curiosity about these questions and their desire to find answers. Academics enjoy the free interplay of ideas; they seek out knowledge through reading and hearing about others' opinions, reasons, and evidence.

- *Critical analysis:* The ability to read and write ideas with an eye to figuring out what is true, what makes sense, and how the ideas are supported by evidence — facts, events, other texts — even when that evidence challenges your own beliefs. The *values* and *beliefs* of both writer and reader (and often their communities) play a significant part in analyzing texts. We call these values and beliefs **assumptions.** Thinking critically also involves questioning your own unexamined beliefs as well as the received wisdom of others.

- *Rhetorical sensitivity:* The understanding of the purposes motivating writers and readers, the expectations of the audience, and the constraints of the **genre** and **medium,** including the ability to recognize different genres, or types, of writing (such as laboratory reports and movie reviews) and media (print or digital, visual or audio) and know when to use them, as well as to recognize and use vocabulary, grammar, punctuation, and spelling that is appropriate to the purpose, audience, genre, and medium in which you are writing. Rhetorical sensitivity also embraces **civility,** the ability to treat the ideas of others fairly and respectfully, even when they challenge your own beliefs and values.

JOINING THE ACADEMIC CONVERSATION

The academic habits of mind we have been discussing are essential to success in all academic areas and disciplines (and most career paths), but these alone are not enough. You may also need to develop skills that will allow you to join the *academic conversation* on topics important to individual disciplines such as economics or sociology. In your first year or two of college, you will enter a variety of academic conversations by reading textbooks and academic articles in different disciplines and by participating in discussions in class and with your instructor. You might join the conversation in some disciplines for a term or a year; you might join the conversation in your major permanently. As you read this text, you will find references to these conversations and your role in them. The habits of mind we discussed above — developing curiosity, thinking and reading critically, and writing well with rhetorical sensitivity and civility — will allow you to develop the skills you need to join these conversations.

ACTIVITY 1

Writing to Learn: Exploring Your Habits of Mind

What habits of mind do you already possess as you approach this course? To determine this, think about your high school study habits or how you mastered a subject, hobby, or technology inside or outside of school. Then write down your answers to the following questions:

- What sparked your interest in the first place?

- What questions did you initially have?

- How did your questions evolve as you learned more?

- How did you go about finding out answers to your questions?

- How did the answers you found lead to further questioning or additional research?

Having looked back on your experience, which habits of mind did you form as you satisfied your curiosity and followed through on your interest? You may see as you read on that you have a head start on the habits expected of college students.

Developing Curiosity

When you read, you develop your critical thinking abilities by asking questions and writing notes in the margins, a process called **annotating.** Reading closely and carefully to figure out the authors' *assumptions* (beliefs and values) about an idea will help you understand their position on a topic and where it comes from. Asking and answering questions like those that follow in this section will help you figure out the authors' *perspectives*, as well as what the authors state in an explicit (or direct) way, and what they leave implicit (implied). Questions like these, in sections called Reading for Meaning, follow each reading throughout this book. We have also annotated the second reading in each chapter, placing these questions in the margins so you can easily consider the questions as you read.

Read the following two passages on bullying in schools.* All of these passages speculate about *causes and effects* (as do the readings in Chapter 9). They also

- *assert* (or *claim*) that bullying is a problem,

- *define* bullying, and

- try to determine the *consequences* of bullying.

---

*A listing of the sources of texts cited can be found at the end of the chapter.

But each differs in how the authors define the term or what the authors believe the consequences of bullying may be.

As you read the excerpts, ask yourself these questions and write down the answers:

- What do you think are the guiding questions the writers asked themselves as they researched and wrote these texts? What in the text specifically leads you to identify these guiding questions?

- What questions do you need to ask as a reader to clarify the meaning of each of these passages?

1. **Ron Banks, "Bullying in Schools"**

   As established by studies in Scandinavian countries, a strong correlation appears to exist between bullying other students during the school years and experiencing legal or criminal troubles as adults. In one study, 60 percent of those characterized as bullies in grades 6–9 had at least one criminal conviction by age 24 (Olweus 1993). Chronic bullies seem to maintain their behaviors into adulthood, negatively influencing their ability to develop and maintain positive relationships (Oliver, Hoover, and Hazler 1994).

   Victims often fear school and consider school to be an unsafe and unhappy place. As many as 7 percent of America's eighth-graders stay home at least once a month because of bullies. The act of being bullied tends to increase some students' isolation because their peers do not want to lose status by associating with them or because they do not want to increase the risks of being bullied themselves. Being bullied leads to depression and low self-esteem, problems that can carry into adulthood (Olweus 1993; Batsche and Knoff 1994).

Note how Banks relies on statistics as evidence to support his assertions. There are many additional strategies writers use to add support, such as the following:

For more information on writers' strategies for providing evidence, see Chapter 2.

- Narrating a story

- Providing facts and statistics

- Describing

- Illustrating (providing examples)

- Classifying

- Comparing and contrasting

- Reporting causes or effects

- Summarizing or paraphrasing

Now take a look at some of the evidence Banks offers and the readers' questions prompted by it:

Is Scandinavia similar enough to the United States that American bullies will have the same rate of criminal conviction? Who is Olweus? Is this source reliable? What's the context of this statistic? Is 7 percent a lot? How many skip to have fun, to avoid a test, etc.?	[I]n Scandinavian countries, . . . 60 percent of those characterized as bullies in grades 6–9 had at least one criminal conviction by age 24 (Olweus 1993). . . . As many as 7 percent of America's eighth-graders stay home at least once a month because of bullies.

The *source* Banks cites — Olweus — is one you could look up and assess for yourself.* When considering the statistics Banks provides, consider the context as well: Statistics have little meaning out of context.

For more on research, see Appendix: Strategies for Research and Documentation, p. 466.

You may have to search for the underlying assumptions by analyzing the *tone* or *connotation* of the words the writer chooses or by thinking critically about the examples the writer uses. Ask yourself whose assumption the writer is giving voice to — her or his own, the wider community's, or a source's. You can see that Banks maintains an objective tone with few or no words that carry emotion, and that he relies primarily on outside sources to make his argument here. One of his assumptions is that bullying hinders the formation of positive relationships, in either childhood or adulthood. This belief is probably true of him and true of his colleagues, who are sociologists and psychologists concerned with human well-being. If it is also true of you, the reader, then he will be successful in his argument. If, however, a reader believes that bullies, despite their antisocial tendencies, can form lasting positive relationships, then Olweus will have to provide more and different kinds of evidence to be fully persuasive. Oliver, Hoover, and Hazler appear to believe that bullies, like those who are bullied, also suffer socially for their behavior, as we can see when they say that bullies, when adults, continue to bully, "negatively influencing their ability to develop and maintain positive relationships."

See Contextualizing in Chapter 2, pp. 29–30.

Here are some additional questions you can ask to bring a writer's assumptions to the surface:

- What are the effects of the assumption, in the context of the essay specifically or in society more generally?

- What do I think about the assumption, and is there anything in the essay that raises doubts about it?

- How does the assumption reinforce or critique commonly held views, and are there any *alternative ideas*, *beliefs*, *or values* that would challenge this assumption?

See Analyzing Assumptions in Chapter 2, pp. 28–29.

*Olweus, Dan. "A Profile of Bullying at School." *Educational Leadership*, vol. 60, no. 6, Mar. 2003, pp. 12–17.

Now read the next excerpt, noting the following:

- The questions the author asks herself
- The assertions (or claims) she makes
- The evidence she supplies to support her assertions / claims
- The assumptions she makes

2. **Tara L. Kuther, "Understanding Bullying"**

Bullying is not a normal part of growing up. Victims of bullying suffer psychological and sometimes physical scars that last a lifetime. Victims report greater fear and anxiety, feel less accepted, suffer from more health problems, and score lower on measures of academic achievement and self-esteem than students who are not bullied. Victims often turn their anger inward, which may lead to depression, anxiety, and even suicide. The experience of bullying is also linked with violence, as the fatal school shootings in Littleton, Colorado; Jonesboro, Arkansas[; and Sandy Hook, Connecticut,] have illustrated.

However, it's not just victims who are hurt by bullying. Bullies fail to learn how to cope, manage their emotions, and communicate effectively — skills vital to success in the adult world. Without intervention, bullies suffer stunted emotional growth and fail to develop empathy. Since bullies are accustomed to achieving their immediate goals by pushing others around, they don't learn how to have genuine relationships with other people. Instead, they externalize and blame others for their problems, never taking responsibility, nor learning how to care for another's needs. Bullies who don't learn other ways of getting what they want develop into adult bullies who are more likely to experience criminal troubles, be abusive toward their spouses, and have more aggressive children, perhaps continuing the cycle of bullying into the next generation.

You can see that even though the authors of the excerpts above did not directly ask questions in their texts, each of them was curious about the long-term effects of bullying, especially on people who later committed crimes or who suffered from difficult psychological adjustments in adult life. The questions you asked as you read allowed you to engage with and think critically about the reading selections, necessary steps to take before you can write productively about a reading selection.

Analyzing Ideas

In college, you will deepen and extend your critical reading and thinking skills by reading a variety of texts that may expose you to wholly new ideas, make you question your own value system, and help you see different points of view. You will also often have opportunities to discuss what you read with your professors and classmates, and doing so will introduce you to additional critical reading strategies that can enhance your existing habits of mind. In order to get the most from texts and discussions, participants in the academic conversation examine all the ideas — their own and others' — critically but also with civility, whether they agree with them or not.

To see this process in action, read the two excerpts below, which include definitions of and discuss the prevalence of bullying in school. The first is from the *Journal of the American Medical Association* — an academic journal — and the second is from a 2004 book on bullying written for the general public and for people who work in schools. As you read, make notes about the following:

- Any ideas that are new to you, especially those that challenge what you currently think about bullying

- Any references to assumptions that are contrary to the writers' beliefs. Look especially for values that may be currently accepted but are open to question.

- How the writers handle assumptions that are contrary to their own

Tonja R. Nansel, Mary Overpeck, Ramani S. Pilla, W. June Ruan, Bruce Simons-Morton, and Peter Scheidt, "Bullying Behaviors among U.S. Youth: Prevalence and Association with Psychosocial Adjustment"

Bullying among school-aged youth is increasingly being recognized as an important problem affecting well-being and social functioning. While a certain amount of conflict and harassment is typical of youth peer relations, bullying presents a potentially more serious threat to healthy youth development. The definition of bullying is widely agreed on in literature on bullying. Bullying is a specific type of aggression in which (1) the behavior is intended to harm or disturb, (2) the behavior occurs repeatedly over time, and (3) there is an imbalance of power, with a more powerful person or group attacking a less powerful one. This asymmetry of power may be physical or psychological, and the aggressive behavior may be verbal (e.g., name-calling, threats), physical (e.g., hitting), or psychological (e.g., rumors, shunning/exclusion). . . .

Bullying takes many forms, and findings about the types of bullying that occur are fairly similar across countries. A British study involving 23 schools found that direct verbal aggression was the most common form of bullying, occurring with similar frequency in both sexes. Direct physical aggression was more common among boys, while indirect forms were more common among girls. Similarly, in a study of several middle schools in Rome, the most common types of bullying reported by boys were threats, physical harm, rejection, and name-calling. The most common forms for girls were name-calling, teasing, rumors, rejection, and taking of personal belongings. . . .

Barbara Coloroso, "The Bully, the Bullied, and the Bystander"

In a study conducted in 2001 by the Kaiser Foundation, a U.S. health care philanthropy organization, in conjunction with the Nickelodeon TV network and Children Now, a youth advocacy group, almost three-quarters of pre-teens interviewed said bullying is a regular occurrence at school and that it becomes even more pervasive as kids start high school; 86 percent of the children between the ages of twelve and fifteen said that they get teased or bullied at school — making bullying more prevalent than smoking, alcohol, drugs, or sex among the same age group. More than half of children between the ages of eight and eleven said that bullying is a "big problem" at school. "It's a big concern on kids' minds. It's something they're dealing with every day," reports Lauren Asher of the Kaiser Foundation . . . (p. 12).

Individual incidents of verbal, physical, or relational bullying can appear trivial or insignificant, nothing to be overly concerned about, part of the school culture. But it is the imbalance of power, the intent to harm, the threat of further aggression, and the creation of an atmosphere of terror that should raise red flags and signal a need for intervention. Sadly, even when the[se] four markers of bullying are clearly in evidence, adults have been known to minimize or dismiss the bullying, underestimate its seriousness, blame the bullied child, and/or heap on additional insult to injury (p. 22).

Considering the ideas that are new to you, think about what you expect from the authors after they have raised these ideas: Do you want more information about what *causes* bullying? About *where* it happens and *what to do about it*? Do you need more evidence of the *problem* before you can be convinced of its importance?

See Looking for Patterns of Opposition in Chapter 2, pp. 35–36.

Reread these two excerpts to consider where and how the authors respond to the statements and assumptions of people with whom they disagree. For example, note that Nansel and her coauthors *acknowledge* the common idea that "boys must be boys" or that "all kids tease each other" when they write, but notice how they introduce this *concession* and then *refute* it.

Cue/*Concession*   While *a certain amount of conflict and harassment is typical*
Refutation   *of youth peer relations,* bullying presents a potentially more
                    serious threat to healthy youth development.

The authors introduce the concession with a transition indicating contrast (like *although, but,* or *however*) to indicate that an exception, refinement, or contradiction is coming. The structure looks something like this:

Look for more examples and sentence strategies in Reading Like a Writer sections following the readings in Chapters 3–10.

▶ While .... may be true, ... is more likely to contribute to ....

▶ Although .... , I think ....

▶ .... may be true in some circumstances, but not in others.

▶ Researchers X and Y provide some evidence that .... occurs in some settings; however, they don't offer sufficient evidence that it occurs in all settings.

See Evaluating the Logic of an Argument in Chapter 2, pp. 40–41.

As a reader, you can decide whether you need more evidence to convince you. Review the excerpt from Coloroso to see if you find a similar concession-refutation structure.

Now consider the tone Nansel et al. use in the example above. Their sentence reflects careful word choices that will not offend the professional writers with whom they disagree or any members of their audience who might share their beliefs. They hedge their statement with *qualifying terms,* such as "a certain amount" and "potentially," to avoid making a stronger claim than they can prove given the evidence. A stronger claim may put off their readers. The hedges also demonstrate the writers' willingness to engage in conversation about this subject.

Barbara Coloroso's text, written for a popular audience, maintains a courteous tone but takes a firmer stance:

> Terms that suggest the writer's point of view and undermine writer's neutrality.
>
> Hedging terms
>
> Sadly, even when the[se] four markers of bullying are clearly in evidence, adults have been known to minimize or dismiss the bullying, underestimate its seriousness, blame the bullied child, and/or heap on additional insult to injury.

Writers, though — even those endeavoring to be rhetorically sensitive and courteous — find that sometimes the authors of alternative arguments use sources that are not convincing. It is then their job to question or challenge those questionable sources. For example, one of the authors cited in the Banks excerpt (p. 4), Olweus, concludes in his own article that while girls suffer from bullying and bully others too, they do not do *more* bullying than boys: "Our research data . . . clearly contradict the view that girls are the most frequent and worst bullies, a view suggested by such recent books as *Queen Bees and Wannabes* (Wiseman 2002) and *Odd Girl Out* (Simmons 2002)."*

ACTIVITY 2

Talking to Learn: Honing Ideas through Discussion

Once you have analyzed the way Nansel and colleagues and Coloroso respond to others, try discussing bullying with your classmates, friends, or family to develop your own definition of bullying, as well as to develop your ideas about what causes it and what schools could do about it. By discussing your reading and speculating about other ways of looking at the problem, you generate and test your *hypotheses,* improving them as you refine them. You also demonstrate your ability to analyze critically, and you practice presenting your ideas to your classmates with rhetorical sensitivity and civility.

---

*Olweus, Dan. "A Profile of Bullying at School." *Educational Leadership,* vol. 60, no. 6, Mar. 2003, pp. 12–17.

Developing Rhetorical Sensitivity

Rhetoric means the ways writers make their ideas understandable and seek to influence their readers. When you develop rhetorical sensitivity, you understand the writer's purpose, audience, context, and genre, and you recognize that the decisions the writer makes — including the types of evidence the writer includes, the kinds of vocabulary he or she chooses, and the *writing strategies* he or she uses — grow out of the *rhetorical situation*.

You probably already have a fairly sophisticated understanding of rhetorical situations: You wouldn't write a thank-you note to your great-aunt using the same tone or vocabulary that you would use when posting a Facebook update about a concert you attended, because you know your purpose, audience, context, and genre are very different in these two situations. Your ability to analyze the **rhetorical situation** — to identify the writer's purpose, audience, context, and genre — and to adapt your writing to your rhetorical situation is central to your success in college and beyond. Your teachers will expect you to analyze the rhetorical situation in each discipline, and by doing so, you will cultivate the skills necessary to join their academic conversation. We explore how to examine the rhetorical situation later in this chapter.

You may have noticed that the excerpts on bullying above were written in different styles. The texts that were written for an academic audience assumed their readers were familiar with the terminology (vocabulary) and concepts characteristic of the discipline — what we call the discipline's **discourse** — as well as its **genre conventions** (typical ways of organizing material and using sources). For example, readers familiar with scientific discourse (biology, for example) would expect a scientific report to include technical descriptions of the methods used and the results obtained and to be organized with separate sections for methods, results, discussion, and references. If the same experiment were discussed in an article for a general audience, however, readers would expect little, if any, technical detail.

Authors of academic discourse try to keep their *tone* objective and courteous, so they will be taken seriously and not provoke an emotional (and perhaps unreasonable) reaction in the reader. Less formal authors may allow passion into their writing, or they may write in a chatty tone, with informal language and direct addresses to the reader. (Note, for instance, how some of the authors refer to bullied people as "kids," while others refer to them as "children." Such words provide a key to the tone.)

Exploring the Rhetorical Situation

Asking and answering the following questions when reading *and* when writing will help you explore the rhetorical situation:

- What is the author's purpose?
- Who is the audience?

- What is the author's stance — perspective and attitude toward the material?
- What is the genre?
- What is the best medium or design for this text?

Asking these questions while reading will help you develop a writer's eye, will help you notice the maneuvers and strategies that writers use to communicate their ideas.

ACTIVITY 3

Writing to Learn: Developing Your Rhetorical Sensitivity

To develop your rhetorical sensitivity for academic writing, look again at the excerpts on bullying above to identify one that you think was written for a general audience and one written for an academic audience. What characteristics can you identify for the two types of writing? List the characteristics of the two excerpts in facing columns:

Excerpt for more general audience	Excerpt for academic audience

Now write a paragraph or two explaining the features that led you to identify the different audiences for these two excerpts.

ACTIVITY 4

Writing to Learn: Pulling It All Together

Look back at what you wrote for Activity 1, where you speculated about the academic habits of mind you already practice. Think now about what you have learned about the habits of mind that lead to successful thinking, reading, and writing in college and beyond. To solidify your understanding, write a note to a person — a friend, a colleague, a sibling, your own child — who is preparing for college. In a page or two, describe the habits of mind you think this person should start (or continue) practicing to ensure his or her success in college and career. Feel free to use examples from this chapter, but try as well to draw on your own experience to support your assertions.

FROM READING CRITICALLY TO WRITING WELL

As the successful novelist Stephen King says: "If you want to be a writer, you must do two things above all others: read a lot and write a lot. There's no way around these two things that I'm aware of, no shortcut." All college students have experience with reading and writing for school, and many of you have extensive experience with informal writing as well, especially in technology-based forums such as blogs, Twitter, and Facebook. This kind of online writing can make you more comfortable with the written word and help you become more aware of who your audience is, because your writing is directed to a variety of people other than your teachers. But for academic writing to be effective, it must grow out of the same habits of mind discussed so far in this chapter: curiosity, critical analysis, rhetorical sensitivity, and civility.

THE WRITING PROCESS

To develop these habits of mind typical of successful college students — curiosity, critical analysis, rhetorical sensitivity, and civility — academic writers can take advantage of the *writing process,* which allows them to shape and hone their writing until it expresses their ideas clearly and effectively, and satisfies (and perhaps even surpasses) the expectations of their audience. In Chapters 3 through 10 of *Reading Critically, Writing Well,* questions following the reading selections help you move from analyzing the selection to writing about it. Each chapter also includes a Guide to Writing to help you write in the genre of the chapter — such as autobiography, concept explanation, or position argument. You can explore and develop these ideas in drafts and then revise those drafts deeply in response to feedback from other readers. Each chapter includes the kinds of writing done in college:

- Analysis of content and meaning of the readings

- Analysis of the rhetorical approach

- Analysis of the kind of writing (genre)

- Writing in different academic genres

In college, much of the writing you submit will be formal, academic discourse in specific genres (such as research reports and essay exams). The activities in the Guides to Writing will help you develop the ideas and language that you will use in those formal writing assignments, with example paragraphs and sentence strategies demonstrating effective methods for presenting your ideas and responding to evidence. As writers, we rarely if ever begin with a complete understanding of our subject or a clear, detailed plan for writing about it. Instead, we write to learn, using the questions and unexpected complexities that arise while writing to inspire more writing and, nearly always, generate further ideas and deeper insights.

As you write, remember that the writing process is *recursive:* it does not proceed smoothly in a straight line from beginning to end, but rather may be chaotic. The steps in the process may include the following:

- Generating and researching ideas
- Drafting your essay
- Getting feedback from others
- Revising deeply
- Editing and proofreading

You may find yourself rethinking, rearranging, and rewriting much of your original text, so you may revisit one or more of these stages several times for one essay. The chart below illustrates some of the options you have when writing an essay.

Generating Ideas	There are many different ways to generate and research ideas. For example, you can • Brainstorm on paper or with a friend or group to get a firmer grasp of your ideas and where they might lead you. • Research to figure out what others have said and how that relates to your ideas. • Determine which genre would be best for presenting your ideas. • Explore what you know about your audience so you can tailor your writing to their needs. • Gather material for your writing so you can support your claim when you figure out what it is.
Planning a Draft	Writers have many different ways of getting started on a draft: • They may just need a first line. • They may make an outline. • They might try an idea map or a scratch copy of the points they want to make.

(continued)

Writing a Draft	Develop your draft by drawing on the language and ideas you generated and researched earlier. You should have • A clear sense of *who* your readers are and what they need to know to be persuaded by your observations. • Some grasp of their values and beliefs, so you can anticipate the *assumptions* they will make and appeal to *common* ground between them and you. • A main idea, sound reasons to support it, and several kinds of evidence. You can always return to idea-generating activities as you determine what else you might need.
Getting Feedback from Others	Writers need feedback from others to determine the strengths and weaknesses of their early draft(s). Pose questions like those below to a friend, classmate, tutor, or instructor so you get the constructive criticism you need: • Is my main idea / thesis clear? • What evidence is most persuasive? Least? • Are there places where you can't follow my reasoning, and can you explain why? • Do I show evidence of having practiced the habits of mind expected of college students: curiosity, critical analysis, rhetorical sensitivity, and civility? Please point it out.
Revising Deeply	Many writers spend more time revising than writing their original draft, another indication that writing generates ideas. You may find that you have to • Revise your whole thesis in light of the feedback you receive from reviewers. • Expand on your ideas, sharpen your reasons, or augment your evidence. • Answer possible objections or questions. • Reorganize in light of readers' confusion. • Rework your ideas into a more reader-friendly form; trim bloated parts. It's important to allow enough time in your schedule for deep revision, since writing is generative, and you may find you have as much work to do mid-essay as you did when you were working on the original writing project.

Editing and Proofreading	To edit and proofread effectively, you need to read your essay through the eyes of your reader. This care and attention to detail yield writing that deserves the careful consideration of those reading it — whether they be specialists, members of the general public, or, in the case of student writing, professors. Rigorously check sentences and paragraphs to make sure your writing includes the following: • A clear thesis in a prominent place • Transitions between sentences and between paragraphs to help your reader follow your line of thinking • Vocabulary appropriate to the subject and audience's needs • Correct grammar and punctuation so you can communicate effectively and not confuse or annoy your reader • Correct spelling so your reader knows exactly what word you mean • Sentence construction that helps your reader understand your points • An appropriate tone given your approach to your subject and your audience

Now you are ready to give your attention to all the strategies available to you to become a critical thinker, reader, and writer.

Sources for Texts on pp. 4, 6, and 7–8

Banks, Ron. *Bullying in Schools. ERIC Digest,* Educational Resources Information Center, Apr. 1997, files.eric.ed.gov/fulltext/ED407154.pdf.

Coloroso, Barbara. *The Bully, the Bullied, and the Bystander: From Preschool to High School: How Parents and Teachers Can Help Break the Cycle of Violence.* Harper-Collins Publishers / Quill, 2004.

Kuther, Tara T. "Understanding Bullying." *Our Children,* vol. 29, no. 2, 2004, pp. 12–13.

Nansel, Tonja R., et al. "Bullying Behaviors Among U.S. Youth: Prevalence and Association with Psychosocial Adjustment." *Journal of the American Medical Association,* vol. 25, Apr. 2001, pp. 2094–2100.

2

A Catalog of Reading Strategies

Here we present fifteen strategies for reading critically that you can apply to the selections in this book as well as to your other college reading. Mastering these strategies will make reading much more satisfying and productive for you and help you handle difficult material with confidence:

- **Annotating:** Recording your reactions to, interpretations of, and questions about a text as you read it

- **Taking inventory:** Listing and grouping your annotations and other notes to find meaningful patterns

- **Outlining:** Listing the text's main ideas to reveal how it is organized

- **Summarizing:** Distilling the main ideas or gist of a text

- **Paraphrasing:** Restating what you have read to clarify or refer to it

- **Synthesizing:** Integrating into your own writing ideas and information gleaned from different sources

- **Analyzing assumptions:** Examining the values and beliefs that underlie the text, either stated directly or implied in the text's word choices

- **Contextualizing:** Placing a text in its historical and cultural context

- **Exploring the significance of figurative language:** Examining how metaphors, similes, and symbols are used in a text to convey meaning and evoke feelings

- **Analyzing visuals:** Thinking about how visual images add meaning to a text

- **Looking for patterns of opposition:** Inferring the values and assumptions embodied in the language of a text

- *Reflecting on challenges to your beliefs and values:* Examining the bases of your personal responses to a text

- *Comparing and contrasting related readings:* Exploring likenesses and differences between texts to understand them better

- *Evaluating the logic of an argument:* Determining whether an argument is well reasoned and adequately supported

- *Recognizing logical fallacies:* Looking for errors in reasoning

- *Recognizing emotional manipulation:* Identifying texts that unfairly and inappropriately use emotional appeals based on false or exaggerated claims

- *Judging the writer's credibility:* Considering whether writers represent different points of view fairly and know what they are writing about

ANNOTATING

Annotations are the marks — underlines, highlights, and comments — you make directly on the page as you read. Annotating can be used to record immediate reactions and questions, outline and summarize main points, and evaluate and relate the reading to other ideas and points of view.

Your annotations can take many forms, such as the following:

- Writing comments, questions, or definitions in the margins; or using comment balloons in a digital space

- Underlining, highlighting, or circling important or questionable words, phrases, or sentences

- Connecting similar or opposing ideas with lines or arrows

- Numbering related points

- Bracketing sections of the text

- Noting anything that strikes you as interesting, important, or questionable

Depending on their purpose for reading, most readers annotate in layers, adding annotations as they think about the ideas and reread key passages.

The following selection, excerpted from Martin Luther King Jr.'s "Letter from Birmingham Jail," illustrates some of the ways you can annotate as you read. Add your own annotations, if you like.

Martin Luther King Jr.

An Annotated Sample from "Letter from Birmingham Jail"

Martin Luther King Jr. (1929–1968) first came to national notice in 1955, when he led a successful boycott against the policy of restricting African American passengers to rear seats on city buses in Montgomery, Alabama, where he was minister of a Baptist church. He subsequently formed the Southern Christian Leadership Conference, which brought people of all races from all over the country to the South to fight nonviolently for racial integration. In 1963, King led demonstrations in Birmingham, Alabama, that were met with violence; a bomb was detonated in an African American church, killing four young girls. King was arrested for his role in organizing the protests, and while in prison, he wrote his "Letter from Birmingham Jail" to justify his strategy of civil disobedience, which he called "nonviolent direct action."

King begins his letter by discussing his disappointment with the lack of support he has received from white moderates, such as the group of clergy who published criticism of his organization in the local newspaper.

- **As you read,** try to infer what the clergy's specific criticisms might have been.
- Notice the tone King uses. Would you characterize the writing as apologetic, conciliatory, accusatory, or something else?

¶1. White moderates block progress.

I must confess that over the past few years I have been gravely disappointed with the white moderate. I have almost reached the regrettable conclusion that the Negro's [great stumbling block in his stride toward freedom] is not the White Citizen's Counciler or the Ku Klux Klanner, but the white moderate, who is more devoted to "order" than to justice; who prefers a negative peace which is the absence of tension to a positive peace which is the presence of justice; who constantly says: "I agree with you in the goal you seek, but I cannot agree with your methods of direct action"; who paternalistically believes he can set the timetable for another man's freedom; who lives by a mythical concept of time and who constantly advises the Negro to wait for a "more convenient season." Shallow understanding from people of good will is more frustrating than absolute misunderstanding from people of ill will. Lukewarm acceptance is much more bewildering than outright rejection.

Contrasts: order vs. justice, negative vs. positive peace, goals vs. methods

(treating others like children)

more contrasts

¶2. What the moderates don't understand

I had hoped that the white moderate would understand that law and order exist for the purpose of establishing justice and that when they fail in

1

2

this purpose they become the [dangerously structured dams that block the flow of social progress.] I had hoped that the white moderate would understand that the present tension in the South is a necessary phase of the transition from an [obnoxious negative peace,] in which the Negro passively accepted his unjust plight, to a [substantive and positive peace,] in which all men will respect the dignity and worth of human personality. Actually, we who engage in nonviolent direct action are not the creators of tension. We merely bring to the surface the hidden tension that is already alive. We bring it out in the open, where it can be seen and dealt with. [Like a boil that can never be cured so long as it is covered up but must be opened with all its ugliness to the natural medicines of air and light, injustice must be exposed, with all the tension its exposure creates, to the light of human conscience and the air of national opinion before it can be cured.]

metaphor: law and order = dams (faulty?)

repeats contrast (negative / positive)

Tension already exists: We help dispel it. (True?)

simile: hidden tension is "like a boil"

3   In your statement you assert that our actions, even though peaceful, must be condemned because they precipitate violence. But is this a logical assertion? Isn't this like condemning (a robbed man) because his possession of money precipitated the evil act of robbery? Isn't this like condemning (Socrates) because his unswerving commitment to truth and his philosophical inquiries precipitated the act by the misguided populace in which they made him drink hemlock? Isn't this like condemning (Jesus) because his unique God-consciousness and never-ceasing devotion to God's will precipitated the evil act of crucifixion? We must come to see that, as the federal courts have consistently affirmed, it is wrong to urge an individual to cease his efforts to gain his basic constitutional rights because the question may precipitate violence. [Society must protect the robbed and punish the robber.]

¶3. Questions clergymen's logic: condemning his actions = condemning robbery victim, Socrates, Jesus.

repetition ("Isn't this like . . .")

(Yes!)

4   I had also hoped that the white moderate would reject the myth concerning time in relation to the struggle for freedom. I have just received a letter from a white brother in Texas. He writes: "All Christians know that the colored people will receive equal rights eventually, but it is possible that you are in too great a religious hurry. It has taken Christianity almost two thousand years to accomplish what it has. The teachings of Christ take time to come to earth." Such an attitude stems from a tragic misconception of time, from the strangely irrational notion that there is something in the very flow of time that will inevitably cure all ills. Actually, time itself is neutral; it can be used either destructively or constructively. More and more I feel that the people of ill will have used time much more effectively than have the people of good will. We will have to repent in this generation not merely for the [hateful words and actions of the bad people] but for the [appalling silence of the good people.] Human progress never rolls in on [wheels of inevitability;] it comes through the tireless efforts of men willing to be co-workers with God, and without this hard work, time itself becomes an ally of the forces of social (stagnation.) [We must use time creatively, in the knowledge that the time is always ripe to do right.] Now is the time to make

example of a white moderate's view

¶4. Time must be used to do right.

Silence / passivity is as bad as hateful words and actions.

metaphor (mechanical?)

(stop developing)

real the promise of democracy and transform our pending [national elegy] into a creative [psalm of brotherhood.] Now is the time to lift our national policy from the [quicksand of racial injustice] to the [solid rock of human dignity.]

metaphors (song, natural world)

You speak of our activity in Birmingham as extreme. At first I was rather 5 disappointed that fellow clergymen would see my nonviolent efforts as those of an extremist. I began thinking about the fact that I stand in the middle of two opposing forces in the Negro community. One is a [force of complacency,] made up in part of Negroes who, as a result of long years of oppression, are so drained of self-respect and a sense of "somebodiness" that they have adjusted to segregation; and in part of a few middle-class Negroes, who because of a degree of academic and economic security and because in some ways they profit by segregation, have become insensitive to the problems of the masses. The other [force is one of bitterness and hatred,] and it comes perilously close to advocating violence. It is expressed in the various black nationalist [groups that are springing up] across the nation, the largest and best-known being Elijah Muhammad's Muslim movement. Nourished by the Negro's frustration over the continued existence of racial discrimination, this movement is made up of people who have lost faith in America, who have absolutely repudiated Christianity, and who have concluded that the white man is an incorrigible "devil."

King accused of being an extremist.

¶5. Puts self in middle of two extremes: complacency and bitterness.

Malcolm X?

I have tried to stand between these two forces, saying that we need emu- 6 late neither the "do-nothingism" of the complacent nor the hatred and despair of the black nationalist. For there is the more excellent way of love and nonviolent protest. I am grateful to God that, through the influence of the Negro church, the way of nonviolence became an integral part of our struggle.

¶6. Offers better choice: nonviolent protest.

(How did nonviolence become part of King's movement?)

If this philosophy had not emerged, by now many streets of the South 7 would, I am convinced, be flowing with blood. And I am further convinced that if our white brothers dismiss as "rabble-rousers" and "outside agitators" those of us who employ nonviolent direct action, and if they refuse to support our nonviolent efforts, millions of Negroes will, out of frustration and despair, seek solace and security in black-nationalist ideologies—a development that would inevitably lead to a frightening racial nightmare.

¶7. Says movement prevents racial violence. (Threat?)

(comfort)

Oppressed people cannot remain oppressed forever. The yearning for 8 freedom eventually manifests itself, and that is what has happened to the American Negro. Something within has reminded him of his birthright of freedom, and something without has reminded him that it can be gained. Consciously or unconsciously, he has been caught up by the Zeitgeist, and with his black brothers of Africa and his brown and yellow brothers of Asia, South America and the Caribbean, the United States Negro is moving with a sense of great urgency toward the [promised land of racial justice.] If one recognizes this [vital urge that has engulfed the Negro community,] one should readily understand why public demonstrations are taking place.

(spirit of the times)

The Negro has many [pent-up resentments] and latent frustrations, and he must release them. So let him march; let him make prayer pilgrimages to the city hall; let him go on freedom rides—and try to understand why he must do so. If his repressed emotions are not released in nonviolent ways, they will seek expression through violence; this is not a threat but a fact of history. So I have not said to my people: "Get rid of your discontent." Rather, I have tried to say that this normal and healthy discontent can be [channeled into the creative outlet of nonviolent direct action.] And now this approach is being termed extremist.

> Not a threat

> ¶8. Discontent is normal, healthy, and historically inevitable, but it must be channeled.

9   But though I was initially disappointed at being categorized as an extremist, as I continued to think about the matter I gradually gained a measure of satisfaction from the label. Was not Jesus an extremist for love: "Love your enemies, bless them that curse you, do good to them that hate you, and pray for them which despitefully use you, and persecute you." Was not Amos an extremist for justice: "Let justice roll down like waters and righteousness like an ever-flowing stream." Was not Paul an extremist for the Christian gospel: "I bear in my body the marks of the Lord Jesus." Was not Martin Luther an extremist: "Here I stand; I cannot do otherwise, so help me God." And John Bunyan: "I will stay in jail to the end of my days before I make a butchery of my conscience." And Abraham Lincoln: "This nation cannot survive half slave and half free." And Thomas Jefferson: "We hold these truths to be self evident, that all men are created equal...." So the question is not whether we will be extremists, but what kind of extremists we will be. Will we be extremists for hate or for love? Will we be extremists for the preservation of injustice or for the extension of justice? In that dramatic scene on Calvary's hill three men were crucified. We must never forget that all three were crucified for the same crime—the crime of extremism. Two were extremists for immorality, and thus fell below their environment. The other, Jesus Christ, was an extremist for love, truth and goodness, and thereby rose above his environment. Perhaps the South, the nation and the world are in dire need of creative extremists.

> ¶9. Redefines "extremism," embraces "extremist" label.

> (Hebrew prophet)

> (Christian apostle)

> (founder of Protestantism)

> (English preacher)

> Compares self to great "extremists"—including Jesus.

10   I had hoped that the white moderate would see this need. Perhaps I was too optimistic; perhaps I expected too much. I suppose I should have realized that few members of the oppressor race can understand the deep groans and passionate yearnings of the oppressed race, and still fewer have the vision to see that [injustice must be rooted out] by strong, persistent and determined action. I am thankful, however, that some of our white brothers in the South have grasped the meaning of this social revolution and committed themselves to it. They are still all too few in quantity, but they are big in quality. Some—such as Ralph McGill, Lillian Smith, Harry Golden, James McBride Dabbs, Ann Braden and Sarah Patton Boyle—have written about our struggle in eloquent and prophetic terms. Others have marched with us down nameless streets of the South. They have languished in filthy, roach-infested

> Disappointed in the white moderate

> ¶10. Praises whites who have supported movement.

> (Who are they?)

> (been left unaided)

jails, <u>suffering the abuse and brutality</u> of policemen who view them as "dirty nigger-lovers." Unlike so many of their moderate brothers and sisters, they have <u>recognized the urgency of the moment and sensed the need</u> for [powerful "action" antidotes] to combat the [disease of segregation.]

Metaphor: segregation is a disease.

CHECKLIST: Annotating

1. Mark the text — for example, circling words to be defined in the margin, underlining key words and phrases, or using arrows to connect related ideas.

2. Write marginal comments — for example, numbering and labeling main ideas, defining unfamiliar words, and noting your responses and questions.

3. Layer additional markings in the text and comments in the margins as you reread.

TAKING INVENTORY

Taking inventory helps you analyze your annotations for different purposes. When you take inventory, you make various kinds of lists to explore patterns of meaning you find in the text. For instance, in reading the annotated passage by Martin Luther King Jr., you might have noticed that certain similes and metaphors are used or that many famous people are named. By listing the names (Socrates, Jesus, Luther, Lincoln, and so on) and then grouping them into categories (people who died for their beliefs, leaders, teachers, and religious figures), you could better understand why the writer refers to these particular people. Taking inventory of your annotations can be helpful if you plan to write about a text you are reading.

CHECKLIST: Taking Inventory

1. Examine the annotations you made for patterns, such as recurring images, repeated words and phrases, related examples or illustrations, and reliance on particular writing strategies.

2. List the items that make up a pattern.

3. Decide what the pattern might reveal about the reading.

OUTLINING

Outlining, which identifies a text's main ideas, is an especially helpful reading strategy for understanding the content and structure of a reading. The key to outlining is distinguishing between the main ideas and the supporting materials, such as reasons, examples, and quotations. You may make either an informal scratch outline or a more formal, multilevel outline. You can easily make a scratch outline summarizing the main idea of each paragraph (as in the marginal annotations on the King excerpt on pages 18–22 that are collected in the scratch outline example below). Or, if you need to analyze a section of a text to write about it, you can take the time to make a formal outline (like the one below, which outlines part of King's essay).

Scratch outline of "Letter from Birmingham Jail"

¶1. White moderates block progress
¶2. What the moderates don't understand
¶3. Questions clergymen's logic
¶4. Time must be used to do right
¶5. Puts self in middle of two extremes: complacency and bitterness
¶6. Offers better choice: nonviolent protest
¶7. Says movement prevents racial violence
¶8. Discontent is normal, healthy, and historically inevitable, but it must be channeled
¶9. Redefines "extremism," embraces "extremist" label
¶10. Praises whites who have supported movement

Formal outline of "Letter from Birmingham Jail" (paragraphs 5–9)

I. Contrary to white moderates' claims, King's civil rights movement is not "extremist" in the usual sense.
   A. It stands between the extremes of passivity and radicalism in the African American community (pars. 5–6).
      1. Passivity illustrated by the oppressed and the self-interested middle class
      2. Violent radicalism illustrated in Elijah Muhammad's followers
   B. In its advocacy of love and nonviolent protest, the movement has forestalled bloodshed and kept more African Americans from joining radicals (pars. 5–7).
   C. The movement helps African Americans channel the urge for freedom that's part of the historical trend and the prevailing *Zeitgeist* (par. 8).
II. The movement can be defined as extremist if the term is redefined: "Creative extremism" is extremism in the service of love, truth, and goodness.
   A. Biblical examples including Amos, Paul, and Jesus (par. 9)
   B. Historical examples including Luther, Bunyan, Lincoln, and Jefferson (par. 9)

CHECKLIST: Outlining

To make a scratch outline of a text:

1. Reread each paragraph, summarizing the main idea or topic of the paragraph. Do not include examples, quotations, or other supporting material.

2. Your scratch outline can be part of your annotations on the text itself or collected on a separate piece of paper or in a file for later reference.

To make a formal outline of a text:

1. Decide what portion of the text you want to analyze closely.

2. Use capital Roman numerals (I, II, III) to identify the main ideas or topics.

3. Use letters (A, B, C) and Arabic numerals (1, 2, 3) to indicate the supporting ideas, examples, comparisons, and such.

SUMMARIZING

For more information on integrating sources responsibly, see the Appendix, pp. 497–508.

A **summary** is a relatively brief restatement, primarily in the reader's own words, of the reading's main ideas. Summarizing helps you understand and remember what is most significant in a reading, and it is one of the main strategies, along with quoting and paraphrasing (p. 25), used to integrate other writers' ideas into your own writing.

Summaries vary in length, depending on the reader's purpose. Some summaries are very brief. For example, if you were referring to the excerpt from "Letter from Birmingham Jail" and simply needed to indicate how it relates to your other sources, your summary might look something like this:

> There have always been advocates of extremism in politics. Martin Luther King Jr., in "Letter from Birmingham Jail," for instance, defends nonviolent civil disobedience as an extreme but necessary means of bringing about racial justice.

If, however, you were surveying the important texts of the civil rights movement, you might write a longer, more detailed summary:

> King expresses his disappointment with white moderates who, by opposing his program of nonviolent direct action, have become a barrier to progress toward racial justice. He acknowledges that his program has raised tension in the South,

but he explains that tension is necessary to bring about change. Furthermore, he argues that tension already exists, but because it has been unexpressed, it is unhealthy and potentially dangerous.

He defends his actions against the clergy's criticisms, particularly their argument that he is in too much of a hurry. Responding to charges of extremism, King claims that he has actually prevented racial violence by channeling the natural frustrations of oppressed African Americans into nonviolent protest. He asserts that extremism is precisely what is needed now — but it must be creative, rather than destructive, extremism. He concludes by again expressing disappointment with white moderates for not joining his effort as some other whites have.

In composing an extended summary, writers usually find it useful to outline the reading as a preliminary to writing a summary. A paragraph-by-paragraph scratch outline (like the one on p. 23) lists the reading's main ideas in the sequence in which they appear in the original. But summarizing requires more than merely stringing together the entries in an outline; it must fill in the logical connections between the author's ideas. Notice also in the preceding example that the reader repeats selected words and phrases and refers to the author by name, indicating, with verbs like *expresses, acknowledges,* and *explains,* the writer's purpose and strategy at each point in the argument.

CHECKLIST: Summarizing

1. Make a scratch outline.

2. Write a paragraph or more that presents the author's main ideas largely in your own words. Use the outline as a guide, but reread parts of the original text as necessary.

3. To make the summary coherent, fill in connections between the ideas you present.

PARAPHRASING

Paraphrasing is restating a text by using mostly your own words. It can help you clarify the meaning of an obscure or ambiguous passage. It is one of the three ways of integrating other people's ideas and information into your own writing, along with **quoting** (reproducing exactly the language of the source text) and **summarizing** (distilling the main ideas or gist of the source text). You might choose to paraphrase rather than quote when the source's language is not especially arresting or memorable. You might paraphrase short passages but summarize longer ones.

Following are two passages. The first is from paragraph 2 of the excerpt from King's "Letter." The second passage is a paraphrase of the first:

Original

I had hoped that the white moderate would understand that law and order exist for the purpose of establishing justice and that when they fail in this purpose they become the dangerously structured dams that block the flow of social progress. I had hoped that the white moderate would understand that the present tension in the South is a necessary phase of the transition from an obnoxious negative peace, in which the Negro passively accepted his unjust plight, to a substantive and positive peace, in which all men will respect the dignity and worth of human personality.

Paraphrase

King writes that he had hoped for more understanding from white moderates — specifically that they would recognize that law and order are not ends in themselves but means to the greater end of establishing justice. When law and order do not serve this greater end, they stand in the way of progress. King expected the white moderate to recognize that the current tense situation in the South is part of a transition process that is necessary for progress. The current situation is bad because although there is peace, it is an "obnoxious" and "negative" kind of peace based on African Americans passively accepting the injustice of the status quo. A better kind of peace — one that is "substantive," real and not imaginary, as well as "positive" — requires that all people, regardless of race, be valued.

When you compare the paraphrase to the original, you can see that the paraphrase contains all the important information and ideas of the original. Notice also that the paraphrase is somewhat longer than the original, refers to the writer by name, and encloses King's original words in quotation marks. The paraphrase tries to be neutral, to avoid inserting the reader's opinions or distorting the original writer's ideas.

CHECKLIST: Paraphrasing

1. Reread the passage, looking up unfamiliar words.

2. Translate the passage into your own words and sentences, putting quotation marks around any words or phrases you quote from the original.

3. Revise to ensure coherence.

SYNTHESIZING

Synthesizing involves presenting ideas and information gleaned from different sources. It can help you see how different sources relate to one another. For example, one reading may provide information that fills out the information in another reading, or a reading could present arguments that challenge arguments in another reading.

When you synthesize material from different sources, you construct a conversation among your sources, a conversation in which you also participate. Synthesizing contributes most when writers use sources, not only to support their idea, but to challenge and extend them as well.

In the following example, the reader uses a variety of sources related to the King passage (pp. 18–22) and brings them together around a central idea. Notice how quotation, paraphrase, and summary are all used.

Synthesis

When King defends his campaign of nonviolent direct action against the clergy-men's criticism that "our actions, even though peaceful, must be condemned because they precipitate violence" (King excerpt, par. 3), he is using what Vinit Haksar calls Mohandas Gandhi's "safety-valve argument" ("Civil Disobedience and Non-Cooperation" 117). According to Haksar, Gandhi gave a "non-threatening warning of worse things to come" if his demands were not met. King similarly makes clear that advocates of actions more extreme than those he advocates are waiting in the wings: "The other force is one of bitterness and hatred, and it comes perilously close to advocating violence" (King excerpt, par. 5). King identifies this force with Elijah Muhammad, and although he does not name him, King's contemporary readers would have known that he was referring also to his disciple Malcolm X, who, according to Herbert J. Storing, "urged that Negroes take seriously the idea of revolution" ("The Case against Civil Disobedience" 90). In fact, Malcolm X accused King of being a modern-day Uncle Tom, trying "to keep us under control, to keep us passive and peaceful and nonviolent" (*Malcolm X Speaks* 12).

CHECKLIST: Synthesizing

1. Find and read a variety of sources on your topic, annotating the passages that give you ideas about the topic.

2. Look for patterns among your sources, possibly supporting or challenging your ideas or those of other sources.

3. Write a paragraph or more synthesizing your sources, using quotation, paraphrase, and summary to present what they say on the topic.

ANALYZING ASSUMPTIONS

Analyzing assumptions involves examining a reading closely to uncover the ideas, beliefs, and values that are taken for granted and assumed to be commonly accepted truths. The assumptions in a text usually reflect the writer's own attitudes or cultural traditions, but they may also represent the views of the writer's sources. Neither good nor bad in themselves, assumptions are often used to make claims and arguments that seem logical, even factual, but may actually be problematic and need to be looked at with a critical eye. Reading to analyze assumptions asks you to uncover these perspectives as well as to probe your own. Sometimes assumptions in a text are stated explicitly, but often they are only implied or hinted at through the writer's choice of words or examples.

For example, Martin Luther King Jr., in paragraph 4 of the excerpt from "Letter from Birmingham Jail" (pp. 19–20), analyzes an assumption in a letter he received. The letter writer criticizes King's civil rights movement for being impatient. According to King, the writer's idea that "the very flow of time . . . will inevitably cure all ills" represents an "attitude" and "irrational notion" that "stems from a tragic misconception of time."

King counters this assumption about time's curative power with his own assumptions about time and progress:

- "Actually, time itself is neutral."

- What counts is whether time is "used . . . destructively or constructively."

- "Human progress never rolls in on wheels of inevitability; it comes through the tireless efforts of men."

- "Now is the time."

Instead of the progress narrative believed by people with good intentions, like the letter writer, King posits an alternative worldview that requires people of goodwill to act as "co-workers with God," and not to wait and expect time to solve problems. King's assumptions lead him to the logical conclusion that failing to act or speak out against injustice is a sin of omission as surely as the sin of commission made by those who use "hateful words and actions" to disrupt progress.

Identifying assumptions in a reading can be challenging. Here are some suggestions that may help:

- Look for questionable assertions of fact, such as claims without proper support.

- Think about the key terms and their assumed definitions or connotations, the cultural assumptions underlying the way things are defined and categorized.

- Examine examples to see what values and beliefs they assume.

- Distinguish what is considered *normal* as opposed to abnormal, unconventional, strange, or deviant.

- Recognize stereotypes, prejudices, preconceptions, preferences, and speculations.
- Be alert to the writer's tone to identify the attitude (for example, dismissive, admiring, pedantic, flippant) toward the subject, sources, and audience.

Then, choose an assumption (or set of assumptions) you think plays an important role in the reading, and use these questions to think about its **rhetoric** — how it tries to achieve its purpose with the audience:

1. What is the effect of the assumption and whose interests does the assumption serve?

2. How does the assumption reinforce or critique commonly held views?

3. What alternative ideas, beliefs, or values could be used to challenge this assumption?

CHECKLIST: Analyzing Assumptions

1. Identify any assumptions — ideas, beliefs, or values — in the reading that seem problematic.

2. Choose one assumption (or set of assumptions) that plays an important role in the reading to analyze in depth.

3. Analyze how the assumption (or set of assumptions) works both in the context of the reading and in society more generally.

CONTEXTUALIZING

Contextualizing is a critical reading strategy that enables you to make inferences about a reading's historical and cultural context and to examine the differences between its context and your own.

The excerpt from King's "Letter from Birmingham Jail" is a good example of a text that benefits from being read contextually. If you knew little about the history of slavery and segregation in the United States, it would be difficult to understand the passion expressed in this passage. To understand the historical and cultural context in which King wrote his "Letter from Birmingham Jail," you could do some library or Internet research. Comparing the situation at the time to situations with which you are familiar would help you understand some of your own attitudes toward King and the civil rights movement.

Notes from a contextualized reading

1. I have seen documentaries showing civil rights demonstrators being attacked by dogs, doused by fire hoses, beaten and dragged by helmeted police.

Such images give me a sense of the violence, fear, and hatred that King was responding to.

The creative tension King refers to comes across in his writing. He uses his anger and frustration to inspire his critics. He also threatens them, although he denies it. I saw a film on Malcolm X, so I could see that King was giving white people a choice between his own nonviolent way and Malcolm's more confrontational way.

2. Things have certainly changed since the 1960s. When I read King's "Letter" today, I feel like I'm reading history. But too frequently today, there are reports of police brutality and hate crimes.

CHECKLIST: Contextualizing

1. Describe the historical and cultural situation as it is represented in the reading and in other sources with which you are familiar. Your knowledge may come from other reading, television or film, school, or library or Internet research.

2. Compare the historical and cultural situation in which the text was written with your own historical and cultural situation. Consider how your understanding and judgment of the reading are affected by your own context.

EXPLORING THE SIGNIFICANCE OF FIGURATIVE LANGUAGE

Figurative language — metaphor, simile, and symbolism — enhances literal meaning by implying abstract ideas through vivid images and by evoking feelings and associations.

Metaphor implicitly compares two different things by identifying them with each other. For instance, when King calls the white moderate "the Negro's great stumbling block in his stride toward freedom" (par. 1), he does not mean that the white moderate literally trips the Negro who is attempting to walk toward freedom. The sentence makes sense only if understood figuratively: The white moderate trips up the Negro by frustrating every effort to achieve justice.

Simile, a more explicit form of comparison, uses the word *like* or *as* to signal the relationship of two seemingly unrelated things. King uses simile when he says that injustice is "[l]ike a boil that can never be cured so long as it is covered up" (par. 2). This simile suggests that injustice is a disease of society as a boil is a disease of the skin, and that injustice, like a boil, must be exposed or it will fester and infect the entire body.

Symbolism compares two things by making one stand for the other. King uses the white moderate as a symbol for supposed liberals and would-be supporters of civil rights who are actually frustrating the cause.

How these figures of speech are used in a text reveals something of the writer's feelings about the subject. Exploring possible meanings in a text's figurative language involves (1) annotating (as on the King essay on pp. 18–22) some of the metaphors, similes, and symbols you find in a reading; (2) grouping and labeling the figures of speech that appear to express related feelings or attitudes; and (3) writing to explore the meaning of the patterns you have found.

Grouping and labeling figures of speech

Sickness: "like a boil" (par. 2); "the disease of segregation" (par. 10)

Underground: "hidden tension" (par. 2); "injustice must be exposed" (par. 2); "injustice must be rooted out" (par. 10)

Blockage: "dams," "block the flow" (par. 2); "Human progress never rolls in on wheels of inevitability" (par. 4); "pent-up resentments," "repressed emotions" (par. 8)

Writing to explore meaning

The patterns labeled *underground* and *blockage* suggest a feeling of frustration. Inertia is a problem; movement forward toward progress or upward toward the promised land is stalled.

The simile of injustice being "like a boil" links the two patterns of underground and sickness, suggesting that a "disease" is inside the people or the society. The cure is to root out the blocked hatred and injustice as well as to release the tension or emotion that has long been repressed.

CHECKLIST: Exploring the Significance of Figurative Language

1. Annotate the figures of speech you find worth examining.

2. Group the figures of speech that appear to express related feelings and attitudes, and label each group.

3. Write one or two paragraphs exploring the meaning of the patterns you have found.

ANALYZING VISUALS

Visuals invite analysis both of their key components and their *rhetorical context*. As we "read" a visual, therefore, we should ask ourselves a series of questions: What image does the visual portray? Who created it? What *audience* is it addressing?

What is it trying to get this audience to think and feel about the subject? How does it attempt to achieve this *purpose?*

Look, for example, at the visual to the right: a public service announcement (PSA) from the World Wildlife Fund (WWF). The central image in this PSA is a photo of an attractive, smiling young couple. Most of us will immediately recognize the dress, posture, and facial expressions of the young man and woman as those of a newly married couple. However, we are immediately struck by the feeling that something is wrong with the picture: a hurricane rages in the background, blowing hair and clothing, and threatening to rip the bouquet from the bride's hand.

FIGURE 2.1 "Wedding," from the WWF's "Beautiful Day U.S." Series

So what do we make of the disruption of the convention (the traditional wedding photo) on which the PSA image is based? The text below the image delivers the message: "Ignoring global warming won't make it go away." The disjunction between the couple's blissful expression and the storm raging around them turns out to be the point of the PSA: Like the young couple in the picture, the PSA implies, we are all blithely ignoring the impending disaster that global warming represents. The reputable, nonprofit WWF's logo and URL, which constitute its "signature," are meant to be an assurance that this threat is real, and not just an idea a profit-seeking ad agency dreamt up to manipulate us.

Criteria for Analyzing Visuals

Key Components

Composition

- Of what elements is the visual composed?
- What is the focal point — that is, the place your eyes are drawn to?

- From what perspective do you view the focal point? Are you looking straight ahead at it, down at it, or up at it? If the visual is a photograph, what angle was the image shot from — straight ahead, looking down or up?

- What colors are used? Are there obvious special effects employed? Is there a frame, or are there any additional graphical elements? If so, what do these elements contribute to your "reading" of the visual?

People / Other Main Figures

- If people are depicted, how would you describe their age, gender, subculture, ethnicity, profession, and socioeconomic class? How stereotypical or surprising are the people?

- Who is looking at whom? Do the people represented seem conscious of the viewer's gaze?

- What do the facial expressions and body language tell you about power relationships (equal, subordinate, in charge) and attitudes (self-confident, vulnerable, anxious, subservient, angry, aggressive, sad)?

Scene

- If a recognizable scene is depicted, what is its setting? What is in the background and the foreground?

- What has happened just before the image was "shot"? What will happen in the next scene?

- What, if anything, is happening just outside the visual frame?

Words

- If text is combined with the visual, what role does the text play? Is it a slogan? A famous quote? Lyrics from a well-known song?

- If the text helps you interpret the visual's overall meaning, what interpretive clues does it provide?

Tone

- What tone, or mood, does the visual convey? Is it lighthearted, somber, frightening, shocking, joyful? What elements in the visual (color, composition, words, people, setting) convey this tone?

- What is the tone of the text? Humorous? Elegiac? Ironic?

(continued)

Context(s)

Rhetorical Context

- **What is the visual's main purpose?** Are we being asked to buy a product? Form an opinion or judgment about something? Support a political party's candidate? Take some other kind of action?

- **Who is its target audience?** Children? Men? Women? Some sub- or super-set of these groups (e.g., African American men, "tweens," seniors)?

- **Who is the author? Who sponsored its publication?** What background/associations do the author and the sponsoring publication have? What other works have they produced?

- **Where was it published, and in what form?** Online? On television? In print? In a commercial publication (a sales brochure, billboard, ad) or an informational one (newspaper, magazine)?

- **If the visual is embedded within a document that is primarily written text, how do the written text and the visual relate to each other?** Do they convey the same message, or are they at odds in any way? What does the image contribute to the written text? Is it essential or just eye candy?

- *Social Context.* **What is the immediate social and cultural context within which the visual is operating?** If we are being asked to support a certain candidate, for example, how does the visual reinforce or counter what we already know about this candidate? What other social/cultural knowledge does the visual assume its audience already has?

- *Historical Context.* **What historical knowledge does it assume the audience already possesses?** Does the visual refer to other historical images, figures, events, or stories that the audience would recognize? How do these historical references relate to the visual's audience and purpose?

- *Intertextuality.* **How does the visual connect, relate to, or contrast with any other significant texts, visual or otherwise, that you are aware of?** How do such considerations inform your ideas about this particular visual?

LOOKING FOR PATTERNS OF OPPOSITION

Looking for **patterns of opposition** can help the reader understand the dialogue of opposing voices and values represented in the text. All texts carry within themselves voices of opposition. These voices may echo the views and values of sources to which the writer is responding or those of potential readers the writer anticipates; they may even reflect the writer's own conflicting values. The excerpt from King's "Letter from Birmingham Jail" (pp. 18–22) is rich in oppositions: *moderate* versus *extremist, order* versus *justice*. These oppositions are not accidental; they form a significant pattern that gives a reader important information about King's argument.

A careful reading will show that King always values one of the two terms in an opposition over the other. For example, *extremist* (par. 9) is valued over *moderate* (par. 10). This preference for extremism is surprising. If King is trying to convince his readers to accept his point of view, why would he represent himself as an extremist? Studying the patterns of opposition in the text enables you to answer this question. You will see that King sets up this opposition to force his readers to examine their own values. Instead of working toward justice, he says, those who support law and order maintain the unjust status quo.

Looking for patterns of opposition involves annotating words or phrases in the reading that indicate oppositions, listing the opposing terms in pairs, deciding which term in each pair is preferred by the writer, and reflecting on the meaning of the patterns. Here is a partial list of oppositions from the King excerpt, with the preferred terms marked by an asterisk:

Listing Patterns of Opposition	
moderate	*extremist
order	*justice
negative peace	*positive peace
absence of justice	*presence of justice
goals	*methods
*direct action	passive acceptance
*exposed tension	hidden tension

CHECKLIST: Looking for Patterns of Opposition

1. Annotate the selection to identify words or phrases indicating oppositions.

2. List the pairs of oppositions. (You may have to paraphrase or even supply the opposite word or phrase if it is not stated directly in the text.)

3. For each pair of oppositions, put an asterisk next to the term that the writer seems to value or prefer over the other.

4. Write to analyze and evaluate the opposing points of view, or, in a reading that does not take a position, the alternative systems of value.

REFLECTING ON CHALLENGES TO YOUR BELIEFS AND VALUES

Reflecting on, or thinking critically about, **your own fundamental beliefs or values** may not be your first reaction when you encounter challenges in a text, such as criticism or misrepresentation. But to read thoughtfully, you need to scrutinize your own assumptions and attitudes as well as those expressed in the text you are reading. If you are like most readers, however, you will find that your assumptions and attitudes are so ingrained that you are not always fully aware of them. A good strategy for getting at these underlying beliefs and values is to identify and reflect on the ways the text challenges you and how it makes you feel — disturbed, threatened, ashamed, combative, pleased, exuberant, or some other way.

For example, here is what one student wrote about the King passage:

Reflections

In paragraph 1, Dr. King criticizes people who are "more devoted to 'order' than to justice." This criticism upsets me because today I think I would choose order over justice. When I reflect on my feelings and try to figure out where they come from, I realize that what I feel most is fear. I am terrified by the violence in society today. I'm afraid of sociopaths who don't respect the rule of law, much less the value of human life.

COMPARING AND CONTRASTING RELATED READINGS

When you **compare** two reading selections, you look for similarities. When you **contrast** them, you look for differences. As critical reading strategies, comparing and contrasting enable you to see both texts more clearly.

Both strategies depend on how imaginative you are in preparing the grounds or basis for comparison. We often hear that it is fruitless, so to speak, to compare apples and oranges. It is true that you cannot add or multiply them, but you can put one against the other and come up with some interesting similarities and differences. For example, comparing apples and oranges in terms of their roles as symbols in Western culture (say, the apple of Adam and Eve compared to the symbol for Apple computers) could be quite productive. The grounds or basis for comparison, like a camera lens, brings some things into focus while blurring others.

To demonstrate how this strategy works, we compare and contrast the excerpt from "Letter from Birmingham Jail" (pp. 18–22) with the following selection by Lewis H. Van Dusen Jr.

Lewis H Van Dusen Jr.

Legitimate Pressures and Illegitimate Results

A respected attorney and legal scholar, Lewis H. Van Dusen Jr. has served as chair of the American Bar Association Committee on Ethics and Professional Responsibility. This selection comes from the essay "Civil

Disobedience: Destroyer of Democracy," which first appeared in the *American Bar Association Journal* in 1969.

As you read, notice the annotations comparing this essay with the one by King.

There are many civil rights leaders who show impatience with the process   1
of democracy. They rely on the sit-in, boycott, or mass picketing to gain speedier solutions to the problems that face every citizen. But we must realize that the legitimate pressures that [won concessions in the past] can easily escalate into the illegitimate power plays that might [extort] demands in the future.] The victories of these civil rights leaders must not shake our confidence in the democratic procedures, as the pressures of demonstration are desirable only if they take place within the limits allowed by law. Civil rights gains should continue to be won by the persuasion of Congress and other legislative bodies and by the decision of courts. Any illegal entreaty for the [rights of some] can be an injury to the [rights of others,] for mass demonstrations often trigger violence.

(to get something
by force or
intimidation)

Those who advocate [taking the law into their own hands] should   2
reflect that when they are disobeying what they consider to be an immoral law, they are deciding on a possibly immoral course. Their answer is that the process for democratic relief is too slow, that only mass confrontation can bring immediate action, and that any injuries are the inevitable cost of the pursuit of justice. Their answer is, simply put, that the end justifies the means. It is this justification of any form of demonstration as a form of dissent that threatens to destroy a society built on the rule of law.

King's concern with
time

Ends vs. means
debate

Any form?

The annotations in the Van Dusen selection above were made in comparison to the annotated King excerpt (pp. 18–22) and focus on contrasts between the two writers' different views on nonviolent direct action. The annotations on the Van Dusen excerpt highlight aspects of his argument against the use of nonviolent direct action. These annotations led directly to the paragraph of contrast below, which summarizes Van Dusen's argument. The second paragraph of the contrast (p. 39) presents King's defense, as well as some of the writer's own ideas on how King could have responded to Van Dusen.

King and Van Dusen present radically different views of legal, nonviolent direct action, such as parades, demonstrations, boycotts, sit-ins, or pickets. Although Van Dusen acknowledges that direct action is legal, he nevertheless fears it; and he challenges it energetically in these paragraphs. He seems most concerned about the ways direct action disturbs the peace, infringes on others' rights, and threatens violence. He worries that, even though some groups make gains through direct action, the end result is that everyone else begins to doubt the validity of the usual democratic procedures of relying on legislation and the courts. He condemns advocates of direct action like King for believing that the end (in this case, racial justice) justifies the means (direct action). Van Dusen argues that demonstrations often end violently and that an organized movement like King's can in the beginning win concessions through direct action but then end up extorting demands through threats and illegal uses of power.

In contrast, King argues that nonviolent direct action preserves the peace by bringing hidden tensions and prejudices to the surface where they can be acknowledged and addressed. Direct action enhances democracy by changing its unjust laws and thereby strengthening it. Since direct action is entirely legal, to forgo it as a strategy for change would be to turn one's back on a basic democratic principle. Although it may inconvenience people, its end (a more just social order) is entirely justified by its means (direct action). King would no doubt insist that the occasional violence that follows direct action results always from aggressive, unlawful interference with demonstrations — interference sometimes led by police officers. He might also argue that neither anarchy nor extortion followed from his group's actions.

Notice that these paragraphs address each writer's argument separately. An alternative plan would have been to compare and contrast the two writers' arguments point by point.

CHECKLIST: Comparing and Contrasting Related Readings

To compare and contrast two related readings,

1. Read them both to decide on a basis or grounds for comparison or contrast.

2. Reread and annotate one selection to identify points of comparison or contrast.

3. Reread the second selection, annotating for the points you have already identified.

4. Write up your analyses of the two selections, revising your analysis of the first selection to reflect any new insights you have gained. Or write a point-by-point comparison or contrast of the two selections.

EVALUATING THE LOGIC OF AN ARGUMENT

An argument includes a thesis backed by reasons and support. The **thesis** asserts a position on a controversial issue or a solution to a problem that the writer wants readers to accept. The **reasons** tell readers why they should accept the thesis, and the **support** (such as examples, statistics, authorities, analogies, and textual evidence) gives readers grounds for accepting it. For an argument to be considered logically acceptable, it must meet the three conditions of what we call the ABC test:

A. The reasons and support must be *appropriate* to the thesis.

B. The reasons and support must be *believable*.

C. The reasons and support must be *consistent* with one another as well as complete.

Testing for Appropriateness

To evaluate the logic of an argument, you first decide whether the argument's reasons and support are appropriate. To test for appropriateness, ask these questions: How does each reason or piece of support relate to the thesis? Is the connection between reasons and support and the thesis clear and compelling?

Readers most often question the appropriateness of reasons and support when the writer argues by analogy or by invoking authority. For example, King uses both analogy and authority in paragraph 3: "Isn't this like condemning Socrates because his unswerving commitment to truth and his philosophical inquiries precipitated the act by the misguided populace in which they made him drink hemlock?" Not only must you judge the appropriateness of the analogy comparing the Greeks' condemnation of Socrates to the white moderates' condemnation of King, but you must also judge whether it is appropriate to accept Socrates as an authority. Since Socrates is generally respected for his teachings on justice, his words and actions are likely to be considered appropriate to King's situation in Birmingham.

Testing for Believability

Believability is a measure of your willingness to accept as true the reasons and support the writer gives in defense of a thesis. To test for believability, ask: On what basis am I being asked to believe this reason or support is true? If it cannot be proved true or false, how much weight does it carry?

For instance, **facts** are statements that can be proved objectively to be true. The believability of facts depends on their *accuracy* (they should not distort or misrepresent reality), their *completeness* (they should not omit important details), and the *trustworthiness* of their sources (sources should be qualified and unbiased).

Examples and **anecdotes** are particular instances used to support a generalization. The believability of examples depends on their *representativeness* (whether they are truly typical and thus generalizable) and their *specificity* (whether particular details make them seem true to life). Even if a vivid example or gripping anecdote does not convince readers, it usually strengthens argumentative writing by clarifying the meaning and dramatizing the point.

Statistics are numerical data. The believability of statistics depends on the *comparability* of the data, the *precision* of the methods employed to gather and analyze data, and the *trustworthiness* of the sources.

Authorities are people to whom the writer attributes expertise on a given subject. Not only must such authorities be appropriate, as mentioned earlier, but they must be *credible* as well — that is, the reader must accept them as experts on the topic at hand. King cites authorities repeatedly throughout his essay — religious leaders as well as American political figures.

Testing for Consistency and Completeness

In looking for consistency, you should be concerned that all the parts of the argument work together and that they are sufficient to convince readers to accept the thesis or at least take it seriously. To test for consistency and completeness, ask: Are any of the reasons and support contradictory? Do they provide sufficient grounds for accepting the thesis? Does the writer fail to acknowledge, concede, or refute any opposing arguments or important objections?

A thoughtful reader might regard as contradictory King's characterizing himself first as a moderate and later as an extremist opposed to the forces of violence. (King attempts to reconcile this apparent contradiction by explicitly redefining extremism in par. 9.) Similarly, the fact that King fails to examine and refute every legal recourse available to his cause might allow a critical reader to question the sufficiency of his argument.

CHECKLIST: Evaluating the Logic of an Argument

Use the ABC test to determine whether an argument makes sense.

A. *Test for appropriateness* by checking that the reasons and support are clearly and directly related to the thesis.

B. *Test for believability* by deciding whether you can accept the reasons and support as likely to be true.

C. *Test for consistency and completeness* by deciding whether the argument has any contradictions and whether any important objections or opposing views have been ignored.

RECOGNIZING LOGICAL FALLACIES

Fallacies are errors in reasoning that seem plausible and often have great persuasive power. Fallacies are not necessarily deliberate efforts to deceive readers. Writers may introduce a fallacy accidentally by not examining their own reasons or underlying assumptions, by failing to establish solid support, or by using unclear or ambiguous words. Here are some of the most common logical fallacies.

Slippery Slope

A **slippery-slope fallacy** occurs when someone asserts that if one thing happens, then a series of bad related consequences will *necessarily* follow. The name comes from the idea that if a person takes one step down a slippery slope, he or she cannot help sliding all the way to the bottom.

EXAMPLE   Marijuana should be banned because it inevitably leads to the use of other illegal drugs.

This is a fallacy because it assumes inevitability.

Post Hoc, Ergo Propter Hoc

The Latin name *post hoc, ergo propter hoc* means "after this, therefore because of this." A **post hoc fallacy** wrongly assumes that an event that occurs *after* another event is *caused* by the first event. This fallacy in causal reasoning often occurs when writers try to attribute to one cause something that has several or many causes. When complex issues are made to seem simple, look for this fallacy.

EXAMPLE   Playing first-person shooter games makes kids violent.

To avoid the *post hoc* fallacy, someone making this argument would have to prove that playing shooter games could actually cause kids to become violent. The person would also need to consider other possible causes, such as membership in gangs, alienation at school, parental abuse, and so on.

False Dilemma (Either/Or Reasoning)

The **false dilemma fallacy,** or either/or reasoning, puts readers in the position of having to choose one of two options as if there were no other choices. Here's an example: Martin Luther King Jr., in paragraph 5 of the excerpt from "Letter from Birmingham Jail" (pp. 18–22), refutes an either/or argument made by others. Arguing that the choice between a "force of complacency" or a force "of bitterness and hatred" is a false dilemma, King points out that there are other alternatives, among them the option of nonviolent protest that he represents.

Hasty Generalization

When someone makes a **hasty generalization,** he or she leaps to a conclusion without providing enough evidence to support the leap.

EXAMPLE   Crime in this city is getting worse and worse. Just yesterday, two people
          were held up at ATMs downtown.

Two crimes, no matter how serious, do not indicate that the overall *rate* of crime is rising. This may indeed be the case, but proving it would require statistics, not just a couple of examples.

Ad Hominem (or Ad Personam) Attack

An ***ad hominem*** (meaning "to the man") or ***ad personam*** ("to the person") **attack** occurs when writers attack the person who propounds the ideas with which they disagree, rather than attacking the ideas themselves.

EXAMPLE   My opponent, one of the richest men in the state, wants to cut taxes for
          himself and his rich friends.

Certainly the character and credibility (and wealth) of the writer making the argument affect how persuasive a reader finds it, but they do not affect the underlying soundness of the argument.

Straw Man

In a **straw man fallacy,** the writer oversimplifies an opponent's position in order to knock it down, like a straw scarecrow.

EXAMPLE   Climate change is nothing to worry about because the weather changes
          all the time.

This example uses the straw man fallacy because it pretends as though worrying about the climate is as pointless as worrying about whether it will rain tomorrow. Equating climate change to the weather makes it seem like people who sound alarms about climate change are just complainers.

Circular Reasoning (Begging the Question)

A **circular reasoning fallacy** merely restates the main claim, often by definition, without actually offering evidence to support the claim.

EXAMPLE   Same-sex marriage is wrong because marriage is between a man and a
          woman.

This example relies on a definition that, if accepted, would end the discussion. But it is the definition of marriage which is at issue in the argument. To support the claim, opponents of same-sex marriage would have to convince readers that their view of marriage is the only correct view.

Red Herring

The **red herring fallacy** distracts readers with irrelevant arguments. Just think of a dead fish (red herring) being dragged across a trail to distract dogs from pursuing the scent of their real target. In this case, writers use irrelevant arguments to distract readers from the real issue, perhaps because their own argument is weak and they don't want the reader to notice.

EXAMPLE   My opponent tries to blame my administration for the high price of prescription drugs, but he supports a government takeover of health care.

That the opponent supports a government takeover of health care (whether true or false) has nothing to do with whether the policies of the speaker's administration are responsible for the high price of prescription drugs.

CHECKLIST: Recognizing Logical Fallacies

1. Annotate places in the text where you stop to think "wait a minute — that doesn't make sense" or where you think the writer has "gone too far."

2. Analyze these places to see if they represent any of the fallacies discussed in this section.

3. Write a few sentences exploring what you discover.

RECOGNIZING EMOTIONAL MANIPULATION

Writers often try to arouse emotions in readers to excite their interest, make them care, or move them to take action. There is nothing wrong with appealing to readers' emotions; what is wrong is manipulating readers with false or exaggerated appeals. Therefore, you should be suspicious of writing that is overly sentimental, that cites alarming statistics and frightening anecdotes, that demonizes others and identifies itself with revered authorities, or that uses potent symbols (for example, the American flag) or emotionally loaded words (such as *racist*).

King, for example, uses the emotionally loaded word *paternalistically* to refer to the white moderate's belief that "he can set the timetable for another man's freedom" (par. 1). In the same paragraph, King uses symbolism to get an emotional reaction from readers when he compares the white moderate to the "Ku Klux Klanner." To get readers to accept his ideas, he also relies on authorities whose names evoke the greatest respect, such as Jesus and Lincoln. But some readers might object that comparing his own crusade to that of Jesus is pretentious and manipulative. A critical reader might also consider King's discussion of African American extremists in paragraph 7 to be a veiled threat designed to frighten readers into agreement.

CHECKLIST: Recognizing Emotional Manipulation

1. Annotate places in the text where you sense emotional appeals are being used.

2. Analyze the emotional appeals, explaining why you think they are or are not manipulative.

JUDGING THE WRITER'S CREDIBILITY

Writers try to persuade readers by presenting an image of themselves in their writing that will gain their readers' confidence. This image must be created indirectly, through the arguments, language, and system of values and beliefs expressed or implied in the writing. Writers establish credibility in their writing in three ways:

- By showing their *knowledge* of the subject
- By building *common ground* with readers
- By responding *fairly* to objections and opposing arguments

Testing for Knowledge

Writers demonstrate their knowledge through the facts and statistics they marshal, the sources they rely on for information, and the scope and depth of their understanding. As a reader, you may not be sufficiently expert on the subject yourself to know whether the facts are accurate, the sources are reliable, and the understanding is sufficient. You may need to do some research to see what others say about the subject. You can also check **credentials** — the writer's educational and professional qualifications, the respectability of the publication in which the selection first appeared, and reviews of the writer's work — to determine whether the writer is a respected authority in the field. For example, King brings with him the authority that comes from being a member of the clergy and a respected leader of the Southern Christian Leadership Conference.

Testing for Common Ground

One way writers can establish **common ground** with their readers is by basing their reasoning on shared values, beliefs, and attitudes. They use language that includes their readers (*we*) and qualify their assertions to keep them from being too extreme. Above all, they acknowledge differences of opinion. You want to notice such appeals.

King creates common ground with readers by using the inclusive pronoun *we*, suggesting shared concerns between himself and his audience. Notice, however, his use of masculine pronouns and other references ("the Negro . . . he," "our brothers"). Although King addressed his letter to male clergy, he intended it to be published in the local newspaper, where it would be read by an audience of both men and women. By using language that excludes women — a common practice at the time the selection was written — King may have missed the opportunity to build common ground with more than half of his readers.

Testing for Fairness

Writers reveal their character by how they handle opposing arguments and objections to their argument. As a critical reader, pay particular attention to how writers treat possible differences of opinion. Be suspicious of those who ignore differences and pretend that everyone agrees with their viewpoints. When objections or opposing views are represented, consider whether they have been distorted in any way; if they are refuted, be sure they are challenged fairly — with sound reasoning and solid support.

One way to gauge the author's credibility is to identify the tone of the argument, for it conveys the writer's attitude toward the subject and toward the reader. Is the text angry? Sarcastic? Evenhanded? Shrill? Condescending? Bullying? Do you feel as if the writer is treating the subject — and you, as a reader — with fairness? King's tone might be characterized in different passages as patient (he doesn't lose his temper), respectful (he refers to white moderates as "people of good will"), or pompous (comparing himself to Jesus and Socrates).

CHECKLIST: Judging the Writer's Credibility

1. As you read and annotate, consider the writer's knowledge of the subject, how well common ground is established, and whether the writer deals fairly with objections and opposing arguments.

2. Decide what in the essay you find credible and what you question.

3

Autobiography

Writing and reading about memorable events and people can pique our curiosity and inspire critical analysis, leading us to think deeply about why certain experiences have meaning for us. They can also help us understand the cultural influences that helped shape who we are and what we value. Whether you are reading or writing, however, it is important to remember that, as a genre, autobiography is public, not private like a diary. Although it involves self-presentation and contributes to self-knowledge, autobiography does not require unwanted self-disclosure. Readers expect autobiographers to portray themselves purposely for their readers — in other words, to write with rhetorical sensitivity. For example, writing about yourself for a college admissions essay, you undoubtedly want to impress readers with such qualities as your thoughtfulness, diligence, social responsibility, and ambition. Writing for friends and family about a dodgy experience, you may want to share your anxieties but also show how you handled the situation — or portray yourself as a daredevil: brave, even reckless.

RHETORICAL SITUATIONS FOR AUTOBIOGRAPHIES

You may think that only politicians and celebrities write their autobiographies, but autobiographical writing is much more common, as the following examples suggest:

- As part of her college application, a high-school senior writes an autobiographical essay that shows what inspired her to want to become a biomedical researcher. She tells what happened when she did her first science experiment on the nutritional effects of different breakfast cereals. Because the mice eating Count Chocula and Froot Loops, and not eating anything else, were dying, she convinced her teacher to let her stop the experiment early. She wants her audience of college admissions officers to appreciate her sense of responsibility and understanding of the ethics of scientific research.

- Asked to post online a few paragraphs reflecting on a significant early child-hood memory, a student in a psychology class writes about a fishing trip he took as a six-year-old. The trip was the first time he spent alone with his father, and he recalls that although he tried hard to win his father's approval, his father criticized everything he did. Looking back on that painful event — now that he knows what a bad relationship his dad had had with his own father — the student reflects on the importance of role models in teaching people how to be good parents. He also refers to an article that helped him understand the impact of toxic parenting.

Thinking about Autobiography

Write a paragraph or two about an occasion when you told, read, heard, or saw an autobiography in school, at work, or in another context.

- Who was the *audience*? Consider how communicating to the particular audience (such as a teacher rather than a friend, a college admissions committee rather than a favorite aunt) affected the tone (for example: playful, informal, satiric), details, even the choice of event or person to focus on.

- What was the main *purpose*? For example, was the goal to illustrate an idea, create a favorable impression, understand why something happened, or arouse sympathy?

- How would you rate the *rhetorical sensitivity* with which the story was presented? What made it appropriate or inappropriate for its particular audience or purpose?

A GUIDE TO READING AUTOBIOGRAPHY

This guide introduces you to autobiography by inviting you to analyze a brief but powerful autobiographical selection by Annie Dillard:

- *Reading for meaning* will help you grasp the event's **significance** for Dillard — what the incident meant to her both at the time she experienced it and years later when she wrote about it. It may also help you explore broader cultural meanings in Dillard's story — for example, ideas about heroism and gender.

- *Reading like a writer* will help you learn how Dillard makes her story exciting and suspenseful, as well as meaningful, by examining how she employs some basic features and strategies typical of autobiographical writing, such as:

  1. Narrating a story dramatically

  2. Presenting people and places vividly

  3. Conveying the significance powerfully

Annie Dillard

An American Childhood

Annie Dillard (b. 1945) is a prolific writer whose first book, *Pilgrim at Tinker Creek* (1974), won the Pulitzer Prize for nonfiction writing. Since then, she has written eleven other books in a variety of genres. They include *Teaching a Stone to Talk* (1988), *The Writing Life* (1989), *Mornings Like This* (1996), and *The Maytrees* (2007). Dillard has also written an autobiography of her early years, *An American Childhood* (1987), from which the following selection comes.

- **Before you read,** notice that Dillard tells us in the opening paragraph why she liked learning to play football. Think about the kinds of play you liked as a child and why.

- **As you read,** consider why Dillard sets the scene in paragraphs 3–8 with so much specificity.

Some boys taught me to play football. This was fine sport. You thought up a new strategy   1
for every play and whispered it to the others. You went out for a pass, fooling everyone. Best, you got to throw yourself mightily at someone's running legs. Either you brought him down or you hit the ground flat out on your chin, with your arms empty before you. It was all or nothing. If you hesitated in fear, you would miss and get hurt: you would take a hard fall while the kid got away, or you would get kicked in the face while the kid got away. But if you flung yourself wholeheartedly at the back of his knees—If you gathered and joined body and soul and pointed them diving fearlessly—then you likely wouldn't get hurt, and you'd stop the ball. Your fate, and your team's score, depended on your concentration and courage. Nothing girls did could compare with it.

Boys welcomed me at baseball, too, for I had, through enthusiastic practice, what   2
was weirdly known as a boy's arm. In winter, in the snow, there was neither baseball nor football, so the boys and I threw snowballs at passing cars. I got in trouble throwing snowballs, and have seldom been happier since.

On one weekday morning after Christmas, six inches of new snow had just fallen. We   3
were standing up to our boot tops in snow on a front yard on trafficked Reynolds

Street, waiting for cars. The cars traveled Reynolds Street slowly and evenly; they were targets all but wrapped in red ribbons, cream puffs. We couldn't miss.

I was seven; the boys were eight, nine, and ten. The oldest two Fahey boys were 4
there—Mikey and Peter—polite blond boys who lived near me on Lloyd Street, and who already had four brothers and sisters. My parents approved Mikey and Peter Fahey. Chickie McBride was there, a tough kid, and Billy Paul and Mackie Kean too, from across Reynolds, where the boys grew up dark and furious, grew up skinny, knowing, and skilled. We had all drifted from our houses that morning looking for action, and had found it here on Reynolds Street.

It was cloudy but cold. The cars' tires laid behind them on the snowy street a complex 5
trail of beige chunks like crenellated castle walls. I had stepped on some earlier; they squeaked. We could not have wished for more traffic. When a car came, we all popped it one. In the intervals between cars we reverted to the natural solitude of children.

I started making an iceball—a perfect iceball, from perfectly white snow, perfectly 6
spherical, and squeezed perfectly translucent so no snow remained all the way through. (The Fahey boys and I considered it unfair actually to throw an iceball at somebody, but it had been known to happen.)

I had just embarked on the iceball project when we heard tire chains come clanking 7
from afar. A black Buick was moving toward us down the street. We all spread out, banged together some regular snowballs, took aim, and, when the Buick drew nigh, fired.

A soft snowball hit the driver's windshield right before the driver's face. It made a 8
smashed star with a hump in the middle.

Often, of course, we hit our target, but this time, the only time in all of life, the car 9
pulled over and stopped. Its wide black door opened; a man got out of it, running. He didn't even close the car door.

He ran after us, and we ran away from him, up the snowy Reynolds sidewalk. At 10
the corner, I looked back; incredibly, he was still after us. He was in city clothes: a suit and tie, street shoes. Any normal adult would have quit, having sprung us into flight and made his point. This man was gaining on us. He was a thin man, all action. All of a sudden, we were running for our lives.

Wordless, we split up. We were on our turf; we could lose ourselves in the neigh- 11
borhood backyards, everyone for himself. I paused and considered. Everyone had vanished except Mikey Fahey, who was just rounding the corner of a yellow brick house. Poor Mikey, I trailed him. The driver of the Buick sensibly picked the two of us to follow. The man apparently had all day.

He chased Mikey and me around the yellow house and up a backyard path we 12
knew by heart: under a low tree, up a bank, through a hedge, down some snowy steps, and across the grocery store's delivery driveway. We smashed through a gap in another hedge, entered a scruffy backyard and ran around its back porch and tight between houses to Edgerton Avenue; we ran across Edgerton to an alley and up our own sliding woodpile to the Halls' front yard; he kept coming. We ran up Lloyd Street and wound through mazy backyards toward the steep hilltop at Willard and Lang.

He chased us silently, block after block. He chased us silently over picket fences, 13
through thorny hedges, between houses, around garbage cans, and across streets. Every time I glanced back, choking for breath, I expected he would have quit. He

must have been as breathless as we were. His jacket strained over his body. It was an immense discovery, pounding into my hot head with every sliding, joyous step, that this ordinary adult evidently knew what I thought only children who trained at football knew: that you have to fling yourself at what you're doing, you have to point yourself, forget yourself, aim, dive.

Mikey and I had nowhere to go, in our own neighborhood or out of it, but away 14 from this man who was chasing us. He impelled us forward; we compelled him to follow our route. The air was cold; every breath tore my throat. We kept running, block after block; we kept improvising, backyard after backyard, running a frantic course and choosing it simultaneously, failing always to find small places or hard places to slow him down, and discovering always, exhilarated, dismayed, that only bare speed could save us—for he would never give up, this man—and we were losing speed.

He chased us through the backyard labyrinths of ten blocks before he caught us by 15 our jackets. He caught us and we all stopped.

We three stood staggering, half blinded, coughing, in an obscure hilltop backyard: 16 a man in his twenties, a boy, a girl. He had released our jackets, our pursuer, our captor, our hero: he knew we weren't going anywhere. We all played by the rules. Mikey and I unzipped our jackets. I pulled off my sopping mittens. Our tracks multiplied in the backyard's new snow. We had been breaking new snow all morning. We didn't look at each other. I was cherishing my excitement. The man's lower pants legs were wet; his cuffs were full of snow, and there was a prow of snow beneath them on his shoes and socks. Some trees bordered the little flat backyard, some messy winter trees. There was no one around: a clearing in a grove, and we the only players.

It was a long time before he could speak. I had some difficulty at first recalling why 17 we were there. My lips felt swollen; I couldn't see out of the sides of my eyes; I kept coughing.

"You stupid kids," he began perfunctorily. 18

We listened perfunctorily indeed, if we listened at all, for the chewing out was 19 redundant, a mere formality, and beside the point. The point was that he had chased us passionately without giving up, and so he had caught us. Now he came down to earth. I wanted the glory to last forever.

But how could the glory have lasted forever? We could have run through every back- 20 yard in North America until we got to Panama. But when he trapped us at the lip of the Panama Canal, what precisely could he have done to prolong the drama of the chase and cap its glory? I brooded about this for the next few years. He could only have fried Mikey Fahey and me in boiling oil, say, or dismembered us piecemeal, or staked us to anthills. None of which I really wanted, and none of which any adult was likely to do, even in the spirit of fun. He could only chew us out there in the Panamanian jungle, after months or years of exalting pursuit. He could only begin, "You stupid kids," and continue in his ordinary Pittsburgh accent with his normal righteous anger and the usual common sense.

If in that snowy backyard the driver of the black Buick had cut off our heads, 21 Mikey's and mine, I would have died happy, for nothing has required so much of me since as being chased all over Pittsburgh in the middle of winter—running terrified, exhausted—by this sainted, skinny, furious redheaded man who wished to have a word with us. I don't know how he found his way back to his car.

READING FOR MEANING

For help with
summarizing,
see Chapter 2,
pp. 24–25.

1. **Read to Summarize.** Write a sentence or two explaining what happened and why.

2. **Read to Respond.** Write a paragraph analyzing your initial reactions to Dillard's story, focusing on anything that seems surprising, such as the iceball scene (pars. 6–7) or the apparent contradiction between Dillard's description of the man who chased her as a "hero" (par. 16) and her dismissal of what he said (par. 19).

For help
analyzing
assumptions,
see Chapter 2,
pp. 28–29.

3. **Read to Analyze Assumptions.** Write a paragraph or two analyzing an assumption you find intriguing in Dillard's story. Here are some ideas:

   Assumptions about the value of rules and fair play. Dillard uses words like *rules* (par. 16) and *unfair* (par. 6) to suggest there are commonly accepted principles of conduct or ethics for childhood games that determine what is considered fair or right. To think critically about the assumptions in this essay related to rules and fairness, consider questions like these:

You may also
try looking for
patterns of
opposition; see
Chapter 2,
pp. 35–36.

   - What unwritten rule do you think the man assumes the kids have broken? Who would agree (or disagree) that what the kids did was wrong? Why?

   - Even though the young Dillard admires his persistence, why might some readers question the man's decision to chase and reprimand the kids? Do you think he was right? Why or why not?

   Assumptions about the superiority of boys' play. Dillard describes the way the neighborhood boys taught her to play football, claiming that "[n]othing girls did could compare with it" (par. 1).

   - What does Dillard seem to be saying about social expectations regarding gender at the time (1950s) and place (Pittsburgh) that she is describing? To what extent do you share these expectations? Why?

   - How have assumptions about the kinds of games considered appropriate for girls and boys changed in American culture today, if at all?

READING LIKE A WRITER

NARRATING THE STORY

Stories of all kinds, including autobiographical stories, try to arouse the reader's curiosity, often by structuring the story around a *conflict* that grows increasingly intense until it reaches a high point or **climax.** The structural elements can be visualized in the form of a *dramatic arc* (see Figure 3.1, p. 53) and can help us analyze narratives like the chase Dillard remembers from her childhood.

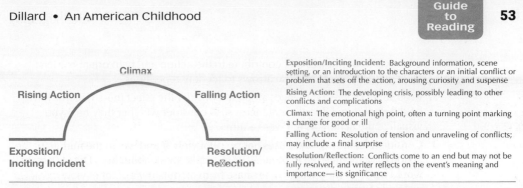

Exposition/Inciting Incident: Background information, scene setting, or an introduction to the characters *or* an initial conflict or problem that sets off the action, arousing curiosity and suspense

Rising Action: The developing crisis, possibly leading to other conflicts and complications

Climax: The emotional high point, often a turning point marking a change for good or ill

Falling Action: Resolution of tension and unraveling of conflicts; may include a final surprise

Resolution/Reflection: Conflicts come to an end but may not be fully resolved, and writer reflects on the event's meaning and importance—its significance

FIGURE 3.1 DRAMATIC ARC   The shape of the arc varies. Not all stories devote the same amount of space to each element, and some may omit elements.

To intensify the rising action of the chase, Dillard constructs a dramatic *action sequence* by using *action verbs* (instead of static verbs like *is* and *was*). In passages, like the one below, the frantic activity signaled by the verbs is amplified by a series of *prepositional phrases* that show movement through space.

Action verbs	He chased Mikey and me around the yellow house and up a backyard
Prepositional phrases	path . . . under a low tree, up a bank, through a hedge. [. . .] We smashed . . . entered . . . and ran. . . . (par. 12)

Other intensifying strategies include the repetition of key words and sentence patterns:

Repetition	He chased us silently, block after block. He chased us silently. . . . (par. 13)
	He impelled us forward; we compelled him to follow our route. (par. 14)

Whereas the exact repetitions in the first example suggest the experience of being chased relentlessly, the sentence pattern repetition in the second example (*He impelled us . . . we compelled him*) emphasizes the connection between the man (*He*) and the children (*we*).

To keep readers oriented, writers often provide pointers such as *transitional words and phrases*, *verb tense*, and *adverbs and prepositions marking location in time and space*:

Time and date	On one weekday morning after Christmas . . . (par. 3)
Adverbs/Prepositions of time	I had just embarked on the iceball project when we heard . . .
Verb tenses showing simultaneous action	(par. 7)

Analyze & Write

Write a paragraph analyzing Dillard's construction of an action sequence.

1. Skim paragraphs 11–13, circling the action verbs, underlining adverbs and prepositions indicating movement in time and space, and highlighting any

other words or phrases that contribute to the action and help orient readers. Note the verb tenses and use arrows to identify repetitions.

2. Read some of these sentences aloud to consider the effect these patterns have on the rhythm of Dillard's sentences. Also consider whether they help you visualize the action, as if it were a film.

3. Consider also how Dillard uses her point of view (*I* and *we*) in the middle of the action to dramatize the narrative. For example, think about how Dillard's story would be different if we saw the chase from an outsider's point of view watching from a distance.

Describing Places

Whether autobiography centers on an event or a person, it may also include some *description* of places. Because Dillard is describing a chase through her neighborhood, she uses a series of prepositional phrases that indicate direction or location in space. To provide specific information about the places and help readers visualize the scene, autobiographers rely on the describing strategies of *naming* objects and *detailing* their colors, shapes, and textures:

Prepositional   . . . around the yellow house and up a backyard path we knew by heart;
phrase   under a low tree, up a bank, through a hedge, down some snowy steps,
Naming   and across the grocery store's delivery driveway. (par. 12)
Detailing

In addition to using these sensory images, writers may characterize and evaluate features of the scene ("perfect iceball" and "scruffy backyard" [pars. 6, 12]). Occasionally, they also use *comparisons* in the form of a *simile* or *metaphor* to add suggestive images that contribute to the overall or *dominant impression*:

Metaphor   The cars traveled Reynolds Street slowly and evenly; they were targets all
                  but wrapped in red ribbons, cream puffs. (par. 3)

Simile   The cars' tires laid behind them on the snowy street a complex trail of
                  beige chunks like crenellated castle walls. (par. 5)

Analyze & Write

Write a paragraph analyzing and evaluating Dillard's use of the describing strategies of naming, detailing, and comparing to make the scene come to life for you.

1. Find an example where Dillard uses naming and detailing to make her description especially vivid and informative. Consider whether the names she gives to the objects in the example you chose are *concrete* or *abstract* and what attributes or sense impressions the details convey. What is the dominant impression you get from this description of the scene?

2. Choose a simile or metaphor that stands out for you. How does it help you imagine what the place looked and felt like to Dillard? How does the comparison reinforce, extend, or complicate the dominant impression?

Presenting People

The describing strategies of naming and detailing are often also used to describe people, as in these brief descriptions of some of Dillard's playmates:

Naming   The oldest two Fahey boys were there — Mikey and Peter — polite blond
Detailing   boys . . . (par. 4)

Writers not only depict what people look like, but they sometimes also characterize or evaluate their behavior and personality. Often, just a few well-chosen details about the way a person looks, dresses, talks, or acts will be sufficient to give readers a vivid impression of the person:

> . . . Billy Paul and Mackie Kean too, from across Reynolds, where the boys grew up dark and furious, grew up skinny, knowing, and skilled. (par. 4)

In this example, the word *dark* may be a literal description as well as a metaphorical marker of ethnicity or race. It may also describe the boys' attitude, making their snowball throwing seem less innocuous than Dillard's.

Analyze & Write

Write a paragraph exploring the dominant impression you get of the man who chased Dillard and Mikey.

1. Underline the words in paragraphs 10, 16, and 21 that describe the man physically, and circle those that characterize or evaluate him.

2. Skim paragraph 18 and the last sentence of paragraph 20, where Dillard presents the man through dialogue. Underline the details Dillard uses to describe how the man looks and sounds. What does Dillard's choice of words like "perfunctorily" (par. 18) and "normal" (par. 20) suggest about her evaluation of him? How does this evaluation affect the impression you get of the man?

Conveying the Autobiographical Significance

Autobiographers convey the significance of an event or a person in two ways: by *showing* or *telling*. Through your analysis of how Dillard narrates the story, presents people, and describes places, you have looked at some of the ways she *shows* the event's significance and creates a dominant impression. Now consider what Dillard *tells* readers. For example, when Dillard writes in the opening paragraphs about boys teaching her to play football and baseball, she is telling why these experiences were memorable and important.

Autobiographers usually tell both what they remember thinking and feeling *at the time* and what they think and feel now *as they write about the past.* Readers must infer from the ideas and the writer's choice of words whether the words convey the writer's *past* or *present perspective* — remembered feelings and thoughts or current ones. For example, consider whether you agree with this analysis, and why or why not.

Remembered feelings and thoughts	Some boys taught me to play football. This was fine sport. You thought up a new strategy for every play and whispered it to the others. (par. 1)
Present perspective	I got in trouble throwing snowballs, and have seldom been happier since. (par. 2)

Analyze & Write

Write a paragraph or two analyzing Dillard's use of showing and telling to create autobiographical significance.

1. Reread paragraphs 19–21. Choose one or two examples that convey Dillard's present perspective as she looks back and reflects on her childhood experience. Also choose one or two examples that seem to be Dillard's remembered feelings and thoughts, how she felt at the time the event occurred. How can you tell the difference?

2. Compare Dillard's remembered and present perspectives. Has her thinking changed over time? If so, how? If you detect a note of self-irony in her tone, a suggestion that she is making fun of her younger self, where do you see it and what does it tell you about Dillard's adult perspective on her younger self?

READINGS

David Sedaris

Me Talk Pretty One Day

David Sedaris, a humorist and social critic, is a prolific essayist, short story writer, and dramatist (in collaboration with his sister, Amy Sedaris), whose radio pieces have been featured on the popular podcast *This American Life*. Recipient of the Thurber Prize for American Humor, his writing appears regularly in the *New Yorker* magazine, and he has published more than a dozen best-selling book collections including *Me Talk Pretty One Day* (2000), from which this selection about his French language class is excerpted.

- **Before you read,** think about whether you have ever been in a "sink or swim" situation, as Sedaris is in this class. If you were in a similar situation, how did you feel at the time?

- **As you read,** notice any places where Sedaris uses humor. How does his use of humor affect your attitude toward Sedaris and the story he tells?

1   I've moved to Paris with hopes of learning the language. My school is an easy ten-minute walk from my apartment, and on the first day of class I arrived early, watching as the returning students greeted one another in the school lobby. Vacations were recounted, and questions were raised concerning mutual friends with names like Kang and Vlatnya. Regardless of their nationalities, everyone spoke in what sounded to me like excellent French. Some accents were better than others, but the students exhibited an ease and confidence I found intimidating. As an added discomfort, they were all young, attractive, and well dressed, causing me to feel not unlike Pa Kettle trapped backstage after a fashion show.

What does this opening exposition *lead you to expect will happen?*

2   The first day of class was nerve-racking because I knew I'd be expected to perform. That's the way they do it here — it's everybody into the language pool, sink or swim. The teacher marched in, deeply tanned from a recent vacation, and proceeded to rattle off a series of administrative announcements. I've spent quite a few summers in Normandy, and I took a month-long French class before leaving New York. I'm not completely in the dark, yet I understood only half of what this woman was saying.

What first impression do you get of Sedaris from his remembered feelings and thoughts?

3   "If you have not *meimslsxp* or *lgpdmurct* by this time, then you should not be in this room. Has everyone *apzkiubjxow*? Everyone? Good, we shall

How do you react to this first bit of dialogue?

begin." She spread out her lesson plan and sighed, saying, "All right, then, who knows the alphabet?"

It was startling because (a) I hadn't been asked that question in a while 4
and (b) I realized, while laughing, that I myself did *not* know the alphabet. They're the same letters, but in France they're pronounced differently. I know the shape of the alphabet but had no idea what it actually sounded like.

"Ahh." The teacher went to the board and sketched the letter *a*. "Do we 5
have anyone in the room whose first name commences with an *ahh*?"

In pars. 6–8, high-light an example of naming, detailing, and comparing. What impression do these describing strategies give of the Annas? Of Sedaris?

Two Polish Annas raised their hands, and the teacher instructed them to 6
present themselves by stating their names, nationalities, occupations, and a brief list of things they liked and disliked in this world. The first Anna hailed from an industrial town outside of Warsaw and had front teeth the size of tombstones. She worked as a seamstress, enjoyed quiet times with friends, and hated the mosquito.

"Oh, really," the teacher said. "How very interesting. I thought that 7
everyone loved the mosquito, but here, in front of all the world, you claim to detest him. How is it that we've been blessed with someone as unique and original as you? Tell us, please."

The seamstress did not understand what was being said but knew that 8
this was an occasion for shame. Her rabbity mouth huffed for breath, and she stared down at her lap as though the appropriate comeback were stitched somewhere alongside the zipper of her slacks.

The second Anna learned from the first and claimed to love sunshine 9
and detest lies. It sounded like a translation of one of those Playmate of the Month data sheets, the answers always written in the same loopy handwriting. "Turn-ons: Mom's famous five-alarm chili! Turnoffs: insecurity and guys who come on too strong!!!!"

The two Polish Annas surely had clear notions of what they loved and 10
hated, but like the rest of us, they were limited in terms of vocabulary, and this made them appear less than sophisticated. The teacher forged on, and we learned that Carlos, the Argentine bandonion player, loved wine, music, and, in his words, "making sex with the womens of the world." Next came a beautiful young Yugoslav who identified herself as an optimist, saying that she loved everything that life had to offer.

In pars. 11–13, how does alternating between the teacher and Sedaris intensify the drama?

The teacher licked her lips, revealing a hint of the saucebox we would 11
later come to know. She crouched low for her attack, placed her hands on the young woman's desk, and leaned close, saying, "Oh yeah? And do you love your little war?"

While the optimist struggled to defend herself, I scrambled to think of an 12
answer to what had obviously become a trick question. How often is one asked what he loves in this world? More to the point, how often is one asked and then publicly ridiculed for his answer? I recalled my mother, flushed with wine, pounding the tabletop late one night, saying, "Love? I love a good steak cooked rare. I love my cat, and I love . . ." My sisters and

I leaned forward, waiting to hear our names. "Tums," our mother said. "I love Tums."

13　　The teacher killed some time accusing the Yugoslavian girl of master-minding a program of genocide, and I jotted frantic notes in the margins of my pad. While I can honestly say that I love leafing through medical text-books devoted to severe dermatological conditions, the hobby is beyond the reach of my French vocabulary, and acting it out would only have invited controversy.

14　　When called upon, I delivered an effortless list of things that I detest: blood sausage, intestinal pâtés, brain pudding. I'd learned these words the hard way. Having given it some thought, I then declared my love for IBM typewriters, the French word for *bruise*, and my electric floor waxer. It was a short list, but still I managed to mispronounce *IBM* and assign the wrong gender to both the floor waxer and the typewriter. The teacher's reaction led me to believe that these mistakes were capital crimes in the country of France.

15　　"Were you always this *palicmkrexis*?" she asked. "Even a *fiuscrzsa tici-welmun* knows that a typewriter is feminine."

16　　I absorbed as much of her abuse as I could understand, thinking—but not saying—that I find it ridiculous to assign a gender to an inanimate object incapable of disrobing and making an occasional fool of itself. Why refer to Lady Crack Pipe or Good Sir Dishrag when these things could never live up to all that their sex implied?

17　　The teacher proceeded to belittle everyone from German Eva, who hated laziness, to Japanese Yukari, who loved paintbrushes and soap. Ital-ian, Thai, Dutch, Korean, and Chinese—we all left class foolishly believing that the worst was over. She'd shaken us up a little, but surely that was just an act designed to weed out the deadweight. We didn't know it then, but the coming months would teach us what it was like to spend time in the presence of a wild animal, something completely unpredictable. Her tem-perament was not based on a series of good and bad days but, rather, good and bad moments. We soon learned to dodge chalk and protect our heads and stomachs whenever she approached us with a question. She hadn't yet punched anyone, but it seemed wise to protect ourselves against the inevitable.

18　　Though we were forbidden to speak anything but French, the teacher would occasionally use us to practice any of her five fluent languages.

19　　"I hate you," she said to me one afternoon. Her English was flawless. "I really, really hate you." Call me sensitive, but I couldn't help but take it personally.

20　　After being singled out as a lazy *kfdtinvfm*, I took to spending four hours a night on my homework, putting in even more time whenever we were assigned an essay. I suppose I could have gotten by with less, but I was determined to create some sort of identity for myself: David the hard

What leads Sedaris to assume the teacher is behaving inappropriately?

Compare Sedaris's initial reaction (par. 16) to his subsequent behav-ior and feelings (pars. 20–24).

worker, David the cut-up. We'd have one of those "complete this sentence" exercises, and I'd fool with the thing for hours, invariably settling on something like "A quick run around the lake? I'd love to! Just give me a moment while I strap on my wooden leg." The teacher, through word and action, conveyed the message that if this was my idea of an identity, she wanted nothing to do with it.

My fear and discomfort crept beyond the borders of the classroom and 21 accompanied me out onto the wide boulevards. Stopping for a coffee, asking directions, depositing money in my bank account: these things were out of the question, as they involved having to speak. Before beginning school, there'd been no shutting me up, but now I was convinced that everything I said was wrong. When the phone rang, I ignored it. If someone asked me a question, I pretended to be deaf. I knew my fear was getting the best of me when I started wondering why they don't sell cuts of meat in vending machines.

How does Sedaris show time passing and also build to the story's climax? Where is the climax? How do you know?

My only comfort was the knowledge that I was not alone. Huddled in 22 the hallways and making the most of our pathetic French, my fellow students and I engaged in the sort of conversation commonly overheard in refugee camps.

"Sometime me cry alone at night."   23

"That be common for I, also, but be more strong, you. Much work and 24 someday you talk pretty. People start love you soon. Maybe tomorrow, okay."

Unlike the French class I had taken in New York, here there was no 25 sense of competition. When the teacher poked a shy Korean in the eyelid with a freshly sharpened pencil, we took no comfort in the fact that, unlike Hyeyoon Cho, we all knew the irregular past tense of the verb *to defeat*. In all fairness, the teacher hadn't meant to stab the girl, but neither did she spend much time apologizing, saying only, "Well, you should have been *vkkdyo* more *kdeynfulh*."

Over time it became impossible to believe that any of us would ever 26 improve. Fall arrived and it rained every day, meaning we would now be scolded for the water dripping from our coats and umbrellas. It was mid-October when the teacher singled me out, saying, "Every day spent with you is like having a cesarean section."

And it struck me that, for the first time since arriving in France, I could 27 understand every word that someone was saying.

Understanding doesn't mean that you can suddenly speak the language. 28 Far from it. It's a small step, nothing more, yet its rewards are intoxicating and deceptive. The teacher continued her diatribe and I settled back, bathing in the subtle beauty of each new curse and insult.

"You exhaust me with your foolishness and reward my efforts with 29 nothing but pain, do you understand me?"

What is the story's significance? Is the teacher good, after all?

The world opened up, and it was with great joy that I responded, "I 30 know the thing that you speak exact now. Talk me more, you, plus, please, plus."

Tom Ruprecht

In Too Deep

Tom Ruprecht is the author of the book *George W. Bush: An Unauthorized Oral History* (2007) and was an Emmy Award–nominated writer for the *Late Show with David Letterman*. With Craig Finn, from the band the Hold Steady, he co-wrote a film adaptation of *Fargo Rock City* based on the book by Chuck Klosterman. His writing has also appeared in periodicals, including the *Wall Street Journal* and the *New York Times Magazine*, where "In Too Deep" appeared in 2011.

Throughout the reading selection, Ruprecht refers to various current events that readers of the *New York Times Magazine* in 2011 would probably have been aware of: that Osama Bin Laden hid in a cave after 9/11/2001; that Aron Ralston amputated his own arm to escape a half-ton boulder pinning him to a canyon wall (an event that was depicted in the 2010 film *127 Hours,* starring James Franco); that the 2010 rescue of Chilean miners trapped underground for six weeks was greeted with worldwide jubilation.

- **Before you read,** think about why Ruprecht expresses concern in the opening paragraph about not looking "cool." What might motivate him?

- **As you read,** consider Ruprecht's references to current events and their likely effect on his original audience and on readers, like you, who read the article years later.

It's impossible to look cool when you're part of a tour group. Instead of bravely explor- 1 ing on your own, you've chosen to be led around like a frightened kindergartner. My wife and I were on a tour bus while in Hawaii recently, and our guide made me feel even more uncool because he was very rugged and handsome. After a couple of hours, he announced we were stopping for what he called "snack break," as if we actually were kindergartners. He then mentioned that down a nearby path there was a cave we could check out. Not being a terrorist mastermind, I've never had a huge desire to hang out in a cave. But the opinion of absolute strangers means a lot to me, and I was desperate to differentiate myself from the other travelers in this cool, rugged guide's eyes.

"I'm going to the cave," I declared and marched down the path to check out its 2 mouth. The mouth. That's as far as I was willing to go.

When I arrived, I found another guy from the group standing there. 3

"Hey, I'm Ernie. I'm a spelunker." 4

Ernie said he was going to take a quick look in the cave and invited me to come 5 along. I politely declined. He insisted. I thought of my dad, who has encouraged me to say "yes!" to every opportunity while traveling. During a trip to Puerto Rico in the '70s, it was this *carpe diem* spirit that led my dad to play tennis all week long with the adult-film star Harry Reems—the same Harry Reems who was in *Deep Throat* (not that you recognized the name, dear reader), though true aficionados prefer his later work, in films like *For Your Thighs Only.* So I entered the mouth of the cave.

Thirty feet in, I began telling Ernie we should probably head back. But he simply   6 rushed ahead, and because he had the flashlight, I had no choice but to follow. I soon found myself slithering through tight spaces in order to get to slightly tighter places. I panicked. It was only a matter of time before I would be wedged between rocks. I began looking around for a knife, so I could pre-emptively chop off my arm like James Franco in that movie I was too scared to see.

Things Ernie did made me question his spelunking expertise. For instance, there   7 was a weird greenish-whitish substance on the cave's roof. "That's probably sodium," Ernie said, and he swabbed a finger on the slimy substance and stuck it in his mouth. He muttered, "That's not sodium." I believe it was Ernie's pride that kept him from adding, "I think it's bat guano."

We were a good mile inside the cave when Ernie looked at me, gave a little laugh   8 and then turned off the flashlight. A mile deep in the cave. "Scared?" he whispered. Then he chuckled, turned the flashlight back on and said, "Nah, the thing you should really be worried about is what would happen if there were an earthquake right now." Seeing my terrified expression, Ernie said, "Oh, hadn't you thought about that?" I had to get out of there. People were waiting for us. More important, my wife was above ground chatting with a ruggedly handsome tour guide. I implored Ernie to turn back. He reluctantly agreed. On the way, we came upon a fork in the cave. I asked if we should go to the right or the left. Ernie, the great spelunker, replied: "Oh, I have a ter-rible sense of direction." So Ernie had me choose. I, of course, picked the wrong way. We wandered aimlessly for 10 minutes, wondering if we were passing the same generic rocks we passed on the way in or if we were passing slightly different generic rocks. If only there had been a spelunker there, I would have asked him.

Eventually Ernie's spelunking expertise did kick in. He realized we were headed   9 down the wrong path. We doubled back, took the other path and, finally, saw a sliver of sunlight. I popped out of the cave, expecting a welcome worthy of a Chilean miner. Instead I was greeted by 11 annoyed people whose trip Ernie and I had hindered. As my wife hugged me, she whispered, "People are kinda mad."

The guide reprimanded us for endangering our lives and delaying the others. But as   10 we started back to the bus, he pulled Ernie and me aside and said in a low voice, "Don't tell anybody, but I think what you guys did was seriously kick-ass!" The rest of the day I walked around with a happy smile, like the proudest little kindergartner you've ever seen.

READING FOR MEANING

For help with summarizing, see Chapter 2, pp. 24–25.

1. **Read to Summarize.** Write a sentence or two explaining what happened in the cave and what it reveals about Ruprecht.

2. **Read to Respond.** Write a paragraph exploring your reactions to Ruprecht's autobiographical story. For example, consider anything that seems contradictory,

such as Ruprecht's comment that "the opinion of absolute strangers means a lot to me" (par. 1) or the guide's saying one thing to the group and something else to Ruprecht and Ernie (par. 10).

3. **Read to Analyze Assumptions.** Write a paragraph or two analyzing an assumption you find intriguing in Ruprecht's essay. For example:

For help analyzing assumptions, see Chapter 2, pp. 28–29.

Assumptions about the **carpe diem** *spirit.* Ruprecht explains that he agreed to enter the cave because he remembered his father's encouragement "to say 'yes!' to every opportunity" (par. 5). *Carpe diem*, Latin for "seize the day," assumes that you should take advantage of an opportunity when it arises because you may not have another chance like it.

- How does Ruprecht's opportunity compare to the one his father did not pass up, of playing tennis with a porn star? Do you think the author is being ironic about his dad or serious? How can you tell?

- Ruprecht says that about thirty feet into the cave, he "had no choice but to follow" Ernie (par. 6). Why would he think this? How does this feeling that he has "no choice" contrast with his earlier decision to seize the day?

Assumptions about wanting to impress others. Ruprecht admits that the person he really wants to impress is the "cool," "very rugged and handsome" guide (par. 1). To think critically about the assumptions in this essay related to the desire to impress others, consider questions like these:

- Why do you think Ruprecht is so concerned about how he appears to others, particularly to the tour guide? What does Ruprecht's description of the guide suggest about his attitude (par. 1)?

- Ruprecht also points out that the guide talks to the tourists "as if we actually were kindergartners" (par. 1). How is his decision to go into the cave with Ernie a reaction to what he sees as the guide's attitude toward the tourists? What does his behavior tell readers about Ruprecht?

READING LIKE A WRITER

DESCRIBING A PLACE

To describe a place, a writer establishes one or more vantage points. In the following examples, we see that Dillard begins with a stationary vantage point to describe the cars coming down the street toward her. When the chase begins, she switches to a moving vantage point to describe where she is in relation to the man following close behind as they move through the neighborhood.

Stationary vantage point — We were standing up to our boot tops in snow on a front yard on trafficked Reynolds Street, waiting for cars. The cars traveled Reynolds Street slowly and evenly; they were targets. (par. 3)

Moving
vantage
point

> He ran after us, and we ran away from him, up the snowy Reynolds
> sidewalk. [. . .] He chased Mikey and me around the yellow house and
> up a backyard path we knew by heart: under a low tree, up a bank,
> through a hedge . . . (pars. 10, 12)

Analyze & Write

Write a paragraph or two analyzing how Ruprecht describes the cave.

1. Reread paragraphs 6–9 to identify the vantage point(s) Ruprecht takes in describing the cave.

2. Also note his use of the describing strategies of naming, detailing, and comparing. What objects in the cave does Ruprecht name and detail? Which sense(s) does he use to give readers an impression of what it was like in the cave?

Saira Shah

Longing to Belong

Saira Shah (b. 1964) is a journalist and documentary filmmaker. The daughter of an Afghan father and Indian mother, she was born and educated in England. After graduating from the School of Oriental and African Studies at London University, Shah began her career as a freelance journalist and eventually became a war correspondent, receiving the Courage under Fire and Television Journalist of the Year awards for her risky reporting on conflicts in some of the world's most troubled areas. She is best known in the United States for her undercover documentary films about the Taliban rule in Afghanistan, *Beneath the Veil* (2001) and *Unholy War* (2002). "Longing to Belong," originally published in the *New York Times Magazine* in 2003, is adapted from Shah's autobiography, *The Storyteller's Daughter* (2003), which relates her search to understand her father's homeland of Afghanistan.

- **Before you read,** think about any experiences you might have had as an outsider longing to belong, such as when you moved to a new school or joined a club.

- **As you read,** think about how Shah conveys her search for her ethnic identity and the sense of cultural dislocation she experiences.

The day he disclosed his matrimonial ambitions for me, my uncle sat me at his right 1 during lunch. This was a sign of special favor, as it allowed him to feed me choice tidbits from his own plate. It was by no means an unadulterated pleasure. He would often generously withdraw a half-chewed delicacy from his mouth and lovingly cram it into mine—an Afghan habit with which I have since tried to come to terms. It was his way of telling me that I was valued, part of the family.

My brother and sister, Tahir and Safia, and my elderly aunt Amina and I were all 2 attending the wedding of my uncle's son. Although my uncle's home was closer than I'd ever been, I was not yet inside Afghanistan. This branch of my family lived in Peshawar, Pakistan. On seeing two unmarried daughters in the company of a female chaperone, my uncle obviously concluded that we had been sent to be married. I was taken aback by the visceral longing I felt to be part of this world. I had never realized that I had been starved of anything. Now, at 17, I discovered that like a princess in a fairy tale, I had been cut off from my origins. This was the point in the tale where, simply by walking through a magical door, I could recover my gardens and palaces. If I allowed my uncle to arrange a marriage for me, I would belong.

Over the next few days, the man my family wished me to marry was introduced 3 into the inner sanctum. He was a distant cousin. His luxuriant black mustache was generally considered to compensate for his lack of height. I was told breathlessly that he was a fighter pilot in the Pakistani Air Force. As an outsider, he wouldn't have been permitted to meet an unmarried girl. But as a relative, he had free run of the house. Whenever I appeared, a female cousin would fling a child into his arms. He'd pose with it, whiskers twitching, while the women cooed their admiration.

A huge cast of relatives had assembled to see my uncle's son marry. The wedding lasted nearly 14 days and ended with a reception. The bride and groom sat on an elevated stage to receive greetings. While the groom was permitted to laugh and chat, the bride was required to sit perfectly still, her eyes demurely lowered. I didn't see her move for four hours.

Watching this *tableau vivant* of a submissive Afghan bride, I knew that marriage would never be my easy route to the East. I could live in my father's mythological homeland only through the eyes of the storyteller. In my desire to experience the fairy tale, I had overlooked the staggeringly obvious: the storyteller was a man. If I wanted freedom, I would have to cut my own path. I began to understand why my uncle's wife had resorted to using religion to regain some control—at least in her own home. Her piety gave her license to impose her will on others.

My putative fiancé returned to Quetta, from where he sent a constant flow of lavish gifts. I was busy examining my hoard when my uncle's wife announced that he was on the phone. My intended was a favorite of hers; she had taken it upon herself to promote the match. As she handed me the receiver, he delivered a line culled straight from a Hindi movie: "We shall have a love-match, *ach-cha*?" Enough was enough. I slammed down the phone and went to find Aunt Amina. When she had heard me out, she said: "I'm glad that finally you've stopped this silly wild goose chase for your roots. I'll have to extricate you from this mess. Wait here while I put on something more impressive." As a piece of Islamic one-upmanship, she returned wearing not one but three head scarves of different colors.

My uncle's wife was sitting on her prayer platform in the drawing room. Amina stormed in, scattering servants before her like chaff. "Your relative . . . ," was Amina's opening salvo, ". . . has been making obscene remarks to my niece." Her mouth opened, but before she could find her voice, Amina fired her heaviest guns: "Over the *telephone*!"

"How dare you!" her rival began.

It gave Amina exactly the opportunity she needed to move in for the kill. "What? Do you support this lewd conduct? Are we living in an American movie? Since when have young people of mixed sexes been permitted to speak to each other *on the telephone*? Let alone to talk—as I regret to inform you your nephew did—of love! Since when has love had anything to do with marriage? What a dangerous and absurd concept!"

My Peshawari aunt was not only outclassed; she was out-Islamed too. "My niece is a rose that hasn't been plucked," Amina said. "It is my task as her chaperone to ensure that this happy state of affairs continues. A match under such circumstances is quite out of the question. The engagement is off." My uncle's wife lost her battle for moral suprem- acy and, it seemed, her battle for sanity as well. In a gruff, slack-jawed way that I found unappealing, she made a sharp, inhuman sound that sounded almost like a bark.

READING FOR MEANING

1. **Read to Summarize.** Write a few sentences explaining what happened and the roles played by Shah's two aunts.

   For help with summarizing, see Chapter 2, pp. 24–25.

2. **Read to Respond.** Write a paragraph about anything that seems surprising, such as Shah's uncle's assumption that she and her sister were sent to Pakistan "to be married" (par. 2) or Shah's realization that "[i]f I wanted freedom, I would have to cut my own path" (par. 5).

3. **Read to Analyze Assumptions.** Write a paragraph or two analyzing an assumption you find intriguing in Shah's essay. For example:

   For help analyzing assumptions, see Chapter 2, pp. 28–29.

   Assumptions about the values underlying cultural differences. Shah begins her story by describing how her uncle feeds her (par. 1). Shah seems ambivalent about this "Afghan habit" — expressing distaste as well as gratitude.

   - What do you think are the beliefs or values underlying Shah's mixed feelings about her uncle's "Afghan habit"?
   - If you have experienced cultural difference, what was your attitude and what values affected your way of thinking?

   Assumptions about the influence of fairy tales. Shah describes herself as "a princess in a fairy tale" (par. 2) in her father's "mythological homeland" (par. 5), but romantic stories about princesses such as *Cinderella* and *The Little Mermaid* are also popular in America.

   - What are girls — and perhaps also boys — taught by the fairy tales with which you are familiar?
   - How does Shah achieve a critical perspective toward her own "desire to experience the fairy tale" (par. 5)?

READING LIKE A WRITER

NARRATING THE STORY

Like most autobiographers, Shah employs elements of the dramatic arc to arouse readers' curiosity and build suspense, leading us to wonder what will result of her uncle and his wife's "matrimonial ambitions" for her (par. 1). The opening scene (par. 1) dramatizes the intimate parental attitude her uncle adopts toward her, initiating the matchmaking story. Paragraph 2 provides exposition, using Shah's remembered feelings and thoughts to explain her internal conflict that is ultimately acted out in the power struggle between her uncle's wife and Aunt Amina.

Analyze & Write

Write a paragraph or two analyzing how Shah constructs her narrative.

1. Look back at the dramatic arc (Figure 3.1, p. 53) and reread Shah's story, noting in the margin where you find additional *exposition*, *rising action*, *climax*, *falling action*, and *resolution* and *reflection*. (Don't be surprised if some of the elements arc very brief or missing altogether.)

2. How useful is the dramatic arc as a tool for analyzing Shah's autobiographical story? How does it help you understand how different scenes relate to one another and how they dramatize the central conflict?

A Special Reading Strategy

Comparing and Contrasting Related Readings: Shah's "Longing to Belong" and Desmond-Harris's "Tupac and My Non-Thug Life"

For help comparing and contrasting related readings, see Chapter 2, pp. 37–39.

Compare and contrast the autobiographical narratives by Saira Shah (p. 65) and Jenée Desmond-Harris (p. 69), thinking about issues such as these:

- Both stories show teenagers in search of their cultural identity. How are their searches similar and different?

- Both authors explore what Desmond-Harris calls "the contradictory textures" of the alternative identity they are trying on (par. 9). How do they resolve their contradictory feelings, if at all?

Jenée Desmond-Harris

Tupac and My Non-Thug Life

Jenée Desmond-Harris is a staff writer at the *Root*, an online magazine dedicated to African American news and culture. She writes about the intersection of race, politics, and culture in a variety of genres. She has also contributed to *Time* magazine, MSNBC's *Powerwall*, and *xoJane* on topics ranging from her relationship with her grandmother, to the political significance of Michelle Obama's hair, to the stereotypes that hinder giving to black-teen mentoring programs. She has provided television commentary on CNN, MSNBC, and Current TV. Desmond-Harris is a graduate of Howard University and Harvard Law School. The selection below was published in the *Root* in 2011. It chronicles Desmond-Harris's reaction to the murder of rap icon Tupac Shakur in a Las Vegas drive-by shooting in 1996. She mentions Tupac's mother, Afeni, as well as the "East Coast–West Coast war" — the rivalry between Tupac and the Notorious B.I.G., who was suspected of being involved in Tupac's murder.

- **Before you read,** recall a public event that affected you. Reflect on why something that didn't affect you personally nevertheless had an emotional impact on you.

- **As you read,** consider how the photograph that appeared in the *Root* article and that is reproduced here contributes to readers' understanding of the young Desmond-Harris's reaction to the news of Tupac's death. How does the photo influence your understanding of the author's persona, or self-presentation?

I learned about Tupac's death when I got home from cheerleading practice that Friday afternoon in September 1996. I was a sophomore in high school in Mill Valley, Calif. I remember trotting up my apartment building's stairs, physically tired but buzzing with the frenetic energy and possibilities for change that accompany fall and a new school year. I'd been cautiously allowing myself to think during the walk home about a topic that felt frighteningly taboo (at least in my world, where discussion of race was avoided as delicately as obesity or mental illness): what it meant to be biracial and on the school's mostly white cheerleading team instead of the mostly black dance team. I remember acknowledging, to the sound of an 8-count that still pounded in my head as I walked through the door, that I didn't really have a choice: I could memorize a series of stiff and precise motions but couldn't actually dance.

My private musings on identity and belonging—not original in the least, but novel to me—were interrupted when my mom heard me slam the front door and drop my bags: *"Your friend died!"* she called out from another room. Confused silence. *"You know, that rapper you and Thea love so much!"*

MOURNING A DEATH IN VEGAS

The news was turned on, with coverage of the deadly Vegas shooting. Phone calls   3
were made. Ultimately my best friend, Thea, and I were left to our own 15-year-old
devices to mourn that weekend. Her mother and stepfather were out of town. Their
expansive, million-dollar home was perched on a hillside less than an hour from
Tupac's former stomping grounds in Oakland and Marin City. Of course, her home
was also worlds away from both places.

We couldn't "pour out" much alcohol undetected for a libation, so we limited our-   4
selves to doing somber shots of liqueur from a well-stocked cabinet. One each. Tipsy,
in a high-ceilinged kitchen surrounded by hardwood floors and Zen flower arrangements, we baked cookies for his mother. We packed them up to ship to Afeni with a
handmade card. ("Did we really do that?" I asked Thea this week. I wanted to ensure
that this story, which people who know me now find hilarious, hadn't morphed into
some sort of personal urban legend over the past 15 years. "Yes," she said. "We put
them in a lovely tin.")

On a sound system that echoed through speakers perched discreetly throughout   5
the airy house, we played "Life Goes On" on a loop and sobbed. We analyzed lyrics
for premonitions of the tragedy. We, of course, cursed Biggie. Who knew that the East
Coast–West Coast war had two earnest soldiers in flannel pajamas, lying on a king-
size bed decorated with pink toe shoes that dangled from one of its posts? There, we
studied our pictures of Tupac and re-created his tattoos on each other's body with a
Sharpie. I got "Thug Life" on my stomach. I gave Thea "Exodus 1811" inside a giant
cross. Both are flanked by "West Side."

A snapshot taken that Monday on our high school's front lawn (seen here) shows   6
the two of us lying side by side, shirts lifted to display the tributes in black marker.
Despite our best efforts, it's the innocent, bubbly lettering of notes passed in class and
of poster boards made for social studies presentations. My hair has recently been
straightened with my first (and last) relaxer and a Gold 'N Hot flatiron on too high a
setting. Hers is slicked back with the mixture of Herbal Essences and Blue Magic that
we formulated in a bathroom laboratory.

My rainbow-striped tee and her white wifebeater capture a transition between our   7
skater-inspired Salvation Army shopping phase and the next one, during which we'd
wear the same jeans slung from our hip bones, revealing peeks of flat stomach, but
transforming ourselves from Alternative Nation to MTV Jams imitators. We would get
bubble coats in primary colors that Christmas and start using silver eyeliner,
trying—and failing—to look something like Aaliyah.[1]

MIXED IDENTITIES: TUPAC AND ME

Did we take ourselves seriously? Did we feel a real stake in the life of this "hard-core"   8
gangsta rapper, and a real loss in his death? We did, even though we were two mixed-
race girls raised by our white moms in a privileged community where we could easily

---

[1]A hit rhythm-and-blues and hip-hop recording artist. Aaliyah Dana Haughton died
in a plane crash at age twenty-two. [Editor's note]

rattle off the names of the small handful of other kids in town who also had one black parent: Sienna. Rashea. Brandon. Aaron. Sudan. Akio. Lauren. Alicia. Even though the most subversive thing we did was make prank calls. Even though we hadn't yet met our first boyfriends, and Shock G's proclamations about putting satin on people's panties sent us into absolute giggling fits. And even though we'd been so delicately cared for, nurtured and protected from any of life's hard edges—with special efforts made to shield us from those involving race—that we sometimes felt ready to explode with boredom. Or maybe because of all that.

I mourned Tupac's death then, and continue to mourn him now, because his music   9 represents the years when I was both forced and privileged to confront what it meant to be black. That time, like his music, was about exploring the contradictory textures of this identity: The ambience and indulgence of the fun side, as in "California Love" and "Picture Me Rollin'." But also the burdensome anxiety and outright anger— "Brenda's Got a Baby," "Changes" and "Hit 'Em Up."

For Thea and me, his songs were the musical score to our transition to high school,   10 where there emerged a vague, lunchtime geography to race: White kids perched on a sloping green lawn and the benches above it. Below, black kids sat on a wall outside the gym. The bottom of the hill beckoned. Thea, more outgoing, with more admirers among the boys, stepped down boldly, and I followed timidly. Our formal invitations came in the form of unsolicited hall passes to go to Black Student Union meetings during free periods. We were assigned to recite Maya Angelou's "Phenomenal Woman" at the Black History Month assembly.

Tupac was the literal sound track when our school's basketball team would come   11 charging onto the court, and our ragtag group of cheerleaders kicked furiously to

The author (left) with her friend Thea
Courtesy of Jenée Desmond-Harris

"Toss It Up" in a humid gymnasium. Those were the games when we might breathlessly join the dance team after our cheer during time-outs if they did the single "African step" we'd mastered for BSU performances.

EVERYTHING BLACK—AND COOL

... Blackness became something cool, something to which we had brand-new access. 12 We flaunted it, buying Kwanzaa candles and insisting on celebrating privately (really, just lighting the candles and excluding our friends) at a sleepover. We memorized "I Get Around"[2] and took turns singing verses to each other as we drove through Marin County suburbs in Thea's green Toyota station wagon. Because he was with us through all of this, we were in love with Tupac and wanted to embody him. On Halloween, Thea donned a bald cap and a do-rag, penciled in her already-full eyebrows and was a dead ringer.

Tupac's music, while full of social commentary (and now even on the Vatican's 13 playlist), probably wasn't made to be a treatise on racial identity. Surely it wasn't created to accompany two girls (*little* girls, really) as they embarked on a coming-of-age journey. But it was there for us when we desperately needed it.

READING FOR MEANING

For help with summarizing, see Chapter 2, pp. 24–25.

1. **Read to Summarize.** Write a sentence or two explaining the conflict that underlies Desmond-Harris's story and how she tries to resolve it.

2. **Read to Respond.** Write a paragraph exploring anything that resonates with your experience — such as Desmond-Harris's claim that Tupac's music was the "sound track" for her youth (par. 11) — or that seems surprising — such as Desmond-Harris's identification with Tupac, perhaps reflecting on why Desmond-Harris and Thea give themselves Sharpie tattoos and take a photograph showing them off (pars. 5–6).

For help analyzing assumptions, see Chapter 2, pp. 28–29.

3. **Read to Analyze Assumptions.** Write a paragraph or two analyzing an assumption you find intriguing in Desmond-Harris's essay. For example:

Assumptions about celebrity. The fifteen-year-old Desmond-Harris apparently thought of Tupac as someone she knew personally, not as some distant star but as a family "friend" (par. 2). To think critically about assumptions regarding celebrity in this essay, consider questions like these:

- How do the media contribute to the sense that we have a personal relationship with certain celebrities?

---

[2] Tupac Shakur's first top-twenty single, released in 1993 on *Strictly 4 My N.I.G.G.A.Z.*, Shakur's second studio album. [Editor's note]

- Critics like Daniel Boorstin argue that celebrities often are admired not because of their special talents or achievements but simply because they are famous. Why do you think Desmond-Harris is so enamored of Tupac?

Assumptions about identity. Desmond-Harris tells us that as a teenager she began to explore what she calls "the contradictory textures" — "the fun side" as well as "the burdensome anxiety and outright anger" — of her biracial identity (par. 9). To think critically about assumptions regarding identity in this essay, consider questions like these:

- Desmond-Harris describes the social and racial divisions in her high school (par. 10). What kinds of divisions existed in your high school and how did they affect how you presented yourself to others?
- In the last paragraph, Desmond-Harris explains that during the period she is writing about, she and her friend had "embarked on a coming-of-age journey" (par. 13). What do you think she learned about herself from Tupac's life and from his death?

READING LIKE A WRITER

CONVEYING THE AUTOBIOGRAPHICAL SIGNIFICANCE

Events that have lasting significance nearly always involve mixed or ambivalent feelings. Therefore, readers expect and appreciate some degree of complexity. Multiple layers of meaning make autobiographical stories more, not less, interesting. Significance that seems simplistic or predictable makes stories less successful.

Analyze & Write

Write a paragraph or two analyzing Desmond-Harris's handling of the complex personal and cultural significance of Tupac's death:

1. Skim the last two sections (pars. 8–13), noting passages where Desmond-Harris tells readers her remembered feelings and thoughts at the time and her present perspective as an adult reflecting on the experience. How does she use this dual perspective to convey complexity?
2. Look closely at paragraph 8, and highlight the following sentence strategies:
   - Rhetorical questions (questions writers answer themselves)
   - Repeated words and phrases
   - Stylistic sentence fragments (incomplete sentences used for special effect)

   What effect do these sentence strategies have on readers? How do they help convey the significance of the event for Desmond-Harris?

Brad Benioff

Rick

Brad Benioff was a first-year college student when he wrote the following essay for an assignment in his composition class. Like Desmond-Harris in the preceding selection, Benioff focuses his essay on a memorable person, but unlike Desmond-Harris, Benioff focuses on someone he knew personally: his high-school water-polo coach, Rick Rezinas.

- **Before you read,** reflect on your own experience of trying to impress someone. What did you do to win that person's approval? Why was it important to you to do so?

- **As you read,** consider the impression Benioff gives readers of himself as a high-school student. What does this way of describing himself tell readers about Benioff?

I walked through the dawn chill, shivering as much from nervousness as from the   1
cold. Steam curled up from the water in the pool and disappeared in the ocher morning light. Athletes spread themselves about on the deck, lazily stretching and whispering to each other as if the stillness were sacred. It was to be my first practice with the high school water polo team. I knew nothing about the game, but a friend had pushed me to play, arguing, "It's the most fun of any sport. Trust me." He had awakened me that morning long before daylight, forced me into a bathing suit, and driven me to the pool.

"Relax," he said. "Rick is the greatest of coaches. You'll like him. You'll have fun."   2

The mythical Rick. I had heard of him many times before. All the older players   3
knew him by his first name and always spoke of him as a friend rather than a coach. He was a math teacher at our school, and his classes were very popular. Whenever class schedules came out, everyone hoped to be placed in Mr. Rezinas's class. He had been known to throw parties for the team or take them on weekend excursions skiing or backpacking. To be Rick's friend was to be part of an exclusive club, and I was being invited to join. And so I looked forward with nervous anticipation to meeting this man.

My friend walked me out to the pool deck and steered me toward a man standing   4
beside the pool.

"Rick," announced my friend, "I'd like you to meet your newest player."   5

Rick was not a friendly looking man. He wore only swim trunks, and his short,   6
powerful legs rose up to meet a bulging torso. His big belly was solid. His shoulders, as if to offset his front-heaviness, were thrown back, creating a deep crease of excess muscle from his sides around the small of his back, a crease like a huge frown. His arms were crossed, two medieval maces placed carefully on their racks, ready to be swung at any moment. His round cheeks and chin were darkened by traces of black whiskers. His hair was sparse. Huge, black, mirrored sunglasses replaced his eyes.

Below his prominent nose was a thin, sinister mustache. I couldn't believe this menacing-looking man was the legendary jovial Rick.

He said nothing at first. In those moments of silence, I felt more inadequate than 7 ever before in my life. My reflection in his glasses stared back at me, accusing me of being too skinny, too young, too stupid, too weak to be on his team. Where did I get the nerve to approach him with such a ridiculous body and ask to play water polo, a man's game? Finally, he broke the silence, having finished appraising my meager body. "We'll fatten him up," he growled.

Thus began a week of torture. For four hours a day, the coach stood beside the pool 8 scowling down at me. I could do nothing right.

"No! No! No!" He shook his head in disgust. "Throw the damn ball with your 9 whole arm! Get your goddamn elbow out of the water!"

Any failure on my part brought down his full wrath. He bellowed at my incompe- 10 tence and punished me with push-ups and wind sprints. Even when I was close to utter exhaustion, I found no sympathy. "What the hell are you doing on the wall?" he would bellow. "Coach . . . my side, it's cramped."

"Swim on it! If you can't take a little pain, then you don't play!" With this, he 11 would push me off the wall.

He seemed to enjoy playing me against the older, stronger players. "Goddamn it, 12 Brad! If someone elbows or hits you, don't look out at me and cry, 'It's not fair.' Push back! Don't be so weak!" I got elbowed around until it seemed that none of my internal organs was unscathed. He worked me until my muscles wouldn't respond, and then he demanded more.

"You're not trying! Push it!" 13

"Would you move? You're too slow! Swim!" 14

"Damn it! Get out and give me twenty!" 15

It took little time for me to hate both the game and the man who ruled it. 16

I reacted by working as hard as I could. I decided to deprive him of the pleasure of 17 finding fault with me. I learned quickly and started playing as flawlessly as possible. I dispensed with looking tired, showing pain, or complaining of cramps. I pushed, hit, and elbowed back at the biggest of players. No matter how flawless or aggressive my performance, though, he would find fault and let me know it. He was never critical of other players. He would laugh and joke with the other players; but whenever he saw me, he frowned.

I decided to quit. 18

After a particularly demanding practice, I walked up to this tyrant. I tried to hold 19 his gaze, but the black glasses forced me to look down.

"Coach Rezinas," I blurted, "I've decided that I don't want to play water polo." His 20 scowl deepened. Then after a moment he said, "You can't quit. Not until after the first game." And he walked away. The dictator had issued his command.

There was no rule to keep me from quitting. Anger flushed through me. Some- 21 how I would get revenge on this awful man. After the first game? Okay. I would play. I would show him what a valuable player I was. He would miss my talents when I quit. I worked myself up before the first game by imagining the hated face: the black glasses, the thin mustache, the open, snarling mouth. I was not surprised that he placed me in the starting lineup because I was certain he would take me out soon. I played furiously. The ball, the goal, the opposition, even the water seemed to be extensions of Rick, his face glaring from every angle, his words echoing loudly in my ears. Time and time again I would get the ball and, thinking of his tortures, fire it toward the goal with a strength to kill. I forgot that he might take me out. No defender could stand up to me. I would swim by them or over them. Anger and the need for vengeance gave me energy. I didn't notice the time slipping by, the quarters ending.

Then, the game ended. My teammates rushed out to me, congratulating and cheering 22
me. I had scored five goals, a school record for one game, and shut out the other team with several key defensive plays. Now I could get revenge. Now I could quit. I stepped out of the pool prepared with the words I would spit into his face: "I QUIT!"

As I approached him, I stopped dead. He was smiling at me, his glasses off. He 23
reached out with his right hand and shook mine with exuberance.

"I knew you had it in you! I knew it!" he laughed.   24

Through his laughter, I gained a new understanding of the man. He had pushed me 25
to my fullest potential, tapping into the talent I may never have found in myself. He was responsible for the way I played that day. My glory was his. He never hated me. On the contrary, I was his apprentice, his favored pupil. He had brought out my best. Could I really hate someone who had done that much for me? He had done what he had promised: he had fattened me up mentally as well as physically. All this hit me in a second and left me completely confused. I tried to speak, but only managed to croak, "Coach . . . uh . . . I, uh. . . ." He cut me off with another burst of laughter. He still shook my hand.

"Call me Rick," he said.   26

READING FOR MEANING

1. **Read to Summarize.** Write a few sentences describing the dramatic arc of this story (see Figure 3.1, p. 53).

2. **Read to Respond.** Write a paragraph reflecting on anything that resonates with your experience, such as Benioff's reaction to the challenge posed by Rick or the high-school students' desire to be "part of an exclusive club" (par. 3).

3. **Read to Analyze Assumptions.** Write a paragraph analyzing an assumption you find intriguing in Benioff's essay. For example:

   Assumptions about the good and bad qualities of coaching. Others describe Rick as "the greatest of coaches" (par. 2) and "a friend rather than a coach" (par. 3). But Benioff calls Rick a "tyrant" (par. 19) and a "dictator" (par. 20).

For help analyzing assumptions, see Chapter 2, pp. 28–29.

He complains that Rick demands too much of him and works him too hard, always finding fault and never giving him praise — at least, until Benioff proves himself to be worthy.

- What does Benioff assume are the good and the bad qualities of coaching? Why does his attitude change after the match?
- In your experience, are coaches like Rick or other authority figures (such as parents, teachers, bosses) expected to be tough and critical rather than sympathetic and encouraging?

Assumptions about the male body and masculinity. Benioff describes his own body before undergoing Rick's makeover as "too skinny . . . too weak," "ridiculous," and "meager" (par. 7). These images are in sharp contrast to those he uses to describe Rick's "powerful," "bulging," "solid" muscular body (par. 6).

- Where do you see evidence that our culture celebrates the same physical qualities that Benioff does?
- Where, if anywhere, does Benioff question the kind of masculinity Rick represents? What other qualities, if any, does our culture (or another culture of which you are aware) associate with masculinity?

READING LIKE A WRITER

PRESENTING PEOPLE

Description and dialogue can help create a vivid portrait and provide readers with insight into the writer's attitude toward and relationship with a person. Effective descriptions name the person and include a few well-chosen details that allow readers to visualize him or her. Dialogue can make readers feel as though they were overhearing what was said and how it was said. It usually includes **speaker tags** that identify the speaker ("he said" [par. 2]) and may also indicate the speaker's tone or attitude ("I blurted" [par. 20]).

Speaker tag
> "Rick," announced my friend, "I'd like you to meet your newest player." (par. 5)
>
> "No! No! No!" He shook his head in disgust. "Throw the damn ball with your whole arm! Get your goddamn elbow out of the water!" (par. 9)

Dialogue that is quoted can be especially expressive and vivid. But when the word choice is not particularly memorable, writers usually summarize dialogue to give readers the gist and move the story along more quickly.

Speaker tag
Summary
> My teammates rushed out to me, congratulating and cheering me. (par. 22)

Analyze & Write

Write a paragraph or two analyzing Benioff's use of description and dialogue (whether quoted, paraphrased, or summarized) to portray Rick and help readers understand why he was such an important figure in Benioff's life.

1. Reread paragraph 6. Circle the parts of Rick's body Benioff names and underline the visual details he uses to describe Rick's body. Also examine the two comparisons: a simile in sentence 4 and a metaphor in sentence 5. What do the naming, detailing, and comparing contribute to the dominant impression you get of Rick from Benioff's visual description?

2. Skim the dialogue between Rick and Benioff. Then pick two or three places where you think the dialogue is illuminating. What does each bit of dialogue tell you about the speaker or the relationship? What feelings or attitudes does it convey?

Writing to Learn Autobiography

Write a brief essay analyzing one of the readings in this chapter (or another selection, perhaps one by a classmate). Explain how (and perhaps, how well) the selection works as an autobiography. Consider, for example, how it uses

- the dramatic arc to make the story engaging or suspenseful;

- naming, detailing, and comparing to make people and places come alive;

- remembered feelings and thoughts, plus present perspective, to convey the personal and cultural significance.

Your essay could also reflect on how you applied one or more of the academic habits of mind as you read the selection:

- **Curiosity** — what questions or ideas did you have as you read the selection?

- **Critical Analysis** — what assumptions in the selection did you find intriguing, and why?

- **Rhetorical Sensitivity** — how effective or ineffective do you think the selection is in achieving its purpose for the intended audience, given the constraints of the medium and the autobiography genre?

A GUIDE TO WRITING AUTOBIOGRAPHY

You have probably done a good deal of analytical writing about your reading. Your instructor may also assign a capstone project to write a brief autobiography of your own. This Guide to Writing offers detailed suggestions and resources to help you meet the special challenges this kind of writing presents.

THE WRITING ASSIGNMENT

Write about a significant event or person in your life.

- Choose an event or person that you feel comfortable writing about for this audience (your instructor and classmates), given your purpose (to present something meaningful).

- Consider how you can tell the story dramatically or describe the person vividly.

- Try to convey the meaning and importance in your life — what we call the **autobiographical significance** — of the event or person you've chosen to write about. Think about how you can lead readers to understand you better, to reflect on their own lives, to become aware of social and cultural influences, or to gain some other insights.

WRITING YOUR DRAFT

CHOOSING A SUBJECT

Rather than limiting yourself to the first subject that comes to mind, take a few minutes to consider your options and list as many subjects as you can. Below are some criteria that can help you choose a promising subject, followed by suggestions for the types of events and people you might consider writing about.

The subject should

- reveal something significant, possibly by centering on a conflict (within yourself or between you and another person or institution)

- express complex or ambivalent feelings (rather than superficial or sentimental ones that oversimplify the subject or make it predictable)

- lead readers to think about their own experience and about the cultural forces that shape their lives and yours

Appropriate events might include

- a difficult situation (for example, a time you had to make a tough choice or struggled to perform a challenging task)

- an incident or encounter with another person that shaped you in a particular way or revealed a personality trait (independence, insecurity, ambition, jealousy, or heroism) that you had not recognized before

- an occasion when something did not turn out as you thought it would (for example, when you expected to be criticized but were praised or ignored instead, or when you were convinced you would succeed but failed)

An appropriate person might be

- someone who made you feel you had something worthwhile to contribute, or someone who made you feel like an outsider

- someone who helped you develop a previously unknown or undeveloped side of yourself or who led you to question assumptions or stereotypes you had about other people

- someone who surprised, pleased, or disappointed you (for example, someone you admired who let you down, or someone you did not appreciate who turned out to be admirable)

Shaping Your Story

Use the elements of the dramatic arc in Figure 3.1 (p. 53) to organize the story:

Sketching Out the Exposition, or Backstory.   Your readers will need to understand what happened. Using the sentence strategies below as a starting point, sketch out the backstory of your event:

- ▶ In .... [year], while I was ....ing in .... [location], ...
- ▶ [Person's name] knew all about .... because s/he was a/an ...., an expert on ....
- ▶ In past years, I had previously .... Now I was starting ....

Drafting the "Inciting Incident."   Sketch out the conflict that triggers the story. To dramatize it, try creating action sequences, using action verbs and prepositional phrases and dialogue, including speaker tags and quotation marks:

Action verb
Prepositional phrase

A black Buick was moving toward us down the street. We all spread out, banged together some regular snowballs, took aim, and, when the Buick drew nigh, fired. (Dillard, par. 7)

Dramatizing the Rising Action and Climax.   The moment of surprise, confrontation, crisis, or discovery — the climax of your story — can be dramatized by using action sequences and by repeating key words. Some writers also include dialogue to dramatize the climax:

> Anger and the need for vengeance gave me energy. [. . .] Now I could get revenge. Now I could quit. [. . .] "I knew you had it in you! I knew it!" he laughed. (Benioff, pars. 21–22, 24)

Experimenting with Endings. Try out a variety of endings. For example, refer in the ending to something from the beginning — repetition with a difference.

> Instead of bravely exploring on your own, you've chosen to be led around like a frightened kindergartner. (Ruprecht, par. 1)

> The rest of the day I walked around with a happy smile, like the proudest little kindergartner you've ever seen. (Ruprecht, par. 10)

Presenting Important People and Places

Using Naming, Detailing, and Comparing. Describe the way important people look, dress, walk, or gesture; their tones of voice and mannerisms — anything that would help readers see the person as you remember her or him.

Naming	Rick was not a friendly looking man. [. . .] His arms were
Detailing	crossed, two medieval maces placed carefully on their racks,
Comparing (metaphor, simile)	ready to be swung at any moment. [. . .] Huge, black, mirrored sunglasses replaced his eyes. (Benioff, par. 6)

Using Dialogue. Reconstruct dialogue, using speaker tags to identify the speaker and possibly indicate the speaker's **tone** or attitude. Dialogue may be quoted to emphasize certain words or give readers a sense of the speaker's personality. It may also be summarized when the gist of what was said is most important.

Summarized dialogue	When called upon, I delivered an effortless list of things that I detest: blood sausage, intestinal pâtés, brain pudding. [. . .] The
Speaker tag	teacher's reaction led me to believe that these mistakes were capital crimes in the country of France.
Quoted dialogue	"Were you always this *palicmkrexis?*" she asked. "Even a *fiuscrzsa ticiwelmun* knows that a typewriter is feminine." (Sedaris, pars. 14–15)

Detailing Important Places. Incorporate descriptions of important places, identifying where the event happened or a place you associate with the person and including specific sensory details — size, shape, color, condition, and texture of the scene or memorable objects in it — that contribute to the dominant impression you want to create. Imagine the place from the front and from the side, from a distance and from up close. Try to keep a consistent point of view, describing the place as if you were walking through the scene or moving from right to left, or front to back.

<table>
<tr><td>

Descriptive naming & detailing

Comparing

Location information
</td><td>

. . . Ultimately my best friend, Thea, and I were left to our own 15-year-old devices to mourn that weekend. Her mother and stepfather were out of town. Their expansive, million-dollar home was perched on a hillside less than an hour from Tupac's former stomping grounds in Oakland and Marin City. Of course, her home was also worlds away from both places. (Desmond-Harris, par. 3)
</td></tr>
</table>

For more on using and analyzing visuals, see Chapter 2, pp. 31–34.

Including Visuals. Including visuals — photographs, postcards, ticket stubs — may strengthen your presentation of the event or person. If you submit your essay electronically or post it on a website, consider including snippets of video with sound as well as photographs or other memorabilia that might give readers a more vivid sense of the time, place, and people about which you are writing. If you want to use any photographs or recordings, though, be sure to request the permission of those depicted.

Reflecting on Your Subject

The following activities will help you think about the significance of your subject and formulate a tentative thesis statement, though the thesis in autobiography tends to be implied rather than stated explicitly.

Reviewing the Dominant Impression Your Description and Narration Create. Write for a few minutes about the kind of impression your writing now conveys and what you would like it to convey.

- Begin by rereading. Look back at the words you chose to describe places and people, as well as the way you dramatized the story.

- Consider the tone and connotations of your word choices. What meanings or feelings do they evoke?

- Note any contradictions or changes in tone or mood that could lead you to a deeper understanding.

Exploring How You Felt at the Time. Write for a few minutes, trying to recall your thoughts and feelings when the event was occurring or when you knew the person:

- What did you feel — in control or powerless, proud or embarrassed, vulnerable, detached, judgmental — and how did you show or express your feelings?

- What were the immediate consequences for you personally?

These sentence strategies may help you put your feelings into words:

▶ As the event started [or during or right after the event], I felt .... and ....

▶ I hoped others would think of me as ....

Exploring Your Present Perspective.   Write for a few minutes, trying to express your present thoughts and feelings as you look back on the event or person:

- How have your feelings changed, and what insights do you now have?

- Try looking at the event or person in broad cultural or social terms. For example, consider whether you or anyone else upset gender expectations or felt out of place in some way.

These sentence strategies may help you put your feelings into words:

- ► My feelings since the event [have/have not] changed in the following ways: ....

- ► At the time, I had been going through ...., which may have affected my experience by ....

Considering Your Purpose and Audience.   Write for several minutes exploring what you want your readers to understand about the significance of the event or person. Use the following questions to help clarify your thoughts:

- What will writing about this event or person enable you to suggest about yourself as an individual?

- What will it let you suggest about the social and cultural forces that helped shape you — for example, how people exercise power over one another, how family and community values and attitudes affect individuals, or how economic and social conditions influence our sense of self?

- What about your subject do you expect will seem familiar to your readers? What do you think will surprise them, perhaps getting them to think in new ways or to question some of their assumptions and stereotypes?

Formulating a Working Thesis.   Write a few sentences trying to articulate a working thesis that explains the significance that you want your writing to convey. Even though readers do not expect autobiographical writing to include an explicit thesis statement, stating a thesis now may help you explore ambivalent feelings and lead you to a deeper understanding of your subject. It also may help you as you continue working on your draft, organizing the story, selecting descriptive details, and choosing words to relate your feelings and thoughts.

Drafting Your Story

By this point, you have done a lot of writing

- to develop a plan for telling a compelling story;

- to present people and places in vivid detail;

- to show or tell the autobiographical significance of your story in a way that will be meaningful for your readers.

Now stitch that material together to create a draft. The next section of this Guide to Writing will help you evaluate and improve your draft.

REVIEWING AND IMPROVING THE DRAFT

This section includes two guides for Peer Review and Troubleshooting Your Draft. Your instructor may arrange a peer review in class or online where you can exchange drafts with a classmate. The Peer Review Guide will help you give each other constructive feedback regarding the basic features and strategies typical of autobiographical writing. (If you want to make specific suggestions for improving the draft, see Troubleshooting Your Draft on pp. 85–86.) Also, be sure to respond to any specific concerns the writer has raised about the draft. The Troubleshooting Your Draft guide that follows will help you reread your own draft with a critical eye, sort through any feedback you've received, and consider a variety of ways to improve your draft.

A PEER REVIEW GUIDE

How effectively does the writer narrate the story?

What's Working Well: Point to a passage where the storytelling is effective—for example, where the dramatic arc is used successfully to engage your interest, arouse your curiosity, or build suspense to a climax.

What Needs Improvement: Identify a passage where the storytelling could be improved—for example, where the story loses focus, gets bogged down in details, lacks drama or suspense.

How vivid are the descriptions of people and places, and how well do the descriptions work together to create a dominant impression?

What's Working Well: Highlight an especially vivid bit of description—for example, where sensory details (sights, sounds, smells, textures) help you imagine the scene or where a photograph gives you a striking impression of a person.

What Needs Improvement: Tell the writer where description could be added, made more vivid, or changed so that it reinforces the dominant impression—for example, where you'd like to know what people look and sound like or where sensory details would help you visualize a place.

How effectively is the autobiographical significance of the event or the person conveyed?

What's Working Well: Mark a passage where the significance is clear and compelling—for example, where remembered thoughts are expressed poignantly, where the present perspective seems insightful, where dialogue helps you understand the underlying conflict, or where the strong dominant impression clarifies the significance.

What Needs Improvement: Note any passages where the significance could be clearer or more fully developed—for example, where the central conflict seems too easily resolved, where a moral seems tacked on at the end, or where more interesting insights could be drawn from the writer's interactions with and feelings about the person.

How clear and easy to follow is the organization?

What's Working Well: Point to any aspect of the organization that seems notably effective—for example, one or more transitions that clearly show how the event unfolded over time or in space.

What Needs Improvement: Let the writer know where the organization can be clearer—for example, where a transition between elements of the dramatic arc is needed or where topic sentences or headings could help orient readers.

Revising Your Draft

Revising means reenvisioning your draft, seeing it in a fresh way, given your purpose, audience, and the review from your peers. Don't hesitate to cut unconvincing or tangential material, add new material, or move passages around. The following chart may help you strengthen your essay.

TROUBLESHOOTING YOUR DRAFT

To Make the Narrative More Dramatic	
If the inciting incident does not arouse curiosity or suspense,	• Tighten the inciting incident by moving background exposition. • Show how the inciting incident stems from an underlying conflict. • Reveal the writer's anxious, fearful, or other intense feelings.
If the dramatic arc flattens and the tension slackens,	• Intensify the rising action by interspersing remembered feelings with action verbs. • Dramatize the climax with quoted dialogue and speaker tags that show strong reactions. • Propel the action through time and space with active verbs, transitions, and prepositional phrases.
If exposition or descriptive detail interrupts the drama,	• Reduce exposition by injecting small bits of background information and detail into the action, or cut it altogether. • Summarize instead of quoting lengthy dialogue, and only quote especially expressive language.

(continued)

To Present People and Places Vividly

If the description of people is vague,	• Add sensory details showing what people look and sound like. • Use speaker tags to reveal the people's attitudes and personality. • Add a comparison to help readers understand the person or relationship.
If it's hard to visualize the place,	• Add more specific nouns to name objects in the scene. • Add more sensory detail to evoke the sense of sight, touch, smell, taste, or hearing. • Use comparison to enrich the description.
If the dominant impression is weak or undercut by contradictory details,	• Add a suggestive comparison to strengthen the dominant impression. • Consider how contradictory details might show complexity in people or their relationships.
If the point of view is confusing,	• Clarify the vantage point from which the scene is described. • Make sure the point of view is consistent.

To Convey the Autobiographical Significance

If the significance is not clear and compelling,	• Sharpen the dominant impression to *show* the significance. • Expand or add passages where you use *telling* to convey the significance directly. • Add remembered thoughts and feelings. • Articulate your present perspective on the event or person.
If the central conflict seems too easily resolved or simplistic,	• Use present perspective to explain why the conflict is so memorable and continues to be important. • Express strong feelings that were—and may still be—complicated and not fully understood. • Explain the conflict in terms of its social, cultural, or historical context.

To Make the Organization More Effective

If there's confusion about what happened when,	• Add or clarify transitions and other time markers. • Review verb tenses to make them consistent.
If too many details seem overwhelming and it's hard to follow,	• Add or revise topic sentences. • Use present perspective to orient readers. • Consider whether headings would help.

Editing and Proofreading Your Draft

Check for errors in usage, punctuation, and mechanics, and consider matters of style. If you keep a list of errors you typically make, begin by checking your draft against this list. Ask someone else to proofread your essay before you submit it to your instructor.

Research on student writing shows that autobiographical writing often has sentence fragments, run-together sentences, and verb tense errors. Check a writer's handbook for help with these potential problems.

Reflecting on Autobiography

In this chapter, you have read critically several pieces of autobiography and have written one of your own. To better remember what you have learned, pause now to reflect on the reading and writing activities you completed in this chapter.

1. Write a page or so reflecting on what you have learned. Begin by describing what you are most pleased with in your essay. Then explain what you think contributed to your achievement. Be specific about this contribution.

   - If it was something you learned from the readings, indicate which readings and specifically what you learned from them.

   - If it came from the writing you did in response to prompts in this chapter, point out the section or sections that helped you most.

2. Reflect more generally on how you tend to interpret autobiographical writing, your own as well as other writers'. Consider some of the following questions:

   - In reading for meaning, do you tend to find yourself interpreting the significance of the event or person in terms of the writer's personal feelings, sense of self-esteem, or psychological well-being? Or do you more often think of significance in terms of larger social or economic influences — for example, in terms of the writer's gender, class, or ethnicity?

   - Where do you think you learned to interpret the significance of people's stories about themselves and their relationships — from your family, friends, television, school?

4

Observation

Observational writing comprises analytical, informative, and thought-provoking portraits, or *profiles*, of a person or a place. These profiles may be cultural ethnographies, ranging from "a day-in-the-life" to an extended immersion study of a community or people at work or at play. They are intensively researched, centering on the field-research techniques of detailed observations and edifying interviews. As a result, observational profiles are generally entertaining to read, sometimes amusing, and often surprising and captivating. Whether written in a college course, for the broader community, or about the workplace, observational writing mobilizes the academic habits of mind, appealing to our curiosity about the world we live in and stimulating critical analysis.

RHETORICAL SITUATIONS FOR OBSERVATIONS

Many people — including bloggers, journalists, psychologists, and cultural anthropologists — write essays based on observations and interviews, as the following examples suggest:

- For an art history course, a student writes a paper about a local artist recently commissioned to paint an outdoor mural for the city. The student visits the artist's studio and talks with him about the process of painting murals. The artist invites the student to spend the following day as a part of a team of local art students and neighborhood volunteers working on the mural under the artist's direction. This firsthand experience helps the student profile the artist, present some of the students on his team, and give readers an intimate understanding of the process and collaboration involved in mural painting.

- For a political science course, a student writes about a controversial urban renewal project to replace decaying houses with a library and park. To learn about the history of the project, she reads newspaper reports and interviews people who helped plan the project as well as some neighborhood residents and activists who oppose it. She also tours the site with the project manager to see what is actually being done.

Thinking about Observation

Recall one occasion when you reported your observations or heard or read the observations of others.

- Who was the *audience?* How did reporting observations to this audience affect the way the writer conveyed his or her perspective? For example, if the audience was already familiar with the subject, did the report arouse curiosity by taking a provocative approach, by going behind the scenes, or in some other way?

- What was the main *purpose?* What did the writer want the audience to learn? For example, was the report primarily intended to teach them something, to show them what the writer had learned, to entertain them, or for some other reason?

- How would you rate the *rhetorical sensitivity* with which the observations were presented? What made the essay appropriate or inappropriate for its particular audience or purpose?

A GUIDE TO READING OBSERVATIONS

This guide introduces you to the strategies typical of observational writing by inviting you to analyze a brief but intriguing profile of Albert Yeganeh and his unique restaurant, Soup Kitchen International:

- *Reading for meaning* will help you understand what we call the writer's **perspective** — the main idea or cultural significance that the writer wants readers to take away from reading the observational profile.

- *Reading like a writer* will help you learn how the writer makes the essay interesting and informative, by examining how he or she uses some of the *basic features* and strategies typical of observational writing:

  1. Deciding whether to take the role of a spectator or a participant

  2. Determining what information to include and how to present it

  3. Organizing the information in a way that will be entertaining to readers

  4. Conveying a perspective on the subject

The *New Yorker*

Soup

"Soup" (1989) was published anonymously in the *New Yorker*, a magazine known for its observational profiles of fascinating people and places. The subject of the article is Albert Yeganeh, the creative and demanding owner/chef of a small take-out restaurant (originally called Soup Kitchen International, now called Soup Man). Yeganeh's restaurant inspired an episode of the then-popular television sitcom *Seinfeld* called "The Soup Nazi." Apparently Yeganeh was so angry that when Jerry Seinfeld went to the restaurant after the episode aired, the chef demanded an apology and told Seinfeld to leave.

- **Before you read,** note the quotations that open the essay: "Soup is my lifeblood" and "I am extremely hard to please." The first quote clearly refers to the kind of food served at the restaurant, but the second quote seems to have a different purpose. What does it lead you to expect from the essay?

- **As you read,** think about how the writer represented Yeganeh to the original *New Yorker* readers. If you have seen the "Soup Nazi" episode, you might compare the way Yeganeh is portrayed in the sitcom to the way he is portrayed in the article. Consider also how Yeganeh is portrayed on his franchise website, *The Original Soup Man*.

When Albert Yeganeh says "Soup is my lifeblood," he means it. And when he says 1 "I am extremely hard to please," he means that, too. Working like a demon alchemist in a tiny storefront kitchen at 259-A West Fifty-fifth Street, Mr. Yeganeh creates anywhere from eight to seventeen soups every weekday. His concoctions are so popular that a wait of half an hour at the lunchtime peak is not uncommon, although there are strict rules for conduct in line. But more on that later.

"I am psychologically kind of a health freak," Mr. Yeganeh said the other day, in a 2 lisping staccato of Armenian origin. "And I know that soup is the greatest meal in the world. It's very good for your digestive system. And I use only the best, the freshest ingredients. I am a perfectionist. When I make a clam soup, I use three different kinds of clams. Every other place uses canned clams. I'm called crazy. I am not crazy. People don't realize why I get so upset. It's because if the soup is not perfect and I'm still selling it, it's a torture. It's *my* soup, and that's why I'm so upset. First you clean and then you cook. I don't believe that ninety-nine per cent of the restaurants in New York know how to clean a tomato. I tell my crew to wash the parsley *eight* times. If they wash it five or six times, I scare them. I tell them they'll go to jail if there is sand in the parsley. One time, I found a mushroom on the floor, and I fired that guy who left it there." He spread his arms and added, "This place is the only one like it in . . . in . . . the whole earth! One day, I hope to learn something from the other places, but so far I haven't. For example, the other day I went to a very fancy restaurant and had borscht. I had to send it back. It was *junk*. I could see all the chemicals in it. I never use chemicals. Last weekend, I had lobster bisque in Brooklyn, a very well-known place. It was *junk*. When I make a lobster bisque, I use a whole lobster. You know, I never advertise. I don't have to. All the big-shot chefs and the kings of the hotels come here to see what *I'm* doing."

As you approach Mr. Yeganeh's Soup Kitchen International from a distance, the first 3 thing you notice about it is the awning, which proclaims "Homemade Hot, Cold, Diet Soups." The second thing you notice is an aroma so delicious that it makes you want to take a bite out of the air. The third thing you notice, in front of the kitchen, is an electric signboard that flashes, saying, "Today's Soups . . . Chicken Vegetable . . . Mexican Beef Chili . . . Cream of Watercress . . . Italian Sausage . . . Clam Bisque . . . Beef Barley . . . Due to Cold Weather . . . For Most Efficient and Fastest Service the Line Must . . . Be Kept Moving . . . Please . . . Have Your Money . . . Ready . . . Pick the Soup of Your Choice . . . Move to Your Extreme . . . Left After Ordering."

"I am not prejudiced against color or religion," Mr. Yeganeh told us, and he jabbed 4 an index finger at the flashing sign. "Whoever follows that I treat very well. My regular customers don't say anything. They are very intelligent and well educated. They know I'm just trying to move the line. The New York cop is very smart—he sees everything but says nothing. But the young girl who wants to stop and tell you how nice you look and hold everyone up—*yah*!" He made a guillotining motion with his hand. "I tell you, I hate to work with the public. They treat me like a slave. My philosophy is: The customer is always wrong and I'm always right. I raised my prices to try to get rid of some of these people, but it didn't work."

The other day, Mr. Yeganeh was dressed in chef's whites with orange smears across 5 his chest, which may have been some of the carrot soup cooking in a huge pot on a little stove in one corner. A three-foot-long handheld mixer from France sat on the sink, looking like an overgrown gardening tool. Mr. Yeganeh spoke to two young helpers in a twisted Armenian-Spanish barrage, then said to us, "I have no overhead, no trained waitresses, and I have the cashier here." He pointed to himself theatrically. Beside the doorway, a glass case with fresh green celery, red and yellow peppers, and purple eggplant was topped by five big gray soup urns. According to a piece of cardboard taped to the door, you can buy Mr. Yeganeh's soups in three sizes, costing from four to fifteen dollars. The order of any well-behaved customer is accompanied by little waxpaper packets of bread, fresh vegetables (such as scallions and radishes), fresh fruit (such as cherries or an orange), a chocolate mint, and a plastic spoon. No coffee, tea, or other drinks are served.

"I get my recipes from books and theories and my own taste," Mr. Yeganeh said. "At 6 home, I have several hundreds of books. When I do research, I find that I don't know anything. Like cabbage is a cancer fighter, and some fish is good for your heart but some is bad. Every day, I should have one sweet, one spicy, one cream, one vegetable soup—and they *must* change, they should always taste a little different." He added that he wasn't sure how extensive his repertoire was, but that it probably includes at least eighty soups, among them African peanut butter, Greek moussaka, hamburger, Reuben, B.L.T., asparagus and caviar, Japanese shrimp miso, chicken chili, Irish corned beef and cabbage, Swiss chocolate, French calf's brain, Korean beef ball, Italian shrimp and eggplant Parmesan, buffalo, ham and egg, short rib, Russian beef

Stroganoff, turkey cacciatore, and Indian mulligatawny. "The chicken and the seafood are an addiction, and when I have French garlic soup I let people have only one small container each," he said. "The doctors and nurses love that one."

A lunch line of thirty people stretched down the block from Mr. Yeganeh's doorway. 7 Behind a construction worker was a man in expensive leather, who was in front of a woman in a fur hat. Few people spoke. Most had their money out and their orders ready.

At the front of the line, a woman in a brown coat couldn't decide which soup to get 8 and started to complain about the prices.

"You talk too much, dear," Mr. Yeganeh said, and motioned her to move to the left. 9 "Next!"

"Just don't talk. Do what he says," a man huddled in a blue parka warned. 10

"He's downright rude," said a blond woman in a blue coat. "Even abusive. But 11 you can't deny it, his soup is the best."

READING FOR MEANING

For help with summarizing, see Chapter 2, pp. 24–25.

1. **Read to Summarize.** Write a sentence or two briefly describing Yeganeh and his views about running a restaurant.

2. **Read to Respond.** Write a paragraph exploring your initial reactions, for example, to Yeganeh's work ethic or his ideas about food quality and health, perhaps in comparison to the quality at fast-food restaurants with which you are familiar.

For more help analyzing assumptions, see Chapter 2, pp. 28–29.

3. **Read to Analyze Assumptions.** Write a paragraph or two analyzing an assumption in this essay. For example:

Assumptions about authority. Yeganeh brags about scaring his employees and defends his right to deny service to anyone who does not follow his rules.

- When Yeganeh talks about scaring and firing his employees (par. 2), does he seem to be holding them to an appropriately high standard or is he just being a bully? In telling the story, is he showing off for the writer, making a serious point, or both?

- When Yeganeh tells a customer she talks too much and then refuses to serve her (par. 9), is he being a tyrant or is he right to use his power in this way?

You may also try reflecting on challenges to your beliefs and values; see Chapter 2, pp. 36–37.

Assumptions about customer service. When Yeganeh says, "The customer is always wrong and I'm always right" (par. 4), he is reversing the popular saying that the customer is always right.

- What seem to be the assumptions of the writer and of Yeganeh's customers about service?

- What influences our assumptions about service — for example, the type of restaurant (take-out or sit-down, family style or formal), how much it costs, our attitudes toward service work and workers?

READING LIKE A WRITER

PRESENTING INFORMATION ABOUT THE SUBJECT

Observational writing, like autobiography (Chapter 3), succeeds in large part by describing people and places vividly. The describing strategies of *naming* objects together with *detailing* their color, shape, size, texture, and other qualities enable readers to imagine what the people and places look, sound, feel, and smell like. Writers also may use *comparing* in the form of simile or metaphor to add a playful or suggestive image to the description:

Naming	The other day, Mr. Yeganeh was dressed in chef's whites with orange
Detailing	smears across his chest, which may have been some of the carrot soup
Comparing	cooking in a huge pot on a little stove in one corner. A three-foot-long
(simile)	handheld mixer from France sat on the sink, looking like an overgrown
	gardening tool. (par. 5)

Writers often use *speaker tags* along with dialogue to characterize people as they talk and interact with others. For example:

Speaker tag   "I am psychologically kind of a health freak," *Mr. Yeganeh said the other day, in a lisping staccato of Armenian origin.* (par. 2)

The author of "Soup" uses dialogue extensively to give readers a vivid impression of the man, his business, and his ideas. Indeed, most of the information in this selection comes from long chunks of an extended interview with Yeganeh, and the profile concludes with a brief overheard exchange between Yeganeh and two people in line.

Analyze & Write

Write a paragraph analyzing the use of naming, detailing, and comparing to present Albert Yeganeh:

1. Find a few examples in paragraphs 1–6 where you think the naming and detailing give an especially vivid description of Yeganeh. What is the dominant impression you get from this description?

2. Also find an example of comparing, either a *simile* (a comparison using *like* or *as*) or a *metaphor* (a comparison that does not use this kind of signaling word). What ideas and associations does this comparison contribute to the impression you got from the other describing strategies? How does it reinforce, extend, change, or complicate the dominant impression?

3. Reflect on what, if anything, you learn from Yeganeh about making soup or operating a restaurant.

Organizing the Information

Writers of observational essays typically rely on three basic organizational plans: *topical*, *narrative*, and *spatial*. As the following examples show, an essay may use all of these ways of arranging information. Note also the kinds of organizational cues — such as transitional words and phrases, calendar and clock time, and prepositional phrases indicating time or location — writers use for each kind of organization.

Topic Organizational cue | "I am psychologically kind of a health freak." . . . "And I know that soup is . . . very good for your digestive system. And I use only the best, the freshest ingredients. I am a perfectionist." (par. 2)

Narrative cue | The other day . . . Mr. Yeganeh spoke to two young helpers in a twisted Armenian-Spanish barrage, then said to us . . . (par. 5)

Spatial cue | *As you approach* Mr. Yeganeh's Soup Kitchen International *from a distance*, the *first thing you notice* about it is . . . *The second thing you notice* is . . . *The third thing you notice, in front of* the kitchen, is . . . (par. 3)

Analyze & Write

Write a paragraph analyzing the use of topical, narrative, and spatial organizing strategies in "Soup":

1. First, make a scratch outline of paragraphs 4, 5, and 6 of "Soup," listing the topics or kinds of information presented. (Some paragraphs include more than one topic. You do not have to list every topic, but try to identify the most important ones.)

2. Then reread paragraphs 7–11, where the writer presents a brief narrative. What, if anything, do you learn from the narrative that illuminates or adds to what you learned from the earlier paragraphs?

3. Finally, scan the essay looking for any other parts that, in addition to the passage quoted above from paragraph 3, organize the information spatially. What cues help you recognize the spatial arrangement?

Adopting an Authorial Role

In making observations and writing them up, writers have a choice of roles to perform: as a *detached spectator* or as a *participant observer*. In the **spectator** role, the writer acts as an independent reporter, watching and listening but remaining outside of the activity. In contrast, the **participant observer** becomes an insider, at least for a short time, joining in the activity with the people being interviewed and observed. We can see examples of both roles in this excerpt from the reading selection by John T. Edge (pp. 102–5):

Participant role   It's just past 4:00 on a Thursday afternoon in June at Jesse's Place . . . I sit alone at the bar, one empty bottle of Bud in front of me, a second in my hand. I drain the beer, order a third, and stare down at the pink juice spreading outward from a crumpled foil pouch and onto the bar.

          I'm not leaving until I eat this thing, I tell myself.

Spectator role   Half a mile down the road, behind a fence coiled with razor wire, Lionel Dufour, proprietor of Farm Fresh Food Supplier, is loading up the last truck of the day, wheeling case after case of pickled pork offal out of his cinder-block processing plant and into a semitrailer bound for Hattiesburg, Mississippi. (pars. 1–3)

Analyze & Write

Write a paragraph discussing the role the writer of "Soup" chose to adopt:

1. Find one or two signs indicating the role the writer has taken, such as the use of the first- or third-person perspective or places where the writer included insider knowledge derived from taking the role of participant observer.

2. What advantages or disadvantages do you see in the role the writer chose to take? What would have been gained (or lost) had the writer chosen a different role?

Conveying a Perspective on the Subject

Writers of observational essays, like autobiographers, convey their perspective on what is significant or intriguing about the subject in two ways: by showing and telling.

One way writers show their perspective is through the dominant impression they create. (See Presenting Information about the Subject, p. 93.) Another way writers use showing is by selecting choice quotes that give readers insight into the speaker, as in this example of Yeganeh's comments about what makes his cooking special:

Does he really want to learn from others?

Do chefs really respect him or does he have delusions of grandeur?

"One day, I hope to learn something from the other places, but so far I haven't. For example, the other day I went to a very fancy restaurant and had borscht. I had to send it back. It was *junk*. . . . All the big-shot chefs and the kings of the hotels come here to see what *I'm* doing." (par. 2)

Observational writers occasionally also use telling to say explicitly what they think of the subject. More often, they imply their judgment of or attitude toward the subject through their word choices. For example, consider whether the writer is praising or criticizing Yeganeh in these opening sentences. Is the tone sarcastic, flattering, or something else?

Telling   When Albert Yeganeh says "Soup is my lifeblood," <u>he means it</u>. And when he says "I am extremely hard to please," <u>he means that, too</u>. (par. 1)

Analyze & Write

Write a paragraph examining how the writer uses showing and/or telling to convey a perspective on Yeganeh and his Soup Kitchen International:

1. Skim paragraphs 3–11, looking for examples of showing in the descriptions and in the choice of quotations. Choose one or two examples and explain what they suggest about the writer's perspective on Yeganeh as a human being, cook, and businessman.

2. Look also for one or two examples of telling. What do they add to your understanding of the writer's perspective?

READINGS

Leslie Jamison

The Immortal Horizon

Leslie Jamison has written a novel, *The Gin Closet* (2010), and a collection of nonfiction essays, *The Empathy Exams* (2014), which thoughtfully explores how we confront pain and care about — and for — each other. A columnist for the *New York Times Book Review*, her writing has been published in various venues such as *Harper's*, *Oxford American*, and the *Virginia Quarterly Review*. This essay focuses on an unusual marathon race that Jamison observed when her brother Julian was a participant.

- **Before you read,** think about any experience you've had as a participant or spectator in a marathon race. What do you expect you will learn from Jamison's essay? What questions would you like her to answer?

- **As you read,** notice that Jamison interweaves information gleaned from a variety of sources. Which information comes from interviews, her own observations, or other research? Which kind of information seems most compelling? Why?

1 On the western edge of Frozen Head State Park, just before dawn, a man in a rust brown trench coat blows a giant conch shell. Runners stir in their tents. They fill their water pouches. They tape their blisters. They eat thousand-calorie breakfasts: Pop-Tarts and candy bars and geriatric energy drinks. Some of them pray. Others ready their fanny packs. The man in the trench coat sits in an ergonomic lawn chair beside a famous yellow gate, holding a cigarette. He calls the two-minute warning.

2   The runners gather in front of him, stretching. They are about to travel more than a hundred miles through the wilderness — if they are strong and lucky enough to make it that far, which they probably aren't. They wait anxiously. We, the watchers, wait anxiously. A pale wash of light is barely visible in the sky. Next to me, a skinny girl holds a skinny dog. She has come all the way from Iowa to watch her father disappear into this gray dawn.

3   All eyes are on the man in the trench coat. At precisely 7:12, he rises from his lawn chair and lights his cigarette. Once the tip glows red, the race known as the Barkley Marathons has begun. . . . The man in the trench coat — Gary Cantrell by birth, self-dubbed Lazarus Lake — has turned this terrain into the stage for a legendary ritual: the Barkley Marathons, held yearly (traditionally on Lazarus Friday or April Fool's Day) outside Wartburg, Tennessee. Lake (known as Laz) calls it "The Race That Eats Its Young." The runners' bibs say something different each year: SUFFERING

Why do you think Jamison repeats the phrase "the man in the trench coat"?

WITHOUT A POINT; NOT ALL PAIN IS GAIN. Only eight men have ever finished. The event is considered extreme even by those who specialize in extremity.

How effective is the rhetorical question and stylistic sentence fragments used to answer it?

What makes it so bad? No trail, for one. A cumulative elevation gain 4 that's nearly twice the height of Everest. Native flora called saw briars that can turn a man's legs to raw meat in meters. The tough hills have names like Rat Jaw, Little Hell, Big Hell, Testicle Spectacle — this last so-called because it inspires most runners to make the sign of the cross (crotch to eyeglasses, shoulder to shoulder) — not to mention Stallion Mountain, Bird Mountain, Coffin Springs, Zip Line, and an uphill stretch, new this year, known simply as "the Bad Thing."

What do you learn about Jamison's perspective from this passage?

The race consists of five loops on a course that's been officially listed at 5 twenty miles, but is probably more like twenty-six. The moral of this slanted truth is that standard metrics are irrelevant. The moral of a lot of Barkley's slanted truths is that standard metrics are irrelevant. The laws of physics and human tolerance have been replaced by Laz's personal whims. Even if the race was really "only" a hundred miles, these would still be "Barkley miles." Guys who could typically finish a hundred miles in twenty hours might not finish a single loop here. If you finish three, you've completed what's known as the Fun Run. If you happen not to finish — and, let's face it, you probably won't — Laz will play taps to commemorate your quitting. The whole camp, shifting and dirty and tired, will listen, except for those who are asleep or too weak to notice, who won't.

It's no easy feat to get here. There are no published entry requirements 6 or procedures. It helps to know someone. Admissions are decided by Laz's personal discretion, and his application isn't exactly standard, with questions like "What is your favorite parasite?" and a required essay with the subject "Why I Should Be Allowed to Run in the Barkley." Only thirty-five entrants are admitted. This year, one of them is my brother.

Julian is a "virgin," one of fifteen newbies who will do their damndest to 7 finish a loop. He has managed to escape the designation of "sacrificial virgin," officially applied to the virgin each year (usually the least experienced ultra-runner) whom Laz has deemed most likely to fail in a spectacular fashion — to get lost for so long, perhaps, that he manages to beat Dan Baglione's course record for slowest pace. At the age of seventy-five, in 2006, Baglione managed two miles in thirty-two hours. Something to do with an unscrewed flashlight cap, an unexpected creek.

How effective is this explanation of "lost"?

It's probably a misnomer to talk about "getting lost" at Barkley. It might 8 be closer to the truth to say you *begin* lost, remain lost through several nights in the woods, and must constantly use your compass, map, instructions, fellow runners, and remaining shards of sanity to perpetually unlose yourself again. First-timers usually try to stay with veterans who know the course, but are often scraped. "Virgin scraping" means ditching the new guy. A virgin bends down to tie his shoelaces, perhaps, and glances up to find his veteran Virgil gone.

9   The day before the race, runners start arriving at camp like rainbow seals, sleekly gliding through the air in multi-colored bodysuits. They come in pickup trucks and rental cars, rusty vans and camper trailers. Their license plates say 100 RUNNR, ULT MAN, CRZY RUN. They bring camouflage tents and orange hunting vests and skeptical girlfriends and acclimated wives and tiny travel towels and tiny dogs. Laz himself brings a little dog (named "Little Dog") with a black spot like a pirate's patch over one eye. . . .

Why do you think Jamison returns to narrating here?

10   It's a male scene. There are a few female regulars, I learn, but they rarely manage more than a loop. Most of the women in sight, like me, are part of someone's support crew. I help sort Julian's supplies in the back of the car. He needs a compass. He needs pain pills and NO-DOZ pills and electrolyte pills and Ginger Chews for when he gets sleepy and a "kit" for popping blisters that basically includes a needle and Band-Aids. He needs tape for when his toenails start falling off. He needs batteries. We pay special attention to the batteries. Running out of batteries is the *must-avoid-at-all-costs worst possible thing that could happen.* But it has happened. It happened to Rich Limacher, whose night spent under a huge buckeye tree earned it the name "Limacher Hilton." Julian's coup de grâce is a pair of duct-tape pants that we've fashioned in the manner of cowboy chaps. They will fend off saw briars, is the idea, and earn Julian the envy of the other runners. . . .

What does Jamison's shift to the participant role here let us see?

11   I watch Laz from across the campfire. He's darkly regal in his trench coat, warming his hands over the flames. I want to meet him, but haven't yet summoned the courage to introduce myself. When I look at him I can't help thinking of *Heart of Darkness*. Like Kurtz, Laz is bald and charismatic, leader of a minor empire, trafficker in human pain. He's like a cross between the Colonel and your grandpa. There's certainly an Inner Station splendor to his orchestration of this whole hormone extravaganza, testosterone spread like fertilizer across miles of barren and brambled wilderness.

How does this comparison help describe Laz?

12   He speaks to "his runners" with comfort and fondness, as if they are a batch of wayward sons turned feral each year at the flick of his lighter. Most have been running "for him" (their phrase) for years. All of them bring offerings. Everyone pays a $1.60 entry fee. Alumni bring Laz a pack of his favorite cigarettes (Camel Filters), veterans bring a new pair of socks, and virgins are responsible for a license plate. These license plates hang like laundry at the edge of camp, a wall of clattering metal flaps. Julian has brought one from Liberia, where—in his non-superhero incarnation as a development economist—he is working on a microfinance project. I asked him how one manages to procure a spare license plate in Liberia. He tells me he asked a guy on the street and the guy said, "Ten dollars," and Julian gave

him five and then it appeared. Laz immediately strings it in a place of honor, near the center, and I can tell Julian is pleased. . . .

The official Barkley requirements read like a treasure hunt: there are ten 13 books placed at various points along the course, and runners are responsible for ripping out the pages that match their race number. Laz is playful in his book choices: *The Most Dangerous Game*, *Death by Misadventure*, *A Time to Die*—even *Heart of Darkness*, a choice that seems to vindicate my associative impulses.

The big talk this year is about Laz's latest addition to the course: a quarter- 14 mile cement tunnel that runs directly under the grounds of the old penitentiary. There's a drop through a narrow concrete shaft to get in, a fifteen-foot climb to get out, and "plenty of" standing water once you're inside. There are also, rumor has it, rats the size of possums and—when it gets warmer—snakes the size of arms. . . .

When Julian comes in from his first loop, it's almost dark. He's been out 15 for twelve hours. I feel like I'm sharing this moment of triumph with Laz . . . Julian is in good spirits. He turns over his pages to be counted. He's gotten 61s, including one from *The Power of Positive Thinking*, which came early in the course, and one from an account of teenage alcoholism called *The Late Great Me*, which came near the end. I notice the duct tape has been ripped from his pants. "You took it off?" I ask.

"Nope," he says. "Course took it off." 16

In camp he eats hummus sandwiches and Girl Scout cookies, barely 17 manages to gulp down a butter pecan Ensure. He is debating another loop. "I'm sure I won't finish," he says. "I'll probably just go out for hours and then drop and have to find my way back in the dark."

Julian pauses. I take one of his cookies. 18

He says, "I guess I'll do it." 19

He takes the last cookie before I can grab it. He takes another bib num- 20 ber, for his second round of pages, and Laz and I send him into the woods. His rain jacket glows silver in the darkness: brother robot, off for another spin.

Julian has completed five hundred-mile races so far, as well as countless 21 "short" ones, and I once asked him why he does it. He explained it like this: He wants to achieve a completely insular system of accountability, one that doesn't depend on external feedback. He wants to run a hundred miles when no one knows he's running, so that the desire to impress people, or the shame of quitting, won't constitute his sources of motivation. Perhaps this kind of thinking is what got him his Ph.D. at the age of twenty-five. It's hard to say. Barkley doesn't offer a pure form of this isolated drive, but it comes pretty close: when it's midnight and it's raining and you're on the steepest hill you've ever climbed and you're bleeding from briars and you're alone and you've been alone for hours, it's only you around to witness yourself quit or continue. . . .

Margin notes:

Why do you think Jamison uses summary instead of quotation to talk about the rumor?

Why do you think Jamison tells how she felt here?

Why do you think Jamison interrupts the narrative to give us this information?

What does Jamison assume motivates Julian?

22   Of course, I have been wondering the whole time: why do people *do* this, anyway? Whenever I pose the question directly, runners reply ironically: I'm a masochist; I need somewhere to put my craziness; type A from birth; etc. I begin to understand that joking about this question is not an evasion but rather an intrinsic part of answering it. Nobody has to answer this question seriously, because they are *already* answering it seriously—with their bodies and their willpower and their pain. The body submits itself in utter earnest, in degradation and commitment, to what words can speak of only lightly. Maybe this is why so many ultra-runners are former addicts: they want to redeem the bodies they once punished, master the physical selves whose cravings they once served.

23   There is a gracefully frustrating tautology to this embodied testimony: Why do I do it? I do it because it hurts so much and I'm still willing to do it. The sheer ferocity of the effort implies that the effort is somehow worth it. This is purpose by implication rather than direct articulation. Laz says, "No one has to ask them why they're out here; they all know."

> Why does Jamison bring up these other possible motives?

24   It would be easy to fix upon any number of possible purposes—conquering the body, fellowship in pain—but it *feels* more like significance dwells in concentric circles of labor around an empty center: commitment to an impetus that resists fixity or labels. The persistence of "why" is the point: the elusive horizon of an unanswerable question, the conceptual equivalent of an un runnable race.

> What is your response to this concluding idea?

John T. Edge

I'm Not Leaving Until I Eat This Thing

John T. Edge (b. 1962) earned an MFA in creative nonfiction from Goucher College as well as an MA in southern studies from the University of Mississippi, where he currently directs the Southern Foodways Alliance at the Center for the Study of Southern Culture. A food writer for outlets such as *Oxford American,* the *New York Times,* and *Garden & Gun,* Edge has also been published in many anthologies. He has coedited several cookbooks and travel guides, and he has written several books, including *Truck Food Cookbook* (2012), a study of American street food; *Southern Belly* (2007), a portrait of southern food told through profiles of people and places; and a series on iconic American foods, including *Hamburgers and Fries: An American Story* (2005) and *Donuts: An American Passion* (2006). This reading first appeared in 1999 in *Oxford American* magazine and was reprinted in the *Utne Reader.*

For more on analyzing visuals, see Chapter 2, pp. 31–34.

- **Before you read,** look at the photo on p. 103. Why do you think Edge includes a picture of a live pig in an essay about making and eating pickled pig lips? What other photos should he have used?

- **As you read,** you will see that Edge moves between two different scenes — notice that whereas Edge uses a chronological narrative to relate what happened at Jesse's Place, he uses a topical organization to present the information he learned from his observations and interview at Farm Fresh Food Supplier processing plant. Why do you think he uses different methods for presenting these two scenes?

1   It's just past 4:00 on a Thursday afternoon in June at Jesse's Place, a country juke 17 miles south of the Mississippi line and three miles west of Amite, Louisiana. The air conditioner hacks and spits forth torrents of Arctic air, but the heat of summer can't be kept at bay. It seeps around the splintered doorjambs and settles in, transforming the squat particleboard-plastered roadhouse into a sauna. Slowly, the dank barroom fills with grease-smeared mechanics from the truck stop up the road and farmers straight from the fields, the soles of their brogans thick with dirt clods. A few weary souls make their way over from the nearby sawmill. I sit alone at the bar, one empty bottle of Bud in front of me, a second in my hand. I drain the beer, order a third, and stare down at the pink juice spreading outward from a crumpled foil pouch and onto the bar.

2   *I'm not leaving until I eat this thing,* I tell myself.

3   Half a mile down the road, behind a fence coiled with razor wire, Lionel Dufour, proprietor of Farm Fresh Food Supplier, is loading up the last truck of the day, wheeling case after case of pickled pork offal out of his cinder-block processing plant and into a semitrailer bound for Hattiesburg, Mississippi.

4   His crew packed lips today. Yesterday, it was pickled sausage; the day before that, pig feet. Tomorrow, it's pickled pig lips again. Lionel has been on the job since 2:45 in

the morning, when he came in to light the boilers. Damon Landry, chief cook and maintenance man, came in at 4:30. By 7:30, the production line was at full tilt: six women in white smocks and blue bouffant caps, slicing ragged white fat from the lips, tossing the good parts in glass jars, the bad parts in barrels bound for the rendering plant. Across the aisle, filled jars clatter by on a conveyor belt as a worker tops them off with a Kool-Aid-red slurry of hot sauce, vinegar, salt, and food coloring. Around the corner, the jars are capped, affixed with a label, and stored in pasteboard boxes to await shipping.

Unlike most offal—euphemistically called "variety meats"—lips belie their prov- 5 enance. Brains, milky white and globular, look like brains. Feet, the ghosts of their cloven hoofs protruding, look like feet. Testicles look like, well, testicles. But lips are different. Loosed from the snout, trimmed of their fat, and dyed a preternatural pink, they look more like candy than like carrion.

At Farm Fresh, no swine root in an adjacent feedlot. No viscera-strewn killing floor 6 lurks just out of sight, down a darkened hallway. These pigs died long ago at some Midwestern abattoir. By the time the lips arrive in Amite, they are, in essence, pig Popsicles, 50-pound blocks of offal and ice.

"Lips are all meat," Lionel told me earlier in the day. "No gristle, no bone, no noth- 7 ing. They're bar food, hot and vinegary, great with a beer. Used to be the lips ended up in sausages, headcheese, those sorts of things. A lot of them still do."

Lionel, a 50-year-old father of three with quick, intelligent eyes set deep in a face 8 the color of cordovan, is a veteran of nearly 40 years in the pickled pig lips business.

© Shannon Brinkman Photo

"I started out with my daddy when I wasn't much more than 10," Lionel told me, his shy smile framed by a coarse black mustache flecked with whispers of gray. "The meatpacking business he owned had gone broke back when I was 6, and he was peddling out of the back of his car, selling dried shrimp, napkins, straws, tubes of plastic cups, pig feet, pig lips, whatever the bar owners needed. He sold to black bars, white bars, sweet shops, snowball stands, you name it. We made the rounds together after I got out of school, sometimes staying out till two or three in the morning. I remember bringing my toy cars to this one joint and racing them around the floor with the bar owner's son while my daddy and his father did business."

For years after the demise of that first meatpacking company, the Dufour family   9
sold someone else's product. "We used to buy lips from Dennis Di Salvo's company down in Belle Chasse," recalled Lionel. "As far as I can tell, his mother was the one who came up with the idea to pickle and pack lips back in the '50s, back when she was working for a company called Three Little Pigs over in Houma. But pretty soon, we were selling so many lips that we had to almost beg Di Salvo's for product. That's when we started cooking up our own," he told me, gesturing toward the cast-iron kettle that hangs from the rafters by the front door of the plant. "My daddy started cooking lips in that very pot."

Lionel now cooks lips in 11 retrofitted milk tanks, dull stainless-steel cauldrons   10
shaped like oversized cradles. But little else has changed. Though Lionel's father has passed away, Farm Fresh remains a family-focused company. His wife, Kathy, keeps the books. His daughter, Dana, a button-cute college student who has won numerous beauty titles, takes to the road in the summer, selling lips to convenience stores and wholesalers. Soon, after he graduates from business school, Lionel's younger son, Matt, will take over operations at the plant. And his older son, a veterinarian, lent his name to one of Farm Fresh's top sellers, Jason's Pickled Pig Lips.

"We do our best to corner the market on lips," Lionel told me, his voice tinged with   11
bravado. "Sometimes they're hard to get from the packing houses. You gotta kill a lot of pigs to get enough lips to keep us going. I've got new customers calling every day; it's all I can do to keep up with demand, but I bust my ass to keep up. I do what I can for my family—and for my customers.

"When my customers tell me something," he continued, "just like when my daddy   12
told me something, I listen. If my customers wanted me to dye the lips green, I'd ask, 'What shade?' As it is, every few years we'll do some red and some blue for the Fourth of July. This year we did jars full of Mardi Gras lips—half purple, half gold," Lionel recalled with a chuckle. "I guess we'd had a few beers when we came up with that one."

Meanwhile, back at Jesse's Place, I finish my third Bud, order my fourth. *Now,* I tell   13
myself, my courage bolstered by booze, *I'm ready to eat a lip.*

They may have looked like candy in the plant, but in the barroom they're carrion   14
once again. I poke and prod the six-inch arc of pink flesh, peering up from my reverie just in time to catch the barkeep's wife, Audrey, staring straight at me. She fixes me with a look just this side of pity and asks, "You gonna eat that thing or make love to it?"

Her nephew, Jerry, sidles up to a bar stool on my left. "A lot of people like 'em with   15
chips," he says with a nod toward the pink juice pooling on the bar in front of me. I
offer to buy him a lip, and Audrey fishes one from a jar behind the counter, wraps it in
tinfoil, and places the whole affair on a paper towel in front of him.

I take stock of my own cowardice, and, following Jerry's lead, reach for a bag of   16
potato chips, tear open the top with my teeth, and toss the quivering hunk of hog flesh
into the shiny interior of the bag, slick with grease and dusted with salt. Vinegar vapors
tickle my nostrils. I stifle a gag that rolls from the back of my throat, swallow hard, and
pray that the urge to vomit passes.

With a smash of my hand, the potato chips are reduced to a pulp, and I feel the   17
cold lump of the lip beneath my fist. I clasp the bag shut and shake it hard in an effort
to ensure chip coverage in all the nooks and crannies of the lip. The technique that
Jerry uses—and I mimic—is not unlike that employed by home cooks mixing up a
mess of Shake 'n Bake chicken.

I pull from the bag a coral crescent of meat now crusted with blond bits of potato   18
chips. When I chomp down, the soft flesh dissolves between my teeth. It tastes like a
flaccid cracklin', unmistakably porcine, and not altogether bad. The chips help, providing texture where there was none. Slowly, my brow unfurrows, my stomach ceases
its fluttering.

Sensing my relief, Jerry leans over and peers into my bag. "Kind of look like Frosted   19
Flakes, don't they?" he says, by way of describing the chips rapidly turning to mush in
the pickling juice. I offer the bag to Jerry, order yet another beer, and turn to eye the
pig feet floating in a murky jar by the cash register, their blunt tips bobbing up through
a pasty white film.

READING FOR MEANING

1. **Read to Summarize.** Write a sentence or two explaining the main idea Edge wants his readers to understand about pickled pig lips and the Dufour family business.

For help with summarizing, see Chapter 2, pp. 24–25.

2. **Read to Respond.** Write a paragraph exploring your initial thoughts about anything that resonates with your experience, such as Lionel Dufour's story about how he "made the rounds" with his father after school (par. 8) or Edge's attempt to eat the pig lip.

3. **Read to Analyze Assumptions.** Write a paragraph or two analyzing an assumption you find intriguing in Edge's essay. For example:

You may also try contextualizing see Chapter 2, pp. 29–30.

Assumptions about culture and food. For many people, foods that they did not eat as children seem strange and sometimes even repulsive. Even though he is a southerner, Edge is squeamish about eating a popular southern delicacy, pickled pig lips. To think critically about

assumptions regarding culture and food, ask yourself questions
like these:

- Why do you suppose Edge uses the words *courage* (par. 13) and
  cowardice (par. 16) to describe his reluctance to try pickled pig lips?

- What do you think causes food anxieties, your own as well as Edge's aversion
  to pickled pig lips?

Assumptions about entrepreneurship. In interviewing Lionel Dufour
and observing the Farm Fresh Food Supplier factory, Edge gives readers
information about one small business and its hands-on proprietor.

- Among the first things Edge tells readers about Farm Fresh is that Lionel is
  the "proprietor" (par. 3) but that he loads trucks and "has been on the job
  since 2:45 in the morning" (par. 4). What does Edge think his readers are
  likely to assume about the kinds of work small-business owners like
  Lionel do?

- Although Americans usually celebrate a strong work ethic, we also tend to
  value entrepreneurship over manual labor. In what ways, if any, do you see
  these values reflected in this essay?

A Special Reading Strategy

Analyzing Visuals

Write a paragraph analyzing the photograph included in Edge's essay and
explaining what it contributes to the essay.

To do the analysis, you can use the Criteria for Analyzing Visuals chart in
Chapter 2 on pp. 32–34. Don't feel you have to answer all of the questions in
the chart; focus on those that seem most productive in helping you write a
paragraph-length analysis. To help you get started, consider adding these
questions that specifically refer to Edge's visual:

- Edge could have included a full-body photograph of a pig, a picture of
  pigs at play, or some other composition. Why do you think he chose a
  close-up of a pig's face taken from one particular angle?

- Given his purpose and audience, why do you think Edge chose a
  photograph of a pig instead of a photograph of pig lips in a jar or being
  eaten at a site like Jesse's Place? Or why didn't he choose a photograph of
  the Farm Fresh company or the Dufour family? What does the choice of
  visual suggest about the subject and the writer's perspective?

READING LIKE A WRITER

PRESENTING INFORMATION ABOUT THE SUBJECT

Like "Soup," much of the information in this profile comes from an extended interview. Edge uses three strategies for presenting what he learned from this interview:

Quotation   "Lips are all meat," Lionel told me earlier in the day. "No gristle, no bone, no nothing." (par. 7)

Paraphrase   By the time the lips arrive in Amite, they are, in essence, pig Popsicles, 50-pound blocks of offal and ice. (par. 6)

Summary   For years after the demise of that first meatpacking company, the Dufour family sold someone else's product. (par. 9)

Writers typically choose to **quote** language that is especially vivid or memorable, giving an impression of the speaker as well as providing important information. **Paraphrase** tends to be used when the writer needs to go into detail but can put the information in a more striking form than the speaker originally used. **Summary** is often used to condense lengthy information.

From his interview with Lionel, Edge gathered a lot of information about the Dufour family history and business as well as about the various products Farm Fresh sells and their production process. In addition, Edge presents information he derived from observations, particularly in paragraphs 3 through 6. Notice how he alternates information from the interview with descriptive details from his firsthand observations. Edge even tells us what he does *not* see — blood and guts on a slaughterhouse floor (par. 6). Letting readers know what he had expected, perhaps feared, appeals to readers who may share his anxieties. Moreover, it encourages readers to embrace Edge's point of view, a process of identification that begins in the opening scene in Jesse's Place and continues through the closing paragraphs.

Analyze & Write

Write a paragraph analyzing and evaluating Edge's use of quoting, paraphrasing, and summarizing information from an interview.

1. Find at least one other example of each of these strategies in paragraphs 3–12.

2. How effective are these ways of presenting information? For example, is there any quotation that could have been better presented as paraphrase or even as summary? What would have been gained or lost?

3. Locate a passage in paragraphs 3–12 where Edge presents his observations. How do you recognize this part as coming from firsthand observations? How does the alternation of information from interviews and observations contribute to your engagement as a reader?

A Special Reading Strategy

Comparing and Contrasting Related Readings: "Soup" and Edge's "I'm Not Leaving Until I Eat This Thing"

Comparing and contrasting related readings is a special critical reading strategy that is useful both in reading for meaning and in reading like a writer. This strategy is particularly applicable when writers present similar subjects, as is the case in the observational essays in this chapter by the *New Yorker* writer (p. 90) and John T. Edge (p. 102). Both writers describe a business they observed and report on their interview with the business owner. In both instances, the business involves food products and their preparation; however, Edge adopts the role of participant observer to relate what he learned, whereas the author of "Soup" maintains a more objective distance. To compare and contrast these two observational essays, think about issues such as these:

- What are the cultural contexts of these two businesses (and the periodicals in which these articles appeared)? What seems most significant about the two business philosophies represented in these essays?

- How did the two writers organize the information derived from interviews and observation? Highlight the places in each essay where information from interviews is quoted or summarized and places where information from direct observation is presented.

- Edge alternates between the participant-observer and spectator roles, while the *New Yorker* writer consistently maintains a spectator role. Note any places in "Soup" where you get a sense of the writer's point of view or judgment. What do the participant observations add to Edge's essay?

See Chapter 2, pp. 37–39 for detailed guidelines on comparing and contrasting related readings.

Gabriel Thompson

A Gringo in the Lettuce Fields

Gabriel Thompson has worked as a community organizer and has written extensively about the lives of undocumented immigrants to the United States. He has published numerous articles in periodicals such as *New York* magazine, the *New York Times,* and the *Nation.* His books include *There's No José Here: Following the Hidden Lives of Mexican Immigrants* (2006), *Calling All Radicals: How Grassroots Organizers Can Help Save Our Democracy* (2007), and *Working in the Shadows: A Year of Doing the Jobs (Most) Americans Won't Do* (2010), from which the selection below is taken. Note the photograph on p. 111 showing lettuce cutters at work, which we added from Thompson's blog, and consider what, if anything, it adds to the essay.

- **Before you read,** consider Thompson's choice of titles: *Working in the Shadows: A Year of Doing the Jobs (Most) Americans Won't Do* and "A Gringo in the Lettuce Fields." What do these titles lead you to expect will be the subject of the observations and the writer's perspective on the subject?

- **As you read,** notice how Thompson as an outsider uses participant observation to get an insider's view of the daily experience of farm workers. What does his outsider status enable him to understand — or prevent him from understanding — about the community he has entered?

I wake up staring into the bluest blue I've ever seen. I must have fallen into a deep 1
sleep because I need several seconds to realize that I'm looking at the Arizona sky, that the pillow beneath my head is a large clump of dirt, and that a near-stranger named Manuel is standing over me, smiling. I pull myself to a sitting position. To my left, in the distance, a Border Patrol helicopter is hovering. To my right is Mexico, separated by only a few fields of lettuce. "*Buenos días,*" Manuel says.

I stand up gingerly. It's only my third day in the fields, but already my 30-year-old 2
body is failing me. I feel like someone has dropped a log on my back. And then piled that log onto a truck with many other logs, and driven that truck over my thighs. "Let's go," I say, trying to sound energetic as I fall in line behind Manuel, stumbling across rows of lettuce and thinking about "the five-day rule." The five-day rule, according to Manuel, is simple: Survive the first five days and you'll be fine. He's been a farmworker for almost two decades, so he should know. I'm on day three of five—the goal is within sight. Of course, another way to look at my situation is that I'm on day three of what I promised myself would be a two-month immersion in the work life of the people who do a job that most Americans won't do. But thinking about the next seven weeks doesn't benefit anyone. *Day three of five.*

"Manuel! Gabriel! Let's go! *¡Vámonos!*" yells Pedro, our foreman. Our short break 3
is over. Two dozen crew members standing near the lettuce machine are already

putting on gloves and sharpening knives. Manuel and I hustle toward the machine, grab our own knives from a box of chlorinated water, and set up in neighboring rows, just as the machine starts moving slowly down another endless field.

Since the early 1980s, Yuma, Ariz., has been the "winter lettuce capital" of Amer- 4 ica. Each winter, when the weather turns cold in Salinas, California—the heart of the nation's lettuce industry—temperatures in sunny Yuma are still in the 70s and 80s. At the height of Yuma's growing season, the fields surrounding the city produce virtually all of the iceberg lettuce and 90 percent of the leafy green vegetables consumed in the United States and Canada.

America's lettuce industry actually needs people like me. Before applying for field- 5 work at the local Dole headquarters, I came across several articles describing the causes of a farmworker shortage. The stories cited an aging workforce, immigration crack-downs, and long delays at the border that discourage workers with green cards who would otherwise commute to the fields from their Mexican homes.[1] Wages have been rising somewhat in response to the demand for laborers (one prominent member of the local growers association tells me average pay is now between $10 and $12 an hour), but it's widely assumed that most U.S. citizens wouldn't do the work at any price. Arizona's own Senator John McCain created a stir in 2006 when he issued a challenge to a group of union members in Washington, D.C. "I'll offer anybody here $50 an hour if you'll go pick lettuce in Yuma this season, and pick for the whole season," he said. Amid jeers, he didn't back down, telling the audience, "You can't do it, my friends."

On my first day I discover that even putting on a lettuce cutter's uniform is chal- 6 lenging (no fieldworkers, I learn, "pick" lettuce). First, I'm handed a pair of black galoshes to go over my shoes. Next comes the *gancho*, an S-shaped hook that slips over my belt to hold packets of plastic bags. A white glove goes on my right hand, a gray glove, supposedly designed to offer protection from cuts, goes on my left. Over the cloth gloves I pull on a pair of latex gloves. I put on a black hairnet, my baseball cap, and a pair of protective sunglasses. Adding to my belt a long leather sheath, I'm good to go. I feel ridiculous.

The crew is already working in the field when Pedro walks me out to them and 7 introduces me to Manuel. Manuel is holding an 18-inch knife in his hand. "Manuel has been cutting for many years, so watch him to see how it's done," Pedro says. Then he walks away. Manuel resumes cutting, following a machine that rolls along just ahead of the crew. Every several seconds Manuel bends down, grabs a head of iceberg lettuce with his left hand, and makes a quick cut with the knife in his right hand, sepa-rating the lettuce from its roots. Next, he lifts the lettuce to his stomach and makes a second cut, trimming the trunk. He shakes the lettuce, letting the outer leaves fall to the ground. With the blade still in his hand, he then brings the lettuce toward the *gancho* at his waist, and with a flick of the wrist the head is bagged and dropped onto

---

[1]A green card is an immigration document that allows noncitizens to work legally in the United States, whether they live here or commute across the border. Undocu-mented workers (or illegal immigrants, depending on your position) lack green cards. [Editor's note]

one of the machine's extensions. Manuel does this over and over again, explaining each movement. "It's not so hard," he says. Five minutes later, Pedro reappears and tells me to grab a knife. Manuel points to a head of lettuce. "Try this one," he says.

I bend over, noticing that most of the crew has turned to watch. I take my knife and make a tentative sawing motion where I assume the trunk to be, though I'm really just guessing. Grabbing the head with my left hand, I straighten up, doing my best to imitate Manuel. Only my lettuce head doesn't move; it's still securely connected to the soil. Pedro steps in. "When you make the first cut, it is like you are stabbing the lettuce." He makes a quick jabbing action. "You want to aim for the center of the lettuce, where the trunk is," he says. 8

Ten minutes later, after a couple of other discouraging moments, I've cut maybe 20 heads of lettuce and am already feeling pretty accomplished. I'm not perfect: If I don't stoop far enough, my stab—instead of landing an inch above the ground—goes right through the head of lettuce, ruining it entirely. The greatest difficulty, though, is in the trimming. I had no idea that a head of lettuce was so humongous. In order to get it into a shape that can be bagged, I trim and trim and trim, but it's taking me upward of a minute to do what Manuel does in several seconds. 9

Pedro offers me a suggestion. "Act like the lettuce is a bomb," he says. "Imagine you've only got five seconds to get rid of it." 10

Surprisingly, that thought seems to work, and I'm able to greatly increase my speed. For a minute or two I feel euphoric. "Look at me!" I want to shout at Pedro; I'm in the zone. But the woman who is packing the lettuce into boxes soon swivels around to face me. "Look, this lettuce is no good." She's right: I've cut the trunk too high, breaking off dozens of good leaves, which will quickly turn brown because they're attached to nothing. With her left hand she holds the bag up, and with her right she smashes it violently, making a loud pop. She turns the bag over and the massacred lettuce falls to the ground. She does the same for the three other bags I've placed on the extension. "It's okay," Manuel tells me. "You shouldn't try to go too fast when you're beginning." Pedro seconds him. "That's right. Make sure the cuts are precise and that you don't rush." 11

Courtesy of Gabriel Thompson

So I am to be very careful and precise, while also treating the lettuce like a bomb 12
that must be tossed aside after five seconds.

That first week on the job was one thing. By midway into week two, it isn't clear to 13
me what more I can do to keep up with the rest of the crew. I know the techniques by
this time and am moving as fast as my body will permit. Yet I need to somehow *double*
my current output to hold my own. I'm able to cut only one row at a time while
Manuel is cutting two. Our fastest cutter, Julio, meanwhile can handle three. But how
someone could cut two rows for an hour—much less an entire day—is beyond me.
"Oh, you will get it," Pedro tells me one day. "You will most definitely get it." Maybe
he's trying to be hopeful or inspiring, but it comes across as a threat.

That feeling aside, what strikes me about our 31-member crew is how quickly they 14
have welcomed me as one of their own. I encountered some suspicion at first, but it
didn't last. Simply showing up on the second day seemed to be proof enough that I was
there to work. When I faltered in the field and fell behind, hands would come across
from adjacent rows to grab a head or two of my lettuce so I could catch up. People
whose names I didn't yet know would ask me how I was holding up, reminding me that
it would get easier as time went by. If I took a seat alone during a break, someone would
call me into their group and offer a homemade taco or two.

Two months in, I make the mistake of calling in sick one Thursday. The day before, 15
I put my left hand too low on a head of lettuce. When I punched my blade through the
stem, the knife struck my middle finger. Thanks to the gloves, my skin wasn't even
broken, but the finger instantly turned purple. I took two painkillers to get through the
afternoon, but when I wake the next morning it is still throbbing. With one call to an
answering machine that morning, and another the next day, I create my own four-day
weekend.

The surprise is that when I return on Monday, feeling recuperated, I wind up having 16
the hardest day of my brief career in lettuce. Within hours, my hands feel weaker than
ever. By quitting time—some 10 hours after our day started—I feel like I'm going to
vomit from exhaustion. A theory forms in my mind. Early in the season—say, after the
first week—a farmworker's body gets thoroughly broken down. Back, legs, and arms
grow sore, hands and feet swell up. A tolerance for the pain is developed, though, and
two-day weekends provide just enough time for the body to recover from the trauma.
My four-day break had been too long; my body actually began to recuperate, and it
wanted more time to continue. Instead, it was thrown right back into the mix and
rebelled. Only on my second day back did my body recover that middle ground. "I
don't think the soreness goes away," I say to Manuel and two other co-workers one
day. "You just forget what it's like not to be sore." Manuel, who's 37, considers this.
"That's true, that's true," he says. "It always takes a few weeks at the end of the year to
get back to normal, to recover."

An older co-worker, Mateo, is the one who eventually guesses that I have joined the 17
crew because I want to write about it. "That is good," he says over coffee at his home
one Sunday. "Americans should know the hard work that Mexicans do in this country."

Mateo is an unusual case. There aren't many other farmworkers who are still in the 18
fields when they reach their 50s. It's simply not possible to do this work for decades

and not suffer a permanently hunched back, or crooked fingers, or hands so swollen that they look as if someone has attached a valve to a finger and pumped vigorously. The punishing nature of the work helps explain why farmworkers don't live very long; the National Migrant Resources Program puts their life expectancy at 49 years.

"Are you cutting two rows yet?" Mateo asks me. "Yes, more or less," I say. "I thought I'd be better by now." Mateo shakes his head. "It takes a long time to learn how to really cut lettuce. It's not something that you learn after only one season. Three, maybe four seasons—then you start understanding how to really work with lettuce." 19

READING FOR MEANING

1. **Read to Summarize.** Write a sentence or two explaining the main idea Thompson wants his readers to understand about his observations.

   For help with summarizing, see Chapter 2, pp. 24–25.

2. **Read to Respond.** Write a paragraph examining anything that seems surprising, such as Thompson's amazement that the other members of the crew "welcomed [him] as one of their own" (par. 14) or his "theory" that farmworkers develop a "tolerance for the pain" (par. 16).

3. **Read to Analyze Assumptions.** Write a paragraph or two analyzing an assumption you find intriguing in Thompson's essay. For example:

   Assumptions about the ethics of undercover observation. Participant observation does not necessarily involve secrecy, but Thompson chose to keep secret his intention to write about his experience as a lettuce cutter.

   For more help analyzing assumptions, see Chapter 2, pp. 28–29.

   - How valuable are immersion experiences like Thompson's to the individual observing, to the group being observed, and to readers in general?

   - What ethical challenges, if any, do you see with this kind of observational writing?

   Assumptions about the kinds of work done by guest or immigrant workers. As the subtitle of his book indicates, Thompson assumes that cutting lettuce falls into the category of *Jobs (Most) Americans Won't Do*. Many of the people who traditionally do these jobs are itinerant farm workers traveling seasonally from field to field (par. 5).

   - Given that wages for farmworkers are "between $10 and $12 an hour," why do you think it is "widely assumed that most U.S. citizens wouldn't do the work at any price" (par. 5)?

   - Thompson seems to be surprised not only by the physical demands of the work but by the high level of skill required to do it well. What do you think most Americans assume about skilled labor versus the "unskilled" manual labor performed by guest and immigrant workers?

READING LIKE A WRITER

ADOPTING AN AUTHORIAL ROLE

Thompson takes on the role of participant observer: He does not watch lettuce cutters from the sidelines but rather works among them for two months. His informal interviews take place during work or on breaks or at the homes of his coworkers during the weekend. Nevertheless, there is a significant difference between a two-month experiment and a personal account written by a lettuce cutter like Mateo after a lifetime at the job. An observational writer may participate but is always to some extent an outsider looking in.

Analyze & Write

Write a paragraph or two analyzing Thompson's use of the participant-observer role:

1. Skim the text, highlighting each time Thompson

    - reminds readers of his status as an outsider—for example, when he refers to a coworker as a "near-stranger" (par. 1)

    - tells readers about something he thinks will be unfamiliar to them—for example, when he explains people do not "'pick' lettuce" (par. 6)

    - calls attention to his own incompetence or failings—for example, when he describes his first attempt to cut lettuce (par. 8)

2. Why do you think Thompson tells us about his errors and reminds us that he is an outsider? What effect are these moves likely to have on his target audience? What are the advantages, if any, of adopting the participant-observer role (as Thompson does) instead of the spectator role (as Brian Cable, in the essay on pp. 122–26, and the author of "Soup" do, for example)?

Amanda Coyne

The Long Good-Bye: Mother's Day in Federal Prison

Amanda Coyne earned a master of fine arts degree in creative writing at the University of Iowa, where she was the recipient of an Iowa Arts Fellowship. She was the cofounder of and a writer for *Alaska Dispatch News,* an award-winning online news site. Her work has appeared in such publications as *Harper's,* the *New York Times Magazine, Bust, Newsweek,* and the *Guardian.* Coyne coauthored a book about oil and politics in Alaska entitled *Crude Awakening: Money, Mavericks, and Mayhem in Alaska* (2011). In 2013, she started an influential blog about Alaska politics, and in 2015, she joined the staff of the new Alaska senator, Dan Sullivan, as a senior adviser and speechwriter. "The Long Good-Bye," her first piece of published writing, originally appeared in *Harper's.* Coyne uses direct observation and interview to study the behavior of a particular community. In this profile, Coyne examines women who have been incarcerated and separated from their children to see how the mothers and children negotiate their difficult relationships.

- **Before you read**, notice how Coyne describes the convict-moms in the opening two paragraphs. What is the dominant impression you get from that description?

- **As you read**, think about the way Coyne compares and contrasts two convict-moms and their sons — Jennifer and Toby, and Stephanie and Ellie. What insights do you get from juxtaposing these two families?

You can spot the convict-moms here in the visiting room by the way they hold and touch their children and by the single flower that is perched in front of them — a rose, a tulip, a daffodil. Many of these mothers have untied the bow that attaches the flower to its silver-and-red cellophane wrapper and are using one of the many empty soda cans at hand as a vase. They sit proudly before their flower-in-a-Coke-can, amid Hershey bar wrappers, half-eaten Ding Dongs, and empty paper coffee cups. Occasionally, a mother will pick up her present and bring it to her nose when one of the bearers of the single flower — her child — asks if she likes it. And the mother will respond the way that mothers always have and always will respond when presented with a gift on this day. "Oh, I just love it. It's perfect. I'll put it in the middle of my Bible." Or, "I'll put it on my desk, right next to your school picture." And always: "It's the best one here." 1

But most of what is being smelled today is the children themselves. While the other adults are plunking coins into the vending machines, the mothers take deep whiffs from the backs of their children's necks, or kiss and smell the backs of their knees, or take off their shoes and tickle their feet and then pull them close to their noses. They hold them tight and take in their own second scent — the scent assuring them that these are still their children and that they still belong to them. 2

The visitors are allowed to bring in pockets full of coins, and today that Mother's   3
Day flower, and I know from previous visits to my older sister here at the Federal
Prison Camp for women in Pekin, Illinois, that there is always an aberrant urge to
gather immediately around the vending machines. The sandwiches are stale, the
coffee weak, the candy bars the ones we always pass up in a convenience store. But
after we hand the children over to their mothers, we gravitate toward those
machines. Like milling in the kitchen at a party. We all do it, and nobody knows
why. Polite conversation ensues around the microwave while the popcorn is popping and the processed-chicken sandwiches are being heated. We ask one another
where we are from, how long a drive we had. An occasional whistle through the
teeth, a shake of the head. "My, my, long way from home, huh?" "Staying at the
Super 8 right up the road. Not a bad place." "Stayed at the Econo Lodge last time.
Wasn't a good place at all." Never asking the questions we really want to ask:
"What's she in for?" "How much time's she got left?" You never ask in the waiting
room of a doctor's office either. Eventually, all of us—fathers, mothers, sisters,
brothers, a few boyfriends, and very few husbands—return to the queen of the day,
sitting at a fold-out table loaded with snacks, prepared for five or so hours of
attempted normal conversation.

Most of the inmates are elaborately dressed, many in prison-crafted dresses and   4
sweaters in bright blues and pinks. They wear meticulously applied makeup in corresponding hues, and their hair is replete with loops and curls—hair that only
women with the time have the time for. Some of the better seamstresses have cro-
cheted vests and purses to match their outfits. Although the world outside would
never accuse these women of making haute-couture fashion statements, the
fathers and the sons and the boyfriends and the very few husbands think they
look beautiful, and they tell them so repeatedly. And I can imagine the hours
spent preparing for this visit—hours of needles and hooks clicking over brightly
colored yards of yarn. The hours of discussing, dissecting, and bragging about
these visitors—especially the men. Hours spent in the other world behind the
door where we're not allowed, sharing lipsticks and mascaras, and unraveling
the occasional hair-tangled hot roller, and the brushing out and lifting and teasing . . . and the giggles that abruptly change into tears without warning—things
that define any female-only world. Even, or especially, if that world is a female
federal prison camp.

While my sister Jennifer is with her son in the playroom, an inmate's mother comes   5
over to introduce herself to my younger sister, Charity, my brother, John, and me. She
tells us about visiting her daughter in a higher-security prison before she was trans-
ferred here. The woman looks old and tired, and her shoulders sag under the weight
of her recently acquired bitterness.

"Pit of fire," she says, shaking her head. "Like a pit of fire straight from hell. Never   6
seen anything like it. Like something out of an old movie about prisons." Her voice is
getting louder and she looks at each of us with pleading eyes. "My *daughter* was
there. Don't even get me started on that place. Women die there."

John and Charity and I silently exchange glances.   7

"My daughter would come to the visiting room with a black eye and I'd think, 'All   8
she did was sit in the car while her boyfriend ran into the house.' She didn't even
touch the stuff. Never even handled it."

She continues to stare at us, each in turn. "Ten years. That boyfriend talked and he   9
got three years. She didn't know anything. Had nothing to tell them. They gave her ten
years. They called it conspiracy. Conspiracy? Aren't there real criminals out there?" She
asks this with hands outstretched, waiting for an answer that none of us can give her.

The woman's daughter, the conspirator, is chasing her son through the maze of   10
chairs and tables and through the other children. She's a twenty-four-year-old blonde,
whom I'll call Stephanie, with Dorothy Hamill hair and matching dimples. She looks
like any girl you might see in any shopping mall in middle America. She catches her
chocolate-brown son and tickles him, and they laugh and trip and fall together onto
the floor and laugh harder.

Had it not been for that wait in the car, this scene would be taking place at home,   11
in a duplex Stephanie would rent while trying to finish her two-year degree in den-
tal hygiene or respiratory therapy at the local community college. The duplex would
be spotless, with a blown-up picture of her and her son over the couch and ceramic
unicorns and horses occupying the shelves of the entertainment center. She would
make sure that her son went to school every day with stylishly floppy pants,
scrubbed teeth, and a good breakfast in his belly. Because of their difference in skin
color, there would be occasional tension — caused by the strange looks from strangers, teachers, other mothers, and the bullies on the playground, who would chant
after they knocked him down, "Your Momma's white, your Momma's white." But if
she were home, their weekends and evenings would be spent together transcending
those looks and healing those bruises. Now, however, their time is spent eating
visiting-room junk food and his school days are spent fighting the boys in the playground who chant, "Your Momma's in prison, your Momma's in prison."

He will be ten when his mother is released, the same age my nephew will be   12
when his mother is let out. But Jennifer, my sister, was able to spend the first five years
of Toby's life with him. Stephanie had Ellie after she was incarcerated. They let her
hold him for eighteen hours, then sent her back to prison. She has done the "tour,"
and her son is a well-traveled six-year-old. He has spent weekends visiting his mother
in prisons in Kentucky, Texas, Connecticut (the Pit of Fire), and now at last here, the
camp — minimum security, Pekin, Illinois.

Ellie looks older than his age. But his shoulders do not droop like his grandmother's.   13
On the contrary, his bitterness lifts them and his chin higher than a child's should be,
and the childlike, wide-eyed curiosity has been replaced by defiance. You can see his
emerging hostility as he and his mother play together. She tells him to pick up the toy
that he threw, say, or to put the deck of cards away. His face turns sullen, but she persists.
She takes him by the shoulders and looks him in the eye, and he uses one of his hands to
swat at her. She grabs the hand and he swats with the other. Eventually, she pulls him
toward her and smells the top of his head, and she picks up the cards or the toy herself.
After all, it is Mother's Day and she sees him so rarely. But her acquiescence makes
him angrier, and he stalks out of the playroom with his shoulders thrown back.

Toby, my brother and sister and I assure one another, will not have these resent- 14 ments. He is better taken care of than most. He is living with relatives in Wisconsin. Good, solid, middle-class, churchgoing relatives. And when he visits us, his aunts and his uncle, we take him out for adventures where we walk down the alley of a city and pretend that we are being chased by the "bad guys." We buy him fast food, and his uncle, John, keeps him up well past his bedtime enthralling him with stories of the monkeys he met in India. A perfect mix, we try to convince one another. Until we take him to see his mother and on the drive back he asks the question that most con- fuses him, and no doubt all the other children who spend much of their lives in prison visiting rooms: "Is my Mommy a bad guy?" It is the question that most seriously disor- ders his five-year-old need to clearly separate right from wrong. And because our own need is perhaps just as great, it is the question that haunts us as well.

Now, however, the answer is relatively simple. In a few years, it won't be. In a few 15 years we will have to explain mandatory minimums, and the war on drugs, and the murky conspiracy laws, and the enormous amount of money and time that federal agents pump into imprisoning low-level drug dealers and those who happen to be their friends and their lovers. In a few years he might have the reasoning skills to ask why so many armed robbers and rapists and child-molesters and, indeed, murderers are punished less severely than his mother. When he is older, we will somehow have to explain to him the difference between federal crimes, which don't allow for parole, and state crimes, which do. We will have to explain that his mother was taken from him for five years not because she was a drug dealer but because she made four phone calls for someone she loved.

But we also know it is vitally important that we explain all this without betraying 16 our bitterness. We understand the danger of abstract anger, of being disillusioned with your country, and, most of all, we do not want him to inherit that legacy. We would still like him to be raised as we were, with the idea that we live in the best country in the world with the best legal system in the world—a legal system care- fully designed to be immune to political mood swings and public hysteria; a system that promises to fit the punishment to the crime. We want him to be a good citizen. We want him to have absolute faith that he lives in a fair country, a country that watches over and protects its most vulnerable citizens: its women and children.

So for now we simply say, "Toby, your mother isn't bad, she just did a bad thing. 17 Like when you put rocks in the lawn mower's gas tank. You weren't bad then, you just did a bad thing."

Once, after being given this weak explanation, he said, "I wish I could have done 18 something really bad, like my Mommy. So I could go to prison too and be with her."

It's now 3:00. Visiting ends at 3:30. The kids are getting cranky, and the adults are both 19 exhausted and wired from too many hours of conversation, too much coffee and candy. The fathers, mothers, sisters, brothers, and the few boyfriends, and the very few husbands are beginning to show signs of gathering the trash. The mothers of the infants are giving their heads one last whiff before tucking them and their paraphernalia into their respective carrying cases. The visitors meander toward the door, leaving the older children with their mothers for one last word. But the mothers never say what they want to say to their children. They say things like, "Do well in school," "Be nice to your sister," "Be good for Aunt Berry, or Grandma." They don't say, "I'm sorry I'm sorry I'm sorry. I love you more than anything else in the world and I think about you every minute and I worry about you with a pain that shoots straight to my heart, a pain so great I think I will just burst when I think of you alone, without me. I'm sorry."

We are standing in front of the double glass doors that lead to the outside world. 20 My older sister holds her son, rocking him gently. They are both crying. We give her a look and she puts him down. Charity and I grasp each of his small hands, and the four of us walk through the doors. As we're walking out, my brother sings one of his banana songs to Toby.

"Take me out to the—" and Toby yells out, "Banana store!" 21

"Buy me some —" 22

"Bananas!!" 23

"I don't care if I ever come back. For it's root, root, root for the—" 24

"Monkey team!" 25

I turn back and see a line of women standing behind the glass wall. Some of them 26 are crying, but many simply stare with dazed eyes. Stephanie is holding both of her son's hands in hers and speaking urgently to him. He is struggling, and his head is twisting violently back and forth. He frees one of his hands from her grasp, balls up his fist, and punches her in the face. Then he walks with purpose through the glass doors and out the exit. I look back at her. She is still in a crouched position. She stares, unblinking, through those doors. Her hands have left her face and are hanging on either side of her. I look away, but before I do, I see drops of blood drip from her nose, down her chin, and onto the shiny marble floor.

READING FOR MEANING

1. **Read to Summarize.** Write a sentence or two explaining the essence of what Coyne observes when she visits her sister in prison.

   For help summarizing, see Chapter 2, pp. 24–25.

2. **Read to Respond.** Write a paragraph exploring your reactions to anything touching or disturbing, such as the mothers smelling their children (par. 2) or their attempts to make themselves beautiful for the visit (par. 4).

3. **Read to Analyze Assumptions.** Write a paragraph or two analyzing an assumption that interests you in Coyne's observational essay. For example:

   For help analyzing assumptions, see Chapter 2, pp. 28–29.

   Assumptions about fairness and the legal system. Near the end of the essay, Coyne reveals that she wishes her nephew Toby would grow up to "have absolute faith that he lives in a fair country" (par. 16).

   - Why do you think Coyne believes her sister's punishment is unfair? Why does Stephanie's mother think Stephanie's punishment is unfair? Do you agree or disagree?

- What does Coyne assume about American culture when she refers to "political mood swings and public hysteria" and when she uses the slogan "make the punishment fit the crime" (par. 16)?

Assumptions about children's rebelliousness. Coyne seems to assume that Ellie's rebellious behavior toward Stephanie is his way of responding to the enforced separation from his mother (par. 13).

- What do you think leads Coyne to make this assumption? How convincing do you think it is to assume that Ellie's behavior is caused by his separation from his mother?

- What other assumptions might one have about the causes of Ellie's behavior? For example, how do you think his grandmother's anger is likely to affect him?

READING LIKE A WRITER

CONVEYING A PERSPECTIVE ON THE SUBJECT

For more on comparing and contrasting, see Chapter 2, pp. 37–39.
Unlike arguments supporting positions or justifying evaluations, which tell readers directly what the writer thinks and why, observational writing often uses comparison/contrast to lead readers to draw their own conclusion. Writers often use transitional words and phrases to make explicit the relationship between the two items being compared or contrasted. For example:

Transition cues contrast	**Although** the world outside would never accuse these women of making haute-couture fashion statements, the fathers and the sons and the boyfriends and the very few husbands think they look beautiful. . . . (par. 4)

Sometimes writers leave out the transition and simply juxtapose the things that are being compared or contrasted by placing them side by side.

Comma cues juxtaposition	He will be ten when his mother is released, the <u>same</u> age my nephew will be when his mother is let out. (par. 12)
Word choice cues comparison	

In this example, the word *same* lets readers know Coyne is pointing out a similarity between the two families. Note that she follows this sentence with an explicit transition to stress that although the two mother-son relationships are comparable, there are significant differences between them:

Transition cues contrast	**But** Jennifer, my sister, was able to spend the first five years of Toby's life with him. Stephanie had Ellie after she was incarcerated. They let her hold him for eighteen hours, then sent her back to prison. (par. 12)

Analyze & Write

Write a paragraph or two analyzing how Coyne uses comparison/contrast cues and juxtapositions to convey her perspective on the plight of convict-moms and their relationships with their kids.

1. Note in the margin which paragraphs focus on Coyne's sister Jennifer and her son Toby and which focus on Stephanie and her son Ellie. Mark where Coyne juxtaposes the two families and where she uses transitions to highlight the comparisons and contrasts. What differences between the two families does Coyne emphasize? What do you think she wants readers to understand about the dilemma of convict-moms and their relationship with their children?

2. Also consider how Coyne sets up a contrast in paragraphs 10–11 between what is and what could have been. What cues does she use to signal this contrast? How does this contrast help convey Coyne's perspective on the plight of women like her sister and children like her nephew?

Brian Cable

The Last Stop

Brian Cable wrote the following observational essay based on a visit to a mortuary, or funeral home, when he was a first-year college student. He records what he sees and interviews two key people, the funeral director and the embalmer. In reporting his observations, he seems equally concerned with the burial process — from the purchase of a casket to the display of the body — and the people who manage this process. Notice also that Cable introduces two pieces of information he got from background research rather than from his own observations and interviews: the photograph of the Promethean casket in paragraph 21 and the information in paragraph 22 about the amount of money spent on funerals. Both came from the Internet. Cable follows academic conventions to reference the photograph as "Fig. 2" with a caption that indicates the content of the photograph. For the statistics, he uses parenthetical citation keyed to a Works Cited list at the end of the essay.

- **Before you read,** notice that Cable opens his essay with a quotation, or epigraph, from Mark Twain. What does this quotation lead you to expect?
- **As you read,** notice passages where Cable tries to use humor. Given his subject and the rhetorical situation of writing for a class, how effective is his choice of tone?

Let us endeavor so to live that when we come to die even the undertaker will be sorry.

— MARK TWAIN, *PUDD'NHEAD WILSON*

Death is a subject largely ignored by the living. We don't discuss it much, not as children (when Grandpa dies, he is said to be "going away"), not as adults, not even as senior citizens. Throughout our lives, death remains intensely private. The death of a loved one can be very painful, partly because of the sense of loss, but also because someone else's mortality reminds us all too vividly of our own.   1

More than a few people avert their eyes as they walk past the dusty-pink building that houses the Goodbody Mortuary. It looks a bit like a church—tall, with gothic arches and stained glass—and somewhat like an apartment complex—low, with many windows stamped out of red brick (see Fig 1).   2

It wasn't at all what I had expected. I thought it would be more like Forest Lawn, serene with lush green lawns and meticulously groomed gardens, a place set apart from the hustle of day-to-day life. Here instead was an odd pink structure set in the middle of a business district. On top of the Goodbody Mortuary sign was a large electric clock. What the hell, I thought. Mortuaries are concerned with time, too.   3

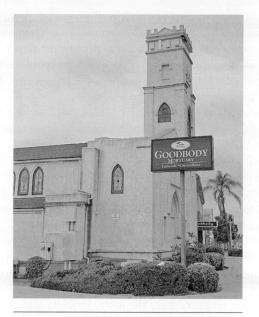

FIGURE 1. The Goodbody Mortuary.
Justin Cressy

I was apprehensive as I climbed the stone steps to the entrance. I feared rejection 4
or, worse, an invitation to come and stay. The door was massive, yet it swung open
easily on well-oiled hinges. "Come in," said the sign. "We're always open." Inside was
a cool and quiet reception room. Curtains were drawn against the outside glare, cutting the light down to a soft glow.

I found the funeral director in the main lobby, adjacent to the reception room. 5
Like most people, I had preconceptions about what an undertaker looked like. Mr.
Deaver fulfilled my expectations entirely. Tall and thin, he even had beady eyes
and a bony face. A low, slanted forehead gave way to a beaked nose. His skin,
scrubbed of all color, contrasted sharply with his jet black hair. He was wearing a
starched white shirt, gray pants, and black shoes. Indeed, he looked like death on
two legs.

He proved an amiable sort, however, and was easy to talk to. As funeral director, 6
Mr. Deaver ("Call me Howard") was responsible for a wide range of services. Goodbody Mortuary, upon notification of someone's death, will remove the remains from
the hospital or home. They then prepare the body for viewing, whereupon features
distorted by illness or accident are restored to their natural condition. The body is
embalmed and then placed in a casket selected by the family of the deceased. Services
are held in one of three chapels at the mortuary, and afterward the casket is placed in
a "visitation room," where family and friends can pay their last respects. Goodbody
also makes arrangements for the purchase of a burial site and transports the body
there for burial.

All this information Howard related in a well-practiced, professional manner. It 7 was obvious he was used to explaining the specifics of his profession. We sat alone in the lobby. His desk was bone clean, no pencils or paper, nothing—just a telephone. He did all his paperwork at home; as it turned out, he and his wife lived right upstairs. The phone rang. As he listened, he bit his lips and squeezed his Adam's apple somewhat nervously.

"I think we'll be able to get him in by Friday. No, no, the family wants him 8 cremated."

His tone was that of a broker conferring on the Dow Jones. Directly behind him 9 was a sign announcing "Visa and Master Charge Welcome Here." It was tacked to the wall, right next to a crucifix.

"Some people have the idea that we are bereavement specialists, that we can han- 10 dle emotional problems which follow a death: Only a trained therapist can do that. We provide services for the dead, not counseling for the living."

Physical comfort was the one thing they did provide for the living. The lobby was 11 modestly but comfortably furnished. There were several couches, in colors ranging from earth brown to pastel blue, and a coffee table in front of each one. On one table lay some magazines and a vase of flowers. Another supported an aquarium. Paintings of pastoral scenes hung on every wall. The lobby looked more or less like that of an old hotel. Nothing seemed to match, but it had a homey, lived-in look.

"The last time the Goodbodies decorated was in '59, I believe. It still makes people 12 feel welcome."

And so "Goodbody" was not a name made up to attract customers but the owner's 13 family name. The Goodbody family started the business way back in 1915. Today, they do over five hundred services a year.

"We're in *Ripley's Believe It or Not*, along with another funeral home whose own- 14 ers' names are Baggit and Sackit," Howard told me, without cracking a smile.

I followed him through an arched doorway into a chapel that smelled musty and old. 15 The only illumination came from sunlight filtered through a stained glass ceiling. Ahead of us lay a casket. I could see that it contained a man dressed in a black suit. Wooden benches ran on either side of an aisle that led to the body. I got no closer. From the red roses across the dead man's chest, it was apparent that services had already been held.

"It was a large service," remarked Howard. "Look at that casket—a beautiful work 16 of craftsmanship."

I guess it was. Death may be the great leveler, but one's coffin quickly reestablishes 17 one's status.

We passed into a bright, fluorescent-lit "display room." Inside were thirty coffins, 18 lids open, patiently awaiting inspection. Like new cars on the showroom floor, they gleamed with high-gloss finishes.

"We have models for every price range." 19

Indeed, there was a wide variety. They came in all colors and various materials. 20 Some were little more than cloth-covered cardboard boxes, others were made of wood, and a few were made of steel, copper, or bronze. Howard told me prices started at $500 and averaged about $1,800. He motioned toward the center of the room: "The top of the line."

This was a solid bronze casket, its seams electronically welded to resist corrosion. 21 Moisture-proof and air-tight, it could be hermetically sealed off from all outside elements. Its handles were plated with 14-karat gold. The Promethean casket made by the Batesville Casket Company is the choice of celebrities and the very wealthy (see Fig 2). The price: a cool $25,000 (Russell).

A proper funeral remains a measure of respect for the deceased. But it is expensive. 22 In the United States, the amount spent annually on funerals is around $12 billion (Grassley). Among ceremonial expenditures, funerals are second only to weddings. As a result, practices are changing. Howard has been in this business for forty years. He remembers a time when everyone was buried. Nowadays, with burials costing more than $7,000 a shot (Grassley), people often opt instead for cremation—as Howard put it, "a cheap, quick, and easy means of disposal." In some areas of the country, according to Howard, the cremation rate is now over 60 percent. Observing this trend, one might wonder whether burials are becoming obsolete. Do burials serve an important role in society?

For Tim, Goodbody's licensed mortician, the answer is very definitely yes. Burials will 23 remain in common practice, according to the slender embalmer with the disarming smile, because they allow family and friends to view the deceased. Painful as it may be, such an experience brings home the finality of death. "Something deep within us demands a confrontation with death," Tim explained. "A last look assures us that the person we loved is, indeed, gone forever."

Apparently, we also need to be assured that the body will be laid to rest in comfort 24 and peace. The average casket, with its innerspring mattress and pleated satin lining, is surprisingly roomy and luxurious. Perhaps such an air of comfort makes it easier for the family to give up their loved one. In addition, the burial site fixes the deceased in the survivors' memory, like a new address. Cremation provides none of these comforts.

FIGURE 2. "The top of the line." The Promethean casket that Michael Jackson was buried in.
© REUTERS/Mario Anzuoni/Landov

Tim started out as a clerk in a funeral home but then studied to become a mortician. 25 "It was a profession I could live with," he told me with a sly grin. Mortuary science might be described as a cross between pre-med and cosmetology, with courses in anatomy and embalming as well as in restorative art.

Tim let me see the preparation, or embalming, room, a white-walled chamber 26 about the size of an operating room. Against the wall was a large sink with elbow taps and a draining board. In the center of the room stood a table with equipment for preparing the arterial embalming fluid, which consists primarily of formaldehyde, a preservative, and phenol, a disinfectant. This mixture sanitizes and also gives better color to the skin. Facial features can then be "set" to achieve a restful expression. Missing eyes, ears, and even noses can be replaced.

I asked Tim if his job ever depressed him. He bridled at the question: "No, it doesn't 27 depress me at all. I do what I can for people and take satisfaction in enabling relatives to see their loved ones as they were in life." He said that he felt people were becoming more aware of the public service his profession provides. Grade-school classes now visit funeral homes as often as they do police stations and museums. The mortician is no longer regarded as a minister of death.

Before leaving, I wanted to see a body up close. I thought I could be indifferent after 28 all I had seen and heard, but I wasn't sure. Cautiously, I reached out and touched the skin. It felt cold and firm, not unlike clay. As I walked out, I felt glad to have satisfied my curiosity about dead bodies, but all too happy to let someone else handle them.

Works Cited

Grassley, Chuck. Opening remarks. *Joint Hearing on Pension Tension: Does the Pension Benefit Guaranty Corporation Deliver for Retirees*, United States, Senate, Special Committee on Aging and the Committee on Small Business, Government Printing Office, 21 Sept. 2000, www.aging.senate.gov/imo/media/doc/publications/9212000.pdf. 106th Congress, 2nd session, Senate Hearing 106–38.

"NFDA Releases Results of Member General Price List Survey." *National Funeral Directors Association*, 1 Aug. 2013, nfda.org/news-a-events/all-press-releases/3719-nfdareleases-results-of-member-general-price-list-survey.html.

Russell, John. "Batesville Casket Is Coy about Starring Role in Jackson Funeral." *ABC News*, 9 July 2009, abcnews.go.com/Business/story?id=8042342.

Twain, Mark. *Pudd'nhead Wilson*. Pocket Books, 2004, p. 45.

READING FOR MEANING

For help with summarizing, see Chapter 2, pp. 24–25.

1. **Read to Summarize.** Write a sentence or two explaining the main idea Cable wants his readers to understand about the Goodbody Mortuary.

2. **Read to Respond.** Write a paragraph exploring anything that resonates with your experience, such as Cable's preconceptions about what an undertaker would look like (par. 5) or his "curiosity about dead bodies" and what one feels like (par. 28).

3. **Read to Analyze Assumptions.** Write a paragraph or two analyzing an assumption you find intriguing in Cable's essay. For example:

For help analyzing your assumptions, see Chapter 2, pp. 28–29.

Assumptions about death. Cable begins his essay by suggesting that people tend not to talk directly and openly about death and that the painfulness of a loved one's death may be in part "because someone else's mortality reminds us all too vividly of our own" (par. 1). Later, he reports Tim's different idea that "[s]omething deep within us demands a confrontation with death" (par. 23).

- What cultural, family, and religious traditions affect your thinking about death?
- As you compare your assumptions with those of other students in your class, particularly students brought up with different traditions, what important differences do you see in the way people view death?

Assumptions about funerals as a status symbol. Comparing the coffin "display room" to a new car "showroom" (par. 18) and describing the top-of-the-line $25,000 "solid bronze casket" with "14-karat gold" handles (par. 21), Cable suggests that "[d]eath may be the great leveler, but one's coffin quickly reestablishes one's status" (par. 17).

You may also try reflecting on challenges to your beliefs and values; see Chapter 2, pp. 36–37.

- Why do you suppose so many people buy expensive caskets, cemetery plots, and newspaper death notices and spend as much money on a funeral as they do on a wedding?
- What messages does an expensive funeral send to the people who attend? What other kinds of assumptions besides those about status might motivate people?

READING LIKE A WRITER

ORGANIZING THE INFORMATION

Observations may be organized **topically,** with the writer bringing up a series of topics about the subject (as in "Soup"); they may be organized **narratively,** with the writer telling a story that extends over a period of time (as Thompson does); or they may be organized **spatially,** with the writer taking readers on a tour of a place, pointing out interesting sights and bringing up various topics about the subject as they move through the scene (as Cable does):

Begins on the sidewalk

Prepositional phrases mark locations

More than a few people avert their eyes as they walk past the dusty-pink building that houses the Goodbody Mortuary. . . . It wasn't at all what I had expected. . . . I was apprehensive as I climbed the stone steps to the entrance. . . . Inside was a cool and quiet reception room. . . . I found the funeral director in the main lobby, adjacent to the reception room. (pars. 2–5)

Cable acts as a tour guide or as the camera in a documentary. He marks his progress with transitional words and phrases such as "I followed him . . . into a chapel" (par. 15). Cable uses each room he enters as a place to introduce a new topic. For example, in the display room, he talks about the commercialization of death. In the embalming room, where he interviews the mortician Tim, Cable discusses cultural attitudes toward death.

Analyze & Write

Write a paragraph analyzing how Cable orients readers as he takes them on a tour of the mortuary.

1. Skim the essay and find the passages where Cable takes readers from one room to another. How does he signal to readers the transition in space?
2. Find an example that shows how these spatial transitions also introduce new topics.
3. How effective or ineffective is a tour as a way of organizing information in a place like a mortuary?

Writing to Learn Observation

Write a brief essay analyzing one of the readings in this chapter (or another selection, perhaps one by a classmate). Explain how (and perhaps, how well) the selection works as an observation. Consider, for example, how it

- presents detailed information about the subject;
- organizes the information topically, narratively, or spatially to make it interesting and clear;
- takes a detached observer or participant-observer role, or alternates between the two;
- conveys the writer's perspective on what makes the subject intriguing and/or culturally significant.

Your essay could also reflect on how you applied one or more of the academic habits of mind as you read the selection:

- **Curiosity** — what questions or ideas did you have as you read the selection?
- **Critical Analysis**—what assumptions in the selection did you find intriguing, and why?
- **Rhetorical Sensitivity** — how effective or ineffective do you think the selection is in achieving its purpose for the intended audience, given the constraints of the medium and the genre of observation?

A GUIDE TO WRITING
OBSERVATIONAL ESSAYS

You have probably done a good deal of analytical writing about your reading. Your instructor may also assign a capstone project to write a brief observation of your own. This Guide to Writing offers detailed suggestions and resources to help you meet the special challenges observational writing presents.

THE WRITING ASSIGNMENT

Write about an intriguing or unusual place, person, or activity.

- Choose a subject that is relatively unfamiliar to your audience or a familiar subject that you can present in a fresh and surprising way.

- Research the subject, gathering detailed information primarily from close observations and interviews, and present that information in a clear, logical way that is entertaining as well as informative.

- Analyze the information you have gathered about the subject so that you can give readers insight into the subject's cultural meaning and importance.

WRITING YOUR DRAFT

Choosing a Subject

Rather than limiting yourself to the first subject that comes to mind, take a few minutes to consider your options and list as many subjects as you can. Below are some criteria that can help you choose a promising subject, followed by suggestions for the types of places, people, and activities you might consider writing about.

The subject should

- spark your — and your readers' — interest and curiosity

- be accessible, allowing you to make detailed observations and conduct in-depth interviews in the time allotted

- lead to ideas about its cultural significance and meanings

Note: Whenever you write an observational report or profile, consider carefully the ethics involved in such research. You will want to treat participants fairly and with respect in the way you both approach and depict them. You may need to obtain permission from your school's ethics review board. Discuss the ethical implications of your research with your instructor, and think carefully about the goals of your research and the effect your research will have on others.

An appropriate person might be

- someone doing work that you might want to do — a city council member, police officer, lab technician, computer programmer, attorney, salesperson

- someone with an unusual job or hobby — a dog trainer, private detective, ham radio operator, race car driver, novelist

- someone recently recognized for academic or community service or achievement

An appropriate place might be

- a place where people come together because they are of the same age, gender, sexual orientation, or ethnic group (for example, a foreign language–speaking residence hall or LGBTQ club) or a place where people have formed a community around a shared interest (for example, a Sunday morning pickup basketball game in the park, political campaign, or barber shop)

- a place where people are trained for a certain kind of work (for example, a police academy, CSI program, or truck driving school)

- a place where a group of people are working together for a particular purpose (for example, a laboratory where scientists are collaborating on a research project)

An appropriate activity might be

- an unconventional sporting event — a dogs' Frisbee tournament, chess match, dog sledding, log sawing and splitting competition; an amateur wrestling or boxing meet, ice-fishing contest

- a team practicing a sport or other activity (one you can observe as a curious outsider, not as an experienced participant)

- a community improvement project — graffiti cleaning, tree planting, house repairing, church painting, road or highway litter collecting

Researching Your Subject

Conducting observations and interviews takes time, so determine whether you can get permission before committing yourself too deeply, and plan your site visits carefully. The most common error students report making on this assignment is waiting too long to make that first call. Be aware, too, that the people and places you contact may not respond immediately (or at all); be sure to follow up if you have not gotten an answer to your request within a few days.

Making a Schedule. Set up a tentative schedule for your observations and interviews. Backward planning is one of the best strategies for scheduling your time so everything gets done by your deadline:

1. Write on a calendar the date the project is due and any other interim due dates (such as the date that your first draft is due).

2. Move backward through the calendar, writing in due dates for other tasks you need to do, such as scheduling initial and follow-up interviews and observations, as well as determining when write-ups and background research should be done.

Setting Up, Preparing for, and Conducting Interviews and Observations. The following activities will help you plan your research:

1. **Make a list of people you would like to interview or the places you would like to observe.** Include a number of possibilities in case your first choice turns you down.

2. **Write out your intentions and goals,** so you can explain them clearly to others. If you would like to take on the participant-observer role, ask permission to take part in a small way for a limited time.

> For a detailed discussion of planning and conducting interviews and observations, see the Appendix, pp. 482–85.

3. **Call or e-mail for an appointment** with your interview subject or to make arrangements to visit the site. Explain who you are and what you are doing. Student research projects are often embraced, but be prepared for your request to be rejected.

4. **Make notes about your assumptions and expectations.** For example: Why do I assume the subject will interest me and my readers? What do I already know and what do I expect to learn about my subject?

5. **Write some interview questions** in advance, or consider how best to conduct the observation.

6. **Make an audio or video recording** — if allowed — during the interview or observation, but also take careful notes, including notes about what you see, hear, and smell, as well as notes about tone, gestures, mannerisms, or overheard conversations.

Ask for stories:

> Tell me how you got into ....
> What surprised/pleased/frustrated you most?

Let subjects correct misconceptions:

> What preconceptions/myths would you most like to bust?

Ask about the subject's past and future:

> How has .... changed over the years, and where do you think it's going?

Reflecting on What You Learned.   Immediately after your interview or observation, be sure to review your notes and write down your first impressions:

▶ My dominant impression of the subject is ....

▶ The most interesting aspect of .... is .... because ....

▶ Although my thoughts about .... were confirmed, I was surprised to learn ....

Focus on *sensory details* that could paint a vivid portrait of the person or people, place, or activity, and write down any questions or concerns you might like to consider for a follow-up interview or observation.

Working with Sources

Integrating Quotations from Interviews

As you write up your interviews and observations and begin drafting your essay, you need to choose quotations that will present information about the subject in an interesting way. To make quotations arresting, use speaker tags (*he shouts, she blurts*). Speaker tags play an important role in observational writing because they help readers visualize the speakers and imagine what they sound like.

To integrate quotations and speaker tags smoothly into your sentences, you may rely on an all-purpose verb, such as *said* or *remarked*:

"I'm sure I won't finish," he says. (Jamison, par. 17)

To depict the speaker's tone or attitude more precisely and vividly, use speaker tags with descriptive verbs, such as *protested* or *yells out*:

I asked Tim if his job ever depressed him. He <u>bridled</u> at the question: "No, it doesn't depress me at all." (Cable, par. 27)

You may also add a word or phrase to a speaker tag to reveal more about how, where, when, or why the speaker speaks:

"Pit of fire," she says, shaking her head. "Like a pit of fire straight from hell. Never seen anything like it. Like something out of an old movie about prisons." <u>Her voice is getting louder and she looks at each of us with pleading eyes.</u> (Coyne, par. 6)

In addition to being carefully introduced, quotations must be precisely punctuated. Fortunately, there are only two general rules:

1. Enclose all quotations in quotation marks. These always come in pairs, one at the beginning and one at the end of the quotation.

2. Separate the quotation from the speaker tag with appropriate punctuation, usually a comma. But if you have more than one sentence, be careful to punctuate the separate sentences properly.

Choosing Your Role

You can take a spectator role (like Cable and Ronson), a participant-observer role (like Thompson), or alternate between being a spectator and a participant (like Jamison and Coyne).

Choose the spectator role to:

- provide readers with a detailed description or guided tour of the scene.

  ► Inside, you could see .... The room was .... and ....

EXAMPLE   The door was massive, yet it swung open easily on well-oiled hinges. "Come in," said the sign. "We're always open." Inside was a cool and quiet reception room. Curtains were drawn against the outside glare, cutting the light down to a soft glow. (Cable, par. 4)

- create an aura of objectivity, making it appear as though you're just reporting what you see and hear without revealing that you have actually made choices about what to include in order to create a dominant impression.

  ► The shiny <u>new/rusty</u> old tools were <u>laid out neatly/piled helter skelter</u> on the workbench, like ....

EXAMPLE   Laz is bald and charismatic, leader of a minor empire, trafficker in human pain. He's like a cross between the Colonel and your grandpa. (Jamison, par. 11)

Caution: The spectator role may cause readers to:

- feel detached, which can lead to a lack of interest in the subject profiled
- suspect a hidden bias behind the appearance of objectivity, undermining the writer's credibility.

Choose the participant-observer role to:

- report on physical activities through the eyes of a novice, so readers can imagine doing the activity themselves:

  ► I picked up the .... It felt like .... and smelled/tasted/sounded like ....

EXAMPLE   The greatest difficulty, though, is in the trimming. I had no idea that a head of lettuce was so humongous. (Thompson, par. 9)

- reveal how others react to you:

  ► X interrupted me as I .... -ed.

EXAMPLE   People whose names I didn't yet know would ask me how I was holding up, reminding me that it would get easier as time went by. (Thompson, par. 14)

Caution: The participant-observer role may cause readers to:

- wonder whether your experience was unique to you, not something they would have experienced
- think the person, place, group, or activity being profiled seemed secondary in relation to the writer's experience.

Developing Your Perspective on the Subject

Explore the cultural significance of your subject. If you are focusing on a *place* (like a mortuary or prison visiting room), consider what intrigues you about its culture by asking yourself questions like these:

- Who are the insiders at this place and why are they there?
- How does the place affect how insiders talk, act, think, feel?
- What function does the place serve in the wider community?
- What tensions are there between insiders and outsiders or between newcomers and veterans?

    ▸ X and Y say .... because they want to .... , but they seem to feel .... because of the way they do ....

EXAMPLE   And I can imagine the hours spent preparing for this visit. . . . The hours of discussing, dissecting, and bragging about these visitors—especially the men. . . . and the giggles that abruptly change into tears without warning—things that define any female-only world. Even, or especially, if that world is a female federal prison camp. (Coyne, par. 4)

If you are focusing on an *activity* (like running a unique marathon or cutting lettuce), ask yourself questions like these:

- Who benefits from it?
- What value does it have for the insider community and for the wider community?
- How has the activity or process changed over time, for good or ill?
- How are outsiders initiated into the activity?

    ▸ .... [date or event] marked a turning point because ....

EXAMPLE   For years after the demise of that first meatpacking company, the Dufour family sold someone else's product. . . . "But pretty soon, we were selling so many lips that we had to almost beg Di Salvo's for product. That's when we started cooking up our own," he told me, gesturing toward the cast-iron kettle that hangs from the rafters by the front door of the plant. "My daddy started cooking lips in that very pot."

> Lionel now cooks lips in 11 retrofitted milk tanks, dull stainless-steel cauldrons shaped like oversized cradles. But little else has changed. (Edge, pars. 9–10)

Define your purpose and audience. Write for five minutes exploring what you want your readers to learn about the subject and why. Use sentence strategies like these to help clarify your thinking:

▶ My readers probably think .... about my subject. I can get them to think about X's social and cultural significance by ....

State your main point. Review what you have written, and summarize in a sentence or two the main idea you want readers to take away from your profile. Readers don't expect a profile to have an explicit thesis statement, but the descriptive details and other information need to work together to convey the main idea.

Formulating a Working Thesis Statement

Review what you have written and try out a few working thesis statements that articulate your insights into, interpretations of, or ideas about the person, place, or activity that you want readers to take away from reading the essay. Like autobiography, observational writing tends not to include an explicit thesis statement, but does include sentences that reinforce and extend the dominant impression you have created.

For example, "Soup" opens and ends with these quotations that capture the writer's main ideas about the subject:

> When Albert Yeganeh says "Soup is my lifeblood," he means it. And when he says "I am extremely hard to please," he means that, too. (par. 1)

> "He's downright rude," said a blond woman in a blue coat. "Even abusive. But you can't deny it, his soup is the best." (par. 12)

Cable uses the opening paragraph to introduce his ideas about death, but he also intersperses his insights throughout the essay.

> Death may be the great leveler, but one's coffin quickly reestablishes one's status. (par. 17)

> Do burials serve an important role in society? . . . [T]hey allow family and friends to view the deceased. Painful as it may be, such an experience brings home the finality of death. (pars. 22–23)

Considering Adding Visuals or Other Media

Think about whether visual or audio elements — photographs, a map of the layout, illustrative materials you picked up at the place or downloaded, still or moving visuals, or audio clips — would strengthen your observational essay. For example, including a photo of a pig in an essay about the production and consumption of pickled pig lips, as Edge does (see p. 103), contributes to the vivid impact of his essay. The fact that the pig seems to be smiling adds a touch of piquant humor.

For more on analyzing visuals, see Chapter 2, pp. 31–34.

Note: Be sure to cite the source of visual or audio elements you didn't create, and get permission from the source if your essay is going to be published on a website that is not password-protected.

Organizing Your Draft

As you have seen, observational profiles often include more than one kind of organization: topical, narrative, spatial. For example, Edge begins and ends with a narrative of his effort to eat a pig lip, but he organizes the middle section of his essay — his observations at Farm Fresh — topically. Nevertheless, it is helpful to consider which plan should predominate:

- To organize topically (like "Soup"), group your observations and information by topic.
- To organize narratively (like Jamison, Thompson, and Coyne), make a timeline and note where the information from your observations and interviews fits.
- To organize spatially (like Cable), sketch the movement from one site to another, noting where you could integrate information from observations and interviews.

For help with outlining, see Chapter 2, pp. 23–24.

For briefer essays, a scratch outline may be sufficient; for longer, more complex essays, a formal outline may be helful.

Drafting Your Observational Essay

By this point, you have done a lot of writing

- to develop something interesting to say about a subject;
- to devise a plan for presenting that information;
- to identify a role for yourself in the essay
- to explore your perspective on the subject.

Now stitch that material together to create a draft. The next section of this Guide to Writing will help you evaluate and improve your draft.

REVIEWING AND IMPROVING THE DRAFT

This section includes two guides for Peer Review and Troubleshooting Your Draft. Your instructor may arrange a peer review in class or online where you can exchange drafts with a classmate. The Peer Review Guide will help you give each other constructive feedback regarding the basic features and strategies typical of observational essays. (If you want to make specific suggestions for improving the draft, see Troubleshooting Your Draft on pp. 138–39.) Also, be sure to respond to any specific concerns the writer has raised about the draft. The Troubleshooting Your Draft guide that follows will help you reread your own draft with a critical eye, sort through any feedback you've received, and consider a variety of ways to improve your draft.

A PEER REVIEW GUIDE

How effective is the presentation of information?

What's Working Well: Let the writer know where information is especially well presented—for example, where the place is described vividly, a process is clearly delineated, or a quotation not only relates information but also portrays the speaker.

What Needs Improvement: Indicate one passage where the presentation of information could be improved—for example, where it's hard to visualize the place or people, a process needs clarification, or you have unanswered questions.

How appropriate is the writer's role?

What's Working Well: Point to any passage where the writer's role works especially well—for example, where the spectator's apparent objectivity adds credibility, the participant observer's insider knowledge enhances interest, or the two roles balance each other.

What Needs Improvement: Note any passage where the writer's role seems unclear or ineffective—for example, where the spectator seems too removed or judgmental, the participant observer's personal experience is distracting, or alternating the two roles gets confusing.

How clear and insightful is the writer's perspective on the subject?

What's Working Well: Indicate a passage where the writer's perspective is especially clear and compelling—for example, where showing creates a strong dominant impression, telling illuminates with a pithy comment or revealing quotation, or the tone toward the subject (respectful, sarcastic, flattering, disapproving) is appropriate and well supported.

What Needs Improvement: Tell the writer where the perspective needs clarification—for example, where showing seems muddied by contradictory details, telling relates the obvious and lacks insight, or the tone (either praising or criticizing) seems inappropriate or unjustified.

How easy to follow is the organization?

What's Working Well: Mark any parts of the essay that seem notably well-organized—for example, where a narratively arranged section orients readers with time markers, a topically arranged section uses topic sentences effectively, or a spatially arranged section employs prepositional phrases to take the reader on a tour of the place.

What Needs Improvement: Identify any aspect of the organization that needs improvement—for example, where a narratively arranged section seems to drag or ramble pointlessly, a topically arranged section seems disorganized or unbalanced, or a spatially arranged section stalls or becomes confusing.

Revising Your Draft

Revising means reenvisioning your draft, trying to see it in a new way, given your purpose and audience, in order to develop an informative and engaging observational essay. Think imaginatively and boldly about cutting unconvincing material, adding new material, and moving material around. The following chart may help you strengthen your essay.

TROUBLESHOOTING YOUR DRAFT

To Organize the Observation More Clearly and Effectively	
If a narratively arranged section drags or rambles,	• Add time markers to clarify the chronology. • Give the narrative shape—for example, by arousing curiosity, or by explaining the sequence of actions in a process narrative.
If a topically arranged section seems disorganized or unbalanced,	• Try rearranging topics to see whether another order makes more sense. • Add logical transitions. • Move, cut, or condense information to restore balance.
If a spatially arranged section is confusing,	• Add transitions to orient readers. • Use prepositional phrases to show direction or movement through space.
If the opening fails to engage readers' attention,	• Think of questions you could open with, or look for an engaging image or dialogue later in the essay to move to the beginning. • Go back to your notes for other ideas. • Recall how the writers in this chapter open their essays.
To Strengthen the Writer's Perspective on the Subject	
If the dominant impression seems vague or contradictory,	• Discuss more directly the contradictions or complexities you see in the subject. • Cut or revise the language that seems vague.
If the perspective is unclear or simplistic,	• Add language or details that strengthen, extend, or clarify the writer's perspective. • Write an explicit thesis statement—and either include it or use quotations and descriptions to convey this idea. • Add sources to explain the social, cultural, or historical context.
If the tone seems inappropriate or unsupported,	• Think about the tone's appropriateness. • Provide support so the tone seems justified.

To Present the Information More Clearly and Vividly	
If people do not come alive,	• Add speaker tags that characterize people's tones, facial expressions, and gestures. • Quote only the language that conveys personality or essential information, and paraphrase or summarize other parts.
If the place is hard to visualize,	• Identify items in the place by name using specific nouns. • Add sensory detail—describe sights, sounds, smells, tastes, textures. • Consider adding a visual—a photograph or sketch, even a film clip if your observation will appear online.
If activities or processes are not clear,	• Make sure the tense of your verbs clearly indicates the sequence of the actions. • Clarify or add transitions showing what happened when.
If the essay could bore or overwhelm readers with too much information about the subject,	• Cut obvious or extraneous information. • Consider alternating blocks of information with descriptive or narrative materials. • Try presenting more of the information through lively dialogue from interviews.
If readers' questions have not been answered,	• Look over your research notes to see if you can answer readers' questions. • If you have time, do follow-up research to find out answers to their questions.

Editing and Proofreading Your Draft

Check for errors in usage, punctuation, and mechanics, and consider matters of style. If you keep a list of errors you typically make, begin by checking your draft against this list. Ask someone else to proofread your essay before you submit it to your instructor.

From our research on student writing, we know that observational essays tend to have errors in the use of quotation marks, when writers quote the exact words of people they have interviewed. Check a writer's handbook for help with these potential problems.

Reflecting on Observation

In this chapter, you have read several observational essays critically and have written one of your own. To better remember what you have learned, pause now to reflect on the reading and writing activities you completed in this chapter.

1. Write a page or so reflecting on what you have learned. Begin by describing what you are most pleased with in your essay. Then explain what you think contributed to your achievement.

   - If it was something you learned from the readings, indicate which readings and specifically what you learned from them.

   - If it came from your research notes and write-ups, point out the parts that helped you most.

   - If you got good advice from a critical reader, explain exactly how the person helped you — perhaps by helping you recognize a problem in your draft or by helping you add a new dimension to your writing.

2. Reflect more generally on how you tend to interpret observational writing, your own as well as other writers'. Consider some of the following questions:

   - In reading for meaning, do you find yourself paying attention to larger cultural or social contexts — for example, thinking of the subject in terms of gender, ethnicity, or class?

   - How do you think the writer's perspective influenced how you saw the subject?

CHAPTER 5

Reflection

L ike autobiographical and observational writing, *reflective writing* is based on the writer's personal experience. Reflective writers present something they did, saw, heard, or read in writing so vivid that the reader can imagine what they experienced. But unlike writers of autobiography and observation, reflective writers help readers imagine the experience and explore its meanings. Reflective writers use events, people, and places as springboards for thinking about society — how people live and what people believe about social change with its many opportunities and challenges; about customs in our culturally diverse society; about traditional virtues and vices; or about common hopes and fears. They do not attempt to exhaust their subjects, nor do they set themselves up as experts. Instead, writers use their reflective essays to explore ideas informally and tentatively. Reading a reflective essay can be as stimulating as having a lively conversation, often surprising us with insights and unlikely connections and encouraging us to look in new ways at even the most familiar things.

RHETORICAL SITUATIONS FOR REFLECTIONS

Writers use a wide range of occasions to reflect on some aspect of contemporary culture, as the following examples indicate:

- A former football player writes a reflective essay for his college alumni magazine about a game in which he sustained a serious injury but continued to play because playing with pain was regarded as a sign of manliness. He reflects on learning this custom from his father and later from coaches and other players, and he wonders why boys are taught not to show pain but encouraged to show aggression and competitiveness. Taking an anthropological view, he sees contemporary sports as equivalent to the kind of training Native American boys traditionally went through to become warriors, and he questions whether playing sports prepares athletes for the kinds of roles they will play in contemporary society.

● Writing a blog post for a political science course, a student reflects on her first experience voting in a presidential election. She contrasts her decision-making process — examining the candidate's experience and voting record and reading endorsements from trusted experts — with those of her acquaintances, one of whom said she chose a candidate because he reminded her of her grandfather, and another who based his choice on his dislike of the way one candidate dressed. The writer then reflects on the implications of such voting decisions.

Thinking about Reflection

Write a paragraph about an occasion when you shared a reflection with others or others shared a reflection with you — friends, classmates, relatives, acquaintances — either orally or in writing.

● Who was the *audience*? How do you think addressing the reflections to this audience affected the way they were "hooked"?

● What was the main *purpose*? How did the writer or speaker want the audience to react? Was the goal to make the audience feel or think in a particular way, or to make an experience seem strange so that audience members could see it differently?

● How would you rate the *rhetorical sensitivity* of the reflection? Did the piece engage the reader or listener? How? Was the insight surprising or motivating?

A GUIDE TO READING REFLECTIVE ESSAYS

This guide introduces you to the basic features and strategies typical of reflective writing by inviting you to analyze a powerful reflective essay by Brent Staples:

● *Reading for meaning* will help you think about the occasions that prompted Staples's reflections — about his attitudes and assumptions regarding racial profiling, and about the broader social implications of, for example, his musical choices.

● *Reading like a writer* will help you learn how Staples employs strategies typical of reflective essays, such as

   1. Presenting the occasion vividly and in a way that prepares readers for the reflections

2. Developing the reflections fully, using appropriate writing strategies

3. Maintaining coherence by providing cues for readers

4. Engaging readers' interest

Brent Staples

Black Men and Public Space

Brent Staples (b. 1951) earned his Ph.D. in psychology from the University of Chicago and went on to become a journalist, writing for several magazines and newspapers. In 1985, he became assistant metropolitan editor of the *New York Times*, where he is now a member of the editorial board. His autobiography, *Parallel Time: Growing Up in Black and White* (1994), won the Anisfield-Wolf Book Award. The following essay originally appeared in *Ms.* magazine under the title "Just Walk on By." Staples revised it slightly for publication in *Harper's* under the present title.

- **Before you read,** think about a time that you frightened others by your presence or that you have been frightened by others.

- **As you read,** think about why Staples changed the title of the essay from "Just Walk on By" to "Black Men and Public Space."

My first victim was a woman—white, well dressed, probably in her early twenties. I   1
came upon her late one evening on a deserted street in Hyde Park, a relatively affluent neighborhood in an otherwise mean, impoverished section of Chicago. As I swung onto the avenue behind her, there seemed to be a discreet, uninflammatory distance between us. Not so. She cast back a worried glance. To her, the youngish black man   a broad six feet two inches with a beard and billowing hair, both hands shoved into the pockets of a bulky military jacket—seemed menacingly close. After a few more quick glimpses, she picked up her pace and was soon running in earnest. Within seconds she disappeared into a cross street.

That was more than a decade ago, I was twenty two years old, a graduate student   2
newly arrived at the University of Chicago. It was in the echo of that terrified woman's footfalls that I first began to know the unwieldy inheritance I'd come into—the ability to alter public space in ugly ways. It was clear that she thought herself the quarry of a mugger, a rapist, or worse. Suffering a bout of insomnia, however, I was stalking sleep, not defenseless wayfarers. As a softy who is scarcely able to take a knife to a raw chicken—let alone hold one to a person's throat—I was surprised, embarrassed, and dismayed all at once. Her flight made me feel like an accomplice in tyranny. It also made it clear that I was indistinguishable from the muggers who occasionally seeped into the area from the surrounding ghetto. That first encounter, and those that followed, signified that a vast, unnerving gulf lay between nighttime pedestrians—particularly

women—and me. And I soon gathered that being perceived as dangerous is a hazard in itself. I only needed to turn a corner into a dicey situation, or crowd some frightened, armed person in a foyer somewhere, or make an errant move after being pulled over by a policeman. Where fear and weapons meet—and they often do in urban America—there is always the possibility of death.

In that first year, my first away from my hometown, I was to become thoroughly 3 familiar with the language of fear. At dark, shadowy intersections, I could cross in front of a car stopped at a traffic light and elicit the thunk, thunk, thunk of the driver—black, white, male, or female—hammering down the door locks. On less traveled streets after dark, I grew accustomed to but never comfortable with people crossing to the other side of the street rather than pass me. Then there were the standard unpleasantries with policemen, doormen, bouncers, cabdrivers, and others whose business it is to screen out troublesome individuals before there is any nastiness.

I moved to New York nearly two years ago and I have remained an avid night walker. 4 In central Manhattan, the near-constant crowd cover minimizes tense one-on-one street encounters. Elsewhere—in SoHo, for example, where sidewalks are narrow and tightly spaced buildings shut out the sky—things can get very taut indeed.

After dark, on the warrenlike streets of Brooklyn where I live, I often see women 5 who fear the worst from me. They seem to have set their faces on neutral, and with their purse straps strung across their chests bandolier-style, they forge ahead as though bracing themselves against being tackled. I understand, of course, that the danger they perceive is not a hallucination. Women are particularly vulnerable to street violence, and young black males are drastically overrepresented among the perpetrators of that violence. Yet these truths are no solace against the kind of alienation that comes of being ever the suspect, a fearsome entity with whom pedestrians avoid making eye contact.

It is not altogether clear to me how I reached the ripe old age of twenty-two with- 6 out being conscious of the lethality nighttime pedestrians attributed to me. Perhaps it was because in Chester, Pennsylvania, the small, angry industrial town where I came of age in the 1960s, I was scarcely noticeable against a backdrop of gang warfare, street knifings, and murders. I grew up one of the good boys, had perhaps a half-dozen fistfights. In retrospect, my shyness of combat has clear sources.

As a boy, I saw countless tough guys locked away; I have since buried several, too. 7 They were babies, really—a teenage cousin, a brother of twenty-two, a childhood friend in his mid-twenties—all gone down in episodes of bravado played out in the streets. I came to doubt the virtues of intimidation early on. I chose, perhaps unconsciously, to remain a shadow—timid, but a survivor.

The fearsomeness mistakenly attributed to me in public places often has a perilous 8 flavor. The most frightening of these confusions occurred in the late 1970s and early 1980s, when I worked as a journalist in Chicago. One day, rushing into the office of a magazine I was writing for with a deadline story in hand, I was mistaken for a burglar. The office manager called security and, with an ad hoc posse, pursued me through the labyrinthine halls, nearly to my editor's door. I had no way of proving who I was. I could only move briskly toward the company of someone who knew me.

Another time I was on assignment for a local paper and killing time before an inter- 9
view. I entered a jewelry store on the city's affluent Near North Side. The proprietor
excused herself and returned with an enormous red Doberman pinscher straining at
the end of a leash. She stood, the dog extended toward me, silent to my questions, her
eyes bulging nearly out of her head. I took a cursory look around, nodded, and bade
her good night.

Relatively speaking, however, I never fared as badly as another black male journal- 10
ist. He went to nearby Waukegan, Illinois, a couple of summers ago to work on a story
about a murderer who was born there. Mistaking the reporter for the killer, police
officers hauled him from his car at gunpoint and but for his press credentials would
probably have tried to book him. Such episodes are not uncommon. Black men trade
tales like this all the time.

Over the years, I learned to smother the rage I felt at so often being taken for a 11
criminal. Not to do so would surely have led to madness. I now take precautions to
make myself less threatening. I move about with care, particularly late in the evening.
I give a wide berth to nervous people on subway platforms during the wee hours, particularly when I have exchanged business clothes for jeans. If I happen to be entering a
building behind some people who appear skittish, I may walk by, letting them clear the
lobby before I return, so as not to seem to be following them. I have been calm and
extremely congenial on those rare occasions when I've been pulled over by the police.

And on late-evening constitutionals I employ what has proved to be an excellent 12
tension-reducing measure: I whistle melodies from Beethoven and Vivaldi and the
more popular classical composers. Even steely New Yorkers hunching toward nighttime destinations seem to relax, and occasionally they even join in the tune. Virtually
everybody seems to sense that a mugger wouldn't be warbling bright, sunny selections from Vivaldi's *Four Seasons*. It is my equivalent of the cow-bell that hikers wear
when they know they are in bear country.

READING FOR MEANING

1. **Read to Summarize.** Write a sentence or two briefly explaining some of
   the occasions that prompted Staples's reflection and how Staples explores
   the actions he took to address these occasions.

   For more
   on summarizing,
   see Chapter 2,
   pp. 24–25.

2. **Read to Respond.** Write a paragraph analyzing your initial reactions
   to Staples's essay. Consider anything that seems surprising, such as Staples's
   reactions to being seen as threatening; or an experience similar to one you
   have had in which race, gender, age, or other differences caused tension.

   You may also
   try reflecting
   on challenges
   to your beliefs
   and values; see
   Chapter 2,
   pp. 36–37.

3. **Read to Analyze Assumptions.** Write a paragraph or two analyzing an
   assumption you find intriguing in Staples's essay. For example:

   Assumptions about the unfairness and danger of racial profiling. The
   example Staples uses to begin his reflection — the young woman who suddenly

becomes frightened of him (par. 1) — illustrates how often he and other black men assume they are the object of racial profiling. He sees that this faulty perception could be a danger to him and to all black men because frightened people can behave violently.

- How did Staples become aware of racial profiling and its consequences?
- To what extent are pedestrians aware of the effects their behavior has on black men? Is Staples right in his assumption that he has been racially profiled? Are there any other possible explanations?

For help analyzing assumptions, see Chapter 2, pp. 28–29.

Assumptions about how musical choices affect others. Staples concludes by writing that to reduce tension on his late-night walks, he whistles Beethoven and Vivaldi along with works of other classical composers (par. 12).

- Why is a classical piece or a "sunny selection" more effective at reducing fear than other kinds of music such as rock, country, or rap?
- Do you think there could be another explanation for how they react to his whistling? For example, could it be that the music calms Staples himself and therefore he sends out a different message?

READING LIKE A WRITER

PRESENTING THE OCCASION

Reflective writers present an occasion — something they experienced or observed — in a vivid and suggestive way that encourages readers to want to know more about the writer's thoughts. Staples begins with an occasion when his mere presence on the street frightened a woman into running away from him. He uses this event to introduce the general subject, fear resulting from racial profiling: "It was in the echo of that terrified woman's footfalls that I first began to know the unwieldy inheritance I'd come into — the ability to alter public space in ugly ways" (par. 2). Throughout the rest of the essay, Staples reflects on this "inheritance" from various angles:

- He expresses his feelings at being misperceived as a threat.
- He gives examples of other occasions when people reacted to him with fear or hostility.
- He explains the effects of racial profiling, including the danger to himself, and the "precautions" he takes to make himself appear "less threatening" (par. 11).

Analyze & Write

Write a paragraph analyzing how Staples uses examples to illustrate and explain his reflections:

1. Reread the opening sentence of paragraph 3, where Staples introduces the idea that there is a "language of fear." Then skim the rest of paragraphs 3, 5–6, and 8–10. What examples does Staples use to help readers understand how this fear is expressed?

2. What have you learned from Staples's essay about how examples can help readers understand or accept a writer's reflections? Choose one or two examples and explain why you think they work especially well to help readers understand what Staples means.

Developing the Reflections

While Staples uses an occasion to introduce his subject, his reflections explore the subject by developing his ideas. Consider, for example, the words he uses to present his "first victim" and the location where he encounters her:

Naming   My first victim was a woman — white, well dressed, probably in her early
Detailing   twenties. I came upon her late one evening on a deserted street in Hyde
            Park, a relatively affluent neighborhood in an otherwise mean, impover-
            ished section of Chicago. (par. 1)

Staples uses a combination of words — some neutral, some with strongly negative connotations — to create a vivid picture. He also uses the word *first* to suggest that this woman was not his only "victim."

Analyze & Write

Write a paragraph analyzing how else Staples makes this occasion vivid for his readers as well as how he prepares them for the reflections that follow.

1. Reread paragraphs 1–2. Underline the names Staples uses to identify himself, and circle the details he uses to describe himself and his actions.

2. Put brackets around words and phrases in these paragraphs that suggest the larger meanings Staples will develop in subsequent paragraphs.

3. Consider Staples's tone. How do the words Staples chooses help you identify (or hinder you from identifying) with him and his "victims"? Use concrete details from the paragraphs to support your claims.

Maintaining Coherence

Reflective essays explore ideas on a subject by examining them first from one perspective and then from another, and sometimes piling up examples to illustrate the ideas. This apparently casual organization is deceptive, however, because in fact the reflective writer has used a number of strategies to create coherence. One way of achieving coherence is to refer to the subject at various points by repeating certain key words or phrases. In the opening anecdote, Staples dramatizes the woman's fear of him. He then repeats the word "fear," or synonyms for it, throughout the essay. Reflective writers also achieve coherence through carefully placed transitions. Staples uses transitions of time and place to introduce a series of examples illustrating the fear he engenders in others simply because of his race and gender:

> Transition of time/place
>
> Synonym for key term
>
> Key term
>
> I only needed to turn a corner into a dicey situation, or crowd some frightened, armed person in a foyer somewhere, or make an errant move after being pulled over by a policeman. Where fear and weapons meet — and they often do in urban America — there is always the possibility of death.
>
> In that first year, my first away from my hometown, I was to become thoroughly familiar with the language of fear. . . . Elsewhere — in SoHo, for example, where sidewalks are narrow and tightly spaced buildings shut out the sky — things can get very taut indeed. (Pars. 2–3)

Analyze & Write

Write a paragraph or two analyzing how Staples uses these strategies of repetition and transitions to maintain coherence throughout the essay:

1. Skim paragraphs 3–12, highlighting the word *fear* each time Staples uses it and circling synonyms or near synonyms for it each time they appear.

2. Now go back through the essay underlining transitions of time and place.

3. Analyze how effectively these strategies work to maintain coherence, supporting your analysis with examples from the reading.

Engaging Readers

Readers of reflective essays expect writers to engage their interest. Readers choose to read an essay because something about it catches their eye — a familiar author's name, an intriguing title, an interesting graphic. Journalists typically begin feature articles with a "hook" designed to catch readers' attention. The occasion that opens many reflective essays often serves this purpose. Staples's opening phrase, "My first victim," certainly grabs attention.

One of the ways reflective writers *keep* readers engaged is by projecting an image of themselves — sometimes called the writer's **persona** or **voice** — that readers can identify with or be curious about. Staples, for example, uses the first-person pronouns *my* and *I* to present himself in his writing and to speak directly to readers. He describes himself as "a softy" (par. 2) and explains how he felt when he realized that the woman was so frightened by him that she ran for her life. Like most reflective writers, Staples tries to make himself sympathetic to readers so that they will listen to what he has to say.

Analyze & Write

Write a paragraph describing the impression you have of Staples from reading this essay and exploring how these impressions affect your curiosity about his ideas.

1. Skim the essay, circling or highlighting words, phrases, or passages that give you a sense of Staples as a person.

2. Consider the impression you have: What engages you or draws you into the essay? What would you add or change to make the essay more effective for you?

A Special Reading Strategy

Comparing and Contrasting Related Readings: Brent Staples's "Black Men and Public Space" and an Excerpt from Staples's Autobiography, *Parallel Time*

Comparing and contrasting related readings is a critical reading strategy that is particularly applicable when writers present similar subjects, as is the case in the two reflective readings by Brent Staples that are compared here. The first, "Black Men and Public Space," the essay you have just read, was originally published nine years before the second, Staples's autobiography, *Parallel Time*. Both readings deal with the same occasion, but the details of this first encounter, as well as Staples's reflections about it, differ significantly in the two readings. As you read, notice what Staples retains from the original and what he changes.

- What seems to you to be the most significant difference between the two descriptions of the occasion? Note, for example, the details about the location and the woman's appearance as well as how Staples describes his immediate reaction.

- What are the main differences between Staples's thoughts and feelings about the situation and the actions he decides to take?

(continued)

For guidelines on comparing and contrasting related readings, see Chapter 2, pp. 37–39.

• What do you think might have changed (in Staples's feelings, in the broader cultural climate, or in some other way) during that period of nine years between versions, leading Staples to share with readers his angry response rather than the image of himself he projects at the end of the original?

From *Parallel Time*

At night, I walked to the lakefront whenever the weather permitted. I was headed home from the lake when I took my first victim. It was late fall, and the wind was cutting. I was wearing my navy pea jacket, the collar turned up, my hands snug in the pockets. Dead leaves scuttled in shoals along the streets. I turned out of Blackstone Avenue and headed west on 57th Street, and there she was, a few yards ahead of me, dressed in business clothes and carrying a brief-case. She looked back at me once, then again, and picked up her pace. She looked back again and started to run. I stopped where I was and looked up at the surrounding windows. What did this look like to people peeking out through their blinds? I was out walking. But what if someone had thought they'd seen something they hadn't and called the police. I held back the urge to run. Instead, I walked south to The Midway, plunged into its darkness, and remained on The Midway until I reached the foot of my street.

I'd been a fool. I'd been walking the streets grinning good evening at people who were frightened to death of me. I did violence to them by just being. How had I missed this? I kept walking at night, but from then on I paid attention.

I became expert in the language of fear. Couples locked arms or reached for each other's hand when they saw me. Some crossed to the other side of the street. People who were carrying on conversations went mute and stared straight ahead, as though avoiding my eyes would save them. This reminded me of an old wives' tale: that rabid dogs didn't bite if you avoided their eyes. The determination to avoid my eyes made me invisible to classmates and professors whom I passed on the street. . . .

READINGS

Dana Jennings

Our Scars Tell the Stories of Our Lives

Dana Jennings (b. 1957), a journalist and editor at the *New York Times* is best known for his novel, *Lonesome Standard Time* (1996); his nonfiction, *Sing Me Back Home: Love, Death and Country Music* (2008); and his blog for the *New York Times* Well section in which he wrote about prostate cancer. In the following essay, which appeared in the *New York Times* on July 21, 2009, Jennings ponders how scars tell stories. He develops his reflection by relating some of the stories prompted by his scars, and speculates about their larger meaning.

- **Before you read,** think about your own scars, what they mean to you, and whether you have memories associated with each scar.

- **As you read,** think about the differences between the scars Jennings first describes and the "heavy hitters, the stitched whips and serpents" (par. 7) to which he devotes the second half of his essay.

1   Our scars tell stories. Sometimes they're stark tales of life threatening catastrophes, but more often they're just footnotes to the ordinary but bloody detours that befall us on the roadways of life. When I parse my body's motley parade of scars, I see them as personal runes and conversation starters. When I wear shorts, the footlong surgical scar on my right knee rarely fails to draw a comment. And in their railroad-track-like appearance, my scars remind me of the startling journeys that my body has taken — often enough to the hospital or the emergency room.

What is the particular occasion (or two) that prompts Jennings to think about the meaning of scars?

2   The ones that intrigue me most are those from childhood that I can't account for. The one on my right eyebrow, for example, and a couple of ancient pockmarks and starbursts on my knees. I'm not shocked by them. To be honest, I wonder why there aren't more.

How does this paragraph illustrate Jennings's curiosity in the topic?

3   I had a full and active boyhood, one that raged with scabs and scrapes, mashed and bloody knees, bumps and lumps, gashes and slashes, cats' claws and dogs' teeth, jagged glass, ragged steel, knots, knobs and shiners. Which raises this question: How do any of us get out of childhood alive?

How does Jennings engage readers' interest?

4   My stubborn chin has sustained a fair bit of damage over the years. On close examination, there's a faint delta of scars that brings back memories of my teenage war on acne. Those frustrating days of tetracycline and gritty soaps left my face not clean and glowing but red and raw. The acne also ravaged my back, scoring the skin there so that it still looks scorched and lunar.

Highlight the details and narrative strategies Jennings uses to develop his reflection in paragraphs 1–8. What is their effect toward engaging readers?

I further cratered my chin as an adult. First, I sprinted into a cast-iron 5 lamppost while chasing a fly ball in a park in Washington; I actually saw a chorus line of stars dance before my eyes as I crumpled to the ground. Second, I hooked one of those old acne potholes with my razor and created an instant dueling scar.

Scanning down from the jut of my chin to the tips of my toes, I've even 6 managed to brand my feet. In high school and college I worked at Kingston Steel Drum, a factory in my New Hampshire hometown that scoured some of the 55-gallon steel drums it cleaned with acid and scalding water. The factory was eventually shut down by the federal government and became a Superfund hazardous waste site, but not before a spigot malfunctioned one day and soaked my feet in acid.

What effect does this one-sentence paragraph have on the audience?

Then there are the heavy hitters, the stitched whips and serpents that 7 make my other scars seem like dimples on a golf ball.

There's that mighty scar on my right knee from when I was 12 years old 8 and had a benign tumor cut out. Then there are the scars on my abdomen from when my colon (devoured by ulcerative colitis) was removed in 1984, and from my radical open prostatectomy last summer to take out my cancerous prostate. (If I ever front a heavy metal band, I think I'll call it Radical Open Prostatectomy.)

What cues does Jennings use to maintain coherence?

But for all the potential tales of woe that they suggest, scars are also 9 signposts of optimism. If your body is game enough to knit itself back together after a hard physical lesson, to make scar tissue, that means you're still alive, means you're on the path toward healing.

How do scars symbolize certain social attitudes to Jennings?

Scars, perhaps, were the primal tattoos, marks of distinction that showed 10 you had been tried and had survived the test. And like tattoos, they also fade, though the one from my surgery last summer is still a fierce and deep purple.

There's also something talismanic about them. I rub my scars the way 11 other people fret a rabbit's foot or burnish a lucky penny. Scars feel smooth and dry, the same way the scales of a snake feel smooth and dry.

I find my abdominal scars to be the most profound. They vividly remind 12 me that skilled surgeons unlocked me with their scalpels, took out what had to be taken, sewed me back up and saved my life. It's almost as if they left their life-giving signatures on my flawed flesh.

The scars remind me, too, that in this vain culture our vanity sometimes 13 needs to be punctured and deflated—and that's not such a bad thing. To paraphrase Ecclesiastes, better to be a scarred and living dog than to be a dead lion.

How would you summarize Jennings's reasons for writing this essay? Do these stories help you rethink your own beliefs about scars?

It's not that I'm proud of my scars—they are what they are, born of acci- 14 dent and necessity—but I'm not embarrassed by them, either. More than anything, I relish the stories they tell. Then again, I've always believed in the power of stories, and I certainly believe in the power of scars.

A Special Reading Strategy

Exploring the Significance of Figurative Language

Figurative language adds color and richness to writing by taking words literally associated with one thing and applying them to something else, often in an unexpected or unconventional way, to create a vivid image or other sensory impression in readers' minds. For example, in "Our Scars Tell the Stories of Our Lives," Jennings refers to his scars as "footnotes to the ordinary but bloody detours that befall us on the roadways of life" (par. 1), and adds that his scars, in their "railroad-track-like appearance" remind him of the "journeys that [his] body has taken" (par. 1). List and label all the figures of speech — metaphors, similes, and symbols — that you find in this essay and look for similar feelings and attitudes. What meanings emerge from the patterns and your writing?

For guidelines on exploring the significance of figurative language, see Chapter 2, pp. 30–31.

Marina Keegan

Stability in Motion

Marina Keegan (1989–2012) graduated from Yale in 2012. Five days after her graduation, she was killed in a car accident. She left behind a remarkable amount of writing from her high school and her college years, both fiction and nonfiction. Her mother, Tracy Keegan, and one of her professors at Yale, Anne Fadiman, gathered several of her essays and stories into a book, *The Opposite of Loneliness* (2014), from which the following essay was taken. Although Keegan was interested in a number of professions, her passion was writing; after she heard a well-known writer speak at Yale saying it was impossible to make a living as a writer, she told a friend, with characteristic resistance and confidence, "I've decided I'm going to be a writer. Like, a real one. With my life."

- **Before you read,** think about a place of your own where you feel comfortable and can relax. What makes it a refuge for you? How did that place come to be your refuge?

- **As you read,** note how Keegan uses her car to disclose information about herself. What word cues does she use to compare her life to her car? Does she use any figurative language to show how her car serves as a "vehicle" for her personality?

My 1990 Camry's DNA was designed inside the metallic walls of the Toyota Multina- 1 tional Corporation's headquarters in Tokyo, Japan; transported via blueprint to the North American Manufacturing nerve center in Hebron, Kentucky; grown organ by organ in four major assembly plants in Alabama, New Jersey, Texas, and New York; trucked to 149 Arsenal Street in Watertown, Massachusetts; and steered home by my grandmother on September 4, 1990. It featured a 200 hp, 3.0 L V6 engine, a four-speed automatic, and an adaptive Variable Suspension System. She deemed the car too "high tech." In 1990 this meant a cassette player, a cup holder, and a manually operated moon roof.

During its youth, the car traveled little. In fifteen years my grandmother accumu- 2 lated a meager twenty-five thousand miles, mostly to and from the market, my family's house, and the Greek jewelry store downtown. The black exterior remained glossy and spotless, the beige interior crisp and pristine. Tissues were disposed of, seats vacuumed, and food prohibited. My grandmother's old-fashioned cleanliness was an endearing virtue—one that I evidently did not inherit.

I acquired the old Camry through an awkward transaction. Ten days before my 3 sixteenth birthday, my grandfather died. He was eighty-six and it had been long expected, yet I still felt a guilty unease when I heard the now surplus car would soon belong to me. For my grandmother, it was a symbolic good-bye. She needed to see only *one* car in her garage—needed to comprehend her loss more tangibly. Grandpa's car was the "nicer" of the two, so that one she would keep. Three weeks after the funeral, my grandmother and I went to the bank, I signed a check for exactly one dollar, and the car was legally mine. That was that. When I drove her home that evening, I manually opened the moon roof and put on a tape of Frank Sinatra. My grandma smiled for the first time in weeks.

Throughout the next three years, the car evolved. When I first parked the Toyota in   4 my driveway, it was spotless, full of gas, and equipped with my grandmother's version of survival necessities. The glove compartment had a magnifying glass, three pens, and the registration in a little Ziploc bag. The trunk had two matching black umbrellas, a first aid kit, and a miniature sewing box for emergency repairs. Like my grandmother's wrists, everything smelled of Opium perfume.

For a while, I maintained this immaculate condition. Yet one Wrigley's wrapper led to   5 two and soon enough my car underwent a radical transformation—the vehicular equivalent of a midlife crisis. Born and raised in proper formality, the car saw me as *that* friend from school, the bad example who washes away naïveté and corrupts the clean and innocent. We were the same age, after all—both eighteen. The Toyota was born again, crammed with clutter, and exposed to decibel levels it had never fathomed. I filled it with giggling friends and emotional phone calls, borrowed skirts and bottled drinks.

The messiness crept up on me. Parts of my life began falling off, forming an eclectic   6 debris that dribbled gradually into every corner. Empty sushi containers, Diet Coke cans, half-full packs of gum, sweaters, sweatshirts, socks, my running shoes. My clutter was nondiscriminatory. I had every variety of newspaper, scratched-up English paper, biology review sheet, and Spanish flash card discarded on the seats after I'd sufficiently studied on my way to school. The left door pocket was filled with tiny tinfoil balls, crumpled after consuming my morning English muffin. By Friday, I had the entire house's supply of portable coffee mugs. By Sunday, someone always complained about their absence and I would rush out, grab them all, and surreptitiously place them in the dishwasher.

My car was not gross; it was occupied, cluttered, cramped. It became an extension   7 of my bedroom, and thus an extension of myself. I had two bumper stickers on the back: REPUBLICANS FOR VOLDEMORT and the symbol for the Equal Rights Campaign. On the back side windows were OBAMA '08 signs that my parents made me take down because they "dangerously blocked my sight lines." The trunk housed my guitar but was also the library, filled with textbooks and novels, the giant tattered copy of *The Complete Works of William Shakespeare* and all one hundred chapters of *Harry Potter* on tape. A few stray cassettes littered the corners, their little brown insides ripped out, tangled and mutilated. They were the casualties of the trunk trenches, sprawled out forgotten next to the headband I never gave back to Meghan.

On average, I spent two hours a day driving. It was nearly an hour each way to   8 school, and the old-fashioned Toyota—regarded with lighthearted amusement by my classmates—came to be a place of comfort and solitude amid the chaos of my daily routine. My mind was free to wander, my muscles to relax. No one was watching or keeping score. Sometimes I let the deep baritone of NPR's Tom Ashbrook lecture me on oil shortages. Other times I played repetitive mix tapes with titles like *Pancake Breakfast, Tie-Dye and Granola,* and *Songs for the Highway When It's Snowing.*

Ravaging my car, I often found more than just physical relics. For two months I   9
could hardly open the side door without reliving the first time he kissed me. His dim-
pled smile was barely visible in the darkness, but it nevertheless made me stumble
backward when I found my way blushingly back into the car. On the backseat there
was the June 3 issue of the *New York Times* that I couldn't bear to throw out. When we
drove home together from the camping trip, he read it cover to cover while I played
Simon and Garfunkel—hoping he'd realize all the songs were about us. We didn't
talk much during that ride. We didn't need to. He slid his hand into mine for the first
time when we got off the highway; it was only after I made my exit that I realized I
should have missed it. Above this newspaper are the fingernail marks I dug into the
leather of my steering wheel on the night we decided to *just be friends*. My car listened to me cry for all twenty-two-and-a-half miles home.

The physical manifestations of my memories soon crowded the car. My right back   10
speaker was broken from the time my older brother and I pulled an all-nighter singing
shamelessly during our rainy drive home from the wedding. I remember the sheer
energy of the storm, the lights, the music—moving through us, transcending the car's
steel shell, and tracing the city. There was the folder left behind from the day I drove
my dad to an interview the month after he lost his job. It was coincidental that *his* car
was in the shop, but I knew he felt more pathetic that it was he, not his daughter, in
the passenger seat. I kept my eyes on the road, feeling the confused sadness of a child
who catches a parent crying.

I talked a lot in my car. Thousands of words and songs and swears are absorbed in   11
its fabric, just like the orange juice I spilled on my way to the dentist. It knows what
happened when Allie went to Puerto Rico, understands the difference between the
way I look at Nick and the way I look at Adam, and remembers the first time I
experimented with talking to myself. I've practiced for auditions, college interviews,
Spanish oral presentations, and debates. There's something novel about swearing
alone in the car. Yet with the pressures of APs and SATs and the other acronyms that
haunt high school, the act became more frequent and less refreshing.

My car has seen three drive-in movies. During *The Dark Knight,* its battery died   12
and, giggling ferociously, we had to ask the overweight family in the next row to jump
it. The smell of popcorn permeated every crevice of the sedan, and all rides for the
next week were like a trip to the movies. There was a variety of smells in the Camry. At
first it smelled like my grandmother—perfume, mint, and mothballs. I went through a
chai-tea phase during which my car smelled incessantly of Indian herbs. Some mornings it would smell slightly of tobacco and I would know immediately that my older
brother had kidnapped it the night before. For exactly three days it reeked of marijuana. Dan had removed the shabbily rolled joint from behind his ear and our fingers
had trembled as the five of us apprehensively inhaled. Nothing happened. Only the
seats seemed to absorb the plant and get high. Mostly, however, it smelled like nothing to me. Yet when I drove my friends, they always said it had a distinct aroma. I
believe this functioned in the same way as not being able to taste your own saliva or
smell your own odor—the car and I were pleasantly immune to each other.

In the Buckingham Browne & Nichols High School yearbook I was voted worst 13
driver, but on most days I will refute this superlative. My car's love for parking tickets
made me an easy target, but I rarely received other violations. My mistakes mostly
harmed me, not others—locking my keys in the car or parking on the wrong side of
the road. Once, last winter, I needed to refill my windshield wiper fluid and in a
rushed frenzy poured an entire bottle of similarly blue antifreeze inside. Antifreeze, as
it turns out, burns out engines if used in excess. I spent the next two hours driving circles around my block in a snowstorm, urgently expelling the antifreeze squirt by thick
blue squirt. I played no music during this vigil. I couldn't find a playlist called *Poison-
ing Your Car.*

It may have been awkward-looking and muddled, but I was attached to my car. It 14
was a portable home that heated my seat in winter and carried me home at night. I
had no diary and rarely took pictures. That old Toyota Camry was an odd documentation of my adolescence. When I was seventeen, the car was seventeen. My younger
brother entered high school last September and I passed my ownership on to him. In
the weeks before I left for college, my parents made me clean it out for his sake. I
spread six trash bags over the driveway, filling them with my car's contents as the
August sun heated their black plastic. The task was strange, like deconstructing a
scrapbook, unpeeling all the pictures and whiting out the captions.

Just like for my grandmother, it was a symbolic good-bye. Standing outside my 15
newly vacuumed car, I wondered, if I tried hard enough, whether I could smell the
Opium perfume again, or if I searched long enough, whether I'd find the matching
umbrellas and the tiny sewing kit. My brother laughed at my nostalgia, reminding me
that I could still drive the car when I came home. He didn't understand that it wasn't
just the driving I'd miss. That it was the tinfoil balls, the *New York Times,* and the
broken speaker; the fingernail marks, the stray cassettes, and the smell of chai. Alone
that night and parked in my driveway, I listened to Frank Sinatra with the moon roof
slid back.

READING FOR MEANING

1. **Read to Summarize.** Write a sentence or two explaining the relationship
   between Keegan and her car, and what Keegan learns about her life when
   she reflects on this relationship.

   For more on summarizing, see Chapter 2, pp. 24–25.

2. **Read to Respond.** Write a paragraph analyzing anything that seems
   interesting or that resonates with your experience, such as Keegan's char-
   acterization of her car having a "midlife crisis" (par. 5) when she begins to
   shed her "eclectic debris" (par. 6) and make the car her own; or the idea of
   "survival necessities" being different things for different people (Keegan,
   her grandmother, her brother). How do Keegan's narrative and descriptions affect your understanding of her relationship with her car—and

with the car's other drivers? Consider your own "debris" and "survival necessities" and what they reveal about you.

You may also try contextualizing; see Chapter 2, pp. 29–30.

3. **Read to Analyze Assumptions.** Write a paragraph or two analyzing an assumption you find intriguing in Keegan's essay. For example:

Assumptions about how memories make us who we are. Keegan explains that she "often found more than just physical relics" (par. 9) in her car. Her memories would flood back just standing by "the side door" where she found herself "reliving the first time he kissed me" (par. 9), or when she saw signs of her fingernail marks in the leather steering wheel from her emotions when their relationship changed to "just friends."

- How do such memories create our inner selves? How might they also create our outer selves?
- Are physical reminders like the car necessary to keep these memories alive? In your view, is it healthy to hold on to these physical reminders, or is nostalgia a crutch or an impediment?

Assumptions that people need a place of their own. Keegan notes that her car "came to be a place of comfort and solitude amid the chaos of [her] daily routine" (par. 8). She saw it as "an extension of [her]self" (par. 7) where "[n]o one was watching or keeping score" (par. 8).

- Do most people have a place of their own? Why might people need a place where no one is watching, where they can just be themselves?
- Consider Keegan's title, "Stability in Motion." What does the title say about the role Keegan's car played in her life?

READING LIKE A WRITER

MAINTAINING COHERENCE

Writers maintain coherence by providing *cues* that help readers move from paragraph to paragraph and from section to section without losing the thread. The most familiar *cohesive device* is probably the transitional word or phrase. Some transitions (*however, because*) alert readers to the logical relationships among ideas, while others indicate relationships in time or space (*next, beyond*). Keegan uses paragraph transitions to maintain coherence. For example, look at the first sentence of the second, third, and fourth paragraphs:

Prepositional
phrases mark
transitions

During its youth, the car traveled little. (par. 2)

I acquired the old Camry through an awkward transaction. (par 3)

Throughout the next three years, the car evolved. (par. 4)

Each sentence refers back to the content of the previous paragraph, and forward to the content of the upcoming paragraph.

Analyze & Write

Write a paragraph or two analyzing how Keegan creates coherence throughout the rest of her essay with paragraph transitions.

1. Highlight the first sentence of each paragraph. Identify which ones serve as a transition, and note how the transition refers back to content in the previous paragraph or forward to the idea in the upcoming paragraph (or both).

2. How effectively does this strategy work to maintain coherence? Support your analysis with examples from the reading.

Jacqueline Woodson

The Pain of the Watermelon Joke

Jacqueline Woodson (b. 1963) is an American writer of young adult fiction. She won the Coretta Scott King Award in 2001 for *Miracle's Boys*
(2000), and Newbery awards for *Show Way* (2005), *Feathers* (2007), *After
Tupac & D Foster* (2008), and *Brown Girl Dreaming* (2014) — a book in
verse for which she also won the 2014 National Book Award for Young
People's Literature. The essay below was published in the *New York Times*
in 2014.

- **Before you read,** think about a joke you have heard that is made at the
  expense of someone or something that you care about. How did the
  joke make you feel?

- **As you read,** consider how Woodson approaches the contentious topic
  of racism with personal stories and references to her family. How do
  her rhetorical choices affect your response to her experience?

As a child in South Carolina, I spent summers like so many children — sitting on my   1
grandparents' back porch with my siblings, spitting watermelon seeds into the garden
or, even worse, swallowing them and trembling as my older brother and sister spoke
of the vine that was probably already growing in my belly.

It was the late '60s and early '70s, and even though Jim Crow was supposed to be   2
far behind us, we spent our days in the all-black community called Nicholtown in a
still segregated South.

One year, we bought a watermelon off the back of a man's pickup truck and placed   3
it in our garden. As my grandfather snapped pictures from his box camera, we laughed
about how we'd fool my mother, who was in New York, by telling her we'd grown it
ourselves. I still have the photo of me in a pale pink dress, beribboned and smiling,
sitting on that melon.

But by the time I was 11 years old, even the smell of watermelon was enough to   4
send me running to the bathroom with my most recent meal returning to my throat.
It seemed I had grown violently allergic to the fruit.

I was a brown girl growing up in the United States. By that point in my life, I had   5
seen the racist representations associated with African-Americans and watermelons,
heard the terrifying stories of black men being lynched with watermelons hanging
around them, watched black migrants from the South try to eke out a living in the big
city by driving through neighborhoods like my own — Bushwick, in Brooklyn — with
trucks loaded down with the fruit.

In a book I found at the library, a camp song about a watermelon vine was illus-   6
trated with caricatures of sleepy-looking black people sitting by trees, grinning and
eating watermelon. Slowly, the hideousness of the stereotype began to sink in. In the
eyes of those who told and repeated the jokes, we were shuffling, googly-eyed and
lesser than.

Perhaps my allergy was actually a deep physical revulsion that came from the psychological impression and weight of the association. Whatever it was, I could no longer eat watermelon. 7

In the midst of observing the world and coming to consciousness, I was becoming a writer, and what I wanted to put on the page were the stories of people who looked like me. I was a child on a mission—to change the face of literature and erase stereotypes. Forever. By the time I was in fifth grade, I was dreaming of the Pulitzer Prize. By the time I was 45, I had won just about every award one could win for young people's literature. Just this month, I received the National Book Award in the young-adult category for my memoir, *Brown Girl Dreaming*. 8

As I walked away from the stage to a standing ovation after my acceptance speech, it was the last place in the world I thought I'd hear the watermelon joke—directed by the M.C., Daniel Handler, at me. "Jackie's allergic to watermelon," he said. "Just let that sink in your mind." Daniel and I have been friends for years. Last summer, at his home on Cape Cod, he served watermelon soup and I let him know I was allergic to the fruit. I was astonished when he brought this up before the National Book Award audience—in the form of a wink-nudge joke about being black. 9

In a few short words, the audience and I were asked to take a step back from everything I've ever written, a step back from the power and meaning of the National Book Award, lest we forget, lest I forget, where I came from. By making light of that deep and troubled history, he showed that he believed we were at a point where we could 10 laugh about it all. His historical context, unlike my own, came from a place of ignorance.

"Brown Girl Dreaming" is the story of my family, moving from slavery through 11 Reconstruction, Jim Crow and the civil rights movement, and ends with me as a child of the '70s. It is steeped in the history of not only my family but of America. As African-Americans, we were given this history daily as weapons against our stories' being erased in the world or, even worse, delivered to us offhandedly in the form of humor.

As I interviewed relatives in both Ohio and Greenville, S.C., I began to piece 12 together the story of my mother's life, my grandparents' lives and the lives of cousins, aunts and uncles. These stories, and the stories I had heard throughout my childhood, were told with the hope that I would carry on this family history and American history, so that those coming after me could walk through the world as armed as I am.

Mr. Handler's watermelon comment was made at a time of change. We Need 13 Diverse Books, a grass-roots organization committed to diversifying all children's literature, had only months before stormed the BookCon conference because of its all-white panels. The world of publishing has been getting shaken like a pecan tree and called to the floor because of its lack of diversity in the workplace. At this year's National Book Awards, many of the books featured nonwhite protagonists, and three of the 20 finalists were people of color. One of those brown finalists (me!), in the very first category, Young People's Literature, had just won.

Just let that sink in your mind.   14

I would have written *Brown Girl Dreaming* if no one had ever wanted to buy it, if 15 it went nowhere but inside a desk drawer that my own children pulled out one day to find a tool for survival, a symbol of how strong we are and how much we've come through. Their great-great-great-grandfather fought in the Civil War. Their great-grandfather, Hope, and great-grandmother, Grace, raised one of the few black families in Nelsonville, Ohio, and saw five children through college. Their grandmother's school in Greenville, Sterling High, was set on fire and burned to the ground.

To know that we African-Americans came here enslaved to work until we died but 16 didn't die, and instead grew up to become doctors and teachers, architects and presidents—how can these children not carry this history with them for those many moments when someone will attempt to make light of it, or want them to forget the depth and amazingness of their journey?

How could I come from such a past and not know that I am on a mission, too?   17

This mission is what's been passed down to me—to write stories that have been 18 historically absent in this country's body of literature, to create mirrors for the people who so rarely see themselves inside contemporary fiction, and windows for those who think we are no more than the stereotypes they're so afraid of. To give young people—and all people—a sense of this country's brilliant and brutal history, so that no one ever thinks they can walk onto a stage one evening and laugh at another's too often painful past.

READING FOR MEANING

1. **Read to Summarize.** Write a sentence or two explaining what happened at the National Book Award ceremony and how that led to Woodson writing an essay on the watermelon joke.

   For help with summarizing, see Chapter 2, pp. 24–25.

2. **Read to Respond.** Write a paragraph exploring anything that resonates with your experience or that seems surprising, such as a friend making a hurtful joke about a watermelon in a public ceremony, or the second appearance of the phrase "just let that sink in your mind" (par. 14).

3. **Read to Analyze Assumptions.** Write a paragraph or two analyzing an assumption you find intriguing in Woodson's essay. For example:

   For help analyzing assumptions, see Chapter 2, pp. 28–29.

   Assumptions about the power of the written word. Woodson notes that she was "a child on a mission — to change the face of literature and erase stereotypes. Forever" (par. 8). In her last paragraph, she adds that her mission is "to create mirrors for the people who so rarely see themselves inside contemporary fiction, and windows for those who think we are no more than the stereotypes they're so afraid of" (par. 18).

   - What makes the written word so powerful? How does its power differ from an aural or visual medium?
   - If the written word creates "mirrors" and "windows," how does it help readers understand stereotyping and racism?

   Assumptions about the importance of learning history. Woodson writes that an understanding of "family history and American history" will allow later generations to "walk through the world as armed" (par. 12). In her essay, she reflects on both her individual experiences as a "brown girl," her ancestors' experiences, and the experiences of African Americans in the nation's troubled past.

   - How do the histories of Woodson's family and of the United States work together in her essay? How does knowing these histories "arm" Woodson to respond to Handler's joke?
   - In your experience, is history remembered the same way by different kinds of people (like Woodson and Handler)? If not, what causes history to be remembered, learned, or used differently — and for what purposes?

READING LIKE A WRITER

ENGAGING READERS

In reflective essays, writers often tell **anecdotes** — brief, entertaining stories — to help engage readers, as Woodson does with the story of taking a picture with an oversized watermelon (par. 3). Woodson believes stories have been used to portray

African Americans in various unflattering ways, and as she was becoming a writer, she "wanted to put on the page . . . the stories of people who looked like" her (par. 8) and to change public perception of them. Consider also what kind of story the illustration tells (p. 161) and how well — and in what ways — it engages Woodson's readers.

| Analyze & Write |

Write a paragraph or two analyzing Woodson's use of an anecdote to set the scene she is trying to change.

1. Reread the opening anecdote (pars. 1–3) to identify how Woodson engages the reader in the "history" of the watermelon joke.

2. Annotate the paragraph to show how Woodson intends to undermine the joke and change the history of the stories and of the joke. Does she succeed in drawing the reader into her purpose?

Manuel Muñoz

Leave Your Name at the Border

Manuel Muñoz (b. 1972) is Associate Professor of Creative Writing at the
University of Arizona. He received his degree from Harvard in 1994 and
his MFA from Cornell in 1998. He is best known for his short stories, collected in *Zigzagger* (2003) and *The Faith Healer of Olive Avenue* (2008),
and his novel *What You See in the Dark* (2011). His stories have won the
PEN/O. Henry Award twice for "Tell Him about Brother John" (2009) and
"The Happiest Girl in the Whole USA" (2015). His writing appears in the
New York Times, Glimmer Train, Epoch, Eleven Eleven, and *Boston Review*
and has aired on National Public Radio's *Selected Shorts*. The essay below
appeared in the *New York Times* in 2007.

- **Before you read,** think about your own name. What does it tell people
  about you? Do you have an opinion about whether names should be
  standardized in the United States?

- **As you read,** pay attention to how Muñoz sets up a contrast between
  English and Spanish. How does this contrast help convey his ideas?

At the Fresno airport, as I made my way to the gate, I heard a name over the intercom. 1
The way the name was pronounced by the gate agent made me want to see what she
looked like. That is, I wanted to see whether she was Mexican. Around Fresno, identity politics rarely deepen into exacting terms, so to say "Mexican" means, essentially,
"not white." The slivered self-identifications Chicano, Hispanic, Mexican-American
and Latino are not part of everyday life in the Valley. You're either Mexican or you're
not. If someone wants to know if you were born in Mexico, they'll ask. Then you're
From Over There—*de allá*. And leave it at that.

The gate agent, it turned out, was Mexican. Well-coiffed, in her 30s, she wore 2
foundation that was several shades lighter than the rest of her skin. It was the kind of
makeup job I've learned to silently identify at the mall when I'm with my mother, who
will say nothing about it until we're back in the car. Then she'll point to the darkness of
her own skin, wondering aloud why women try to camouflage who they are.

I watched the Mexican gate agent busy herself at the counter, professional and 3
studied. Once again, she picked up the microphone and, with authority, announced
the name of the missing customer: "Eugenio Reyes, please come to the front desk."

You can probably guess how she said it. Her Anglicized pronunciation wouldn't be 4
unusual in a place like California's Central Valley. I didn't have a Mexican name there
either: I was an instruction guide.

When people ask me where I'm from, I say Fresno because I don't expect them to 5
know little Dinuba. Fresno is a booming city of nearly 500,000 these days, with a
diversity—white, Mexican, African-American, Armenian, Hmong and Middle East-
ern people are all well represented—that shouldn't surprise anyone. It's in the small
towns like Dinuba that surround Fresno that the awareness of cultural difference is

stripped down to the interactions between the only two groups that tend to live there: whites and Mexicans. When you hear a Mexican name spoken in these towns, regardless of the speaker's background, it's no wonder that there's an "English way of pronouncing it."

I was born in 1972, part of a generation that learned both English and Spanish. 6 Many of my cousins and siblings are bilingual, serving as translators for those in the family whose English is barely functional. Others have no way of following the Spanish banter at family gatherings. You can tell who falls into which group: Estella, Eric, Delia, Dubina, Melanie.

It's intriguing to watch "American" names begin to dominate among my nieces and 7 nephews and second cousins, as well as with the children of my hometown friends. I am not surprised to meet 5-year-old Brandon or Kaitlyn. Hardly anyone questions the incongruity of matching these names with last names like Trujillo or Zepeda. The English-only way of life partly explains the quiet erasure of cultural difference that assimilation has attempted to accomplish. A name like Kaitlyn Zepeda doesn't completely obscure her ethnicity, but the half-step of her name, as a gesture, is almost understandable.

Spanish was and still is viewed with suspicion: Always the language of the vilified 8 illegal immigrant, it segregated schoolchildren into English-only and bilingual programs; it defined you, above all else, as part of a lower class. Learning English, though, brought its own complications. It was simultaneously the language of the white population and a path toward the richer, expansive identity of "American." But it took getting out of the Valley for me to understand that "white" and "American" were two very different things.

Something as simple as saying our names "in English" was our unwittingly com- 9 plicit gesture of trying to blend in. Pronouncing Mexican names correctly was never encouraged. Names like Daniel, Olivia and Marco slipped right into the mutability of the English language.

I remember a school ceremony at which the mathematics teacher, a white man, 10 announced the names of Mexican students correctly and caused some confusion, if not embarrassment. Years later we recognized that he spoke in deference to our Spanish-speaking parents in the audience, caring teacher that he was.

These were difficult names for a non-Spanish speaker: Araceli, Nadira, Luis (a beauti- 11 ful name when you glide the *u* and the *i* as you're supposed to). We had been accustomed to having our birth names altered for convenience. Concepción was Connie. Ramón was Raymond. My cousin Esperanza was Hope—but her name was pronounced "Hopie" because any Spanish speaker would automatically pronounce the *e* at the end.

Ours, then, were names that stood as barriers to a complete embrace of an American 12 identity, simply because their pronunciations required a slip into Spanish, the otherness that assimilation was supposed to erase. What to do with names like Amado, Lucio or Élida? There are no English "equivalents," no answer when white teachers asked, "What does your name mean?" when what they really wanted to know was "What's the English one?" So what you heard was a name butchered beyond recognition, a pronunciation that pointed the finger at the Spanish language as the source of clunky sound and ugly rhythm.

My stepfather, from Ojos de Agua, Mexico, jokes when I ask him about the names 13 of Mexicans born here. He deliberately stumbles over pronunciations, imitating our elders who have difficulty with Bradley and Madelyn. "Ashley Sánchez. *¿Tú crees?*"[1] He wonders aloud what has happened to the *"nombres del rancho"*—traditional Mexican names that are hardly given anymore to children born in the States: Heraclio, Madaleno, Otilia, Dominga.

My stepfather's experience with the Anglicization of his name—Antonio to Tony— 14 ties into something bigger than learning English. For him, the erasure of his name was about deference and subservience. Becoming Tony gave him a measure of access as he struggled to learn English and get more fieldwork.

This isn't to say that my stepfather welcomed the change, only that he could not 15 put up much resistance. Not changing put him at risk of being passed over for work. English was a world of power and decisions, of smooth, uninterrupted negotiation. Clear communication meant you could go unsupervised. Every gesture made toward convincing an employer that English was on its way to being mastered had the potential to make a season of fieldwork profitable.

It's curious that many of us growing up in Dinuba adhered to the same rules. 16 Although as children of farm workers we worked in the fields at an early age, we'd also had the opportunity to stay in one town long enough to finish school. Most of us had learned English early and splintered off into a dual existence of English at school, Spanish at home. But instead of recognizing the need for fluency in both languages, we turned it into a peculiar kind of battle. English was for public display. Spanish was for privacy—and privacy quickly turned to shame.

The corrosive effect of assimilation is the displacement of one culture over another, 17 the inability to sustain more than one way of being. It isn't a code word for racial and ethnic acculturation only. It applies to needing to belong, of seeing from the outside and wondering how to get in and then, once inside, realizing there are always those still on the fringe.

When I went to college on the East Coast, I was confronted for the first time by 18 people who said my name correctly without prompting; if they stumbled, there was a quick apology and an honest plea to help with the pronunciation. But introducing myself was painful: already shy, I avoided meeting people because I didn't want to say my name, felt burdened by my own history. I knew that my small-town upbringing and its limitations on Spanish would not have been tolerated by any of the students of color who had grown up in large cities, in places where the sheer force of their native languages made them dominant in their neighborhoods.

It didn't take long for me to assert the power of code-switching in public, the trans- 19 ferring of words from one language to another, regardless of who might be listening. I was learning that the English language composed new meanings when its constrictions were ignored, crossed over or crossed out. Language is all about manipulation, or not listening to the rules.

When I come back to Dinuba, I have a hard time hearing my name said incor- 20 rectly, but I have an even harder time beginning a conversation with others about why the pronunciation of our names matters. Leaving a small town requires an embrace of a larger point of view, but a town like Dinuba remains forever embedded in an either/or way of life. My stepfather still answers to Tony and, as the United States–born

---

[1]*¿Tú crees?:* Can you believe it? [Ed.]

children grow older, their Anglicized names begin to signify who does and who does not "belong"—who was born here and who is *de allá*.

My name is Manuel. To this day, most people cannot say it correctly, the way it was 21 intended to be said. But I can live with that because I love the alliteration of my full name. It wasn't the name my mother, Esmeralda, was going to give me. At the last minute, my father named me after an uncle I would never meet. My name was to have been Ricardo. Growing up in Dinuba, I'm certain I would have become Ricky or even Richard, and the journey toward the discovery of the English language's extraordinary power in even the most ordinary of circumstances would probably have gone unlearned.

I count on a collective sense of cultural loss to once again swing the names back to 22 our native language. The Mexican gate agent announced Eugenio Reyes, but I never got a chance to see who appeared. I pictured an older man, cowboy hat in hand, but I made the assumption on his name alone, the clash of privileges I imagined between someone *de allá* and a Mexican woman with a good job in the United States. Would she speak to him in Spanish? Or would she raise her voice to him as if he were hard of hearing?

But who was I to imagine this man being from anywhere, based on his name alone? 23 At a place of arrivals and departures, it sank into me that the currency of our names is a stroke of luck: because mine was not an easy name, it forced me to consider how language would rule me if I allowed it. Yet I discovered that only by leaving. My step-father must live in the Valley, a place that does not allow that choice, every day. And Eugenio Reyes—I do not know if he was coming or going.

READING FOR MEANING

For help with summarizing, see Chapter 2, pp. 24–25.

1. **Read to Summarize.** Write a few sentences explaining the message Manuel Muñoz is trying to convey about language and names.

2. **Read to Respond.** Write a paragraph exploring anything that resonates with your experience or that seems surprising, such as how the Mexican gate agent pronounced Eugenio Reyes's name, or the sentence "But it took getting out of the Valley for me to understand that 'white' and 'American' were two very different things" (par. 8).

For help analyzing assumptions, see Chapter 2, pp. 28–29.

3. **Read to Analyze Assumptions.** Write a paragraph or two analyzing an assumption you find intriguing in Muñoz's essay. For example:

   Assumptions about the differences between small towns and cities. Muñoz points out differences between Fresno and Dinuba (par. 5), the Valley (par. 8), and "college on the East Coast" (par. 18).

   - Why does Muñoz call attention to these differences? How does acknowledging them highlight his reflections on language and names? Are these differences helpful, harmful, or somewhere in between?
   - What do you think the residents of these varied areas believe about cultural differences? What experiences, texts, or people have influenced how you think about people in these places and their beliefs?

Assumptions about the significance of names. Names give information about background, ethnicity, and perhaps allegiances. Muñoz points out that in the Valley, Spanish "defined you, above all else, as part of a lower class" (par. 8). Anglicizing names, while springing from "deference and subservience" (par. 14), gave access to more work, as it did for his stepfather, who shifted from Antonio to Tony (par. 14).

- Why does the origin or pronunciation of a name matter?
- Are Muñoz's views about names universal? Are there cultures where names have more or less significance? How do you know?

READING LIKE A WRITER

MAINTAINING COHERENCE WITH CUES

Authors can maintain coherence in reflective writing by calling on repetition of key words or phrases to keep the reader returning to important concepts. Muñoz repeats the word *name* throughout his essay (including in the title).

Analyze & Write

Write a paragraph or two analyzing how Muñoz uses the strategy of repetition to maintain coherence throughout his essay.

1. Skim the essay, underlining or highlighting the word *name* whenever it appears.
2. Examine the different contexts in which the word appears, and analyze the meanings of its varied uses. What do you conclude about why Muñoz repeats the word so often and what this repetition means to the reader?

Katherine Haines

Whose Body Is This?

Katherine Haines wrote this essay for an assignment in her first-year college composition course. As the title suggests, the writer reflects on her dismay and anger about American society's obsession with the perfect body — especially the perfect female body.

- **Before you read,** think about your own attitude toward the female body as it is portrayed in the media. Do you find anything disturbing about it?

- **As you read,** consider Haines's rhetorical situation; she is writing about a sensitive topic for many women. What strategies does she use to develop her reflection, support her opinions, and remain sensitive to her audience?

"Hey Rox, what's up? Do you wanna go down to the pool with me? It's a gorgeous day."   1
   "No thanks, you go ahead without me."   2
   "What? Why don't you want to go? You've got the day off work, and what else are   3
you going to do?"
   "Well, I've got a bunch of stuff to do around the house . . . pay the bills, clean the   4
bathroom, you know. Besides, I don't want to have to see myself in a bathing suit — I'm
so fat."

Why do so many women seem obsessed with their weight and body shape? Are they   5
really that unhappy and dissatisfied with themselves? Or are these women continually
hearing from other people that their bodies are not acceptable?

   In today's society, the expectations for women and their bodies are all too evident.   6
Fashion, magazines, talk shows, "lite" and fat-free food in stores and restaurants, and
diet centers are all daily reminders of these expectations. For instance, the latest fashions for women reveal more and more skin: shorts have become shorter, to the point
of being scarcely larger than a pair of underpants, and the bustier, which covers only a
little more skin than a bra, is making a comeback. These styles are flattering on only
the slimmest of bodies, and many women who were previously happy with their bodies may emerge from the dressing room after a run-in with these styles and decide that
it must be diet time again. Instead of coming to the realization that these clothes are
unflattering for most women, how many women will simply look for different and
more flattering styles, and how many women will end up heading for the gym to burn
off some more calories or to the bookstore to buy the latest diet book?

   When I was in junior high, about two-thirds of the girls I knew were on diets.   7
Everyone was obsessed with fitting into the smallest-size miniskirt possible. One of
my friends would eat a carrot stick, a celery stick, and two rice cakes for lunch. Junior
high (and the onset of adolescence) seemed to be the beginning of the pressure for
most women. It is at this age that appearance suddenly becomes important, especially

for those girls who want to be "popular" and those who are cheerleaders or on the drill team. The pressure is intense; some girls believe no one will like them or accept them if they are "overweight," even by a pound or two. The measures these girls will take to attain the body that they think will make them acceptable are often debilitating and life threatening.

My sister was on the drill team in junior high. My sister wanted to fit in with the right 8 crowd—and my sister drove herself to the edge of becoming anorexic. I watched as she came home from school, having eaten nothing for breakfast and at lunch only a bag of pretzels and an apple (and she didn't always finish that), and began pacing the Oriental carpet that was in our living room. Around and around and around, without a break, from four o'clock until dinnertime, which was usually at six or seven o'clock. And then at dinner, she would take minute portions and only pick at her food. After several months of this, she became much paler and thinner but not in any sort of attractive sense. Finally, after catching a cold and having to stay in bed for three days because she was so weak, she was forced to go to the doctor. The doctor said she was suffering from malnourishment and was to stay in bed until she regained some of her strength. He advised her to eat lots of fruits and vegetables until the bruises all over her body had healed (these were a result of vitamin deficiency). Although my sister did not develop anorexia, it was frightening to see what she had done to herself. She had little strength, and the bruises she had made her look like an abused child.

This mania to lose weight and have the "ideal" body is not easily avoided in our 9 society. It is created by television and magazines as they flaunt their models and latest diet crazes in front of our faces. And then there are the Nutri-System and Jenny Craig commercials, which show hideous "before" pictures and glamorous "after" pictures and have smiling, happy people dancing around and talking about how their lives have been transformed simply because they have lost weight. This propaganda that happiness is in large part based on having the "perfect" body shape is a message that the media constantly sends to the public. No one seems to be able to escape it.

My mother and father were even sucked in by this idea. One evening, when I was in 10 the fifth grade, I heard Mom and Dad calling me into the kitchen. Oh no, what had I done now? It was never good news when you got summoned into the kitchen alone. As I walked into the kitchen, Mom looked up at me with an anxious expression; Dad was sitting at the head of the table with a pen in hand and a yellow legal pad in front of him. They informed me that I was going on a diet. A diet!? I wanted to scream at them, "I'm only ten years old, why do I have to be on a diet?" I was so embarrassed, and I felt so guilty. Was I really fat? I guess so, I thought, otherwise why would my parents do this to me?

It seems that this obsession with the perfect body and a woman's appearance has 11 grown to monumental heights. It is ironic, however, that now many people feel that this problem is disappearing. People have begun to assume that women want to be thin because they just want to be "healthy." But what has happened is that the sickness slips in under the guise of wanting a "healthy" body. The demand for thin bodies is anything but "healthy." How many anorexics or bulimics have you seen that are healthy?

It is strange that women do not come out and object to society's pressure to become 12 thin. Or maybe women feel that they really do want to be thin and so go on dieting endlessly (they call it "eating sensibly"), thinking this is what they really want. I think if these women carefully examined their reasons for wanting to lose weight—and were not allowed to include reasons that relate to society's demands, such as a weight chart, a questionnaire in a magazine, a certain size in a pair of shorts, or even a scale—they would find that they are being ruled by what society wants, not what they want. So why do women not break free from these standards? Why do they not demand an end to being judged in such a demeaning and senseless way?

Self-esteem plays a large part in determining whether women succumb to the will of   13
society or whether they are independent and self-assured enough to make their own decisions. Lack of self-esteem is one of the things the women's movement has had to fight the hardest against. If women didn't think they were worthy, then how could they even begin to fight for their own rights? The same is true with the issue of body size. If women do not feel their body is worthy, then how can they believe that it is okay to just let it stay that way? Without self-esteem, women will be swayed by society and will continue to make themselves unhappy by trying to maintain whatever weight or body shape society is dictating for them. It is ironic that many of the popular women's magazines (*Cosmopolitan*, *Mademoiselle*, *Glamour*) often feature articles on self-esteem, how essential it is, and how to improve it—and then in the same issue give the latest diet tips. This mixed message will never give women the power they deserve over their bodies and will never enable them to make their own decisions about what type of body they want.

"Rox, why do you think you're fat? You work out all the time, and you just bought   14
that new suit. Why don't you just come down to the pool for a little while?"

"No, I really don't want to. I feel so self-conscious with all those people around. It   15
makes me want to run and put on a big, baggy dress so no one can tell what size I am!"

"Ah, Rox, that's really sad. You have to learn to believe in yourself and your own   16
judgment, not other people's."

READING FOR MEANING

For help with
summarizing and
analyzing
assumptions,
see Chapter 2,
pp. 24–25 and
28–29.

1. **Read to Summarize.** Write a sentence or two explaining what you think Haines wants readers to understand about the occasion she describes.

2. **Read to Respond.** Write a paragraph analyzing anything that seems contradictory, such as Haines's response to women who claim they maintain a thin body for "health" (pars. 11–12) or whether men have similar perfect-body issues that are also worth considering.

You may also
try recognizing
emotional
manipulation;
see Chapter 2,
pp. 44–45.

3. **Read to Analyze Assumptions**. Write a paragraph or two analyzing an assumption you find intriguing in Haines's essay. For example:

   Assumptions about high self-esteem enabling women to make their own decisions. According to Haines, "[s]elf-esteem plays a large part in determining whether women succumb to the will of society or whether they are independent and self-assured enough to make their own decisions" (par. 13).

- Is a woman's size always an indication of her self-esteem?
- What are the qualities of self-esteem that enable men and women to be independent and to make their own decisions?

Assumptions that media have a strong effect on human behavior. Haines writes that "[f]ashion, magazines, talk shows, 'lite' and fat-free food in stores and restaurants, and diet centers are all daily reminders of . . . expectations" (par. 6) for women to be thin.

- Which examples in the essay rest on an assumption about the media's effect?
- Are fat-free foods and diet centers related to the media? Why or why not?

READING LIKE A WRITER

DEVELOPING THE REFLECTIONS

In reflective writing, insights and ideas are central. Yet writers cannot merely list ideas, regardless of how fresh and daring their ideas might be. Instead, writers must work imaginatively to develop their ideas, to explain and elaborate on them, and to view them from one angle and then another. One way writers develop their reflections and make them compelling for readers is by drawing on examples from their personal experiences. For example, Haines uses current fashions in paragraph 6 and a junior-high-school friend's lunch ("a carrot stick, a celery stick, and two rice cakes") in paragraph 7 to make her point about the effects of fashion trends on self-esteem and the lengths women (and girls) will go to achieve the bodies society seems to be demanding.

Analyze & Write

Write a paragraph or two analyzing Haines's use of extended examples to convey her insights and ideas about the destructive power of unreasonable social ideals.

1. Skim paragraphs 1–4 and 14–16. How does Haines use dialogue to help readers understand the effects of unreasonable standards on women? What effect does this example have on you as a reader?

2. Reread paragraphs 8 and 10. How does Haines use examples from her own and her family's experience? Does the use of personal examples strengthen or undermine Haines's message that our culture puts an unnatural emphasis on what women's bodies should look like?

Writing to Learn Reflection

Write a brief essay analyzing one of the readings in this chapter (or another selection, perhaps one by a classmate). Explain how (and perhaps, how well) the selection works as a reflection. Consider, for example, how it uses

- an occasion to prompt the reflection and prepare the reader;

- varied writing strategies to develop the reflection;

- cues to maintain coherence;

- strategies to engage readers' interest.

Your essay could also reflect on how you applied one or more of the academic habits of mind as you read the selection:

- **Curiosity**—what questions or ideas did you have as you read the selection?

- **Critical Analysis**—what assumptions in the selection did you find intriguing, and why?

- **Rhetorical Sensitivity**—how effective or ineffective do you think the selection is in achieving its purpose for the intended audience, given the constraints of the medium and the reflection genre?

A GUIDE TO WRITING REFLECTIVE ESSAYS

You have probably done a good deal of analytical writing about your reading. Your instructor may also assign a capstone project to write a brief reflection of your own. This Guide to Writing offers detailed suggestions and resources to help you meet the special challenges reflective writing presents.

THE WRITING ASSIGNMENT

Write a reflective essay that grows out of a specific occasion or event.

- Choose an occasion or event that you feel comfortable writing about for this audience (your instructor and classmates). You may want to select the general subject that you want to reflect on first, and then choose an event or occasion that effectively particularizes this subject.

- Consider how you can depict the occasion or event vividly so that readers can imagine what you experienced. Try to create a voice or persona that will appeal to your audience.

- Develop your reflections, including insights that interest, surprise, or enlighten your readers.

- Organize your reflection so that readers will be able to follow your train of thought.

WRITING YOUR DRAFT

Choosing an Occasion and General Subject

Writers of reflections often connect an occasion to a subject or a subject to an occasion. Sometimes writers choose a general subject (such as envy or friendship) and then search for the right occasion (an image or anecdote) with which to particularize it. Sometimes the occasion prompts the subject.

To get started, use a chart like the one below to list several possible occasions and the general subjects they suggest (or start with the "General Subjects" column and then list the occasions they suggest).

Particular Occasions	*General Subjects*
I had an experience on the train.	The social benefits of mass transit
I met someone (or am someone) with a disability.	Measures taken for people with disabilities
I had a great time skiing.	The importance of exercise or of time away from work

For occasions, consider the following:

- conversations you have had or overheard
- memorable scenes you observed, read about, or saw in a movie or other media
- incidents in your own or someone else's life that led you to reflect more generally

Also consider the general subjects suggested by the occasions:

- human qualities such as compassion, vanity, jealousy, and faithfulness
- customs for socializing and working
- abstract notions such as fate, free will, and imagination

Shaping Your Reflection

Write up the initial occasion that prompted your reflection. Use specific details and choose evocative words to make your description vivid; use active, specific verbs to make your writing lively; and use time markers to give immediacy and color to your narration of the occasion. The example paragraph below demonstrates how one writer in this chapter used these strategies to shape their reflections:

Vivid description Active verb Time marker	My <u>first</u> victim was a woman — white, well dressed, probably in her early twenties. I came upon her <u>late one evening</u> on a deserted street in Hyde Park, a relatively affluent neighborhood in an otherwise mean, impoverished section of Chicago. As I swung onto the avenue behind her, there seemed to be a discreet, uninflammatory distance between us. Not so. She cast back a worried glance. To her, the youngish black man — a broad six feet two inches with a beard and billowing hair, both hands shoved into the pockets of a bulky military jacket — seemed menacingly close. <u>After a few more quick</u> glimpses, she picked up her pace and was <u>soon</u> running in earnest. <u>Within seconds</u> she disappeared into a cross street. (Staples, par. 1)

Developing Your Reflection

The following activities will help you recall details about the occasion for your reflection.

Narrating and Describing an Event.   Write for five to ten minutes narrating what happened during the event. Try to make your story vivid so that readers can imagine what it was like. Describe the people involved in the event — what they looked like, how they acted, what they said — and the place where it occurred.

Cubing. To explore your ideas about the subject, try an invention strategy called *cubing*. This approach encourages you to examine your subject as you would turn over a cube, looking at it in six different ways. You can use some of the eight options below or come up with your own. Whichever six you choose, write about your subject for five minutes from each of the six perspectives to invent new ways of considering it.

- **Analyzing.** What is your subject composed of? How are the parts related to one another? Are they all of equal importance?

- **Applying.** How can you use your subject or act on it? What difference would it make to you and to others?

- **Comparing and Contrasting.** What subject could you compare with yours? What are the similarities and the differences between them?

- **Describing.** What details would you use to describe the people or places involved in the occasion that gave rise to your reflections?

- **Extending.** What are the implications of your subject? Where does it lead?

- **Generalizing.** What does the occasion suggest about people in general or about the society in which you live?

- **Giving Examples.** What examples would best characterize or help your readers understand your reflection?

- **Visualizing.** What would your occasion look like from the perspective of an outside observer?

Exploring How You Felt at the Time and What the Occasion Made You Realize Later. Write for a few minutes, recalling your thoughts and feelings when the occasion was occurring.

- What did you feel at the moment the occasion was occurring — in control or powerless, proud or embarrassed, vulnerable, detached, judgmental? For example, Staples uses phrases like "swung onto the avenue" to indicate a light mood (par. 1). Sentence strategies like these might help you describe your initial experience of the occasion:

  ▸ As soon as I [saw/did/imagined] ...., I felt ...., ..., and ....

  ▸ .... [describe occasion] made me feel as if ....

- What larger reflection was prompted by your occasion? Muñoz, for example, suggests "[m]y stepfather's experience with the Anglicization of his name — Antonio to Tony — ties into something bigger than learning English. For him, the erasure of his name was about deference and subservience" (par. 14). These sentence strategies may help you put your reflection into words:

  ▸ Since then, I realize ...., but also ....

  ▸ Now that I have seen ...., I know that .... and ....

Considering Your Purpose and Audience. Write for several minutes exploring what you want your readers to think about your reflection after reading your essay. Your answer may change as you write, but thinking about your goals may help you decide which of your ideas to include in the essay. Answering the following questions may help you clarify your purpose:

- Which of your ideas are most important to you? Why?

- How do your ideas relate to one another? If your ideas seem contradictory, how could you use the contradictions to convey the complexity of your ideas and feelings on the subject?

- Is the occasion for your reflection likely to resonate with your readers' experience and observation?

Formulating a Working Thesis. Review what you wrote for Considering Your Purpose and Audience and add another two or three sentences to bring your reflection into focus. Write sentences that indicate what is most important or interesting about the subject. Readers may not expect reflective essays to begin with an explicit thesis statement — but stating the main point of your reflective essay now may lead you to a deeper understanding of your occasion and the reflection it inspired, and it may guide your selection of ideas to develop.

To learn more about citing visuals, see Chapter 2, pp. 31–34.

Considering Visuals. Think about whether visuals — cartoons, photographs, drawings, charts — would help readers understand and appreciate your reflections. For example, look at the visual at the beginning of Woodson's essay on the watermelon joke (p. 161). How does this drawing illuminate the point she is making about the history of her family and of her race in this country and about the role of the watermelon in that history? Does it give you a perspective that augments her writing, or perhaps shifts how you see her point?

If you submit your essay electronically to other students and your instructor, or if you post it on a website, you may even consider including snippets of video or audio files. You could import your own photographs or drawings, or you could scan materials from books and magazines or download them from the Internet, but remember that you will need to cite any visuals you borrow from another source.

Drafting Your Reflective Essay

By this point, you have done a lot of writing

- to present an occasion that prompts a reflection

- to present the reflection and develop it using a variety of approaches

- to relate the significance of your reflection in a way meaningful to your readers

Now stitch that material together to create a draft. The next section of this Guide to Writing will help you evaluate and improve it.

REVIEWING AND IMPROVING THE DRAFT

This section includes two guides for Peer Review and Troubleshooting Your Draft. Your instructor may arrange a peer review in class or online where you can exchange drafts with a classmate. The Peer Review Guide will help you give each other constructive feedback regarding the basic features and strategies typical of reflective essays. (If you want to make specific suggestions for improving the draft, see Troubleshooting Your Draft on pp. 180–81.) Also, be sure to respond to any specific concerns the writer has raised about the draft. The Troubleshooting Your Draft guide that follows will help you reread your own draft with a critical eye, sort through any feedback you've received, and consider a variety of ways to improve your draft.

A PEER REVIEW GUIDE

How effectively does the writer present the occasion?

What's Working Well: Identify a passage where the writer presents the occasion that prompted the reflection, perhaps suggesting the occasion's significance. Tell the writer if the occasion arouses interest and leads logically to the reflection.

What Needs Improvement: Let the writer know if there are details of the occasion that dominate the essay too much or are scant and need development.

How appropriate are the methods of developing the reflection?

What's Working Well: Point to a passage that is particularly effective in helping you understand the purpose of the reflection. To develop it, does the writer try compare/contrast, examples, consideration of social implications, or connections to other ideas?

What Needs Improvement: Identify any ideas or anecdotes you find lackluster or irrelevant to the broader association, explaining briefly why you think so.

How could the writer strengthen coherence?

What's Working Well: Highlight cues—strong transitions, time markers, or repeated words and ideas—that help hold the essay together.

What Needs Improvement: Point to areas where you get lost or don't understand the connection from one sentence or paragraph to the next. Note any section that seems out of place, and suggest where it might fit better.

(continued)

> **How could the readers be more engaged?**
>
> **What's Working Well:** Mark a part of the essay that especially draws you in, holds your interest, inspires you to think, challenges your attitudes or values, or keeps you wanting to read to the end.
>
> **What Needs Improvement:** Note passages where you lose interest or don't understand the significance to your own ideas and experiences. Suggest ways for the writer to liven up the essay by considering what aspects of the essays you read in this chapter inspired your own reflections.

Revising Your Draft

Revising means reenvisioning your draft, trying to see it in a new way, given your purpose and audience, in order to develop a more engaging, more coherent reflective essay. Think imaginatively and boldly about cutting unconvincing material, adding new material, and moving material around. The suggestions in the following chart may help you strengthen your essay.

TROUBLESHOOTING YOUR DRAFT

To Present the Subject More Effectively

If the occasion doesn't seem interesting or is too general or abstract,	• Add details for drama and surprise. • Make it into a story. • Try using the first person. • Try the present tense, and make your verbs active. • Choose another occasion that is more interesting and specific.
If the occasion is not clearly related to the reflection that follows,	• Make transitions clearer. • Explain how the two are related. • Choose another occasion that prepares readers by providing a context for your reflection.

To Clarify and Strengthen the Argument

If promising ideas are not fully developed,	• Provide more examples. • Compare or contrast your ideas with other ideas. • Consult Chapter 2 on reading strategies, and see whether you could use some of them to develop your reflection.

If your reflection does not move beyond personal association,	• Consider adding visuals. • Extend it into a broader association, such as social, political, scientific, or educational. • Comment on its larger implications for people in general.

To Improve the Response to Objections and/or Alternative Judgments

If there are gaps between sentences or paragraphs,	• Reorder the sequence of actions. • Add explicit transitions. • Revise pairs or a series of related ideas or examples into parallel form.
If the reflection seems scattered or disorganized,	• Repeat words and phrases to help readers follow your reflection. • Try time markers to show a clear sequence.

To Make the Organization Clearer

If the reflection doesn't encourage readers to reflect on their own lives,	• Think about your audience and tie your reflection to their values and beliefs. • Expand beyond the personal with more generalized stories or anecdotes. • Consider the broader social implications of your ideas. • Express the significance more directly.

Editing and Proofreading Your Draft

Check for errors in usage, punctuation, and mechanics, and consider matters of style. If you keep a list of errors you typically make, begin by checking your draft against this list. Ask someone else to proofread your essay before you submit it to your instructor.

From our research on student writing, we know that reflective essays have a high frequency of unnecessary shifts in verb tense and mood. Check a writer's handbook for help with these potential problems.

Reflecting on Reflection

In this chapter, you have read critically several reflective essays and have written one of your own. To better remember what you have learned, pause now to reflect on the reading and writing activities you completed in this chapter.

1. Write a page or so reflecting on what you have learned. Begin by describing what you are most pleased with in your essay. Then explain what you think contributed to your achievement. Be specific about this contribution.

   - If it was something you learned from the readings, indicate which readings and specifically what you learned from them.

   - If it came from the writing you did in response to prompts in this chapter, point out the section or sections that helped you most.

2. Reflect more generally on how you tend to interpret reflective writing, your own as well as other writers'. Consider some of the following questions:

   - Did you find rich enough material from your own personal ideas on a subject, or did you conduct research or interview people to collect their ideas?

   - How might your gender, social class, or ethnic group have influenced the ideas you came up with for your essay?

   - What contribution might reflective essays make to our society that other genres cannot make?

Explaining Concepts

A concept is a major idea. Concepts include abstract ideas, phenomena, and processes. We create concepts, name them, communicate them, and think with them in every field of study. Psychology, for example, has *schizophrenia* and *narcissism*; business has *micromanagement* and *direct marketing*; and nursing has *gerontology* and *whole-person caring*. Explaining concepts is a kind (or genre) of explanatory writing that is especially important for college students because it involves widely applicable strategies for critical reading, essay exams, and paper assignments. We learn new concepts by connecting them to what we have previously learned. Writing that explains concepts facilitates such connections through a range of writing strategies, including, among others, *definition*, *illustration*, *cause effect*, and *comparison-contrast*.

RHETORICAL SITUATIONS FOR CONCEPT EXPLANATIONS

Writing that explains concepts is familiar in college and professional life, as the following examples show:

- For a presentation at the annual convention of the American Medical Association, an anesthesiologist writes a report on the concept of *awareness during surgery*. He presents evidence that patients under anesthesia, as in hypnosis, can hear, and he reviews research demonstrating that they can perceive and carry out instructions that speed their recovery. He describes how he applies the concept in his own work — how he prepares patients before surgery, what he tells them while they are under anesthesia, and what happens as they recover.

- As part of a group assignment, a college student at a summer biology camp in the Sierra Nevada mountains reads about the condition of mammals at birth. She learns the distinction between infant mammals that are *altricial* (born nude and helpless within a protective nest) and those that are *precocial* (born well formed with eyes open and ears erect). In her part of a group report, she develops this contrast point by point, giving many examples of specific mammals but focusing in detail on altricial mice and precocial porcupines.

Thinking about Concept Explanation

Write a paragraph or two about an occasion when you told, read, heard, or saw an explanation of a concept in school, at work, or in another context.

- Who was the *audience?* How educated was the audience in the field of the concept? How did the writer tailor the explanation to help familiarize the audience with the concept, given their age, level of expertise, and experience?

- What was the main *purpose?* Why did the writer (or speaker) want the audience to understand the concept? For example, was the goal for the audience to demonstrate their understanding on a test, or the importance of the concept in their own lives?

- How would you rate the *rhetorical sensitivity* with which the explanation was presented? How was it appropriate or inappropriate for its audience or purpose?

A GUIDE TO READING CONCEPT EXPLANATIONS

This guide introduces you to concept explanations by inviting you to analyze an intriguing selection by Susan Cain that explains *introversion:*

- *Reading for meaning* will help you understand the topic and its significance for Cain. Why does Cain see our culture's attitude toward introversion as a long-term danger?

- *Reading like a writer* will help you learn how Cain employs strategies typical of concept explanations, such as

  1. using appropriate writing strategies: defining, illustrating, comparing and contrasting, and showing causes and effects

  2. organizing the information clearly and logically

  3. integrating sources smoothly

  4. engaging readers' interest

Susan Cain

Shyness: Evolutionary Tactic?

Susan Cain (b. 1968) attended Princeton University and Harvard Law School, and worked for several years as an attorney and a negotiations consultant. She is the author of the book *Quiet: The Power of Introverts in a World That Can't Stop Talking* (2012). She also writes a popular blog about introversion and has contributed articles on this topic to such journals and magazines as *Psychology Today* and *Time*, and her TED talk has broken viewing records. The op-ed that appears below was published in the *New York Times*.

- **Before you read,** notice the title of this reading and the title of Cain's book (above). What do these titles lead you to expect?
- **As you read,** think about the rhetorical sensitivity with which Cain is writing. How effective is the opening paragraph as a hook to catch readers' attention?

1   A beautiful woman lowers her eyes demurely beneath a hat. In an earlier era, her gaze might have signaled a mysterious allure. But this is a 2003 advertisement for Zoloft, a selective serotonin reuptake inhibitor (SSRI) approved by the FDA to treat social anxiety disorder. "Is she just shy? Or is it Social Anxiety Disorder?" reads the caption, suggesting that the young woman is not alluring at all. She is sick.

2   But is she?

3   It is possible that the lovely young woman has a life-wrecking form of social anxiety. There are people too afraid of disapproval to venture out for a job interview, a date or even a meal in public. Despite the risk of serious side effects—nausea, loss of sex drive, seizures—drugs like Zoloft can be a godsend for this group.

4   But the ad's insinuation aside, it's also possible the young woman is "just shy," or introverted—traits our society disfavors. One way we manifest this bias is by encouraging perfectly healthy shy people to see themselves as ill.

5   This does us all a grave disservice, because shyness and introversion—or more precisely, the careful, sensitive temperament from which both often spring—are not just normal. They are valuable. And they may be essential to the survival of our species.

6   Theoretically, shyness and social anxiety disorder are easily distinguishable. But a blurry line divides the two. Imagine that the woman in the ad enjoys a steady paycheck, a strong marriage and a small circle of close friends—a good life by most measures—except that she avoids a needed promotion because she's nervous about leading meetings. She often criticizes herself for feeling too shy to speak up.

7   What do you think now? Is she ill, or does she simply need public-speaking training?

8   Before 1980, this would have seemed a strange question. Social anxiety disorder did not officially exist until it appeared in that year's Diagnostic and Statistical Manual,

the DSM-III, the psychiatrist's bible of mental disorders, under the name "social phobia." It was not widely known until the 1990s, when pharmaceutical companies
received FDA approval to treat social anxiety with SSRI's and poured tens of millions
of dollars into advertising its existence. The current version of the Diagnostic and Statistical Manual, the DSM-IV, acknowledges that stage fright (and shyness in social situations) is common and not necessarily a sign of illness. But it also says that diagnosis
is warranted when anxiety "interferes significantly" with work performance or if the
sufferer shows "marked distress" about it. According to this definition, the answer to
our question is clear: the young woman in the ad is indeed sick.

The DSM inevitably reflects cultural attitudes; it used to identify homosexuality as   9
a disease, too. Though the DSM did not set out to pathologize shyness, it risks doing
so, and has twice come close to identifying introversion as a disorder, too. (Shyness
and introversion are not the same thing. Shy people fear negative judgment; introverts
simply prefer quiet, minimally stimulating environments.)

But shyness and introversion share an undervalued status in a world that prizes   10
extroversion. Children's classroom desks are now often arranged in pods, because
group participation supposedly leads to better learning; in one school I visited, a sign
announcing "Rules for Group Work" included, "You can't ask a teacher for help
unless everyone in your group has the same question." Many adults work for organizations that now assign work in teams, in offices without walls, for supervisors who
value "people skills" above all. As a society, we prefer action to contemplation, risk-
taking to heed-taking, certainty to doubt. Studies show that we rank fast and frequent
talkers as more competent, likable and even smarter than slow ones. As the psychologists William Hart and Dolores Albarracin point out, phrases like "get active," "get
moving," "do something" and similar calls to action surface repeatedly in recent
books.

Yet shy and introverted people have been part of our species for a very long time,   11
often in leadership positions. We find them in the Bible ("Who am I, that I should go
unto Pharaoh?" asked Moses, whom the Book of Numbers describes as "very meek,
above all the men which were upon the face of the earth.") We find them in recent
history, in figures like Charles Darwin, Marcel Proust and Albert Einstein, and, in contemporary times: think of Google's Larry Page, or Harry Potter's creator, J. K. Rowling.

In the science journalist Winifred Gallagher's words: "The glory of the disposition   12
that stops to consider stimuli rather than rushing to engage with them is its long association with intellectual and artistic achievement. Neither $E = mc^2$ nor *Paradise Lost*
was dashed off by a party animal."

We even find "introverts" in the animal kingdom, where 15 percent to 20 percent   13
of many species are watchful, slow-to-warm-up types who stick to the sidelines
(sometimes called "sitters") while the other 80 percent are "rovers" who sally forth
without paying much attention to their surroundings. Sitters and rovers favor different
survival strategies, which could be summed up as the sitter's "Look before you leap"
versus the rover's inclination to "Just do it!" Each strategy reaps different rewards.

In an illustrative experiment, David Sloan Wilson, a Binghamton evolutionary biol-   14
ogist, dropped metal traps into a pond of pumpkinseed sunfish. The "rover" fish

couldn't help but investigate—and were immediately caught. But the "sitter" fish stayed back, making it impossible for Professor Wilson to capture them. Had Professor Wilson's traps posed a real threat, only the sitters would have survived. But had the sitters taken Zoloft and become more like bold rovers, the entire family of pumpkin-seed sunfish would have been wiped out. "Anxiety" about the trap saved the fishes' lives.

Next, Professor Wilson used fishing nets to catch both types of fish; when he car-   15
ried them back to his lab, he noted that the rovers quickly acclimated to their new environment and started eating a full five days earlier than their sitter brethren. In this situation, the rovers were the likely survivors. "There is no single best . . . [animal] personality," Professor Wilson concludes in his book, *Evolution for Everyone,* "but rather a diversity of personalities maintained by natural selection."

The same might be said of humans, 15 percent to 20 percent of whom are also   16
born with sitter-like temperaments that predispose them to shyness and introversion. (The overall incidence of shyness and introversion is higher—40 percent of the population for shyness, according to the psychology professor Jonathan Cheek, and 50 percent for introversion. Conversely, some born sitters never become shy or intro-verted at all.)

Once you know about sitters and rovers, you see them everywhere, especially   17
among young children. Drop in on your local Mommy and Me music class: there are the sitters, intently watching the action from their mothers' laps, while the rovers march around the room banging their drums and shaking their maracas.

Relaxed and exploratory, the rovers have fun, make friends and will take risks, both   18
rewarding and dangerous ones, as they grow. According to Daniel Nettle, a New-castle University evolutionary psychologist, extroverts are more likely than introverts to be hospitalized as a result of an injury, have affairs (men) and change relationships (women). One study of bus drivers even found that accidents are more likely to occur when extroverts are at the wheel.

In contrast, sitter children are careful and astute, and tend to learn by observing   19
instead of by acting. They notice scary things more than other children do, but they also notice more things in general. Studies dating all the way back to the 1960s by the psychologists Jerome Kagan and Ellen Siegelman found that cautious, solitary chil-dren playing matching games spent more time considering all the alternatives than impulsive children did, actually using more eye movements to make decisions. Recent studies by a group of scientists at Stony Brook University and at Chinese uni-versities using functional MRI technology echoed this research, finding that adults with sitter-like temperaments looked longer at pairs of photos with subtle differences and showed more activity in brain regions that make associations between the photos and other stored information in the brain.

Once they reach school age, many sitter children use such traits to great effect.   20
Introverts, who tend to digest information thoroughly, stay on task, and work accu-rately, earn disproportionate numbers of National Merit Scholarship finalist positions and Phi Beta Kappa keys, according to the Center for Applications of Psychological Type, a research arm for the Myers-Briggs personality type indicator—even though

their IQ scores are no higher than those of extroverts. Another study, by the psychologists Eric Rolfhus and Philip Ackerman, tested 141 college students' knowledge of 20 different subjects, from art to astronomy to statistics, and found that the introverts knew more than the extroverts about 19 subjects—presumably, the researchers concluded, because the more time people spend socializing, the less time they have for learning.

21 The psychologist Gregory Feist found that many of the most creative people in a range of fields are introverts who are comfortable working in solitary conditions in which they can focus attention inward. Steve Wozniak, the engineer who founded Apple with Steve Jobs, is a prime example: Mr. Wozniak describes his creative process as an exercise in solitude. "Most inventors and engineers I've met are like me," he writes in *iWoz*, his autobiography. "They're shy and they live in their heads. They're almost like artists. In fact, the very best of them are artists. And artists work best alone. . . . Not on a committee. Not on a team."

22 Sitters' temperaments also confer more subtle advantages. Anxiety, it seems, can serve an important social purpose; for example, it plays a key role in the development of some children's consciences. When caregivers rebuke them for acting up, they become anxious, and since anxiety is unpleasant, they tend to develop pro-social behaviors. Shy children are often easier to socialize and more conscientious, according to the developmental psychologist Grazyna Kochanska. By six they're less likely than their peers to cheat or break rules, even when they think they can't be caught, according to one study. By seven they're more likely to be described by their parents as having high levels of moral traits such as empathy.

23 When I shared this information with the mother of a "sitter" daughter, her reaction was mixed. "That is all very nice," she said, "but how will it help her in the tough real world?" But sensitivity, if it is not excessive and is properly nurtured, can be a catalyst for empathy and even leadership. Eleanor Roosevelt, for example, was a courageous leader who was very likely a sitter. Painfully shy and serious as a child, she grew up to be a woman who could not look away from other people's suffering—and who urged her husband, the constitutionally buoyant F.D.R., to do the same; the man who had nothing to fear but fear itself relied, paradoxically, on a woman deeply acquainted with it.

24 Another advantage sitters bring to leadership is a willingness to listen to and implement other people's ideas. A groundbreaking study led by the Wharton management professor Adam Grant, to be published this month in *The Academy of Management Journal*, found that introverts outperform extroverts when leading teams of proactive workers—the kinds of employees who take initiative and are disposed to dream up better ways of doing things. Professor Grant notes that business self-help guides often suggest that introverted leaders practice their communication skills and smile more. But, he told me, it may be extrovert leaders who need to change, to listen more and say less.

25 What would the world look like if all our sitters chose to medicate themselves? The day may come when we have pills that "cure" shyness and turn introverts into social butterflies—without the side effects and other drawbacks of today's medications.

(A recent study suggests that today's SSRI's not only relieve social anxiety but also induce extroverted behavior.) The day may come—and might be here already—when people are as comfortable changing their psyches as the color of their hair. If we continue to confuse shyness with sickness, we may find ourselves in a world of all rovers and no sitters, of all yang and no yin.

As a sitter who enjoys an engaged, productive life, and a professional speaking career, but still experiences the occasional knock-kneed moment, I can understand why caring physicians prescribe available medicine and encourage effective non-pharmaceutical treatments such as cognitive-behavioral therapy. 26

But even non-medical treatments emphasize what is wrong with the people who use them. They don't focus on what is right. Perhaps we need to rethink our approach to social anxiety: to address the pain, but to respect the temperament that underlies it. The act of treating shyness as an illness obscures the value of that temperament. Ridding people of social unease need not involve pathologizing their fundamental nature, but rather urging them to use its gifts. 27

It's time for the young woman in the Zoloft ad to rediscover her allure. 28

READING FOR MEANING

1. **Read to Summarize.** Write a sentence or two explaining what Cain means by *introversion* and why she thinks it is important.

For help with summarizing, see Chapter 2, pp. 24–25.

2. **Read to Respond.** Write a paragraph or two, focusing on anything that seems surprising, such as the way psychiatrists and the pharmaceutical industry may be pathologizing shyness or introversion; or Cain's assertion that "[o]nce you know about sitters and rovers, you see them everywhere" (par. 17). Which of the characteristics of shyness, sitters, or rovers seemed truest of your experience? Why?

3. **Read to Analyze Assumptions.** Write a paragraph or two analyzing an assumption you find intriguing in Cain's essay. For example:

For help analyzing assumptions, see Chapter 2, pp. 28–29.

   Assumptions about medical conditions. Cain attempts to overturn the assumption that treatments focus on what is wrong rather than what is right about introverts. Examine two or three of the paragraphs that develop the idea that introverts are not sick but are instead assets to society (for example, pars. 11–13, 14, and 19–24).

   - Do they alter your assumptions about medical conditions and how or whether to treat them?

   - If they do, what assumptions made you believe the evidence?

You may also try looking for patterns of opposition; see Chapter 2, pp. 35–36.

   Assumptions that what is true of other animals is true of humans. Cain supports her title's assumption — that shyness is an evolutionary tactic — by demonstrating how different temperaments in animals are important to their survival (pars. 13–15). Evolution assumes that offspring who inherit beneficial traits are more likely to survive and reproduce than those who do not.

- What are some of the human traits Cain examines by drawing comparisons to animal behavior?
- Are there human traits that animal behavior would not illuminate? What are they?

READING LIKE A WRITER

Using Appropriate Writing Strategies

For more on reading and writing strategies, see Chapter 2.

When writers present information, they rely on explanatory strategies such as defining, illustrating, comparing and contrasting, and showing causes or effects. Writers narrow the **focus** — either eliminating qualities that the concept does not have, or defining and elaborating on the qualities the concept does have, with explanatory strategies. Comparing and contrasting, for example, allows the writer to show how the concept is similar to and different from other concepts that might be familiar to the reader.

Consider the passage below, in which Cain uses contrast to point out how shyness and introversion differ from social anxiety:

Repeated sentence pattern

Concept B

Transition

Concept A

It is possible that the lovely young woman has a life-wrecking form of social anxiety. . . .

But the ad's insinuation aside, it's *also* possible the young woman is "just shy," or introverted. . . . (pars. 3–4)

Analyze & Write

Write a paragraph or two analyzing how Cain uses contrast to explain her concept:

1. Find and highlight two or three of the sentence patterns she uses for cueing contrast in paragraphs 9, 10, 13, 18, and 19.
2. Analyze what is being contrasted and how each contrast works.

Organizing the Information Clearly and Logically

Experienced writers know that readers often have a hard time following explanations of unfamiliar concepts, so they provide "road signs" — forecasting statements, topic sentences, transitions, pronouns that refer to nouns that appear earlier in the sentence, synonyms, and summaries — to guide readers through the explanation.

Transition and
pronoun referent

Key term or
synonym

Summary

*Forecasting
statement*

> But the ad's insinuation aside, it's also possible the young woman is "just shy," or introverted — traits our society disfavors. One way we manifest this bias is by encouraging perfectly healthy shy people to see themselves as ill.
>   This does us all a grave disservice, because shyness and introversion — or more precisely, the careful, sensitive tempera-ment from which both often spring — *are not just normal. They are valuable. And they may be essential to the survival of our species.* (pars. 4–5)

Forecasting statements usually appear early in an essay, often in the thesis, to announce the main points the writer will address; they may also appear at the beginning of major sections. Topic sentences announce each main idea as it comes up, transitions (such as *in contrast* and *another*) and pronoun referents relate what is coming to what came before, and summaries remind readers of what has been explained already.

| Analyze & Write |

Write a paragraph or two analyzing the strategies Cain uses to make her concept explanation easy to follow:

1. Skim the rest of the essay (pars. 6–28), underlining other places Cain forecasts and summarizes main ideas or provides topic sentences, transitions, and pro-noun referents. How do the strategies she uses make her concept explanation easier to follow?

2. Examine any places in the essay that you found hard to follow. How might Cain have used one or more of these strategies to make her concept explanation clearer?

Integrating Sources Smoothly

In addition to drawing on personal knowledge and fresh observations, writers often do additional research about the concepts they are trying to explain. Doing research in the library and on the Internet, writers immediately confront the ethical respon-sibility to their readers of locating relevant sources, evaluating them critically, and representing them without distortion. Like the authors of other articles published in popular periodicals, Cain names her sources and mentions their credentials, but she does not cite them formally as you must do when writing a paper for a college class. While you cannot use Cain's approach to citation as a model for your own academic writing, you can follow her lead by doing the following:

For more information on finding and using sources, see the Appendix, pp. 474–81.

- Making a claim of your own and supporting it with appropriate, relevant evidence.

- Explaining how the evidence you provide supports your claim.
- Naming your source author(s) in a **signal phrase** (name plus an appropriate verb) and mentioning the author's (or authors') credentials.

Cain's idea	*As a society, we prefer action to contemplation, risk-taking to heed-taking, certainty to doubt.* Studies show that we rank fast and frequent talkers as more competent, likable and even smarter than slow ones. As the psychologists William Hart and Dolores Albarracin point out, phrases like "get active," "get moving," "do something" and similar calls to action surface repeatedly in recent books. (par. 10)
Research findings supporting Cain's idea	
Author and credentials in signal phrase	
Links between Cain's idea and research findings	

Analyze & Write

Write a paragraph analyzing another passage in which Cain integrates source material to support her explanation:

1. Review paragraphs 19, 20, or 21 to see how Cain uses a similar pattern. Mark the following elements: Cain's idea; the name(s) and credentials of the source or sources; what the source found; text linking the source's findings to the original idea or extending the idea in some way.

2. Explain why writers, when using information from sources, often begin by stating their own idea (even if they got the idea from a source). What would be the effect on readers if the opening sentence of paragraph 18 or 20 began with the source instead of with Cain's topic sentence?

Engaging Readers' Interest

Writers explaining concepts may engage readers' interest in a variety of ways. For example, they may

- remind readers of what they already know about the concept;
- show readers a new way of using or regarding a familiar concept;
- connect the concept, sometimes through *metaphor* or *analogy*, to common human experiences; or
- present the concept in a humorous way to convince readers that learning about a concept can be pleasurable.

Analyze & Write

Write a paragraph analyzing how Cain engages her readers:

1. Note the strategies Cain uses in three or four of the following paragraphs: 1, 4, 7, 8, 11–12, 21–22, 25, and 27.

2. Explain how Cain engages her readers' interest in the concept of introversion, using examples from your notes to support your explanation.

READINGS

John Tierney

Do You Suffer from Decision Fatigue?

John Tierney (b. 1953) has written for the *New York Times* since 1990 as a reporter and regular columnist for columns such as "Findings" for the Science Times section. He has written for several other magazines and newspapers, among them the *Atlantic Monthly, Discover, Esquire, Newsweek, Outside,* and the *Wall Street Journal.* In collaboration with novelist Christopher Buckley, Tierney co-wrote the comic novel, *God Is My Broker* (2012). The essay below, originally published in 2011 in the *New York Times Magazine,* was adapted from a book he wrote with Roy F. Baumeister, *Willpower: Rediscovering the Greatest Human Strength* (2011).

- **Before you read,** think about your own views about willpower. Is yours strong, weak, or in between? What conditions affect the strength of your willpower?

- **As you read,** think about the assumptions many people have about decisions. For example, which decisions are more difficult than others? How are these assumptions borne out or challenged in this essay?

Three men doing time in Israeli prisons recently appeared before a parole   1
board consisting of a judge, a criminologist and a social worker. The three prisoners had completed at least two-thirds of their sentences, but the parole board granted freedom to only one of them. Guess which one:

> Case 1 (heard at 8:50 a.m.): An Arab Israeli serving a 30-month sentence for fraud.
> Case 2 (heard at 3:10 p.m.): A Jewish Israeli serving a 16-month sentence for assault.
> Case 3 (heard at 4:25 p.m.): An Arab Israeli serving a 30-month sentence for fraud.

There was a pattern to the parole board's decisions, but it wasn't related   2
to the men's ethnic backgrounds, crimes or sentences. It was all about timing, as researchers discovered by analyzing more than 1,100 decisions over the course of a year. Judges, who would hear the prisoners' appeals and then get advice from the other members of the board, approved parole in about a third of the cases, but the probability of being paroled fluctuated wildly throughout the day. Prisoners who appeared early in the morning received parole about 70 percent of the time, while those who appeared late in the day were paroled less than 10 percent of the time.

How is Tierney arousing curiosity in the reader in these first few paragraphs?

3   The odds favored the prisoner who appeared at 8:50 a.m.—and he did in fact receive parole. But even though the other Arab Israeli prisoner was serving the same sentence for the same crime—fraud—the odds were against him when he appeared (on a different day) at 4:25 in the afternoon. He was denied parole, as was the Jewish Israeli prisoner at 3:10 p.m, whose sentence was shorter than that of the man who was released. They were just asking for parole at the wrong time of day.

Referring to time is often used as a cue to help readers follow the author's line of thinking. Underline and analyze the references to time in paragraphs 1–6. How do they work to unify the paragraphs?

4   There was nothing malicious or even unusual about the judges' behavior, which was reported . . . by Jonathan Levav of Stanford and Shai Danziger of Ben-Gurion University.[1] The judges' erratic judgment was due to the occupational hazard of being, as George W. Bush once put it, "the decider." The mental work of ruling on case after case, whatever the individual merits, wore them down. This sort of decision fatigue can make quarterbacks prone to dubious choices late in the game and C.F.O.'s prone to disastrous dalliances late in the evening. It routinely warps the judgment of everyone, executive and nonexecutive, rich and poor—in fact, it can take a special toll on the poor. Yet few people are even aware of it, and researchers are only beginning to understand why it happens and how to counteract it.

How have the introductory paragraphs helped define and explain this key term so far?

5   Decision fatigue helps explain why ordinarily sensible people get angry at colleagues and families, splurge on clothes, buy junk food at the supermarket and can't resist the dealer's offer to rustproof their new car. No matter how rational and high-minded you try to be, you can't make decision after decision without paying a biological price. It's different from ordinary physical fatigue—you're not consciously aware of being tired—but you're low on mental energy. The more choices you make throughout the day, the harder each one becomes for your brain, and eventually it looks for shortcuts, usually in either of two very different ways. One shortcut is to become reckless: to act impulsively instead of expending the energy to first think through the consequences. (Sure, tweet that photo! What could go wrong?) The other shortcut is the ultimate energy saver: do nothing. Instead of agonizing over decisions, avoid any choice. Ducking a decision often creates bigger problems in the long run, but for the moment, it eases the mental strain. You start to resist any change, any potentially risky move—like releasing a prisoner who might commit a crime. So the fatigued judge on a parole board takes the easy way out, and the prisoner keeps doing time.

How does Tierney use the writing strategy of compare/contrast in this paragraph? How do these comparisons affect the reader's understanding of the concept?

6   Decision fatigue is the newest discovery involving a phenomenon called ego depletion, a term coined by the social psychologist Roy F. Baumeister[2] . . . [who] began studying mental discipline in a series of experiments, first at Case Western and then at Florida State University. These experiments demonstrated that there is a finite store of mental energy for exerting self-control. When people fended off the temptation to scarf down M&M's or freshly baked chocolate-chip cookies, they were then less able to resist other temptations. When they forced themselves to remain stoic during a tearjerker movie, afterward they gave up more

What is Tierney's assumption about the validity of experiments conducted at universities? Do you share his assumption?

What writing strategies does Tierney use in paragraphs 6–9 to introduce the concept of decision fatigue? (See Chapter 2 for a list of possible strategies.)

quickly on lab tasks requiring self-discipline, like working on a geometry puzzle or squeezing a hand-grip exerciser. Willpower turned out to be more than a folk concept or a metaphor. It really was a form of mental energy that could be exhausted. The experiments confirmed the 19th-century notion of willpower being like a muscle that was fatigued with use, a force that could be conserved by avoiding temptation. To study the process of ego depletion, researchers concentrated initially on acts involving self-control—the kind of self-discipline popularly associated with willpower, like resisting a bowl of ice cream. They weren't concerned with routine decision-making, like choosing between chocolate and vanilla, a mental process that they assumed was quite distinct and much less strenuous. Intuitively, the chocolate-vanilla choice didn't appear to require willpower.

But then a postdoctoral fellow, Jean Twenge, started working at 7 Baumeister's laboratory right after planning her wedding. As Twenge studied the results of the lab's ego-depletion experiments, she remembered how exhausted she felt the evening she and her fiancé went through the ritual of registering for gifts. Did they want plain white china or something with a pattern? Which brand of knives? How many towels? What kind of sheets? Precisely how many threads per square inch?

Highlight the first sentence of the next several paragraphs to see how Tierney uses paragraph transitions to organize his ideas. Where does he place old information, and where new?

"By the end, you could have talked me into anything," Twenge told her 8 new colleagues. The symptoms sounded familiar to them too, and gave them an idea. A nearby department store was holding a going-out-of-business sale, so researchers from the lab went off to fill their car trunks with simple products—not exactly wedding-quality gifts, but sufficiently appealing to interest college students. When they came to the lab, the students were told they would get to keep one item at the end of the experiment, but first they had to make a series of choices. Would they prefer a pen or a candle? A vanilla-scented candle or an almond-scented one? A candle or a T-shirt? A black T-shirt or a red T-shirt? A control group, meanwhile—let's call them the nondeciders—spent an equally long period contemplating all these same products without having to make any choices. They were asked just to give their opinion of each product and report how often they had used such a product in the last six months.

Afterward, all the participants were given one of the classic tests of self- 9 control: holding your hand in ice water for as long as you can. The impulse is to pull your hand out, so self-discipline is needed to keep the hand underwater. The deciders gave up much faster; they lasted 28 seconds, less than half the 67-second average of the nondeciders. Making all those choices had apparently sapped their willpower. . . .

Any decision, whether it's what pants to buy or whether to start a war, 10 can be broken down into what psychologists call the Rubicon model of action phases, in honor of the river that separated Italy from the Roman province of Gaul. When Caesar reached it in 49 BC, on his way home after conquering the Gauls, he knew that a general returning to Rome was forbidden to take his legions across the river with him, lest it be considered an invasion of Rome. Waiting on the Gaul side of the river, he was in the "predecisional phase" as he contemplated the risks and benefits of starting a civil war. Then he stopped calculating and crossed the Rubicon, reaching the "postdecisional phase," which Caesar defined much more felicitously: "The die is cast."

11   The whole process could deplete anyone's willpower, but which phase of the decision-making process was most fatiguing? To find out, Kathleen Vohs, a former colleague of Baumeister's now at the University of Minnesota, performed an experiment [that] showed that crossing the Rubicon is more tiring than anything that happens on either bank—more mentally fatiguing than sitting on the Gaul side contemplating your options or marching on Rome once you've crossed. As a result, someone without Caesar's willpower is liable to stay put. To a fatigued judge, denying parole seems like the easier call not only because it preserves the status quo and eliminates the risk of a parolee going on a crime spree but also because it leaves more options open: the judge retains the option of paroling the prisoner at a future date without sacrificing the option of keeping him securely in prison right now.

12   Once you're mentally depleted, you become reluctant to make trade-offs, which involve a particularly advanced and taxing form of decision making. In the rest of the animal kingdom, there aren't a lot of protracted negotiations between predators and prey. To compromise is a complex human ability and therefore one of the first to decline when willpower is depleted. You become what researchers call a cognitive miser, hoarding your energy. If you're shopping, you're liable to look at only one dimension, like price: just give me the cheapest. Or you indulge yourself by looking at quality: I want the very best (an especially easy strategy if someone else is paying).

13   Decision fatigue leaves you vulnerable to marketers who know how to time their sales, as Jonathan Levav, the Stanford professor, demonstrated in experiments involving . . . new cars. . . . The car buyers . . . had to choose, for instance, among 4 styles of gearshift knobs, 13 kinds of wheel rims, 25 configurations of the engine and gearbox and a palette of 56 colors for the interior. As they started picking features, customers would carefully weigh the choices, but as decision fatigue set in, they would start settling for whatever the default option was. And the more tough choices they encountered early in the process—like going through those 56 colors to choose the precise shade of gray or brown—the quicker people became fatigued and settled for the path of least resistance by taking the default option. By manipulating the order of the car buyers' choices, the researchers found that the customers would end up settling for different kinds of options. . . . Whether the customers paid a little extra for fancy wheel rims

How does this analogy between the anecdote of the Rubicon and the process of deciding illuminate the concept of decision fatigue?

Why does Tierney provide this information about his source?

In your opinion, has Tierney "earned" his conclusions about the consumerism and willpower in this paragraph? How and why?

Tierney realizes this solution cannot extend to all of society for all of the situations in which decision fatigue exists. (See Chapter 2, pp. 42–44, for more on logical fallacies.) What could be some solutions for contemporary society?

Have your assumptions about willpower — who has it, who doesn't, and why some seem to have more than others — changed from reading this essay? In what way? Why?

or a lot extra for a more powerful engine depended on when the choice was offered and how much willpower was left in the customer. . . .

It's simple enough to imagine reforms for the parole board in Israel — like,   14
say, restricting each judge's shift to half a day, preferably in the morning, interspersed with frequent breaks for food and rest. But it's not so obvious what to do with the decision fatigue affecting the rest of society. . . . Today we feel overwhelmed because there are so many choices. . . . Choosing what to have for breakfast, where to go on vacation, whom to hire, how much to spend — these all deplete willpower, and there's no telltale symptom of when that willpower is low. It's not like getting winded or hitting the wall during a marathon.

Ego depletion manifests itself not as one feeling but rather as a propen-   15
sity to experience everything more intensely. When the brain's regulatory powers weaken, frustrations seem more irritating than usual. Impulses to eat, drink, spend and say stupid things feel more powerful (and alcohol causes self-control to decline further). . . . Like the depleted parole judges, [ego-depleted humans] become inclined to take the safer, easier option even when that option hurts someone else.

Links

1. Danziger, Shai, et al. "Extraneous Factors in Judicial Decisions." *Proceedings of the National Academy of Sciences for the United States of America,* vol. 108, no. 17, 26 Apr. 2011, pp. 6889–92.

2. "Dr. Roy Baumeister." *Faculty Directory*, Psychology Dept., Florida State U, 2013, psy.fsu.edu/faculty/baumeister.dp.html.

Alexis C. Madrigal

The Machine Zone

Alexis Madrigal graduated from Harvard and was a visiting scholar for the Center for Science, Technology, Medicine, and Society at the University of California at Berkeley. He has written for *Wired Digital*, was a senior editor at the *Atlantic*, and is currently editor in chief of *Fusion*, an ABC-Univision online "digital and television platform show." He is the author of *Powering the Dream: The History and Promise of Green Technology* (2011). The essay below was published in the *Atlantic* in 2013. Because Madrigal was publishing for a national magazine online, he included hyperlinks but not a bibliography. We have converted the links to in-text citations and provided a list of works cited at the end of the selection, using MLA style. (See Appendix, pp. 509–36, for help with citing sources.)

- **Before you read,** think about how you feel when you look at Facebook or similar online platforms. Do you get caught up in the experience or maintain a distance?

- **As you read,** pay attention to the sources of Madrigal's information. How do they enhance his credibility? How do they illustrate his rhetorical sensitivity?

"People love Facebook. They really love it," Biz Stone[1] wrote earlier this month. "My 　1 mother-in-law looks hypnotized when she decides to put in some Facebook time" (Stone).

She is not the only one. ComScore estimates Facebook eats up 11 percent of all the 　2 time spent online in the United States. Its users have been known to spend an average of 400 minutes a month on the site (McGee).

I know the hypnosis, as I'm sure you do, too. You start clicking through photos 　3 of your friends of friends and next thing you know an hour has gone by. It's oddly soothing, but unsatisfying. Once the spell is broken, I feel like I've just wasted a bunch of time. But while it's happening, I'm caught inside the machine, a human animated GIF: I. Just. Cannot. Stop. Or maybe it'll come on when I'm scrolling through tweets at night before bed. I'm not even clicking the links or responding to people. I'm just scrolling down, or worse, pulling down with my thumb, reloading, reloading. Or sometimes, I get caught in the melancholy of Tumblr's infinite scroll.

Are these experiences, as Stone would have it, love? The tech world generally 　4 measures how much you like a service by how much time you spend on it. So a lot of time equals love. My own intuition is that this is not love. It's something much more technologically specific that MIT anthropologist Natasha Schüll calls *"the machine zone."*

[1]Christopher Isaac "Biz" Stone (b. 1972), co-founder of Twitter. [Editor's note]

"IT'S NOT ABOUT WINNING, IT'S ABOUT GETTING INTO THE ZONE"

Schüll spent more than a decade going to Las Vegas and talking with gamblers and   5
casino operators about slot machines, which have exploded in profitability during the
digital era as game designers have optimized them to keep people playing. What she
discovered is that most people playing the machines aren't there to make money. They
know they're not going to hit the jackpot and go home (Schüll). As Roman Mars put it
in a recent episode of his awesome podcast, *99% Invisible*, on Schüll's research: "It's
not about winning; it's about getting into the zone" (Mars).

What is the machine zone? It's a rhythm. It's a response to a fine-tuned feedback   6
loop. It's a powerful space-time distortion. You hit a button. Something happens. You
hit it again. Something similar, but not exactly the same happens. Maybe you win,
maybe you don't. Repeat. Repeat. Repeat. Repeat. Repeat. It's the pleasure of the
repeat, the security of the loop.

"Everything else falls away," Schüll says to Mars. "A sense of monetary value, time,   7
space, even a sense of self is annihilated in the extreme form of this zone that you
enter." In Schüll's book, *Addiction by Design*, a gambler named Lola tells her: "I'm
almost hypnotized into *being* that machine. It's like playing against yourself: You are
the machine; the machine is you."

There's that word again: hypnotized, like Stone's grandmother. Many gamblers used   8
variations on the phrase. "To put the zone into words," Schüll writes, "the gamblers I
spoke with supplemented an exotic, nineteenth-century terminology of hypnosis and
magnetism with twentieth-century references to television watching, computer processing, and vehicle driving." They said things like, "You're in a trance, you're on auto-
pilot. The zone is like a magnet, it just pulls you in and holds you there."

Why these words, these metaphors? We don't cognitively grasp the state we fall   9
into—we only feel its grip on us—the way we've merged circuits with the inanimate.
You are the machine; the machine is you. And it feels . . . the words fail. In fact, it feels
like words failing because it is at the edge of human experience, bleeding over into a
cybernetic realm best expressed in data and code.

The machine zone is the dark side of "flow," a psychological state proposed by   10
Mihály Csíkszentmihályi. In a flow state, there is a goal, rules for getting to the goal,
and feedback on how that's going. Importantly, the task has to match your skills, so
there's a feeling of "simultaneous control and challenge" (Bogost). In a 1996 *Wired*
interview, Csíkszentmihályi described the state like this: "Being completely involved
in an activity for its own sake. The ego falls away. Time flies. Every action, movement,
and thought follows inevitably from the previous one, like playing jazz" (Geirland,
1996).

Schüll sees a twist on this phenomenon in front of the new slot machines of Vegas,   11
which incorporate tiny squirts of seeming control to amp up their feedback loops. But
instead of the self-fulfillment and happiness that Csíkszentmihályi describes, many
gamblers feel deflated and sad about their time on the slots. The games exploit the
human desire for flow, but without the meaning or mastery attached to the state. The
machine zone is where the mind goes as the body loses itself in the task. "You can

erase it all at the machines," a gambler tells Schüll. "You can even erase yourself." You can get away from it all in the machine zone, but only as long as you stay there.

THE FACEBOOK ZONE

When we get wrapped up in a repetitive task on our computers, I think we can 12 enter some softer version of the machine zone. Obviously, if you're engaged in banter with friends or messaging your mom on Facebook, you're not in that zone. If you're reading actively and writing poems on Twitter, you're not in that zone. If you're making art on Tumblr, you're not in that zone. The machine zone is antisocial, and it's characterized by a lack of human connection. You might be looking at people when you look through photos, but your interactions with their digital presences are mechanical, repetitive, and reinforced by computerized feedback.

I'm not claiming that people are "addicted" to Facebook. Some of the gamblers 13 quoted in Schüll's research do in fact have serious problems. But I am using their stories as Schüll did—as sources of expertise on the zone, not to say their experience with slot machines is exactly like your average user's time on Facebook.

I'm not making an argument about the totality of services like Facebook. This is 14 a criticism of specific behavioral loops that can arise within them. The purest example of an onramp into the machine zone is clicking through photo albums on Facebook. There's nothing particularly rewarding or interesting about it. And yet, show me the Facebook user who hasn't spent hours and hours doing just that. Why? You can find the zone. Click. Photo. Click. Photo. Click. Photo. And perhaps, somewhere in there, you find something cool ("My friend knows my cousin.") or cute ("Kitten."). Great. Jackpot! Click. Photo. Click. Photo. Click. Photo.

Facebook is the single largest photo sharing service in the world. In 2008, 15 when the site had 10 billion photographs archived, users pulled up 15 billion images *per day* (Beaver). The process was occurring 300,000 *per second*. Click. Photo. Click. In 2010, Facebook had uploaded 65 billion images, and they were served up at a peak rate of 1 million per second (Beaver et al.). By 2012, Facebook users were uploading 300 million photos per day ("Facebook"). And early this year, Facebook announced users had entrusted them with 240 billion photos (Constine "Facebookers").

If we assume the ratio of photos uploaded to photos viewed has not declined pre- 16 cipitously, users are probably pulling up *billions of Facebook photos per day* at a rate of millions per second. Click. Photo. Click. It all adds up to a lot of time spent in the loop. According to a 2011 ComScore report, users spend 17 percent of their time on the site exclusively browsing photos (which as Inside Facebook notes, doesn't include "time spent reading news feed stories and notifications generated by photo uploads") (Constine "ComScore Report"). To put these numbers in perspective, ComScore's 2013 Digital Focus report found that Facebook took 83 percent of the time spent on *all* social networks on the web. That means that of all the time spent on social networks, 14 percent of it occurs within this one behavioral loop. That's more than all the time spent on Tumblr, Pinterest, Twitter, and LinkedIn combined!

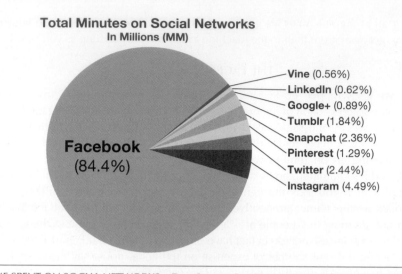

Total Minutes on Social Networks
In Millions (MM)

Vine (0.56%)
LinkedIn (0.62%)
Google+ (0.89%)
Tumblr (1.84%)
Snapchat (2.36%)
Pinterest (1.29%)
Twitter (2.44%)
Instagram (4.49%)

Facebook
(84.4%)

TIME SPENT ON SOCIAL NETWORKS   Data Source: ComScore U.S. Digital Future in Focus, 2015

If all technological artifacts contain certain "prescriptions" within them, if 17
designers can inscribe intentions into the things they build, as in sociologist Bruno
Latour's theory, then we can say that some engagement mechanisms are more pre-
scriptive than others (Brookhenkel). What Facebook and slot machines share is the
ability to provide fast feedback to simple actions; they deliver tiny rewards on an
imperfectly predictable "payout" schedule. These are coercive loops, distorting
whatever the original intention of the user was. What began as "See a picture of
person X" becomes "keep seeing more pictures." The mechanism itself becomes
the point.

What would it mean for the project of social media if we understood it to 18
induce similar psychological states to machine-based gambling? Would Silicon
Valley employees struggle with their product the way slot-machine designers do? I
know a lot of coders and people who've worked for various social companies;
they certainly don't see themselves as being in the same core business as a casino.
Most of them think they're "doing well by doing good." As a thought experiment,
imagine there were incontrovertible proof that certain web service designs caused
people to enter the machine zone, quadrupling time on site for a subset of users.
Would designers outlaw their use or would they all deploy the tricks for their
startups?

Things could be different. A site could encourage a different ethic of consumption. 19
To be a little absurd: Why not post a sign after someone has looked through 100 pictures that says, "Why not write a friend or family member a note instead?" Shouldn't
these things be part of what web companies think about? Not just encouraging users
to consume more and more, but helping them stop.

THE PROBLEM OF "GIVING PEOPLE WHAT THEY WANT"

You could argue that designers are simply *giving the people what they want*. The data   20
says people spend a lot of time looking at pictures; so, Facebook serves up the pictures. Simple as that.

Engagement is usually the currency of the social network realm. Since it's much   21
harder to measure whether someone is actually enjoying an experience than it is to
measure the number of minutes someone spends doing it, engagement is typically
measured by time. And so, Silicon Valley has made the case to itself (and to the users
of its software) that we are voting with our clicks.

But there's a problem. A definition of "what people want" got smuggled in with the   22
data. The definition starts logically: People go to sites they like. But then it gets wob-
blier. They say that the more time you spend on a site or part of a site, the more you
like it. Of course, that completely elides the role the company itself plays in shaping
user behavior to increase consumption. And it ignores that people sometimes (often?)
do things to themselves that they don't like. Who "likes" spending hours flipping
channels—and yet it's been a core part of the American experience for decades.
What if the 400 minutes a month people spend on Facebook is mostly (or even partly)
spent in the machine zone, hypnotized, accumulating ad impressions for the
company?

Here's my contention: Thinking about the machine zone and the coercive loops   23
that initiate it has great explanatory power. It explains the "lost time" feeling I've had
on various social networks, and that I've heard other people talk about. It explains
how the more Facebook has tuned its services, the more people seem to dislike the
experiences they have, even as they don't abandon them.

At the very least, the phenomenon of the machine zone has to become a part of the   24
way we talk about the pleasures of the Internet. Perhaps, over the long run, these
problems will self-correct. I'm not so sure, though: The economic forces at the heart of
ad-supported social networks basically require maximizing how much time people
spend on a site, generating ad impressions. It just so happens that the user behavioral
patterns that are most profitable for Facebook and other social networks are precisely
the patterns that they've interpreted to mean that people love them. It's almost as if
they determined what would be most profitable and then figured out how to justify
that as serving user needs.

But I actually don't believe that. You can say many things about the entrepreneurs,   25
designers, and coders who create social networking companies, but they believe in
what they do. They're more likely to be ideologues than craven financial triangulators.
And they spend all day on Facebook, Instagram, Twitter, Tumblr, and Pinterest, too.
I bet they know the machine zone, too. And that's why I have hope they might actually
stop designing traps.

In any case, fighting the great nullness at the heart of these coercive loops should   26
be one of the goals of technology design, use, and criticism. In the great tradition of
the Valley, we'll make a t-shirt: Just Say No To The Machine Zone.

Links

Beaver, Doug. "10 Billion Photos." *Facebook*, 14 Oct. 2008, www.facebook.com/note
.php?note_id=30695603919.

Beaver, Doug, et al. "Finding a Needle in Haystack: Facebook's Photo Storage." Usenix,
2015, www.usenix.org/legacy/event/osdi10/tech/full_papers/Beaver.pdf.

Bogost, Ian. "A Portrait of the Artist as a Game Studio." *The Atlantic*, 15 Mar. 2012, www
.theatlantic.com/technology/archive/2012/03/a-portrait-of-the-artist-as-a-game
-studio/254494/.

Brookhenkel. "Session 10: The Collective." *Thing Theory*, 1 Apr. 2009, thingtheory2009
.wordpress.com/author/brookhenkel/.

Constine, Josh. "ComScore Report: 27% of Facebook Browsing on News Feed, Just 10% on
Apps." *SocialTimes*, Mediabistro Holdings, 26 July 2011, www.adweek.com
/socialtimes/most-facebook-browsing-on-news-feed/266098.

---. "Facebookers Feed Graph Search And Set A Record By Uploading 1.1B Photos On New
Year's Day/Eve." *TechCrunch*, AOL, 17 Jan. 2013, techcrunch.com/2013/01/17
/facebook-photos-record/.

Csikszentmihályi, Mihály. "Go with the Flow." Interview by John Gierland. *Wired*, Condé
Nast, 1 Sept. 1996, www.wired.com/1996/09/czik/.

"Facebook Data Center Hosts 220 Billion Photos and May Reach 500 Billion Count by 2014."
StorageServers, 18 Dec. 2012, storageservers.wordpress.com/2012/12/18/facebook-data
-center-hosts-220-billion-photos-and-may-reach-500-billion-count-by-2014/.

Mars, Roman. "Episode 78: No Armed Bandit." *99% Invisible*, 30 Apr. 2013,
99percentinvisible.org/episode/episode-78-no-armed-bandit/.

McGee, Matt. "Facebook's Time-On-Site Back Above 400 Minutes Per User in June,
com- Score Says." *Marketing Land*, Third Door Media, 12 July 2012, marketingland
.com/facebooks-time-on-site-back-above-400-minutes-per-user-16305.

Schüll, Natasha. *Addiction by Design: Machine Gambling in Las Vegas*. Princeton UP, 2012.

Stone, Biz. "Facebook Premium." *Medium*, 19 July 2013, medium.com/the-biz-stone
-collection/facebook-premium-47715441d0be#.hlonkskpd.

READING FOR MEANING

For more
help with
summarizing,
see Chapter 2,
pp. 24–25.

1. **Read to Summarize.** Write a sentence or two explaining what the "machine zone" is and the "problem" Madrigal sees with it.

2. **Read to Respond.** Write a paragraph analyzing anything that resonates with your experience or that seems to support or refute Madrigal's concern with the "machine zone," such as whether the machine zone does seem like "hypnosis" (par. 3); or whether you agree that it is "the dark side of 'flow ' " (par. 10), a state of being that is normally all positive.

You may also
try reflecting
on challenges
to your beliefs
and values;
see Chapter 2,
pp. 36–37.

3. **Read to Analyze Assumptions.** Write a paragraph or two analyzing an assumption you find intriguing in Madrigal's essay, such as:

   The assumption that the choice to spend time on a given site is purely the consumer's choice. Madrigal notes that "they say that the more time you spend on a site or part of a site, the more you like it" (par. 22). He questions this assumption when he wonders whether the *company* that sponsors the site is "shaping user behavior to increase consumption" (par. 22).

- When you spend time on a site such as Facebook, do you feel you are the one choosing the amount of time, or do you think it might be Facebook and its advertisers manipulating you into spending more time than you would really like?

- Madrigal assumes you will know the origin of Ronald Reagan's phrase "just say no" (to drugs) when he ends his essay with "Just Say No To The Machine Zone." Is his assumption that we actually could "just say no" to spending time on something we like, or is it more complicated, as it was with resisting drugs? What do you think are his real assumptions about the ease of such a solution?

For help analyzing assumptions, see Chapter 2, pp. 28–29.

The assumption that looking at photos is frivolous. Madrigal says his argument is "a criticism of specific behavioral loops . . . the purest example [of which] is clicking through photo albums on Facebook" (par. 14). He cites statistics to show that "users spend 17 percent of their time on the site exclusively browsing photos" (par. 16).

- Why would Madrigal think that looking at photos for such a length of time is a waste? Do you agree?

- What do photos convey that other forms of visuals do not? What difference could that make to the viewers?

READING LIKE A WRITER

INTEGRATING SOURCES SMOOTHLY

Writers of concept explanations usually conduct research and incorporate information (summaries, paraphrases, and quotations) from sources. They provide information about their sources to indicate why they should be trusted. For example, when describing a study to support her claim that "[w]e even find 'introverts' in the animal kingdom" (par. 13), Cain names the researcher and identifies his academic specialty: "In an illustrative experiment, David Sloan Wilson, a Binghamton evolutionary biologist, dropped metal traps into a pond of pumpkinseed sunfish" (par. 14). In "The Machine Zone," Alexis Madrigal introduces his key source by providing her academic credentials:

Credentials   It's something much more technologically specific that MIT anthropologist Natasha Schüll calls "*the machine zone.*"

Analyze & Write

Write a paragraph or two analyzing the kinds of material Madrigal incorporates from sources, and how he identifies his sources so that his readers know that they are relevant and **credible** (reliable and believable).

1. Skim the essay, highlighting places where Madrigal quotes, paraphrases, or summarizes information from sources. How does he identify those sources? What information does he provide, and how does this information help readers know the source is relevant and reliable?

2. Now look at the material that is in quotations. Why would Madrigal choose to quote these sources, rather than summarize or paraphrase them?

A Special Reading Strategy

Synthesizing Information from Sources

Synthesizing information is a strategy academic writers use regularly as they read sources to discover, support, challenge, or extend their ideas. It is also a skill writers use to support their ideas in research-based writing. Alexis C. Madrigal, for example, uses information from a variety of sources to explain the concept of the "machine zone."

To analyze how Madrigal synthesizes information from sources to support his claims, skim paragraphs 10 and 11, highlighting the sources he quotes, paraphrases, or summarizes. Look for signal phrases (made up of a reference to a speaker or source author and an appropriate verb), such as "In a 1996 *Wired* interview, Csíkszentmihályi described the state like this," and parenthetical citations. What is Madrigal's central idea in these two paragraphs? How does he use information from the different sources he cites to support this central idea?

For synthesizing as a reading and writing strategy, see Chapter 2, p. 27. For detailed guidelines on synthesizing information from sources, see p. 27 and pp. 230–231; for guidance on using information to support your claims, see pp. 230–31; and for coverage of using signal phrases and parenthetical citations to cite sources, see p. 231.

Melanie Tannenbaum

The Problem When Sexism Just Sounds So Darn Friendly

Melanie Tannenbaum received her Ph.D. in quantitative psychology from the University of Illinois at Urbana–Champaign, where she also teaches. She is a freelance science communications consultant, science writer, and psychology blogger who has contributed pieces to *The Complete Guide to Science Blogging* (2015), *The Open Laboratory Anthology for the Best Science Writing Online* (2012, 2013), the *British Psychological Society Research Digest*, and *In-Mind Magazine*, as well as in six peer-reviewed scientific journals. She founded *PsySociety* on the *Scientific American* blog network, where the following essay was published in 2013. Because she wrote for a scientific blog, Tannenbaum uses APA-citation style (see the Appendix, pp. 527–36); accordingly, we have adapted the original hyperlinks as in-text citations.

- **Before you read,** recall times when you may have been a victim of sexism (whether you are a man or woman). What were the situations in which you felt you were being judged merely on the basis of your gender, and nothing else?

- **As you read,** consider how Tannenbaum's presentation of the "benevolent sexism" concept and the key words she uses makes you react. Do you identify with her word choice and examples, or do they make you feel confused or offended? Identify ways that Tannenbaum anticipates and acknowledges the sensitivity of the topic.

Something can't *actually* be sexist if it's really, really nice, right? 1

I mean, if someone compliments me on my looks or my cooking, that's not sexist. 2 That's awesome! I should be thrilled that I'm being noticed for something positive!

Yet there are many comments that, while seemingly complimentary, somehow still 3 feel wrong. These comments may focus on an author's appearance rather than the content of her writing, or mention how surprising it is that she's a woman, being that her field is mostly filled with men. Even though these remarks can sometimes feel good to hear—and no one is denying that this type of comment *can* feel good, especially in the right context—they can also cause a feeling of unease, particularly when one is in the position of trying to draw attention towards her work rather than personal qualities like her gender or appearance.

In social psychology, these seemingly-positive-yet-still-somewhat-unsettling com- 4 ments and behaviors have a name: *Benevolent Sexism.* Although it is tempting to brush this experience off as an overreaction to compliments or a misunderstanding of benign intent, benevolent sexism is both real and insidiously dangerous.

WHAT IS BENEVOLENT SEXISM?

In 1996, Peter Glick and Susan Fiske wrote a paper on the concept of *ambivalent sex-*   5
ism, noting that despite common beliefs, there are actually two different kinds of sexist attitudes and behavior. *Hostile sexism* is what most people think of when they
picture "sexism" — angry, explicitly negative attitudes towards women. However, the
authors note, there is also something called *benevolent sexism*:

> We define benevolent sexism as a set of interrelated attitudes toward
> women that are sexist in terms of viewing women stereotypically and in
> restricted roles but that are subjectively positive in feeling tone (for the per-
> ceiver) and also tend to elicit behaviors typically categorized as prosocial
> (e.g., helping) or intimacy-seeking (e.g., self-disclosure) (Glick & Fiske,
> 1996, p. 491).
>
> [Benevolent sexism is] a subjectively positive orientation of protection,
> idealization, and affection directed toward women that, like hostile sexism,
> serves to justify women's subordinate status to men (Glick et al., 2000, p. 763).

Yes, there's actually an official name for all of those comments and stereotypes that   6
can somehow feel both nice and wrong at the same time, like the belief that women
are "delicate flowers" who need to be protected by men, or the notion that women
have the special gift of being "more kind and caring" than their male counterparts. It
might sound like a compliment, but it still counts as sexism.

For a very recent example of how benevolent sexism might play out in our everyday   7
lives, take a look at Jennie Dusheck's "Family Man Who Invented Relativity and Made
Great Chili Dies," a satirical piece which jokingly re-writes Albert Einstein's obituary.
To quote: 8

> He made sure he shopped for groceries every night on the way home from
> work, took the garbage out, and hand washed the antimacassars. But to his
> step daughters he was just Dad. "He was always there for us," said his step
> daughter and first cousin once removed Margo.
>
> Albert Einstein, who died on Tuesday, had another life at work, where
> he sometimes slipped away to peck at projects like showing that atoms really
> exist. His discovery of something called the photoelectric effect won him a
> coveted Nobel Prize.

Looks weird, right? Kind of like something you would never actually see in print?   9
Yet the author of rocket scientist Yvonne Brill's obituary didn't hesitate before writ- 10
ing the following about her last week:

> She made a mean beef stroganoff, followed her husband from job to job, and
> took eight years off from work to raise three children. "The world's best
> mom," her son Matthew said.
>
> But Yvonne Brill, who died on Wednesday at 88 in Princeton, N.J., was
> also a brilliant rocket scientist, who in the early 1970s invented a propulsion
> system to help keep communications satellites from slipping out of their
> orbits. (Comparing: Yvonne Brill, 2013)

In fact, Obituaries editor William McDonald still sees nothing wrong with it. In his 11 words, he's "surprised . . . [because] it never occurred to [him] that this would be read as sexist," and if he had to re-write it again, he still "wouldn't do anything differently."

I want to make one thing perfectly clear. There's not a problem with mentioning 12 Brill's family, friends, and loved ones. It's not a problem to note how wonderfully Brill balanced her domestic and professional lives. Brill was a female scientist during a time when very few women could occupy that role in society, and that means something truly important.

But the *problem* here is really that if "Yvonne" were "Yvan," the obit would have 13 looked fundamentally different. If we're talking up the importance of work-life balance and familial roles for women but we're not also mentioning those things about men, that's a problem. If a woman's accomplishments must be accompanied by a reassurance that she really was "a good Mom," but a man's accomplishments are allowed to stand on their own, that's a problem. And lest you think that I only care about women, let's not act like this doesn't have a real and dangerous impact on men, too. If a man spends years of his life as a doting father and caring husband, yet his strong devotion to his family is not considered an important fact for his obituary because he's male . . . then yes, that's also a **big** problem.

The fact that so many people don't understand why it might be unnerving that the 14 writer's idea for a good story arc in Brill's obituary was to lead with her role as a wife and mother, and then let the surprise that she was *actually a really smart rocket scientist* come in later as a shocking twist? That's benevolent sexism.

WHY IS BENEVOLENT SEXISM A PROBLEM?

Admittedly, this research begs an obvious question. If benevolently sexist comments 15 seem like nothing more than compliments, why are they problematic? Is it really "sexism" if the content of the statements seems positive towards women?

After all, the obituary noted nothing more than how beloved Brill was as a wife and 16 a mother. Why should anyone be upset by that? Sure, men wouldn't be written about in the same way, but who cares? It's so nice!

Well, for one thing, benevolently sexist statements aren't *all* sunshine and butter- 17 flies. They often end up implying that women are weak, sensitive creatures that need to be "protected." While this may seem positive to some, for others — especially women in male-dominated fields — it creates a damaging stereotype.

As Glick and Fiske themselves note in their seminal paper: 18

> We do not consider benevolent sexism a good thing, for despite the positive feelings it may indicate for the perceiver, its underpinnings lie in traditional stereotyping and masculine dominance (e.g., the man as the provider and woman as his dependent), and its consequences are often damaging. Benevolent sexism is not necessarily experienced as benevolent by the recipient. For example, a man's comment to a female coworker on how "cute" she looks, however well-intentioned, may undermine her feelings of being taken seriously as a professional (Glick & Fiske, 1996, p. 491–492).

In a later paper, Glick and Fiske went on to determine the extent to which 15,000   19
men and women across 19 different countries endorse both hostile and benevolently
sexist statements. First of all, they found that hostile and benevolent sexism tend to
correlate highly across nations. So, it is *not* the case that people who endorse hostile
sexism don't tend to endorse benevolent sexism, whereas those who endorse benevolent sexism look nothing like the "real" sexists. On the contrary, those who endorsed
benevolent sexism were likely to admit that they *also* held explicit, hostile attitudes
towards women (although one does not necessarily *have* to endorse these hostile attitudes in order to engage in benevolent sexism).

Secondly, they discovered that benevolent sexism was a significant predictor of   20
nationwide gender inequality, **independent of the effects of hostile sexism**. In countries where the men were more likely to endorse benevolent sexism, *even when con-
trolling for hostile sexism*, men also lived longer, were more educated, had higher
literacy rates, made significantly more money, and actively participated in the political and economic spheres more than their female counterparts. The warm, fuzzy feelings surrounding benevolent sexism come at a cost, and that cost is often actual,
objective gender equality.

THE INSIDIOUS NATURE OF BENEVOLENT SEXISM

A recent paper by Julia Becker and Stephen Wright details even more of the insidi-   21
ous ways that benevolent sexism might be harmful for both women and social
activism. In a series of experiments, women were exposed to statements that either
illustrated hostile sexism (e.g., "Women are too easily offended") or benevolent
sexism (e.g., "Women have a way of caring that men are not capable of in the
same way"). The results are quite discouraging; when the women read statements
illustrating benevolent sexism, they were less willing to engage in anti-sexist collective action, such as signing a petition, participating in a rally, or generally "acting against sexism." Not only that, but this effect was partially mediated by the fact
that women who were exposed to benevolent sexism were more likely to think
that there are many advantages to being a woman and were also more likely to
engage in *system justification*, a process by which people justify the status quo and
believe that there are no longer problems facing disadvantaged groups (such as
women) in modern day society. Furthermore, women who were exposed to hostile
sexism actually displayed the opposite effect — they were *more* likely to intend to
engage in collective action, and *more* willing to fight against sexism in their everyday lives.

How might this play out in a day-to-day context? Imagine that there's an anti-   22
female policy being brought to a vote, like a regulation that would make it easier for
local businesses to fire pregnant women once they find out that they are expecting.
If you are collecting signatures for a petition or trying to gather women to protest
this policy and those women were recently exposed to a group of men making comments about the policy in question, it would be significantly easier to gain their support and vote down the policy if the men were commenting that pregnant women

should be fired because they were dumb for getting pregnant in the first place. However, if they instead happened to mention that women are much more compassionate than men and make better stay-at-home parents as a result, these remarks might actually lead these women to be less likely to fight an objectively sexist policy.

"I MEAN, IS SEXISM REALLY STILL A PROBLEM?"

We often hear people claiming that sexism, racism, or other forms of discrimination   23
that seem to be outdated are "no longer really a problem." Some people legitimately believe this to be true, while others (particularly women and racial minorities) find it ridiculous that others could be so blind to the problems that still exist. So why does this disparity exist? Why is it so difficult for so many people to see that sexism and racism are still alive and thriving?

Maybe the answer lies right here, on the benevolent side of prejudice. While   24
"old fashioned" forms of discrimination may have died down quite a bit (after all, it really isn't quite as socially acceptable in most areas of the world to be as explicitly sexist and/or racist as people have been in the past), more "benevolent" forms of discrimination still very much exist, and they have their own sneaky ways of suppressing equality. Unaffected bystanders (or perpetrators) may construe benevolently sexist sentiments as harmless or even beneficial; in fact, as demonstrated by Becker and Wright, targets may even feel better about themselves after exposure to benevolently sexist statements. This could be, in some ways, even worse than explicit, hostile discrimination; because it hides under the guise of compliments, it's easy to use benevolent sexism to demotivate people against collective action or convince people that there is no longer a need to fight for equality.

However, to those people who *still* may be tempted to argue that benevolent sex-   25
ism is nothing more than an overreaction to well-intentioned compliments, let me pose this question: What happens when there is a predominant stereotype saying that women are better stay-at-home parents than men because they are inherently more caring, maternal, and compassionate? It seems nice enough, but how does this ideology affect the woman who wants to continue to work full time after having her first child and faces judgment from her colleagues who accuse her of neglecting her child? How does it affect the man who wants to stay at home with his newborn baby, only to discover that his company doesn't offer paternity leave because they assume that women are the better candidates to be staying at home?

At the end of the day, "good intent" is not a panacea. Benevolent sexism may very   26
well seem like harmless flattery to many people, but that doesn't mean it isn't insidiously dangerous.

To conclude, I'll now ask you to think about recent events surrounding Elise   27
Andrew, creator of the wildly popular "I F—king Love Science" Facebook page (https://www.facebook.com/IFeakingLoveScience). When she shared her personal Twitter account with the page's 4.4 million fans, many commented on the link

because they were absolutely **SHOCKED** . . . about what? Why, of course, about the fact that she is female:

> "I had no idea that IFLS had such a beautiful face!"
>
> "holy hell, youre a HOTTIE!"
>
> "you mean you're a girl, AND you're beautiful? wow, i just liked science a lil bit more today ^^"
>
> "I thought that because of all the ways you were so proud to spout off "I f — king love science" in a difient swary manner against people who hated sware words being used that you was a dude."
>
> "you're a girl!? I always imagined you as a guy; don't know why; well, nice to see to how you look like i guess"
>
> "What?!!? Gurlz don't like science! LOL Totally thought you were a dude."
>
> "It's not just being a girl that's the surprise, but being a fit girl! (For any non-Brits, fit, in this context, means hot/bangable/shagtastic/attractive)."

Right. See, that's the thing. Elise felt uncomfortable with this, as did many others 28 out there who saw it—and rightfully so. Yet many people would call her (and others like her) oversensitive for feeling negatively about statements that appear to be compliments. Many thought that Elise should have been happy that others were calling her attractive, or pointing out that it's idiosyncratic for her to be a female who loves science. What Elise (and many others) felt was the benevolently sexist side of things—the side that perpetuates a stereotype that women (especially *attractive* women) don't "do" science, and that the most noteworthy thing to comment on about a female scientist is what she looks like.

Unfortunately, it's very likely that no one walked away from this experience having 29 learned anything. People who could tell that this was offensive were obviously willing to recognize it as such, but people who endorsed those statements just thought they were being nice. Because they weren't calling her incompetent or unworthy, none of them were willing to recognize it as sexism, even when explicitly told that that's what it was—even though, based on research, we know that this sort of behavior has actual, meaningful consequences for society and for gender equality.

That right there?   30

That's the ***real*** problem with benevolent sexism.   31

References

Becker, J., & Wright, S. (2011). Yet another dark side of chivalry: Benevolent sexism undermines and hostile sexism motivates collective action for social change. *Journal of Personality and Social Psychology, 101*(1), 62–77. doi:10.1037/a0022615

Dusheck, J. (2013, April 1). Guest Post: Family Man Who Invented Relativity and Made Great Chili Dies. *The Last Word on Nothing.* Retrieved from http://www.lastwordonnothing.com/2013/04/01/guest-post-physicist-dies-made-great-chili/

Glick, P., & Fiske, S. (1996). The Ambivalent Sexism Inventory: Differentiating hostile and benevolent sexism. *Journal of Personality and Social Psychology, 70*(3), 491–512. doi:10.1037/0022-3514.70.3.491

Glick, P., Fiske, S., Mladinic, A., Saiz, J., Abrams, D., Masser, B., ... López, W. (2000). Beyond prejudice as simple antipathy: Hostile and benevolent sexism across cultures. *Journal of Personality and Social Psychology, 79*(5), 763–775. doi:10.1037/0022-3514.79.5.763

Yvonne Brill, a pioneering rocket scientist, dies at 88. (2013). *News Diffs*. Retrieved from http://www.newsdiffs.org/diff/192021/192137/www.nytimes.com/2013/03/31/science/space/yvonne-brill-rocket-scientist-dies-at-88.html

READING FOR MEANING

1. **Read to Summarize.** Write a sentence or two explaining what Tannenbaum means when she defines "benevolent sexism" and where she sees evidence of it in society.

For more on summarizing, see Chapter 2, pp. 24–25.

2 **Read to Respond.** Write a paragraph analyzing anything that seems surprising, such as the Obituaries editor's refusal to see benevolent sexism as problematic, even after it was pointed out to him (par. 11); or the finding by Glick and Fiske that "those who endorsed benevolent sexism were likely to admit that they *also* held explicit, hostile attitudes towards women" (par. 19). Does this response or the finding confuse or baffle you? Why?

3. **Read to Analyze Assumptions.** Write a paragraph or two analyzing an assumption you find intriguing in Tannenbaum's essay. For example:

You may also try contextualizing; see Chapter 2, pp. 29–30.

Assumptions about the dangers benevolent sexism poses. Tannenbaum uses the word *dangerous* to describe benevolent sexism in paragraphs 4, 13, and 26. She goes further, adding the word *insidious* to imply that this brand of sexism is more dangerous because it is often hidden and gradually harmful — to both women and men.

- What social values does benevolent sexism threaten?
- What kinds of danger does it pose to those who have been the objects of benevolent sexism or who are "tempt[ed] to brush this experience off as an overreaction . . . or a misunderstanding" (par. 4)? What should people do in the face of danger?

For help analyzing assumptions, see Chapter 2, pp. 28–29.

The assumption that men and women should be treated equally in any and all situations. Tannenbaum points out that even compliments, if they bow to stereotypes, are sexist — they "feel wrong," and, even if they make you "feel good," they "cause a feeling of unease" (par. 3). She notes that different treatment — such as believing that women need to be protected or are more caring — may "sound like a compliment, but it still counts as sexism" (par. 6).

- Can you think of similar stereotypes that apply to men? What situations could lead men to complain of benevolent sexism? (See par. 25.)
- Is being *treated* equally in all situations the same as *being* equal in all situations? What would Tannenbaum say? Explain.

READING LIKE A WRITER

USING APPROPRIATE WRITING STRATEGIES

For help with more reading and writing strategies, see Chapter 2.

When explaining concepts, writers use several strategies to support their explanation. Tannenbaum, for example, uses comparing and/or contrasting when explaining "ambivalent" and "hostile" sexism (par. 5); illustrating the responses to the "I F—king Love Science" author's identity (par. 27); speculating about causes or effects of benevolent sexism (pars. 20–21); and defining (pars. 5–6). Choose one of these strategies and analyze its use in Tannenbaum's essay.

| Analyze & Write |

Write a paragraph or two analyzing the rhetorical strategies that Tannenbaum uses to cultivate academic habits of mind.

1. How does the strategy you chose arouse curiosity in the topic or enable critical analysis of the concept of "benevolent sexism"?

2. Who are Tannenbaum's readers, and how does the strategy you chose enable Tannenbaum to demonstrate rhetorical sensitivity to her audience?

Michael Pollan

Altered State: Why "Natural" Doesn't Mean Anything

Michael Pollan (b. 1955) is a contributing writer for the *New York Times Magazine* and a former executive editor for *Harper's*. His essays have appeared in numerous anthologies, and he is the author of seven books, including *The Omnivore's Dilemma: A Natural History of Four Meals* (2006) and *In Defense of Food: An Eater's Manifesto* (2008). Pollan has won numerous prizes for his journalism and his books, among them the President's Citation Award from the American Institute of Biological Sciences (2009) and the Voices of Nature Award from the Natural Resources Defense Council (2009). Since 2003, he has been the John S. and James L. Knight Professor of Journalism at the University of California, Berkeley's Graduate School of Journalism, and the director of the Knight Program in Science and Environmental Journalism. The essay below was published in the *New York Times Magazine* in 2015.

- **Before you read,** think about how you react when you hear the word *natural*. Do you attach it as an adjective to any particular noun, such as *natural childbirth*, or do you have a ready definition or association in your mind?

- **As you read,** consider how Pollan engages his readers: Is it the subject matter, the writing style, or something else?

It isn't every day that the definition of a common English word that is ubiquitous in common parlance is challenged in federal court, but that is precisely what has happened with the word "natural." During the past few years, some 200 class-action suits have been filed against food manufacturers, charging them with misuse of the adjective in marketing such edible oxymorons as "natural" Cheetos Puffs, "all-natural" Sun Chips, "all-natural" Naked Juice, "100 percent all-natural" Tyson chicken nuggets and so forth. The plaintiffs argue that many of these products contain ingredients — high-fructose corn syrup, artificial flavors and colorings, chemical preservatives and genetically modified organisms — that the typical consumer wouldn't think of as "natural." 1

Judges hearing these cases — many of them in the Northern District of California — have sought a standard definition of the adjective that they could cite to adjudicate these claims, only to discover that no such thing exists. 2

Something in the human mind, or heart, seems to need a word of praise for all that humanity hasn't contaminated, and for us that word now is "natural." Such an ideal can be put to all sorts of rhetorical uses. Among the antivaccination crowd, for example, it's not uncommon to read about the superiority of something called "natural immunity," brought about by exposure to the pathogen in question rather than to the 3 deactivated (and therefore harmless) version of it made by humans in laboratories. "When you inject a vaccine into the body," reads a post on an antivaxxer website, Campaign for Truth in Medicine, "you're actually performing an unnatural act." This, of course, is the very same term once used to decry homosexuality and, more recently, same-sex marriage, which the Family Research Council has taken to comparing unfavorably to what it calls "natural marriage."

So what are we really talking about when we talk about natural? It depends; the 4 adjective is impressively slippery, its use steeped in dubious assumptions that are easy to overlook. Perhaps the most incoherent of these is the notion that nature consists of everything in the world except us and all that we have done or made. In our heart of hearts, it seems, we are all creationists.

In the case of "natural immunity," the modifier implies the absence of human inter- 5 vention, allowing for a process to unfold as it would if we did nothing, as in "letting nature take its course." In fact, most of medicine sets itself *against* nature's course, which is precisely what we like about it—at least when it's saving us from dying, an eventuality that is perhaps more natural than it is desirable.

Yet sometimes medicine's interventions are unwelcome or go overboard, and 6 nature's way of doing things can serve as a useful corrective. This seems to be especially true at the beginning and end of life, where we've seen a backlash against humanity's technological ingenuity that has given us both "natural childbirth" and, more recently, "natural death."

This last phrase, which I expect will soon be on many doctors' lips, indicates the 7 enduring power of the adjective to improve just about anything you attach it to, from cereal bars all the way on up to dying. It seems that getting end-of-life patients and their families to endorse "do not resuscitate" orders has been challenging. To many ears, "D.N.R." sounds a little too much like throwing Grandpa under the bus. But according to a paper in the *Journal of Medical Ethics*, when the orders are reworded to say "allow natural death," patients and family members and even medical professionals are much more likely to give their consent to what amounts to exactly the same protocols.

The word means something a little different when applied to human behavior 8 rather than biology (let alone snack foods). When marriage or certain sexual practices are described as "natural," the word is being strategically deployed as a synonym for "normal" or "traditional," neither of which carries nearly as much rhetorical weight. "Normal" is by now too obviously soaked in moral bigotry; by comparison, "natural" seems to float high above human squabbling, offering a kind of secular version of what used to be called divine law. Of course, that's exactly the role that "natural law" played for America's founding fathers, who invoked nature rather than God as the granter of rights and the arbiter of right and wrong.

"Traditional" marriage might be a more defensible term, but traditional is a much 9 weaker modifier than natural. Tradition changes over time and from culture to culture, and so commands a fraction of the authority of nature, which we think of as timeless and universal, beyond the reach of messy, contested history.

Implicit here is the idea that nature is a repository of abiding moral and ethical   10
values—and that we can say with confidence exactly what those values are. Philoso-
phers often call this the "naturalistic fallacy": the idea that whatever *is* (in nature) is
what *ought to be* (in human behavior). But if nature offers a moral standard by which
we can measure ourselves, and a set of values to which we should aspire, exactly
what sort of values are they? Are they the brutally competitive values of "nature, red in
tooth and claw," in which every individual is out for him- or herself? Or are they the
values of cooperation on display in a beehive or ant colony, where the interests of the
community trump those of the individual? Opponents of same-sex marriage can find
examples of monogamy in the animal kingdom, and yet to do so they need to look
past equally compelling examples of animal polygamy as well as increasing evidence
of apparent animal homosexuality. And let's not overlook the dismaying rates of what
looks very much like rape in the animal kingdom, or infanticide, or the apparent
sadism of your average house cat.

The American Puritans called nature "God's Second Book," and they read it for moral   11
guidance, just as we do today. Yet in the same way we can rummage around in the Bible
and find textual support for pretty much whatever we want to do or argue, we can ran-
sack nature to justify just about anything. Like the maddening whiteness of Ahab's whale,
nature is an obligingly blank screen on which we can project what we want to see.

So does this mean that, when it comes to saying what's natural, anything goes? I   12
don't think so. In fact, I think there's some philosophical wisdom we can harvest from,
of all places, the Food and Drug Administration. When the federal judges couldn't
find a definition of "natural" to apply to the class-action suits before them, three of
them wrote to the F.D.A., ordering the agency to define the word. But the F.D.A. had
considered the question several times before, and refused to attempt a definition. The
only advice the F.D.A. was willing to offer the jurists is that a food labeled "natural"
should have "nothing artificial or synthetic" in it "that would not normally be expected
in the food." The F.D.A. states on its website that "it is difficult to define a food product
as 'natural' because the food has probably been processed and is no longer the product of the earth," suggesting that the industry might not want to press the point too
hard, lest it discover that *nothing* it sells is natural.

The F.D.A.'s philosopher-bureaucrats are probably right: At least at the margins, it's   13
impossible to fix a definition of "natural." Yet somewhere between those margins
there lies a broad expanse of common sense. "Natural" has a fairly sturdy antonym—
artificial, or synthetic—and, at least on a scale of relative values, it's not hard to say
which of two things is "more natural" than the other: cane sugar or high-fructose corn
syrup? Chicken or chicken nuggets? G.M.O.s or heirloom seeds? The most natural
foods in the supermarket seldom bother with the word; any food product that feels
compelled to tell you it's natural in all likelihood is not.

But it is probably unwise to venture beyond the shores of common sense, for it isn't   14
long before you encounter either Scylla or Charybdis. At one extreme end of the spectrum of possible meanings, there's nothing *but* nature. Our species is a result of the same
process—natural selection—that created every other species, meaning that we and

whatever we do are natural, too. So go ahead and call your nuggets natural: It's like saying they're made with matter, or molecules, which is to say, it's like saying nothing at all.

And yet at the opposite end of the spectrum of meaning, where humanity in some   15
sense stands outside nature—as most of us still unthinkingly believe—what is left of the natural that we haven't altered in some way? We're mixed up with all of it now, from the chemical composition of the atmosphere to the genome of every plant or animal in the supermarket to the human body itself, which has long since evolved in response to cultural practices we invented, like agriculture and cooking. Nature, if you believe in human exceptionalism, is over. We probably ought to search elsewhere for our values.

READING FOR MEANING

For help with
summarizing,
see Chapter 2,
pp. 24–25.

1. **Read to Summarize.** Write a few sentences explaining what the definition of *natural* means to Pollan and how he thinks our culture has shaped the word.

2. **Read to Respond.** Write a paragraph analyzing anything that seems fascinating, such as the word *natural* having "the enduring power of the adjective to improve just about anything you attach it to, from cereal bars all the way on up to dying" (par. 7), and think about the power of language to influence your responses to an object or idea.

For help
analyzing
assumptions,
see Chapter 2,
pp. 28–29.

3. **Read to Analyze Assumptions.** Write a paragraph or two analyzing an assumption you find intriguing in Pollan's essay. For example:

   The assumption that "nature is a repository of abiding moral and ethical values" (par. 10). As Pollan asks, "what sort of values are they?"

   - Pollan considers the word *natural* as a "modifier [that] implies the absence of human intervention" (par. 5), which implies that association with humans is somehow wrong. Do you agree? How does this understanding affect people's approach to their food and other purchases?

   - Think about how you use the word *natural*. Does your use fall into any of the definitions Pollan provides, and what values does your definition assume?

   Assumptions that "common sense" (par. 13) dictates a path worth following—that extremes do not help us figure out what is important or how to behave well. Pollan explains that it's impossible to define *natural* "at the margins" (par. 13), but that if we consider its antonyms — artificial, synthetic — we can figure out what is truly "natural."

You might try
looking for
patterns of
opposition.
See Chapter 2,
pp. 35–36.

   - Is common sense easily come by? How do we know it when we see it?

   - Consider examples of "natural" in Pollan's essay and in your own experience. Can common sense serve us well as guidance in the context of determining what is natural?

READING LIKE A WRITER

ENGAGING READERS' INTEREST

While the content of an essay can be interesting in and of itself, writers explaining concepts try to engage readers' interest with a variety of strategies, such as telling stories or anecdotes, or asking questions. Pollan uses humor and **tone** (attitude or mood) to engage his readers. He starts his essay using exaggeratedly fancy vocabulary — "ubiquitous," "parlance," and "edible oxymorons" — to explain a plain-sounding word, "natural" (par. 1). He develops his examination of *natural* by giving several definitions: "Something in the human mind, or heart, seems to need a word of praise for all that humanity hasn't contaminated, and for us that word now is 'natural'" (par. 3).

Analyze & Write

Write a paragraph or two analyzing Pollan's tone and its effect on his audience.

1. Skim the essay, highlighting examples of Pollan's tone. Is it friendly? Meditative? Ironic? Bitter?

2. How does Pollan's tone engage readers? Does this strategy work well for you? Why or why not?

Linh Kieu Ngo

Cannibalism: It Still Exists

Linh Kieu Ngo wrote this essay when he was a college student. He
explains a concept of importance in anthropology and of wide general
interest — cannibalism, the eating of human flesh by other humans. Most
Americans may have heard about survival cannibalism, but few may
know about dietary and ritual cannibalism and their historical importance. Ngo explains these concepts in his essay.

- **Before you read,** think about any examples of survival cannibalism
  you may know about (the people in the book *Alive*, the members of
  the Donner Party, etc.). Under what conditions has survival
  cannibalism been practiced?

- **As you read,** pay attention to any cues Ngo gives to keep readers on
  track. Consider his need for rhetorical sensitivity: writing about what
  could be a repulsive practice for some members of his audience. What
  strategies does he use to keep his audience engaged and on track?

Fifty-five Vietnamese refugees fled to Malaysia on a small fishing boat to escape com- 1
munist rule in their country following the Vietnam War. During their escape attempt,
the captain was shot by the coast guard. The boat and its passengers managed to out-
run the coast guard to the open sea, but they had lost the only person who knew the
way to Malaysia, the captain.

The men onboard tried to navigate the boat, but after a week fuel ran out and they 2
drifted farther out to sea. Their supply of food and water was gone; people were starv-
ing, and some of the elderly were near death. The men managed to produce a small
amount of drinking water by boiling salt water, using dispensable wood from the boat
to create a small fire near the stern. They also tried to fish, but had little success.

A month went by, and the old and weak died. At first, the crew threw the dead 3
overboard, but later, out of desperation, the crew turned to human flesh as a source of
food. Some people vomited as they attempted to eat it, while others refused to resort
to cannibalism and see the bodies of their loved ones sacrificed for food. Those who
did not eat died of starvation, and their bodies in turn became food for others. Human
flesh was cut out, washed in salt water, and hung to dry for preservation. The liquids
inside the cranium were eaten to quench thirst. The livers, kidneys, heart, stomach,
and intestines were boiled and eaten.

Five months passed before a whaling vessel discovered the drifting boat, looking 4
like a graveyard of bones. There was only one survivor.

Cannibalism, the act of human beings eating human flesh (Sagan 2), has a long his- 5
tory and continues to hold interest and create controversy. Many books and research
reports offer examples of cannibalism, but a few scholars have questioned whether
cannibalism was ever practiced anywhere, except in cases of ensuring survival in
times of famine or isolation (Askenasy 43–54). Recently, some scholars have tried to

understand why people in the West have been so eager to attribute cannibalism to non-Westerners (Barker et al.). Cannibalism has long been a part of American popular culture. For example, Mark Twain's "Cannibalism in the Cars" tells a humorous story about cannibalism by well-to-do travelers on a train stranded in a snowstorm, and cannibalism is still a popular subject for jokes.

If we assume there is some reality to the reports about cannibalism, how can we   6 best understand this concept? Cannibalism can be broken down into two main categories: exocannibalism, the eating of outsiders or foreigners, and endocannibalism, the eating of members of one's own social group (Shipman 70). Within these categories are several functional types of cannibalism, three of the most common being survival cannibalism, dietary cannibalism, and religious and ritual cannibalism.

Survival cannibalism occurs when people trapped without food have to decide   7 "whether to starve or eat fellow humans" (Shipman 70). In the case of the Vietnamese refugees, the crew and passengers on the boat ate human flesh to stay alive. They did not kill people to get human flesh for nourishment, but instead waited until the people had died. Even after human carcasses were sacrificed as food, the boat people ate only enough to survive. Another case of survival cannibalism occurred in 1945, when General Douglas MacArthur's forces cut supply lines to Japanese troops stationed in the Pacific Islands. In one incident, Japanese troops were reported to have sacrificed the Arapesh people of northeastern New Guinea for food in order to avoid death by starvation (Tuzin 63). The most famous example of survival cannibalism in American history comes from the diaries, letters, and interviews of survivors of the California-bound Donner Party, who in the winter of 1846 were snowbound in the Sierra Nevada Mountains for five months. Thirty-five of eighty-seven adults and children died, and some of them were eaten (Hart 116–17; Johnson).

Unlike survival cannibalism, in which human flesh is eaten as a last resort after a   8 person has died, in dietary cannibalism, humans are purchased or trapped for food and then eaten as a part of a culture's traditions. In addition, survival cannibalism often involves people eating other people of the same origins, whereas dietary cannibalism usually involves people eating foreigners.

In the Miyanmin society of the west Sepik interior of Papua New Guinea, villagers do   9 not value human flesh over that of pigs or marsupials because human flesh is part of their diet (Poole 17). The Miyanmin people observe no differences in "gender, kinship, ritual status, and bodily substance"; they eat anyone, even their own dead. In this respect, then, they practice both endocannibalism and exocannibalism; and to ensure a constant supply of human flesh for food, they raid neighboring tribes and drag their victims back to their village to be eaten (Poole 11). Perhaps, in the history of this society, there was at one time a shortage of wild game to be hunted for food, and because people were more plentiful than fish, deer, rabbits, pigs, or cows, survival cannibalism was adopted as a last resort. Then, as their culture developed, the Miyanmin may have retained the practice of dietary cannibalism, which has endured as a part of their culture.

Similar to the Miyanmin, the people of the Leopard and Alligator societies in South   10 America eat human flesh as part of their cultural tradition. Practicing dietary exocannibalism, the Leopard people hunt in groups, with one member wearing the skin of a leopard to conceal the face. They ambush their victims in the forest and carry their victims back to their village to be eaten. The Alligator people also hunt in groups, but they hide themselves under a canoelike submarine that resembles an alligator, then swim close to a fisherman's or trader's canoe to overturn it and catch their victims (MacCormack 54).

Religious or ritual cannibalism is different from survival and dietary cannibalism in that it has a ceremonial purpose rather than one of nourishment. Sometimes only a single victim is sacrificed in a ritual, while at other times many are sacrificed. For example, the Bangala tribe of the Congo River in central Africa honors a deceased chief or leader by purchasing, sacrificing, and feasting on slaves (Sagan 53). The number of slaves sacrificed is determined by how highly the tribe members revered the deceased leader. 11

Ritual cannibalism among South American Indians often serves as revenge for the dead. Like the Bangalas, some South American tribes kill their victims to be served as part of funeral rituals, with human sacrifices denoting that the deceased was held in high honor. Also like the Bangalas, these tribes use outsiders as victims. Unlike the Bangalas, however, the Indians sacrifice only one victim instead of many in a single ritual. For example, when a warrior of a tribe is killed in battle, the family of the warrior forces a victim to take the identity of the warrior. The family adorns the victim with the deceased warrior's belongings and may even force him to marry the deceased warrior's wives. But once the family believes the victim has assumed the spiritual identity of the deceased warrior, the family kills him. The children in the tribe soak their hands in the victim's blood to symbolize their revenge of the warrior's death. Elderly women from the tribe drink the victim's blood and then cut up his body for roasting and eating (Sagan 53–54). By sacrificing a victim, the people of the tribe believe that the death of the warrior has been avenged and the soul of the deceased can rest in peace. 12

In the villages of certain African tribes, only a small part of a dead body is used in ritual cannibalism. In these tribes, where the childbearing capacity of women is highly valued, women are obligated to eat small, raw fragments of genital parts during fertility rites. Elders of the tribe supervise this ritual to ensure that the women will be fertile. In the Bimin-Kuskusmin tribe, for instance, a widow eats a small, raw fragment of flesh from the penis of her deceased husband in order to enhance her future fertility and reproductive capacity. Similarly, a widower may eat a raw fragment of flesh from his deceased wife's vagina along with a piece of her bone marrow; by eating her flesh, he hopes to strengthen the fertility capacity of his daughters borne by his dead wife, and by eating her bone marrow, he honors her reproductive capacity. Also, when an elder woman of the village who has shown great reproductive capacity dies, her uterus and the interior parts of her vagina are eaten by other women who hope to further benefit from her reproductive power (Poole 16–17). 13

Members of developed societies in general practice none of these forms of cannibalism, with the occasional exception of survival cannibalism when the only alternative is starvation. It is possible, however, that our distant-past ancestors were cannibals who through the eons turned away from the practice. We are, after all, descended from the same ancestors as the Miyanmin, the Alligator, and the Leopard people, and survival cannibalism shows that people are capable of eating human flesh when they have no other choice. 14

Works Cited

Askenasy, Hans. *Cannibalism: From Sacrifice to Survival*. Prometheus Books, 1994.

Barker, Francis, et al., editors. *Cannibalism and the New World*. Cambridge UP, 1998.

Brown, Paula, and Donald Tuzin, editors. *The Ethnography of Cannibalism*. Society for Psychological Anthropology, 1983.

Hart, James D. *A Companion to California*. U of California P, 1987.

Johnson, Kristin. *New Light on the Donner Party*. Kristin Johnson, www.utahcrossroads.org /DonnerParty/.

MacCormack, Carol. "Human Leopard and Crocodile." Brown and Tuzin, pp. 54–55.

Poole, Fitz John Porter. "Cannibals, Tricksters, and Witches." Brown and Tuzin, pp. 11, 16–17.

Sagan, Eli. *Cannibalism*. Harper, 1976.

Shipman, Pat. "The Myths and Perturbing Realities of Cannibalism." *Discover*, vol. 8, no. 3, Mar. 1987, pp. 70–76.

Tuzin, Donald. "Cannibalism and Arapesh Cosmology." Brown and Tuzin, pp. 61–63.

Twain, Mark. "Cannibalism in the Cars." *The Complete Short Stories of Mark Twain*, edited by Charles Neider, Doubleday, 1957, pp. 9–16.

READING FOR MEANING

1. **Read to Summarize.** Write a few sentences explaining the concept of cannibalism in its different forms.

   For help with summarizing, see Chapter 2, pp. 24–25.

2. **Read to Respond.** Write a paragraph analyzing anything that seems surprising, such as the anecdotes about the Vietnamese refugees (pars. 1–4) and the Donner Party in California (par. 7) or the idea that cannibalism may be performed for ceremonial or ritual purposes (par. 11).

3. **Read to Analyze Assumptions.** Write a paragraph or two analyzing an assumption you find intriguing in Ngo's essay. For example:

   You may also try reflecting on challenges to your beliefs and values; see Chapter 2, pp. 36–37.

   Assumptions about how to deal with the dead. Ngo discusses several tribes that practice cannibalism in some form to honor the dead or to take on the good traits of the dead (pars. 11–13). Many cultures and religions of the world practice a form of this belief, although they may substitute another substance to represent the human. Yet the practice of cannibalism, even of people who are already dead, is controversial (par. 5).

   - What beliefs and values come into play among those who find cannibalism disgusting?
   - How do people comfort themselves with portions of the bodies of the dead?

   Assumptions about what constitutes "developed societies." Ngo does not define "developed societies" (par. 14), so he must assume that readers know what he means. Many of the tribes he describes, though, might think our society is anything but "developed."

   For help analyzing assumptions, see Chapter 2, pp. 28–29.

- What might people in Western industrialized societies do that would make people in "undeveloped societies" uncomfortable?

- How do you feel about the assumptions behind the idea of some societies' being "developed" while others are not?

READING LIKE A WRITER

ORGANIZING THE INFORMATION CLEARLY AND LOGICALLY

Think of an essay explaining a concept as a logical, interrelated sequence of topics. Each topic or main idea follows the preceding topic in a way that makes sense to readers and is cued by one or more of the following: a forecasting statement, a topic sentence, a brief summary of what came before, or one or more transitions.

We see all of these *cueing devices* in Ngo's essay. Note how in the first several paragraphs Ngo cues readers by using time markers:

> . . . following the Vietnam War. During their escape attempt . . . (par. 1)
>
> A month went by . . . At first . . . (par. 3)
>
> Five months passed . . . (par. 4)

He also guides readers with strong transitions in the first sentence of every paragraph. These transitions refer to the content of the previous paragraph, often including brief summaries, and forecast the content of the upcoming paragraph. Usually, the first sentence in the paragraph is also the **topic sentence,** a sentence announcing the idea the paragraph (or a series of paragraphs) will develop. For example, look at the last sentence of paragraph 6 and the first sentence of paragraph 7:

Forecast	Within these categories are several functional types of cannibalism, three
Paragraph topic	of the most common being survival cannibalism, dietary cannibalism, and religious and ritual cannibalism.
Topic sentence	Survival cannibalism occurs when people trapped without food have to decide "whether to starve or eat fellow humans" (Shipman 70).

Analyze & Write

Write a paragraph or two analyzing how Ngo uses these strategies elsewhere to guide readers:

1. Skim paragraphs 8–14, underlining or highlighting transitions, forecasting statements, and topic sentences.

2. Make an outline of the transitions. How do they help readers follow the logic of the essay?

Writing to Learn Concept Explanation

Write a brief essay analyzing one of the readings in this chapter (or another selection, perhaps one by a classmate). Explain how (and perhaps, how well) the selection works as a concept explanation. Consider, for example, how it uses

- writing strategies such as definition, compare/contrast, example, and illustration to develop the concept thoroughly;

- reliable, appropriate sources to explain and support the concept;

- cues to signal transitions and repetition to organize explanation of the concept;

- strategies to engage and hold the reader's interest.

Your essay could also reflect on how you applied one or more of the academic habits of mind:

- **Curiosity** — what questions or ideas did you have as you read the selection?

- **Critical Analysis** — what assumptions in the selection did you find intriguing, and why?

- **Rhetorical Sensitivity** — how effective or ineffective do you think the selection is in achieving its purpose for the intended audience, given the constraints of the medium and the concept genre?

A GUIDE TO WRITING ESSAYS EXPLAINING CONCEPTS

You have probably done a good deal of analytical writing about your reading. Your instructor may also assign a capstone project to explain a concept of your own. This Guide to Writing offers detailed suggestions and resources to help you meet the special challenges this kind of writing presents.

THE WRITING ASSIGNMENT

Write an explanation of a concept that interests you enough to study further.

- Choose a concept that you know a good deal about or about which you'd like to learn.

- Consider what your readers already know about the concept and how your explanation can add to their knowledge.

- Research material that helps clarify or provides examples of your concept.

- Consider the most effective writing strategies to convey your concept.

- Think about how to engage your readers' interest in your concept and guide them through your explanation.

WRITING YOUR DRAFT

Choosing a Concept

Rather than limiting yourself to the first concept that comes to mind, take a few minutes to consider your options. Below are some criteria that can help you choose a promising concept to explain, followed by suggestions for the types of concepts you might consider writing about.

Choose a concept that

- you think is important and will interest your readers;

- you can research sufficiently in the allotted time;

- provides you with a clear purpose, such as to inform readers about an important idea or theory, to show how the concept has promoted original thinking and research, to help readers better understand the concept, or to demonstrate knowledge of the concept and the ability to apply it.

Below are some concepts from various fields of study:

- *Literature, philosophy, and art:* figurative language, postcolonialism, modernism, postmodernism; existentialism, nihilism, determinism; cubism, iconography, pop art, conceptual art, performance art, graffiti, surrealism, expressionism

- *Business management:* autonomous work group, quality circle, management by objectives, zero-based budgeting, benchmarking, focus group, pods

- *Psychology:* phobia, narcissism, fetish, emotional intelligence, divergent and convergent thinking, behaviorism, Jungian archetype, visualization

- *Government and law:* one person/one vote, federalism, socialism, theocracy, separation of church and state, political action committee, Electoral College; arbitration, liability, reasonable doubt, sexual harassment, nondisclosure agreement

- *Biology and environmental studies:* ecosystem, plasmolysis, DNA, homozygosity, diffusion; acid rain, recycling, ozone depletion, toxic waste, endangered species, greenhouse effect, climate change, hydrologic cycle, El Niño, xeriscape

- *Nutrition and public health:* vegetarianism, bulimia, food allergy, aerobic exercise, obesity, Maillard reaction, sustainability, locavore, epidemic, drug abuse, contraception, disability, autism

- *Physical sciences and math:* gravity, mass, energy, quantum theory, law of definite proportions, osmotic pressure, first law of thermodynamics, entropy, free energy, fusion, boundedness; complex numbers, exponent, polynomial, factoring, derivative, infinity

Analyzing Your Readers

Write for a few minutes, analyzing your potential readers:

- What might my potential readers already know about the concept or the field of study to which it applies?

- What kinds of examples or information could I provide that readers will find new, useful, interesting, or amusing? How might I clarify misconceptions or faulty assumptions?

- What kinds of sources will my readers find credible?

Researching the Concept

You will probably need to research your concept in three stages:

1. Gain an overview of the concept by considering what you already know and what you need to learn, and by conducting some preliminary research.

2. Choose an aspect of your concept to focus on, an aspect that you can explore thoroughly in the space and time you have.

3. Conduct enough research to learn about this aspect of the concept.

Determining What You Know (and Don't Know).   You can determine what you already know about your concept by explaining it briefly, using one or more of the strategies below as a starting point:

- ▶ My concept can be divided into .... types or categories: ...., ..., ..., and ....
- ▶ Examples of my concept include ...., ..., and ....
- ▶ My concept is a .... [member of a larger category] that is/does/has .... [defining characteristics].
- ▶ My concept is [similar to/different from] .... in these ways: ...., ..., and ....

Try to answer the questions you think your readers will have.

Conducting Background Research.   Talk to experts, such as a professor or teaching assistant for an academic topic, or your supervisor for a work-related topic. You could also post a question on a blog devoted to this subject.

You may want to consult some general reference sources or databases, such as the Gale Virtual Reference Library, SAGE Knowledge, or Web of Science, to conduct a preliminary search on your concept. (Check with a librarian to find out which reference databases your school subscribes to.) After reading articles in several relevant reference sources, list the following:

- names of scholars, experts, or respected authors on your subject;

- terms, phrases, or synonyms that you might use as search terms later;

- interesting aspects of the concept that you might want to focus on.

To learn more about conducting research and assessing reliability, see the Appendix, pp. 491–96.
To conduct an Internet search on your concept, start by entering the word *overview* or *definition* with the name of your concept, and then skim the top ten search results to get a general sense of your topic.

Choosing an Aspect of Your Concept to Focus On.   List two or three aspects of your concept that interest you and then answer these questions:

- Why does this aspect of the concept interest me or my readers?

- How is it relevant to my family, community, work, studies, or readers?

- What are my readers likely to know about the concept? How can I build on what they already know?

Conducting Additional Research on Your Focused Concept. Your instructor may expect you to do in-depth research or may limit the number and type of sources you can use. Readers will want to be sure that your sources are reliable and relevant, and may want to read your sources for themselves, so include enough information in your notes to put your sources in context and to cite them accurately.

Formulating a Working Thesis Statement

A working thesis will help you begin drafting your essay purposefully. Your thesis should announce the concept and focus of the explanation, and may also forecast the main topics. Here are two example thesis statements from the readings.

Concept	This does us all a grave disservice, because shyness and introver-
Focus	sion — or more precisely, the careful, sensitive temperament from
Forecast	which both often spring — are not just normal. They are valuable.
	And they may be essential to the survival of our species. (Cain, par. 5)

In social psychology, these seemingly-positive-yet-still-somewhat-unsettling comments and behaviors have a name: *Benevolent Sexism*. Although it is tempting to brush this experience off as an overreaction to compliments or a misunderstanding of benign intent, benevolent sexism is both real and insidiously dangerous. (Tannenbaum, par. 4)

Using Appropriate Explanatory Strategies

To explain your concept effectively, consider how you would define it, what examples you can provide, how similar or different it is from other concepts, how it happens or gets done, and what its causes or effects are. Your goal is not only to inform but also to engage. The following sentence strategies may help you find the best ways to explain your concept.

- What are the concept's defining characteristics? What broader class does it belong to, and how does it differ from other members of its class? (*definition*)

  ▶ .... [Concept] is a .... in which .... [list defining characteristics].

- What examples or anecdotes can make the concept less abstract, more focused, and more understandable? (*example*)

  ▸ [Experts/scientists/etc.] first became aware of [concept] in [year], when .... (citation).

- How is this concept like or unlike related concepts with which your readers may be more familiar? (*comparison and contrast*)

  ▸ Many people think the term .... [concept] means .... , but it might be more accurate to say it means ....

- How can an explanation of this concept be divided into parts to make it easier for readers to understand? (*classification*)

  ▸ Experts like .... [name of expert] say there are .... [number] [categories, types, subtypes, versions] of .... [concept], ranging from .... ([citation]) to .... ([citation]).

- How does this concept happen, or how does one go about doing it? (*process narration*)

  ▸ To perform .... [concept or task related to concept], a [person, performer, participant, etc.] starts by .... Then [he/she/it] must .... [verb], ... [verb], and .... [verb].

- What are this concept's known causes or effects? (*cause and effect*)

  ▸ Experts disagree over the causes of .... [concept]. Some, like .... [name 1], believe .... ([citation]). Others, like .... [name 2], contend that .... ([citation]).

Including Visuals

For more on analyzing visuals, see Chapter 2, pp. 31–34.

Think about whether visuals — tables, graphs, drawings, photographs — would make your explanation clearer. You could construct your own visuals, download materials from the Internet, or scan and import visuals from books and magazines. Visuals are not a requirement of an essay explaining a concept, but they sometimes add a new dimension to your writing. If you include visuals you did not create yourself, be sure to cite the source(s) from which you borrow them. For an example, see the chart "Time on Social Networks" in the essay by Alexis Madrigal on p. 202. Consider what the visual data add to your understanding of the "machine zone."

Integrating Information from Sources

Summaries, paraphrases, and quotations from sources are frequently used to explain concepts or reinforce an explanation:

- Use a summary to give the gist of a research report or other information.

- Use a paraphrase to provide specific details or examples when the language of the source is not especially memorable.

- Use a quotation to emphasize source material that is particularly vivid or clear, to convey an expert's voice, or to discuss the source's choice of words.

Your readers will want you to explain how the ideas from the sources you cite reinforce the points you are making. Make sure you comment on your sources, clearly defining the relationship between your own ideas and the supporting information from sources. For more help with integrating sources, see the Appendix, pp. 499–508.

When introducing quotations, paraphrases, or summaries, writers often use a signal phrase — the source author's name plus an appropriate verb — to alert readers to the fact that they are borrowing someone else's words or ideas. Often the verb is neutral, as with the following example:

Credentials of source author Signal phrase (name + <u>verb</u>)	The psychologist Gregory Feist <u>found</u> that many of the most creative people in a range of fields are introverts who are comfortable working in solitary conditions in which they can focus attention inward. (Cain, par. 21)

Notice in the example above that the writer also mentions the source's credentials, which is often an option when introducing sources with a signal phrase. Sometimes, however, writers choose a descriptive adjective or verb to introduce a source, such as *stresses, approvingly reports, vividly details, disparagingly writes, emphasizes, extols,* or *stays firm.* By choosing carefully among a wide variety of precise verbs, you can convey the attitude or approach of the source as you integrate supporting information.

Notice that Linh Kieu Ngo does not use signal phrases to introduce his sources in the body of "Cannibalism: It Still Exists." Instead, he simply integrates the information from them into his sentences and uses parenthetical citations and entries in the Works Cited list to show readers where the information he borrows comes from. Here is an example from paragraph 9, in which Ngo includes a quotation together with information he paraphrases from his source:

Parenthetical citation (name & page number)	The Miyanmin people observe no differences in "gender, kinship, ritual status, and bodily substance"; they eat anyone, even their own dead. In this respect, then, they practice both endocannibalism and exocannibalism; and to ensure a constant supply of human flesh for food, they raid neighboring tribes and drag their victims back to their village to be eaten (<u>Poole 11</u>).

This strategy of integrating source material without using a signal phrase is useful when you want to emphasize the information and play down the source.

Organizing Your Concept Explanation Effectively for Your Readers

For help with
outlining, see
Chapter 2,
pp. 23–24.
The forecasting statement from your thesis can act as an informal outline when writing about simpler concepts, but for more complex concepts a tentative formal outline may be more useful.

Try to introduce new material in stages, so that readers' understanding of the concept builds slowly but steadily. Including a topic sentence for each paragraph or group of paragraphs on a single topic may help readers follow your explanation.

An essay explaining a concept is made up of four basic parts:

1. an attempt to engage readers' interest in the explanation

2. the thesis statement, announcing the concept and perhaps also forecasting the sequence of topics

3. a description or definition of the concept

4. the information about the concept, organized around a series of topics that reflect how the information has been divided up

An initial attempt to gain your readers' interest — by starting with an intriguing question or surprising example, for instance — could take as little space as two or three sentences or as much as four or five paragraphs, but you will want to maintain your readers' interest throughout the essay by providing examples or information that readers will find new, useful, interesting, or amusing.

Consider any outline you create tentative before you begin drafting. As you draft, you will usually see ways to improve on your original plan. Be ready to revise your outline, shift parts around, or drop or add parts as you draft.

Drafting Your Concept Explanation

By this point, you have done a lot of writing

- to focus your explanation and develop a working thesis statement;

- to organize your explanation clearly for your readers;

- to try out writing strategies that can help you explain your concept;

- to integrate information into your explanation smoothly and in a way that supports your own ideas.

Now stitch that material together to create a draft. The next section of this Guide to Writing will help you evaluate and improve it.

REVIEWING AND IMPROVING THE DRAFT

This section includes two guides for Peer Review and Troubleshooting Your Draft. Your instructor may arrange a peer review in class or online where you can exchange drafts with a classmate. The Peer Review Guide will help you give each other constructive feedback regarding the basic features and strategies typical of explaining a concept. (If you want to make specific suggestions for improving the draft, see Troubleshooting Your Draft on p. 234.) Also, be sure to respond to any specific concerns the writer has raised about the draft. The Troubleshooting Your Draft guide that follows will help you reread your own draft with a critical eye, sort through any feedback you've received, and consider a variety of ways to improve your draft.

A PEER REVIEW GUIDE

How effectively does the writer explain the concept?

What's Working Well: Point to a passage where the explanation of the concept is effective. For example, identify where the focus seems appropriate, or note where the strategy used to support the explanation—such as an example or a comparison is helpful. (See Chapter 2 for more strategies.)

What Needs Improvement: Identity any passage where the explanation could be improved—for example, where the focus is too broad or too narrow, where you lose track of the concept description, or where you need an additional strategy to fill out the explanation.

How well is the essay arranged to help the reader understand the concept?

What's Working Well: Highlight especially effective sentences or paragraphs that help move the reader from topic to topic or advance an explanation that moves from general to specific (or from specific to general). Note strong uses of forecasting statements or topic sentences that keep the reader oriented through the explanation.

What Needs Improvement: Show the writer where transitions might be needed for material that appears suddenly, or where a forecasting statement or topic sentence might announce the main ideas more clearly.

How effectively is information from sources integrated into the concept explanation?

What's Working Well: Mark a passage where a source is clearly identified and the material is introduced with an appropriate signal phrase and perhaps a particularly engaging verb.

(continued)

What Needs Improvement: Note any passages where you need more information about a source, or where the information from a source doesn't effectively explain or support the concept.

How engaging is the explanation of the concept?

What's Working Well: Point to a passage where you find the explanation most interesting or compelling, or where you felt drawn to keep reading to find out more. Was it the vividness of the language, the appropriateness of the explanation, or some other strategy that worked so well?

What Needs Improvement: Let the writer know where information might seem obvious or too complicated. Write down any questions you still have, and note whether there are some writing strategies that could improve your understanding of the concept.

Revising Your Draft

Revising means reenvisioning your draft and seeing it in a fresh way given your purpose, audience, and the review from your peers. Don't hesitate to cut unconvincing or tangential material, add new material, or move passages around. The following chart may help you strengthen your essay.

TROUBLESHOOTING YOUR DRAFT

To Focus the Concept and Explain It Clearly and Fully	
If the concept is confusing, unclear, or vague,	• Define the concept more precisely. • Give more examples. • Compare the concept to something familiar. • Apply the concept to a real-world experience.
If the focus seems too broad or too narrow,	• Concentrate on only one aspect of the concept. • Review your invention and research notes for a larger or more significant aspect of the concept.
If the content seems thin,	• Use explanatory writing strategies. • Develop your strategies more fully. • Explain how they relate to more familiar terms.

If some words are new to most readers,	• Define them or explain how they relate to more familiar terms. • Add analogies and examples to make them less abstract. • Place them in a context that clarifies their meaning.
To Improve the Organization	
If the essay as a whole is difficult to follow,	• Forecast the topics you will cover in the order in which they will appear. • Rearrange your topics so readers can follow your logic. • Revise or add topic sentences to clarify the content of each paragraph or section. • Outline your essay to see if the connections are clear; then reorganize as needed.
If connections from one sentence or paragraph to the next are vague or unclear,	• Make the connections clearer by improving or adding transitions. • Revise or add topic sentences to make connections between paragraphs clear.
To Integrate Information from Sources Smoothly	
If quotations, paraphrases, or summaries are not smoothly integrated into the text,	• Add appropriate signal phrases, using verbs that clarify the writer's position, approach, or attitude. • Explain how the quotation supports your point. • Contextualize the source to show its relevance and establish its reliability.
If some quotations could just as effectively be expressed in your own words,	• Paraphrase or summarize the quotation (with an appropriate citation).
If sources are not acknowledged properly,	• Include a signal phrase to identify the source. • Include the author's last name and a page number in parentheses following the borrowed material, and cite the source in a list at the end of the essay. (Check the Appendix, pp. 509–36, for the correct citation form.)

(continued)

To Engage Readers	
If readers are not interested in the concept or focus,	• Select examples that readers are already familiar with or that may be relevant to their lives. • Dramatize the concept to show its importance or relevance. • Show readers a new way of using or understanding a familiar concept.

Editing and Proofreading Your Draft

Check for errors in usage, punctuation, and mechanics, and consider matters of style. If you keep a list of errors you typically make, begin by checking your draft against this list. Ask someone else to proofread your essay before you submit it to your instructor.

From our research on student writing, we know that essays explaining concepts tend to have errors in essential or nonessential clauses beginning with *who*, *which*, or *that*. They also have errors in the use of commas to set off appositives. Check a writer's handbook for help with these potential problems.

Reflecting on Concept Explanation

In this chapter, you have read critically several pieces explaining a concept and have written one of your own. To better remember what you have learned, pause now to reflect on the reading and writing activities you completed in this chapter.

1. Write a page or so reflecting on what you have learned. Begin by describing what you are most pleased with in your essay. Then explain what you think contributed to your achievement. Be specific about this contribution.

   • If it was something you learned from the readings, indicate which readings and specifically what you learned from them.

   • If it came from your research notes and the writing you did in response to prompts in this chapter, point out the parts that helped you most.

2. Reflect more generally on explaining concepts, a genre of writing important in education and in society. Consider some of the following questions:

- When doing research, did you discover that some of the information on concepts was challenged by experts? What were the grounds for the challenge? Did you think your readers might question your information? How did you decide what information might seem new or surprising to readers?

- Did you feel comfortable in your roles as the selector and giver of knowledge? Describe how you felt in these roles.

Evaluation

Before you buy a computer, phone, or video game, do you take a look at the reviews? Brief reviews, written by consumers, are easy to find, but some are more helpful than others. The best reviewers know what they're talking about. They don't just say what they like, but they also justify *why* they like it, giving examples or other evidence. Moreover, their judgment is based not on individual taste alone but on commonly held standards or **criteria.** For example, no one would consider it appropriate to judge an action film by its poetic dialogue or its subtle characterizations; people judge such films by whether they deliver an exciting roller-coaster ride. The usefulness of an evaluation — be it a brief consumer comment or an expert's detailed review — depends on readers sharing, or at least respecting, the writer's criteria.

RHETORICAL SITUATIONS
FOR EVALUATIONS

Many people — including managers, reviewers, bloggers, and ordinary consumers — write evaluations, as the following examples suggest:

- A supervisor reviews the work of a probationary employee. She judges the employee's performance as being adequate overall but still needing improvement in several key areas, particularly completing projects on time and communicating clearly with others. To support her judgment, she describes several problems that the employee has had over the six-month probationary period.

- An older brother, a college junior, sends an e-mail message to his younger brother, a high-school senior, who is trying to decide which college to attend. Because the older brother attends one of the colleges being considered and has friends at another, he feels competent to offer advice. He centers his message on the question of what standards to use in evaluating colleges. He argues that if playing football is the primary goal, then college number one is the clear choice. But if having the opportunity to work in an award-winning scientist's genetics lab is more important, then the second college is the better choice.

Thinking about Evaluation

Recall a time when you evaluated something you had seen, heard, read, or tried (such as a film, live performance, novel, sports team, restaurant, television show, game, computer, or cell phone) or a time that you read or heard an evaluation someone else had made.

- Who was the *audience?* How do you think presenting the evaluation to this audience affected the writer's (or speaker's) judgment or the way the evaluation was supported? For example, did the audience's knowledge of the subject, or of subjects like it, influence the reasons or examples given?

- What was the main *purpose?* What did the writer (or speaker) want the audience to learn? For example, did he or she want to influence the actions of audience members, get them to think differently about the criteria or standards they should use when judging subjects of this kind, get them to look at the subject in a new way, or accomplish some other purpose?

- How would you rate the *rhetorical sensitivity* with which the evaluation was presented? What made the essay appropriate or inappropriate for its particular audience or purpose?

A GUIDE TO READING EVALUATIONS

This guide introduces you to the basic features and strategies typical of evaluative writing by inviting you to analyze an intriguing selection by Amitai Etzioni that evaluates McDonald's-type fast-food jobs for high-school students:

- *Reading for meaning* will help you understand Etzioni's judgment and his reasoning.

- *Reading like a writer* will help you learn how Etzioni employs strategies typical of evaluative writing, such as

    1. presenting the subject in enough detail so that readers know what is being judged

2. supporting an overall judgment based on appropriate criteria with credible evidence

3. responding to objections and alternative judgments readers might prefer

4. organizing the evaluation in a way that will be clear and logical to readers

Amitai Etzioni

Working at McDonald's

Amitai Etzioni (b. 1929) earned his Ph.D. in sociology from the University of California at Berkeley and has taught at Berkeley, Columbia, Harvard, and George Washington universities. A respected scholar, he served as president of the American Sociological Association and has written more than two dozen books, including *Privacy in a Cyber Age* (2015) and *Hot Spots: American Foreign Policy in a Post Human-Rights World* (2012). A highly visible public intellectual, Etzioni often writes for the *Huffington Post*. Among his many awards is the Simon Wiesenthal Center's 1997 Tolerance Book Award. "Working at McDonald's" was originally published in the *Miami Herald* with a headnote explaining that Etzioni's son Dari helped him write the essay.

- **Before you read,** think about any jobs you have had during high school or college (voluntary or for pay). Consider what you learned that might have made you a better student and prepared you for the kind of work you hope to do in the future.

- **As you read,** think about how the standards or criteria that Etzioni uses to evaluate jobs at fast-food restaurants would apply to the kinds of jobs you have held, and whether they are criteria you would apply.

McDonald's is bad for your kids. I do not mean the flat patties and the white-flour buns; I refer to the jobs teen-agers undertake, mass-producing these choice items. 1

As many as two-thirds of America's high school juniors and seniors now hold down part-time paying jobs, according to studies. Many of these are in fast-food chains, of which McDonald's is the pioneer, trend-setter, and symbol. 2

At first, such jobs may seem right out of the Founding Fathers' educational manual for how to bring up self-reliant, work-ethic-driven, productive youngsters. But in fact, these jobs undermine school attendance and involvement, impart few skills that will be useful in later life, and simultaneously skew the values of teen-agers—especially their ideas about the worth of a dollar. 3

It has been a longstanding American tradition that youngsters ought to get paying jobs. In folklore, few pursuits are more deeply revered than the newspaper route and the sidewalk lemonade stand. Here the youngsters are to learn how sweet are the fruits of labor and self-discipline (papers are delivered early in the 4 morning, rain or shine), and the ways of trade (if you price your lemonade too high or too low . . .).

Roy Rogers, Baskin Robbins, Kentucky Fried Chicken, et al. may at first seem noth- 5
ing but a vast extension of the lemonade stand. They provide very large numbers of teen jobs, provide regular employment, pay quite well compared to many other teen jobs, and, in the modern equivalent of toiling over a hot stove, test one's stamina.

Closer examination, however, finds the McDonald's kind of job highly uneducational 6
in several ways. Far from providing opportunities for entrepreneurship (the lemonade stand) or self-discipline, self-supervision, and self-scheduling (the paper route), most teen jobs these days are highly structured—what social scientists call "highly routinized."

True, you still have to have the gumption to get yourself over to the hamburger 7
stand, but once you don the prescribed uniform, your task is spelled out in minute detail. The franchise prescribes the shape of the coffee cups; the weight, size, shape, and color of the patties; and the texture of the napkins (if any). Fresh coffee is to be made every eight minutes. And so on. There is no room for initiative, creativity, or even elementary rearrangements. These are breeding grounds for robots working for yesterday's assembly lines, not tomorrow's high-tech posts.

There are very few studies of the matter. One of the few is a 1984 study by Ivan 8
Charper and Bryan Shore Fraser. The study relies mainly on what teen-agers write in response to questionnaires rather than actual observations of fast-food jobs. The authors argue that the employees develop many skills such as how to operate a food-preparation machine and a cash register. However, little attention is paid to how long it takes to acquire such a skill, or what its significance is.

What does it matter if you spend 20 minutes to learn to use a cash register, and 9
then—"operate" it? What skill have you acquired? It is a long way from learning to work with a lathe or carpenter tools in the olden days or to program computers in the modern age.

A 1980 study by A. V. Harrell and P. W. Wirtz found that, among those students 10
who worked at least 25 hours per week while in school, their unemployment rate four years later was half of that of seniors who did not work. This is an impressive statistic. It must be seen, though, together with the finding that many who begin as part-time employees in fast-food chains drop out of high school and are gobbled up in the world of low-skill jobs.

Some say that while these jobs are rather unsuited for college-bound, white, 11
middle-class youngsters, they are "ideal" for lower-class, "non-academic," minority youngsters. Indeed, minorities are "over-represented" in these jobs (21 percent of fast-food employees). While it is true that these places provide income, work, and even some training to such youngsters, they also tend to perpetuate their disadvantaged status. They provide no career ladders, few marketable skills, and undermine school attendance and involvement.

The hours are often long. Among those 14 to 17, a third of fast-food employees 12
(including some school dropouts) labor more than 30 hours per week, according to the Charper-Fraser study. Only 20 percent work 15 hours or less. The rest: between 15 and 30 hours.

Often the stores close late, and after closing one must clean up and tally up. In afflu- 13
ent Montgomery County, Md., where child labor would not seem to be a widespread
economic necessity, 24 percent of the seniors at one high school in 1985 worked as
much as five to seven days a week; 27 percent, three to five. There is just no way such
amounts of work will not interfere with school work, especially homework. In an informal survey published in the most recent yearbook of the high school, 58 percent of the
seniors acknowledged that their jobs interfere with their school work.

The Charper-Fraser study sees merit in learning teamwork and working under 14
supervision. The authors have a point here. However, it must be noted that such learning is not automatically educational or wholesome. For example, much of the supervision in fast-food places leans toward teaching one the wrong kinds of compliance:
blind obedience, or shared alienation with the "boss."

Supervision is often both tight and woefully inappropriate. Today, fast-food chains 15
and other such places of work (record shops, bowling alleys) keep costs down by having teens supervise teens with often no adult on the premises.

There is no father or mother figure with which to identify, to emulate, to provide a 16
role model and guidance. The work-culture varies from one place to another: Sometimes it is a tightly run shop (must keep the cash registers ringing); sometimes a rather
loose pot party interrupted by customers. However, only rarely is there a master to
learn from, or much worth learning. Indeed, far from being places where solid adult
work values are being transmitted, these are places where all too often delinquent
teen values dominate. Typically, when my son Oren was dishing out ice cream for
Baskin Robbins in upper Manhattan, his fellow teen-workers considered him a sucker
for not helping himself to the till. Most youngsters felt they were entitled to $50 sever-
ance "pay" on their last day on the job.

The pay, oddly, is the part of the teen work-world that is most difficult to evaluate. 17
The lemonade stand or paper route money was for your allowance. In the old days,
apprentices learning a trade from a master contributed most, if not all, of their income
to their parents' household. Today, the teen pay may be low by adult standards, but it
is often, especially in the middle class, spent largely or wholly by the teens. That is,
the youngsters live free at home ("after all, they are high school kids") and are left with
very substantial sums of money.

Where this money goes is not quite clear. Some use it to support themselves, espe- 18
cially among the poor. More middle-class kids set some money aside to help pay for
college, or save it for a major purchase—often a car. But large amounts seem to flow
to pay for an early introduction into the most trite aspects of American consumerism:
flimsy punk clothes, trinkets, and whatever else is the last fast-moving teen craze.

One may say that this is only fair and square; they are being good American con- 19
sumers and spend their money on what turns them on. At least, a cynic might add,
these funds do not go into illicit drugs and booze. On the other hand, an educator
might bemoan that these young, yet unformed individuals, so early in life driven to
buy objects of no intrinsic educational, cultural, or social merit, learn so quickly the
dubious merit of keeping up with the Joneses in ever-changing fads, promoted by
mass merchandising.

Many teens find the instant reward of money, and the youth status symbols it 20
buys, much more alluring than credits in calculus courses, European history, or foreign languages. No wonder quite a few would rather skip school—and certainly
homework—and instead work longer at a Burger King. Thus, most teen work these
days is not providing early lessons in work ethic; it fosters escape from school and
responsibilities, quick gratification, and a short cut to the consumeristic aspects of
adult life.

Thus, parents should look at teen employment not as automatically educational. It 21
is an activity—like sports—that can be turned into an educational opportunity. But it
can also easily be abused. Youngsters must learn to balance the quest for income with
the needs to keep growing and pursue other endeavors that do not pay off instantly—
above all education.

Go back to school. 22

READING FOR MEANING

1. **Read to Summarize.** Write a sentence or two briefly stating Etzioni's main point about the value of part-time jobs for teenagers.

   For help with summarizing, see Chapter 2, pp. 24–25.

2. **Read to Respond.** Write a paragraph analyzing anything that resonates for you, such as the "longstanding American tradition that youngsters ought to get paying jobs" (par. 4); or Etzioni's argument that working while attending school interferes with schoolwork (par. 13), perhaps in relation to your own work and school experience.

3. **Read to Analyze Assumptions.** Write a paragraph or two analyzing an assumption you find intriguing in Etzioni's essay. For example:

   For more help analyzing assumptions, see Chapter 2, pp. 28–29.

   Assumptions about the usefulness of certain skills. Etzioni asserts that fast-food jobs "impart few skills that will be useful in later life" (par. 3). For example, he claims they do not provide "opportunities for entrepreneur-ship . . . or self-discipline, self-supervision, and self-scheduling" (par. 6) and "[t]here is no room for initiative, creativity" (par. 7).

   - How different, really, is delivering newspapers from working at McDonald's in terms of the skills learned about discipline, scheduling, and so on?

   - What other kinds of skills do teens learn when working at fast-food restau-rants, and what potential use do you think these skills have in future life?

   Assumptions about the culture of consumerism. Toward the end of the essay, Etzioni complains that the things teenagers choose to buy with the money they earn from fast-food jobs represent "the most trite aspects of American consumerism: flimsy punk clothes, trinkets, and whatever else is the last fast-moving teen craze" (par. 18). His focus on what teens buy and

   You may also try reflecting on challenges to your beliefs and values; see Chapter 2, pp. 36–37.

why they buy it reveals Etzioni's ideas about teenagers' indoctrination into a consumerist culture.

- Etzioni uses the words *trite*, *flimsy*, and *trinkets* to criticize the things teens buy, but if teens purchased items that were original, well-made, and valuable, do you think he would still object? What might he be criticizing other than teenagers' taste?

- In referring to "fads" and "mass merchandising," he seems to assume teens are especially vulnerable to the influence of advertising (par. 19). To what extent, if any, do you agree?

READING LIKE A WRITER

Presenting the Subject

Writers must present the subject so readers know what is being judged and so that they can decide whether the criteria for evaluation they offer are appropriate. Writers often name the subject in the title and then describe it in some detail. A film reviewer, for example, might name the film in the title and then, in the review, indicate the category, or genre, of film he or she is critiquing as well as identify the actors, describe the characters they play, and tell some of the plot.

Similarly, Etzioni identifies the subject of his evaluation in his title: "Working at McDonald's"; he then specifies the type of work that concerns him, and explains why he focuses his attention on this company:

Subject	As many as two-thirds of America's high school juniors and seniors
Reasons why he uses McDonald's	now hold down part-time paying jobs, according to studies. Many of these are in fast-food chains, of which McDonald's is the pioneer, trend-setter, and symbol. (par. 2)

For information on documenting sources, see the Appendix, pp. 509–36.

Although the fact that many teenagers hold fast-food jobs is common knowledge, Etzioni cites statistics to establish how widespread it is: "As many as two-thirds of America's high school juniors and seniors. . . ." (par. 2). Notice that he refers generally to "studies" without providing any detail that would help readers follow up on his sources. Later, however, he uses researchers' names and the publication dates to cite his sources more specifically, although still informally. Etzioni's original newspaper readers would have been used to such informal references, but if he were writing for an academic audience, he would be expected to use a conventional documentation style.

Etzioni also names several other "fast-food chains" (par. 5) to make the point that he is not singling out McDonald's but using it as an example and "symbol." He spends a good portion of the rest of his evaluation describing the kind of job he objects to.

Analyze & Write

Write a paragraph analyzing how Etzioni describes McDonald's-type jobs:

1. First, underline the factual details in paragraphs 5–7, 9, 12, 15, and 16 that describe the people who work at fast-food restaurants and what they do.

2. How do the details Etzioni provides in these paragraphs help you understand the subject of his essay as important or worth reading about?

3. Which of the details in these paragraphs do you accept as valid, inaccurate, or only partially true? How fair does Etzioni's description seem to you?

Supporting the Judgment

Evaluations analyze the subject, but they also present an argument designed to convince readers that the writer's judgment is trustworthy because the reasons are

- based on criteria, such as shared values, that are appropriate to the subject
- backed by reliable evidence

Writers usually declare their overall judgment early in the essay and may repeat it in the essay's conclusion. This judgment is the main idea or thesis, asserting that the subject is good or bad, or better or worse than something comparable. For example, Etzioni opens with the straightforward judgment:

Judgment   McDonald's is bad for your kids. (par. 1)

Although readers expect a definitive judgment, they also appreciate a balanced one that acknowledges good as well as bad qualities, so Etzioni acknowledges the benefits of fast-food jobs for teenagers:

Good qualities of   They provide very large numbers of teen jobs, provide regular
fast-food job   employment, pay quite well compared to many other teen jobs,
                     and, in the modern equivalent of toiling over a hot stove, test one's
                     stamina. (par. 5)

Etzioni makes two additional moves typical of strong reviews:

1. He reaches out to readers to establish shared values.

2. He gives reasons backed by evidence to support his judgment:

Shared value   At first, such jobs may seem right out of the Founding Fathers' educa-
Reason   tional manual for how to bring up self-reliant, work-ethic-driven, pro-
                ductive youngsters. But in fact, these jobs undermine school
                attendance and involvement, impart few skills that will be useful in
                later life, and simultaneously skew the values of teen-agers — especially
                their ideas about the worth of a dollar. (par. 3)

By referring to "the Founding Fathers" and using familiar phrases (such as "self-reliant" and "work-ethic") that connote traditional values, Etzioni builds his argument on values he expects his audience will share. But to be convincing, the reasons also must be supported by **evidence** such as facts, *s*tatistics, expert testimony, research studies, relevant examples, or personal anecdotes.

Analyze & Write

Write a paragraph analyzing how Etzioni supports one of his reasons:

1. First, choose *one* of the reasons Etzioni introduces in paragraph 3 and find the passage later in the essay where you think he supports that part of the argument.

For more on evaluating the logic of an argument, see Chapter 2, pp. 40–41.

2. Then analyze Etzioni's argument. For example, what kinds of evidence does he provide? Is the evidence appropriate and believable? Why or why not?

3. Would Etzioni's original *Miami Herald* readers have found this part of the argument convincing? Explain why you think so.

Responding to Objections or Alternative Judgments

Writers of evaluations often respond to possible objections and alternative judgments their readers may be likely to raise. They may **refute** (argue against) objections or alternative judgments they believe are weak or flawed, or they may **concede** (accept) objections and judgments they think are valid. To alert readers that a response is coming, reviewers may provide a transition or other cue. Here's an example of a refutation from Etzioni:

> Alternative judgment
> Cue
> Refutation
>
> The authors argue that the employees develop many skills such as how to operate a food-preparation machine and a cash register. However, little attention is paid to how long it takes to acquire such a skill, or what its significance is.
>
> What does it matter if you spend 20 minutes to learn to use a cash register, and then — "operate" it? What skill have you acquired? It is a long way from learning to work with a lathe or carpenter tools in the olden days or to program computers in the modern age. (pars. 8–9)

Notice the basic structure of a refutation. (The cue signaling refutation is highlighted.)

▶ X says _____, but I think _____ because _____.

Here's an example of conceding valid concerns or objections:

> [Fast-food jobs] provide very large numbers of teen jobs, provide regular employment, pay quite well compared to many other teen jobs, and, in the modern equivalent of toiling over a hot stove, test one's stamina. (par. 5)

Below are some typical sentence strategies for conceding, with cues signaling concession highlighted:

▶ Of course, ... is an important factor.
▶ Granted, ... must be taken into consideration.

Frequently, though, reviewers reach out to those who hold an opposing position by first conceding a portion of that position but then going on to indicate where they differ:

Cue signaling concession   True, you still have to have the gumption to get yourself over to the hamburger stand, but once you don the prescribed uniform, your task
Cue signaling refutation   is spelled out in minute detail. (par. 7)

Etzioni often uses this strategy of concession followed by refutation when citing research that initially appears to undermine his claim. For example, he begins by conceding when he cites a study by Harrell and Wirtz (par. 10) that links work as a student with greater likelihood of employment later on. However, he then refutes the significance of this finding, reinterpreting the data to suggest that the high likelihood of future employment could be an indication that workers in fast-food restaurants are more likely to drop out of school than an indication that workers are learning important employment skills. This strategy of conceding and then refuting by reinterpreting evidence can be especially effective in college writing, as Etzioni (a professor) well knows.

Analyze & Write

Write a paragraph analyzing how Etzioni responds to objections or alternative judgments.

1. First, find and highlight the alternative judgment or objection in paragraphs 8–11, 14, and 19.

2. Then choose *one* of these objections or alternative judgments and determine whether Etzioni responds by refuting or conceding or both.

3. Finally, evaluate the effectiveness of Etzioni's response. What made his response convincing (or unconvincing) for his original readers? How about for you reading today?

Organizing the Evaluation

Writers of evaluation usually try to make their writing clear, logical, and easy for readers to follow by providing cues or road signs. For example, they may

● forecast their reasons early in the essay and repeat key terms (or synonyms) from these reasons later in the evaluation

- use topic sentences to announce the subject of each paragraph or group of paragraphs
- use transitions (such as *but, however, on the other hand, thus*) to guide readers from one point to another

These strategies are all helpful and are often expected in college writing.

As we've seen, Etzioni forecasts his reasons in paragraph 3:

Forecasting statement
: . . . these jobs undermine school attendance and involvement, impart few skills that will be useful in later life, and simultaneously skew the values of teen-agers — especially their ideas about the worth of a dollar.

He develops the argument supporting each of these reasons in subsequent paragraphs. His essay would be easier to follow if he addressed the reasons in the order he first introduced them in paragraph 3. Nevertheless, he helps readers find the reasons by repeating key terms, as when he uses the phrase "marketable *skills*" (par. 11) to refer to "few skills" from his forecasting statement; or he uses a close substitute, as when he uses the phrase "drop out of *high school*" (par. 10) to refer to "*undermine school attendance*" in paragraph 3.

Topic sentences are also used to orient readers. Often placed at the beginning of a paragraph or related sequence of paragraphs, they announce the topic that will be developed in the subsequent sentences. For example:

Topic sentence
Examples of traditional kids' jobs
What these jobs teach
: It has been a longstanding American tradition that youngsters ought to get paying jobs. In folklore, few pursuits are more deeply revered than the newspaper route and the sidewalk lemonade stand. Here the youngsters are to learn how sweet are the fruits of labor and self-discipline (papers are delivered early in the morning, rain or shine), and the ways of trade (if you price your lemonade too high or too low . . .). (par. 4)

Notice that Etzioni focuses this paragraph on the topic of useful skills he introduced in the preceding forecasting statement. The next two paragraphs use topic sentences to make the argument that fast-food jobs "seem" like traditional jobs, but they do not teach really valuable skills. Skimming the sequence of topic sentences in paragraphs 5 and 6, you can get an idea of the outline of Etzioni's argument:

Transitions
: Roy Rogers, Baskin Robbins, Kentucky Fried Chicken, et al. may at first seem nothing but a vast extension of the lemonade stand. . . .

Closer examination, however, finds the McDonald's kind of job highly uneducational in several ways. . . .

As the two topic sentences above suggest, transitions (and other cues) also play an important role in clarifying the logic of a sequence. For example, *at first* suggests that what follows is only a tentative conclusion, especially when combined with the hedging words *may* and *seem*; *however* firmly establishes a contrast or contradiction to that provisional conclusion.

Analyze & Write

Write a paragraph analyzing how Etzioni helps readers track his argument and how effective the cues he uses are.

1. Look at the way Etzioni uses topic sentences in the rest of his essay to announce the subject of individual paragraphs or groups of paragraphs.

2. Find a couple of examples that you think work well. What makes these topic sentences effective?

READINGS

Molly McHugh

This App Digitally Curates Your Messiest Past Relationships. Yay?

Molly McHugh is a digital journalist and opinion writer whose work has been featured on *Yahoo*, *Salon*, *Slate*, and the *Week*, among other online publications. McHugh served as Technology Sections Editor of the *Daily Dot*, where she also wrote on controversial topics related to privacy and voyeur pornography. As Products Editor at *Wired*, McHugh writes reviews, how-to videos, and appears on Gadget Lab podcasts. This review of the Shryne App originally appeared in *Wired*.

- **Before you read,** think about any mementos you keep from your past and consider why you keep them.

- **As you read,** reflect on the way technology makes it possible to save—indeed, hard *not* to save—mementos from your past, even if you don't think of yourself as someone who saves such things.

What are the pros and cons of beginning with this anecdote?

Years ago, a boyfriend and I drunkenly wandered into a construction site, where each of us stole a doorknob for no reason other than it would be "a thing" we'd done together. It sounds stupid in hindsight, but it was at that point in the relationship where everything is a little blurry because you're emotionally hurtling toward each other, so you just go with it. The doorknobs sat on the mantel in the apartment we shared, and when we split up three years later, my doorknob went into a box, and the box went under my bed. Even now, coming across that doorknob is like a fishhook tugging at my gut. And so it goes back into the box, with everything else from my past that is important, if occasionally painful. 1

We all have a box. And if you're anything like me, you open it from time to time and after some momentary, futile resistance, gingerly go through it. Maybe you start with a card. Or a photo. Or whatever it is that's your version of my doorknob. Hours later, you'll realize you've dissected every memento you pointedly keep hidden from yourself. 2

Shryne is the digital version of that box and the obsession it compels. The app collects data from your social media and email and other accounts and creates something akin to a digital scrapbook. Rather than letting you stumble upon these things in your Facebook feed or Gmail history, Shryne encourages you to seek them out so it can label and organize them. It's like 3 a beautiful filing system for your digital past, a box for everyone in your life. . . . The idea is to collate and curate just about everything you say and share online. It will gather images from Facebook, Instagram, or your camera roll, as well as your texting, Gchat, Gmail, and Messenger histories. Broadly speaking, Shryne allows you to create a beautiful landing page and timeline for all your digital interactions with someone.

4   "I realized that a surprisingly complete index of our social lives exists in our communication records with others, so understanding one's past through individual relationships felt like an intuitive step," says Aldo Cherdabayev, who came up with the idea for Shryne while working as an architect. "It can be quite surreal to see a relationship from start to finish in one feed, and each archive becomes a powerful biographical milestone."

5   Shryne isn't entirely predicated on the idea of reliving failed romances. In large part, its core mission is to unite all the digital ephemera you've scattered across the Internet. "Shryne's objective is to make getting files from all these sources as painless as possible," Cherdabayev says. But while Shryne is about collecting all the files related to any relationship—mom, co-worker, best friend—everyone should just assume the ex category is going to be a popular one. . . .

6   It isn't the easiest tool to use (something Cherdabayev readily admits), and there are several things Shryne doesn't include but should (WhatsApp, for example). A forthcoming update should address some of its early bugs. But the bigger problem isn't how Shryne works, but whether you really want it to. As much as we all like to occasionally sift through our box, doing so digitally might do us more harm that good. A box can be hidden away. An app is always right there.

7   Still, as someone who loves digital organization and traipsing into emotional minefields, I had to try it. I tiptoed into Shryne by making an archive for my sister. It was easy and fun, and I felt no fishhook tug. Which is why I knew I had to dive in and make an archive for my ex.

8   The problem with any relationship organizer is that it tries to do something really, really hard: create a record of our past. The past is messy, especially when it comes to relationships—so messy that we sometimes delete it. We delete Gmail archives and Facebook Messages. We delete people from our phones, because simply seeing the number is too much to bear. We delete photos because even an accidental glimpse might send us reeling.

9   Even the stuff we keep can be messy, even meaningless. It can be a little depressing when nearly all the archived emails from your most recent relationship read something like "Can you get bread? Do we have milk?" followed by a Kanye shrug GIF. It might have been a great relationship, but seeing that all your communication was so banal makes you wonder if it wasn't. Shryne can minimize some interactions, while giving others outsized emotional heft.

On what criteria does McHugh base her judgment of Shryne's beauty and efficiency?

Why do you think McHugh focuses on "the ex category"?

If this is a positive evaluation, why does McHugh acknowledge problems?

Is personal experience a good way to support your evaluation? Why or why not?

What's repeated in these sentence openings—and what's the effect?

What assumptions does McHugh make about relationships and the things we leave behind?

There's also the fact that even the best curator will inevitably leave　10 something out. Yes, it's a safe bet Facebook, Instagram, and Gmail preserved great swaths of your relationship, but there are many things Shryne completely ignores. Your Amazon history is but one example. Even now, whenever I peruse my order history, I come across gifts bought for an ex. My Google Maps is another; the timeline pinpoints our adventures together. Spotify playlists— the ones made while we were together and when we were breaking up. WhatsApp chats, Flickr photos. None of these things make it into the box Shryne creates for you.

What else is not likely to be covered by Shryne? Does it really matter how thorough the archive is?

What does make it in, though, is hard to argue with. You can't remember　11 things with rose-tinted glasses like you would when you pick up a photo or a T-shirt, and you can certainly warp your mind into believing you were the better half. But seeing things in plain old pixels should make things starkly accurate.

But it's simultaneously sobering and heady to see it all contained in your　12 phone: You can't reinvent how a conversation went, because it's just there in black and white. Here's the thing though: The parts that are missing— what was deleted or what happened in real life moments after—those holes are what your brain tries to fill in when you're scrolling through Shryne. And that's a dangerous game.

Don't we always "fill in" memories? Why does McHugh think Shryne makes remembering more dangerous?

In any relationship, romantic or otherwise, there are things we keep and　13 things we discard, and we make those choices for a reason. The problem with Shryne, or maybe love in the Internet age, is it allows us to keep far more than we should (or knew we kept) while not allowing us to hide it. It is always right there. After all, an app on my phone screen begs for my attention far more loudly than a box under my bed.

A recent study asked more than 200 Facebook users nearly 80 questions　14 about their relationship with their exes on Facebook. "People who accepted former partners' invitations to become Facebook friends," it found, "were much more depressed than those who did not." Time heals all wounds, but it doesn't help when you're constantly seeing updates in your feed.

It's more than just Facebook photos making you sad. Another oft-cited　15 study on Facebook's impact on breakups found that the fact we cannot physically touch (or hide) our digital mementos makes them far more volatile than physical ones. "Unlike objects in a shoebox, these cannot be put away in a closet," the study states. "On Facebook, it is easy to stumble across, or actively seek, old pictures that one may be better off not seeing." In other words, if you have an app that beautifully collates your digital memories of someone, you're going to look at it and it's going to hurt.

How do the Facebook research studies McHugh cites relate to her evaluation?

"You can look at Shryne all the time on a smartphone, but a shoebox full　16 of old mementos is probably tucked away some place and only looked at occasionally," says Dr. Tara Marshall, who studied how Facebook surveillance impacts breakups. "The more reminders you have of your ex, the harder it is to get over them; out of sight, out of mind." This is especially true right after a breakup; the first two or three months are especially raw and probably not the time to make or peruse a Shryne archive. Marshall's research found that people who kept tabs on an ex's Facebook profile experience "greater distress, lower personal growth, more negative feelings toward the ex . . . but also greater longing and sexual desire for the ex" than those who cut digital ties.

17   Of course, there's some chicken-and-egg thinking at work here. "People who use Shryne for an ex-partner may report worse post-breakup recovery, but it's also likely that people who have worse post-breakup recovery would be more likely to use Shryne," Marshall says. It's difficult to determine whether something like Shryne might cause someone to have a hard time moving on or simply make an already difficult process that much harder.

18   It's not all bad news, though. Marshall says people who dwell on a breakup can grow from it, and Shryne might help them move on. "Something like Shryne might allow some people to reflect on the past relationship and breakup, piecing together a narrative about what went wrong," she says. . . . To fully explore what Shryne can do, I created an archive of my ex (he of doorknob fame). Looking at my archive, I saw patterns emerge. I saw myself picking the same fights, using the same defenses. I've got some level of emotional maturity and I am aware of my habits, but seeing the exact same wording in two different arguments was a revelation. The silver lining to the heartache Shryne (and digital memorabilia in general) can create is perhaps it can keep us from repeating the same mistakes in subsequent relationships. The risk you take for this insight, of course, is navigating some dull emotional torture. But pain is the touchstone of all growth.

> How does McHugh use her personal experience to support her evaluation?

19   What surprised me most, though, is how incomplete my digital past is, and how much of it I'd thrown away. I'd long since deleted untold gigabytes of our Gchat and Gmail history. It was the same story with our SMS. And the app can't access all your Facebook photo albums, so I had only a handful to include. Once Shryne did collect everything, reading it was downright shocking: I watched us go from flirting to fighting and then breaking up—something that occurred over the course of four years—within a minute or two of scrolling. So now, the archive sitting in my Shryne app is a pitiful synopsis of what was a rich, formative, and incredibly important experience. Its incompleteness is just a reminder of how much information I suppressed and distanced myself from.

20   In concept, Shryne makes a lot of sense. For family and friends and even acquaintances, a beautiful landing page of your most important relationships is a novel idea. It's wonderful seeing a friendship evolve, or remembering a loved one who's passed. But if you're going to wade into these tricky emotional waters, there is one category that should be avoided by all but the strongest swimmers: your exes. Leave them in that box under the bed and whatever corner of the Internet deleted data is banished to.

> How effective is this way of concluding an evaluation?

Emily Nussbaum

The Aristocrats: The Graphic Arts of *Game of Thrones*

Emily Nussbaum has written for numerous publications including the *New York Times, Slate,* and *New York* magazine, for which she worked as culture editor. Currently, she is the Pulitzer Prize–winning television critic for the *New Yorker,* in which this review originally appeared. Her initial fascination with analyzing and critiquing television programs sprang from an obsession with *Buffy the Vampire Slayer.* Her reviews and commentary have become influential particularly in discussions about the effects of technology and social media on television as a medium and on our viewing habits.

- **Before you read,** notice that Nussbaum begins with a little narrative about her job as a television reviewer. How does this story prepare you for what follows?

- **As you read,** consider how effectively Nussbaum establishes her credibility as a reviewer. What in her evaluation, if anything, helps demonstrate her expertise?

For critics, sorting through television pilots is an act of triage. Last year, when *Game of Thrones* landed on my desk, I skimmed two episodes and made a quick call: we'd have to let this one go. The HBO series, based on the best-selling fantasy books by George R. R. Martin, looked as if it were another guts-and-corsets melodrama, like *The Borgias.* In the première, a ten-year-old boy was shoved out of a tower window. The episode climaxed with what might be described as an Orientalist gang rape/wedding dance. I figured I might catch up later, if the buzz was good.

It was the right decision, even if I made it for the wrong reason. *Game of Thrones* is an ideal show to binge-watch on DVD: with its cliffhangers and Grand Guignol[1] dazzle, it rewards a bloody, committed immersion in its foreign world—and by this I mean not only the medieval-ish landscape of Westeros (the show's mythical realm) but the genre from which it derives. Fantasy—like television itself, really—has long been burdened with audience condescension: the assumption that it's trash, or juvenile, something intrinsically icky and low. Several reviews of *Game of Thrones* have taken this stance, including two notable writeups in the *Times:* Ginia Bellafante sniffed that the show was "boy fiction" and Neil Genzlinger called it "vileness for voyeurism's sake," directed at "Dungeons & Dragons[2] types."

It's true that *Game of Thrones* is unusually lurid, even within the arms race of pay cable: the show is so graphic that it was parodied on *Saturday Night Live,* with a

---

[1]An over-the-top style of entertainment designed to shock and thrill viewers, originally of the kind produced at the Grand Guignol Theater in Paris. [Editor's note]

[2]A role-play war game in a fantasy setting. [Editor's note]

"behind-the-scenes" skit in which a horny thirteen-year-old boy acted as a consultant. To watch it, you must steel yourself for baby-stabbing, as well as rat torture and murder by molten gold. But, once I began sliding in disks in a stupor, it became clear that, despite the show's Maltese vistas and asymmetrical midriff tops, this was not really an exotic property. To the contrary, *Game of Thrones* is the latest entry in television's most esteemed category: the sophisticated cable drama about a patriarchal subculture. This phenomenon launched with *The Sopranos*, but it now includes shows such as *Deadwood*, *Mad Men*, *Downton Abbey*, and *Big Love*. Each of these acclaimed series is a sprawling, multi-character exploration of a closed, often violent hierarchical system. These worlds are picturesque, elegantly filmed, and ruled by rigid etiquette—lit up, for viewers, by the thrill of seeing brutality enforced (or, in the case of *Downton Abbey*, a really nice house kept in the family). And yet the undergirding strength of each series is its insight into what it means to be excluded from power: to be a woman, or a bastard, or a "half man."

The first season of *Game of Thrones* built up skillfully, sketching in ten episodes a conflict among the kingdoms of Westeros, each its own philosophical ecosystem. There were the Northern Starks, led by the gruffly ethical Ned Stark and his dignified wife, Catelyn, and their gruffly ethical and dignified children. There were the Southern Lannisters, a crowd of high-cheekboned beauties (and one lusty dwarf, played by the lust-worthy Peter Dinklage), who form a family constellation so twisted, charismatic, and cruel that it rivals *Flowers in the Attic*[3] for blond dysfunction. Across the sea, there were the Dothraki, a Hun-like race of horseman warriors, whose brutal ruler, Drogo, took the delicate, unspellable Daenerys as a bride. A teen girl traded like currency by her brother, Daenerys was initiated into marriage through rape; in time, she began to embrace both that marriage and her desert queenhood. (Although the cast is mostly white, the dusky-race aesthetics of the Dothraki sequences are head-clutchingly problematic.) By the finale, she was standing naked in the desert—widowed, traumatized, but triumphant, with three baby dragons crawling over her like vines. (This quick summary doesn't capture the complexity of the series' ensemble, which rivals a Bosch painting: there's also the whispery eunuch Spider; a scheming brothel owner named Littlefinger; and a ketchup-haired sorceress who gives birth to shadow babies.)

In the season's penultimate episode, the show made a radical move: it killed off the protagonist. On a public stage, Ned Stark was beheaded, on the orders of the teen-age sadist King Joffrey, a sequence edited with unusual beauty and terror—birds fluttering in the air, a hushed soundtrack, and a truly poignant shot from Ned's point of view, as he looked out toward his two daughters. This primal act suggested the limits of ethical behavior in a brutalized universe, and also dramatized the show's vision of what aristocracy means: a succession of domestic traumas, as each new regent dispatches

---

[3]A popular novel by V. C. Andrews in which a newly widowed (and indebted) mother moves her children into the attic of her estranged parents' home, while she tries to win back their affections so she will inherit their fortune. This novel has formed the basis of a number of movies and made-for-TV movies since it was published in 1979. [Editor's note]

threats to his bloodline. (Or, as Joffrey's mother, Cersei, puts it, kinghood means "lying on a bed of weeds, ripping them out one by one, before they strangle you in your sleep.") It demonstrated, too, a willingness to risk alienating its audience. . . .

Still, the most compelling plots remain those of the subalterns, who are forced to 6
wield power from below. These characters range from heroic figures like the tomboy Arya Stark to villains like Littlefinger, but even the worst turn out to have psychic wounds that complicate their actions. If the show has a hero, it's Tyrion (Dinklage), who is capable of cruelty but also possesses insight and empathy, concealed beneath a carapace of Wildean wit. So far, his strategic gifts have proved more effective than the torture-with-rats approach. Power is "a trick, a shadow on the wall," the eunuch tells Tyrion. "And a very small man can cast a very large shadow."

Then, of course, there are the whores. From the start, the show has featured copious 7
helpings of pay-cable nudity, much of it in scenes that don't strictly require a woman to display her impressive butt dimples as the backdrop for a monologue about kings. (The most common fan idiom for these sequences is "sexposition," but I've also seen them referred to as "data humps.") These scenes are at once a turn-on and a turn-off. At times, I found myself marveling at the way that HBO has solved the riddle of its own economic existence, merging *Hookers at the Point*[4] with quasi-Shakespearean narrative. In the most egregious instance so far, Littlefinger tutored two prostitutes in how to moan in fake lesbianism for their customers, even as they moaned in fake lesbianism for us.

Viewed in another light, however, these sex scenes aren't always so gratuitous. Like 8
Mad Men, Game of Thrones is elementally concerned with the way that meaningful consent dissolves when female bodies are treated as currency. War means raping the enemy's women; princesses go for a higher price, because their wombs are the coin of the realm, cementing strategic alliances. It helps that the narrative is equally fascinated by the ways in which women secure authority, and even pleasure, within these strictures, and that in the second season its bench of female characters has got even deeper—among them, a seafaring warrior princess, a butch knight, and Tyrion's prostitute girlfriend.

Game of Thrones is not coy about the way the engine of misogyny can grind the 9
fingers of those who try to work it in their favor. An episode two weeks ago featured a sickening sequence in which King Joffrey ordered one prostitute—a character the audience had grown to care about—to rape another. The scenario . . . seemed designed not to turn viewers on but to confront them with the logical endgame of this pornographic system. . . . But while the scene may have been righteous in theory, in practice it was jarring, and slightly incoherent, particularly since it included the creamy nudity we've come to expect as visual dessert.

As with *True Blood*, the show's most graphic elements—the cruel ones, the fantasy 10
ones, and the cruel-fantasy ones—speak to female as well as male viewers. (One of the nuttiest quotes I've ever read came from Alan Ball, *True Blood's* showrunner,[5] who

---

[4]A 2002 HBO documentary about prostitutes working the Hunts Point neighborhood in New York's South Bronx. [Editor's note]

[5]The producer responsible for day-to-day management of a television program. [Editor's note]

said that a focus group had revealed that men watched his series for the sex and women for the romance. Please.) But there is something troubling about this sea of C.G.I.[6]-perfect flesh, shaved and scentless and not especially medieval. It's unsettling to recall that these are not merely pretty women; they are unknown actresses who must strip, front and back, then mimic graphic sex and sexual torture, a skill increasingly key to attaining employment on cable dramas. During the filming of the second season, an Irish actress walked off the set when her scene shifted to what she termed "soft porn." Of course, not everyone strips: there are no truly explicit scenes of gay male sex, fewer lingering shots of male bodies, and the leading actresses stay mostly buttoned up. Artistically, *Game of Thrones* is in a different class from *House of Lies*, *Californication*, and *Entourage*. But it's still part of another colorful patriarchal subculture, the one called Los Angeles.

READING FOR MEANING

1. **Read to Summarize.** Write a sentence or two restating in your own words Nussbaum's evaluation of *Game of Thrones* and her supporting reasons.

For more on summarizing, see Chapter 2, pp. 24–25.

2. **Read to Respond.** Write a paragraph analyzing anything in the essay that you find surprising, such as the assertion that the genre of fantasy is "trash, or juvenile" (par. 2) or "the most compelling plots remain those of the subalterns" (par. 6).

3. **Read to Analyze Assumptions.** Write a paragraph or two analyzing an assumption you find intriguing in Nussbaum's essay. For example:

For help analyzing assumptions, see Chapter 2, pp. 28–29.

   Assumptions about binge watching. "*Game of Thrones* is an ideal show to binge-watch," Nussbaum proclaims (par. 2). Her reason is that "with its cliffhangers and Grand Guignol dazzle, it rewards a bloody, committed immersion in its foreign world."

   • Nussbaum assumes that a program like *Game of Thrones* is "ideal" for binge watching because it draws viewers into a complex imaginary world (par. 2). Why do you think being immersed in an imagined world is a—or even *the*—main attraction of binge watching? Or do you think something else matters more, and if so, what?

   • Nussbaum suggests that the kinds of imagined worlds viewers gravitate toward (at least at the time she was writing) portray "a closed, often violent hierarchical system" that shows "what it means to be excluded from power" (par. 3). Why do you imagine viewers might be enticed by this theme?

   Assumptions about sexploitation. Nussbaum does not use the term *sexploitation* — exploiting or profiting from sexual images in the media — but she does apparently assume her readers are aware of the concept. These images, Nussbaum notes, range from what she calls "the creamy nudity we've come to

[6]Computer-generated imagery. [Editor's note]

expect as visual dessert" (par. 9) to the graphic violence of rape and "sexual torture" (par. 10).

- If you are familiar with *Game of Thrones* or a similar program, do you think it is fair to apply the label *sexploitation* to the series? Why or why not? Given your viewing experience of other television or cable programs, how prevalent is sexploitation in the media?

- In the concluding paragraphs, Nussbaum suggests that the creators of *Game of Thrones* are trying to have it both ways: critiquing "this pornographic system" (par. 9), while still participating in the entertainment industry's exploitation of "unknown actresses who must strip, front and back, then mimic graphic sex and sexual torture" (par. 10). How do the programs with which you are familiar try to critique the system, if indeed you think they do?

READING LIKE A WRITER

PRESENTING THE SUBJECT

Writers of evaluative essays usually begin by identifying the subject being evaluated. The strategies used to present the subject include naming it (often in the title, as Etzioni does). But if, as in Etzioni's case, the name (*McDonald's*) is meant to stand for a general category or genre (fast-food restaurant jobs), then naming other familiar examples of the genre may also be necessary ("Roy Rogers, Baskin Robbins, Kentucky Fried Chicken" [par. 5]). Later in this chapter, Christine Romano uses the same two strategies when she names her subject ("organized competitive sports" for kids) and cites two examples of the genre ("Peewee Football and Little League Base- ball" [par. 1]). Identifying the genre is important for all subjects, but crucial for story-based subjects because different genres — of film, for example — have differ- ent criteria to meet. All films may be evaluated on the basis of factors such as acting and direction. But comedies have to be funny, and action films have to be exciting. Therefore, as a critical reader, you will want to think about how Nussbaum classifies *Game of Thrones* and whether the genre and therefore the criteria she applies are appropriate.

Analyze & Write

Write a paragraph analyzing how Nussbaum presents *Game of Thrones*.

1. Reread paragraphs 1–3, noting the various ways Nussbaum describes *Game of Thrones*. What kinds of information does she tell her audience about the program?

2. What genres does Nussbaum use to categorize *Game of Thrones?*

3. What other examples of these genres does she use for comparison? What crite- ria does Nussbaum indicate are usually used to evaluate works in these genres?

Malcolm Gladwell

What College Rankings Really Tell Us

Malcolm Gladwell (b. 1963) has a BA in history from the University of Toronto. He is a staff writer for the *New Yorker* magazine and has written a number of best-selling books, including *Outliers: The Story of Success* (2008) and *Blink: The Power of Thinking without Thinking* (2005). He received the American Sociological Association Award for Excellence in the Reporting of Social Issues and was named one of the hundred most influential people by *Time* magazine. "What College Rankings Really Tell Us" (2011) evaluates the popular *U.S. News* "Best Colleges" annual guide. You may be familiar with this guide and may have even consulted it when selecting a college. Excerpted from a longer *New Yorker* article, Gladwell's evaluation focuses on the *U.S. News* ranking system.

- **Before you read,** think about the criteria that are important to you for choosing a college.

- **As you read** Gladwell's review, consider who, besides prospective college students, would be likely to think the criteria *U.S. News* uses to rank colleges are important, and why.

Car and Driver conducted a comparison test of three sports cars, the Lotus Evora, the Chevrolet Corvette Grand Sport, and the Porsche Cayman S. . . . Yet when you inspect the magazine's tabulations it is hard to figure out why *Car and Driver* was so sure that the Cayman is better than the Corvette and the Evora. The trouble starts with the fact that the ranking methodology *Car and Driver* used was essentially the same one it uses for all the vehicles it tests—from S.U.V.s to economy sedans. It's not set up for sports cars. Exterior styling, for example, counts for four per cent of the total score. Has anyone buying a sports car ever placed so little value on how it looks? Similarly, the categories of "fun to drive" and "chassis"—which cover the subjective experience of driving the car—count for only eighty-five points out of the total of two hundred and thirty-five. That may make sense for S.U.V. buyers. But, for people interested in Porsches and Corvettes and Lotuses, the subjective experience of driving is surely what matters most. In other words, in trying to come up with a ranking that is heterogeneous—a methodology that is broad enough to cover all vehicles—*Car and Driver* ended up with a system that is absurdly ill-suited to some vehicles. . . .

A heterogeneous ranking system works if it focuses just on, say, how much fun a car is to drive, or how good-looking it is, or how beautifully it handles. The magazine's ambition to create a comprehensive ranking system—one that considered cars along twenty-one variables, each weighted according to a secret sauce cooked up by the editors—would also be fine, as long as the cars being compared were truly similar. It's only when one car is thirteen thousand dollars more than another that juggling twenty-one variables starts to break down, because you're faced with the impossible task of deciding how much a difference of that degree ought to matter. A ranking can be heterogeneous, in other words, as long as it doesn't try to be too comprehensive. And it can be comprehensive as long as it doesn't try to measure things that are heterogeneous. But it's an act of real audacity when a ranking system tries to be comprehensive and heterogeneous—which is the first thing to keep in mind in any consideration of *U.S. News & World Report*'s annual "Best Colleges" guide.

The *U.S. News* rankings . . . relies on seven weighted variables: 3

1. Undergraduate academic reputation, 22.5 per cent
2. Graduation and freshman retention rates, 20 per cent
3. Faculty resources, 20 per cent
4. Student selectivity, 15 per cent
5. Financial resources, 10 per cent
6. Graduation rate performance, 7.5 per cent
7. Alumni giving, 5 per cent

From these variables, *U.S. News* generates a score for each institution on a scale of 1 to 100. . . . This ranking system looks a great deal like the *Car and Driver* methodology. It is heterogeneous. It doesn't just compare U.C. Irvine, the University of Washington, the University of Texas–Austin, the University of Wisconsin–Madison, Penn State, and the University of Illinois, Urbana–Champaign—all public institutions of roughly the same size. It aims to compare Penn State—a very large, public, land-grant university with a low tuition and an economically diverse student body, set in a rural valley in central Pennsylvania and famous for its football team—with Yeshiva University, a small, expensive, private Jewish university whose undergraduate program is set on two campuses in Manhattan (one in midtown, for the women, and one far uptown, for the men) and is definitely not famous for its football team.

The system is also comprehensive. It doesn't simply compare schools along one   4 dimension—the test scores of incoming freshmen, say, or academic reputation. An algorithm takes a slate of statistics on each college and transforms them into a single score: it tells us that Penn State is a better school than Yeshiva by one point. It is easy to see why the *U.S. News* rankings are so popular. A single score allows us to judge between entities (like Yeshiva and Penn State) that otherwise would be impossible to compare. . . .

A comprehensive, heterogeneous ranking system was a stretch for *Car and*   5 *Driver*—and all it did was rank inanimate objects operated by a single person. The Penn State campus at University Park is a complex institution with dozens of schools and departments, four thousand faculty members, and forty-five thousand students. How on earth does anyone propose to assign a number to something like that?

The first difficulty with rankings is that it can be surprisingly hard to measure the   6 variable you want to rank—even in cases where that variable seems perfectly objective. . . . There's no direct way to measure the quality of an institution—how well a college manages to inform, inspire, and challenge its students. So the *U.S. News* algorithm relies instead on proxies for quality—and the proxies for educational quality turn out to be flimsy at best.

Take the category of "faculty resources," which counts for twenty per cent of an   7 institution's score (number 3 on the chart above). "Research shows that the more satisfied students are about their contact with professors," the College Guide's explanation of the category begins, "the more they will learn and the more likely it is they will graduate." That's true. According to educational researchers, arguably the most important variable in a successful college education is a vague but crucial concept called student "engagement"—that is, the extent to which students immerse themselves in the intellectual and social life of their college—and a major component of engagement is the quality of a student's contacts with faculty. . . . So what proxies does *U.S. News* use to measure this elusive dimension of engagement? The explanation goes on:

> We use six factors from the 2009–10 academic year to assess a school's commitment to instruction. Class size has two components, the proportion of classes with fewer than 20 students (30 percent of the faculty resources score) and the proportion with 50 or more students (10 percent of the score). Faculty salary (35 percent) is the average faculty pay, plus benefits, during the 2008–09 and 2009–10 academic years, adjusted for regional differences in the cost of living. . . . We also weigh the proportion of professors with the highest degree in their fields (15 percent), the student-faculty ratio (5 percent), and the proportion of faculty who are full time (5 percent).

This is a puzzling list. Do professors who get paid more money really take their   8 teaching roles more seriously? And why does it matter whether a professor has the highest degree in his or her field? Salaries and degree attainment are known to be predictors of research productivity. But studies show that being oriented toward research has very little to do with being good at teaching. Almost none of the *U.S. News* variables, in fact, seem to be particularly effective proxies for engagement. As the educational researchers Patrick Terenzini and Ernest Pascarella concluded after analyzing twenty-six hundred reports on the effects of college on students:

> After taking into account the characteristics, abilities, and backgrounds students bring with them to college, we found that how much students grow or change has only inconsistent and, perhaps in a practical sense, trivial relationships with such traditional measures of institutional "quality" as educational expenditures per student, student/faculty ratios, faculty salaries, percentage of faculty with the highest degree in their field, faculty research productivity, size of the library, [or] admissions selectivity. . . .

There's something missing from that list of variables, of course: it doesn't include   9 price. That is one of the most distinctive features of the *U.S. News* methodology. Both its college rankings and its law-school rankings reward schools for devoting lots of financial resources to educating their students, but not for being affordable. Why? [Director of Data Research Robert] Morse admitted that there was no formal reason for that position. It was just a feeling. "We're not saying that we're measuring educational outcomes," he explained. "We're not saying we're social scientists, or we're subjecting our rankings to some peer-review process. We're just saying we've made this judgment. We're saying we've interviewed a lot of experts, we've developed these academic indicators, and we think these measures measure quality schools."

As answers go, that's up there with the parental "Because I said so." But Morse is   10
simply being honest. If we don't understand what the right proxies for college quality
are, let alone how to represent those proxies in a comprehensive, heterogeneous
grading system, then our rankings are inherently arbitrary. . . . *U.S. News* thinks that
schools that spend a lot of money on their students are nicer than those that don't, and
that this niceness ought to be factored into the equation of desirability. Plenty of
Americans agree: the campus of Vanderbilt University or Williams College is filled
with students whose families are largely indifferent to the price their school charges
but keenly interested in the flower beds and the spacious suites and the architecturally
distinguished lecture halls those high prices make possible. Of course, given that the
rising cost of college has become a significant social problem in the United States in
recent years, you can make a strong case that a school ought to be rewarded for being
affordable. . . .

The *U.S. News* rankings turn out to be full of these kinds of implicit ideological   11
choices. One common statistic used to evaluate colleges, for example, is called
"graduation rate performance," which compares a school's actual graduation rate
with its predicted graduation rate given the socioeconomic status and the test scores
of its incoming freshman class. It is a measure of the school's efficacy: it quantifies
the impact of a school's culture and teachers and institutional support mechanisms.
Tulane, given the qualifications of the students that it admits, ought to have a graduation rate of eighty-seven per cent; its actual 2009 graduation rate was seventy-three
per cent. That shortfall suggests that something is amiss at Tulane. Another common
statistic for measuring college quality is "student selectivity." This reflects variables
such as how many of a college's freshmen were in the top ten per cent of their high-
school class, how high their S.A.T. scores were, and what percentage of applicants a
college admits. Selectivity quantifies how accomplished students are when they first
arrive on campus.

Each of these statistics matters, but for very different reasons. As a society, we   12
probably care more about efficacy: America's future depends on colleges that make
sure the students they admit leave with an education and a degree. If you are a
bright high-school senior and you're thinking about your own future, though, you
may well care more about selectivity, because that relates to the prestige of your
degree. . . .

There is no right answer to how much weight a ranking system should give to these   13
two competing values. It's a matter of which educational model you value more—and
here, once again, *U.S. News* makes its position clear. It gives twice as much weight to
selectivity as it does to efficacy. . . .

Rankings are not benign. They enshrine very particular ideologies, and, at a time   14
when American higher education is facing a crisis of accessibility and affordability,
we have adopted a de facto standard of college quality that is uninterested in both
of those factors. And why? Because a group of magazine analysts in an office building in Washington, D.C., decided twenty years ago to value selectivity over
efficacy.

READING FOR MEANING

1. **Read to Summarize.** Write a sentence or two identifying Gladwell's overall judgment and his main reasons.

For help with summarizing, see Chapter 2, pp. 24–25.

2. **Read to Respond.** Write a paragraph analyzing anything that reso- nates with your experience, such as the research finding that "student 'engagement' — that is, the extent to which students immerse themselves in the intellectual and social life of their college" may be "the most important variable in a successful" educational experience (par. 7); or the fact that "price" was not included as a variable in the *U.S. News* college rankings.

3. **Read to Analyze Assumptions.** Write a paragraph or two analyzing an assumption you find intriguing in Gladwell's essay. For example:

Assumptions about ideology. **Ideology** means the ideas, beliefs, values, and concerns of an individual or a group, and it often centers on issues concern- ing power and equality. Gladwell asserts that "The *U.S. News* rankings turn out to be full of . . . implicit ideological choices" (par. 11), such as not includ- ing affordability, and valuing "selectivity over efficacy" in its ranking formula (par. 14).

For help analyzing assumptions, see Chapter 2, pp. 28–29.

- Gladwell criticizes rankings in general and the *U.S. News* ranking system in particular for having harmful effects. Who does a ranking system like that of the *U.S. News* benefit? Who does it potentially harm?

- In paragraph 14, Gladwell specifies "affordability" as an important factor or criterion. In light of "the rising cost of college," he calls affordability "a significant social problem" (par. 10). What does the omission of price indi- cate about the ideology behind the *U.S. News* ranking system? Who should care that some highly qualified students cannot afford to attend the best colleges? Why?

Assumptions about efficacy and selectivity. Gladwell explains that judging a school's efficacy is often at odds with judging its selectivity. Efficacy refers to the effectiveness in graduating the students the school accepted: in other words, the graduation rate. Selectivity refers to who is accepted in the first place, and therefore "quantifies how accomplished students are when they first arrive on campus" (par. 11).

You may also try reflecting on challenges to your beliefs and values; see Chapter 2, pp. 36–37.

- Why do you think Gladwell claims that "[a]s a society, we probably care more about efficacy" . . . but "a bright high-school senior . . . may well care more about selectivity" (par. 12)? What added benefits are there to attending a highly selective, prestigious college?

- What assumptions do we make about the value of a college education? What is its value to you personally and to society in general?

READING LIKE A WRITER

RESPONDING TO OBJECTIONS AND ALTERNATIVE JUDGMENTS

Because it is a negative evaluation, one could say that Gladwell's entire essay is an implied refutation of those who think well of the *U.S. News* college rankings. However, Gladwell also responds specifically to comments made by Robert Morse, the director of data research for *U.S. News & World Report*. Gladwell cues his refutation with the rhetorical question "Why?" and he goes on to answer by quoting Morse:

Cue
Words conveying
tone

> Why? [Director of Data Research Robert] Morse admitted that there was no formal reason for that position. It was just a feeling. "We're not saying that we're measuring educational outcomes," he explained. (par. 9)

Not only does he present his reasons for disagreeing with Morse, but Gladwell also expresses his attitude toward Morse's explanation through his choice of words. He continues in this *tone* when he comments at the beginning of the next paragraph: "As answers go, that's up there with the parental 'Because I said so'" (par. 10).

A writer's tone, especially when sarcastic or mocking, can have a strong effect on readers. Those who agree may appreciate it, but those who disagree or are uncertain may be put off by it.

| Analyze & Write |

Write a paragraph analyzing Morse's response to Gladwell and Gladwell's response to Morse:

1. Reread paragraph 9. How would you describe Morse's response to Gladwell's criticism: Which of Gladwell's points does Morse concede or refute?

2. Now reread paragraphs 10–12. How does Gladwell respond to Morse? How does he concede or refute Morse's response? How would you describe the tone, or emotional resonance, of Gladwell's response? Is he fair, mean, sarcastic, something else?

3. Given Gladwell's purpose and audience, how do you imagine readers would react to Morse's response to criticism as well as to Gladwell's handling of Morse's response? How did you respond?

A Special Reading Strategy

Judging the Writer's Credibility

Encountering an evaluation like Malcolm Gladwell's "What College Rankings Really Tell Us," readers typically consider the writer's credibility in order to determine whether what we are being told is worth taking seriously. We often take into account what we know—for example, the writer's academic and professional credentials as well as whether the text appeared in a reputable publication. But we also need to think about how the writer comes across in the text itself. In an evaluative argument, we especially want to see whether the writer is knowledgeable about the subject and fair in handling objections and alternative judgments, and also whether the writer shares our values or criteria for evaluating this kind of subject.

Follow the instructions in Chapter 2, pp. 45–46, for Judging the Writer's Credibility. As you reread Gladwell's essay, consider the questions below to help you analyze whether he comes across as a trustworthy judge of the *U.S. News & World Report* college ranking system. Then write a paragraph or two about your analysis and evaluation of Gladwell's credibility in this essay.

- If you already worked on the Reading Like a Writer activity, you've analyzed Gladwell's response to Robert Morse, the person responsible for the *U.S. News* ranking system. Now consider whether his tone makes Gladwell more or less credible. Does he seem fair or not, and why?

- Consider also how authoritative and knowledgeable Gladwell seems about ranking systems in general and the *U.S. News* system in particular. Point to any place in the essay that either instills confidence in his knowledge or makes you wonder whether he knows enough to make a judgment.

- Finally, review Gladwell's criteria. For example, do you agree or disagree that price or affordability ought to be a consideration in evaluating colleges? Do you agree with Gladwell that a college cannot be both selective and concerned with efficacy or helping students to graduate?

Christine Rosen

The Myth of Multitasking

Christine Rosen (b. 1973) holds a Ph.D. in history from Emory University and has been a scholar at the New America Foundation and the American Enterprise Institute. She has written several books, including *The Extinction of Experience* (2016), *My Fundamentalist Education* (2005), and *The Feminist Dilemma* (2001). She also coedited *Acculturated: 23 Savvy Writers Find Hidden Virtue in Reality TV, Chic Lit, Video Games, and Other Pillars of Pop Culture* (2011). A commentator on bioethics and the social effects of technology, she has frequently appeared on National Public Radio, CNN, and Fox News and in other venues. Rosen's essays have appeared in such prestigious publications as the *New York Times Magazine, Washington Post, Wall Street Journal, National Review*, and *New Atlantis: A Journal of Technology & Society*, where she is a senior editor and where this essay originally appeared in 2008.

- **Before you read,** think about what Rosen might mean by her title, "The Myth of Multitasking." What does the word *myth* lead you to expect her judgment to be?

- **As you read,** think about your own experience with multitasking and what you think its advantages and disadvantages are. How well does Rosen's essay resonate with your experience?

In one of the many letters he wrote to his son in the 1740s, Lord Chesterfield offered the following advice: "There is time enough for everything in the course of the day, if you do but one thing at once, but there is not time enough in the year, if you will do two things at a time." To Chesterfield, singular focus was not merely a practical way to structure one's time; it was a mark of intelligence. "This steady and undissipated attention to one object, is a sure mark of a superior genius; as hurry, bustle, and agitation, are the never-failing symptoms of a weak and frivolous mind." 1

In modern times, hurry, bustle, and agitation have become a regular way of life for many people—so much so that we have embraced a word to describe our efforts to respond to the many pressing demands on our time: *multitasking*. Used for decades to describe the parallel processing abilities of computers, multitasking is now shorthand for the human attempt to do simultaneously as many things as possible, as quickly as possible, preferably marshaling the power of as many technologies as possible. 2

In the late 1990s and early 2000s, one sensed a kind of exuberance about the possibilities of multitasking. Advertisements for new electronic gadgets—particularly the first generation of handheld digital devices—celebrated the notion of using technology to accomplish several things at once. The word *multitasking* began appearing in the "skills" sections of résumés, as office workers restyled themselves as high-tech, high-performing team players. "We have always multitasked—inability to walk and 3 chew gum is a time-honored cause for derision—but never so intensely or self-consciously as now," James Gleick wrote in his 1999 book *Faster*. "We are multitasking connoisseurs—experts in crowding, pressing, packing, and overlapping distinct activities in our all-too-finite moments." An article in the *New York Times Magazine* in 2001 asked, "Who can remember life before multitasking? These days we all do it." The article offered advice on "How to Multitask" with suggestions about giving your brain's "multitasking hot spot" an appropriate workout.

But more recently, challenges to the ethos of multitasking have begun to 4 emerge. Numerous studies have shown the sometimes-fatal danger of using cell phones and other electronic devices while driving, for example, and several states have now made that particular form of multitasking illegal. In the business world, where concerns about time-management are perennial, warnings about workplace distractions spawned by a multitasking culture are on the rise. In 2005, the BBC reported on a research study, funded by Hewlett-Packard and conducted by the Institute of Psychiatry at the University of London, that found, "Workers distracted by e-mail and phone calls suffer a fall in IQ more than twice that found in marijuana smokers." The psychologist who led the study called this new "infomania" a serious threat to workplace productivity. One of the *Harvard Business Review*'s "Breakthrough Ideas" for 2007 was Linda Stone's notion of "continuous partial attention," which might be understood as a subspecies of multitasking: using mobile computing power and the Internet, we are "constantly scanning for opportunities and staying on top of contacts, events, and activities in an effort to miss nothing."

Dr. Edward Hallowell, a Massachusetts-based psychiatrist who specializes in the 5 treatment of attention deficit/hyperactivity disorder and has written a book with the self-explanatory title *CrazyBusy*, has been offering therapies to combat extreme multitasking for years; in his book he calls multitasking a "mythical activity in which people believe they can perform two or more tasks simultaneously." In a 2005 article, he described a new condition, "Attention Deficit Trait," which he claims is rampant in the business world. ADT is "purely a response to the hyperkinetic environment in which we live," writes Hallowell, and its hallmark symptoms mimic those of ADD. "Never in history has the human brain been asked to track so many data points," Hallowell argues, and this challenge "can be controlled only by creatively engineering one's environment and one's emotional and physical health." Limiting multitasking is essential. Best-selling business advice author Timothy Ferriss also extols the virtues of "single-tasking" in his book, *The 4-Hour Workweek*.

Multitasking might also be taking a toll on the economy. One study by researchers 6 at the University of California at Irvine monitored interruptions among office workers; they found that workers took an average of twenty-five minutes to recover from interruptions such as phone calls or answering e-mail and return to their original task. Discussing multitasking with the *New York Times* in 2007, Jonathan B. Spira, an analyst at the business research firm Basex, estimated that extreme multitasking—information overload—costs the U.S. economy $650 billion a year in lost productivity.

CHANGING OUR BRAINS

To better understand the multitasking phenomenon, neurologists and psychologists 7
have studied the workings of the brain. In 1999, Jordan Grafman, chief of cognitive
neuroscience at the National Institute of Neurological Disorders and Stroke (part of
the National Institutes of Health), used functional magnetic resonance imaging
(fMRI) scans to determine that when people engage in "task-switching"—that is,
multitasking behavior—the flow of blood increases to a region of the frontal cortex
called Brodmann area 10. (The flow of blood to particular regions of the brain is
taken as a proxy indication of activity in those regions.) "This is presumably the last
part of the brain to evolve, the most mysterious and exciting part," Grafman told the
New York Times in 2001—adding, with a touch of hyperbole, "It's what makes us
most human."

It is also what makes multitasking a poor long-term strategy for learning. Other 8
studies, such as those performed by psychologist René Marois of Vanderbilt University,
have used fMRI to demonstrate the brain's response to handling multiple tasks. Marois
found evidence of a "response selection bottleneck" that occurs when the brain is
forced to respond to several stimuli at once. As a result, task-switching leads to time
lost as the brain determines which task to perform. Psychologist David Meyer at the
University of Michigan believes that rather than a bottleneck in the brain, a process of
"adaptive executive control" takes place, which "schedules task processes appropriately to obey instructions about their relative priorities and serial order," as he
described to the *New Scientist*. Unlike many other researchers who study multitasking, Meyer is optimistic that, with training, the brain can learn to task-switch more
effectively, and there is some evidence that certain simple tasks are amenable to such
practice. But his research has also found that multitasking contributes to the release of
stress hormones and adrenaline, which can cause long-term health problems if not
controlled, and contributes to the loss of short-term memory.

In one recent study, Russell Poldrack, a psychology professor at the University of 9
California, Los Angeles, found that "multitasking adversely affects how you learn.
Even if you learn while multitasking, that learning is less flexible and more specialized, so you cannot retrieve the information as easily." His research demonstrates that
people use different areas of the brain for learning and storing new information when
they are distracted: brain scans of people who are distracted or multitasking show
activity in the striatum, a region of the brain involved in learning new skills; brain
scans of people who are not distracted show activity in the hippocampus, a region
involved in storing and recalling information. Discussing his research on National
Public Radio recently, Poldrack warned, "We have to be aware that there is a cost to
the way that our society is changing, that humans are not built to work this way. We're
really built to focus. And when we sort of force ourselves to multitask, we're driving
ourselves to perhaps be less efficient in the long run even though it sometimes feels
like we're being more efficient."

If, as Poldrack concluded, "multitasking changes the way people learn," what 10
might this mean for today's children and teens, raised with an excess of new entertain-

ment and educational technology, and avidly multitasking at a young age? Poldrack calls this the "million-dollar question." Media multitasking—that is, the simultaneous use of several different media, such as television, the Internet, video games, text messages, telephones, and e-mail—is clearly on the rise, as a 2006 report from the Kaiser Family Foundation showed: in 1999, only 16 percent of the time people spent using any of those media was spent on multiple media at once; by 2005, 26 percent of media time was spent multitasking. "I multitask every single second I am online," confessed one study participant. "At this very moment I am watching TV, checking my e-mail every two minutes, reading a newsgroup about who shot JFK, burning some music to a CD, and writing this message."

The Kaiser report noted several factors that increase the likelihood of media multi- 11 tasking, including "having a computer and being able to see a television from it." Also, "sensation-seeking" personality types are more likely to multitask, as are those living in "a highly TV-oriented household." The picture that emerges of these pubescent multitasking mavens is of a generation of great technical facility and intelligence but of extreme impatience, unsatisfied with slowness and uncomfortable with silence: "I get bored if it's not all going at once, because everything has gaps—waiting for a website to come up, commercials on TV, etc.," one participant said. The report concludes on a very peculiar note, perhaps intended to be optimistic: "In this media-heavy world, it is likely that brains that are more adept at media multitasking will be passed along and these changes will be naturally selected," the report states. "After all, information is power, and if one can process more information all at once, perhaps one can be more powerful." This is techno-social Darwinism, nature red in pixel and claw.

Other experts aren't so sure. As neurologist Jordan Grafman told *Time* magazine: 12 "Kids that are instant messaging while doing homework, playing games online and watching TV, I predict, aren't going to do well in the long run." "I think this generation of kids is guinea pigs," educational psychologist Jane Healy told the *San Francisco Chronicle*; she worries that they might become adults who engage in "very quick but very shallow thinking." Or, as the novelist Walter Kirn suggests in a deft essay in *The Atlantic*, we might be headed for an "Attention-Deficit Recession."

PAYING ATTENTION

When we talk about multitasking, we are really talking about attention: the art of 13 paying attention, the ability to shift our attention, and, more broadly, to exercise judgment about what objects are worthy of our attention. People who have achieved great things often credit for their success a finely honed skill for paying attention. When asked about his particular genius, Isaac Newton responded that if he had made any discoveries, it was "owing more to patient attention than to any other talent."

William James, the great psychologist, wrote at length about the varieties of human 14 attention. In *The Principles of Psychology* (1890), he outlined the differences among "sensorial attention," "intellectual attention," "passive attention," and the like, and noted the "gray chaotic indiscriminateness" of the minds of people who were incapable of paying attention. James compared our stream of thought to a river, and his observations presaged the cognitive "bottlenecks" described later by neurologists: "On the whole easy simple flowing predominates in it, the drift of things is with the pull of gravity, and effortless attention is the rule," he wrote. "But at intervals an obstruction, a set-back, a log-jam occurs, stops the current, creates an eddy, and makes things temporarily move the other way."

To James, steady attention was thus the default condition of a mature mind, an 15 ordinary state undone only by perturbation. To readers a century later, that placid portrayal may seem alien—as though depicting a bygone world. Instead, today's multitasking adult may find something more familiar in James's description of the youthful mind: an "extreme mobility of the attention" that "makes the child seem to belong less to himself than to every object which happens to catch his notice." For some people, James noted, this challenge is never overcome; such people only get their work done "in the interstices of their mind-wandering." Like Chesterfield, James believed that the transition from youthful distraction to mature attention was in large part the result of personal mastery and discipline—and so was illustrative of character. "The faculty of voluntarily bringing back a wandering attention, over and over again," he wrote, "is the very root of judgment, character, and will."

Today, our collective will to pay attention seems fairly weak. We require advice 16 books to teach us how to avoid distraction. In the not-too-distant future we may even employ new devices to help us overcome the unintended attention deficits created by today's gadgets. As one *New York Times* article recently suggested, "Further research could help create clever technology, like sensors or smart software that workers could instruct with their preferences and priorities to serve as a high tech 'time nanny' to ease the modern multitasker's plight." Perhaps we will all accept as a matter of course a computer governor—like the devices placed on engines so that people can't drive cars beyond a certain speed. Our technological governors might prompt us with reminders to set mental limits when we try to do too much, too quickly, all at once.

Then again, perhaps we will simply adjust and come to accept what James called 17 "acquired inattention." E-mails pouring in, cell phones ringing, televisions blaring, podcasts streaming—all this may become background noise, like the "din of a foundry or factory" that James observed workers could scarcely avoid at first, but which eventually became just another part of their daily routine. For the younger generation of multitaskers, the great electronic din is an expected part of everyday life. And given what neuroscience and anecdotal evidence have shown us, this state of constant intentional self-distraction could well be of profound detriment to individual and cultural well-being. When people do their work only in the "interstices of their mind-wandering," with crumbs of attention rationed out among many competing tasks, their culture may gain in information, but it will surely weaken in wisdom.

READING FOR MEANING

1. **Read to Summarize.** Write a sentence or two summarizing Rosen's reasons for critiquing multitasking.

   For help summarizing, see Chapter 2, pp. 24–25.

2. **Read to Respond.** Write a paragraph analyzing anything that resonates with your own experience, such as your experience multitasking compared to "single-tasking" — and what the advantages or disadvantages are of focusing your attention on one task at a time (par. 5); or the suggestion that multitaskers are impatient and "uncomfortable with silence," and that they quickly get bored (par. 11).

3. **Read to Analyze Assumptions.** Write a paragraph or two analyzing an assumption you find intriguing in Rosen's essay. For example:

   Assumptions about the causes of not focusing attention. Quoting Lord Chesterfield's writing from the eighteenth century and William James's from the nineteenth, Rosen suggests that not focusing one's attention may indicate "a weak and frivolous mind" (par. 1) or the lack of "a mature mind" or of "judgment, character, and will" (par. 15). Such language makes a moral judgment about a person's lack of seriousness or self-discipline. In contrast, quoting Edward Hallowell, Rosen suggests that not focusing attention may be a sign of illness akin to attention deficit/hyperactivity disorder (par. 5).

   For help analyzing assumptions, see Chapter 2, pp. 28–29.

   - Why might people, particularly young people, who do not focus their attention be labeled as lacking in character or intelligence or as suffering from a medical malady?

   - Are critics less likely today than in the past to make judgments about intelligence or character, and perhaps more likely to make medical diagnoses about the same kinds of behavior? Why or why not?

   You may also want to try reflecting on challenges to your beliefs and values; see Chapter 2, pp. 36–37.

   Assumptions about the role of media in multitasking. According to Rosen, the Kaiser Family Foundation has reported a substantial increase in multitasking on media. She cites the foundation's finding that, in 1999, 16 percent of media time (for example, watching television, surfing the Internet, or texting friends) was spent doing two or more of such tasks simultaneously. By 2005, the time spent multitasking had increased to 26 percent.

   - When you are multitasking, is some kind of electronic medium always involved, or do you ever multitask without using media?

   - Do you primarily use media multitasking to fill or kill time, or for some other reason? What percentage of time spent multitasking do you think the Kaiser Family Foundation would find if they did their report today?

READING LIKE A WRITER

SUPPORTING THE JUDGMENT

Rosen relies primarily on authorities and research studies to support her argument about the value of multitasking. Because she is not writing for an academic audience, however, she does not have to include formal citations, as you will be expected to do in your college writing. Nevertheless, note that Rosen does provide many of the same kinds of information about her sources that formal citations offer — the source author or lead researcher's name, the title of the publication in which the borrowed material appeared, and the year of publication of the source — so that readers can locate and read the source themselves. Notice in the following examples how Rosen presents this information.

Bibliographical information
> In one of the many letters he wrote to his son in the 1740s, Lord Chesterfield offered the following advice: "There is time enough for everything. . . ." (par. 1)

> "We have always multitasked . . . but never so intensely or self-consciously as now," James Gleick wrote in his 1999 book *Faster*. "We are multitasking connoisseurs. . . ." (par. 3)

Writers often begin with the source's name to provide context and establish credibility. In the third example, Rosen places the source information in the middle of the quotation, possibly because she wants to emphasize the opening phrases of both sentences.

Not all sources are quoted, of course. Writers sometimes summarize the main idea or paraphrase what the source has said:

Summary
> One study by researchers at the University of California at Irvine monitored interruptions among office workers; they found that workers took an average of twenty-five minutes to recover from interruptions. . . . (par. 6)

Paraphrase
> The psychologist who led the study called this new "infomania" a serious threat to workplace productivity. (par. 4)

Analyze & Write

Write a paragraph analyzing and evaluating how Rosen uses material from other authorities and research studies to support her argument:

1. First, skim paragraphs 4–9 and highlight the names of authorities and the research studies Rosen cites.
2. Then choose two sources, and determine how Rosen uses them to support her judgment about the value of multitasking. Also notice how she integrates these sources into her text.
3. Finally, consider why these sources might or might not be convincing for Rosen's readers. How convincing are they for you, and why?

A Special Reading Strategy

Looking for Patterns of Opposition

To refute a favorable judgment she expects readers to have made about multitasking, Rosen tries to reframe the argument about its value. Reframing is a common strategy writers use to help readers see the subject in a new way. Rosen tries to set up an opposition between focused attention and multitasking that makes multitasking seem less preferable. She uses Lord Chesterfield's letter advising his son and William James's ideas about psychology to associate focused attention with maturity and intelligence, and multitasking with immaturity and a lack of intelligence, or at least the inability to think properly. To see how Rosen reframes the subject, use the critical reading strategy looking for patterns of opposition (see Chapter 2, pp. 35–36).

- Reread paragraphs 1–3 and 13–16, highlighting the words Rosen uses to develop this opposition.

- Analyze the system of oppositions Rosen sets up by making a two-column chart and placing the words Rosen associates with focused attention in one column and the words she associates with multitasking in the other column. Then put an asterisk next to the word that Rosen values more highly — for example, *maturity* as opposed to *immaturity*.

- Write a couple of sentences describing the way that Rosen uses this system of oppositions to reframe readers' ideas about multitasking.

Christine Romano

Jessica Statsky's "Children Need to Play, Not Compete": An Evaluation

Christine Romano wrote the following essay when she was a first-year college student. In it, she evaluates a position paper written by another student, Jessica Statsky's "Children Need to Play, Not Compete," which appears in Chapter 8 of this book (pp. 334–39). Romano focuses not on the writing strategies Statsky uses but rather on her logic — that is, on whether Statsky's argument is likely to convince her intended readers. She evaluates the logic of the argument according to the criteria or standards presented in Chapter 2 (pp. 40–41).

- **Before you read** Romano's evaluation, you might want to read Statsky's essay, thinking about what seems most and least convincing to you about her argument that competitive sports can be harmful to young children.

- **As you read,** think about Romano's criteria. How important is it that the supporting evidence for an argument be "appropriate, believable, consistent, and complete" (par. 2)?

Parents of young children have a lot to worry about and to hope for. In "Children Need   1
to Play, Not Compete," Jessica Statsky appeals to their worries and hopes in order to convince them that organized competitive sports may harm their children physically and psychologically. Statsky states her thesis clearly and fully forecasts the reasons she will offer to justify her position: Besides causing physical and psychological harm, competitive sports discourage young people from becoming players and fans when they are older and inevitably put parents' needs and fantasies ahead of children's welfare. Statsky also carefully defines her key terms. By *sports*, for example, she means to include both contact and noncontact sports that emphasize competition. The sports may be organized locally at schools or summer sports camps or nationally, as in the examples of Peewee Football and Little League Baseball. She is concerned only with children six to twelve years of age.

In this essay, I will evaluate the logic of Statsky's argument, considering whether   2
the support for her thesis is appropriate, believable, consistent, and complete. While her logic *is* appropriate, believable, and consistent, her argument also has weaknesses. It seems incomplete because it neglects to anticipate parents' predictable questions and objections and because it fails to support certain parts fully.

Statsky provides appropriate support for her thesis. Throughout her essay, she relies   3
for support on different kinds of information (she cites thirteen separate sources, including books, newspapers, and websites). Her quotations, examples, and statistics all support the reasons she believes competitive sports are bad for children. For example, in paragraph 3, Statsky offers the reason that competitive sports may damage

children's bodies and that contact sports may be especially injurious. She supports this reason by paraphrasing Koppett's statement that muscle strain or even permanent injury may result when a twelve-year-old throws curve balls. She then quotes Tutko on the dangers of tackle football. The opinions of both experts are obviously appropriate. They are relevant to her reason, and we can easily imagine that they would worry many parents.

Not only is Statsky's support appropriate but it is also believable. Statsky quotes or 4 summarizes authorities to support her argument in nearly every paragraph. The question is whether readers would find these authorities believable or credible. Since Statsky relies almost entirely on authorities to support her argument, readers must believe these authorities for her argument to succeed. I have not read Statsky's sources, but I think there are good reasons to consider them authoritative. First of all, the newspaper writers she quotes write for two of America's most respected newspapers, *The New York Times* and *The Los Angeles Times*. Both of these newspapers have sports reporters who not only report on sports events but also take a critical look at sports issues. In addition, both newspapers have reporters who specialize in children's health and education. Second, Statsky gives background information about the authorities she quotes, information intended to increase the person's believability in the eyes of parents of young children. In paragraph 3, she tells readers that Thomas Tutko is "a psychology professor at San Jose State University and coauthor of the book *Winning Is Everything and Other American Myths*." In paragraph 5, she announces that Martin Rablovsky is "a former sports editor for *The New York Times*," and she notes that he has watched children play organized sports for many years. Third, Statsky quotes from a number of websites, including the official Little League site and the American Orthopaedic Society for Sports Medicine. Parents are likely to accept the authority of these sites.

In addition to quoting authorities, Statsky relies on examples and anecdotes to 5 support the reasons for her position. If examples and anecdotes are to be believable, they must seem representative to readers, not bizarre or highly unusual or completely unpredictable. Readers can imagine a similar event happening elsewhere. For anecdotes to be believable, they should, in addition, be specific and true to life. All of Statsky's examples and anecdotes fulfill these requirements, and her readers would likely find them believable. For example, early in her argument, in paragraph 4, Statsky reasons that fear of being hurt greatly reduces children's enjoyment of contact sports. The anecdote comes from Tosches's investigative report on Peewee Football, as does the quotation by the mother of an eight-year-old player who says that the children become frightened and pretend to be injured in order to stay out of the game. In the anecdote, a seven-year-old makes himself vomit to avoid playing. Because these echo the familiar "I feel bad" or "I'm sick" excuse children give when they do not want to go somewhere (especially school) or do something, most parents would find them believable. They could easily imagine their own children pretending to be hurt or ill if they were fearful or depressed. The anecdote is also specific. Tosches reports what the boy said and did and what the coach said and did.

Other examples provide support for all the major reasons Statsky gives for her   6
position:

- That competitive sports pose psychological dangers—children becoming serious
  and unplayful when the game starts (par. 5)

- That adults' desire to win puts children at risk—parents fighting each other at a
  Peewee Football game and a baseball coach setting fire to an opposing team's
  jersey (par. 8)

- That organized sports should emphasize cooperation and individual performance
  instead of winning—a coach wishing to ban scoring but finding that parents
  would not support him and a New York City basketball league in which all children play an equal amount of time and scoring is easier (pars. 10–11)

All of these examples are appropriate to the reasons they support. They are also believable. Together, they help Statsky achieve her purpose of convincing parents that organized, competitive sports may be bad for their children and that there are
alternatives.

If readers are to find an argument logical and convincing, it must be consistent and   7
complete. While there are no inconsistencies or contradictions in Statsky's argument,
it is seriously incomplete because it neglects to support fully one of its reasons, it fails
to anticipate many predictable questions parents would have, and it pays too little
attention to noncontact competitive team sports. The most obvious example of thin
support comes in paragraphs 10–11, where Statsky asserts that many parents are ready
for children's team sports that emphasize cooperation and individual performance.
Yet the example of a Little League official who failed to win parents' approval to ban
scores raises serious questions about just how many parents are ready to embrace
noncompetitive sports teams. The other support, a brief description of City Sports for
Kids in New York City, is very convincing but will only be logically compelling to
those parents who are already inclined to agree with Statsky's position. Parents
inclined to disagree with Statsky would need additional evidence. Most parents know
that big cities receive special federal funding for evening, weekend, and summer rec-
reation. Brief descriptions of six or eight noncompetitive teams in a variety of sports in
cities, rural areas, suburban neighborhoods—some funded publicly, some funded
privately—would be more likely to convince skeptics. Statsky is guilty here of failing
to accept the burden of proof, a logical fallacy.

Statsky's argument is also incomplete in that it fails to anticipate certain objections   8
and questions that some parents, especially those she most wants to convince, are
almost sure to raise. In the first sentences of paragraphs 10 and 12, Statsky does show
that she is thinking about her readers' questions. She does not go nearly far enough,
however, to have a chance of influencing two types of readers: those who themselves
are or were fans of and participants in competitive sports and those who want their
six- to twelve-year-old children involved in mainstream sports programs despite the
risks, especially the national programs that have a certain prestige. Such parents might
feel that competitive team sports for young children create a sense of community with

a shared purpose, build character through self-sacrifice and commitment to the group, teach children to face their fears early and learn how to deal with them through the support of coaches and team members, and introduce children to the principles of social cooperation and collaboration. Some parents are likely to believe and to know from personal experience that coaches who burn opposing teams' jerseys on the pitching mound before the game starts are the exception, not the rule. Some young children idolize teachers and coaches, and team practice and games are the brightest moments in their lives. Statsky seems not to have considered these reasonable possibilities, and as a result her argument lacks a compelling logic it might have had. By acknowledging that she was aware of many of these objections—and perhaps even accommodating more of them in her own argument, as she does in paragraph 12, while refuting other objections—she would have strengthened her argument.

Finally, Statsky's argument is incomplete because she overlooks examples of non-contact team sports. Track, swimming, and tennis are good examples that some readers would certainly think of. Some elementary schools compete in track meets. Public and private clubs and recreational programs organize competitive swimming and tennis competitions. In these sports, individual performance is the focus. No one gets trampled. Children exert themselves only as much as they are able to. Yet individual performances are scored, and a team score is derived. Because Statsky fails to mention any of these obvious possibilities, her argument is weakened. 9

The logic of Statsky's argument, then, has both strengths and weaknesses. The support she offers is appropriate, believable, and consistent. The major weakness is incompleteness—she fails to anticipate more fully the likely objections of a wide range of readers. Her logic would prevent parents who enjoy and advocate competitive sports from taking her argument seriously. Such parents and their children have probably had positive experiences with team sports, and these experiences would lead them to believe that the gains are worth whatever risks may be involved. Many probably think that the risks Statsky points out can be avoided by careful monitoring. For those parents inclined to agree with her, Statsky's logic is likely to seem sound and complete. An argument that successfully confirms readers' beliefs is certainly valid, and Statsky succeeds admirably at this kind of argument. Because she does not offer compelling counterarguments to the legitimate objections of those inclined not to agree with her, however, her success is limited. 10

READING FOR MEANING

1. **Read to Summarize.** Write a sentence or two briefly summarizing the strengths and weaknesses of Statsky's argument, according to Romano.

2. **Read to Respond.** Write a paragraph analyzing your initial reactions to Romano's evaluation of Statsky's argument. For example, based on your experience or observation of organized sports for kids, do you agree with Romano's judgment that Statsky's reasons seem believable?

For help with summarizing, see Chapter 2, pp. 24–25.

For help
analyzing
assumptions,
see Chapter 2,
pp. 28–29.

3. **Read to Analyze Assumptions.** Write a paragraph or two analyzing an assumption you find intriguing in Romano's essay. For example:

Assumptions about the relative value of competition or cooperation. Romano gives an example supporting Statsky's argument that team sports for young children "should emphasize cooperation and individual performance instead of winning" (par. 6). In paragraph 8, however, Romano suggests that some parents believe that team sports may teach cooperation together with competition and that the two skills and attitudes may be more closely related than Statsky acknowledges.

- What do you think leads Romano to suggest that children learn both competition and cooperation when they participate in team sports?
- How is learning to cooperate and collaborate beneficial for us as individuals and as a society? Is competition also beneficial?

Assumptions about the importance of facing fear. As Romano notes in paragraph 5, "Statsky reasons that fear of being hurt greatly reduces children's enjoyment of contact sports," and as support she cites Tosches's anecdote about the child who "makes himself vomit to avoid playing." Nevertheless, Romano suggests that some parents think facing fear is a good thing:

- In what contexts, other than sports, do people typically experience physical or psychological fear?
- Why might learning how to deal with fear (presumably by doing something even though it causes us to be fearful) be a good thing?

READING LIKE A WRITER

ORGANIZING THE EVALUATION

Transitions or cues play an important role in helping readers follow the logic of the argument. Logical transitions serve a variety of specific purposes:

- To list items consecutively

Consecutive cues	. . . there are good reasons to consider them authoritative. First of all, the newspaper writers. . . . Second, Statsky gives. . . . Third, Statsky quotes. . . . (par. 4)

- To call attention to additional points

Other examples provide support for all the major reasons Statsky gives for her position:

Note that items in list are parallel.	That competitive sports pose . . .
	That adults' desire to win puts . . .
	That organized sports should emphasize . . . (par. 6)

- To introduce a contrast or an opposing point

  I have not read Statsky's sources, but I think . . . (par. 4)

- To signal a cause or effect

  Transition indi-   It seems incomplete because it . . . (par. 2)
  cating a cause
  Transition indi-   Statsky seems . . . , and as a result her argument lacks . . . (par. 8)
  cating an effect

- To conclude

  The logic of Statsky's argument, then, has . . . (par. 10)

Analyze & Write

Write a paragraph analyzing and evaluating the effectiveness of Romano's cueing strategies.

1. First, find Romano's thesis and forecasting statement, underlining the reasons supporting her argument.
2. Then skim the essay, noting where each of her reasons is brought up again, underlining topic sentences and any cues she uses to help readers follow her argument.
3. How effectively does Romano use these devices to orient readers? Where, if anywhere, would you appreciate more cueing?

Writing to Learn Evaluation

Write a brief essay analyzing one of the readings in this chapter (or another selection, perhaps one by a classmate). Explain how (and, perhaps, how well) the selection works as an evaluation. Consider, for example, how it

- presents the subject in a way that is appropriate for the purpose and audience;

- supports the judgment with reasons and evidence based on shared criteria;

- responds sensitively to possible objections and alternative judgments;

- organizes the review clearly and logically, helping readers follow the argument.

(*continued*)

Your essay could also reflect on how you applied one or more of the academic habits of mind as you read the selection:

- **Curiosity** — what questions or ideas did you have as you read the selection?

- **Critical Analysis** — what assumptions does the author make about the appropriate criteria for evaluating that kind of subject?

- **Rhetorical Sensitivity** — how effective or ineffective do you think the selection is in achieving its purpose for the intended audience, given the constraints of the medium and the evaluation genre?

A GUIDE TO WRITING EVALUATIONS

You have probably done a good deal of analytical writing about your reading. Your instructor may also assign a capstone project to write a brief evaluation of your own. This Guide to Writing offers detailed suggestions and resources to help you meet the special challenges this kind of writing presents.

THE WRITING ASSIGNMENT

Write an evaluation supporting your judgment.

- Choose a subject that you can analyze in detail.

- Base your judgment on widely recognized criteria for evaluating a subject like yours.

- Marshal evidence to support your judgment.

- Consider possible objections your readers might raise as well as alternative judgments they might prefer.

- Organize your evaluation clearly and logically.

WRITING YOUR DRAFT

Choosing a Subject to Evaluate

Rather than limiting yourself to the first subject that comes to mind, take a few minutes to consider your options and list as many subjects as you can. Below are some guidelines to help you choose a promising subject, followed by suggestions for the types of subjects you might consider writing about.

Choose a subject that

- you can view and review (for example, a location you can visit; a printed text; or a website or digital recording from which you can capture stills or video clips to use as examples);

- is typically evaluated according to criteria or standards of judgment that you understand and share with your readers;

- has strengths and/or weaknesses you could illustrate.

Below are some categories and ideas for possible subjects:

- *Culture:* a film or group of films, a television show or series, a computer game, a song, a live or recorded performance, an art museum or individual work of art, a park

- *Written work:* an essay in this book or another your instructor approves, a short story, website, magazine, campus publication, textbook in a course you've taken

- *Education:* your high school, a course you have taken, a laboratory you have worked in, a library or campus support service, a teacher or program

- *Government:* an elected official or candidate for public office, a proposed or existing law, an agency or program

- *Social:* a club or organized activity such as a camping trip, sports team, debate group

Assessing Your Subject and Considering How to Present It to Your Readers

Once you have made a preliminary choice of a subject, consider how you can frame it so that readers will be open to your evaluation. To do this, consider first how you regard the subject and what your readers are likely to think. Use the following questions and sentence strategies as a jumping-off point. You can make the sentences you generate your own later, as you revise.

What Do I Think?   List those qualities of your subject that you like and dislike, or list its strengths and weaknesses or advantages and disadvantages.

- ▶ What makes .... [good/bad] is ...., ..., and ....
- ▶ Although .... is stellar in [these ways], it falls short in [these other ways].

What genre or kind of subject is it?

- ▶ The .... is a [genre or category of subject, such as romantic comedy or horror movie].
- ▶ It is an innovative [category in which the subject belongs] that combines elements of .... and ....

What criteria or standards of judgment do you usually use to evaluate things of this kind?

- ▶ I expect .... to be .... or ....
- ▶ I dislike it when .... are ....

How does your subject compare to other examples of the genre?

- ▶ Compared to [other subjects], ... has the [best or worst] .... [name trait].
- ▶ Whereas other [comparable subjects] can be [faulted/praised for] ...., this subject ....

What Do My Readers Think?   Who are your readers, and why will they be reading your evaluation? Is the subject new or familiar to them?

▶ My readers are .... and are probably reading my review [to learn about the subject or to decide whether to see it, play it, or buy it].

How might factors such as the readers' age, gender, cultural background, or work experience affect their judgment of the subject?

▶ People who work in .... or who are familiar with .... may be [more/less critical, or apply different standards] to a subject like this one.

What criteria or standards of judgment do you expect your readers to use when evaluating subjects of this kind? What other examples of the genre would they be familiar with?

▶ If they [like/dislike] [comparable subject], they are sure to [like/dislike] ....

▶ Judging [this kind of subject] on the basis of .... is likely to surprise readers because they probably are more familiar with .... and ....

Considering Your Purpose for Your Audience

Write for a few minutes exploring your purpose in writing to your particular audience. Ask yourself questions like these:

- What do I want my readers to believe or do after they read my essay?

- How can I connect to their experience with my subject (or subjects like it)? How can I interest them in a subject that is outside their experience?

- Can I assume that readers will share my standards for judging the subject, or must I explain and justify the standards?

- How can I offer a balanced evaluation that will enhance my credibility with readers?

Formulating a Working Thesis Statement

A working thesis will help you begin drafting your essay purposefully. Your thesis should announce your subject and make your overall judgment clear: stating whether your subject is good or bad, or better or worse than something else in the same genre or category.

Remember that evaluations can be mixed — you can concede shortcomings in a generally favorable review or concede admirable qualities in a mostly negative assessment. If you feel comfortable drafting a working thesis statement now, do so. You may use the sentence strategies below as a jumping-off point — you can always revise them later — or use language of your own. (Alternatively, if you prefer to develop your argument before trying to formulate a thesis, skip this activity now and return to it later.)

A good strategy is to begin by naming the subject and identifying the kind of subject it is, and then using value terms to state your judgment of the subject's strengths and weaknesses:

> ▸ .... is a brilliant embodiment of [the genre/category], especially notable for its superb .... and thorough ....

> ▸ .... has many good qualities, including .... and .... ; however, the pluses do not outweigh its one major drawback, namely that ....

As you develop your argument, you may want to rework your thesis to make it more compelling by sharpening the language and perhaps also by forecasting your reasons. You may also need to *qualify* your judgment with words like *generally, may,* or *in part.*

Here are two sample thesis statements from the readings:

McDonald's is bad for your kids. . . . [T]hese jobs undermine school attendance and involvement, impart few skills that will be useful in later life, and simultaneously skew the values of teen-agers — especially their ideas about the worth of a dollar. (Etzioni, pars. 1, 3)

While her logic *is* appropriate, believable, and consistent, her argument also has weaknesses. It seems incomplete because it neglects to anticipate parents' predictable questions and objections and because it fails to support certain parts fully. (Romano, par. 2)

Both of these thesis statements assert the writer's judgment clearly and also forecast the reasons that will support the argument. But whereas Etzioni's thesis is unmistakably negative in its overall judgment, Romano's is mixed.

Developing the Reasons and Evidence Supporting Your Judgment

The following activities will help you find reasons and evidence to support your evaluation. Begin by writing down what you already know. You can do some focused research later to fill in the details.

List the good and bad qualities of the subject. Begin by reviewing the criteria and the value terms you have already used to describe the good and bad qualities of the subject. These are the potential reasons for your judgment. Try restating them using this basic sentence strategy,

> ▸ .... is [your overall judgment] because .... , ... , and ....

Write steadily for at least five minutes, developing your reasons. Ask yourself questions like these:

> ▸ Why are the characteristics I'm pointing out for praise or criticism so important in judging my subject?

▶ How can I prove to readers that the value terms I'm using to evaluate these characteristics are fair and accurate?

Make notes of the evidence you will use to support your judgment. Evidence you might use to support each reason may include the following:

- examples

- quotations from authorities

- textual evidence (quotations, paraphrases, or summaries)

- illustrations, such as screenshots, video clips, or photographs

- statistics

- comparisons or contrasts

You may already have some evidence you could use. If you lack evidence for any of your reasons, make a *Research to Do* note for later.

Researching Your Evaluation

Consult your notes to determine what you need to find out. If you are evaluating a subject that others have written about, try searching for articles or books on your topic. Enter keywords or phrases related to the subject, genre, or category into the search box of

- an all-purpose database — such as *Academic OneFile* (InfoTrac) or *Academic Search Complete* (EBSCOHost) — to find relevant articles in magazines and journals;

- the database *Lexis/Nexis* to find newspaper reviews;

- a search engine like *Google* or *Bing;*

- your library's catalog to locate books on your topic.

Turn to databases and search engines for information on recent items, like films and popular novels; use books, databases, and search engines to find information on classic topics. (Books are more likely to provide in-depth information, but articles in print or online are more likely to be current.) For more about searching a database or catalog, see the Appendix, pp. 474–78.

Responding to a Likely Objection or Alternative Judgment

Start by identifying an objection or an alternative judgment you expect some readers to raise. To come up with likely objections or alternative judgments, you might try the following:

- *Brainstorm* a list on your own or with fellow students.

- *Freewrite* for ten minutes on this topic.

- Conduct research to learn what others have said about your subject.

- Conduct interviews with experts.

- Distribute a survey to a group of people similar to your intended readers.

Then figure out whether to concede or refute a likely objection or alternative judgment. You may be able simply to acknowledge it, but if the criticism is serious, consider conceding the point and qualifying your judgment. You might also try to refute an objection or alternative judgment by arguing that the standards you are using are appropriate and important. Use the following strategies for generating ideas and sentences as a jumping-off point, and revise them later to make them your own.

1. Start by listing objections you expect readers to have as well as their preferred alternative judgments. You have already considered your readers and the criteria they are likely to favor (pp. 246–247). If their criteria differ from yours, you may need to explain or defend your criteria.

2. Analyze your list of objections and alternative judgments to determine which are likely to be most powerful for your readers.

3. Draft refutations and concession statements:

To refute

▸ Some people think .... [alternative judgment] because of ...., ..., and .... [reasons]. Although one can see why they might make this argument, the evidence does not back it up because ....

To concede

▸ Indeed, the more hard-core enthusiasts may carp that .... is not sufficiently .... [shortcomings].

▸ The one justifiable criticism that could be made against .... is ....

To concede and refute

Frequently, writers concede a point only to come back with a refutation. To make this move, follow concessions like those above with sentences that begin with a transition emphasizing contrast, like *but*, *however*, *yet*, or *nevertheless*, and then explain why you believe that your judgment is more powerful or compelling.

▸ As some critics have pointed out, ... follows the tried-and-true formula of .... In this case, however, the [director/writer/artist] is using the formula effectively to ....

Including Visuals or Other Media

If appropriate to your rhetorical situation, consider whether visual or audio illustrations — screenshots, photographs, film clips, background music, or sound bites — would help you present your subject more effectively to readers or strengthen your evaluation of it, especially if you're publishing your review online. Visual and audio materials are not at all a requirement of an effective evaluation, but they could provide strong support to your argument.

For more on strategies for visuals, see Chapter 2, pp. 31–34.

Note: Be sure to cite the source of visual or audio elements you did not create, and get permission from the source if your essay is going to be published on a website that is not password-protected.

Organizing Your Evaluation Effectively for Your Readers

The forecasting statement from your thesis can act as a rough outline when you are writing a simpler evaluation, but for complex evaluations, a scratch outline of your argument may be more useful for organizing your evaluation effectively for your readers. You might even want to make two or three different outlines before choosing the organization that looks most promising.

An evaluative essay contains as many as four basic parts:

1. Presentation of the subject

2. Judgment of the subject

3. Presentation of reasons and support

4. Consideration of readers' objections and alternative judgments

These parts can be organized in various ways: If you are writing primarily for readers who disagree with your judgment, you could start by showing them what you think they have overlooked or misjudged about the subject. Then you could anticipate and refute their likely objections before presenting your own reasons. If you expect some readers to disagree with your judgment even though they share your standards, you could begin by restating these standards and then demonstrate how the subject fails to meet them. Then you could present your reasons and support before responding to alternative judgments.

Whether you choose either of these approaches or an approach of your own, be flexible: As you draft, you may see ways to improve your original plan, and you should be ready to revise your outline, shift parts around, or drop or add parts as needed.

┌───┐

─────────── **Working with Sources** ───────────

Using Summary to Support Your Evaluative Argument

Writers of evaluation often use summary to support their argument. For example, evaluations may summarize an expert source (as Etzioni and Rosen do), the plot of a film or television show (as Nussbaum does), or an aspect of a written text (as Romano and Gladwell do). Let's look closely at how Romano uses summary.

Romano's summary

Quotes Paraphrases *Describes Statsky's moves*	For example, in paragraph 3, *Statsky offers the reason* that competitive sports may <u>damage children's bodies</u> and that <u>contact sports may be especially injurious</u>. *She supports this reason* by paraphrasing Koppett's statement that <u>muscle strain or even permanent injury may</u> result when a <u>twelve-year-old throws curve balls</u>. *She then quotes* Tutko on the dangers of tackle football. (Romano, par. 3)

Statsky's original (see pp. 334–35, par. 3)

Language para-phrased &/ or quoted	One readily understandable danger of overly competitive sports is that they entice children into physical actions that are <u>bad for growing bodies</u>. . . . Although the official Little League website acknowledges that children do risk injury playing baseball, it insists that "severe injuries . . . are infrequent," the risk "far less than the risk of riding a skateboard, a bicycle, or even the school bus" ("Little League Parent Responsibilities"). Nevertheless, Leonard Koppett in *Sports Illusion, Sports Reality* claims that a <u>twelve-year-old</u> trying to throw a <u>curve ball</u>, for example, may put abnormal <u>strain on developing arm and shoulder muscles,</u> <u>sometimes resulting in lifelong injuries</u> (294). Contact sports like <u>football</u> can be even more <u>hazardous</u>. Thomas Tutko . . . writes:

> I am strongly opposed to young kids playing <u>tackle football</u>. . . .

Romano's summarizing strategies

- Repeats Statsky's main ideas in a condensed form, summarizing the gist.

- Paraphrases central ideas using her own words and sentence structures. Note that because some words are basic or not readily replaceable (words such as *curve ball*, *football*, and *muscle strain*), Romano's vocabulary does overlap with Statsky's, but this is to be expected.

- Provides a play-by-play description of Statsky's strategic moves to show readers exactly how she uses paraphrase and quotation to support her argument.

└───┘

Drafting Your Evaluation

By this point, you have done a lot of writing

- to devise a well-presented subject and make a judgment about it;
- to support your judgment with reasons and evidence that your readers will find persuasive;
- to refute or concede objections and alternative judgments;
- to organize your ideas to make them clear, logical, and effective for readers.

Now stitch that material together to create a draft. The next two parts of this Guide to Writing will help you evaluate and improve it.

REVIEWING AND IMPROVING THE DRAFT

This section includes two guides for Peer Review and Troubleshooting Your Draft. Your instructor may arrange a peer review in class or online where you can exchange drafts with a classmate. The Peer Review Guide will help you give each other constructive feedback regarding the basic features and strategies typical of evaluative writing. (If you want to make specific suggestions for improving the draft, see Troubleshooting Your Draft on pp. 290–92.) Also, be sure to respond to any specific concerns the writer has raised about the draft. The Troubleshooting Your Draft guide that follows will help you reread your own draft with a critical eye, sort through any feedback you've received, and consider a variety of ways to improve your draft.

A PEER REVIEW GUIDE

How effective is the presentation of the subject?

What's Working Well: Point to a passage where the subject is presented effectively—for example, where the subject is identified by name or genre, briefly summarized, or compared to one or more familiar examples of the genre.

What Needs Improvement: Identify a passage where presentation of the subject could be improved—for example, where the subject could be classified more definitively or examples of the genre could be given for comparison.

How well supported is the evaluation?

What's Working Well: Indicate a passage where the argument is well developed—for example, where the overall judgment is balanced, criticizing the subject's weaknesses but also praising its strengths, or where one of the criteria on which the argument is based is likely to be convincing to readers.

What Needs Improvement: Identify a passage where the evaluative argument could be improved—for example, where additional examples, facts, statistics, or research studies could be used as evidence to support the writer's judgment.

(*continued*)

> **How effective is the writer's response to objections and alternative judgments?**
>
> **What's Working Well:** Identify a passage where the writer responds effectively—for example, refuting an objection with concrete evidence or recognized authorities.
>
> **What Needs Improvement:** Tell the writer where a response is needed or could be made more effective—for example, explaining what's wrong with the criteria behind an alternative judgment or offering facts and examples that refute an objection.
>
> **Is the evaluation clearly and logically organized?**
>
> **What's Working Well:** Give an example of a passage where the essay succeeds in being readable—in its clear presentation of the thesis, in its effective opening or closing, or by its use of logical transitions.
>
> **What Needs Improvement:** Tell the writer where the readability could be improved—for example, by suggesting a better beginning or a more effective ending, or a way to rearrange parts or strengthen connections.

Revising Your Draft

Revising means reenvisioning your draft, seeing it in a new way given your purpose and audience, and the feedback from your peer review. Don't hesitate to cut unconvincing material, add new material, and move passages around. The following chart may help you strengthen your evaluation.

TROUBLESHOOTING YOUR DRAFT

To Present the Subject More Effectively	
If the subject is not identified clearly,	• Identify the subject (such as by naming the director and main actors of a film). • Describe the subject by summarizing it and giving examples. • Establish the subject's importance by citing statistics or quoting authorities. • Consider adding illustrations—photographs, graphs, tables, or charts—to help clarify the subject.

	• Classify the subject into a genre or category.
If it is not clear what kind of subject it is,	• Compare your subject to other, better-known examples of the genre.
	• Refer to other reviews or reviewers of subjects of this kind.

To Support the Evaluation and Strengthen the Argument

	• Assert your overall judgment early in the essay, making clear if your judgment is mixed.
If the overall judgment is not clear,	• Qualify your judgment if it seems overstated or is not supported by your argument.
	• Make sure that your judgment is consistent throughout, even when you point out good as well as bad qualities.

	• Explain the criteria you are using and why they are appropriate for the kind of subject you are reviewing.
If the argument is not based on what readers consider appropriate criteria,	• Justify your criteria—for example, by making comparisons or citing authorities.

	• Add support by quoting or summarizing experts or research studies, providing facts or statistics, or giving specific examples.
If support is not provided, not convincing, or not clear,	• Cite your sources and indicate why they can be depended on.
	• Explain more fully why the evidence, including visuals, supports your judgment.

To Improve the Response to Objections and/or Alternative Judgments

	• Refute an objection that undermines your argument—for example, by showing that it is not based on widely held or appropriate criteria, or that it misunderstands your argument or the subject itself.
If a likely objection has not been responded to adequately,	• Concede an objection that cannot be refuted, but try to show it is only a minor concern that does not invalidate your evaluation, using sentence strategies like *It is true that . . . , but my point is. . . .*

(continued)

If a likely alternative judgment has not been responded to adequately,	• Mention good or bad qualities of the subject that others emphasize, even if your overall judgment is different. • Cite authorities to justify your criteria or give reasons why the alternative criteria are inappropriate.
To Make the Organization Clearer	
If the thesis and forecast statements are missing, inaccurate, or unclear,	• Add or revise the thesis and forecast statements. • Make sure your thesis and forecast are placed early in the essay to guide readers. • Repeat key terms in your topic sentences.
If the essay seems disorganized or is hard to follow,	• Move, add, or delete sections to strengthen coherence. • Add appropriate transitions or improve the existing ones.
If the conclusion seems abrupt or awkward,	• Add a transition to signal the conclusion. • Try restating your judgment or summarizing your argument. • Consider whether you can echo something from the opening.

Editing and Proofreading Your Draft

Check for errors in usage, punctuation, and mechanics, and consider matters of style. If you keep a list of errors you typically make, begin by checking your draft against this list. Ask someone else to proofread your essay before you submit it to your instructor.

From our research on student writing, we know that evaluative essays have frequent problems in sentences that set up comparisons. The comparisons can be incomplete, illogical, or unclear. Check a writer's handbook for help with these potential problems.

Reflecting on Evaluation

In this chapter, you have read critically several evaluative essays and have written one of your own. To better remember what you have learned, pause now to reflect on the reading and writing activities you completed in this chapter.

1. Write a page or so reflecting on what you have learned. Begin by describing what you are most pleased with in your essay. Then explain what you think contributed to your achievement.

   - If it was something you learned from the readings, indicate which readings and specifically what you learned from them.

   - If it came from your explorations of alternative points of view, point out the strategies that helped you most.

   - If you got good advice from a critical reader, explain exactly how the person helped you — perhaps by identifying a problem in your draft or by helping you add a new dimension to your writing.

2. Reflect more generally on evaluative essays, a genre of writing important in education and in society. Consider some of the following questions:

   - How confident do you feel about asserting a judgment and supporting it?

   - How comfortable are you playing the role of judge and jury on the subject?

   - How do your personal preferences and values influence your judgment?

   - How might your gender, ethnicity, religious beliefs, age, or social class influence your ideas about the subject?

   - What contribution might evaluative essays make to our society that other genres cannot make?

8

Arguing for a Position

P osition arguments take a position on controversial issues that have no obvious "right" answer, no truth everyone accepts, no single authority everyone trusts. Consequently, simply gathering information — finding the facts or learning from experts — will not settle these disputes because ultimately they are matters of opinion and judgment for which writers must argue.

You may associate arguing with quarreling or with the in-your-face debating we often hear on radio and television talk shows. These ways of arguing may let us vent strong feelings, but they seldom lead us to consider seriously other points of view, let alone to look critically at our own thinking or learn anything new. This chapter presents a more deliberative way of arguing that we call *reasoned argument* because it depends on giving reasons rather than raising voices. Although it is not possible to prove that a position on a controversial issue is right or wrong, it is possible to convince others to consider a particular position seriously or to accept or reject a position. A **position essay** must give readers strong reasons and solid support. It also must anticipate opposing arguments.

Because arguing for and defending a position can muster up strong feelings (especially if it is on a controversial subject), it is important to know the circumstances and your audience — in other words, to write with rhetorical sensitivity and civility.

RHETORICAL SITUATIONS FOR POSITION ARGUMENTS

Writing that takes a position on a controversial issue plays a significant role in college work and professional life, as the following examples indicate:

- A committee made up of business and community leaders investigates the issue of regulating urban growth. After reviewing the arguments for and against government regulation, committee members argue against it on the grounds that supply and demand alone will regulate development, that landowners should be permitted to sell their property to the highest bidder, and that developers are guided by the needs of the market and thus serve the people.

- For an economics class, a student writes a term paper on the controversies surrounding the rising cost of public education. Online and in the library, she finds several blogs, newspaper and magazine articles, and contemporary books that help her understand the debate over the issues. She presents the strongest arguments on the different sides and takes the position that, to be economically viable, public education needs more financial support from various sectors, including business, government, and nonprofit organizations.

Thinking about Position Argument

Write a paragraph or two about an occasion when you read, heard, or took a position in school, at work, or in another context.

- Who was the *audience*? Consider how communicating to the particular audience (such as a friend rather than a teacher, or a group of your peers rather than a gathering of their parents) shaped the argument. How much did the audience already know about the topic, and had they already taken their own position? Did you or the author choose particular details or evidence because you knew it would be convincing to your audience? How was the tone tailored to appeal to them — informal, perhaps, for friends, more formal for parents or teachers?

- What was the main *purpose*? Was the goal to convince the audience of the rightness of the position, to show several points of view, or perhaps simply to shift their perspective on a controversial topic?

- How would you rate the *rhetorical sensitivity* with which the argument was presented? What made it appropriate or inappropriate for its particular audience or purpose?

A GUIDE TO READING
ESSAYS ARGUING FOR A POSITION

This guide introduces you to writing that takes a position by inviting you to analyze a brief but impassioned essay about science by Brian Greene:

- *Reading for meaning* will help you understand the scope of the issue as well as understand and respond to Greene's argument — for example, your own feelings about science and the way it is taught.

- *Reading like a writer* will help you learn how Greene makes the essay interesting, informative, and compelling by examining how the basic features and strategies typical of position writing are employed, such as

  1. presenting the controversial issue *fairly* and *credibly*

  2. asserting a *clear position*

  3. arguing directly for it with reasonable *evidence*

  4. *responding to objections and alternative positions* fairly

Brian Greene

Put a Little Science in Your Life

Brian Greene (b. 1963) earned his Ph.D. from Oxford University as a Rhodes Scholar. He is currently a professor of mathematics and physics at Columbia University, where he is also codirector of the Institute for Strings, Cosmology, and Astroparticle Physics (ISCAP). Greene is the author of numerous professional and popular essays, as well as four books about physics for a general audience: *The Elegant Universe: Superstrings, Hidden Dimensions, and the Quest for the Ultimate Theory* (1999); *The Fabric of the Cosmos: Space, Time, and the Texture of Reality* (2004); *Icarus at the Edge of Time* (2008); and *The Elegant Universe: Parallel Universes and the Deep Laws of the Cosmos* (2011). As he reveals in the following essay, published in the *New York Times*, Greene believes science should be placed alongside music, art, and literature as fields that give life meaning.

- **Before you read,** think about your own experiences with science, either in school or out of it. Do you understand science easily, or only with difficulty?

- **As you read,** think about Greene's assertion that "[l]ike a life without music, art or literature, a life without science is bereft of something that gives experience a rich and otherwise inaccessible dimension" (par. 11). Does Greene persuade you of the truth of this statement?

A couple of years ago I received a letter from an American soldier in Iraq. The letter 1 began by saying that, as we've all become painfully aware, serving on the front lines is physically exhausting and emotionally debilitating. But the reason for his writing was to tell me that in that hostile and lonely environment, a book I'd written had become a kind of lifeline. As the book is about science—one that traces physicists' search for nature's deepest laws—the soldier's letter might strike you as, well, odd.

But it's not. Rather, it speaks to the powerful role science can play in giving life 2 context and meaning. At the same time, the soldier's letter emphasized something I've increasingly come to believe: our educational system fails to teach science in a way that allows students to integrate it into their lives.

Allow me a moment to explain.   3

When we consider the ubiquity of cellphones, iPods, personal computers and the   4 Internet, it's easy to see how science (and the technology to which it leads) is woven into the fabric of our day-to-day activities. When we benefit from CT scanners, M.R.I. devices, pacemakers and arterial stents, we can immediately appreciate how science affects the quality of our lives. When we assess the state of the world, and identify looming challenges like climate change, global pandemics, security threats and diminishing resources, we don't hesitate in turning to science to gauge the problems and find solutions.

And when we look at the wealth of opportunities hovering on the horizon— stem   5 cells, genomic sequencing, personalized medicine, longevity research, nanoscience, brain-machine interface, quantum computers, space technology—we realize how crucial it is to cultivate a general public that can engage with scientific issues; there's simply no other way that as a society we will be prepared to make informed decisions on a range of issues that will shape the future.

These are the standard—and enormously important—reasons many would give in   6 explaining why science matters.

But here's the thing. The reason science really matters runs deeper still. Science is a   7 way of life. Science is a perspective. Science is the process that takes us from confusion to understanding in a manner that's precise, predictive and reliable—a transformation, for those lucky enough to experience it, that is empowering and emotional. To be able to think through and grasp explanations—for everything from why the sky is blue to how life formed on earth—not because they are declared dogma but rather because they reveal patterns confirmed by experiment and observation, is one of the most precious of human experiences.

As a practicing scientist, I know this from my own work and study. But I also know   8 that you don't have to be a scientist for science to be transformative. I've seen children's eyes light up as I've told them about black holes and the Big Bang. I've spoken with high school dropouts who've stumbled on popular science books about the human genome project, and then returned to school with newfound purpose. And in that letter from Iraq, the soldier told me how learning about relativity and quantum physics in the dusty and dangerous environs of greater Baghdad kept him going because it revealed a deeper reality of which we're all a part.

It's striking that science is still widely viewed as merely a subject one studies in the   9 classroom or an isolated body of largely esoteric knowledge that sometimes shows up in the "real" world in the form of technological or medical advances. In reality, science is a language of hope and inspiration, providing discoveries that fire the imagination and instill a sense of connection to our lives and our world.

If science isn't your strong suit—and for many it's not—this side of science is   10 something you may have rarely if ever experienced. I've spoken with so many people over the years whose encounters with science in school left them thinking of it as cold, distant and intimidating. They happily use the innovations that science makes possible, but feel that the science itself is just not relevant to their lives. What a shame.

Like a life without music, art or literature, a life without science is bereft of some- 11 thing that gives experience a rich and otherwise inaccessible dimension.

It's one thing to go outside on a crisp, clear night and marvel at a sky full of stars. It's 12 another to marvel not only at the spectacle but to recognize that those stars are the result of exceedingly ordered conditions 13.7 billion years ago at the moment of the Big Bang. It's another still to understand how those stars act as nuclear furnaces that supply the universe with carbon, oxygen and nitrogen, the raw material of life as we know it.

And it's yet another level of experience to realize that those stars account for less 13 than 4 percent of what's out there—the rest being of an unknown composition, so-called dark matter and energy, which researchers are now vigorously trying to divine.

As every parent knows, children begin life as uninhibited, unabashed explorers of 14 the unknown. From the time we can walk and talk, we want to know what things are and how they work—we begin life as little scientists. But most of us quickly lose our intrinsic scientific passion. And it's a profound loss.

A great many studies have focused on this problem, identifying important opportu- 15 nities for improving science education. Recommendations have ranged from increasing the level of training for science teachers to curriculum reforms.

But most of these studies (and their suggestions) avoid an overarching systemic 16 issue: in teaching our students, we continually fail to activate rich opportunities for revealing the breathtaking vistas opened up by science, and instead focus on the need to gain competency with science's underlying technical details.

In fact, many students I've spoken to have little sense of the big questions those 17 technical details collectively try to answer: Where did the universe come from? How did life originate? How does the brain give rise to consciousness? Like a music curriculum that requires its students to practice scales while rarely if ever inspiring them by playing the great masterpieces, this way of teaching science squanders the chance to make students sit up in their chairs and say, "Wow, that's science?"

In physics, just to give a sense of the raw material that's available to be leveraged, 18 the most revolutionary of advances have happened in the last 100 years—special relativity, general relativity, quantum mechanics—a symphony of discoveries that changed our conception of reality. More recently, the last 10 years have witnessed an upheaval in our understanding of the universe's composition, yielding a wholly new prediction for what the cosmos will be like in the far future.

These are paradigm-shaking developments. But rare is the high school class, and 19 rarer still is the middle school class, in which these breakthroughs are introduced. It's much the same story in classes for biology, chemistry and mathematics.

At the root of this pedagogical approach is a firm belief in the vertical nature of sci- 20 ence: you must master *A* before moving on to *B*. When *A* happened a few hundred years ago, it's a long climb to the modern era. Certainly, when it comes to teaching the technicalities—solving this equation, balancing that reaction, grasping the discrete parts of the cell—the verticality of science is unassailable.

But science is so much more than its technical details. And with careful attention 21 to presentation, cutting-edge insights and discoveries can be clearly and faithfully communicated to students independent of those details; in fact, those insights and discoveries are precisely the ones that can drive a young student to want to learn the details. We rob science education of life when we focus solely on results and seek to train students to solve problems and recite facts without a commensurate emphasis on transporting them out beyond the stars.

Science is the greatest of all adventure stories, one that's been unfolding for thou- 22 sands of years as we have sought to understand ourselves and our surroundings. Science needs to be taught to the young and communicated to the mature in a manner that captures this drama. We must embark on a cultural shift that places science in its rightful place alongside music, art and literature as an indispensable part of what makes life worth living.

It's the birthright of every child, it's a necessity for every adult, to look out on the 23 world, as the soldier in Iraq did, and see that the wonder of the cosmos transcends everything that divides us.

READING FOR MEANING

1. **Read to Summarize.** Write a sentence or two explaining the author's position on science's contribution to education.

   For help with summarizing, see Chapter 2, pp. 24–25.

2. **Read to Respond.** Write a paragraph analyzing your initial reactions to anything that seems surprising, such as Greene's assertion that "in teaching our students, we continually fail to activate rich opportunities for revealing the breathtaking vistas opened up by science, and instead focus on the need to gain competency with science's underlying technical details" (par. 16); or why you think Greene chooses to begin his essay with a letter from a soldier in Iraq (par. 1).

   You may also try recognizing emotional manipulation; see Chapter 2, pp. 44–45.

3. **Read to Analyze Assumptions.** Write a paragraph or two analyzing an assumption you find intriguing in Greene's essay. For example:

   For help analyzing assumptions, see Chapter 2, pp. 28–29.

   Assumptions about the intrinsic excitement and pleasure of discovery. Greene asserts the idea not only that science matters but also that it is "a language of hope and inspiration, providing discoveries that fire the imagination and instill a sense of connection to our lives and our world" (par. 9).

   - What kinds of discoveries does Greene mention, and what do they mean to you? Are your discoveries (if you have made them) scientific, or are they in other fields? How do you feel when you've made a discovery?

   - Why does Greene group science with music, art, and literature? Does this suggest parallels among them, or underscore qualities they have in common?

Assumptions about the transforming role of education. Greene uses language like "transformation" (par. 7) and "transporting them out beyond the stars" (par. 21) to describe the effect he thinks science should have on children. He points out that children "begin life as little scientists" (par. 14) but that most of them lose their "intrinsic scientific passion" (par. 14) because schools "fail to activate rich opportunities for revealing the breathtaking vistas opened up by science, and instead focus on the need to gain competency with science's underlying technical details" (par. 16).

- What view of education is held by those who teach science as a "vertical" (par. 20) subject? Do you think Greene's view of science as "the greatest of all adventure stories" (par. 22) is held by most people? Is it the duty of education to be transforming — "to make students sit up in their chairs and say, 'Wow . . .'" (par. 17)? What value, if any, is there to gaining "competency with science's underlying technical details" (par. 16)?

You may also try evaluating the logic of an argument; see Chapter 2, pp. 40–41.

- Greene criticizes schooling that doesn't teach the "big questions" (par. 17): "But rare is the high school class, and rarer still is the middle school class, in which these breakthroughs are introduced. It's much the same story in classes for biology, chemistry and mathematics" (par. 19). Greene seems to assume that exposure to contemporary scientific discoveries would benefit education. What evidence does he offer to persuade you?

READING LIKE A WRITER

Presenting the Controversial Issue Fairly and Credibly

For position papers published during an ongoing public debate, writers may need only to mention the issue. In most cases, however, writers need to explain the issue to readers. They may, for example, place the issue in its historical or cultural context, cite specific instances to make the issue seem less abstract, show their personal interest in the debate, or establish or redefine the terms of the debate. Greene uses a common sentence pattern for redefining the terms of the debate. First he presents the issue as he believes it is commonly perceived, and then he contrasts this common perception with his own view:

▶ When _____ [issue/event] happens, most people think _____, but I think _____.

Here's an example from the reading selection:

These are the standard — and enormously important — reasons many would give in explaining why science matters.
But here's the thing. The reason science really matters runs deeper still. (pars. 6–7)

Note how civil — how rhetorically sensitive — Greene is in the first sentence; he respects those who have the standard reasons for explaining why science matters. Then in the second sentence he proposes that science matters for even "deeper" reasons.

Analyze & Write

Write a paragraph analyzing how Greene presents the issue for his readers and gives them a reason to listen to him:

1. Reread paragraphs 1–7, where Greene introduces the issue, and underline phrases that connect you to the issue. For example, Greene notes that "as we've all become painfully aware, serving on the front lines is physically exhausting and emotionally debilitating" (par. 1). How does using the first-person plural (*we*) help readers make a link to their own experience? Does Greene use other strategies in these paragraphs to present the issue in a way readers will find engaging and prompt their curiosity?

2. Reread paragraphs 4–5. Look at Greene's lists of everything connected to science. For example, "the ubiquity of cellphones, iPods, personal computers and the Internet" (par. 4). How does his listing demonstrate the importance of the issue? What other strategies does he use here or elsewhere in the essay to demonstrate the importance of science education?

3. Now reread paragraph 8 to see how Greene establishes his credibility as a writer on the issue of science education. His last line in paragraph 7 heralds the scientific method as a way of enabling us to "think through and grasp explanations . . . not because they are declared dogma but rather because they reveal patterns confirmed by experiment and observation," and asserts that this is "one of the most precious of human experiences." What words and phrases in paragraph 8 establish Greene not only as a scientist but also as a teacher and remind the reader of important discoveries with which Greene is familiar?

You might also try recognizing emotional manipulation; see Chapter 2, pp. 44–45.

Asserting a Clear Position

Writers of position papers take sides. Their primary purposes are to assert a position of their own and to influence readers' thinking. The assertion is the main point of the essay — its **thesis.** Presented simply and directly, the thesis statement often forecasts the stages of the argument as well, identifying the main reason or reasons that will be developed and supported in the essay.

Many writers place the thesis early in the essay to let readers know right away where they stand. But if they need to present the issue at length or define the terms of the debate, writers can postpone introducing their own position. Restating the thesis in different words at various points in the body of the essay and at the end can help keep readers oriented.

Analyze & Write

Write a paragraph analyzing how and why Greene states and restates his position:

1. Underline the sentence in which Greene explicitly asserts his position (at the end of par. 2). Note any key words he uses there.

2. Skim paragraphs 7–9, 11, 14, 16–17, 19, and 21–22, and put brackets around the sentences in these paragraphs that restate the thesis in various ways.

3. Now examine *how* Greene restates his thesis. Look closely at the language he uses to see whether he repeats key words, uses synonyms for them, or adds new phrasing. What do you learn from Greene's repetition and his variations?

Arguing Directly for the Position, and Supporting the Position with Reasonable Evidence

Not only do writers of position papers explicitly assert their positions, but they also give reasons for them. They usually support their reasons with facts, statistics, examples, anecdotes, expert opinions, and analogies:

- **Facts** are statements that can be proven objectively to be true, but readers may need to be reassured that the facts come from trustworthy sources.

- **Statistics** may be mistaken for facts, but they are only interpretations or compilations of numerical data. Their reliability depends on how and by whom the information was collected and interpreted.

- **Examples** are not usually claimed to be proof of the writer's position or to be evidence that the position applies in every case. Examples help a reader understand the situations in which the position is valid. Powerful examples are often the reason readers change their minds or at least grant that the position is true in the case of a particular example.

- **Anecdotes** tell stories and recall vivid images to help readers imagine themselves in the position of the writer. Anecdotes are also memorable, as many stories are, so readers remember why the author has taken a certain position.

- **Expert opinions** and **analogies** are also useful for support. Readers must decide whether to regard quotations from experts as credible and authoritative. They must also decide how much weight to give analogies — comparisons that encourage readers to assume that what is true about one thing is also true about something to which it is compared.

Position arguments are most convincing when writers are able to appeal to readers on three levels:

- **logos:** Appeals to readers' intellect, presenting them with logical reasoning and reliable evidence

- **ethos:** Appeals to readers' perception of the writer's credibility and fairness

- **pathos:** Appeals to readers' values and feelings

Analyze & Write

Write a paragraph or two analyzing Greene's strategy of arguing by example:

1. Reread paragraph 7 and paragraphs 17–18, where Greene develops his argument that the study of science should include the big questions as well as the technical details, and put brackets around the sentence or sentences in each paragraph that state this part of his argument.

2. Look closely at the examples in paragraphs 17–18, where Greene supports this reason with appropriate questions to ask and the scientific theories developed in the last one hundred years. Underline these questions and theories throughout both paragraphs, and then compare them to each other. Do you think that some readers would find the argument in this part of the essay compelling and other readers would not? If so, why or why not?

Responding to Objections and Alternative Positions Fairly and Credibly

Writers of position papers often try to anticipate the likely objections, questions, and alternative positions that readers might raise. Writers may concede points with which they agree and may even modify a thesis to accommodate valid objections. A typical way of conceding is to use sentence strategies like these:

▶ I agree that .... is certainly an important factor.

But when they think that the criticism is groundless or opposing arguments are flawed, writers respond assertively. They refute the challenges to their argument by pointing out the flaws in their opponents' reasoning and support. A typical refutation states the problem with the opposing view and then explains why the view is problematic, using sentence strategies like these:

▶ One problem with .... [opposing view] is that ....
▶ Some claim .... [opposing view], but in reality ....

Notice that writers often introduce the refutation with a transition that indicates contrast, such as *but, although, nevertheless,* or *however.* When writers deal with alternative viewpoints, they enhance their own fairness and credibility by treating those who hold these views with civility and respect.

Frequently, writers reach out to readers by making a concession, but then go on to point out where they differ. Writers conceding and then refuting often use sentence strategies like these:

▶ .... may be true for ...., *but* not for ....

▶ *Although* ...., I think ....

▶ .... insists that .... *Nevertheless, in spite of her good* intentions, ...

Not all writers use transition words to signal a response to alternative views, however. Consider, for example, the way Greene concedes and then refutes the existing approach to science education:

Cues signaling concession	These are the standard — and enormously important — reasons many would give in explaining why science matters.
Cues signaling refutation	But here's the thing. The reason science really matters runs deeper still. (pars. 6–7)

Analyze & Write

Write a paragraph or two analyzing how Greene responds to alternative views and evaluating Greene's credibility and likely success with his readers:

1. Reread paragraphs 9–10, 15–16, and 20–21, where Greene introduces alternative arguments to his position. Underline the sentence in each paragraph that best states the alternative position.

2. Now highlight the sentences in which Greene responds to these opposing arguments. Where does he concede and where does he refute these alternatives? What seems to be his attitude toward those who disagree with him or who object to parts of his argument? How effective are his strategies in persuading readers to accept his position?

READINGS

David Z. Hambrick and Christopher Chabris

Yes, IQ Really Matters

David Z. Hambrick received his Ph.D. from Georgia Institute of Technology and is a professor of psychology at Michigan State University. He has published numerous professional and popular articles on brain theory and learning. He is an associate editor of the *Journal of Experimental Psychology: General* and has received research grants from the U.S. Department of Naval Research and the National Science Foundation.

Christopher Chabris received his Ph.D. in psychology from Harvard. He is an associate professor of psychology and codirector of the Neuroscience Program at Union College as well as a visiting fellow at the Institute for Advanced Study in Toulouse, France. He has published numerous articles in professional journals such as *Science, Nature, Perception,* and *Cognitive Science.* He is a contributor to the *New York Times,* the *Wall Street Journal,* and other national magazines, and is coauthor with Daniel Simons of *The Invisible Gorilla: How Our Intuitions Deceive Us* (2010).

The essay below was published on *Slate,* an online current affairs and cultural magazine, in 2015. We have converted Hambrick and Chabris's links to in-text citations where needed and have provided a list of the links at the end of the selection; citations appear in APA Style, which is the documentation style preferred by social sciences. (For more on APA Style, see the Appendix, pp. 527–36.)

- **Before you read,** think about your own experience with the SAT, IQ tests, or other standardized exams. Have they impacted your educational opportunities or life so far? How?

- **As you read,** note how the authors present the arguments of those with whom they disagree, and how they then deal with those arguments. Are their strategies effective?

1 The College Board — the standardized testing behemoth that develops and administers the SAT and other tests — has redesigned its flagship product again. Beginning in spring 2016, the writing section will be optional, the reading section will no longer test "obscure" vocabulary words, and the math section will put more emphasis on solving problems with real-world relevance. Overall, as the College Board explains on its website, "The redesigned SAT will more closely reflect the real work of college and career, where a flexible command of evidence — whether found in text or graphic [sic] — is more important than ever."

Does this opening paragraph arouse your curiosity? Why or why not?

2 A number of pressures may be behind this redesign. Perhaps it's competition from the ACT, or fear that unless the SAT is made to seem more

relevant, more colleges will go the way of Wake Forest, Brandeis, and Sarah Lawrence and join the "test optional admissions movement," which already boasts several hundred members (850+ Colleges and Universities, 2016). Or maybe it's the wave of bad press that standardized testing, in general, has received over the past few years.

Critics of standardized testing are grabbing this opportunity to take their   3 best shot at the SAT. They make two main arguments. The first is simply that a person's SAT score is essentially meaningless—that it says nothing about whether that person will go on to succeed in college. Leon Botstein, president of Bard College and longtime standardized testing critic (2000), wrote in *Time* that the SAT "needs to be abandoned and replaced," and added:

> The blunt fact is that the SAT has never been a good predictor of academic achievement in college. High school grades adjusted to account for the curriculum and academic programs in the high school from which a student graduates are. The essential mechanism of the SAT, the multiple choice test question, is a bizarre relic of long outdated 20th century social scientific assumptions and strategies. (Botstein, "Tyranny"; Botstein, "College President")

Calling use of SAT scores for college admissions a "national scandal,"   4 Jennifer Finney Boylan (2014), an English professor at Colby College, argued in the *New York Times* that:

> The only way to measure students' potential is to look at the complex portrait of their lives: what their schools are like; how they've done in their courses; what they've chosen to study; what progress they've made over time; how they've reacted to adversity.

Along the same lines, Elizabeth Kolbert (2015) wrote in *The New Yorker* that "the SAT measures those skills—and really only those skills—necessary for the SATs."

But this argument is wrong. The SAT *does* predict success in   5 college—not perfectly, but relatively well, especially given that it takes just a few hours to administer. And, unlike a "complex portrait" of a student's life, it can be scored in an objective way. (In a recent *New York Times* op-ed, "We Need More Tests, Not Fewer," the University of New Hampshire psychologist John D. Mayer aptly described the SAT's validity as an "astonishing achievement.") In a 2012 study published in *Psychological Science,* University of Minnesota researchers Paul Sackett, Nathan Kuncel, and their colleagues investigated the relationship between SAT scores and college grades in a very large sample: nearly 150,000 students from 110 colleges and universities. SAT scores predicted first-year college GPA about as well as high school grades did, and the best prediction was achieved by considering *both* factors. Botstein, Boylan, and Kolbert are either unaware of this directly relevant, easily accessible, and widely disseminated empirical evidence, or they have decided to ignore it and base their claims on

Paragraphs 2–4 present the arguments of the opposition to Hambrick and Chabris's thesis that the SAT is a valid predictor of college performance. Why did they choose to present the opposition before they present directly for their own argument? How does this decision impact or influence their readers?

intuition and anecdote—or perhaps on their beliefs about the way the world should be rather than the way it is.

6   Furthermore, contrary to popular belief, it's not just first-year college GPA that SAT scores predict. In a four-year study that started with nearly 3,000 college students, a team of Michigan State University researchers led by Neal Schmitt (2009) found that test score (SAT or ACT—whichever the student took) correlated strongly with cumulative GPA at the end of the fourth year. If the students were ranked on both their test scores and cumulative GPAs, those who had test scores in the top half (above the 50th percentile, or median) would have had a roughly two-thirds chance of having a cumulative GPA in the top half. By contrast, students with bottom-half SAT scores would be only one-third likely to make it to the top half in GPA.

7   Test scores also predicted whether the students graduated: A student who scored in the 95th percentile on the SAT or ACT was about 60 percent more likely to graduate than a student who scored in the 50th percentile. Similarly impressive evidence supports the validity of the SAT's graduate school counterparts: the Graduate Record Examinations, the Law School Admissions Test, and the Graduate Management Admission Test. A 2007 *Science* article summed up the evidence succinctly: "Standardized admissions tests have positive and useful relationships with subsequent student accomplishments" (Kuncel & Hezlett, 2007).

8   SAT scores even predict success beyond the college years. For more than two decades, Vanderbilt University researchers [Kimberly Robertson, Stijn Smeets,] David Lubinski, and Camilla Benbow (2010) have tracked the accomplishments of people who, as part of a youth talent search, scored in the top 1 percent on the SAT by age 13. Remarkably, even within this group of gifted students, higher scorers were not only more likely to earn advanced degrees but also more likely to succeed outside of academia. For example, compared with people who "only" scored in the top 1 percent, those who scored in the top *one-tenth* of 1 percent—the extremely gifted—were more than twice as likely as adults to have an annual income in the top 5 percent of Americans.

9   The second popular anti-SAT argument is that, if the test measures anything at all, it's not cognitive skill but socioeconomic status. In other words, some kids do better than others on the SAT not because they're smarter, but because their parents are rich. Boylan (2014) argued in her *Times* article that the SAT "favors the rich, who can afford preparatory crash courses" like those offered by Kaplan and the Princeton Review. Leon Botstein (2014) claimed in his *Time* article that "the only persistent statistical result from the SAT is the correlation between high income and high test scores." And according to a *Washington Post Wonkblog* infographic (which is really more of a disinfographic) "your SAT score says more about your parents than about you" (http://knowmore .washingtonpost.com/2014/03/06/why-your-sat-score-says-more-about-your -parents -than-about-you/).

How do you respond to the last sentence in paragraph 5? Do you think the authors are being rhetorically sensitive to their audience and exhibiting civility within the essay? (See p. 10 for more on these academic habits of mind.)

What kinds of evidence are presented in paragraphs 6–9 to support the contention that the opposing arguments are "wrong"? (See Chapter 2 to help you analyze different writing strategies for presenting evidence.)

What information do the authors provide about their sources? Keep in mind that they are writing for a popular online audience. Do you share the assumptions of Hambrick and Chabris that the credentials are adequate to make these sources believable? Why or why not?

FIGURE 8.1   2015 College-bound seniors' SAT scores by family income

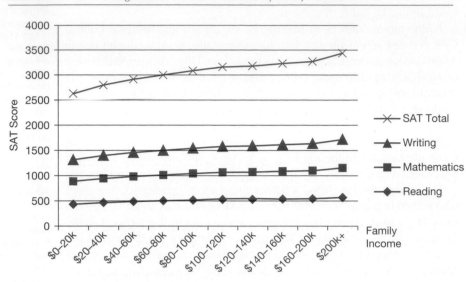

Data from: College Board, 2015 College-Bound Seniors Total Group Profile Report

The sequence in paragraphs 10 and 11 is called *concession/refutation*. What is the effect on the reader when a writer first concedes the claim of the opposition but then refutes its accuracy?

It's true that economic background correlates with SAT scores. Kids from well-off families tend to do better on the SAT. However, the correlation is far from perfect. In the University of Minnesota study (Sackett et al., 2012) of nearly 150,000 students, the correlation between socioeconomic status, or SES, and SAT was not trivial but not huge. (A perfect correlation has a value of 1; this one was .25.) What this means is that there are plenty of low-income students who get good scores on the SAT; there are even likely to be low-income students among those who achieve a *perfect score* on the SAT.   10

Thus, just as it was originally designed to do, the SAT in fact goes a long way toward leveling the playing field, giving students an opportunity to distinguish themselves regardless of their background. Scoring well on the SAT may in fact be the *only* such opportunity for students who graduate from public high schools that are regarded by college admissions offices as academically weak. In a letter to the editor (2014), a reader of Elizabeth Kolbert's *New Yorker* article on the SAT made this point well: 11

Does this first-person example convince you, or do you think one personal example is not enough evidence to be convincing? Why or why not?

The SAT may be the bane of upper-middle-class parents trying to launch their children on a path to success. But sometimes one person's obstacle is another person's springboard. I am the daughter of a single, immigrant father who never attended college, and a good SAT score was one of the achievements that catapulted me into my state's flagship university and, from there, on to medical school. Flawed though it is, the SAT afforded me, as it has thousands of others, a way to prove that a poor, public-school kid who never had any test prep can do just as well as, if not better than, her better-off peers.

12   The sort of admissions approach that Botstein advocates—adjusting high school GPA "to account for the curriculum and academic programs in the high school from which a student graduates" and abandoning the SAT—would do the *opposite* of leveling the playing field (2014). A given high school GPA would be adjusted down for a poor, public-school kid, and adjusted up for a rich, private-school kid.

13   Furthermore, contrary to what Boylan (2014) implies in her *Times* piece, "preparatory crash courses" don't change SAT scores much. Research has consistently shown that prep courses have only a small effect on SAT scores—and a *much* smaller effect than test prep companies claim they do (Briggs, 2001). For example, in one study of a random sample of more than 4,000 students, average improvement in overall score on the "old" SAI, which had a range from 400 to 1600, was no more than about 30 points (Powers & Rock, 1999).

14   Finally, it is clear that SES is *not* what accounts for the fact that SAT scores predict success in college. In the University of Minnesota study, the correlation between high school SAT and college GPA was virtually unchanged after the researchers statistically controlled for the influence of SES (Sackett et al., 2012). If SAT scores were just a proxy for privilege, then putting SES into the mix should have removed, or at least dramatically decreased, the association between the SAT and college performance. But it didn't. This is more evidence that Boylan overlooks or chooses to ignore.

15   What this all means is that the SAT measures something—some stable characteristic of high school students other than their parents' income—that translates into success in college. And what could that characteristic be? General intelligence. The content of the SAT is practically indistinguishable from that of standardized intelligence tests that social scientists use to study individual differences, and that psychologists and psychiatrists use to determine whether a person is intellectually disabled—and even whether a person should be spared execution in states that have the death penalty. Scores on the SAT correlate very highly with scores on IQ tests—so highly that the Harvard education scholar Howard Gardner (1999), known for his theory of multiple intelligences, once called the SAT and other scholastic measures "thinly disguised" intelligence tests (p. 18).

16   One could of course argue that IQ is also meaningless—and many have. For example, in his bestseller *The Social Animal,* David Brooks (2001) claimed that "once you get past some pretty obvious correlations (smart people make better mathematicians), there is a very loose relationship between IQ and life outcomes." And in a recent *Huffington Post* article, psychologists Tracy Alloway and Ross Alloway (2013) wrote that

> IQ won't help you in the things that really matter: It won't help you find happiness, it won't help you make better decisions, and it won't help you manage your kids' homework and the accounts at the same time. It isn't even that useful at its raison d'être: predicting success.

The authors are performing a critical analysis of the arguments claiming that IQ predicts success. What kinds of evidence do they provide to support their assumption? Do you share their assumption that the SAT essentially equals the IQ test?

But this argument is wrong, too. Indeed, we know as well as anything 17 we know in psychology that IQ predicts many different measures of success. Exhibit A is evidence from research on job performance by the University of Iowa industrial psychologist Frank Schmidt and his late colleague John Hunter. Synthesizing evidence from nearly a century of empirical studies, Schmidt and Hunter established that general mental ability—the psychological trait that IQ scores reflect—is the single best predictor of job training success, and that it accounts for differences in job performance even in workers with more than a decade of experience (2008, 2014). It's more predictive than interests, personality, reference checks, and interview performance. Smart people don't just make better mathematicians, as Brooks (2001) observed—they make better managers, clerks, salespeople, service workers, vehicle operators, and soldiers.

IQ predicts other things that matter, too, like income, employment, 18 health, and even longevity. In a 2001 study published in the *British Medical Journal,* Scottish researchers Lawrence Whalley and Ian Deary identified more than 2,000 people who had taken part in the Scottish Mental Survey of 1932, a nationwide assessment of IQ. Remarkably, people with high IQs at age 11 were considerably more likely to survive to old age than were people with lower IQs. For example, a person with an IQ of 100 (the average for the general population) was 21 percent more likely to live to age 76 than a person with an IQ of 85. And the relationship between IQ and longevity remains statistically significant even after taking SES into account. Perhaps IQ reflects the mental resources—the reasoning and problem-solving skills—that people can bring to bear on maintaining their health and making wise decisions throughout life. This explanation is supported by evidence that higher-IQ individuals engage in more positive health behaviors, such as deciding to quit smoking (Goffredson & Dreary, 2004).

How are you affected by this shift in focus from predictive success in a career to longer and better life?

IQ is of course not the only factor that contributes to differences in out- 19 comes like academic achievement and job performance (and longevity). Psychologists have known for many decades that certain personality traits also have an impact. One is conscientiousness, which reflects a person's self-control, discipline, and thoroughness. People who are high in conscientiousness delay gratification to get their work done, finish tasks that they start, and are careful in their work, whereas people who are low in conscientiousness are impulsive, undependable, and careless (compare Lisa and Bart Simpson). The University of Pennsylvania psychologist Angela Duckworth has proposed a closely related characteristic that she calls "grit," which she defines as a person's "tendency to sustain interest in and effort toward very long-term goals," like building a career or family (Home, 2016).

Duckworth has argued that such factors may be even more important as 20 predictors of success than IQ. In one study, she and UPenn colleague Martin Seligman (2005) found that a measure of self-control collected at the start of eighth grade correlated more than twice as strongly with year-end grades than IQ did. However, the results of meta-analyses, which are more telling than the results of any individual study, indicate that these factors do not have a larger effect than IQ does on measures of academic achievement and job performance (Poropoat, 2009). So, while it seems clear that factors like conscientiousness—not to mention social skill, creativity, interest, and motivation—do influence success, they cannot take the place of IQ.

21   None of this is to say that IQ, whether measured with the SAT or a traditional intelligence test, is an indicator of value or worth. Nobody should be judged, negatively or positively, on the basis of a test score. A test score is a prediction, not a prophecy, and doesn't say anything specific about what a person will or will not achieve in life. A high IQ doesn't guarantee success, and a low IQ doesn't guarantee failure. Furthermore, the fact that IQ is at present a powerful predictor of certain socially relevant outcomes doesn't mean it always will be. If there were less variability in income—a smaller gap between the rich and the poor—then IQ would have a weaker correlation with income. For the same reason, if everyone received the same quality of health care, there would be a weaker correlation between IQ and health.

Why do you think the authors offer this disclaimer?

22   But the bottom line is that there are large, measurable differences among people in intellectual ability, and these differences have consequences for people's lives. Ignoring these facts will only distract us from discovering and implementing wise policies.

23   Given everything that social scientists have learned about IQ and its broad predictive validity, it is reasonable to make it a factor in decisions such as whom to hire for a particular job or admit to a particular college or university. In fact, disregarding IQ—by admitting students to colleges or hiring people for jobs in which they are very likely to fail—is harmful both to individuals and to society. For example, in occupations where safety is paramount, employers could be incentivized to incorporate measures of cognitive ability into the recruitment process. Above all, the policies of public and private organizations should be based on evidence rather than ideology or wishful thinking.

This paragraph follows the strategy of arguing through cause and effect (see Ch. 9). Does the essay help you understand and accept this conclusion, or do you feel the authors have not been convincing?

Links

850+ colleges and universities that do not use SAT/ACT scores for admitting substantial numbers of students into bachelor degree programs. (2016). *FairTest*. Retrieved from http://www.fairtest.org/

Alloway, T., & Alloway, R. (2013, October 28). The end of IQ (and the dawn of working memory). *The Huffington Post*. Retrieved from http://www.huffingtonpost.com/

Botstein, L. (2000, May 28). A tyranny of standardized tests. *The New York Times*. Retrieved from http://www.nytimes.com/

Botstein, L. (2014, March 7). College president: SAT is part hoax, part fraud. *Time*. Retrieved from http://time.com/

Briggs, D. C. (2001). The effect of admissions test preparation: evidence from NELS:88. *Chance 14*(1), 10–18. Retrieved from http://nepc.colorado.edu/files/Briggs_Theeffectofadmissionstestpreparation.pdf

Brooks, David. (2011). *The social animal: the hidden sources of love, character, and achievement*. Retrieved from https://books.google.com/

Boylan, J. F. (2014, March 6). Save us from the SAT. *The New York Times*. Retrieved from http://www.nytimes.com/

Duckworth, A. (2013, April). *The key to success? Grit.* [Video file]. Retrieved from http://www.ted.com/

Duckworth, A., & Seligman, M. E. P. (2005). Self-discipline outdoes IQ in predicting academic performance of adolescents. *Psychological Science 16*(12), 939–44. doi:10.1111/j.1467-9280.2005.01641.x

Gardner, H.E. (1999). *Intelligence reframed: Multiple intelligences for the 21st century.* Retrieved from https://books.google.com/

Goffredson, L. S., & Dreary, I. J. (2004). Intelligence predicts health and longevity, but why? *Current Directions in Psychological Science 13*(1), 1–4. doi:10.1111/j.0963-7214.2004.01301001.x

Home. (2016). *The Duckworth Lab*. Retrieved from https://sites.sas.upenn.edu/

Kolbert, E. (2015, December 16). Big score. *The New Yorker*. Retrieved from http://www.newyorker.com/

Kuncel, N. R., & Hezlett, S. A. (2007). Standardized tests predict graduate students' success." *Science 315*(5815), 1080–81. doi:10.1177/0956797612438732

Letters to the Editor. (2014, March 14). *The New Yorker*. Retrieved from http://www.newyorker.com/

Mayer, J. D. (2015, December 16). We need more tests, not fewer. *The New York Times*. Retrieved from http://www.nytimes.com/

The New SAT. (n.d.). *The College Board*. Retrieved from https://www.collegeboard.org

Poropat, A. E. (2009). A meta-analysis of the five-factor model of personality and academic performance. *Psychological Bulletin 135*(2), 322–38. doi:10.1037/a0014996

Powers, D. E., & Rock, D. A. (1999). Effects of coaching on SAT I: Reasoning test scores. *Journal of Educational Measurement 36*(2), 93–118. doi: 10.1111/j.1745-3984.1999.tb00549.x

Robertson, K. F., Smeets, S., Lubinski, D., & Benbow, C. (2010). Beyond the threshold hypothesis: Even among the gifted and top math/science graduate students, cognitive abilities, vocational interests, and lifestyle preferences matter for career choice, performance, and persistence. *Current Directions in Psychological Science 19*(6), 346–351.

Sackett, P. R., Kuncel, N. R., Beatty, A. S., Rigdon, J. L., Shen, W., & Kiger, T.B. (2012). The role of socioeconomic status in SAT-grade relationships and in college admissions decisions. *Psychological Science 23*(9), 1000–1007. doi:10.1177/0956797612438732

Schmidt, F. L., & Hunter, J. E. (2008). The validity and utility of selection methods in personnel psychology: practical and theoretical implications of 85 years of research findings. *Psychological Bulletin 124*(2), 262–74. doi:10.1037/0033-2909.124.2.262

Schmidt, F. L., & Hunter, J. E. (2014). General mental ability in the world of work: occupational attainment and job performance. *Journal of Personality and Social Psychology 86*(1), 162–73. doi:10.1037/0022-3514.86.1.162

Schmitt, N., Keeney, J., Oswald, F.L., Pleskac, T.J., Billington, A.Q., Sinha, R., Zorzie, M. (2009). Prediction of 4-year college student performance using cognitive and noncognitive predictors and the impact on demographic status of admitted students. *Journal of Applied Psychology 94*(6), 1479–97. doi:10.1037/a0016810

Whalley, L. J., & Dreary, I. J. (2001). Longitudinal cohort study of childhood IQ and survival up to age 76. *British Medical Journal 322*(819), 1–5. Retrieved from http://www.bmj.com/

Sherry Turkle

The Flight from Conversation

Sherry Turkle (b. 1948), professor of the social studies of science and technology at the Massachusetts Institute of Technology, earned her Ph.D. from Harvard University. She is the author of *Psychoanalytic Politics: Jacques Lacan and Freud's French Revolution* (1978); *Second Self: Computers and the Human Spirit* (1984); *Life on the Screen: Identity in the Age of the Internet* (1995); and *Simulation and Its Discontents* (2009). Turkle's most recent book is *Alone Together: Why We Expect More from Technology and Less from Each Other* (2011). Turkle is a media commentator on the social and psychological effects of technology. The article below was published in the Sunday Review section of the *New York Times* in 2012.

- **Before you read,** think about how much time you spend communicating with friends and family via "texting and e-mail and posting" (par. 10) versus how much time you spend talking with friends and family over the phone or face-to-face.

- **As you read,** pay attention to the kinds of evidence Turkle provides to support her assertions, such as quotations from interviews and written sources, examples, statistics, illustrations, and so on.

We live in a technological universe in which we are always communicating. And yet 1 we have sacrificed conversation for mere connection.

At home, families sit together, texting and reading e-mail. At work executives text 2 during board meetings. We text (and shop and go on Facebook) during classes and when we're on dates. My students tell me about an important new skill: it involves maintaining eye contact with someone while you text someone else; it's hard, but it can be done.

Over the past 15 years, I've studied technologies of mobile connection and talked 3 to hundreds of people of all ages and circumstances about their plugged-in lives. I've learned that the little devices most of us carry around are so powerful that they change not only what we do, but also who we are.

We've become accustomed to a new way of being "alone together." Technology- 4 enabled, we are able to be with one another, and also elsewhere, connected to wherever we want to be. We want to customize our lives. We want to move in and out of where we are because the thing we value most is control over where we focus our attention. We have gotten used to the idea of being in a tribe of one, loyal to our own party.

Our colleagues want to go to that board meeting but pay attention only to what 5 interests them. To some this seems like a good idea, but we can end up hiding from one another, even as we are constantly connected to one another.

A businessman laments that he no longer has colleagues at work. He doesn't stop 6 by to talk; he doesn't call. He says that he doesn't want to interrupt them. He says they're "too busy on their e-mail." But then he pauses and corrects himself. "I'm not telling the truth. I'm the one who doesn't want to be interrupted. I think I should. But I'd rather just do things on my BlackBerry."

A 16-year-old boy who relies on texting for almost everything says almost wist- 7 fully, "Someday, someday, but certainly not now, I'd like to learn how to have a conversation."

In today's workplace, young people who have grown up fearing conversation show 8 up on the job wearing earphones. Walking through a college library or the campus of a high-tech start-up, one sees the same thing: we are together, but each of us is in our own bubble, furiously connected to keyboards and tiny touch screens. A senior part-ner at a Boston law firm describes a scene in his office. Young associates lay out their suite of technologies: laptops, iPods and multiple phones. And then they put their earphones on. "Big ones. Like pilots. They turn their desks into cockpits." With the young lawyers in their cockpits, the office is quiet, a quiet that does not ask to be broken.

In the silence of connection, people are comforted by being in touch with a lot of 9 people — carefully kept at bay. We can't get enough of one another if we can use tech-nology to keep one another at distances we can control: not too close, not too far, just right. I think of it as a Goldilocks effect.

Texting and e-mail and posting let us present the self we want to be. This means we 10 can edit. And if we wish to, we can delete. Or retouch: the voice, the flesh, the face, the body. Not too much, not too little — just right.

Human relationships are rich; they're messy and demanding. We have learned the 11 habit of cleaning them up with technology. And the move from conversation to con-nection is part of this. But it's a process in which we shortchange ourselves. Worse, it seems that over time we stop caring, we forget that there is a difference.

We are tempted to think that our little "sips" of online connection add up to a big 12 gulp of real conversation. But they don't. E-mail, Twitter, Facebook, all of these have their places — in politics, commerce, romance and friendship. But no matter how valuable, they do not substitute for conversation.

Connecting in sips may work for gathering discrete bits of information or for saying, 13 "I am thinking about you." Or even for saying, "I love you." But connecting in sips doesn't work as well when it comes to understanding and knowing one another. In con-versation we tend to one another. (The word itself is kinetic; it's derived from words that mean to move, together.) We can attend to tone and nuance. In conversation, we are called upon to see things from another's point of view.

Face-to-face conversation unfolds slowly. It teaches patience. When we communi- 14 cate on our digital devices, we learn different habits. As we ramp up the volume and velocity of online connections, we start to expect faster answers. To get these, we ask one another simpler questions; we dumb down our communications, even on the most important matters. It is as though we have all put ourselves on cable news. Shakespeare might have said, "We are consum'd with that which we were nourish'd by."

And we use conversation with others to learn to converse with ourselves. So our 15 flight from conversation can mean diminished chances to learn skills of self-reflection. These days, social media continually asks us what's "on our mind," but we have little motivation to say something truly self-reflective. Self-reflection in conversation requires trust. It's hard to do anything with 3,000 Facebook friends except connect.

As we get used to being shortchanged on conversation and to getting by with less, 16 we seem almost willing to dispense with people altogether. Serious people muse about the future of computer programs as psychiatrists. A high school sophomore confides to me that he wishes he could talk to an artificial intelligence program instead of his dad about dating; he says the A.I. would have so much more in its database. Indeed, many people tell me they hope that as Siri, the digital assistant on Apple's iPhone, becomes more advanced, "she" will be more and more like a best friend—one who will listen when others won't.

During the years I have spent researching people and their relationships with tech- 17 nology, I have often heard the sentiment "No one is listening to me." I believe this feeling helps explain why it is so appealing to have a Facebook page or a Twitter feed—each provides so many automatic listeners. And it helps explain why—against all reason—so many of us are willing to talk to machines that seem to care about us. Researchers around the world are busy inventing sociable robots, designed to be companions to the elderly, to children, to all of us.

One of the most haunting experiences during my research came when I brought 18 one of these robots, designed in the shape of a baby seal, to an elder-care facility, and an older woman began to talk to it about the loss of her child. The robot seemed to be looking into her eyes. It seemed to be following the conversation. The woman was comforted.

And so many people found this amazing. Like the sophomore who wants advice 19 about dating from artificial intelligence and those who look forward to computer psychiatry, this enthusiasm speaks to how much we have confused conversation with connection and collectively seem to have embraced a new kind of delusion that accepts the simulation of compassion as sufficient unto the day. And why would we want to talk about love and loss with a machine that has no experience of the arc of human life? Have we so lost confidence that we will be there for one another?

We expect more from technology and less from one another and seem increasingly 20 drawn to technologies that provide the illusion of companionship without the demands of relationship. Always-on/always-on-you devices provide three powerful fantasies: that we will always be heard; that we can put our attention wherever we want it to be; and that we never have to be alone. Indeed our new devices have turned being alone into a problem that can be solved.

When people are alone, even for a few moments, they fidget and reach for a 21 device. Here connection works like a symptom, not a cure, and our constant, reflexive impulse to connect shapes a new way of being.

Think of it as "I share, therefore I am." We use technology to define ourselves by 22 sharing our thoughts and feelings as we're having them. We used to think, "I have a feeling; I want to make a call." Now our impulse is, "I want to have a feeling; I need to send a text."

So, in order to feel more, and to feel more like ourselves, we connect. But in our   23
rush to connect, we flee from solitude, our ability to be separate and gather ourselves.
Lacking the capacity for solitude, we turn to other people but don't experience them
as they are. It is as though we use them, need them as spare parts to support our
increasingly fragile selves.

We think constant connection will make us feel less lonely. The opposite is true. If   24
we are unable to be alone, we are far more likely to be lonely. If we don't teach our
children to be alone, they will know only how to be lonely.

I am a partisan for conversation. To make room for it, I see some first, deliberate   25
steps. At home, we can create sacred spaces: the kitchen, the dining room. We can
make our cars "device-free zones." We can demonstrate the value of conversation to
our children. And we can do the same thing at work. There we are so busy communicating that we often don't have time to talk to one another about what really matters.
Employees asked for casual Fridays; perhaps managers should introduce conversa-
tional Thursdays. Most of all, we need to remember—in between texts and e-mails
and Facebook posts—to listen to one another, even to the boring bits, because it is
often in unedited moments, moments in which we hesitate and stutter and go silent,
that we reveal ourselves to one another.

I spend the summers at a cottage on Cape Cod, and for decades I walked the same   26
dunes that Thoreau once walked. Not too long ago, people walked with their heads
up, looking at the water, the sky, the sand and at one another, talking. Now they often
walk with their heads down, typing. Even when they are with friends, partners, children, everyone is on their own devices.

So I say, look up, look at one another, and let's start the conversation.   27

READING FOR MEANING

For help with
summarizing,
see Chapter 2,
pp. 24–25.

1. **Read to Summarize.** Write a sentence or two explaining Turkle's position
   on digitally mediated communication (texting, e-mailing, and posting)
   versus conversation.

2. **Read to Respond.** Write a paragraph analyzing anything that seems contradictory, such as Turkle's claim about the messiness (par. 11) of relationships
   conducted face-to-face or via telephone conversations versus via texting,
   posting, and e-mailing; or Turkle's denial that "our little 'sips' of online
   connection add up to a big gulp of real conversation" (par. 12).

You may also try
looking for
patterns of
opposition; see
Chapter 2,
pp. 35–36.

3. **Read to Analyze Assumptions.** Write a paragraph or two analyzing an
   assumption you find intriguing in Turkle's essay. For example:

   Assumptions about the role of conversation in our well-being and our lives.
   Turkle writes that "conversation unfolds slowly. It teaches patience. . . .
   [W]e use conversation with others to learn to converse with ourselves"
   (pars. 14–15).

- What pattern is revealed in the examples Turkle offers when arguing in favor of the benefits of conversation on our thinking and our emotions? What does this pattern reveal?
- According to Turkle, conversation helps a person be alone, but not lonely, a seeming paradox (pars. 20–24). What is your experience? Does texting friends and family enhance closeness? Does not texting make you anxious or lonely?

Assumptions about control of our selves. Turkle believes we use technology to keep ourselves separate, at a distance from others, and that we have come to value the way we can edit ourselves in our interactions with others through technology.

- Turkle writes that "people are comforted by being in touch with a lot of people — carefully kept at bay" (par. 9). What are the advantages and disadvantages of keeping each other "at bay"? How does your communication style vary from that of close friends to acquaintances?
- What does Turkle think we lose when we allow technology to dictate the way our relationships are conducted? What do you think we lose — and gain?

READING LIKE A WRITER

ARGUING DIRECTLY FOR THE POSITION, AND SUPPORTING
THE POSITION WITH REASONABLE EVIDENCE

A strong argument needs to present reasons and support for the writer's position on an issue. Writers may use facts, statistics, examples, anecdotes, expert opinion, or analogies to make their case. Turkle uses several of these types of evidence to support her reasons, and she also includes quotations (presumably gleaned from interviews) to support her assertion that by using modern technologies, we have "sacrificed conversation for mere connection" (par. 1).

| Analyze & Write |

Write a paragraph or two analyzing how Turkle uses quotations to support her claims:

1. Reread paragraphs 6–8, highlighting the words she uses to introduce and contextualize quotations and underlining the quotations themselves. What do the quotations add — perhaps something compelling that the use of other strategies would not provide? If so, what is it?

2. Now skim the rest of her essay, noting where Turkle quotes sources elsewhere in her position argument. What kind of pattern does she follow for introducing these quotations? How effective is it for you as a reader?

A Special Reading Strategy

Reflecting on Challenges to Your Beliefs and Values

Often when we read critically, we find ourselves uneasy, disturbed, or upset about something the author is writing about. It may be the presentation, the ideas, or the examples. Usually when we are upset by a reading, it's because our fundamental values and beliefs are being challenged. Sometimes we don't even know we *have* these beliefs until we pay attention to our uneasiness. When we do, we may find that probing them helps us understand ourselves and the reading better.

Follow the instructions in Chapter 2, pp. 36–37, to reflect on challenges to your values and beliefs. As you reread Turkle's essay, think about your initial response and consider whether any of the three passages below make you feel resistant. Then write a paragraph or two about your feelings, not defending them but instead analyzing their source.

- "I've learned that the little devices most of us carry around are so powerful that they change not only what we do, but also who we are" (par. 3).

- "In the silence of connection, people are comforted by being in touch with a lot of people — carefully kept at bay. We can't get enough of one another if we can use technology to keep one another at distances we can control: not too close, not too far, just right. I think of it as a Goldilocks effect" (par. 9).

- "We think constant connection will make us feel less lonely. The opposite is true. If we are unable to be alone, we are far more likely to be lonely. If we don't teach our children to be alone, they will know only how to be lonely" (par. 24).

Daniel J. Solove

Why Privacy Matters Even If You Have "Nothing to Hide"

Daniel J. Solove (b. 1972), currently John Marshall Harlan research professor of law at the George Washington University Law School, earned his J.D. at Yale Law School. In addition to writing numerous books and articles on issues of privacy and the Internet, Solove is the founder of a company that provides privacy and data security training to corporations and universities. Among his books are *The Future of Reputation: Gossip, Rumor, and Privacy on the Internet* (2007), and *Nothing to Hide: The False Tradeoff Between Privacy and Security* (2011). An earlier and longer version of this essay in a law review journal included citations that had to be eliminated for publication in the *Chronicle of Higher Education* in 2011, but we have restored them so that you can see how Solove uses a variety of sources to support his position.

- **Before you read,** think about how (or whether) you make an effort to protect your privacy on social networking and other websites.

- **As you read,** notice the sources cited in the opening paragraphs, and consider how they contribute to your understanding of why many people think privacy is not something they should be concerned about.

When the government gathers or analyzes personal information, many people say 1 they're not worried. "I've got nothing to hide," they declare. "Only if you're doing something wrong should you worry, and then you don't deserve to keep it private." The nothing-to-hide argument pervades discussions about privacy. The data-security expert Bruce Schneier calls it the "most common retort against privacy advocates." The legal scholar Geoffrey Stone refers to it as an "all-too-common refrain." In its most compelling form, it is an argument that the privacy interest is generally minimal, thus making the contest with security concerns a foreordained victory for security.

The nothing-to-hide argument is everywhere. In Britain, for example, the govern- 2 ment has installed millions of public surveillance cameras in cities and towns, which are watched by officials via closed-circuit television. In a campaign slogan for the program, the government declares: "If you've got nothing to hide, you've got nothing to fear" (Rosen 36). Variations of nothing-to-hide arguments frequently appear in blogs, letters to the editor, television news interviews, and other forums. One blogger in the United States, in reference to profiling people for national-security purposes, declares: "I don't mind people wanting to find out things about me, I've got nothing to hide! Which is why I support [the government's] efforts to find terrorists by monitoring our phone calls!" (greatcarrieoakey).

On the surface, it seems easy to dismiss the nothing-to-hide argument. Everybody 3 probably has something to hide from somebody. As Aleksandr Solzhenitsyn declared,

"Everyone is guilty of something or has something to conceal. All one has to do is look hard enough to find what it is" (192). . . . One can usually think of something that even the most open person would want to hide. As a commenter to my blog post noted, "If you have nothing to hide, then that quite literally means you are willing to let me photograph you naked? And I get full rights to that photograph—so I can show it to your neighbors?" (Andrew) . . .

But such responses attack the nothing-to-hide argument only in its most extreme   4
form, which isn't particularly strong. In a less extreme form, the nothing-to-hide argument refers not to all personal information but only to the type of data the government is likely to collect. Retorts to the nothing-to-hide argument about exposing people's naked bodies or their deepest secrets are relevant only if the government is likely to gather this kind of information. In many instances, hardly anyone will see the information, and it won't be disclosed to the public. Thus, some might argue, the privacy interest is minimal, and the security interest in preventing terrorism is much more important. In this less extreme form, the nothing-to-hide argument is a formidable one. However, it stems from certain faulty assumptions about privacy and its value. . . .

Most attempts to understand privacy do so by attempting to locate its essence—its   5
core characteristics or the common denominator that links together the various things we classify under the rubric of "privacy." Privacy, however, is too complex a concept to be reduced to a singular essence. It is a plurality of different things that do not share any one element but nevertheless bear a resemblance to one another. For example, privacy can be invaded by the disclosure of your deepest secrets. It might also be invaded if you're watched by a peeping Tom, even if no secrets are ever revealed. With the disclosure of secrets, the harm is that your concealed information is spread to others. With the peeping Tom, the harm is that you're being watched. You'd probably find that creepy regardless of whether the peeper finds out anything sensitive or discloses any information to others. There are many other forms of invasion of privacy, such as blackmail and the improper use of your personal data. Your privacy can also be invaded if the government compiles an extensive dossier about you. Privacy, in other words, involves so many things that it is impossible to reduce them all to one simple idea. And we need not do so. . . .

To describe the problems created by the collection and use of personal data, many   6
commentators use a metaphor based on George Orwell's *Nineteen Eighty-Four.* Orwell depicted a harrowing totalitarian society ruled by a government called Big Brother that watches its citizens obsessively and demands strict discipline. The Orwell metaphor, which focuses on the harms of surveillance (such as inhibition and social control), might be apt to describe government monitoring of citizens. But much of the data gathered in computer databases, such as one's race, birth date, gender, address, or marital status, isn't particularly sensitive. Many people don't care about concealing the hotels they stay at, the cars they own, or the kind of beverages they drink. Frequently, though not always, people wouldn't be inhibited or embarrassed if others knew this information.

Another metaphor better captures the problems: Franz Kafka's *The Trial.* Kafka's   7
novel centers around a man who is arrested but not informed why. He desperately

tries to find out what triggered his arrest and what's in store for him. He finds out that a mysterious court system has a dossier on him and is investigating him, but he's unable to learn much more. *The Trial* depicts a bureaucracy with inscrutable purposes that uses people's information to make important decisions about them, yet denies the people the ability to participate in how their information is used.

The problems portrayed by the Kafkaesque metaphor are of a different sort than the problems caused by surveillance. They often do not result in inhibition. Instead they are problems of information processing — the storage, use, or analysis of data — rather than of information collection. They affect the power relationships between people and the institutions of the modern state. They not only frustrate the individual by creating a sense of helplessness and powerlessness, but also affect social structure by altering the kind of relationships people have with the institutions that make important decisions about their lives. 8

Legal and policy solutions focus too much on the problems under the Orwellian metaphor — those of surveillance — and aren't adequately addressing the Kafkaesque problems — those of information processing. The difficulty is that commentators are trying to conceive of the problems caused by databases in terms of surveillance when, in fact, those problems are different. Commentators often attempt to refute the nothing-to-hide argument by pointing to things people want to hide. But the problem with the nothing-to-hide argument is the underlying assumption that privacy is about hiding bad things. By accepting this assumption, we concede far too much ground and invite an unproductive discussion about information that people would very likely want to hide. As the computer-security specialist Schneier aptly notes, the nothing-to-hide argument stems from a faulty "premise that privacy is about hiding a wrong." Surveillance, for example, can inhibit such lawful activities as free speech, free association, and other First Amendment rights essential for democracy. 9

The deeper problem with the nothing-to-hide argument is that it myopically views privacy as a form of secrecy. In contrast, understanding privacy as a plurality of related issues demonstrates that the disclosure of bad things is just one among many difficulties caused by government security measures. To return to my discussion of literary metaphors, the problems are not just Orwellian but Kafkaesque. Government information-gathering programs are problematic even if no information that people want to hide is uncovered. In *The Trial*, the problem is not inhibited behavior but rather a suffocating powerlessness and vulnerability created by the court system's use of personal data and its denial to the protagonist of any knowledge of or participation in the process. The harms are bureaucratic ones — indifference, error, abuse, frustration, and lack of transparency and accountability. 10

One such harm, for example, which I call aggregation, emerges from the fusion of small bits of seemingly innocuous data. When combined, the information becomes much more telling. By joining pieces of information we might not take pains to guard, the government can glean information about us that we might indeed wish to conceal. For example, suppose you bought a book about cancer. This purchase isn't very revealing on its own, for it indicates just an interest in the disease. Suppose you bought a wig. The purchase of a wig, by itself, could be for a number of reasons. But combine those 11 two pieces of information, and now the inference can be made that you have cancer and are undergoing chemotherapy. That might be a fact you wouldn't mind sharing, but you'd certainly want to have the choice.

Another potential problem with the government's harvest of personal data is one I 12 call exclusion. Exclusion occurs when people are prevented from having knowledge about how information about them is being used, and when they are barred from accessing and correcting errors in that data. Many government national-security measures involve maintaining a huge database of information that individuals cannot access. Indeed, because they involve national security, the very existence of these programs is often kept secret. This kind of information processing, which blocks subjects' knowledge and involvement, is a kind of due-process problem. It is a structural problem, involving the way people are treated by government institutions and creating a power imbalance between people and the government. To what extent should government officials have such a significant power over citizens? This issue isn't about what information people want to hide but about the power and the structure of government.

A related problem involves secondary use. Secondary use is the exploitation of 13 data obtained for one purpose for an unrelated purpose without the subject's consent. How long will personal data be stored? How will the information be used? What could it be used for in the future? The potential uses of any piece of personal information are vast. Without limits on or accountability for how that information is used, it is hard for people to assess the dangers of the data's being in the government's control.

Yet another problem with government gathering and use of personal data is distor- 14 tion. Although personal information can reveal quite a lot about people's personalities and activities, it often fails to reflect the whole person. It can paint a distorted picture, especially since records are reductive—they often capture information in a standardized format with many details omitted. For example, suppose government officials learn that a person has bought a number of books on how to manufacture methamphetamine. That information makes them suspect that he's building a meth lab. What is missing from the records is the full story: The person is writing a novel about a character who makes meth. When he bought the books, he didn't consider how suspicious the purchase might appear to government officials, and his records didn't reveal the reason for the purchases. Should he have to worry about government scrutiny of all his purchases and actions? Should he have to be concerned that he'll wind up on a suspicious-persons list? Even if he isn't doing anything wrong, he may want to keep his records away from government officials who might make faulty inferences from them. He might not want to have to worry about how everything he does will be perceived by officials nervously monitoring for criminal activity. He might not want to have a computer flag him as suspicious because he has an unusual pattern of behavior. . . .

Privacy is rarely lost in one fell swoop. It is usually eroded over time, little bits dissolv- 15 ing almost imperceptibly until we finally begin to notice how much is gone. When the government starts monitoring the phone numbers people call, many may shrug their shoulders and say, "Ah, it's just numbers, that's all." Then the government might start monitoring some phone calls. "It's just a few phone calls, nothing more." The government might install more video cameras in public places. "So what? Some more cameras watching in a few more places. No big deal." The increase in cameras might lead to a more elaborate network of video surveillance. Satellite surveillance might be added to help track people's movements. The government might start analyzing people's bank records. "It's just my deposits and some of the bills I pay—no problem." The government may then start combing through credit-card records, then expand to Internet-service providers' records, health records, employment records, and more. Each step may seem incremental, but after a while, the government will be watching and knowing everything about us.

"My life's an open book," people might say. "I've got nothing to hide." But now the 16 government has large dossiers of everyone's activities, interests, reading habits, finances, and health. What if the government leaks the information to the public? What if the government mistakenly determines that based on your pattern of activities, you're likely to engage in a criminal act? What if it denies you the right to fly? What if the government thinks your financial transactions look odd—even if you've done nothing wrong—and freezes your accounts? What if the government doesn't protect your information with adequate security, and an identity thief obtains it and uses it to defraud you? Even if you have nothing to hide, the government can cause you a lot of harm. . . .

Works Cited

greatcarrieoakey (Carrie Oakey). "Look All You Want! I've Got Nothing to Hide!" *Reach for the Stars*, Blogger, 14 May 2006, greatcarrieoakey.blogspot.com/2006_05_01_archive.html.

Rosen, Jeffrey. *The Naked Crowd: Reclaiming Security and Freedom in an Anxious Age.* Random House Books, 2004.

Schneier, Bruce. "The Eternal Value of Privacy." *Wired*, 18 May 2006. *Schneier on Security*, www.schneier.com/essays/archives/2006/05/the_eternal_value_of.html.

Solzhenitsyn, Aleksandr. *Cancer Ward*. Translated by Nicholas Bethell and David Burg, Farrar, Straus and Giroux, 1969.

Stone, Geoffrey R. "Freedom and Public Responsibility." *Chicago Tribune*, 21 May 2006, p. 11.

READING FOR MEANING

1. **Read to Summarize.** Write a few sentences explaining why Solove is worried about the attitude many people share — that they have "nothing to hide" and are therefore unconcerned about government surveillance.

   For help with summarizing, see Chapter 2, pp. 25–26.

2. **Read to Respond.** Write a paragraph about anything that seems interesting, such as Solove's division of violations of privacy into two types: Orwellian, "which focuses on the harms of surveillance (such as inhibition and social control)" (par. 6) and Kafkaesque "problems of information processing — the storage, use, or analysis of data — rather than of information collection" (par. 8); or Solove's argument that the loss of privacy is usually incremental, "eroded over time" (par. 15). Do the divisions or stages seem logical to you, and are they valid stepping-stones to more alarming consequences?

3. **Read to Analyze Assumptions**. Write a paragraph or two analyzing an assumption in Solove's essay. For example:

For help
analyzing
assumptions,
see Chapter 2,
pp. 28–29.

Assumptions that "privacy is about hiding bad things" (par. 9). Solove quotes "data-security expert" (par. 1) Bruce Schneier to make explicit a commonly held assumption, that privacy is "'about hiding a wrong'" (par. 9).

- Are "one's race, birth date, gender, address, or marital status [not] particularly sensitive," as Solove asserts (par. 6)? Can you think of situations in which this kind of information could be used to injure someone?

- Solove counters the assumption that privacy is about bad things by stating that this assumption is not the only way to think about privacy. What alternatives does he offer? Are they convincing to you?

Assumptions that people would take steps to curb violations of privacy if they knew how the information could be used. Solove brings two kinds of privacy violation to our attention because he believes that doing so will change our point of view that we have "nothing to hide."

- Solove compares privacy violations to Franz Kafka's *The Trial*, in which information is withheld from a man who is arrested but not told why (par. 7). He adds that the problems are not from surveillance, but "are problems of information processing — the storage, use, or analysis of data — rather than of information collection" (par. 8). Why does Solove think this is a much bigger problem?

- In his final paragraph (par. 16), Solove speculates about the consequences to invasions of privacy that may not have occurred to readers. What is he assuming readers will value, now that he has opened their eyes? Do his examples reflect consequences that could make people change their behavior?

READING LIKE A WRITER

PRESENTING THE CONTROVERSIAL ISSUE FAIRLY AND CREDIBLY

Writers sometimes have to remind their readers why an issue is controversial. Beginning with the title, Solove works to undermine the widely held assumption that the erosion of privacy should not be a concern. He does this primarily by contrasting two different ways of thinking about threats to privacy, which he calls Orwellian and Kafkaesque. To present this contrast, Solove uses sentence patterns like these:

- ▶ Not ...., but ....

- ▶ .... focus on ...., which is characterized by ...., and they don't even notice ...., which is characterized by ....

Here is an example from Solove's position argument:

> Legal and policy solutions focus too much on the problems under the Orwellian metaphor — those of surveillance — and aren't adequately addressing the Kafkaesque problems — those of information processing. . . . [T]he problems are not just Orwellian but Kafkaesque. (pars. 9–10)

Analyze & Write

Write a few paragraphs analyzing and evaluating the effectiveness of Solove's use of contrast to *reframe* the issue for readers:

1. Notice how Solove uses sources in his first three paragraphs. Given his purpose to reframe a commonly held view of privacy, why do you think he begins this way?

2. Reread paragraphs 6–7 to see how Solove explains the two contrasting metaphors. Then skim paragraphs 8–10, highlighting any sentence patterns he uses to mark the contrast.

3. Has Solove's reframing of the discussion affected your understanding of privacy and your concerns about its loss? Why or why not?

Miya Tokumitsu

In the Name of Love

Miya Tokumitsu earned her Ph.D. in art history from the University of Pennsylvania and teaches art history and art curatorship at the University of Melbourne, Australia. She is a contributing editor of *Jacobin,* an online and print quarterly of the American left, where the following essay was published in 2015. In it, she critiques the clichéd idea that people can only be happy if they pursue a career they love. The essay's success led to her book, *Do What You Love and Other Lies about Success and Happiness* (2015).

- **Before you read,** think about your expectations of your future job or career. Do you think you will love what you do? Or do you think a job is a job, and not necessarily something that needs to be rewarding and fulfilling?

- **As you read,** consider how clearly Tokumitsu presents her argument. Can you find her thesis easily? Identify the strategies she uses to remind you of her position throughout her argument and consider how effective they are.

Mario De Armas

"Do what you love. Love what you do."   1

The commands are framed and perched in a living room that can only be described   2
as "well-curated." A picture of this room appeared first on a popular design blog, but
has been pinned, tumbl'd, and liked thousands of times by now.

Lovingly lit and photographed, this room is styled to inspire *Sehnsucht*, roughly   3
translatable from German as a pleasurable yearning for some utopian thing or place.
Despite the fact that it introduces exhortations to labor into a space of leisure, the "do
what you love" living room—where artful tchotchkes abound and work is not drudgery but love—is precisely the place all those pinners and likers long to be. The dip-
tych arrangement suggests a secular version of a medieval house altar.

There's little doubt that "do what you love" (DWYL) is now the unofficial work   4
mantra for our time. The problem is that it leads not to salvation, but to the devaluation of actual work, including the very work it pretends to elevate—and more importantly, the dehumanization of the vast majority of laborers.

Superficially, DWYL is an uplifting piece of advice, urging us to ponder what it is   5
we most enjoy doing and then turn that activity into a wage-generating enterprise. But
why should our pleasure be for profit? Who is the audience for this dictum? Who is
not?

By keeping us focused on ourselves and our individual happiness, DWYL distracts   6
us from the working conditions of others while validating our own choices and reliev-
ing us from obligations to all who labor, whether or not they love it. It is the secret
handshake of the privileged and a worldview that disguises its elitism as noble self-
betterment. According to this way of thinking, labor is not something one does for
compensation, but an act of self-love. If profit doesn't happen to follow, it is because
the worker's passion and determination were insufficient. Its real achievement is making workers believe their labor serves the self and not the marketplace.

Aphorisms have numerous origins and reincarnations, but the generic and hack-   7
neyed nature of DWYL confounds precise attribution. Oxford Reference links the
phrase and variants of it to Martina Navratilova and François Rabelais, among others.
The internet frequently attributes it to Confucius, locating it in a misty, Orientalized
past. Oprah Winfrey and other peddlers of positivity have included it in their reper-
toires for decades, but the most important recent evangelist of the DWYL creed is
deceased Apple CEO Steve Jobs.

His graduation speech to the Stanford University class of 2005 provides as good an   8
origin myth as any, especially since Jobs had already been beatified as the patron saint
of aestheticized work well before his early death. In the speech, Jobs recounts the
creation of Apple, and inserts this reflection:

> You've got to find what you love. And that is as true for your work as it is for your
> lovers. Your work is going to fill a large part of your life, and the only way to be truly
> satisfied is to do what you believe is great work. And the only way to do great work is
> to love what you do.

In these four sentences, the words "you" and "your" appear eight times. This focus   9
on the individual is hardly surprising coming from Jobs, who cultivated a very specific

image of himself as a worker: inspired, casual, passionate—all states agreeable with ideal romantic love. Jobs telegraphed the conflation of his besotted worker-self with his company so effectively that his black turtleneck and blue jeans became metonyms for all of Apple and the labor that maintains it.

But by portraying Apple as a labor of his individual love, Jobs elided the labor of 10 untold thousands in Apple's factories, conveniently hidden from sight on the other side of the planet—the very labor that allowed Jobs to actualize his love.

The violence of this erasure needs to be exposed. While "do what you love" sounds 11 harmless and precious, it is ultimately self-focused to the point of narcissism. Jobs' formulation of "do what you love" is the depressing antithesis to Henry David Thoreau's utopian vision of labor for all. In "Life Without Principle," Thoreau wrote,

> . . . it would be good economy for a town to pay its laborers so well that they would not feel that they were working for low ends, as for a livelihood merely, but for scientific, even moral ends. Do not hire a man who does your work for money, but him who does it for the love of it.

Admittedly, Thoreau had little feel for the proletariat (it's hard to imagine someone 12 washing diapers for "scientific, even moral ends," no matter how well-paid). But he nonetheless maintains that society has a stake in making work well-compensated and meaningful. By contrast, the twenty-first-century Jobsian view demands that we all turn inward. It absolves us of any obligation to or acknowledgment of the wider world, underscoring its fundamental betrayal of all workers, whether they consciously embrace it or not.

One consequence of this isolation is the division that DWYL creates among work- 13 ers, largely along class lines. Work becomes divided into two opposing classes: that which is lovable (creative, intellectual, socially prestigious) and that which is not (repetitive, unintellectual, undistinguished). Those in the lovable work camp are vastly more privileged in terms of wealth, social status, education, society's racial biases, and political clout, while comprising a small minority of the workforce.

For those forced into unlovable work, it's a different story. Under the DWYL credo, 14 labor that is done out of motives or needs other than love (which is, in fact, most labor) is not only demeaned but erased. As in Jobs' Stanford speech, unlovable but socially necessary work is banished from the spectrum of consciousness altogether.

Think of the great variety of work that allowed Jobs to spend even one day as CEO: 15 his food harvested from fields, then transported across great distances. His company's goods assembled, packaged, shipped. Apple advertisements scripted, cast, filmed. Lawsuits processed. Office wastebaskets emptied and ink cartridges filled. Job creation goes both ways. Yet with the vast majority of workers effectively invisible to elites busy in their lovable occupations, how can it be surprising that the heavy strains faced by today's workers (abysmal wages, massive child care costs, et cetera) barely register as political issues even among the liberal faction of the ruling class?

In ignoring most work and reclassifying the rest as love, DWYL may be the most 16 elegant anti-worker ideology around. Why should workers assemble and assert their class interests if there's no such thing as work?

"Do what you love" disguises the fact that being able to choose a career primarily 17 for personal reward is an unmerited privilege, a sign of that person's socioeconomic class. Even if a self-employed graphic designer had parents who could pay for art school and cosign a lease for a slick Brooklyn apartment, she can self-righteously bestow DWYL as career advice to those covetous of her success.

If we believe that working as a Silicon Valley entrepreneur or a museum publicist 18 or a think-tank acolyte is essential to being true to ourselves—in fact, to loving ourselves—what do we believe about the inner lives and hopes of those who clean hotel rooms and stock shelves at big-box stores? The answer is: nothing.

Yet arduous, low-wage work is what ever more Americans do and will be doing. 19 According to the US Bureau of Labor Statistics, the two fastest-growing occupations projected until 2020 are "Personal Care Aide" and "Home Care Aide," with average salaries of $19,640 per year and $20,560 per year in 2010, respectively. Elevating certain types of professions to something worthy of love necessarily denigrates the labor of those who do unglamorous work that keeps society functioning, especially the crucial work of caregivers.

If DWYL denigrates or makes dangerously invisible vast swaths of labor that 20 allow many of us to live in comfort and to do what we love, it has also caused great damage to the professions it portends to celebrate, especially those jobs existing within institutional structures. Nowhere has the DWYL mantra been more devastating to its adherents than in academia. The average PhD student of the mid 2000s forwent the easy money of finance and law (now slightly less easy) to live on a meager stipend in order to pursue their passion for Norse mythology or the history of Afro-Cuban music.

The reward for answering this higher calling is an academic employment market- 21 place in which around 41 percent of American faculty are adjunct professors— contract instructors who usually receive low pay, no benefits, no office, no job security, and no long-term stake in the schools where they work.

There are many factors that keep PhDs providing such high-skilled labor for such 22 extremely low wages, including path dependency and the sunk costs of earning a PhD, but one of the strongest is how pervasively the DWYL doctrine is embedded in academia. Few other professions fuse the personal identity of their workers so intimately with the work output. This intense identification partly explains why so many proudly left-leaning faculty remain oddly silent about the working conditions of their peers. Because academic research should be done out of pure love, the actual conditions of and compensation for this labor become afterthoughts, if they are considered at all.

In "Academic Labor, the Aesthetics of Management, and the Promise of Autono- 23 mous Work," Sarah Brouillette writes of academic faculty,

> . . . our faith that our work offers non-material rewards, and is more integral to our identity than a "regular" job would be, makes us ideal employees when the goal of management is to extract our labor's maximum value at minimum cost.

Many academics like to think they have avoided a corporate work environment 24
and its attendant values, but Marc Bousquet notes in his essay "We Work" that academia may actually provide a model for corporate management:

> How to emulate the academic workplace and get people to work at a high level of
> intellectual and emotional intensity for fifty or sixty hours a week for bartenders'
> wages or less? Is there any way we can get our employees to swoon over their desks,
> murmuring "I love what I do" in response to greater workloads and smaller pay-
> checks? How can we get our workers to be like faculty and deny that they work at all?
> How can we adjust our corporate culture to resemble campus culture, so that our
> workforce will fall in love with their work too?

No one is arguing that enjoyable work should be less so. But emotionally satisfying 25
work is still work, and acknowledging it as such doesn't undermine it in any way.
Refusing to acknowledge it, on the other hand, opens the door to the most vicious
exploitation and harms all workers.

Ironically, DWYL reinforces exploitation even within the so-called lovable profes- 26
sions where off-the-clock, underpaid, or unpaid labor is the new norm: reporters
required to do the work of their laid-off photographers, publicists expected to Pin and
Tweet on weekends, the 46 percent of the workforce expected to check their work
email on sick days. Nothing makes exploitation go down easier than convincing
workers that they are doing what they love.

Instead of crafting a nation of self-fulfilled, happy workers, our DWYL era has seen 27
the rise of the adjunct professor and the unpaid intern—people persuaded to work for
cheap or free, or even for a net loss of wealth. This has certainly been the case for all
those interns working for college credit or those who actually purchase ultra-desirable
fashion-house internships at auction. (Valentino and Balenciaga are among a handful
of houses that auctioned off month-long internships. For charity, of course.) The latter is
worker exploitation taken to its most extreme, and as an ongoing Pro Publica investiga-
tion[1] reveals, the unpaid intern is an ever larger presence in the American workforce.

It should be no surprise that unpaid interns abound in fields that are highly socially 28
desirable, including fashion, media, and the arts. These industries have long been
accustomed to masses of employees willing to work for social currency instead of
actual wages, all in the name of love. Excluded from these opportunities, of course, is
the overwhelming majority of the population: those who need to work for wages. This
exclusion not only calcifies economic and professional immobility, but insulates
these industries from the full diversity of voices society has to offer.

And it's no coincidence that the industries that rely heavily on interns—fashion, 29
media, and the arts—just happen to be the feminized ones, as Madeleine Schwartz
wrote in *Dissent*.[2] Yet another damaging consequence of DWYL is how ruthlessly it

[1]"Internships." *Pro Publica: Journalism in the Public Interest,* www.propublica.org
/series/internships. [Ed.]

[2]Schwartz, Madeleine. "Opportunity Costs: The True Price of Internships." *Dissent
Magazine,* www.dissentmagazine.org/article/opportunity-costs-the-true-price-of-
internships. [Ed.]

works to extract female labor for little or no compensation. Women comprise the majority of the low-wage or unpaid workforce; as care workers, adjunct faculty, and unpaid interns, they outnumber men. What unites all of this work, whether performed by GEDs or PhDs, is the belief that wages shouldn't be the primary motivation for doing it. Women are supposed to do work because they are natural nurturers and are eager to please; after all they've been doing uncompensated childcare, elder care, and housework since time immemorial. And talking money is unladylike anyway.

The DWYL dream is, true to its American mythology, superficially democratic. 30 PhDs can do what they love, making careers that indulge their love of the Victorian novel and writing thoughtful essays in the *New York Review of Books*. High school grads can also do it, building prepared food empires out of their Aunt Pearl's jam recipe. The hallowed path of the entrepreneur always offers this way out of disadvantaged beginnings, excusing the rest of us for allowing those beginnings to be as miserable as they are. In America, everyone has the opportunity to do what he or she loves and get rich.

Do what you love and you'll never work a day in your life! Before succumbing to 31 the intoxicating warmth of that promise, it's critical to ask, "Who, exactly, benefits from making work feel like non-work?" "Why *should* workers feel as if they aren't working when they are?" Historian Mario Liverani reminds us that "ideology has the function of presenting exploitation in a favorable light to the exploited, as advantageous to the disadvantaged."

In masking the very exploitative mechanisms of labor that it fuels, DWYL is, in fact, 32 the most perfect ideological tool of capitalism. It shunts aside the labor of others and disguises our own labor to ourselves. It hides the fact that if we acknowledged all of our work as work, we could set appropriate limits for it, demanding fair compensation and humane schedules that allow for family and leisure time.

And if we did that, more of us could get around to doing what it is we *really* love. 33

READING FOR MEANING

1. **Read to Summarize.** Write a few sentences explaining how, according to Tokumitsu, doing "what you love" for a living is unrealistic for most people and can be downright harmful to those who can't.

   For help with summarizing, see Chapter 2, pp. 24–25.

2. **Read to Respond.** Write a paragraph about anything surprising, such as Tokumitsu's assertion that doing what you love leads to the "devaluation of actual work" and the "dehumanization of the vast majority of laborers" (par. 4); or that DWYL is, in Tokumitsu's view, undemocratic (pars. 30–32).

3. **Read to Analyze Assumptions.** Write a paragraph or two analyzing an assumption you find intriguing in Tokumitsu's essay. For example:

   For help analyzing assumptions, see Chapter 2, pp. 28–29.

   Assumptions about work as part of our lives — not our whole lives. Tokumitsu begins her essay with a description of a "living room" that is also a work room, where "work is not drudgery but love" (par. 3). The room serves as a metaphor for a life, where work has entered the "private" living space.

- If the living room/work room described in paragraphs 2–3 is exceptional because it is for work that is pleasant, not drudgery, what does Tokumitsu assume about *most* work — or, at least, people's attitudes toward their work? How does she support this assumption?

- Tokumitsu criticizes companies "within the so-called lovable professions" for exploiting their workforce, who are expected to engage in technology for work (pins, Tweets, e-mails) on weekends (par. 26). What are her assumptions about the relationship between work and weekends?

Assumptions about the relationship between socioeconomic status and work that is valued. Tokumitsu asserts that " 'Do what you love' disguises the fact that being able to choose a career primarily for personal reward is an unmerited privilege, a sign of that person's socioeconomic class" (par. 17).

- Do you share this assumption that people who can choose work they love are generally in a comfortable socioeconomic bracket? Does anything in your experience support or disprove this assumption?

- Tokumitsu believes that "emotionally satisfying work is still work, and . . . refusing to acknowledge it . . . opens the door to the most vicious exploitation and harms all workers" (par. 25). Think of examples from the media or your own experience that illustrate or refute her point about "exploitation." How does refusing to acknowledge that satisfying work is still work damage workers who don't necessarily love what they do?

READING LIKE A WRITER

ASSERTING A CLEAR POSITION

Writers usually (but not always) assert their positions early in an essay and, to help readers focus, may reassert the position later and in the conclusion. The position is the *thesis*, and a restatement of the thesis can occur regularly as the writer develops reasons and evidence to support it. Tokumitsu's thesis appears in paragraph 4: "The problem is that [the mantra 'do what you love'] leads not to salvation, but to the devaluation of actual work, including the very work it pretends to elevate — and more importantly, the dehumanization of the vast majority of laborers."

| Analyze & Write |

Write a paragraph or two analyzing how effectively Tokumitsu asserts her position.

1. Skim her essay and highlight all the places where she restates her thesis—for example, "While 'do what you love' sounds harmless and precious, it is ultimately self-focused to the point of narcissism" (par. 11).

2. Underline any sentences that assert a reason in support of her thesis. (The word *because* often has a reason following it.) For example, she explains why DWYL is implicitly elitist: "labor is not something one does for compensation, but an act of self-love. If profit doesn't happen to follow, it is because the worker's passion and determination were insufficient" (par. 6). How do the reasons support her thesis? Are there any reasons that undermine her position or make it unclear? If so, what are they?

Jessica Statsky

Children Need to Play, Not Compete

Jessica Statsky was a college student when she wrote this position paper, in which she argues that organized sports are not good for children between the ages of six and twelve. Annotate the text, paying special attention to the features of a position paper — presenting the issue fairly and credibly, asserting a clear position, arguing directly for the position with reasonable evidence, and responding to objections and alternative positions fairly.

- **Before you read,** recall your own experiences as an elementary-school student playing competitive sports, either in or out of school. If you were not actively involved yourself, did you know anyone who was? Was winning emphasized? What about having a good time? Getting along with others? Developing athletic skills and confidence?

- **As you read,** notice how Statsky sets forth her position clearly, supports the reasons for her position, and handles readers' likely objections. Also note the visible cues that Statsky provides to guide you through her argument step-by-step.

"Organized sports for young people have become an institution in North America," 1 reports sports journalist Steve Silverman, attracting more than 44 million youngsters according to a recent survey by the National Council of Youth Sports ("History"). Though many adults regard Little League Baseball and Peewee Football as a basic part of childhood, the games are not always joyous ones. When overzealous parents and coaches impose adult standards on children's sports, the result can be activities that are neither satisfying nor beneficial to children.

I am concerned about all organized sports activities for children between the ages 2 of six and twelve. The damage I see results from noncontact as well as contact sports, from sports organized locally as well as those organized nationally. Highly organized competitive sports such as Peewee Football and Little League Baseball are too often played to adult standards, which are developmentally inappropriate for children and can be both physically and psychologically harmful. Furthermore, because they eliminate many children from organized sports before they are ready to compete, they are actually counterproductive for developing either future players or fans. Finally, because they emphasize competition and winning, they unfortunately provide occasions for some parents and coaches to place their own fantasies and needs ahead of children's welfare.

One readily understandable danger of overly competitive sports is that they entice 3 children into physical actions that are bad for growing bodies. "There is a growing epidemic of preventable youth sports injuries," according to the STOP Sports Injuries campaign. "Among athletes ages 5 to 14, 28 percent of football players, 25 percent of baseball players, 22 percent of soccer players, 15 percent of basketball players, and 12 percent of softball players were injured while playing their respective sports." Although Little League Baseball and Softball acknowledges that children do risk injury playing baseball, it insists that "severe injuries . . . are infrequent," the risk "far less than the risk of riding a skateboard, a bicycle, or even the school bus" ("Little League Parent"). Nevertheless, Leonard Koppett in *Sports Illusion, Sports Reality* claims that a twelve-year-old trying to throw a curve ball, for example, may put abnormal strain on developing arm and shoulder muscles, sometimes resulting in lifelong injuries (294). Contact sports like football can be even more hazardous. Thomas Tutko, a psychology professor at San Jose State University and coauthor of the book *Winning Is Everything and Other American Myths*, writes:

> I am strongly opposed to young kids playing tackle football. It is not the right stage of development for them to be taught to crash into other kids. Kids under the age of fourteen are not by nature physical. Their main concern is self-preservation. They don't want to meet head on and slam into each other. But tackle football absolutely requires that they try to hit each other as hard as they can. And it is too traumatic for young kids. (qtd. in Tosches A1)

As Tutko indicates, even when children are not injured, fear of being hurt detracts   4 from their enjoyment of the sport. The Little League ranks fear of injury as the seventh of seven reasons children quit ("Little League Parent"). One mother of an eight-year-old Peewee Football player explained, "The kids get so scared. They get hit once and they don't want anything to do with football anymore. They'll sit on the bench and pretend their leg hurts . . ." (qtd. in Tosches A1). Some children are driven to even more desperate measures. For example, in one Peewee Football game, a reporter watched the following scene as a player took himself out of the game:

> "Coach, my tummy hurts. I can't play," he said. The coach told the player to get back onto the field. "There's nothing wrong with your stomach," he said. When the coach turned his head the seven-year-old stuck a finger down his throat and made himself vomit. When the coach turned back, the boy pointed to the ground and told him, "Yes there is, coach. See?" (Tosches A33)

Besides physical hazards and anxieties, competitive sports pose psychological   5 dangers for children. Martin Rablovsky, a former sports editor for the *New York Times*, says that in all his years of watching young children play organized sports, he has noticed very few of them smiling. "I've seen children enjoying a spontaneous pre-practice scrimmage become somber and serious when the coach's whistle blows," Rablovsky says. "The spirit of play suddenly disappears, and sport becomes joblike" (qtd. in Coakley 94). The primary goal of a professional athlete—winning—is not appropriate for children. Their goals should be having fun, learning, and being with friends. Although winning does add to the fun, too many adults lose sight of what matters and make winning the most important goal. Several studies have shown that when children are asked whether they would rather be warming the bench on a winning team or playing regularly on a losing team, about 90 percent choose the latter (Smith et al. 11). According to Mark Hyman, professor of sports management at George Washington University and author of several books on youth sports: "If we wiped the slate clean and reinvented youth sports from scratch by putting the physical and emotional needs of kids first, how different would it look? Nothing would be recognizable" (qtd. in Rosenwald).

Winning and losing may be an inevitable part of adult life, but they should not be 6 part of childhood. Too much competition too early in life can affect a child's development. Children are easily influenced, and when they sense that their competence and worth are based on their ability to live up to their parents' and coaches' high expectations—and on their ability to win—they can become discouraged and depressed. Little League advises parents to "keep winning in perspective," noting that the most common reasons children give for quitting, aside from change in interest, are lack of playing time, failure and fear of failure, disapproval by significant others, and psychological stress ("Little League Parent"). According to Dr. Glyn C. Roberts, a professor of kinesiology at the Institute of Child Behavior and Development at the University of Illinois, 80 to 90 percent of children who play competitive sports at a young age drop out by sixteen (Kutner).

This statistic illustrates another reason I oppose competitive sports for children: 7 because they are so highly selective, very few children get to participate. Far too soon, a few children are singled out for their athletic promise, while many others, who may be on the verge of developing the necessary strength and ability, are screened out and discouraged from trying out again. Like adults, children fear failure, and so even those with good physical skills may stay away because they lack self-confidence. Consequently, teams lose many promising players who with some encouragement and experience might have become stars. The problem is that many parent-sponsored, out-of-school programs give more importance to having a winning team than to developing children's physical skills and self-esteem.

Indeed, it is no secret that too often scorekeeping, league standings, and the drive 8 to win bring out the worst in adults who are more absorbed in living out their own fantasies than in enhancing the quality of the experience for children (Smith et al. 9). Recent newspaper articles on children's sports contain plenty of horror stories. *Los Angeles Times* reporter Rich Tosches, for example, tells the story of a brawl among seventy-five parents following a Peewee Football game (A33). As a result of the brawl, which began when a parent from one team confronted a player from the other team, the teams are now thinking of hiring security guards for future games. Another example is provided by a *Los Angeles Times* editorial about a Little League manager who intimidated the opposing team by setting fire to one of their team's jerseys on the pitcher's mound before the game began. As the editorial writer commented, the manager showed his young team that "intimidation could substitute for playing well" ("The Bad News Pyromaniacs?"). This phenomenon, according to Ken Reed, author of

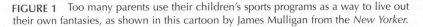

"Please, Mrs. Enright, if I let you pinch-hit for Tommy, all the mothers will want to pinch-hit."

FIGURE 1 Too many parents use their children's sports programs as a way to live out their own fantasies, as shown in this cartoon by James Mulligan from the *New Yorker*.

How We Can Save Sports: A Game Plan, is known as the "Achievement by Proxy Syndrome—adults living vicariously through the exploits of their children" (1). Reed acknowledges that the "issue of overbearing parents and coaches in youth sports isn't a new one," but "things are definitely getting worse. Adults are taking their seriousness about youth sports to new unhealthy extremes" (1).

Although not all parents or coaches behave so inappropriately, the seriousness of 9 the problem is illustrated by the fact that Adelphi University in Garden City, New York, offers a sports psychology workshop for Little League coaches, designed to balance their "animal instincts" with "educational theory" in hopes of reducing the "screaming and hollering," in the words of Harold Weisman, manager of sixteen Little Leagues in New York City (Schmitt). In a three-and-one-half-hour Sunday morning workshop, coaches learn how to make practices more fun, treat injuries, deal with irate parents, and be "more sensitive to their young players' fears, emotional frailties, and need for recognition." Little League is to be credited with recognizing the need for such workshops.

Some parents would no doubt argue that children cannot start too soon preparing 10 to live in a competitive free-market economy. After all, secondary schools and colleges require students to compete for grades, and college admission is extremely competitive. And it is perfectly obvious how important competitive skills are in finding a job. Yet the ability to cooperate is also important for success in life. Before children are psychologically ready for competition, maybe we should emphasize cooperation and individual performance in team sports rather than winning.

Many people are ready for such an emphasis. In 1988, one New York Little League 11 official who had attended the Adelphi workshop tried to ban scoring from six- to eight-year-olds' games—but parents wouldn't support him (Schmitt). An innovative children's sports program in New York City, City Sports for Kids, emphasizes fitness, self-esteem, and sportsmanship. In this program's basketball games, every member on a team plays at least two of six eight-minute periods. The basket is seven feet from the floor, rather than ten feet, and a player can score a point just by hitting the rim (Bloch). I believe this kind of local program should replace overly competitive programs like Peewee Football and Little League Baseball. As one coach explains, significant improvements can result from a few simple rule changes, such as including every player in the batting order and giving every player, regardless of age or ability, the opportunity to play at least four innings a game (Frank).

Some children *want* to play competitive sports; they are not being forced to 12 play. These children are eager to learn skills, to enjoy the camaraderie of the team, and earn self-respect by trying hard to benefit their team. I acknowledge that some children may benefit from playing competitive sports. While some children do benefit from these programs, however, many more would benefit from programs that avoid the excesses and dangers of many competitive sports programs and instead emphasize fitness, cooperation, sportsmanship, and individual performance.

Works Cited

"The Bad News Pyromaniacs? Fiery Anaheim Little Manager Is, Rightly, Fired." Editorial. *Los Angeles Times,* 16 June 1990, p. B6, articles.latimes.com/1990-06-16/local/me-31 _1_team-manager.

Bloch, Gordon B. "Thrill of Victory Is Secondary to Fun." *The New York Times,* 2 Apr. 1990, p. C12.

Coakley, Jay J. *Sport in Society: Issues and Controversies.* Mosby, 1982.

Frank, L. "Contributions from Parents and Coaches." *CYB Message Board,* AOL, 8 July 1997, www.aol.com/. Accessed 14 May 2008.

Koppett, Leonard. *Sports Illusion, Sports Reality.* Boston: Houghton MIfflin, 1981. Print.

Kutner, Lawrence. "Athletics, through a Child's Eyes." *The New York Times* 23 Mar. 1989, p. C8, www.nytimes.com/1989/03/23/garden/parent-child.html.

Little League Parent Responsibilities." *Warwick National Little League 2007 Safety Plan,* Little League Baseball and Softball, 17 Apr. 2007, www.littleleague.org/Assets/forms_pubs /asap/Warwick_LL_safetyplan08.pdf.

Reed, Ken. "Youth Sports Burnout Driven by Achievement by Proxy Syndrome." *The Huffington Post,* 10 Oct. 2015, www.huffingtonpost.com/ken-reed/youth-sports-burnout-driv _b_8274078.html.

Rosenwald, Michael S. "Are Parents Ruining Youth Sports? Fewer Kids Play Amid Pressure." *The Washington Post,* 4 Oct. 2015, www.washingtonpost.com/local/are-parents-ruining -youth-sports-fewer-kids-play-amid-pressure/2015/10/04/eb1460dc-686e-11e5-9ef3 -fde182507eac_story.html.

Schmitt, Eric. "Psychologists Take Seat on Little League Bench." *The New York Times,* 14 Mar. 1988, late ed., p. B2. *LexisNexis Academic,* www.lexisnexis.com.

Silverman, Steve. "The History of Youth Sports." *Livestrong*, Demand Media, Inc., 01 Sept., 2015, www.livestrong.com/article/353963-the-history-of-youth-sports/.

Smith, Nathan, et al. *Kidsports: A Survival Guide for Parents*. Addison-Wesley, 1983.

Tosches, Rich. "Peewee Football: Is It Time to Blow the Whistle?" *The Los Angeles Times*, 3 Dec. 1988, pp. A1+. *LexisNexis*, articles.latimes.com/1988-12-03/news/mn-936_1_ youth -football-games.

"Youth Sports Injuries Statistics." STOP Sports Injuries: Community Outreach Toolkit, American Orthopaedic Society for Sports Medicine, www.sportsmed.org/aossmimis/stop/downloads /CommunityOutreachToolkit.pdf.

READING FOR MEANING

1. **Read to Summarize.** Write a sentence or two explaining what you learned about children and sports from Statsky's argument.

   For help with summarizing, see Chapter 2, pp. 25–26.

2. **Read to Respond.** Write a paragraph analyzing anything that resonates with your experience or that seems surprising, such as Statsky's claim that children can become discouraged and depressed "when they sense that their competence and worth are based on their ability to live up to their parents' and coaches' high expectations — and on their ability to win" (par. 6); or Statsky's assertion that "it is no secret that too often scorekeeping, league standings, and the drive to win bring out the worst in adults . . ." (par. 8). Was this true of your experience or that of your friends? What kinds of values do overzealous parents demonstrate? Are there any that are positive?

3. **Read to Analyze Assumptions.** Write a paragraph or two analyzing an assumption you find intriguing in Statsky's essay. For example:

   You may also try looking for patterns of opposition; see Chapter 2, pp. 35–36.

   Assumptions that cooperation is as important a skill to develop as competition. Statsky explicitly states this assumption when she writes that the ability to cooperate is as important as competitive skills for success (par. 10).

   - Statsky asserts that "overzealous parents and coaches impose adult standards on children's sports, [leading to] activities that are neither satisfying nor beneficial to children" (par. 1). Do you agree that coaches and parents impose the desire to win on children? Should children's sports have different standards?

   - Statsky acknowledges how important competitive skills are for getting into college and finding a job, but immediately follows with a response: "Yet the ability to cooperate is also important for success in life. Before children are psychologically ready for competition, maybe we should emphasize cooperation and individual performance in team sports rather than winning" (par. 10). Do you think Statsky provides enough evidence that most children are not psychologically ready for competition? If so, which kinds of evidence are most compelling for you? Why?

For help
analyzing
assumptions,
see Chapter 2,
pp. 28–29.

Assumptions that children's sports should be inclusive. Statsky argues that children's competitive sports should be reformed because they favor the most coordinated and strongest children (par. 7) to the exclusion of children who are weaker or less skilled.

- What evidence does Statsky offer to support this claim, especially for the youngest participants in PeeWee Football and Little League? Is it possible that the stronger and better-coordinated children might be drawn to organized sports because they enjoy playing more? Might children who enjoy physical activity have developed the skills needed to succeed on the playing field through practice rather than through the process of development?

- Should those who organize children's sports have an obligation to include all children who want to participate? Why or why not?

READING LIKE A WRITER

RESPONDING TO OBJECTIONS AND ALTERNATIVE POSITIONS FAIRLY

An effective argument concedes valid objections, concerns, or reasons and refutes opposing views that are weak or flawed. Consider this passage from Statsky's essay:

Concession   Some parents would no doubt argue that children cannot start too soon preparing to live in a competitive free-market economy. After all, secondary schools and colleges require students to compete for grades, and college admission is extremely competitive. And it is perfectly obvious how important competitive skills are in finding a job.

Refutation   Yet the ability to cooperate is also important for success in life. Before children are psychologically ready for competition, maybe we should emphasize cooperation and individual performance in team sports rather than winning. (par. 10)

Notice how Statsky treats alternative views with civility and respect, enhancing her credibility, or **ethos**.

| **Analyze & Write** |

Write a paragraph analyzing other passages in which Statsky responds to alternative points of view:

To review the
meaning of
rhetorical
sensitivity, see
Chapter 1,
p. 10.

1. Reread the first sentence in paragraph 6, the first and last sentences in paragraph 9, and the first sentence in paragraph 12, highlighting the words that signal Statsky's acknowledgment of objections to her thesis.

2. Now reread the sentences following those you highlighted, to see how Statsky deals with her opposition. Does she seem to practice rhetorical sensitivity here? Why or why not?

A Special Reading Strategy

Analyzing Visuals

Write a paragraph analyzing the cartoon included in Statsky's position argument (Fig. 1) and explaining what it contributes to the essay. To help you get started, consider these questions:

For more on analyzing visuals, see Chapter 2, pp. 31–34.

- How does the cartoon illustrate Statsky's concerns about parents' involvement in their children's competitive sports?

- What does the cartoon's caption — what the coach is saying to Mrs. Enright — say about parents as role models for their children?

- Two schools of thought about how to raise children are (1) to show them what to do and (2) to allow them to learn on their own, including making mistakes. Clearly this cartoon illustrates the first school, taken to an extreme. How might you illustrate the second school?

Writing to Learn Position Argument

Write a brief essay analyzing one of the readings in this chapter (or another selection, perhaps one by a classmate). Explain how (and perhaps, how well) the selection works as a position argument. Consider, for example, how it

- presents a controversial issue fairly and credibly by putting it in context and being specific about the terms of the debate;

- asserts a clear position in a thesis that forecasts the stages of the argument and the reasons that support it;

- argues directly for the position with writing strategies such as facts, statistics, examples, anecdotes, expert opinions, and analogies;

- responds to objections, conceding where necessary and refuting when possible.

(continued)

Your essay could also reflect on how you applied one or more of the academic habits of mind as you read the selection:

- **Curiosity**—what questions or ideas did you have as you read the selection?

- **Critical Analysis**—what assumptions in the selection did you find intriguing, and why?

- **Rhetorical Sensitivity**—how effective or ineffective do you think the selection is in achieving its purpose for the intended audience, given the constraints of the medium and the position argument genre?

A GUIDE TO WRITING POSITION ARGUMENTS

You have probably done a good deal of analytical writing about your reading. Your instructor may also assign a capstone project to write a brief position argument of your own. This Guide to Writing offers detailed suggestions and resources to help you meet the special challenges this kind of writing presents.

THE WRITING ASSIGNMENT

Write an essay arguing a position on a controversial issue.

- Choose an issue on which you either have a position or would like to investigate further.

- Consider what your readers might know about the issue, and what stance they might take toward it.

- Conduct research on the issue so you can support and clarify your own argument, and address the objections your readers might raise as well as the alternative positions they might prefer.

- Adopt a reasonable tone, one that will lend credibility to your position.

WRITING YOUR DRAFT

Choosing a Controversial Issue

Rather than limiting yourself to the first subject that comes to mind, take a few minutes to consider your options. When choosing an issue, keep in mind that the issue must be

- controversial — an issue that people disagree about;

- arguable — a matter of opinion on which there is no absolute proof or authority;

- one that you can research, as necessary, in the time you have;

- one that you care about but for which you can be fair and reasonable.

Choosing an issue about which you have special knowledge usually works best, and it's important to focus the issue so that you can write a brief paper on it.

For example, if you are thinking of addressing an issue of national concern, focus on a local or a specific aspect of it: Instead of addressing censorship in general, write about a recent lawmaker's effort to propose a law censoring the Internet, a city council attempt to block access to Internet sites at a public library, or a school board's ban on certain textbooks.

You may already have an issue in mind. If you do not, the topics that follow may suggest one you can make your own. Note that they are in the form of questions, the answers to which could be positions.

- Should particular courses, community service, or an internship be a graduation requirement at your high school or college?

- Should children raised in this country whose parents entered illegally be given an opportunity to become citizens upon finishing college or serving in the military?

- Should you look primarily for a job that is well paid, or for a job that is personally fulfilling or socially responsible?

- Should the racial, ethnic, or gender makeup of the police force resemble the makeup of the community it serves?

- Should your large lecture or online courses have frequent (weekly or biweekly) exams instead of only a midterm and final?

- Should the football conference your school (or another school in the area) participates in be allowed to expand?

- Should the state or federal government provide job training for those who are unemployed but able to work?

For help conducting and using research, see the Appendix.

Before making a final decision about the issue on which you will take a position, try writing nonstop about it for a few minutes. Doing so will help stimulate your memory, letting you see what you already know about the issue and how much research you will need to do.

Developing Your Argument

The writing and research activities that follow will enable you to test your choice and discover good ways to argue for your position on the issue.

Presenting the Issue.   The following questions and sentence strategies can help you explore the issue and consider how best to present it to your readers.

How can I present the issue effectively?

What is the issue and why should your readers be concerned about it?

▶ I'm concerned about .... because ....

Why are popular approaches or attitudes inappropriate or inadequate?

▶ Although some argue ...., I think .... because ....

How can I explore the issue?

What groups or notable individuals have shaped the debate on this issue? What positions have they taken?

▶ Whereas supporters of ...., such as ...., ..., and ...., have argued that ...., opponents such as .... [list individuals/groups] contend that ....

How has the issue, or people's opinions about the issue, changed? What makes the issue important now?

▶ The debate over whether .... should .... was initially concerned that ...., but the main concern now seems to be that ....

What do my readers think?

What values and concerns do you and your readers share regarding the issue?

▶ Concern about .... leads many of us to oppose .... We worry that .... will happen if ....

What fundamental differences in worldview or experience might keep you and your readers from agreeing?

▶ Those who disagree about .... often see it as a choice between and .... But both are important. We don't have to choose between them because ....

▶ While others may view it as a matter of ...., for me, the issue hinges on ....

Drafting a Working Thesis. You may already have a position on the issue; if so, try drafting a working thesis statement now. (If you have not yet taken a position on the issue, you may want to skip ahead to the section on researching an issue below. Researching the positions others have taken and their reasons may help you decide on your own position.) Begin by describing the issue, possibly indicating where others stand on it or what's at stake, and then saying what you think. These sentence strategies may help you get started:

▶ On this issue, ... and .... [list individuals/groups] say .... Although I understand and to some degree sympathize with their point of view, this is ultimately a question of .... What's at stake is not ...., but .... Therefore, we must ....

▶ This issue is dividing our community. Some people argue .... Others contend .... And still others believe .... It is in all of our interests to ...., however, because ....

Here are four examples from the readings:

- "[O]ur educational system fails to teach science in a way that allows students to integrate it into their lives." (Greene, par. 2)

- "There's little doubt that 'do what you love' (DWYL) is now the unofficial work mantra for our time. The problem is that it leads not to salvation, but to the devaluation of actual work, including the very work it pretends to elevate — and more importantly, the dehumanization of the vast majority of laborers." (Tokomitsu, par. 4)

- "The deeper problem with the nothing-to-hide argument is that it myopically views privacy as a form of secrecy. In contrast, understanding privacy as a plurality of related issues demonstrates that the disclosure of bad things is just one among many difficulties caused by government security measures." (Solove, par. 10)

- "When overzealous parents and coaches impose adult standards on children's sports, the result can be activities that are neither satisfying nor beneficial to children." (Statsky, par. 1)

Developing the Reasons Supporting Your Position.   The following activities will help you find plausible reasons and evidence for your position. Begin by writing down what you already know. (If you did this when choosing your issue, look back at what you wrote.) You can do some focused research later to fill in the details or skip ahead to conduct research now. At this point, don't worry about the exact language you will use in your final draft. Instead, just write the reasons you hold your position and the evidence (such as anecdotes, examples, statistics, expert testimony) that supports it. Keep your readers in mind — what will they find most convincing?

Writers sometimes prefer to brainstorm a list of reasons:

1. Write your position at the top of the page.

2. List as many reasons as you can to support your position. If you think of a bit of supporting evidence, such as a good example or a research study, but you're not sure how to formulate the reason, simply list the support so you can work on it later.

3. Organize your reasons into related groups. For example, which reasons make an argument based on moral values, political ideology, or self-interest, and which are realistic or idealistic? Which would be most and least convincing for your readers?

Once you have listed several reasons in support of your position, write steadily for at least five minutes exploring how best to present them. Ask yourself questions like these:

- How could I show readers that my reasons lead logically to my position?

- How could I arouse my readers' curiosity?

- How could I appeal to my readers' values and beliefs and show my rhetorical sensitivity?

Where you need supporting evidence, fill in the gaps with research.

Researching the Issue.   Research can help you look critically at your own thinking and help you anticipate your readers' arguments and possible objections to your argument.

- Enter keywords or phrases related to the issue or your position in the search box of an all-purpose database such as *Academic OneFile* (InfoTrac) or *Academic Search Complete* (EBSCOHost) to find relevant articles in magazines and journals, or a database like *LexisNexis* to find articles in newspapers. For example, Statsky could have tried a combination of keywords such as *children's competitive sports* or variations on her terms (such as *youth team sports*) to find relevant articles. A similar search could also be conducted in your library's catalog to locate books and other resources on your topic.

- If you think your issue has been dealt with by a government agency, explore the state, local, or tribal sections of the U.S. government's official website, or visit the Library of Congress page on State Government Information and follow the links.

- Bookmark or keep a record of the URLs of promising sites. You may want to download or copy information you could use in your essay. When available, download PDF files rather than HTML files because PDFs are likely to retain the visuals.

> To learn more about finding and documenting sources, see Appendix: Strategies for Research and Documentation.

Remember to record source information and to cite and document any sources, including visuals, that you use in your essay.

Including Visuals.   Consider whether visuals — drawings, photographs, tables, or graphs — would strengthen your argument. You could construct your own visuals, scan materials from books and magazines, or download them from the Internet. If you submit your essay electronically to other students and your instructor or if you post it on a website, consider including snippets of film or sound as well. Visual and auditory materials are not a requirement of a successful position argument, as you can tell from the readings in this chapter, but they could add a new dimension to your writing. If you want to use photographs or recordings of people, though, be sure to obtain permission.

Responding Fairly to Objections Your Readers Are Likely to Raise.   The activity below will help you anticipate alternative positions your readers may hold or objections they may have.

1. List the positions you expect your readers will hold and the objections you expect them to raise. To think of readers' concerns, consider their values, beliefs, and priorities.

2. Which objections can you refute? Which may you need to concede?

Considering Your Purpose.   Write for several minutes about your purpose for writing this position paper. The following questions will help you:

- How do I want to influence my readers' thinking? What one big idea do I want them to grasp?

- How can I help my readers see the significance of the issue — both to society at large and to them personally?

- How can I present myself as fair and ethical?

Organizing Your Position Argument Effectively for Your Readers

For more on outlining, see Chapter 2, pp. 23–24.

Whether you have rough notes or a complete draft, making an outline of what you have written can help you organize your essay effectively for your audience. You may want to draft a sentence that forecasts the elements of your argument to alert your readers to your main points (and give yourself a tentative outline). Putting your points in a logical order (from least to most effective, for example) will make it easier for you to guide your readers from point to point.

Keep in mind that a position argument has five basic parts:

- presentation of the issue

- thesis statement

- your most plausible reasons and evidence

- concessions or refutation of opposing reasons or objections to your argument

- a conclusion that reaffirms your position

These parts can be organized in various ways: If your readers are not likely to agree with your position, you may want to anticipate and respond to their possible objections right before you present the evidence in favor of your own position. If you expect readers *are* likely to favor your position, you may want to concede or refute alternatives after offering your own reasons. Either way, you may want to emphasize the common ground you share and conclude by emphasizing that your position takes into account your shared values.

As you draft, you may see ways to improve your original plan, and you should be ready to revise your outline, shift parts around, or drop or add parts as needed.

Drafting Your Position Argument

By this point, you have done a lot of writing

- to choose an arguable issue and draft a working thesis that asserts your position on it;

- to support your position with reasons and evidence;

- to respond to your readers' likely objections and alternative positions;

- to establish your credibility as thoughtful and fair.

Now stitch that material together to create a draft. The next section of this Guide to Writing will help you evaluate and improve it.

Working with Sources

Using Sources to Reinforce Your Credibility

How you represent your sources can quickly establish your credibility (ethos) — or the reverse. For example, by briefly describing the author's credentials the first time you summarize, paraphrase, or quote from a source, you establish the source's authority and demonstrate that you have selected sources appropriately. (Make sure the author's credentials are relevant to the topic you are discussing.) For example, in paragraph 5 of "Children Need to Play, Not Compete," Statsky writes:

> Martin Rablovsky, a former sports editor for the *New York Times,* says that in all his years of watching young children play organized sports, he has noticed very few of them smiling. "I've seen children enjoying a spontaneous pre-practice scrimmage become somber and serious when the coach's whistle blows," Rablovsky says . . . (qtd in Coakley 94).

Notice how Statsky integrates Rablovsky's credentials (underlined in green) and a summary of his main idea (black) into her own sentence. By doing so, she not only demonstrates her credibility but also provides context for the quotation and demonstrates its relevance to her claim.

In the example below, from her third paragraph, Statsky demonstrates her fairness by quoting from the website of Little League, a well-known organization, and establishes her credibility by illustrating that even those who disagree with her recognize that injuries occur:

> Although the official Little League website acknowledges that children do risk injury playing baseball, it insists that "severe injuries . . . are infrequent . . . far less than the risk of riding a skateboard, a bicycle, or even the school bus" ("Little League Parent").

In both examples, Statsky also introduces the source to her readers, demonstrating the relevance of the source material for readers rather than leaving readers to figure out its relevance for themselves.

Whenever you borrow information from sources, be sure to double-check that you are summarizing, paraphrasing, and quoting accurately and

(continued)

fairly. Compare Statsky's sentences with the source passage, shown below. (The portions she uses are underlined.) Notice that she has inserted an ellipsis to indicate that she has left out words from her source's second sentence.

Source

Injuries seem to be inevitable in any rigorous activity, especially if players are new to the sport and unfamiliar with its demands. But because of the safety precautions taken in Little League, <u>severe injuries</u> such as bone fractures <u>are infrequent</u>. Most injuries are sprains and strains, abrasions and cuts and bruises. The risk of serious injury in Little League Baseball is <u>far less than the risk of riding a skateboard, a bicycle,</u> or even the school bus.

In both examples above, Statsky uses quotation marks to indicate that she is borrowing the words of a source, and she provides an in-text citation so readers can locate her sources in her list of works cited. Both are essential to avoid plagiarism; doing one or the other is not enough.

For more on integrating language from sources into your own sentences and avoiding plagiarism, see Using Information from Sources to Support Your Claims in the Appendix, pp. 497–508.

REVIEWING AND IMPROVING THE DRAFT

This section includes two guides for Peer Review and Troubleshooting Your Draft. Your instructor may arrange a peer review in class or online where you can exchange drafts with a classmate. The Peer Review Guide will help you give each other constructive feedback regarding the basic features and strategies typical of writing a position argument. (If you want to make specific suggestions for improving the draft, see Troubleshooting Your Draft on p. 352.) Also, be sure to respond to any specific concerns the writer has raised about the draft. The Troubleshooting Your Draft guide that follows will help you reread your own draft with a critical eye, sort through any feedback you've received, and consider a variety of ways to improve your draft.

A PEER REVIEW GUIDE

How effective is the presentation of the issue?

What's Working Well: Let the writer know where the issue is especially well presented—for example, where the issue is given historical or cultural context, or where the terms of the debate are given clearly.

What Needs Improvement: Indicate one passage where the presentation of the issue could be improved—for example, where the issue or controversy is not presented fully, or where the key terms could be clarified.

How well does the thesis present the position and forecast its stages?

What's Working Well: Identify the thesis and point to a particularly convincing reason that supports the thesis.

What Needs Improvement: Tell the writer if the thesis seems unclear—too general or too narrow, for example—or alert the writer to reasons that are not on target or that undermine the thesis.

How well does the writer develop the position with appropriate writing strategies?

What's Working Well: Indicate passages where the writer has supported the thesis with facts, statistics, examples, anecdotes, expert opinions, or analogies that are particularly accurate or persuasive.

What Needs Improvement: Tell the writer where an omitted writing strategy might be helpful, or point to a strategy that seems inappropriate or unnecessary for the position to be persuasive. (Consult Chapter 2 for strategy ideas.)

How effective is the response to objections?

What's Working Well: Mark any parts of the argument where objections to the position are acknowledged. Note whether the writer simply acknowledges, concedes, or refutes effectively.

What Needs Improvement: If you think an objection or point of view that should be noted has been ignored, point it out. Note whether a concession or refutation seems weak or inaccurate, or could use more support.

Revising Your Draft

Revising means reenvisioning your draft, trying to see it in a new way, given your purpose and audience, to develop a well-argued position argument. Think imaginatively and boldly about cutting unconvincing or tangential material, adding new material, and moving material around.

TROUBLESHOOTING YOUR DRAFT

To Present the Issue More Effectively	
If readers don't understand what is at stake with the issue,	• Add anecdotes, examples, facts, quotations, or visuals to make the issue more specific and vivid. • Explain systematically why you see the issue as you do.
If your terms are surprising or are antagonistic to readers who disagree with your position,	• Use terms that are more familiar. • Use terms that are more neutral.

To Assert the Position More Clearly	
If your position on the issue is unclear,	• Rephrase it or spell it out in more detail.
If the thesis statement is hard to find,	• State it more directly or position it more boldly. • Repeat it in different words throughout your essay.
If the thesis is not qualified to account for valid opposing arguments or objections,	• Limit the scope of your thesis. • Use qualifying terms, such as *many*, *often*, or *in some cases*.

To Strengthen the Argument for the Position	
If a reason given for the position seems unconvincing,	• Clarify its relevance to the argument. • Add support for your reasoning.
If the support for a reason is inadequate,	• Review your invention notes or do more research to find facts, statistics, quotations, examples, or other types of support to add.

To Improve the Response to Alternative Arguments	
If your argument ignores a strong opposing position or reasonable objection,	• Address the criticism directly, perhaps using the sentence strategy of concession and refutation. • If necessary, modify your position to accommodate the criticism.
If your refutation of a criticism is unconvincing or attacks opponents on a personal level,	• Provide more or better support (such as facts and statistics from reputable sources). • Revise to eliminate personal attacks.

For an explanation of the *ad hominem* fallacy, see Chapter 2, p. 43.

To Enhance Credibility	
If readers consider some of your sources questionable,	• Establish the sources' credibility by providing background information about them. • Choose more reputable sources.
If you ignore likely objections or opposing arguments,	• Demonstrate to readers that you know and understand, even if you do not accept, the criticisms of those who hold alternative views. • Use the sentence strategy of concession and refutation or acknowledgment and refutation.
If your tone is harsh or offensive,	• Check your rhetorical sensitivity by finding ways to show respect for and establish common ground with readers. • Revise your word choices to create a more civil tone. • Consider the concession-refutation strategy.
To Improve Readability	
If the beginning is dull or unfocused,	• Rewrite it, perhaps by adding a surprising or vivid anecdote or visual.
If your argument is disorganized or hard to follow,	• Add a brief forecast of your main points at the beginning of the essay. • Reorder your points in a logical arrangement, such as least to most important. • Announce each reason explicitly in a topic sentence. • Add logical sentence and paragraph transitions to make the connections between points clearer.
If the end is weak or trails off,	• Search your invention and research notes for a memorable quotation or a vivid example to end with. • Explain the consequences if your position is adopted. • Reiterate the shared values that underlie your position.

Editing and Proofreading Your Draft

Check for errors in usage, punctuation, and mechanics, and consider matters of style. If you keep a list of errors you typically make, begin by checking your draft against this list. Ask someone else to proofread your essay before you submit it to your instructor.

From our research on student writing, we know that essays arguing positions have a high percentage of sentence fragment errors involving *subordinating conjunctions* as well as punctuation errors involving *conjunctive adverbs*. Because arguing a position often requires you to use subordinating conjunctions (such as *because*, *although*, and *since*) and conjunctive adverbs (such as *therefore*, *however*, and *thus*), be sure you know the conventions for punctuating sentences that include these types of words. Check a writer's handbook for help with avoiding sentence fragments and using punctuation correctly in sentences with these potential problems.

Reflecting on Position Argument

In this chapter, you have read critically several position arguments and have written one of your own. To better remember what you have learned, pause now to reflect on the reading and writing activities you completed in this chapter.

1. Write a page or so reflecting on what you have learned. Begin by describing what you are most pleased with in your essay. Then explain what you think contributed to your achievement.

   - If it was something you learned from the readings, indicate which readings and specifically what you learned from them.

   - If it came from your invention writing, point out the section or sections that helped you most.

   - If it came from your research notes and write-ups, point out the parts that helped you most.

2. Reflect more generally on position arguments, a genre of writing that plays an important role in our society. Consider some of the following questions:

   - How important are reasons and supporting evidence? When people argue positions on television, on radio talk shows, and in online discussion forums like blogs, do they tend to emphasize reasons and support? If not, what do they emphasize?

   - How does the purpose of television, radio, and online position arguments differ from the purpose of the writers you read in this chapter and from your own purpose in writing a position argument?

   - What contribution might position arguments make to our society that other genres of writing cannot make?

Speculating about Causes or Effects

W hen a surprising event occurs, we ask, "Why did that happen?" Whether we want to understand the event, prevent its recurrence, or make it happen again, we need to speculate about what caused it. Sometimes our focus may shift from "Why did that happen?" to "What is going to happen?" so that we can plan or make decisions. Such speculations are the natural result of our curiosity about origins and consequences. In many cases, the connections between causes and effects can be answered by experimentation. For example, through experimentation, scientists discovered that greenhouse gases are causing the temperature of the Earth's atmosphere to rise — a phenomenon we now know as global warming. When we cannot be certain of causes or effects, the best we can do is **speculate,** or make educated guesses. For example, at this point we cannot be certain what other causes or long-term effects there are for global warming.

RHETORICAL SITUATIONS FOR
SPECULATING ABOUT CAUSES OR EFFECTS

Many people, including analysts, economists, sportswriters, and college students, write essays speculating about causes or effects, as the following examples suggest:

- For an introductory psychology class, a student speculates about the effects of extensive video-game playing among preteens. Based on his own experience and observation, he hypothesizes that video games may improve children's hand-eye coordination and their ability to concentrate on a single task but also that some children may spend too much time playing video games, to the detriment of their physical fitness, social-skills development, and academic performance.

- After her son is disciplined in school, a science reporter comes up with an idea for an article speculating on the reasons for intolerance of "boyish behavior" in school. She reviews recent research in sociological and medical journals and conjectures that adults attempt to stamp out signs of aggression in boys for several reasons: because of concern about bullying; because boys' behavior is perceived as disruptive, especially in group-oriented classrooms; and because boys' fidgeting at their desks is seen as a threat to their eventual success in an economy that values sitting still and concentrating for seven or more hours a day.

Thinking about Speculations about Causes or Effects

You may have speculated with friends or family about the causes or effects of a phenomenon, event, or trend, or composed speculations for science or history exams — or even about a stunning upset for the sports pages. Recall a time when you speculated about a cause or effect or read or heard others doing so. Think about how you (or another writer or speaker) engaged the audience in the subject, presented a credible case for the preferred cause or effect, and ruled out alternative explanations.

- Who was the *audience?* How do you think addressing this audience affected the choice of phenomenon, event, or trend, or the type of evidence presented? For example, did the audience's familiarity with the topic influence the number or type of causes or effects that were presented?

- What was the main *purpose?* Why did you (or the other writer or speaker) want the audience to understand these causes or effects? For example, was it so that they could demonstrate their own understanding on a test or take action in the future?

- How would you rate the *rhetorical sensitivity* with which the speculation was presented? What made the essay appropriate or inappropriate for its particular audience and purpose?

A GUIDE TO READING ESSAYS SPECULATING ABOUT CAUSES OR EFFECTS

This guide introduces you to cause-and-effect writing by inviting you to analyze a brief but powerful causal argument by Stephen King.

- *Reading for meaning* will help you think about the subject that prompted King's essay, as well as understand and respond to King's speculations about why horror movies are so popular.

- *Reading like a writer* will help you learn how King employs strategies typical of speculations about causes or effects, such as

1. presenting the subject fairly

2. making a logical, well-supported cause or effect argument

3. responding to objections or alternative speculations

4. establishing credibility to present the writer as thoughtful and fair

Stephen King

Why We Crave Horror Movies

Stephen King (b. 1947) is America's best-known writer of horror fiction. He received his B.A. from the University of Maine. He has won many awards, including the Lifetime Achievement Award from the Horror Writers Association and the 2003 National Book Foundation Medal for Distinguished Contribution to American Letters. In 2015, King was awarded a National Medal of Arts from the United States National Endowment for the Arts. A prolific writer in many genres and media, King's recent publications include *End of Watch* (2016); his tenth collection of short stories, *The Bazaar of Bad Dreams* (2015); and *Finders Keepers* (2015). Many films and television movies have been based on King's work, including the classics *The Shawshank Redemption* (1994), *Stand by Me* (1986), *The Shining* (1980), and *Carrie* (1976). The following selection is a classic essay that attempts to explain the causes for a common phenomenon: many people's liking — even craving — for horror movies.

- **Before you read,** think about the horror movie that you remember best and consider why it appeals to you (or doesn't).

- **As you read,** test King's argument about the appeal of horror movies against your own experience. On first reading, how convincing are his causal speculations?

I think that we're all mentally ill; those of us outside the asylums only hide it a little 1
better — and maybe not all that much better, after all. We've all known people who talk to themselves, people who sometimes squinch their faces into horrible grimaces when they believe no one is watching, people who have some hysterical fear — of snakes, the dark, the tight place, the long drop . . . and, of course, those final worms and grubs that are waiting so patiently underground.

When we pay our four or five bucks and seat ourselves at tenth-row center in a 2
theater showing a horror movie, we are daring the nightmare.

Why? Some of the reasons are simple and obvious. To show that we can, that we 3
are not afraid, that we can ride this roller coaster. Which is not to say that a really

good horror movie may not surprise a scream out of us at some point, the way we may scream when the roller coaster twists through a complete 360 or plows through a lake at the bottom of the drop. And horror movies, like roller coasters, have always been the special province of the young; by the time one turns 40 or 50, one's appetite for double twists or 360-degree loops may be considerably depleted.

We also go to re-establish our feelings of essential normality; the horror movie is 4 innately conservative, even reactionary. Freda Jackson as the horrible melting woman in *Die, Monster, Die!* confirms for us that no matter how far we may be removed from the beauty of a Robert Redford or a Diana Ross, we are still light-years from true ugliness.

And we go to have fun. 5

Ah, but this is where the ground starts to slope away, isn't it? Because this is a very 6 peculiar sort of fun, indeed. The fun comes from seeing others menaced—sometimes killed. One critic has suggested that if pro football has become the voyeur's version of combat, then the horror film has become the modern version of the public lynching.

It is true that the mythic, "fairy tale" horror film intends to take away the shades of 7 gray. . . . It urges us to put away our more civilized and adult penchant for analysis and to become children again, seeing things in pure blacks and whites. It may be that horror movies provide psychic relief on this level because this invitation to lapse into simplicity, irrationality, and even outright madness is extended so rarely. We are told we may allow our emotions a free rein . . . or no rein at all.

If we are all insane, then sanity becomes a matter of degree. If your insanity leads 8 you to carve up women like Jack the Ripper or the Cleveland Torso Murderer, we clap you away in the funny farm (but neither of those two amateur-night surgeons was ever caught, heh-heh-heh); if, on the other hand, your insanity leads you only to talk to yourself when you're under stress or to pick your nose on your morning bus, then you are left alone to go about your business . . . though it is doubtful that you will ever be invited to the best parties.

The potential lyncher is in almost all of us (excluding saints, past and present; but 9 then, most saints have been crazy in their own ways), and every now and then, he has to be let loose to scream and roll around in the grass. Our emotions and our fears form their own body, and we recognize that it demands its own exercise to maintain proper muscle tone. Certain of these emotional muscles are accepted—even exalted—in civilized society; they are, of course, the emotions that tend to maintain the status quo of civilization itself. Love, friendship, loyalty, kindness—these are all the emotions that we applaud, emotions that have been immortalized in the couplets of Hallmark cards and in the verses (I don't dare call it poetry) of Leonard Nimoy.

When we exhibit these emotions, society showers us with positive reinforcement; 10 we learn this even before we get out of diapers. When, as children, we hug our rotten little puke of a sister and give her a kiss, all the aunts and uncles smile and twit and cry, "Isn't he the sweetest little thing?" Such coveted treats as chocolate-covered graham crackers often follow. But if we deliberately slam the rotten little puke of a sister's fingers in the door, sanctions follow—angry remonstrance from parents, aunts, and uncles; instead of a chocolate-covered graham cracker, a spanking.

But anticivilization emotions don't go away, and they demand periodic exercise. 11
We have such "sick" jokes as "What's the difference between a truckload of bowling
balls and a truckload of dead babies?" (You can't unload a truckload of bowling balls
with a pitchfork . . . a joke, by the way, that I heard originally from a ten-year-old.)
Such a joke may surprise a laugh or a grin out of us even as we recoil, a possibility
that confirms the thesis: If we share a brotherhood of man, then we also share an
insanity of man. None of which is intended as a defense of either the sick joke or
insanity but merely as an explanation of why the best horror films, like the best
fairy tales, manage to be reactionary, anarchistic, and revolutionary all at the
same time.

The mythic horror movie, like the sick joke, has a dirty job to do. It deliberately 12
appeals to all that is worst in us. It is morbidity unchained, our most base instincts let
free, our nastiest fantasies realized . . . and it all happens, fittingly enough, in the dark.
For those reasons, good liberals often shy away from horror films. For myself, I like to
see the most aggressive of them—*Dawn of the Dead*, for instance—as lifting a trap
door in the civilized forebrain and throwing a basket of raw meat to the hungry alliga-
tors swimming around in that subterranean river beneath.

Why bother? Because it keeps them from getting out, man. It keeps them down 13
there and me up here. It was Lennon and McCartney who said that all you need is
love, and I would agree with that.

As long as you keep the gators fed. 14

READING FOR MEANING

1. **Read to Summarize.** Write a sentence or two explaining the main reasons
   King thinks we crave horror movies.

2. **Read to Respond.** Write a paragraph analyzing anything that seems
   fascinating, such as King's assertion that "[i]f we are all insane, then sanity
   becomes a matter of degree" (par. 8); or the difference between prociviliza-
   tion and "anticivilization" emotions (pars. 10–13), indicating what you
   think about King's distinction between these two kinds of emotions.

3. **Read to Analyze Assumptions.** Write a paragraph or two analyzing an
   assumption in King's essay, such as

   Assumptions about the universality and range of human emotions. King
   asserts that "[t]he mythic horror movie . . . has a dirty job to do. It deliberately appeals to all that is worst in us" (par. 12). He adds, "It is morbidity
   unchained, our most base instincts let free, our nastiest fantasies realized . . ."
   (par. 12).

   - What if we don't watch horror movies, don't like them, or don't believe they rep-
     resent our "nastiest fantasies"? If you don't share King's assumption about uni-
     versal human nastiness, how do you respond to his essay?

For help with
summarizing,
see Chapter 2,
pp. 24–25.

You may also try
contextualizing;
see Chapter 2,
pp. 29–30.

● What alternatives to King's thinking occur to you? In a culture that has a different view of the human mind, what other causes of horror movies' popularity might be just as believable?

Assumptions about differences between younger and older people. King asserts that "horror movies . . . have always been the special province of the young" (par. 3) and that we go to see them "to put away our more civilized and adult penchant for analysis and to become children again" (par. 7).

You may also try recognizing emotional manipulation; see Chapter 2, pp. 44–45.

● What viewpoints do children have that adults do not have or have outgrown?

● What does King assume distinguishes children and adults in their attitude toward scary situations (par. 3) or complex ones (par. 7)? Why would adults want to become children again?

READING LIKE A WRITER

Presenting the Subject Fairly

In writing an essay speculating about causes or effects, writers try to present their subject in an intriguing way that makes readers curious about it. Writers also must judge whether or not they need to explain the subject for their audience before examining causes or effects. When writers decide they need to prove that the event, trend, or phenomenon exists, they may describe it in detail, give examples, offer factual evidence, cite statistics, or quote statements by authorities. They may frame or reframe their subjects: **Framing** (or **reframing**) is like cropping and resizing a photograph to focus the viewer's eye on one part of the picture. Writers typically frame or reframe a subject in a way that sets the stage for their argument and promotes their point of view.

Analyze & Write

Write a couple of paragraphs analyzing and evaluating how King reframes his subject:

1. The subject of this essay is horror movies, but the key term in the title is the word "crave." Look up "crave" and "craving" to see what they mean. Then highlight some of the other words and phrases King associates with the appeal of horror movies, such as "mentally ill" and "hysterical fear" (par. 1). How do the words you highlighted relate to the word *crave*?

2. Given these key terms, how would you describe the way King reframes the subject for readers? How do these key terms enable him to plant the seed of his main idea at the beginning of the essay?

Making a Logical, Well-Supported Cause or Effect Argument

At the heart of an essay speculating about causes or effects is an argument with two essential elements:

1. the logical analysis of the proposed causes or effects
2. the reasoning and support offered for each cause or effect

Writers of essays speculating about causes or effects sometimes rely on certain sentence strategies to present these cause-effect relationships:

▸ When .... happens, ... is the result.
▸ If [I/he/she/we/they] [do/say/act] ...., then [others] [do/say/act] ....

These two types of sentences can be seen in King's essay:

Causes
Effects

> When we exhibit these emotions, society showers us with positive reinforcement; we learn this even before we get out of diapers. When, as children, we hug our rotten little puke of a sister and give her a kiss, all the aunts and uncles smile and twit and cry, "Isn't he the sweetest little thing?" Such coveted treats as chocolate-covered graham crackers often follow. But if we deliberately slam the rotten little puke of a sister's fingers in the door, sanctions follow — angry remonstrance from parents, aunts, and uncles; instead of a chocolate-covered graham cracker, a spanking. (par. 10)

Both of these sentence patterns establish a **chronological relationship** — one thing happens after another in time. They also establish a **causal relationship** — one thing *makes* another thing happen. (Chronology and causality do not always go together, however; see Recognizing Logical Fallacies in Chapter 2, pp. 42–44.)

Analyze & Write

Write a paragraph or two analyzing and evaluating how King uses these sentence patterns elsewhere in this reading selection:

1. Skim paragraphs 1–9 and 11–14 and mark the sentences that use these strategies. Does each present a cause-effect relationship as well as a chronological sequence? How do you know?
2. Why do you think King repeats these sentence strategies so often in this essay? How effective or ineffective is this strategy?

Responding to Objections and Alternative Speculations

When causes or effects cannot be known for certain, there is bound to be disagreement. Consequently, writers may consider an array of possibilities before focusing on one or two serious probabilities. They may concede that certain possible causes play some role; they may refute them by providing reasons and supporting evidence for why they play no role (or only a minor role); or they may simply dismiss them as trivial or irrelevant, as King does. "Some of the reasons," King explicitly declares, "are simple and obvious" (par. 3).

Analyze & Write

Write a couple of paragraphs analyzing and evaluating how effectively King concedes or refutes alternative causes for the popularity of horror movies:

1. Look at the causes King considers in the opening paragraphs to determine how he responds to them. For example, how does he support the assertion that some of them are "simple and obvious" (par. 3)? What other arguments does he use to refute these causes?

2. Given his purpose and audience, why do you think King begins by presenting reasons he regards as "simple and obvious"? (par. 3)

Establishing Credibility to Present the Writer as Thoughtful and Fair

Because cause or effect writing is highly speculative, its effectiveness depends in large part on whether readers trust the writer. Writers seek to establish their credibility with readers by making their reasoning clear and logical, their evidence relevant and trustworthy, and their handling of objections fair and balanced. They try to be **authoritative** (knowledgeable) without appearing **authoritarian** (opinionated and dogmatic).

Analyze & Write

Write a paragraph or two analyzing King's **persona** (the personality he wants readers to infer) and assessing how it helps him establish credibility with his readers:

1. Reread the headnote that precedes King's essay, and reflect on what else his readers might already know about him.

2. Skim the essay to decide whether the reasoning is clear and logical and the examples and analogies relevant and trustworthy. Because King's reasoning is psychological (he argues that mental and emotional needs explain why some people crave horror films), you can evaluate King's credibility in light of your own personal experience—that is, your understanding of the role horror movies (and novels) play in your own life.

3. Describe the impression readers might get from King from reading both the headnote and his essay. What details in the headnote might make them trust or distrust what he says about his subject? What word choices or other details in the essay might make him a credible authority on the subject?

READINGS

Eve Fairbanks

How Did Sleep Become So Nightmarish?

Eve Fairbanks holds a degree from Yale in political philosophy. She has received fellowships from the Institute of Current World Affairs, the Daniel Pearl Investigative Journalism Initiative, the Pulitzer Center on Crisis Reporting, and the Writing Invisibility Project at the Max Planck Institute. She has written for the *New Republic, Foreign Policy,* and the *New York Times Magazine,* where the essay below was published in 2014.

- **Before you read,** think about your sleep patterns and how much sleep means to you. Do you think you need more or less than the average person? Does the amount and/or quality of your sleep affect your work? How?

- **As you read,** consider the shift in Fairbanks's thinking about sleep: from childhood to adulthood; from employment by others to employment by oneself; from before her research to after it. How does this shifting structure help you understand her speculations about causes for insomnia?

My experience with insomnia began when I was 6 or 7, though I didn't   1 recognize it as such. In those days, I thought of it as a gift. I had a window that faced east, and in the mornings, a sweet, clear light would pour over my bed, rousing me from the middle of my dreams. I went to bed late and woke up early, and when I did sleep, I slept lightly, waking many times in the night to register the clocklike clicking of a raccoon's claws on the roof, an especially noisy frog or the breathing and muttering of the house as it rolled and shifted position with the temperature, my fellow restless sleeper.

This time I spent lying half-awake made up the most precious moments   2 of my existence. All the ideas of the day moved in like soft clouds, then broke apart into fantasies; I felt both a gathering and an exhilarating dissolving of my identity. But my pleasure wouldn't last long. After a few years of working life, all my perceptions of sleep and rest changed, and I began to hate and fear my insomnia. Desperate, I lined up at the pharmacy to fill one of the 60 million prescriptions written every year for chemical sleep aids in America; I became part of what the Centers for Disease Control and Prevention have declared a full-blown "public-health epidemic." It was amazing: What had been my life's strangest blessing became its greatest curse.

Fairbanks moves from regarding sleep as an adventure — a "blessing" — to sleep as a "curse" here; how does this arouse your curiosity?

3   In the last year or two, an obsessive fixation on getting sleep—not just any sleep, but *good* sleep—has crept into our public consciousness. In the early 2000s, the small number of *New York Times* articles that referred to sleep mostly instructed new mothers on how to get their babies to nod off. Not so in 2013 and early '14, when there were articles on how insomnia makes you fat, sleep seminars, exercising for better sleep, napping for success, sleep as depression cure and an array of new, supposedly soporific devices and products, including dozens of sleep-monitoring smartphone apps, alarm clocks that won't wake you during REM stages, sleep-inducing chocolates, candles that crackle like fireplaces, technologically enhanced sleep masks that "switch off your mind," fitness bracelets that give you a sleep score ("I really want to do well in terms of sleep, I want to maintain my streak!" one user wrote) and a $12,000 sleep-enhancing mattress containing soothing seaweed and coconut husks.

4   There were also books, like *Effortless Sleep* and *Prime Your Mind for Sleep* and *The Secret World of Sleep;* radio specials; a *Harper's* symposium; and major surveys of sleep science in the *Atlantic* and the *New Yorker*. And in keeping with the times, there are endless listicles: 10 Foods to Avoid for Better Sleep, 10 Signs You May Be Sleep Deprived, 12 Simple Steps to Improve Your Sleep, the purposes of five-, 20-, 45-, versus 60-minute naps. There's even a website called Sleepyti.me, which helps users calculate an optimal bedtime or wake-up time, to avoid interrupting their 90 minute sleep cycles.

5   It would be easy to dismiss all this as a byproduct of aging baby boomers' collective obsession with health news and the media's willingness to indulge them, were it not for the fact that sleep in the U.S. has become a $32 billion business, according to the health-marketing analytics firm IMS Health; this includes the hugely lucrative Ambien-type drugs, sleep clinics and those candles that crackle like fireplaces (available from DayNa Decker for up to $75 apiece).

6   If this onslaught of coverage has an underlying ideology, it is this: First, that sleep is absolutely critical for high performance; and second, that you can improve your sleep—but only with intense effort.

7   It was actually an uptick in effort and microscheduling that brought on a darker insomnia for me. I had quit my staff-writing job at a magazine and decided to write freelance for a while. When you're a freelancer, though, productivity becomes everything. It became my obsession. The longer hours I worked, the more it meant I loved my writing. I looked down on sleep as an indulgence for the indolent. Any time off from pitching articles or researching was time spent not growing my little business. I was ashamed of my tiny income, which subsequently made me ashamed of taking any rest—even an evening. I stayed up late to work, woke up early to work, got up in the middle of the night to work.

[marginal notes]

In the next few paragraphs, note what kinds of sources Fairbanks uses. What is their effect?

Fairbanks describes the *effects* of the current "full-blown 'public-health epidemic'" (par. 2) that lack of sleep has become. Do paragraphs 3 and 4 present the subject fairly? Why or why not?

What is Fairbanks's purpose in mentioning how easy it would be to dismiss this epidemic as just a baby boomers' "obsession"?

Some assumptions are only implied, but here Fairbanks makes explicit assumptions about the need for sleep to perform well and that sleep can be improved. How do you respond to her assertions in this paragraph?

Soon enough, though, I found I couldn't fall asleep even when I was 8
willing. All my projects and how to prioritize them circled endlessly in my
mind, giving me no rest. Some nights I didn't sleep at all. This went on for
months. Everything started to suffer. One night, after rolling over and over
in bed until 4:30 without a wink of slumber, I burst into howling tears, waking my boyfriend, a deep sleeper who once nearly slept through a robbery
in our bedroom. He begged me to relax, to prioritize rest for a change.

Why does Fairbanks
decide to use her
own transformation
as key evidence?
What is the effect
on you, the reader?

And I did—but not before I found the scientific studies showing that 9
good sleep and rest would actually boost my productivity. I was captivated
by the writings of a mindfulness guru named Tony Schwartz, author of *Be
Excellent at Anything: The Four Keys to Transforming the Way We Work and
Live*. Schwartz specializes in peddling the idea that sleep and rest, paradoxically, don't diminish our capacity for activity but actually make us better worker bees. As the chief executive of the Energy Project, he "helps
companies fuel sustainable high-performance by better meeting the needs
of their employees." And mostly that means sleep.

"In a world of rising demand, rest should no longer be demonized but 10
celebrated for its intimate connection to sustainable high performance," he
wrote in *The Times* last November. Full of excitement, I showed my boyfriend a Schwartz article titled, "Relax! You'll Be More Productive." I told
him we could now take a vacation because Schwartz had shown that "for
each additional 10 hours of vacation employees took, their year-end performance ratings . . . improved by 8 percent."

Why would
Fairbanks present
this important point
in the words of her
boyfriend instead of
her own? Is he the
"opposition," or is
he serving another
role?

My boyfriend, a South African, was completely disgusted. "You 11
Americans don't know how to rest," he said. "You rest only to work better."

It's true. And it underpins our current obsession with sleep: We want to 12
sleep more now not because we value sleep more on its own terms, but
because we are so fixated on productivity. In a fascinating short book *24/7:
Late Capitalism and the Ends of Sleep*, which came out last June, the culture critic Jonathan Crary writes that capitalism continually corrodes the
value of sleep, positing "continuous functioning" as the ideal and pushing
us to pursue "mastery" over the need to stop and rest.

Sleep, he argues, is perhaps the only area of human existence yet to be 13
conquered by the productivity-maximizing logic of capitalism. Twentieth-
century capitalism already squeezed our sleep into an artificially compact
period of eight hours. Scientific, historical and even literary evidence
(pulled from Chaucer's *Canterbury Tales*) suggest that two separate chunks
of nighttime sleep, plus daytime naps, are the more natural pattern for
human beings. Electric lighting has irrevocably altered our circadian
rhythms, and newer technologies and modes of production have done
more damage. Siestas are incompatible with the assembly line or the all-
night box store. (Just ask Spain, which is considering doing away with the
tradition.)

Fairbanks alludes to
ongoing conversa-
tions about sleep
from different fields:
economics, science,
history, and litera-
ture. How does this
strategy support her
ideas? (Read about
contextualizing in
Ch. 2, pp. 29–30.)

14   The Pentagon has even been funding studies of the physiology of migratory birds to figure out how soldiers can go up to seven days sans sleep without experiencing a decline in cognitive functioning. Pills or genetic modifications that allow us to go days without sleep might sound far-fetched now, but Crary notes how many innovations by the military—microwaves, satellites, the Internet—have been widely adopted in civilian life.

15   But in the last year or so, we've actually conquered sleep in a more insidious way. We've shown that sleep *is* an element of continuous functioning. Instead of being a strange, wild, mysterious Land of Nod whose purpose we don't fully understand, sleep has been colonized by our ambition, becoming just another zone of the day to be farmed for productivity, generating new components necessary for performance like serotonin and healthy glial cells. Crary suggests that we despise sleep because "the stunning, inconceivable reality is that nothing of value can be extracted from it," but with our new science and the interventions of folks like Tony Schwartz, that no longer appears to be true. We can now sleep in order to maximize our economic value.

16   And thus sleep becomes just another burden. A review of one of the new sleep books says it's "for sleep strivers," which is, when you step back from it, one of the most insane phrases ever written. But I was striving for sleep for a while there. In my quest to improve my sleep, I tried restrictive diets (gluten-free, dairy-free, ayurvedic), special (and expensive) teas and drugs and meditation. I applied great concentration to this meditation, separating every thought into restful or nonrestful and volleying the nonrestful ones away, as if I were in a game of mental badminton. Needless to say, this was not actually very relaxing. But at least I felt as if I were *doing* something.

> Fairbanks is exploring the *effects* of striving for sleep: how does her first-person account help or hinder the effectiveness of her argument? How does it add to her credibility?

17   There is another side to life. The side in which we don't do, but just be. Sleep best represents this side of life. We cannot control our dreams; so often we appear in them other than we wish to be, or fear we are. It's what I loved most about drifting in and out of sleep as a child: the sense that I was falling apart, my acting and willing self collapsing under a curious influx of thoughts and fantasies whose provenance I couldn't figure out. By day, my life had to be purpose-driven; by night, it was reigned by mystery. The night life seemed all the more wondrous for its ungovernability.

> Notice Fairbanks's return to the theme of sleep as wondrous, mysterious, and its own master. What is the benefit of this organizational choice for the reader?

18   I'm not too sure about all these studies that promise to unlock the physiological purpose of sleep. They ultimately seek to make it activity's dutiful handmaiden. I'd rather leave sleep shrouded in its aura of mystery. After all, I got a measure of peace only when I finally stopped caring so much—when I stopped trying to discern how my sleep affected my work and let it be a wholly separate realm of experience. I said to myself: Maybe I can lie awake and still do my work fine in the morning; maybe my journey in the nighttime has nothing to do with my day's work at all. There was a certain abandonment of ego in there, too.

Fairbanks seems to conclude that one of our driving forces is to "release our true potential," no matter how we get there. Has her support throughout the essay convinced you of the logic and accuracy of her argument?

The premise of all this research is that we all have greatness locked 19
inside of us, and if only we could release our true potential, we could all be
Richard Branson[1]. In decades past, the secret was said to lie with those who
worked harder. Now it's with those who rest more effectively. But it's all the
same thing.

[1]*Sir Richard Branson* (b. 1950): humanitarian, inventor, and business mogul, best
known as the founder of the Virgin Group. [Ed.]

Shankar Vedantam

The Telescope Effect

Shankar Vedantam (b. 1969) graduated from Stanford University with a master's degree in journalism. He is a science correspondent for National Public Radio and has worked for a number of major newspapers, including the *Philadelphia Inquirer, Washington Post,* and *Newsday.* He has been honored with fellowships and awards by Harvard University, the World Health Organization, the Society of Professional Journalists, and the American Public Health Association. In addition to many articles, Vedantam has written plays and fiction, including his short-story collection *The Ghosts of Kashmir* (2005). "The Telescope Effect" is excerpted from his book *The Hidden Brain: How Our Unconscious Minds Elect Presidents, Control Markets, Wage Wars, and Save Our Lives* (2010).

- **Before you read,** think about your own degree of **empathy,** the ability to feel the emotions and think the thoughts of beings other than yourself. You "get inside their skin." Is this quality something that comes naturally to you?

- **As you read,** pay attention to how Vedantam supports his hypothesis about the "telescope effect." What kinds of evidence does he use?

The *Insiko 1907* was a tramp tanker that roamed the Pacific Ocean. Its twelve-man 1 Taiwanese crew hunted the seas for fishing fleets in need of fuel; the *Insiko* had a cargo of tens of thousands of gallons of diesel. It was supposed to be an Indonesian ship, except that it was not registered in Indonesia because its owner, who lived in China, did not bother with taxes. In terms of international law, the *Insiko 1907* was stateless, a two-hundred-sixty-foot microscopic speck on the largest ocean on earth. On March 13, 2002, a fire broke out in the *Insiko*'s engine room. . . . The ship was about eight hundred miles south of Hawaii's Big Island, and adrift. Its crew could not call on anyone for help, and no one who could help knew of the *Insiko*'s existence, let alone its problems.[1]

Drawn by wind and currents, the *Insiko* eventually got within two hundred twenty 2 miles of Hawaii, where it was spotted by a cruise ship called the *Norwegian Star* on April 2. The cruise ship diverted course, rescued the Taiwanese crew, and radioed the United States Coast Guard. But as the *Norwegian Star* pulled away from the *Insiko* and steamed toward Hawaii, a few passengers on the cruise ship heard the sound of barking. The captain's puppy had been left behind on the tanker.

It is not entirely clear why the cruise ship did not rescue the Jack Russell mixed ter- 3 rier, or why the Taiwanese crew did not insist on it. . . . Whatever the reason, the burned-out tanker and its lonely inhabitant were abandoned on the terrible immensity of the Pacific. The *Norwegian Star* made a stop at Maui. A passenger who heard the barking dog called the Hawaiian Humane Society in Honolulu. . . . The Humane

Society alerted fishing boats about the lost tanker. Media reports began appearing about the terrier, whose name was Hokget.

Something about a lost puppy on an abandoned ship on the Pacific gripped people's imaginations. Money poured into the Humane Society to fund a rescue. One check was for five thousand dollars. . . . "It was just about a dog," [Hawaiian Humane Society president Pamela] Burns told me. . . . "This was an opportunity for people to feel good about rescuing a dog. People poured out their support. A handful of people were incensed. These people said, 'You should be giving money to the homeless.'" But Burns felt the great thing about America was that people were free to give money to whatever cause they cared about, and people cared about Hokget. . . .

On April 26, nearly one and a half months after the puppy's ordeal began, the *American Quest* found the *Insiko* and boarded the tanker. The forty-pound female pup was still alive, and hiding in a pile of tires. It was a hot day, so Brian Murray, the *American Quest*'s salvage supervisor, went in and simply grabbed the terrier by the scruff of her neck. The puppy was terrified and shook for two hours. Her rescuers fed her, bathed her, and applied lotion to her nose, which was sunburned.

Hokget, the rescued dog, with Dr. Becky Rhoades, a veterinarian with the Kauai (Hawaii) Humane Society

© Craig T. Kojima, Honolulu Star-Advertiser

The story of Hokget's rescue is comical, but it is also touching. Human beings from around the world came together to save a dog. The vast majority of people who sent money to the Humane Society knew they would never personally see Hokget, never have their hands licked in gratitude. Saving the dog, as Pamela Burns suggested to me, was an act of pure altruism, and a marker of the remarkable capacity human beings have to empathize with the plight of others.

There are a series of disturbing questions, however. Eight years before Hokget was rescued, the same world that showed extraordinary compassion in the rescue of a dog sat on its hands as a million human beings were killed in Rwanda. . . . The twentieth century reveals a shockingly long list of similar horrors that have been ignored by the world as they unfolded. . . . Why have successive generations of Americans—a people with extraordinary powers of compassion—done so little to halt suffering on such a large scale? . . .

There are many explanations for the discrepancy between our response to Hokget 8 and our response to genocide. Some argue that Americans care little about foreign lives—but then what should we make about their willingness to spend thousands of dollars to rescue a dog, a foreign dog on a stateless ship in international waters? Well, perhaps Americans care more about pets than people? But that does not stand up to scrutiny, either. Hokget's rescue was remarkable, but there are countless stories about similar acts of compassion and generosity that people show toward their fellow human beings every day. No, there is something about genocide, about mass death in particular, that seems to trigger inaction.

I believe our inability to wrap our minds around large numbers is responsible for 9 our apathy toward mass suffering. We are unconsciously biased in our moral judgment, in much the same way we are biased when we think about risk. Just as we are blasé about heart disease and lackadaisical about suicide, but terrified about psychopaths and terrorists, so also we make systematic errors in thinking about moral questions—especially those involving large numbers of people.

The philosopher Peter Singer once devised a dilemma that highlights a central contradiction in our moral reasoning. If you see a child drowning in a pond, and you 10 know you can save the child without any risk to your own life—but you would ruin a fine pair of shoes worth two hundred dollars if you jumped into the water—would you save the child or save your shoes?[2] Most people react incredulously to the question; obviously, a child's life is worth more than a pair of shoes. If this is the case, Singer asked, why do large numbers of people hesitate to write a check for two hundred dollars to a reputable charity that could save the life of a child halfway around the world—when there are millions of such children who need our help? Even when people are absolutely certain their money will not be wasted and will be used to save a child's life, fewer people are willing to write the check than to leap into the pond.

Our moral responsibilities feel different in these situations even though Singer is 11 absolutely right in arguing they are equivalent challenges; one feels immediate and visceral, the other distant and abstract. We feel personally responsible for one child, whereas the other is one of millions who need help. Our responsibility feels diffused when it comes to children in distant places—there are many people who could write that check. But distance and diffusion of responsibility do not explain why we step forward in some cases—why did so many people come forward to save Hokget? Why did they write checks for a dog they would never meet? Why did they feel a single abandoned dog on a stateless ship was *their* problem?

I want to offer a disturbing idea. The reason human beings seem to care so little 12 about mass suffering and death is precisely *because* the suffering is happening on a mass scale. The brain is simply not very good at grasping the implications of mass suffering. Americans would be far more likely to step forward if only a few people were suffering, or a single person were in pain. Hokget did not draw our sympathies because we care more about dogs than people; she drew our sympathies because she was a *single* dog lost on the biggest ocean in the world. If the hidden brain biases our perceptions about risk toward exotic threats, it shapes our compassion into a telescope. We are best able to respond when we are focused on a single victim. We don't feel twenty times sadder when we hear that twenty people have died in a disaster than when we hear that one person has died, even though the magnitude of the tragedy *is* twenty times larger. . . . We can certainly reach such a conclusion abstractly, in our conscious minds, but we cannot *feel it viscerally*, because that is the domain of the hidden brain, and the hidden brain is simply not calibrated to deal with the difference between a single death and a million deaths.

But the paradox does not end there. Even if ten deaths do not make us feel ten   13 times as sad as a single death, shouldn't we feel five times as sad, or even at least twice as sad? There is disturbing evidence that shows that in many situations, not only do we not care twice as much about ten deaths as we do about one, but we may actually care *less*. I strongly suspect that if the *Insiko* had been carrying a hundred dogs, many people would have cared less about their fate than they did about Hokget. A hundred dogs do not have a single face, a single name, a single life story around which we can wrap our imaginations—and our compassion. . . .

The evidence for what I am going to call the telescope effect comes from a series of   14 fascinating experiments.[3] At the University of Oregon, the psychologist Paul Slovic asked . . . groups of volunteers to imagine they were running a philanthropic foundation. Would they rather spend ten million dollars to save 10,000 lives from a disease that caused 15,000 deaths a year, or save 20,000 lives from a disease that killed 290,000 people a year? Overwhelmingly, volunteers preferred to spend money saving the ten thousand lives rather than the twenty thousand lives. Rather than tailor their investments to saving the largest number of lives, people sought to save the largest *proportion* of lives among the different groups of victims. An investment directed toward disease A could save two-thirds of the victims, whereas an investment directed at disease B could save "only" seven percent of the victims.

We respond to mass suffering in much the same way we respond to most things in   15 our lives. We fall back on rules of thumb, on feelings, on intuitions. People who choose to spend money saving ten thousand lives rather than twenty thousand lives are not bad people. Rather, like those who spend thousands of dollars rescuing a single dog rather than directing the same amount of money to save a dozen dogs, they are merely allowing their hidden brain to guide them.

I have often wondered why the hidden brain displays a telescope effect when it   16 comes to compassion. Evolutionary psychology tends to be an armchair sport, so please take my explanation for the paradox as one of several possible answers. The telescope effect may have arisen because evolution has built a powerful bias into us to preferentially love our kith and kin. It is absurd that we spend two hundred dollars on a birthday party for our son or our daughter when we could send the same money to a charity and save the life of a child halfway around the world. How can one child's birthday party mean more to us than another child's life? When we put it in those terms, we sound like terrible human beings. The paradox, as with the rescue of Hokget, is that our impulse springs from love, not callousness. Evolution has built a fierce loyalty toward our children into the deepest strands of our psyche. Without the unthinking telescope effect in the unconscious mind, parents would not devote the immense time and effort it takes to raise children; generations of our ancestors would not have braved danger and cold, predators and hunger, to protect their young. The fact that you and I exist testifies to the utility of having a telescope in the brain that caused our ancestors to care intensely about the good of the few rather than the good of the many.

17   This telescope is activated when we hear a single cry for help—the child drowning in the pond, the puppy abandoned on an ocean. When we think of human suffering on a mass scale, our telescope does not work, because it has not been designed to work in such situations.

18   What makes evolutionary sense rarely makes moral sense. (One paradox of evolution is that ruthless natural selection has produced a species that recoils at the ruthlessness of natural selection.) Humans are the first and only species that is even aware of large-scale suffering taking place in distant lands; the moral telescope in our brain has not had a chance to evolve and catch up with our technological advances. When we are told about a faraway genocide, we can apply only our conscious mind to the challenge. We can reason, but we cannot feel the visceral compassion that is automatically triggered by the child who is drowning right before us. Our conscious minds can tell us that it is absurd to spend a boatload of money to save one life when the same money could be used to save ten—just as it can tell us it is absurd to be more worried about homicide than suicide. But in moral decision-making, as in many other domains of life where we are unaware of how unconscious biases influence us, it is the hidden brain that usually carries the day.

Editor's Notes

1. Chris Lee and George Butler, "Complex Response to Tankship *Insiko 1907*," *Proceedings of the Marine Safety Council*, Vol. 60, No. 1 (January–March 2003), pp. 49–51.
2. Peter Singer has mentioned the story about the drowning child in a number of publications, including his 2009 book, *The Life You Can Save*, Random House, Inc.
3. Paul Slovic, "'If I Look at the Mass I Will Never Act': Psychic Numbing and Genocide," *Judgment and Decision Making*, Vol. 2, No. 2 (April 2007), pp. 79–95.

READING FOR MEANING

1. **Read to Summarize.** Write a sentence or two explaining what you think Vedantam wants his readers to understand about the impulse behind the "telescope effect."

    For help with summarizing, see Chapter 2, pp. 24–25.

2. **Read to Respond.** Write a paragraph analyzing anything that seems contradictory, such as the rescue of Hokget. Pamela Burns is quoted as saying, "This was an opportunity for people to feel good about rescuing a dog." But she also notes, "A handful of people were incensed. These people said, 'You should be giving money to the homeless'" (par. 4). Which side do you come down on? Why? Or you might consider Vedantam's speculation that "just as we are blasé about heart disease and lackadaisical about suicide, but terrified about

    You may also try reflecting on challenges to your beliefs and values; see Chapter 2, pp. 36–37.

psychopaths and terrorists, so also we make systematic errors in thinking about moral questions — especially those involving large numbers of people" (par. 9). Are you persuaded by Vedantam's reasoning? Why or why not?

3. **Read to Analyze Assumptions.** Write a paragraph or two analyzing an assumption you find intriguing in Vedantam's essay. For example:

Assumptions about the effects of the "hidden brain" on our moral choices. Vedantam speculates that our "hidden brain" — his term for a host of unconscious mental processes that subtly bias our judgment — "shapes our compassion into a telescope. We are best able to respond when we are focused on a single victim" (par. 12).

- Why does such brain behavior lead to more empathy for a few than the many? Do you agree with Vedantam that this is the result of our evolutionary past, or is it possible that we feel more empathy for the few because we believe we can more realistically help a single individual?

- Why does Vedantam call the telescope effect a form of "bias" (par. 12)?

For help analyzing assumptions, see Chapter 2, pp. 28–29.

Assumptions about money as a measure of compassion. Vedantam provides several examples to illustrate that donating money is evidence of human compassion: money for the dog, Hokget (par. 6); money (or the lack of money) for Rwanda genocide (par. 7); and money (or the lack of it) for children around the world (par. 10). He speculates that "many people could write that check" for faraway children, and that "distance and diffusion of responsibility do not explain why we step forward in some cases — why did so many people come forward to save Hokget?" (par. 11).

- If compassion correlates with generosity, then are people who make large donations more compassionate than those who make small donations or none at all? What other kinds of donations (of time, for example) might indicate generosity?

- Pamela Burns suggests that "the great thing about America was that people were free to give money to whatever cause they cared about . . ." (par. 4). Does this suggest that the Americans who donated to rescue Hokget are generally more compassionate than others?

READING LIKE A WRITER

MAKING A LOGICAL, WELL-SUPPORTED CAUSE
OR EFFECT ARGUMENT

Although Vedantam is writing for a general audience, he does acknowledge his sources. In fact, Vedantam states at the beginning of paragraph 14 that psychologist Paul Slovic's research provides the main "evidence" supporting his favored cause and cites Slovic's research in the Editor's Notes (p. 373).

| Analyze & Write |

Write a paragraph or two analyzing how Vedantam uses Slovic's research:

1. Reread paragraph 14. How does Vedantam use Slovic's research to support his causal analysis?
2. Reread paragraph 12 and paragraphs 15–18. What could Vedantam have added, if anything, to clarify the connection between Slovic's research and Vedantam's ideas about "the telescope effect" and "the hidden brain"?

Nicholas Carr

Is Google Making Us Stupid?

Nicholas Carr (b. 1959) received his master's degree in English and American literature and language from Harvard. He writes on the social, economic, and business implications of technology. He is the author of *Does IT Matter?* (2004), *The Big Switch: Rewiring the World, from Edison to Google* (2008), and *The Shallows: What the Internet Is Doing to Our Brains* (2010). Carr has also written for many periodicals, including the *Atlantic Monthly*, the *New York Times Magazine*, *Wired*, the *Financial Times*, the *Futurist*, and *Advertising Age*, and has been a columnist for the *Guardian* and the *Industry Standard*. The essay below was the cover story of the *Atlantic Monthly*'s Ideas issue in 2008.

- **Before you read,** think about your own habits of concentration, considering whether you are able to focus deeply for long periods of time or whether you move from one idea to another fairly swiftly. Also think about whether concentration has to be sacrificed for the sake of acquiring more information.

- **As you read,** note how Carr mentions and responds to alternative ideas about the effect of the Internet on our thinking.

"Dave, stop. Stop, will you? Stop, Dave. Will you stop, Dave?" So the supercomputer 1 HAL pleads with the implacable astronaut Dave Bowman in a famous and weirdly poignant scene toward the end of Stanley Kubrick's *2001: A Space Odyssey*. Bowman, having nearly been sent to a deep-space death by the malfunctioning machine, is calmly, coldly disconnecting the memory circuits that control its artificial "brain." "Dave, my mind is going," HAL says, forlornly. "I can feel it. I can feel it."

I can feel it, too. Over the past few years I've had an uncomfortable sense that 2 someone, or something, has been tinkering with my brain, remapping the neural circuitry, reprogramming the memory. My mind isn't going—so far as I can tell—but it's changing. I'm not thinking the way I used to think. I can feel it most strongly when I'm reading. Immersing myself in a book or a lengthy article used to be easy. My mind would get caught up in the narrative or the turns of the argument, and I'd spend hours strolling through long stretches of prose. That's rarely the case anymore. Now my concentration often starts to drift after two or three pages. I get fidgety, lose the thread, begin looking for something else to do. I feel as if I'm always dragging my wayward brain back to the text. The deep reading that used to come naturally has become a struggle.

I think I know what's going on. For more than a decade now, I've been spending a 3 lot of time online, searching and surfing and sometimes adding to the great databases of the Internet. The Web has been a godsend to me as a writer. Research that once required days in the stacks or periodical rooms of libraries can now be done in minutes. A few Google searches, some quick clicks on hyperlinks, and I've got the telltale

$$Ax^2 + Bx + C = 0$$
$$A^2 + B^2 = C^2$$

"The Cloud ate my homework."

©Tom Cheney/The New Yorker Collection/cartoonbank.com

fact or pithy quote I was after. Even when I'm not working, I'm as likely as not to be foraging in the Web's info-thickets, reading and writing e-mails, scanning headlines and blog posts, watching videos and listening to podcasts, or just tripping from link to link to link. (Unlike footnotes, to which they're sometimes likened, hyperlinks don't merely point to related works; they propel you toward them.)

For me, as for others, the Net is becoming a universal medium, the conduit for   4
most of the information that flows through my eyes and ears and into my mind. The advantages of having immediate access to such an incredibly rich store of information are many, and they've been widely described and duly applauded. "The perfect recall of silicon memory," *Wired*'s Clive Thompson has written, "can be an enormous boon to thinking." But that boon comes at a price. As the media theorist Marshall McLuhan pointed out in the 1960s, media are not just passive channels of information. They supply the stuff of thought, but they also shape the process of thought. And what the Net seems to be doing is chipping away my capacity for concentration and contemplation. My mind now expects to take in information the way the Net distributes it: in

a swiftly moving stream of particles. Once I was a scuba diver in the sea of words. Now I zip along the surface like a guy on a Jet Ski.

I'm not the only one. When I mention my troubles with reading to friends and acquaintances—literary types, most of them—many say they're having similar experiences. The more they use the Web, the more they have to fight to stay focused on long pieces of writing. Some of the bloggers I follow have also begun mentioning the phenomenon. Scott Karp, who writes a blog about online media, recently confessed that he has stopped reading books altogether. "I was a lit major in college, and used to be [a] voracious book reader," he wrote. "What happened?" He speculates on the answer: "What if I do all my reading on the web not so much because the way I read has changed, i.e., I'm just seeking convenience, but because the way I THINK has changed?"

Bruce Friedman, who blogs regularly about the use of computers in medicine, also has described how the Internet has altered his mental habits. "I now have almost totally lost the ability to read and absorb a longish article on the web or in print," he wrote earlier this year. A pathologist who has long been on the faculty of the University of Michigan Medical School, Friedman elaborated on his comment in a telephone conversation with me. His thinking, he said, has taken on a "staccato" quality, reflecting the way he quickly scans short passages of text from many sources online. "I can't read *War and Peace* anymore," he admitted. "I've lost the ability to do that. Even a blog post of more than three or four paragraphs is too much to absorb. I skim it."

Anecdotes alone don't prove much. And we still await the long-term neurological and psychological experiments that will provide a definitive picture of how Internet use affects cognition. But a recently published study of online research habits, conducted by scholars from University College London, suggests that we may well be in the midst of a sea change in the way we read and think. As part of the five-year research program, the scholars examined computer logs documenting the behavior of visitors to two popular research sites, one operated by the British Library and one by a U.K. educational consortium, that provide access to journal articles, e-books, and other sources of written information. They found that people using the sites exhibited "a form of skimming activity," hopping from one source to another and rarely returning to any source they'd already visited. They typically read no more than one or two pages of an article or book before they would "bounce" out to another site. Sometimes they'd save a long article, but there's no evidence that they ever went back and actually read it. The authors of the study report:

> It is clear that users are not reading online in the traditional sense; indeed there are signs that new forms of "reading" are emerging as users "power browse" horizontally through titles, contents pages and abstracts going for quick wins. It almost seems that they go online to avoid reading in the traditional sense.

Thanks to the ubiquity of text on the Internet, not to mention the popularity of text-messaging on cell phones, we may well be reading more today than we did in the 1970s or 1980s, when television was our medium of choice. But it's a different kind of reading, and behind it lies a different kind of thinking—perhaps even a new sense of the self. "We are not only *what* we read," says Maryanne Wolf, a developmental psychologist at Tufts University and the author of *Proust and the Squid: The Story and Science of the Reading Brain.* "We are *how* we read." Wolf worries that the style of reading promoted by the Net, a style that puts "efficiency" and "immediacy" above all else, may be weakening our capacity for the kind of deep reading that emerged when an earlier technology, the printing press, made long and complex works of prose commonplace. When we read online, she says, we tend to become "mere decoders of information." Our ability to interpret text, to make the rich mental connections that form when we read deeply and without distraction, remains largely disengaged.

Reading, explains Wolf, is not an instinctive skill for human beings. It's not etched 9 into our genes the way speech is. We have to teach our minds how to translate the symbolic characters we see into the language we understand. And the media or other technologies we use in learning and practicing the craft of reading play an important part in shaping the neural circuits inside our brains. Experiments demonstrate that readers of ideograms, such as the Chinese, develop a mental circuitry for reading that is very different from the circuitry found in those of us whose written language employs an alphabet. The variations extend across many regions of the brain, including those that govern such essential cognitive functions as memory and the interpretation of visual and auditory stimuli. We can expect as well that the circuits woven by our use of the Net will be different from those woven by our reading of books and other printed works. . . .

The human brain is almost infinitely malleable. People used to think that our men- 10 tal meshwork, the dense connections formed among the 100 billion or so neurons inside our skulls, was largely fixed by the time we reached adulthood. But brain researchers have discovered that that's not the case. James Olds, a professor of neuroscience who directs the Krasnow Institute for Advanced Study at George Mason University, says that even the adult mind "is very plastic." Nerve cells routinely break old connections and form new ones. "The brain," according to Olds, "has the ability to reprogram itself on the fly, altering the way it functions." . . .

The process of adapting to new intellectual technologies is reflected in the chang- 11 ing metaphors we use to explain ourselves to ourselves. When the mechanical clock arrived, people began thinking of their brains as operating "like clockwork." Today, in the age of software, we have come to think of them as operating "like computers." But the changes, neuroscience tells us, go much deeper than metaphor. Thanks to our brain's plasticity, the adaptation occurs also at a biological level.

The Internet promises to have particularly far-reaching effects on cognition. In a 12 paper published in 1936, the British mathematician Alan Turing proved that a digital computer, which at the time existed only as a theoretical machine, could be programmed to perform the function of any other information-processing device. And that's what we're seeing today. The Internet, an immeasurably powerful computing system, is subsuming most of our other intellectual technologies. It's becoming our map and our clock, our printing press and our typewriter, our calculator and our telephone, and our radio and TV.

When the Net absorbs a medium, that medium is re-created in the Net's image. It 13 injects the medium's content with hyperlinks, blinking ads, and other digital gewgaws, and it surrounds the content with the content of all the other media it has absorbed. A new e-mail message, for instance, may announce its arrival as we're glancing over the latest headlines at a newspaper's site. The result is to scatter our attention and diffuse our concentration.

The Net's influence doesn't end at the edges of a computer screen, either. As 14 people's minds become attuned to the crazy quilt of Internet media, traditional media have to adapt to the audience's new expectations. Television programs add text crawls and pop-up ads, and magazines and newspapers shorten their articles, introduce capsule summaries, and crowd their pages with easy-to-browse info-snippets. When, in March of this year, the *New York Times* decided to devote the second and third pages of every edition to article abstracts, its design director, Tom Bodkin, explained that the "shortcuts" would give harried readers a quick "taste" of the day's news, sparing them the "less efficient" method of actually turning the pages and reading the articles. Old media have little choice but to play by the new-media rules.

Never has a communications system played so many roles in our lives—or exerted 15 such broad influence over our thoughts—as the Internet does today. Yet, for all that's been written about the Net, there's been little consideration of how, exactly, it's reprogramming us. The Net's intellectual ethic remains obscure. . . .

Google's headquarters, in Mountain View, California—the Googleplex—is the Inter- 16 net's high church. . . . Google, says its chief executive, Eric Schmidt, is "a company that's founded around the science of measurement," and it is striving to "systematize everything" it does. Drawing on the terabytes of behavioral data it collects through its search engine and other sites, it carries out thousands of experiments a day, according to the *Harvard Business Review*, and it uses the results to refine the algorithms that increasingly control how people find information and extract meaning from it. . . .

The company has declared that its mission is "to organize the world's information 17 and make it universally accessible and useful." It seeks to develop "the perfect search engine," which it defines as something that "understands exactly what you mean and gives you back exactly what you want." In Google's view, information is a kind of commodity, a utilitarian resource that can be mined and processed with industrial efficiency. The more pieces of information we can "access" and the faster we can extract their gist, the more productive we become as thinkers.

Where does it end? Sergey Brin and Larry Page, the gifted young men who founded 18 Google while pursuing doctoral degrees in computer science at Stanford, speak frequently of their desire to turn their search engine into an artificial intelligence, a HAL-like machine that might be connected directly to our brains. "The ultimate search engine is something as smart as people—or smarter," Page said in a speech a few years back. "For us, working on search is a way to work on artificial intelligence." In a 2004 interview with *Newsweek*, Brin said, "Certainly if you had all the world's information directly attached to your brain, or an artificial brain that was smarter than your brain, you'd be better off." Last year, Page told a convention of scientists that Google is "really trying to build artificial intelligence and to do it on a large scale."

Such an ambition is a natural one, even an admirable one, for a pair of math whiz-   19
zes with vast quantities of cash at their disposal and a small army of computer scientists in their employ. A fundamentally scientific enterprise, Google is motivated by a
desire to use technology, in Eric Schmidt's words, "to solve problems that have never
been solved before," and artificial intelligence is the hardest problem out there. Why
wouldn't Brin and Page want to be the ones to crack it?

Still, their easy assumption that we'd all "be better off" if our brains were supple-   20
mented, or even replaced, by an artificial intelligence is unsettling. It suggests a belief
that intelligence is the output of a mechanical process, a series of discrete steps that
can be isolated, measured, and optimized. In Google's world, the world we enter
when we go online, there's little place for the fuzziness of contemplation. Ambiguity
is not an opening for insight but a bug to be fixed. The human brain is just an outdated
computer that needs a faster processor and a bigger hard drive.

The idea that our minds should operate as high-speed data-processing machines is   21
not only built into the workings of the Internet, it is the network's reigning business
model as well. The faster we surf across the Web—the more links we click and pages
we view—the more opportunities Google and other companies gain to collect information about us and to feed us advertisements. Most of the proprietors of the commercial Internet have a financial stake in collecting the crumbs of data we leave
behind as we flit from link to link—the more crumbs, the better. The last thing these
companies want is to encourage leisurely reading or slow, concentrated thought. It's
in their economic interest to drive us to distraction.

Maybe I'm just a worrywart. Just as there's a tendency to glorify technological prog-   22
ress, there's a countertendency to expect the worst of every new tool or machine. . . .
Perhaps those who dismiss critics of the Internet as Luddites or nostalgists will be
proved correct, and from our hyperactive, data-stoked minds will spring a golden age
of intellectual discovery and universal wisdom. Then again, the Net isn't the alphabet,
and although it may replace the printing press, it produces something altogether different. The kind of deep reading that a sequence of printed pages promotes is valuable not
just for the knowledge we acquire from the author's words but for the intellectual vibra-
tions those words set off within our own minds. In the quiet spaces opened up by the
sustained, undistracted reading of a book, or by any other act of contemplation, for that
matter, we make our own associations, draw our own inferences and analogies, foster
our own ideas. Deep reading, as Maryanne Wolf argues, is indistinguishable from deep
thinking. If we lose those quiet spaces, or fill them up with "content," we will sacrifice
something important not only in our selves but in our culture. In a recent essay, the
playwright Richard Foreman eloquently described what's at stake:

> I come from a tradition of Western culture, in which the ideal (my ideal) was
> the complex, dense and "cathedral-like" structure of the highly educated
> and articulate personality—a man or woman who carried inside them-
> selves a personally constructed and unique version of the entire heritage of
> the West. [But now] I see within us all (myself included) the replacement of
> complex inner density with a new kind of self—evolving under the pressure
> of information overload and the technology of the "instantly available."

As we are drained of our "inner repertory of dense cultural inheritance," Foreman 23
concluded, we risk turning into "'pancake people'—spread wide and thin as we
connect with that vast network of information accessed by the mere touch of a
button."

I'm haunted by that scene in *2001*. What makes it so poignant, and so weird, is the 24
computer's emotional response to the disassembly of its mind: its despair as one cir-
cuit after another goes dark, its childlike pleading with the astronaut—"I can feel it. I
can feel it. I'm afraid"—and its final reversion to what can only be called a state of
innocence. HAL's outpouring of feeling contrasts with the emotionlessness that char-
acterizes the human figures in the film, who go about their business with an almost
robotic efficiency. Their thoughts and actions feel scripted, as if they're following the
steps of an algorithm. In the world of *2001*, people have become so machinelike that
the most human character turns out to be a machine. That's the essence of Kubrick's
dark prophecy: as we come to rely on computers to mediate our understanding of the
world, it is our own intelligence that flattens into artificial intelligence.

READING FOR MEANING

For help with
summarizing,
see Chapter 2,
pp. 24–25.

You may also
try reflecting
on challenges
to your beliefs
and values; see
Chapter 2,
pp. 36–37.

1. **Read to Summarize.** Write a sentence or two explaining Carr's concern
   regarding the Internet's effect on our ability to concentrate and think deeply.

2. **Read to Respond.** Write a paragraph analyzing anything that seems interesting, such as the role of Carr's anecdotes in the first six paragraphs. Do they
   draw the reader into the essay? Present the subject? Help readers identify
   with Carr? Provide hard evidence? What role(s) do they play? Or consider
   your own experience with reading on the Internet, and whether you share
   Carr's concern that the kind of reading fostered there is undermining "deep
   reading" (par. 2).

3. **Read to Analyze Assumptions.** Write a paragraph or two analyzing an
   assumption you find intriguing in Carr's essay. For example:

   Assumptions about the value of sustained concentration. Carr returns again
   and again to ways the Internet is reducing our ability to sustain concentration
   and focus for an extended period of time. He reports that he and his friends
   "have to fight to stay focused on long pieces of writing" (par. 5), cites a study
   about "power browsing" (par. 7), and states that "[t]he last thing these companies [Google and others] want is to encourage leisurely reading or slow,
   concentrated thought" (par. 21).

   - How does Carr support his contention that we lose something valuable if we
     lose sustained concentration?

   - Is there a compromise — a way to have both sustained concentration and all
     the knowledge we need?

Assumptions about the value of the human over the machine. Carr seems concerned that machines will replace human thought, and that we will lose something important to our humanity as a result. He says that in "Google's world," the human brain is "just an outdated computer that needs a faster processor and a bigger hard drive" (par. 20). In his conclusion, Carr laments that in the movie *2001*, "people have become so machinelike that the most human character turns out to be a machine" (par. 24).

- What do you think of Carr's concerns about the danger that machines pose to humans, especially machines that mimic the human mind?

- What could be the long-lasting consequences of *not* prizing human qualities, like the ability to contemplate?

You may also want to try recognizing emotional manipulation; see Chapter 2, pp. 44–45.

READING LIKE A WRITER

RESPONDING TO OBJECTIONS OR ALTERNATIVE SPECULATIONS

Writers speculating about effects must support their proposed effects, using all the relevant resources available to them — quoting authorities, citing statistics and research findings, comparing and contrasting, posing rhetorical questions, offering literary allusions, and crafting metaphors, among other strategies. (Carr uses all of these resources in his essay.) Writers know that at every point in the argument their readers will have objections, questions, and alternative effects in mind, and that they must anticipate and respond to them. Just as imaginatively as they argue for their proposed effects, writers in this genre attempt to answer readers' questions, react to their objections, and evaluate their preferred effects.

Analyze & Write

Write a paragraph or two analyzing how Carr anticipates his readers' objections and supports his response:

1. Reread paragraphs 4, 7, 8, 10, 17, 18, 19, and 22, in which Carr responds to alternative arguments, underlining the main objections that he anticipates his readers will have to his argument. For example, in paragraph 4, he antici-pates readers' likely objection that having access to so much information is a terrific advantage.

2. Now examine how Carr manages readers' possible objections and questions. For at least three of the objections or questions you identified in the paragraphs you reread, notice the kinds of support he relies on to argue against each objec-tion. How appropriate and believable do you find his support? Why?

You may also try looking for patterns of opposition; see Chapter 2, pp. 35–36.

A Special Reading Strategy

Analyzing Visuals

For more on analyzing visuals, see Chapter 2, pp. 31–34.

Write a paragraph analyzing the cartoon included in Carr's essay and explaining what it contributes to the essay. To do the analysis, consider these questions that specifically refer to the cartoon:

- Recall the old excuse, "The dog ate my homework." How does the cartoon play on that parody of an excuse for turning work in late?

- Consider the traditional appearance of the teacher, student, and classroom. How does the contrast between that traditional look and the caption help generate the cartoon's humor?

- The cartoon originally appeared in the *New Yorker* magazine, a periodical that appeals to a middle-aged, fairly well-to-do, and sophisticated readership. How does the cartoon appeal to this audience?

Sendhil Mullainathan

The Mental Strain of Making Do with Less

Sendhil Mullainathan (b. 1972) received his Ph.D. from Harvard and is a professor of economics there. He has published many articles in professional economics journals and has the distinction of being a MacArthur Fellow. He is the author, with Jeffrey R. Kling and William J. Congdon, of *Policy and Choice: Public Finance through the Lens of Behavioral Economics* (2011), and he is the author, with Eldar Shafir, of *Scarcity: Why Having Too Little Means So Much* (2013). The essay below is based on the work described in *Scarcity*. For your reference, we have converted Mullainathan's sources to in-text citations and a list of Works Cited at the end of the selection.

- **Before you read,** think about your own experiences with **scarcity** — with having less than you need to achieve a goal. Were you aware of any physiological or emotional challenges to "making do with less"?

- **As you read,** note places where Mullainathan establishes his credibility, such as where he presents his issue thoughtfully and fairly, and consider why you think so.

Diets don't just reduce weight, they can reduce mental capacity. In other words, diet- 1 ing can make you dumber. Understanding why this is the case can illuminate a range of experiences, including something as far removed from voluntary calorie restriction as the ordeal of outright poverty.

Imagine that you are attending a late-afternoon meeting. Someone brings in a plate 2 of cookies and places them on the other side of the conference table. Ten minutes later you realize you've processed only half of what has been said. Why? Only half of your mind was in the meeting. The other half was with the cookies: "Should I have one? I worked out yesterday. I deserve it. No, I should be good." That cookie threatened to strain your waistline. It succeeded in straining your mind.

This can happen even with no cookie in sight. Dieters conjure their own cookies: 3 psychologists find that dieters have spontaneous self-generated cravings at a much higher rate than nondieters (Hill). And these cravings are not the dieters' only distraction. Diets force trade-offs: If you eat the cookie, should you skip the appetizer at dinner? But that restaurant looked so good!

Many diets also require constant calculations to determine calorie counts. All this 4 clogs up the brain. Psychologists measure the impact of this clogging on various tasks: logical and spatial reasoning, self-control, problem solving, and absorption and retention of new information. Together these tasks measure "bandwidth," the resource that underlies all higher-order mental activity. Inevitably, dieters do worse than nondieters on all these tasks; they have less bandwidth.

One particularly clever study by Janey Polivy, Julie Coleman, and C. Peter Herman 5 went further. It tested how dieters and nondieters reacted to eating a chocolate bar.

Even though the bar provided calories, eating it widened the bandwidth gap between dieters and nondieters. Nondieters ate and moved on, but dieters started wondering how to make up for the calories they had just ingested or, even more fundamentally, pondered, "Why did I eat the bar?"

In other words, diets do not just strain bandwidth because they leave us hungry. 6 They have psychological, not just physiological, effects.

The basic insight extends well beyond the experience of calorie counting. Some- 7 thing similar happens whenever we make do with less, as when we feel that we have too little time, or too little money. Just as the cookie tugs at the dieter, a looming dead-line preoccupies a busy person, and the prospect of a painful rent payment shatters the peace of the poor. Just as dieters constantly track food, the hyper-busy track each minute and the poor track each dollar.

A similar psychology of scarcity operates across these examples but with varying 8 degrees of force. If a cookie can tax our mental resources, imagine how much more psychological impact other forms of scarcity can have (Mullainathan and Shafir).

Take the case of poverty. In a paper published September 16, 2015 in *Science*, Profs. 9 Anandi Mani at the University of Warwick, Jiaying Zhao at the University of British Columbia, Professor Eldar Shafir at Princeton University, and I waded into politically charged territory. Some people argue that the poor make terrible choices and do so because they are inherently less capable. But our analysis of scarcity suggests a different perspective: perhaps the poor are just as capable as everyone else. Perhaps the problem is not poor people but the mental strain that poverty imposes on anyone who must endure it.

One of our studies focused on Indian sugar cane farmers, who typically feel them- 10 selves to be both poor and rich, depending on the season. They are paid once a year at harvest time. When the crop is sold, they are flush with cash. But the money runs out quickly, and by the time the next harvest arrives they are stretched thin: they are, for example, 20 times as likely to pawn an item before harvest as after it. Rather than compare poor and rich farmers, we compare each farmer to himself: when he is rich against when he is poor. This kind of comparison is important because it addresses valid concerns that differences in psychological tests merely reflect differences in cul-ture or test familiarity.

We measured farmers' mental function—on what psychologists call fluid intelli- 11 gence and executive control—one month before and one month after harvest. And the effects were large: preharvest I.Q., for example, was lower by about nine to 10 points, which in a common descriptive classification is the distance between "aver-age" and "superior" intelligence. To put that in perspective, a full night without sleep has a similar effect on I.Q. (Mani et al.).

Bandwidth scarcity has far-reaching consequences, whether we are talking about 12 poor farmers or affluent dieters. We all use bandwidth to make decisions at work, to resist the urge to yell at our children when they annoy us, or even to focus on a con-versation during dinner or in a meeting. The diversity of these behaviors—combined with the size of the measurable effects—suggests a very different way to interpret the choices and behaviors of the poor. Just picture how distracting that cookie was, and multiply that experience by a factor of 10.

For dieters, bandwidth scarcity has one particularly important consequence, illus- 13
trated in a study by Baba Shiv and Alexander Fedorikhin that gave people a choice between fruit salad and cake. Before choosing, half of the subjects had their bandwidth taxed: they were asked to remember a seven-digit number. The other half had a mentally less-demanding task: they were asked to remember a two-digit number. Those with less available bandwidth ate more cake: they were 50 percent more likely to choose cake than the others. There is a paradox here: diets create mental conditions that make it hard to diet.

This may sound defeatist. But there are positive lessons for how to manage the dif- 14
ferent kinds of scarcity. The United States government, laudably, offers financial aid for low-income students to attend college. Qualifying for it, though, requires completing a densely packed 10-page booklet, mentally taxing for anyone. A one-page version would not only be simpler but it would also recognize that the poor are short on bandwidth as well as cash.

The same tactic—economizing on bandwidth—can be used in dieting. Take the 15
Atkins diet, which effectively bans many foods, including bread and a lot of desserts. A ban is less complex than the trade-offs and calorie accounting required by many other diets. While all diets require self-control, Atkins requires less thinking. This might explain its popularity, and even its effectiveness: a recent study shows that people persist longer with diets that require less thought. The same study had another interesting finding: it was the perceived complexity of a diet—not its actual complexity—that determined persistence (Mata, et al.).

So keep this in mind the next time you're picking a diet to shed a few pounds. Try 16
one that won't also shed a few I.Q. points.

Works Cited

Hill, Andrew J. "The Psychology of Food Craving." *Proceedings of the Nutrition Society,* vol. 66, no. 2, May 2007, pp. 277–85.

Mani, Anandi, et al. "Poverty Impedes Cognitive Function." *Science,* vol. 341, no. 6149, 30 Aug. 2013, pp. 976–90.

Mata, Jutta, et al. "When Weight Management Lasts. Lower Perceived Rule Complexity Increases Adherence." *Appetite,* vol. 54, no. 1, Feb. 2010, pp. 37–43.

Mullainathan, Sendhil, and Eldar Shafir. *Scarcity: The New Science of Having Less and How it Defines Our Lives.* Picador, 2013.

Polivy, Janet, et al. " The Effect of Deprivation on Food Cravings and Eating Behavior in Restrained and Unrestrained Eaters." *International Journal of Eating Disorders,* vol. 38, no. 4, Dec. 2005, pp. 301–9, doi:10.1002/eat.20195.

Shiv, Baba, and Alexander Fedorikhin. "Heart and Mind in Conflict: The Interplay of Affect and Cognition in Consumer Decision Making." *Journal of Consumer Research,* vol. 26, no. 3, Dec. 1999, pp. 278–92.

READING FOR MEANING

For help with
summarizing,
see Chapter 2,
pp. 24–25.

1. **Read to Summarize.** Write a sentence or two defining *scarcity* and explaining the effect of "bandwidth" on our mental capacities and behavior, according to Mullainathan.

2. **Read to Respond.** Write a paragraph analyzing anything that seems contradictory, such as Mullainathan's "paradox" that "diets create mental conditions that make it hard to diet" (par. 13) or his observation that "Indian sugar cane farmers . . . typically feel themselves to be both poor and rich, depending on the season" (par. 10).

3. **Read to Analyze Assumptions.** Write a paragraph or two analyzing an assumption you find intriguing in Mullainathan's essay. For example:

For help
analyzing
assumptions,
see Chapter 2,
pp. 28–29.

The assumption that the brain can perform only a limited number of functions at one time. Mullainathan uses counting calories as an activity that "clogs up the brain" (par. 4) to such an extent that the brain suffers losses on "logical and spatial reasoning, self-control, problem solving, and absorption and retention of new information" (par. 4).

- Can you think of instances in which you have experienced or seen someone else experience a loss of mental function as a result of a seemingly unrelated distraction?

- Can you think of other causes for this mental malfunctioning that might explain it convincingly?

The assumption that the stress of dieting is familiar enough to illuminate a more unfamiliar and difficult concept — bandwidth scarcity. As Mullainathan notes, "dieting can make you dumber. Understanding why this is the case can illuminate a range of experiences, including something as far removed from voluntary calorie restriction as the ordeal of outright poverty" (par. 1). He shows how dieting impedes you from successfully completing mental tasks and therefore has "psychological, not just physiological, effects" (par. 6).

- Before you read this essay, did you believe that diets have psychological effects? Did reading about dieting stresses help you understand how bandwidth scarcity affects people who have too little money as well as too few calories?

- Choosing dieting as a primary example suggests that more readers will identify with dieting than other examples. Do you think this is true? Why or why not? Mullainathan also reports that diets with fewer rules are more successful (par. 15). Do you think this is true of all successful diets, or does it depend on the individual dieter? If the latter, does Mullainathan's example still work to explain the effects of bandwidth scarcity?

READING LIKE A WRITER

ESTABLISHING CREDIBILITY TO PRESENT THE WRITER AS THOUGHTFUL AND FAIR

On a topic of international interest like the causes of mental strain or the effects of scarcity on the mind, writers either have to be expert in the subject or have to do research to become expert enough to convince their readers that they should be taken seriously. To seem credible, For help judging the writer's credibility, see Chapter 2, pp. 45–46.

- they must not oversimplify, trivialize, or stereotype their subject;

- they must not overlook possible objections or alternative causes or effects that will occur to readers

- they must show that they have thought about their subject deeply and seriously.

Analyze & Write

Write a paragraph or two analyzing Mullainathan's strategies to establish his credibility:

1. Reread "The Mental Strain of Making Do with Less," and annotate it for evidence of credibility or lack of it. How knowledgeable does Mullainathan seem about the subject? Look especially at paragraphs 3, 5, 9–12, and 15. Which paragraphs most impress you with his authority? Why?

2. What evidence do you find that Mullainathan has thought deeply about his subject? Do you think that dieting is the most important subject in his essay, or is he really alerting his audience to something more pervasive? If so, how would you explain his approach?

For more on
evaluating the
logic of an
argument,
see Chapter 2,
pp. 40–41.

A Special Reading Strategy

Evaluating the Logic of an Argument

To **evaluate the logic of an argument** speculating about causes or effects, ask yourself three basic questions:

- How appropriate is the support for each cause or effect being speculated about?

- How believable is the support?

- How consistent and complete is the overall argument?

Such an evaluation requires a comprehensive and thoughtful critical reading, but your efforts will help you understand more fully what makes a causal argument successful. To evaluate the logic of Mullainathan's argument, follow the guidelines in Chapter 2, pp. 40–41. There you will find definitions and explanations as well as an illustration based on an excerpt from a famous essay by Martin Luther King Jr. (The excerpt appears on pp. 18–22).

Clayton Pangelinan

#socialnetworking: Why It's *Really* So Popular

Clayton Pangelinan wrote this essay in his first-year college composition course. He was curious about why social networking had become so popular and has sustained its popularity over some time, and he wanted to examine the causes for this sustained interest.

- **Before you read,** think about why you engage in social networking, and why you think it has maintained its popularity after it was initially invented.

- **As you read,** pay attention to how Pangelinan tries to present his subject fairly, to establish his causes, and to understand the larger significance of the trend he examines.

Complain about problems in a *tweet* over Twitter. Add a *friend*, virtually *poke* each   1 other, and *like* friends' postings and ramblings on Facebook. Send images and videos to each other using Snapchat. Capture a *selfie* with Instagram, edit it, add hashtags, and share it for your friends to see and comment on. Social networking is only a click away with apps like Vine and YouTube, Twitter, Facebook, Snapchat, Instagram, and Whatsapp on smartphones and tablets everywhere. Over the last decade or so, there has been a remarkable increase in the popularity of social networking. As Figure 1 below [p. 393] shows, the rise in popularity cuts across all age groups. The most dramatic growth has been among young adults. The percentage of 18–29 year olds using social media rose from 9% to 49% in just 18 months, from February 2005 to August 2006 (Fig. 1). Like young adults, teenagers have flocked to social media. A 2015 survey reported that 71% of all teens use Facebook, along with sites like Instagram and Snapchat (Lenhart). Facebook has tended to outpace other networking outlets for adults as well, with 71% of online adults reporting they use Facebook (Social Networking Fact Sheet). Preferences among social networking sites have changed over the years, but the bottom line is that social networking continues to be enormously popular.

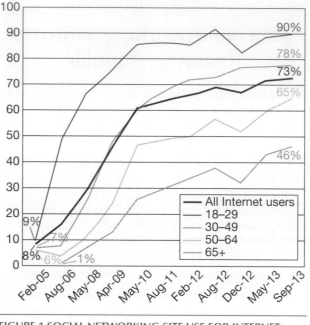

FIGURE 1 SOCIAL NETWORKING SITE USE FOR INTERNET USERS BY AGE GROUP, 2005–2013. "Social Networking Fact Sheet." *Internet Project Library Survey*, Pew Research Center, www.pewinternet.org/data-trend/social-media/social-media-use-by-age-group/.

"Social Media Use by Age Group Over Time," Pew Research Center, Washington, DC (January 2014) http://www.pewinternet.org/data-trend/social-media/social-media-use-by-age-group/.

The fact *that* social networking is popular is well established. The question is *why* is it so popular? The most basic answer is that social networking is popular because it's available. Without the technological advances that transformed the static read-only Web into the dynamic, interactive virtual community known as Web 2.0, none of the social networking we all engage in today would have been possible. A better answer, though, is that social media offer people a way to satisfy their desire to connect with others and maybe also be "world-famous for fifteen minutes" (as Andy Warhol supposedly remarked). When people were asked what their motivations were for using social networking sites like Facebook and Twitter, two-thirds of those surveyed reported that they go online primarily to connect with friends and family and meet new people (see Fig. 2). As social animals, people have an inherent need for human connection. Professor Matthew Lieberman, in his recent book *Social: Why Our Brains Are Wired to Connect,*   2

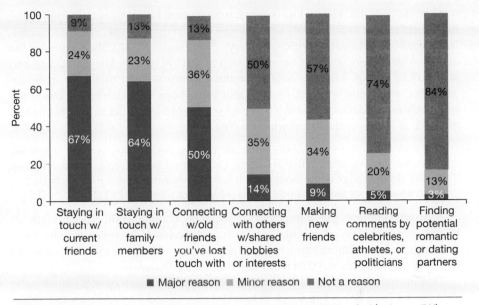

FIGURE 2 MOTIVATIONS FOR USING SOCIAL NETWORKING SITES.   Smith, Aaron. "Why Americans Use Social Media." *Pew Research Center*, 15 Nov. 2011, www.pewinternet .org/2011/11/15/why-americans-use-social-media/

"Why Americans Use Social Media," Pew Research Center, Washington, DC (November, 2011) http://pewinternet.org/2011/11/15/ why-americans-use-social-media.

reports experiments using fMRIs to prove that the need to connect is hard-wired. According to Lieberman, our wiring impels us not only to share, but also to hear. Communication naturally flows both ways: Not only are we "driven by deep motivations to stay connected with friends and family" but we are also "naturally curious about what is going on in the minds of other people" (ix).

Social media outlets offer a way to satisfy both impulses. Consider the story of Emmalene Pruden, a YouTube sensation who began posting her video blogs on YouTube after moving and feeling "cut off from her friends" (Niedzviecki 37). Emmalene is one example of how social media allow individuals to feel connected to a larger community: "If nothing else," as Niedzviecki claims, "peeping your problem, suspicion, or outrage is guaranteed to make you feel less alone" (142). But Emmalene's popularity also suggests that—as Hal Niedzviecki, author of *The Peep Diaries: How We're Learning to Love Watching Ourselves and Our Neighbors*, puts it—"it is these quotidian revelations that make her enticing to her viewers" (39). Viewers may feel less lonely knowing that their own everyday struggles and daily trivialities are no different than Emmalene's.

Consider also the story of Lisa Sargese, who "started blogging as a way to tell the   4
truth about her life as a morbidly obese, single woman determined to return to mobility and health via stomach-shrinking surgery" (Niedzviecki 51-52). She chronicled the
effects of her surgery, growing her readership as she lost weight. Like Emmalene and
her YouTube videos, Lisa was able to produce something that made her audience
adore her: the sympathy effect. Readers also found hope by watching her overcome
her problems. Niedzviecki makes a powerful statement that applies to both Emmalene
and Lisa, as well as to their fans, when he concludes:

> We're alone all the time. We're alone on the bus, we're alone walking down the
> street, we're alone at the office and in the classroom, alone waiting in line at Disney
> World. We're tired of being alone, which is why increasingly we are barely hesitating
> to do whatever we feel we need to do to push out of solitude. (212-213)

This statement rings true throughout the social networking world but especially on   5
Facebook, where users often post whatever is on their minds, however intimate. From
the status of their relationships to pornographic home videos, social networkers can
find it in a Facebook post. What motivates the extreme sharers?

One answer might be a desire for celebrity. Consider the story of a woman who   6
calls herself Padme. For her, social networking has turned into an obsession apparently motivated by her need for fame: "In our case you get to 1.6 million readers it's
really hard to just walk away from that" (qtd. in Niedzviecki 26). Padme appears to be
a typical suburban housewife and mother, except that she is also a fantastically popular writer of a sexually explicit Star Wars–themed blog, *Journey to the Darkside*. Padme's popularity appears to come not only from her sexual confessions (and visuals),
but also from her story of living a double life, as both a mother and as a Star Wars sex
slave. In addition to recording her rather ordinary day-to-day activities as a stay-at-
home mom, she also writes "about her need to be dominated by the man she calls
Master Anakin, the man she's been . . . 'married to for 4 years, living with for 12 years,
and best friends with for 18 years'" (Niedzviecki 23).

Writing in the American Psychological Association journal *Psychology of Popu-*   7
lar Media Culture, Dara Greenwood reviews research showing that "a craving for
positive feedback and validation may be a common thread that links a desire for
fame with social media use" (223). More specifically, she points to the correlation
between the desire to be seen and valued and the need to feel connected, "to feel
meaningfully embedded in social networks," as Greenwood puts it (223). While
Padme carries her blogging to extremes that Emmalene and Lisa don't reach, what
Greenwood writes applies to all three. The underlying cause of this need for visibility
may be narcissism, fairly obvious in all three cases but especially so in Padme's as
demonstrated by the "increased tendency to engage in exhibitionist postings on social
media sites" (224).

Of course, most of us participate in social networks without getting as carried away as 8
Emmalene, Lisa, or Padme. In fact, if you understood the first paragraph in this essay, then
chances are you sign in, sign up, tune in, and engage in many of these forms of social
media. So ask yourself: What are your reasons for joining in? To connect? To tune in
to what others are up to? To show off? Whatever your reasons, you can be sure you are
not alone.

Works Cited

Greenwood, Dara N. "Fame, Facebook, and Twitter: How Attitudes about Fame Predict the
　　Frequency and Nature of Social Media Use." *Psychology of Popular Media Culture,* vol.
　　2, no. 4, 2013, pp. 222–36. *PsycINFO,* doi:10.1037/ppm0000013.

Lenhart, Amanda. "Teens, Social Media & Technology Overview 2015." *Pew Research Center,*
　　9 Apr. 2015, www.pewinternet.org/2015/04/09/teens-social-media-technology-2015/.

Lieberman, Matthew. *Social: Why Our Brains Are Wired to Connect.* Crown Publishing,
　　2013.

Niedzviecki, Hal. *The Peep Diaries: How We're Learning to Love Watching Ourselves and
　　Our Neighbors.* City Lights Books, 2009.

Smith, Aaron. "Why Americans Use Social Media." *Pew Research Center,* 15 Nov. 2011,
　　www.pewinternet.org/2011/11/15/why-americans-use-social-media/.

"Social Networking Fact Sheet." *Internet Project Library Survey.* Pew Research Center, www
　　.pewinternet.org/fact-sheets/social-networking-fact-sheet/. Accessed 15 Oct. 2015.

READING FOR MEANING

For help with
summarizing,
see Chapter 2,
pp. 24–25.

1. **Read to Summarize.** Write a few sentences explaining the reasons Pangelinan gives to account for the trend of the continuing popularity of social media.

2. **Read to Respond.** Write a paragraph about anything that seems surprising, such as Facebook's reigning position as the most popular social media site — by an overwhelming lead (par. 1; Fig. 1)—or Pangelinan's speculation that the need for celebrity is a motivating factor in the popularity of social networking (pars. 6–7). Why would you find this factor surprising?

For help
analyzing
assumptions,
see Chapter 2,
pp. 28–29.

3. **Read to Analyze Assumptions.** Write a paragraph analyzing an assumption you find intriguing in Pangelinan's essay. For example:

   Assumptions about the validity of findings from an international research center. Pangelinan includes two charts in his essay: one on social networking by age group (par. 1), and one on "motivations for using social networking sites" (par. 2). Both are by the Pew Research Center, one from its Internet Project Library Survey (2013), and one from its Internet & American Life Project (2011).

   - Is the name "Pew" familiar to you as a valid source for facts about social trends in America? Do you associate it with credibility or with something else?

   - Do these two charts provide enough information from this source to convince you that Pangelinan's interpretation of them is correct and useful?

   Assumptions about what level of sharing is considered "normal." Pangelinan establishes a distinction between simple sharing and extreme sharing (par. 7). He seems to think that the stories of Lisa and Emmalene are just normal sharing, in an effort to connect and to be "meaningfully embedded in social networks", but that Padme is an "exhibitionist" (Greenwood, qtd. in par. 7).

   - Do you agree with the distinction between the two types of sharing? Are there examples from your own experience that would support — or complicate — the distinction?

   - Does sharing carry a stigma when it reaches a certain level? Where would a stigma come from on a social media site? How do people's responses change to the different degrees of sharing, and how can you tell?

READING LIKE A WRITER

PRESENTING THE SUBJECT FAIRLY

One effective strategy for proving that an event, phenomenon, or trend exists is framing (or reframing) the topic to help readers understand it and engage their interest. When writers use **framing,** they focus the reader's eye on one angle or viewpoint that is important and might have a larger significance. Pangelinan spends some time establishing that the trend of social networking does in fact exist, and then speculates about the reasons for its persistence/popularity.

| Analyze & Write |

Write a paragraph or two analyzing and evaluating how fairly and effectively Pangelinan presents his subject.

1. Reread paragraphs 1–4. How does each paragraph serve the goal of establishing the existence of a trend and presenting the questions about it fairly?

2. Now skim the subsequent paragraphs that develop his ideas. What kind of evidence does Pangelinan present to support his speculations? Does this evidence help you understand why social networking has maintained its popularity?

A Special Reading Strategy

Comparing and Contrasting Related Readings: Turkle's "The Flight from Conversation" and Pangelinan's "#socialnetworking: Why It's *Really* So Popular"

Compare and contrast the cause or effect strategies used by Sherry Turkle (p. 313) and Clayton Pangelinan (p. 391), thinking about issues such as these:

- Compare how the two writers discuss the effects of modern technology on our relationships and the ways we interact. How are their arguments similar and different?

- Turkle opens her essay with the assertion "we have sacrificed conversation for mere connection" (par. 1), while Pangelinan offers that social media is so popular because it will "satisfy [people's] desire to connect with others" (par. 2). These two writers seem to have quite different opinions on connection. Do you think they contradict each other, or is there some meeting point for them? Do they share any common assumptions about our culture or the way we relate to one another? Explain your answer.

For help with comparing and contrasting related readings, see Chapter 2, pp. 37–39.

Writing to Learn Speculations about Causes or Effects

Write a brief essay analyzing one of the readings in this chapter (or another selection, perhaps one by a classmate). Explain how (and perhaps, how well) the selection works as an argument speculating about causes or effects. Consider, for example, how it

- presents the argument fairly to help readers know the issue and enhance the writer's credibility;

- uses writing strategies, such as definition, compare/contrast, example, illustration, and analogy to make a logical, well-supported argument

- responds to objections or alternative speculations that are fair and appropriate.

Your essay could also reflect on how you applied one or more of the academic habits of mind as you read the selection:

- **Curiosity** — what questions or ideas did you have as you read the selection?

- **Critical Analysis** — what assumptions in the selection did you find intriguing, and why?

- **Rhetorical Sensitivity** — how effective or ineffective do you think the selection is in achieving its purpose for the intended audience, given the constraints of the medium and the speculative argument genre?

A GUIDE TO WRITING ESSAYS SPECULATING ABOUT CAUSES OR EFFECTS

You have probably done a good deal of analytical writing about your reading. Your instructor may also assign a capstone project to write a brief speculative essay of your own [for parity with wording of other chapters] arguing for your preferred causes or effects of an event, a phenomenon, or a trend. This Guide to Writing offers detailed suggestions and resources to help you meet the special challenges this kind of writing presents.

THE WRITING ASSIGNMENT

Write an essay arguing for your preferred causes or effects for an event, a phenomenon, or a trend.

- Choose a subject that invites you to speculate about its causes or effects: why it may have happened or what its effects may be.

- Research the subject, gathering detailed information from appropriate sources, and present that information in a clear, logical way.

- Establish the existence and significance of the subject.

- Convince readers that the causes or effects you propose are more plausible than the alternatives.

WRITING YOUR DRAFT

Choosing a Subject

Rather than limiting yourself to the first subject that comes to mind, take a few minutes to consider your options. Keep in mind that it must be

- one that you can show exists (such as with examples or statistics);

- one that has no definitive, proven cause or effect;

- one that you can research, as necessary, in the time you have;

- one that will puzzle — or at least interest — you and your readers.

Here are some ideas that may help you find a subject.

Trends

- changing patterns in leisure, entertainment, lifestyle, religious life, health, or technology
- completed artistic or historical trends (art movements or historical changes)
- long-term changes in economic conditions or political behavior or attitudes

Events

- a recent national or international event that is surrounded by confusion or controversy
- a recent surprising or controversial event at your college or in your community
- a historical event about which there is still some dispute as to its causes or effects

Phenomena

- a social problem, such as discrimination, homelessness, high-school or college dropout rates, youth suicides, or teenage pregnancy
- one or more aspects of college life, such as noisy libraries, large classes, lack of financial aid, difficulties in scheduling classes, or insufficient availability of housing
- a human trait, such as anxiety, selfishness, fear of success or failure, leadership, jealousy, insecurity, envy, opportunism, or curiosity

Because an authoritative essay arguing for preferred causes or effects requires sustained thinking, drafting, revising, and possibly research, you will want to choose a subject for which you have enough time and interest.

Consider carefully whether you are more interested in the causes or the effects of the event, trend, or phenomenon. For example, you could speculate about the causes of increasing membership in your church, whereas the effects of the increase might for now be so uncertain as to discourage plausible speculation. Some subjects invite speculation about both their causes and their effects. For this assignment, however, you need not do both.

You may find it useful to frame your topic in question form:

- ▶ Cause: Why is .... the most popular major at College X?
- ▶ Effect: How will the cancellation of the .... at X University affect students' employment prospects after graduation?

Making a chart listing subjects that interest you and their possible causes or effects can help you decide which subject is most promising.

Subject	Possible Causes or Effects
Example: Why do students often procrastinate in writing papers or studying for exams?	• They have better things to do. • The project seems overwhelming. • They have many responsibilities and the one with the latest deadline suffers/the most difficult task gets done last. • They are lazy. • They may not be mature enough to meet deadlines.
Example: What would be the effect of making all science classes in middle school gender-specific?	• Children might perform better. • Courses for boys (or girls) might receive better funding. • Children may not get used to studying side by side with children of the other sex and face more difficulties in high school or college. • The types of instruction boys and girls receive may differ.

Analyzing Your Readers

Now that you have a potential subject, write for a few minutes, analyzing your potential readers.

- What might my potential readers already know about the event, phenomenon, or trend? (Even if you are writing only for your instructor, you should consider what he or she knows about your subject.)

- What kinds of examples or information could I provide that readers will find new, useful, interesting, or amusing? How might I clarify misconceptions or faulty assumptions?

- Will a more or less formal writing style be appropriate for my readers?

- What kinds of sources will my readers find credible?

- What questions might they ask? What might they be interested in learning more about?

Exploring Your Subject

You may discover that you know more about your subject than you suspect if you write about it for a few minutes without stopping. This brief sustained writing will stimulate your memory and help you probe your interest in the subject. As you write, consider the following questions:

- What about this subject interests me? What about it will interest my readers?

  ▶ I think the [subject] is important because ....

  ▶ My readers are likely to be curious about the subject because .... [Examples: it affects them personally/it raises important moral, psychological, or other questions they will find intriguing].

- What do I already know about the subject? What do my readers already know?

  ▶ I know what the obvious causes of [the subject] are, but I'm curious about the underlying [cultural/psychological/ideological] causes because ....

  ▶ The subject [has been in the news or is so well-known] that I expect my readers will know .... but not ....

Considering Causes or Effects

Discovering and analyzing the causes or effects you can already imagine can give your research (should you need to conduct research) direction and can also help you develop a list of the most (and least) plausible ones.

Discovering Causes or Effects.   Brainstorm a list of possible causes or effects. For causes, consider underlying or background causes as well as immediate or instigating causes. For example, say you have noticed that the number of students in your classes has increased sharply in the past year.

- An underlying cause could be that a few years ago the voters in your state passed a bill that sharply reduced income for public colleges, and now the effects are beginning to show;

- An immediate cause could be that the college has had to lay off one-third of its faculty.

For effects, consider both short-term and long-term consequences, as well as how one effect may lead to another in a kind of chain reaction. Try to think of obvious causes or effects and also of those that might be overlooked.

Considering how your subject is similar to or different from related subjects may also help you come up with causes or effects to add to your list:

  ▶ .... [name subject] is like .... [name other subject] in that they are both caused by ....

  ▶ Whereas .... [the other subject] is .... , ... [my subject] is ....

Conducting Research. Research can give you a greater understanding of an event, trend, or phenomenon and may suggest to you plausible causes or effects you have overlooked. (In addition, you may find support for your responses to readers' objections or to others' proposed causes or effects.) Enter keywords or phrases related to your cause or effect subject into the search box of

- an all-purpose database such as *Academic OneFile* (InfoTrac) or *Academic Search Complete* (EBSCOHost) to find relevant articles in magazines and journals

- a database like *LexisNexis* to find articles in newspapers

- a search engine like *Google* or *Yahoo!* to find relevant websites, blogs, podcasts, and discussion lists

- your library's catalog or WorldCat to find books and other resources on your topic

To learn more about finding sources, consult the Appendix, pp. 474–81.

To locate numerical or statistical evidence that you could use as evidence or to draw graphs or tables, try the following sites:

- U.S. government official Web portal for information about the federal government

- Library of Congress page on state government information (follow the links for information on both state and local government)

- U.S. Census Bureau, especially the Quick Facts and Fact Finder pages and the Statistical Abstracts for various years (to compare years), for demographic information

- Centers for Disease Control and Prevention, especially the FastStats pages, for statistics about diseases and illnesses

- National Center for Education Statistics for reports such as "America's Youth: Transitions to Adulthood"

- Pew Research Center for research data or public opinion polling data

- Rasmussen Reports or Gallup for public opinion polling data

Bookmark or keep a record of the URLs of promising sites. If you find useful information, you may want to download or copy it to use in your essay. When available, download PDF files rather than HTML files because PDFs are likely to include visuals such as graphs and charts. If you copy and paste relevant information from sources into your notes, be careful to distinguish carefully between all material from sources and your own ideas. Remember to record source information with care and to cite and document any sources you use, including visuals and interviews.

Another option is to conduct field research and use personal experience.

For more on field research, turn to the Appendix, pp. 482–89.

Analyzing Causes or Effects. Once you have come up with a number of causes or effects, identify the most convincing (and surprising) ones. Remember that cause or effect essays often speculate about several possible causes or effects but usually also argue for one that is especially interesting or plausible. You may want to try several of the sentence strategies below to help you determine which of your causes or effects will be most convincing:

▸ Why do I/my readers think .... [cause/effect] could have resulted in/ caused .... [name subject]?

▸ Is .... [cause] necessary to bring about .... [effect]; that is, could .... [effect] not happen without it? Is .... [cause] sufficient—enough in itself—to cause .... [effect]?

▸ Is .... [effect] inevitable for .... [cause]; are other effects more plausible?

▸ If .... [cause] is one of several contributing factors, what role does it play? For example, is it a minor or major cause, an obvious or hidden cause, a triggering cause (the one that got the cause-effect process started), or a continuing cause (the one that keeps it going)?

▸ If .... [effect] is one of several, what role does it play? Is it a minor effect, or is it a major effect not given proper attention?

▸ What kinds of evidence could I use to argue in favor of or to argue against .... [cause/effect]?

Now classify the causes or effects you plan to discuss in your essay into three categories: plausible cause(s) or effect(s) you want to argue for, causes or effects your readers may favor that you can concede but put aside as obvious or minor, and causes or effects you should refute because your readers are likely to think they are important.

Plausible Causes to Argue For	Readers' Causes to Concede/Put Aside	Readers' Causes to Refute

Remember that the only category you *must* include in your essay is the first: one or more causes or effects you will argue played a major, and perhaps, surprising role.

Considering Your Purpose

Write for several minutes about your purpose for writing this essay. The following questions will help you think about your purpose:

- What do I hope to accomplish with my readers? What one big idea do I want them to grasp and remember?

- How can I interest readers in my subject? How can I help them see its importance or significance?

- How much resistance should I expect from readers to each of the causes or effects I propose? Will my readers be largely receptive? Skeptical but convincible? Resistant and perhaps even antagonistic?

Formulating a Working Thesis Statement

To get an idea about how you might formulate your thesis, take a look at the thesis statements from the reading selections you've studied in this chapter. Here are two:

> The mythic horror movie, like the sick joke, has a dirty job to do. It deliberately appeals to all that is worst in us. It is morbidity unchained, our most base instincts let free, our nastiest fantasies realized . . . and it all happens, fittingly enough, in the dark. (King, par. 12)

> The question is why is [social networking] so popular? The most basic answer is that social networking is popular because it's available. . . . A better answer, though, is that social media offer people a way to satisfy their desire to connect with others and maybe also be "world-famous for fifteen minutes" . . . (Pangelinan, par. 2)

Now draft your own thesis statement, either using the sentence strategies below as a jumping-off point (you can put them into your own words when you revise) or using your own words and sentence patterns:

- ▶ The cause(s)/effect(s) of .... may be [surprising/alarming/disturbing/amazing], but they are clear: .... [state cause(s) or effect(s)].

- ▶ For many years, [name group] has believed that .... Now there is research supporting this claim, but not for the reasons you may think. It's not .... that has been causing this phenomenon but .... / It's not .... that has resulted from ...., it's ....

Working with Sources

Citing a Variety of Sources

Writers of essays speculating about causes or effects often rely on evidence from experts to support some causes or effects and refute others. You will have to decide whether sources will make your speculations more convincing, what types of sources might be appropriate, and how many would be sufficient.

Look, for example, at Clayton Pangelinan's essay, "#socialnetworking: Why It's *Really* So Popular" (pp. 391–96). Pangelinan uses a number of different sources to support his causal analysis. Because he is writing for a class, Pangelinan includes both in-text citations and a list of works cited. He uses signal phrases to provide the credentials of his sources. Pangelinan also uses statistics from research institutions, but he does not rely solely — or even primarily — on one kind of source. He cites independent sources his readers are likely to find credible, such as the Pew Research Center, a popular book, and an academic article. Pangelinan also refers to his own observations. The number of sources, their authority, and their variety lend credibility to Pangelinan's speculations.

As you determine how many and what kinds of sources to cite in your essay, keep in mind that readers of essays speculating about causes or effects are more likely to be persuaded if the sources you rely on are neither too few nor too narrowly focused. If, when you begin to draft, you find that your research seems skimpy, you may need to do further research.

Responding to Readers' Likely Objections or Preferred Causes

Start by analyzing your readers' likely objections, and then consider ways you might respond:

Analyzing and Responding to Your Readers' Likely Objections. For each of your preferred causes or effects, consider the questions your readers might raise.

▶ Even if you can prove that .... and .... increased/decreased at the same time, how do you know .... actually caused/resulted from ....?

▶ .... seems to have been a cause/effect of ...., but was it really a major cause/effect or just one of many contributing factors?

Now consider how you might respond to the strongest of your readers' likely objections:

- ▶ The objection that .... can be caused by/can result from things other than .... may be true. But there is strong evidence showing that .... played a central role by ....

- ▶ Researchers studying .... have shown a causal connection between .... and .... They claim .... [quote/paraphrase/summarize information from source] (cite source).

- ▶ A large number of people have been polled on this question, and it appears that .... was an important factor in their decision to ....

Refuting or Conceding Readers' Preferred Causes or Effects. Choose an alternative cause or effect, and summarize it. Be sure to summarize it accurately and fairly. Do not commit the **"straw man" fallacy** of knocking down something that no one really takes seriously. Also, decide whether you can *refute* the alternative cause or effect or you need to *concede* it.

To learn more about fallacies, see Chapter 2, pp. 42–44.

Refute it if you can show that it lacks credible support or if the reasoning underlying the cause or effect is flawed:

- ▶ The .... [scenario or anecdote] others sometimes give to support this cause/effect certainly helps dramatize the subject, but it doesn't really explain

   ....

- ▶ If .... caused/resulted from .... , then one would expect .... to happen, but [it hasn't/the opposite has happened].

- ▶ The research showing .... is questionable because it is based on [a small or unrepresentative sample/anecdotal evidence].

Concede it by pointing out that the cause or effect is obvious and setting it aside, or by showing that it plays a less important role than the cause or effect you are championing.

- ▶ An obvious explanation is .... But if we dig deeper, we find that

   ....

- ▶ .... is one of the answers but may actually not play as central a role as most people think it does.

Including Visuals or Other Media

Consider whether visuals — especially tables and static or animated graphics — would strengthen your argument. You could construct your own visuals, scan materials from books and magazines, or download them from the Internet. Be sure to cite the source of visual or audio elements you did not create, and get permission from the source if your essay is going to be published on a website.

Organizing Your Speculative Argument Effectively for Your Readers

Outlining what you have written can help you organize your essay effectively for your audience. You may want to draft a sentence that forecasts the elements of your argument to alert your readers to your main points (and give yourself a tentative outline). Putting your points in a logical order (from least to most effective, for example) will make it easier for you to guide your readers from point to point. A cause or effect analysis may contain as many as four basic parts:

1. a presentation of the subject

2. plausible causes or effects, logically sequenced

3. convincing support for each cause or effect

4. a consideration of readers' questions, objections, and alternative causes or effects

These parts can be organized in various ways: If your readers are not likely to agree with your speculations about causes or effects, you may want to anticipate and respond to their possible objections just before you present the evidence in favor of your argument. If you expect readers *are* likely to favor your speculations, you may want to concede or refute alternatives after offering your own reasons. Either way, you may want to emphasize the common ground you share.

As you draft, you may see ways to improve your original plan, and you should be ready to revise your outline, shift parts around, or drop or add parts as needed.

For more on outlining, see Chapter 2, pp. 23–24.

Drafting Your Cause or Effect Argument

By this point, you have done a lot of writing

- to present the subject fairly;

- to make a logical argument and support your preferred causes or effects with evidence your readers will find persuasive;

- to respond to objections and alternative speculations;

- to establish your credibility by presenting yourself as thoughtful and fair.

Now stitch that material together to create a draft. The next two parts of this Guide to Writing will help you evaluate and improve it.

REVIEWING AND IMPROVING THE DRAFT

This section includes two guides for Peer Review and Troubleshooting Your Draft. Your instructor may arrange a peer review in class or online where you can exchange drafts with a classmate. The Peer Review Guide will help you give each other constructive feedback regarding the basic features and strategies typical of writing a cause or effect argument. (If you want to make specific suggestions for improving the draft, see Troubleshooting Your Draft on p. 410.) Also, be sure to respond to any specific concerns the writer has raised about the draft. The Troubleshooting Your Draft guide that follows will help you reread your own draft with a critical eye, sort through any feedback you've received, and consider a variety of ways to improve your draft.

A PEER REVIEW GUIDE

How fairly is the subject presented?

What's Working Well: Let the writer know where the subject is presented especially fairly—for example, where the issue is framed so the reader's curiosity is aroused, or it's presented clearly and objectively before the writer presents a point of view about the causes or effects. Note where the writer seems particularly knowledgeable and responds to differing points of view with well-thought-out insights.

What Needs Improvement: Indicate one passage where the presentation of the subject could be improved—for example, where it is not presented fully enough to provide context, or there isn't enough indication of causes or effects that will be developed. If you think the writer seems biased or is ignoring a logical point of view, indicate where the perspective could change or a point of view should be included and responded to.

How logical and well supported is the cause or effect argument?

What's Working Well: Identify the causes or effects for the subject of the argument. Note where a point is well supported or uses a particularly convincing kind of evidence, such as statistics, examples, anecdotes, expert opinions, or analogies.

What Needs Improvement: Note any passage where the cause or effect does not seem logical, where a reader unfamiliar with the subject might need more information, or where an outside source could help convince a reader of the writer's point.

How well does the writer respond to objections or alternative speculations?

What's Working Well: Indicate passages where the writer has cited differing opinions about the causes or effects of the subject, and has responded to them with solid information that supports the writer's thesis and main points.

What Needs Improvement: Tell the writer if you think of alternative speculations that he or she might consider, or different ways to respond to objections.

Revising Your Draft

Revising means reenvisioning your draft, trying to see it in a new way, given your purpose and readers, in order to strengthen your cause or effect argument. Think imaginatively and boldly about cutting unconvincing material, adding new material, and moving material around.

TROUBLESHOOTING YOUR DRAFT

To Present the Subject More Effectively	
If readers unfamiliar with the subject don't understand it readily,	• Provide more introductory information about the subject.
If the significance of the subject is not clear,	• Dramatize its significance with an anecdote. • Highlight its social or cultural implications.
If the subject is a trend, but its existence is not established,	• Show evidence of a significant increase or decrease over time. • Include a graphic to make the trend visible.

To Strengthen the Cause or Effect Argument	
If there are too many proposed causes or effects,	• Clarify the role of each one and the way it is related to others. • Drop one or more that seem too obvious, obscure, or minor.
If a cause or effect lacks adequate support,	• Provide further examples, anecdotes, statistics, or quotations from authorities. • Drop it if you cannot find more support.

To Strengthen the Responses to Alternative Views	
If a likely question or objection readers will have is not addressed,	• Add information to answer the question. • Accommodate the objection by conceding the point and making it part of your own argument. • Refute the objection, arguing that it need not be taken seriously and providing the reasons why.
If an alternative cause or effect readers would propose is not addressed,	• Present it fairly and concede or refute it.
If readers are attacked or ridiculed in a refutation,	• Refute ideas decisively while showing respect for your readers as people. • Use the sentence strategy of concession and refutation (Chapter 9, pp. 303–4).

To Enhance Credibility

If the essay does not establish common ground with readers,	• Figure out what you might have in common with your audience—some shared values, attitudes, or beliefs— and include them in your argument.
If readers question your credibility,	• Learn more about your subject, and support your argument more fully. • Address more of readers' likely questions, objections, and alternatives. • Talk with others who can help you think more imaginatively about your speculations. • Check your rhetorical sensitivity by adjusting your tone to make it civil and to clarify that you respect those who hold alternative views.

To Make the Organization More Effective

If the causes or effects are not presented in a logical sequence,	• Change the sequence into some kind of logical order, such as chronological or least to most effective. You may find that you need to add or drop certain causes or effects.
If connections between ideas are not clear,	• Provide clearer transitions (*first, second, moreover, in addition*) to guide readers from one step in the argument to the next. • Use clear topic sentences to signal the stages of your argument and the support you provide for each cause or effect.
If your responses to alternative arguments are introduced awkwardly or unexpectedly,	• Move them around or add transitions to integrate them more smoothly.

Editing and Proofreading Your Draft

Check for errors in usage, punctuation, and mechanics, and consider matters of style. If you keep a list of errors you typically make, begin by checking your draft against this list. Ask someone else to proofread your essay before you submit it to your instructor.

From our research on student writing, we know that essays speculating about causes or effects have a high percentage of errors in the use of numbers and "reason is because" sentences. Because writers are usually drawn into "reason is because" sentences when making a causal argument, you will need to know options for revising such sentences. And, because you must usually rely on numbers to present statistics when you support your argument or demonstrate the existence of a trend, you will need to learn and follow the conventions for presenting different kinds of numbers. Check a writer's handbook for help with these potential problems.

Reflecting on Speculations about Causes or Effects

In this chapter, you have read critically several essays that speculate about causes or effects and have written one of your own. To better remember what you have learned, pause now to reflect on the reading and writing activities you completed in this chapter.

1. Write a page or so reflecting on what you have learned. Begin by describing what you are most pleased with in your essay. Then explain what you think contributed to your achievement.

   - If it was something you learned from the readings, indicate which readings and specifically what you learned from them.

   - If it came from your invention writing, point out the section or sections that helped you most.

   - If you got good advice from a critical reader, explain exactly how the person helped you — perhaps by helping you understand a problem in your draft or by helping you add a new dimension to your writing.

2. Reflect more generally on speculating about causes or effects, a genre of writing that plays an important role in social life and public policy in the United States. Consider some of the following questions:

   - Do you tend to adopt a tentative or an assertive stance when making such speculations about public issues? Why?

   - How might your personal preferences and values influence your speculations about, for example, the causes of health-care cost inflation or the effects of same-sex marriage? How about your gender, ethnicity, religious beliefs, age, or social class?

   - What contribution might writing that speculates about causes or effects make to our society that other genres cannot make?

10

Proposal to Solve a Problem

A proposal can help us analyze a problem, evaluate the feasibility of alternative solutions, and ultimately move readers to take particular actions to solve the problem. Whether the proposal is written in college (for example, to research an indigenous language or to prohibit the sale of genetically manufactured foods on campus), in the broader community (for example, to install audible traffic signals for the visually impaired or to improve community policing), or in the workplace (for example, to bid for a service contract or to institute an employee wellness program), proposals enable us to take pragmatic action to address pressing problems. To be effective, proposals use the academic habits of mind. They arouse readers' curiosity and concern, use critical analysis to invent imaginative solutions, and apply rhetorical sensitivity to communicate with readers and persuade them to consider new ideas.

RHETORICAL SITUATIONS FOR PROPOSALS

Proposals appear in a wide variety of contexts and media. Here are just a couple examples:

- A blogger posts a proposal to solve the problem of the rising college loan default rate, which she illustrates with statistics and graphs from the U.S. Department of Education. She concedes one reason why the problem is worst at for-profit colleges: they enroll a larger proportion of working parents and first-generation college students — who have greater financial challenges compared to the majority of traditional public and private college students. Nevertheless, the blogger argues that many for-profit colleges make the problem worse by using advertising to lure potential students with the promise of a college program many students cannot complete and a well-paying job the colleges cannot guarantee. She proposes that truth-in-advertising laws be used to crack down on the aggressive recruiting tactics of for-profits that target low-income students.

- For a political science class, a college student proposes that a direct popular vote replace the Electoral College system for electing the president because the Electoral College is undemocratic. He points out that several times in our history, for example in 2000, a candidate who lost the popular vote has become president. The fact that most states allocate electors on a winner-take-all basis, with all of the state's votes going to the winner even if the margin of victory is 50.1 percent to 49.9 percent, makes the system especially undemocratic. The student argues that using the direct popular vote instead would be the surest and simplest way to solve the problem, and voters would be likely to support this solution because it is based on the core American principle of "one person, one vote."

Thinking about Proposal

Recall one occasion when you heard or read a proposal, or proposed a solution yourself orally or in writing. Use the following questions to develop your thoughts.

- Who was the *audience*? How do you think communicating to this audience influenced what was told or how it was told? For example, if the audience was not personally affected by the problem, how were they inspired to care about solving the problem?

- What was the main *purpose*? What did you — or the other writer or speaker — hope to achieve? For example, was the primary purpose to inspire the audience to vote a certain way or to urge people in a position of power to take a particular action?

- How would you rate the *rhetorical sensitivity* with which the proposal was presented? What made the essay appropriate or inappropriate for its particular audience or purpose?

A GUIDE TO READING PROPOSALS

This guide introduces you to proposal writing by inviting you to analyze a proposal by David Bornstein that offers a surprising way to help prevent bullying.

- *Reading for meaning* will help you understand how Bornstein proposes to solve the problem of bullying.

- *Reading like a writer* will help you learn how Bornstein employs the strategies typical of proposal writing to makes his essay persuasive, such as

    1. demonstrating that the problem exists and is serious

    2. showing how his proposal would help solve the problem and is feasible

    3. responding to objections and alternative solutions

    4. organizing the proposal in a way that is clear, logical, and convincing

David Bornstein

Fighting Bullying with Babies

David Bornstein (b. 1940) blogs regularly for the *New York Times*, and his articles have appeared in other major venues as well. He has written several books about solving social problems, including *How to Change the World: Social Entrepreneurs and the Power of New Ideas* (2007) and *Social Entrepreneurship: What Everyone Needs to Know* (2010). The recipient of several awards (for example, from Duke University's Fuqua School of Business), Bornstein also co-wrote the PBS documentary *To Our Credit*. Bornstein originally posted his proposal "Fighting Bullying with Babies" in 2010. We have converted Bornstein's links to in-text citations and have provided a list of the links at the end of the selection.

- **Before you read,** think about Bornstein's title and the tone created by his opening journalistic hook: "Imagine there was a cure for meanness. Well, maybe there is." Given his original *New York Times* blog audience, why do you think Bornstein begins his proposal this way?

- **As you read,** notice the photograph we added from the Roots of Empathy site and consider what, if anything, it contributes to Bornstein's essay.

Imagine there was a cure for meanness. Well, maybe there is. Lately, the issue of bul-   1
lying has been in the news, sparked by the suicide of Tyler Clementi ("Tyler"), a gay college student who was a victim of cyber-bullying, and by a widely circulated *New York Times* article that focused on "mean girl" bullying in kindergarten (Paul). The federal government has identified bullying as a national problem. In August, it organized the first-ever "Bullying Prevention Summit," and it is now rolling out an anti-bullying campaign aimed at 5- to 8-year-old children (United States, Department of Health). This past month the Department of Education released a guidance letter (United States, Department of Education) urging schools, colleges and universities to take bullying seriously, or face potential legal consequences.

The typical institutional response to bullying is to get tough. In the Tyler Clementi 2 case, prosecutors are considering bringing hate-crime charges (Dolnick).[1] But programs like the one I want to discuss today show the potential of augmenting our innate impulses to care for one another instead of just falling back on punishment as a deterrent. And what's the secret formula? A baby.

We know that humans are hardwired to be aggressive and selfish. But a growing 3 body of research is demonstrating that there is also a biological basis for human compassion (Angier). Brain scans reveal that when we contemplate violence done to others we activate the same regions in our brains that fire up when mothers gaze at their children, suggesting that caring for strangers may be instinctual. When we help others, areas of the brain associated with pleasure also light up. Research by Felix Warneken and Michael Tomasello indicates that toddlers as young as 18 months behave altruistically. (If you want to feel good, watch one of their 15-second video clips [Warneken]. . . .)

More important, we are beginning to understand how to nurture this biological 4 potential. It seems that it's not only possible to make people kinder, it's possible to do it systematically at scale — at least with school children. That's what one organization based in Toronto called Roots of Empathy has done. Roots of Empathy was founded in 1996 by Mary Gordon, an educator who had built Canada's largest network of school-based parenting and family-literacy centers after having worked with neglectful and abusive parents (Toronto District School Board). Gordon had found many of them to be lacking in empathy for their children. They hadn't developed the skill because they hadn't experienced or witnessed it sufficiently themselves. She envisioned Roots as a seriously proactive parent education program — one that would begin when the mothers- and fathers-to-be were in kindergarten. Since then, Roots has worked with more than 12,600 classes across Canada, and in recent years, the program has expanded to the Isle of Man, the United Kingdom, New Zealand, and the United States, where it currently operates in Seattle. Researchers have found that the program increases kindness and acceptance of others and decreases negative aggression.

Here's how it works: Roots arranges monthly class visits by a mother and her baby 5 (who must be between two and four months old at the beginning of the school year). Each month, for nine months, a trained instructor guides a classroom using a standard curriculum that involves three 40-minute visits — a pre-visit, a baby visit, and a post-visit. The program runs from kindergarten to seventh grade. During the baby visits, the children sit around the baby and mother (sometimes it's a father) on a green blanket (which represents new life and nature) and they try to understand the baby's feelings. The instructor helps by labeling them. "It's a launch pad for them to understand their own feelings and the feelings of others," explains Gordon. "It carries over to the rest of class" (Gordon).

I have visited several public schools in low-income neighborhoods in Toronto to 6 observe Roots of Empathy's work. What I find most fascinating is how the baby actually changes the children's behavior. Teachers have confirmed my impressions: tough kids

---

[1]Tyler Clementi's roommate, Dharun Ravi, was found guilty in March 2010 of fifteen counts, including invasion of privacy, tampering with evidence, and bias intimidation. [Editor's note]

Elementary school students are taught empathy with a visit from Baby
Leo, five months, through the Roots of Empathy program.
Chris So/Getty Images

smile, disruptive kids focus, shy kids open up. In a seventh grade class, I found 12-year-olds unabashedly singing nursery rhymes. The baby seems to act like a heart-softening magnet. No one fully understands why. Kimberly Schonert-Reichl, an applied developmental psychologist who is a professor at the University of British Columbia, has evaluated Roots of Empathy in four studies. "Do kids become more empathic and understanding? Do they become less aggressive and kinder to each other? The answer is yes and yes," she explained. "The question is why?" (Schonert-Reichl)

C. Sue Carter, a neurobiologist based at the University of Illinois at Chicago, who has 7 conducted pioneering research into the effects of oxytocin, a hormone that has been linked with caring and trusting behavior, suspects that biology is playing a role in the program's impact (Angier). "This may be an oxytocin story," Carter told me. "I believe that being around the baby is somehow putting the children in a biologically different place. We don't know what that place is because we haven't measured it. However, if it works here as it does in other animals, we would guess that exposure to an infant would create a physiological state in which the children would be more social."

To parent well, you must try to imagine what your baby is experiencing. So the kids 8 do a lot of "perspective taking." When the baby is too small to raise its own head, for example, the instructor asks the children to lay their heads on the blanket and look around from there. Perspective taking is the cognitive dimension of empathy—and like any skill it takes practice to master. Children learn strategies for comforting a crying baby. They learn that one must never shake a baby. They discover that everyone comes into the world with a different temperament, including themselves and their classmates. They see how hard it can be to be a parent, which helps them empathize with their own mothers and fathers. And they marvel at how capacity develops. Each month, the baby does something that it couldn't do during its last visit: roll over, crawl, sit up, maybe even begin walking. Witnessing the baby's triumphs—even something as small as picking up a rattle for the first time—the children will often cheer.

Ervin Staub, professor emeritus of psychology at the University of Massachusetts, has studied altruism in children and found that the best way to create a caring climate is to engage children collectively in an activity that benefits another human being ("Ervin Staub's Biographical Note"). In Roots, children are enlisted in each class to do something to care for the baby, whether it is to sing a song, speak in a gentle voice, or make a "wishing tree." The results can be dramatic. In a study of first- to third-grade classrooms, Schonert-Reichl focused on the subset of kids who exhibited "proactive aggression"—the deliberate and cold-blooded aggression of bullies who prey on vulnerable kids (Schonert-Reichl et al.). Of those who participated in the Roots program, 88 percent decreased this form of behavior over the school year, while in the control group, only 9 percent did, and many actually increased it. Schonert-Reichl has reproduced these findings with fourth- to seventh-grade children in a randomized controlled trial. She also found that Roots produced significant drops in "relational aggression"—things like gossiping, excluding others, and backstabbing. Research also found a sharp increase in children's parenting knowledge. "Empathy can't be taught, but it can be caught," Gordon often says—and not just by children. "Programmatically my biggest surprise was that not only did empathy increase in children, but it increased in their teachers," she added. "And that, to me, was glorious, because teachers hold such sway over children." 9

When the program was implemented on a large scale across the province of Manitoba—it's now in 300 classrooms there—it achieved an "effect size" that Rob Santos, the scientific director of Healthy Child Manitoba, said translates to reducing the proportion of students who get into fights from 15 percent to 8 percent, close to a 50 percent reduction ("Putting Children"). "For a program that costs only hundreds of dollars per child, the cost-benefit of preventing later problems that cost thousands of dollars per child, is obvious," said Santos. Follow-up studies have found that outcomes are maintained or enhanced three years after the program ends. "When you've got emotion and cognition happening at the same time, that's deep learning," explains Gordon. "That's learning that will last." 10

Links

Angier, Natalie. "The Biology Behind the Milk of Human Kindness." *The New York Times,* 23 Nov. 2009, www.nytimes.com/2009/11/24/science/24angier.html.

Carter, Sue C. Personal interview. 2010.

Dolnick, Sam. "2 Linked to Suicide Case Withdraw from Rutgers." *The New York Times,* 29 Oct. 2010, www.nytimes.com/2010/10/30/nyregion/30rutgers.html.

Gordon, Mary. Personal interview. 2010.

"Putting Children and Families First." *Healthy Child Manitoba,* www.gov.mb.ca /healthychild/.

Paul, Pamela. "The Playground Gets Even Tougher." *The New York Times,* 8 Oct. 2010, www .nytimes.com/2010/10/10/fashion/10Cultural.html.

"Roots of Empathy: From Research to Recognition." *Roots of Empathy,* 2012, www .rootsofempathy.org/en/component/content/article/25-public-pages/front-page/237-roots -of-empathy-from-research-to-recognition.html.

Schonert-Reichl, Kimberly. Personal interview. 2010.

Schonert-Reichl, Kimberly, et al. "Contextual Considerations in the Evaluation of a School-Based Social Emotional Competence Program." American Educational Research Association, April 2009.

Staub, Ervin. "Ervin Staub's Biographical Note." Ervin Staub, Ervinstaub.com.

Toronto District School Board. "Parenting and Family Literacy Centres." Toronto District School Board, 2014, www.tdsb.on.ca/earlyyears/preschoolyears/parentingandfamilyliteracy.aspx.

"Tyler Clementi." The New York Times, www.nytimes.com/topic/person/tyler-clementi.

United States, Department of Education. "Guidance Targeting Harassment Outlines Local and Federal Responsibility." U.S. Department of Education, 26 Oct. 2010, www.ed.gov/news/press-releases/guidance-targeting-harassment-outlines-local-and-federal-responsibility.

---. Department of Health and Human Services, Health Resources and Services Administration. "Stop Bullying Now." Stopbullying.gov, Department of Health and Human Services, www.stopbullying.gov/.

Warneken, Felix. "Study Videos." Department of Developmental and Comparative Psychology, Max Planck Institute for Evolutionary Anthropology, www.eva.mpg.de/psycho/publications-and-videos/study-videos.html.

Warneken, Felix, and Michael Tomasello. "Altruistic Helping in Human Infants and Young Chimpanzees." Science, vol. 311, no. 5765, 3 Mar. 2006, pp. 1301–3. Academic Search Complete, www.ebscohost.com/academic/academic-search-complete.

READING FOR MEANING

1. **Read to Summarize.** Write a sentence or two explaining how the proposed solution will help solve the bullying problem.

   For help with summarizing, see Chapter 2, pp. 24–25.

2. **Read to Respond.** Write a paragraph analyzing your initial reactions to Bornstein's blog post. For example, consider the fact that "a guidance letter" was sent to urge "schools, colleges and universities to take bullying seriously" (par. 1); or the research Bornstein cites to show that the children taking part in the Roots program "become less aggressive and kinder to each other" (par. 6), focusing on one of the program's methods you find intriguing.

3. **Read to Analyze Assumptions.** Write a paragraph or two analyzing an assumption you find in Bornstein's essay. For example:

   For help analyzing assumptions, see Chapter 2, pp. 28–29.

   Assumptions about bullying. When Bornstein asserts as common knowledge the idea that "humans are hardwired to be aggressive and selfish," he seems to assume that meanness or bullying has a "biological," even an evolutionary, basis in human development (par. 3).

   - How might traits like aggressiveness and selfishness have been beneficial to us in the past? In our society today, how are they advantageous or disadvantageous?

   - What does Bornstein assume about nature and nurture? Does he see them as opposite or complementary? What role does nurture play in causing bullying and what role could it play in preventing bullying?

You may also try contextualizing; see Chapter 2, pp. 29–30.

Assumptions about empathy. The goal of Bornstein's model solution to the problem of bullying — Roots of Empathy — is to cultivate empathy, to plant a seed, and to help it grow.

- Bornstein quotes Roots of Empathy founder Mary Gordon as frequently saying: "Empathy can't be taught, but it can be caught" (par. 9). What do you think she means?
- One of the tools the Roots of Empathy program uses to cultivate empathy is "perspective taking" (par. 8). Is it really possible to see things from another person's point of view and to understand their feelings? Why or why not?

READING LIKE A WRITER

Demonstrating the Problem Exists and Is Serious

Every proposal begins with a problem. What writers say about the problem and how much space they devote to it depend on what they assume their readers know and think about the problem. Some problems require more explanation than others. Obviously, if readers are already immersed in discussing the problem and possible solutions, then the writer may not have to say much to introduce the problem. Nevertheless, savvy proposal writers try to present even familiar problems in a way that alerts readers to a problem's seriousness and prepares them for the writer's preferred solution.

| Analyze & Write |

Write a paragraph or two analyzing and evaluating how Bornstein presents the problem and establishes its seriousness:

1. Reread the title and first paragraph. How do the title and the opening sentences hook readers?

2. Why do you think Bornstein refers to a White House conference and the Department of Education's "guidance letter" (par. 1)? How do these references help him define the problem and excite readers' interest in his solution?

3. Note that Bornstein does not directly define *bullying*. Assuming that bullying is a rather wide and varied class of behaviors, how important is it that Bornstein clarify what he means by bullying? How does he give readers a sense of what bullying involves?

Showing How the Proposed Solution Would Help Solve the Problem and Is Feasible

The proposal writer's primary purposes are twofold:

1. To convince readers that the proposed solution would be **effective** — that it would help solve the problem, even if it would not eliminate it altogether

2. To convince readers that the proposed solution is **feasible** — that it can be implemented fairly easily and is cost-effective

For proposed solutions that already exist, the writer may need only to give the solution a name and give examples of where it is being applied successfully. For example, in "Fighting Bullying with Babies," Bornstein centers his argument on the example of the Roots of Empathy program in Toronto. Writers may also support their claims about the solution's effectiveness and feasibility with such evidence as statistics, research studies, and quotations from authorities.

Analyze & Write

Write a paragraph or two analyzing and evaluating Bornstein's use of evidence, particularly his use of the Roots of Empathy program, to support his proposal:

1. Reread paragraph 5, noting the details Bornstein shares with readers about how the Roots of Empathy program works.

2. Also skim paragraphs 6–10 to see what kinds of evidence Bornstein uses to support his argument that the Roots of Empathy model really can help to solve the problem of bullying and can be implemented on a wide scale fairly easily and inexpensively.

3. What do you think is most and least convincing about Bornstein's argument? Why?

Responding to Objections and Alternative Solutions

As they introduce the problem and then argue for the solution, proposal writers need to anticipate readers' possible objections to their argument as well as alternative solutions readers may prefer. Ignoring likely objections or alternative solutions is not a wise strategy because it gives the impression that the writer either does not fully understand the issue or cannot counter criticism. Writers have two options. They may:

1. *Concede* (or acknowledge) that an objection or alternative solution has some value and modify their proposed solution to accommodate it

2. *Refute* (or argue against) objections and alternative solutions by demonstrating that an objection is mistaken or that an alternative solution would not solve the problem or is inferior to the solution being proposed

Analyze & Write

Write a paragraph analyzing and evaluating how Bornstein responds to an alternative solution:

1. Reread paragraph 2, looking closely at the way Bornstein introduces and describes "the typical institutional response to bullying." Notice that he labels this alternative solution as "typical," but he doesn't specify what getting tough involves. What do

(continued)

you imagine Bornstein's original *New York Times* readers assumed were the ways a school usually gets tough with bullies? What would your school do? Note that Bornstein singles out only one extreme example of punishment. Why?

2. Consider the words Bornstein uses to describe getting tough: "just falling back on punishment as a deterrent" (par. 2). *Deterrent* may remind older readers of the cold war strategy of mutual assured destruction (appropriately called MAD), the threat to use nuclear weapons in retaliation if the other side used them first. What effect would this connotation be likely to have on Bornstein's *New York Times* readers' ideas about the alternative solution Bornstein is refuting? What effect do they have on you?

3. Finally, reread paragraph 3. How does Bornstein use the fact that "humans are hardwired to be aggressive and selfish" to argue against getting tough? Why is this a strong or a weak argument?

Organizing the Proposal in a Way That Is Clear, Logical, and Convincing

To help readers identify the parts of the proposal, writers often use *cues* or signposts. For example, Bornstein introduces the problem and solution in his title — "Fighting Bullying with Babies." He uses a **rhetorical question** (a question he answers for readers) to reiterate this solution: "what's the secret formula? A baby" (par. 2). But Bornstein makes this assertion early in the essay as a teaser to keep people reading. His thesis statement requires a couple of paragraphs to explain because it not only asserts the solution but also the reasoning behind it:

Transitions   We know that humans are hardwired to be aggressive and selfish. But a growing body of research is demonstrating that there is also a biological basis for human compassion. . . .

More important, we are beginning to understand how to nurture this biological potential. (pars. 3–4)

Notice how the transitions help orient readers to the twists and turns of Bornstein's argument. "More important," for example, emphasizes the crucial part of the proposal: that something can be done to influence human behavior even if it is "hardwired."

Topic sentences, sentences that state the main idea of a paragraph or group of paragraphs, can be especially helpful to readers trying to follow the logic of a proposal. For example, notice how Bornstein uses topic sentences to indicate the alternative solution he is refuting (par. 2) and the explanation of how his proposed solution can be implemented (par. 5):

The typical institutional response to bullying is . . . (par. 2)

Here's how it works: (par. 5)

Analyze & Write

Write a couple of paragraphs analyzing and evaluating Bornstein's uses of cueing to help readers follow his argument:

1. Reread paragraphs 7–9 to see how Bornstein answers the rhetorical question "Why does the solution work?"

2. Look particularly at each of the topic sentences in these paragraphs to see how well he announces the answers.

3. Given Bornstein's purpose and audience, how clear and comprehensible is the logic of this proposal argument? If you were to give Bornstein advice on revising this proposal, what, if anything, would you recommend?

A Special Reading Strategy

Comparing and Contrasting Related Readings: David Bornstein's "Fighting Bullying with Babies" and Excerpts on Bullying in Chapter 1

Comparing and contrasting related readings is a critical reading strategy useful both in reading for meaning and in reading like a writer. This strategy is particularly applicable when writers present similar subjects, as is the case in the essay by David Bornstein and the excerpts on bullying in Chapter 1 by Ron Banks (p. 4), Tara L. Kuther (p. 6), Tonja R. Nansel, et al (p. 7), and Barbara Coloroso (pp. 7–8). The genres differ — the excerpts are cause-effect analyses and Bornstein's is a proposal — but like many proposals, "Fighting Bullying with Babies" includes causal analysis. Choose one of the excerpts from Chapter 1 to compare and contrast to "Fighting Bullying with Babies," considering topics such as these:

• The way the authors define bullying and establish that it exists and is serious. For example, what do they assume readers already know about bullying? Do they cite examples of bullying, and if so, how much detail do they give? What kinds of evidence do they provide to persuade readers that the problem is serious?

• The causes and/or effects bullying has on the victims and/or the bullies themselves. What similarities and differences do you find in how the two readings analyze causes and effects? How do they support their cause-effect analysis?

For detailed guidelines on comparing and contrasting related readings, see Chapter 2, pp. 37–39.

READINGS

Harold Meyerson

How to Raise Americans' Wages

Harold Meyerson (b. 1950) writes a weekly opinion column for the *Washington Post* and contributes to its PostPartisan blog. He also serves as executive editor of the progressive magazine, *The American Prospect*, in which his proposal "How to Raise Americans' Wages" first appeared in 2015. A senior fellow at the Center for American Progress, Meyerson often writes about politics, labor, and economics for major publications like the *New Yorker*, the *Atlantic*, and the *New York Times*. He has also hosted a weekly radio show and written a biography of *The Wizard of Oz* lyricist Yip Harburg.

- **Before you read,** think about why Meyerson opens his proposal as if it were a fairy tale, with the conventional "once upon a time" beginning.

- **As you read,** notice that Meyerson's proposal offers several different but related solutions to the problem. Consider how each solution would help to raise wages for American workers.

Once upon a time in a faraway land—the United States following World 1 War II—workers reaped what they sowed. From 1947 through 1973, their income rose in lockstep with increases in productivity. Their median compensation (wages plus benefits) increased by 95 percent as their productivity increased by 97 percent. Then, abruptly, the rewards for greater productivity started going elsewhere—to shareholders, financiers, and top corporate executives. Today, for the vast majority of American workers, the

Why is the disconnect between productivity and compensation a problem?

link between their productivity and their compensation no longer exists. As economists Robert Gordon and Ian Dew-Becker have established, the gains in workers' productivity for the past three decades have gone entirely to the wealthiest 10 percent . . .

Today, the drive to restore workers' share has been narrowed down to 2 the campaign to raise the minimum wage. That raise is long overdue. . . . But even raising that wage wouldn't do much for most workers; they make well more than the minimum, but their own wages have been stagnating or shrinking for decades as well. What, then, do we do for American workers

How well do rhetorical questions work here?

more generally? How do we raise their wages? How do we re-create a growing and vibrant middle class?

For many business leaders, politicians, and commentators, workers' 3 declining share is the inevitable result of globalization and technological change—forces of nature that nations, much less individuals, are powerless to stop. They also tend to blame the victim: According to conventional wisdom, workers lack the education and training to fill the new high-tech jobs the economy now demands. Globalization and technological change have indeed played key roles in weakening workers' bargaining power, and a more educated workforce surely commands better pay than workers without the requisite skills. Nonetheless, the business leaders and their apologists are fundamentally wrong in both their diagnoses and prescriptions. To begin, at least one major nation every bit as subject to globalization and technological change as ours hasn't seen the evisceration of its middle class and the redistribution of income from labor to capital that we've endured. Germany has a greater level of foreign trade than the U.S. and a comparable level of technological change, but it has managed to retain its best manufacturing jobs, because of the greater power that its workers exercise and the diminished role its shareholders play. In Germany, law and custom have enabled labor and required management to collaborate on making sure that the most highly skilled and compensated jobs remain at home. The claim that American workers lack the skills they need is belied by workers in low-skilled jobs (those that pay two-thirds or less of the median wage) having much more education than equivalent workers four decades ago: 46 percent of low-skilled workers today have attended college; in the 1960s, just 17 percent had. Moreover, the incomes of many professionals, including lawyers and college teachers, have declined in recent years as well.

How effectively does Meyerson refute alternative views of the problem?

4   What corporate apologists won't acknowledge is that workers' incomes have been reduced by design. American business has adamantly opposed workers' efforts to organize unions. Millions of jobs have been outsourced, offshored, franchised out, reclassified as temporary or part-time, or had their wages slashed, in a successful, decades-long campaign to increase the return to capital. Indeed, the only way to explain the soaring profit margins and stock values of recent years despite anemic increases in corporate revenues is that profits have come at the expense of labor . . .

5   The transfer of income from labor to capital, then, is chiefly the consequence of capitalists' design. But precisely because that transfer has been so thorough, reversing it will be exquisitely difficult. Traditionally, American workers were able to raise their wages by collective bargaining or through the clout they could wield in a full-employment economy. But the ability of private-sector workers to bargain collectively has been destroyed by the evisceration of unions, which now represent just 6.7 percent of private-sector workers. The labor movement has tried . . . to strengthen protections for workers in organizing campaigns. Each time, however, the unions failed to surmount the Senate's supermajority threshold. Until they can, the most direct way to raise workers' wages will remain a dead letter. Re-creating the other avenue for bolstering workers' leverage—a full-employment economy—looks just as remote. Historically, workers won some of their biggest wage gains when the unemployment rate dipped beneath 4 percent. . . . During the New Deal, the federal

Why do you think Meyerson repeats this idea about "design"?

government embarked on massive public-works and employment programs. Now, confronted with a growing share of working-age Americans who have given up on finding employment, government needs to take up that task again. Such a project should combine a program to rebuild the nation's sagging infrastructure with increased public investment in home care, child care, and preschool. But such a project also requires far greater public belief in the necessity and efficacy of governmental endeavors and the election of a president and a sufficient number of legislators who share that belief. However devoutly progressives may wish it, this is not likely to happen any time soon.

In a nation where workers have lost the power they once had to raise 6 their incomes, what can be done to make those incomes rise? Here are [four] proposals . . .

What strategies does Meyerson use to help readers follow this multi-part proposal?

1. LEGISLATE WAGE HIKES IN STATES AND CITIES

In poll after poll, raising the federal minimum wage emerges as one of the 7 most popular policy options on the political landscape, supported by an overwhelming majority of Democrats, a sizable majority of independents, about 50 percent of Republicans, and an increasing number of major retailers. Nonetheless, such is the influence of small business (of restaurants, especially) and the Tea Party that prospects for getting a raise through Congress remain dim. . . . In a number of states, the wage already substantially exceeds the federal minimum, and some have raised their standard even more in the past year (in California, to $10). Cities and counties in certain states have the right to set their own minimum wage higher than that of their state. In Maryland, the two counties bordering the District of Columbia recently increased the wage, in tandem with the District, to $11.50. . . .

How does Meyerson support his argument that this solution is feasible?

Since the late 1990s, local progressive governments have been able to lift 8 wage levels for private-sector workers in government-owned facilities (such as airports or museums) and projects that receive government assistance (such as property-tax abatements or infrastructure improvements) or require special governmental approvals (such as sports arenas). Advocates of these "living wage" ordinances argue that governments should not be using taxpayer dollars to subsidize poverty-wage jobs. . . . Currently, at least 150 cities have established living-wage ordinances or community-benefit agreements. . . .

2. LINK CORPORATE TAX RATES TO WORKER PRODUCTIVITY INCREASES AND CEO-EMPLOYEE PAY RATIOS

Congress could create a lower tax rate for those corporations that increased 9 their median wage in line with the annual national productivity increase. . . . Constructing a tax code that gives corporations an incentive to pass on productivity increases to their employees is admittedly a complex task. The tax break would have to be big enough to be attractive to the companies' directors and managers. The break would also have to be withheld from corporations that game the system by initially cutting their workers' pay to reduce

How does Meyerson handle objections to this solution?

the median wage, then restore it through a productivity increase. Devising a process for monitoring and assessing corporate conduct would not be easy. But with unionization—the straightforward means of linking employee pay to productivity gains—off the table, complexity is the price we'd have to pay to create a more prosperous economy. . . .

10   They should also promote legislation that would link corporate tax rates to the ratio between CEO pay and the firm's median pay: the lower the ratio, the lower the tax. This is sure to elicit a backlash from corporate elites and the financial sector, but it should gain popular support. A poll conducted this February showed that 66 percent of the public believed that "executive pay is generally too high"—an assessment shared by 79 percent of Democrats, 61 percent of independents, and 58 percent of Republicans. The rise in the ratio of CEO to median-worker pay began about the time that workers' compensation was detached from increases in productivity. In 1978, CEOs made 28 times the pay of their median-paid employee; by 2012, CEOs made 273 times the median.

11   Were this proposal to become law, CEOs and their boards would face a fundamental choice: They could persist in excessive executive compensation at the expense of forcing their company to shell out considerably more in corporate taxes. Or they could reduce executive pay to levels the American people see as a more legitimate reflection of executive worth. They would also have a self-interest in raising their workers' wages. Indeed, if enacted in conjunction with the proposal linking the median worker's pay to productivity increases, this proposal would limit corporations' incentive to game that system by reducing workers' pay before the median is calculated.

Why is "choice" likely to strengthen this solution?

12   What kind of ratio should progressives set as an appropriate valuation of a CEO's worth? In 1977, the celebrated management guru Peter Drucker wrote in the *Wall Street Journal* that a ratio of 15 to 1 seemed right for a small or midsize business, and 25 to 1 for a large business. By that standard, a CEO at a sizable firm where the average employee makes $60,000 a year would make $1.5 million.

3. MAKE CORPORATIONS RESPONSIBLE FOR ALL THEIR WORKERS

13   Many of the problems American workers encounter in making a decent wage stem from a confusion about who employs them. In recent decades, companies have routinely shifted the production and delivery of their goods and services and other tasks needed to run their businesses from their own employees to workers employed by contractors, subcontractors, franchisees, or temporary job agencies or to workers who are labeled independent contractors. In many cases, these workers are the same workers the parent company once employed. In most cases, they could be employed directly by the parent company, but they're not, chiefly because having the labor done by nonemployees saves the parent company money.

14   Inevitably, all this reduces the workers' wages and benefits. By outsourcing work, Boston University economist David Weil explains in an important new

How convincing are
the sources in pars.
10, 12, 14, and 15?
What makes them
convincing (or not)?

book, *The Fissured Workplace*, an employer trades a wage-setting problem for a pricing problem. Rather than pay his own employees a low wage, he can choose from a range of contractors, who compete with one another on price—a process that advantages the contractor with the lowest labor costs. . . . Nissan's temp workers do the same jobs as the Nissan employees next to them on the line, only for a good deal less. Wal-Mart, master of the logistics universe, specifies which products are to be moved through its warehouses and sent to which destinations, at which times, and at what cost. Most of the "independent contractors" who move goods from the port rent their trucks from one company, drive exclusively for that company, with orders and routes set by that company. But neither Nissan, Wal-Mart, nor the trucking companies directly pay these workers, who, of course, are not eligible for any of the parent companies' benefits. If these workers put in uncompensated overtime to complete their work, or are paid less than the minimum wage, or are injured on the job, their parent company is held harmless, though the parent company dictates the conditions of their work and the amount they are paid. . . . A radical amendment to the radical reforms I proposed in the preceding section: Count the parent company's contract workers as employees in calculating corporate tax rates.

4. RAISE TAXES ON CAPITAL INCOME AND REDISTRIBUTE IT TO LABOR

Another solution to the rise of investment income and the decline of income   15 from work would be to use the tax code to explicitly redistribute capital income to labor. The current tax code comes close to doing the reverse. Capital income—income from qualified dividends and capital gains—can

How clearly does
Meyerson explain
the difference
between capital
income and wages?

be taxed at a rate no higher than 20 percent, while income from wages and salaries is subjected to a progressive tax that tops out at 39.6 percent. As Warren Buffett frequently notes, upper-middle-class and middle-class Americans sometimes pay more taxes on their wages and salaries than billionaires pay on their investments.

The justification for the low rate on capital—that it boosts the American   16 economy by promoting domestic investment—has been rendered absurd

How effectively
does Meyerson
refute alternative
views in this
paragraph?

by the globalization of American businesses. The disparity between capital and labor tax rates also means that the government has diminished its take from that part of the national income that is growing, while maintaining a higher rate on that part of the nation's income that is shrinking.

For all those reasons, the tax rates on capital should be raised to the level of   17 the rates on labor; indeed, given that taxable labor must be domestic while taxable capital can be derived from anywhere, the rate on capital should be

How effective is this
way of concluding a
multi-part proposal?
What else could
Meyerson have
done?

higher than that on labor. But what to do with this new revenue? As shareholder capital comes more and more at labor's expense, it should be taxed for the purpose of boosting labor income. One option would be to devote some of it to increase labor income through a major expansion of the Earned Income Tax Credit, a tax rebate that supplements the income of the working poor.

Naomi Rose

Captivity Kills Orcas

Naomi Rose is a scientist specializing in marine mammals at the Animal Welfare Institute in Washington, D.C. Author of numerous articles and book chapters for scientists and the general public, Rose regularly presents university lectures, serves on task forces, and testifies before Congress. She has also worked with the Merlin Entertainments Group to build sanctuaries for bottlenose dolphins. This proposal is based on research Rose conducted for the Humane Society International and published in *Killer Controversy: Why Orcas Should No Longer Be Kept in Captivity* (2011). "Captivity Kills Orcas" first appeared on CNN.com in 2013, shortly after the release of the controversial documentary *Blackfish*, which depicts the devastating results — to both the animals and their trainers — of keeping wild orcas in captivity. We have converted Rose's links to in-text citations and have provided a list of the links at the end of the selection.

- **Before you read,** think about the audience Rose could expect to read this proposal on the CNN website and what they could do to help solve the problem.

- **As you read,** take into account the fact that in mid-2016, SeaWorld announced that it would stop breeding orcas and phase out theatrical orca shows in at least one of its theme parks. How do these changes affect your reading of Rose's proposal?

The film *Blackfish* compellingly describes many of the reasons why keeping orcas in 1 captivity is — and always has been — a bad idea ("*Blackfish*—Official Trailer"). The main premise of the film is that these large, intelligent, social predators are dangerous to their trainers. But orcas are also directly harmed by being confined in concrete tanks and the science is growing to support this common sense conclusion.

The latest data (Rose) show that orcas are more than three times as likely to die at 2 any age in captivity as they are in the wild. This translates into a shorter life span and is probably the result of several factors. First, orcas in captivity are out of shape; they are the equivalent of couch potatoes, as the largest orca tank in the world is less than one ten-thousandth of one percent (0.0001%) the size of the smallest home range of wild orcas. Second, they are in artificial and often incompatible social groups. This contributes to chronic stress, which can depress the immune system and leave captive orcas susceptible to infections they would normally fight off in the wild. Third, they often break their teeth chewing compulsively on metal gates. These broken teeth, even drilled and cleaned regularly by irrigation, are clear routes for bacteria to enter the bloodstream. These are the obvious factors; there are almost certainly others contributing to the elevated mortality seen in captivity. These factors boil down simply to this: Captivity kills orcas.

Yes, they may survive for years entertaining audiences, but eventually the stressors 3 of captivity catch up to them. Very few captive orcas make it to midlife (approximately

Tilikum, a bull orca, performing at SeaWorld in a scene from *Blackfish* (2013).
Everett Collection, Inc.

30 years for males and 45 for females) and not one out of more than 200 held in captivity has ever come close to old age (60 for males, 80 for females) ("Killer Whale"). Most captive orcas die while they are still very young by wild orca standards.

There is a solution to both the trainer safety and orca welfare dilemmas facing 4 marine theme parks around the world, including SeaWorld in the United States. These facilities can work with experts around the world to create sanctuaries where captive orcas can be rehabilitated and retired. These sanctuaries would be sea pens or netted-off bays or coves, in temperate to cold water natural habitat. They would offer the animals respite from performing and the constant exposure to a parade of strangers (an entirely unnatural situation for a species whose social groupings are based on family ties and stability—"strangers" essentially do not exist in orca society). Incompatible animals would not be forced to cohabit the same enclosures and family groups would be preserved. Show business trainers would no longer be necessary. Expert caretakers would continue to train retired whales for veterinary procedures, but would not get in the water and would remain at a safe distance (this is known in zoo parlance as "protected contact"). And the degree to which they interact directly with the whales would be each whale's choice.

A fundamental premise of these sanctuaries, however, is that eventually they 5 would empty. Breeding would not be allowed and captive orcas would no longer exist within the next few decades. Many wildlife sanctuaries, for circus, roadside zoo and backyard refugees, exist around the globe for animals such as big cats, elephants and chimpanzees. The business (usually non-profit) model for these types of facilities is therefore well-established for terrestrial species and can be adapted for orcas. Wildlife sanctuaries are sometimes open to the public, although public interaction with the animals is usually minimized. A visitor's center can offer education, real-time remote viewing of the animals, a gift shop, and in the case of whales and dolphins can even be a base for responsible whale watching if the sanctuary is in a suitable location for that activity. Marine theme parks do not need to lose out financially by phasing out orca shows; this is a transformative proposal, not a punitive one.

Creating a whale or dolphin sanctuary is not entirely theoretical. Merlin Entertain- 6 ments is pursuing the establishment of the world's first bottlenose dolphin sanctuary with Whale and Dolphin Conservation ("WDCS"), a nonprofit environmental group. Whale and Dolphin Conservation put together a team to determine the feasibility of such a concept and the company has now identified potential sites and is studying the infrastructure that will be needed to support a group of retired dolphins.

Before the tragic death of SeaWorld trainer Dawn Brancheau in 2010 ("Sea- 7 World"), the ethical arguments against keeping orcas in captivity came largely from the animal welfare/animal rights community, with the marine theme parks basically ignoring or dismissing their opponents as a vocal and out-of-touch minority. Now even staunch SeaWorld supporters are wondering if the time has come to think out-side the (concrete) box.

Furthermore, the marine mammal science community, which has long maintained 8 a neutral stance on the question of whether orcas are a suitable species for captive display, has finally recognized the need to engage. An informal panel discussion on captive orcas is scheduled at the 20th Biennial Conference on the Biology of Marine Mammals in December, the first time this topic will be openly addressed by the world's largest marine mammal science society.

The first orca was put on public display in 1964. The debate on whether that was a 9 good idea—for people or the whales—began the next day but didn't really heat up until the 1970s. It raged mostly on the fringe for the next 25 years. It picked up steam in the mid-1990s, with the release of the film *Free Willy* and the rehabilitation of its orca star Keiko. And now, thanks in part to *Blackfish*, it is mainstream and consensus is building that orcas don't belong in captivity. The marine theme parks can shift with the paradigm or be left behind—it is up to them.

Links

"Killer Whale (Orcinus orca)." *Office of Protected Resources*, United States, Department of Commerce, NOAA Fisheries, 25 June 2014, www.nmfs.noaa.gov/pr/species/mammals /whales/killer-whale.html.

"Blackfish—Official Trailer." *YouTube,* uploaded by Magnolia Pictures and Magnet Releasing, 3 June 2013, www.youtube.com/watch?v=G93beiYiE74.

Rose, Naomi A. *Killer Controversy: Why Orcas Should No Longer Be Kept in Captivity.* Humane Society International / Humane Society of the United States, Sept. 2011, www.hsi.org/assets /pdfs/orca_white_paper.pdf.

"SeaWorld Trainer Killed by Killer Whale." *CNN,* 25 Feb. 2010, 4:57 p.m., www.cnn.com/2010 /US/02/24/killer.whale.trainer.death/.

"WDCS to Work with Merlin Entertainments on Better Future for Captive Dolphins." *Whale and Dolphin Conservation,* 17 Mar. 2009, 12:00 a.m., us.whales.org/news/2009/03 /wdcs-to-work-with-merlin-entertainments-on-better-future-for-captive-dolphins.

READING FOR MEANING

For help with summarizing, see Chapter 2, pp. 24–25.

1. **Read to Summarize.** Write a sentence or two summarizing Rose's proposed solution to the problems associated with orca captivity.

2. **Read to Respond.** Write a paragraph responding to any of Rose's ideas that strike you as surprising, such as that the presence of "strangers" — non-family orcas as well as people — upsets orcas (par. 4), or that the sanctuary proposal aims ultimately to have no orcas in captivity (par. 5).

For help analyzing assumptions, see Chapter 2, pp. 28–29.

3. **Read to Analyze Assumptions.** Write a paragraph or two analyzing an assumption you find intriguing in Rose's essay. For example:

Assumptions about corporate and consumer responsibility. Rose argues that for-profit marine parks should eliminate orca performances and create "sanctuaries" for their captive orcas.

- Why does Rose assume corporations like SeaWorld have a responsibility to care for the animals they have used to make a profit? What, if anything, does she suggest about the consumer's responsibility toward animals held in captivity? What can consumers do to influence corporations like SeaWorld?

- What does Rose assume when she compares her proposed marine sanctuaries to "wildlife sanctuaries" that already "exist around the globe for animals such as big cats, elephants and chimpanzees" (par. 5)? Why do you think she claims that marine sanctuaries "do not need to lose out financially," even though the wildlife sanctuaries she compares them to are "usually non-profit"?

Assumptions about the role of the scientific community. Rose points out that "the marine mammal science community . . . has long maintained a neutral stance on the question of whether orcas are a suitable species for captive display" (par. 8).

- Rose points out that there has been a lively "debate" among scientists on this issue. What assumptions do you think drive each side of this debate?

- Why is it surprising that the films *Free Willy* and *Blackfish* have helped heat up the debate among scientists?

READING LIKE A WRITER

DEMONSTRATING THE PROBLEM EXISTS AND IS SERIOUS

Proposal writers use a variety of strategies to alert readers to the problem. The title, "Captivity Kills Orcas," is likely to capture readers' attention because it goes against the image of orcas happily performing tricks for adoring audiences. This is the image marine park visitors get from watching orca shows and the impression fostered by advertisements. Although orcas are often called "killer whales," the title announces orcas are not the killers — the marine parks themselves are.

In addition, Rose opens her essay by referring to the documentary film *Blackfish*. The film portrays the horrific death of SeaWorld trainer Dawn Brancheau in what Michael O'Sullivan called in his *Washington Post* review, "a damning documentary about the treatment of the animals by marine parks." *Blackfish* set off a heated controversy. Animal advocates signed petitions to boycott SeaWorld and its stock plunged as a result. SeaWorld criticized the film as "shamefully dishonest, deliberately misleading and scientifically inaccurate." The following activity invites you to examine how Rose, described on the CNN website simply as a "marine mammal scientist," responds to the accusation about scientific inaccuracy.

Analyze & Write

Write a paragraph analyzing how Rose uses science to frame the problem and establish its seriousness:

1. Reread paragraphs 1–3, marking where Rose uses science to explain the problem and tries to convince readers that it is serious and worth solving.

2. How does Rose present herself as an authority whose expertise can be relied upon? How credible does she seem to you?

A Special Reading Strategy

Analyzing Visuals

Write a paragraph analyzing the visual in "Captivity Kills Orcas" and explaining what, if anything, it contributes to Rose's argument. To do the analysis, you can use the Criteria for Analyzing Visuals chart in Chapter 2 on pp. 32–34. Don't feel you have to answer all of the questions in the chart; focus on those that seem most productive in helping you write a paragraph-length analysis. To help you get started, consider adding these questions that specifically refer to the visual in Rose's proposal:

- Why do you think Rose chose an image from the film *Blackfish*? What impression of the orca do you think readers are likely to get from this visual whether or not they've seen the film?

- Notice that the caption under the photo identifies the orca by name. Why is identifying the orca by name important?

William F. Shughart II

Why Not a Football Degree?

William F. Shughart II (b. 1947) is a distinguished professor at the Utah State University School of Business who specializes in public choice theory that uses the tools of economics to study political attitudes and behavior. Shughart has been highly influential as editor-in-chief of the *Public Choice* journal and as research director and senior fellow at the Independent Institute, a libertarian conservative think tank. Shughart has written many books and articles addressing a broad array of social issues that range from sin taxes to taxing the Internet, campaign finance to terrorism. Sports are among Shughart's many interests, as reflected in these articles: "Moral Hazard and the Effects of the Designated Hitter Rule Revisited," "Close Look Shows College Sports No Drain on Schools' Resources," and this proposal "Why Not a Football Degree?" which was originally published in the *Wall Street Journal*.

- **Before you read,** note that the title asks the question "Why Not a Football Degree?" What problem do you imagine a college degree in football would solve?

- **As you read,** consider that this proposal was written originally for the *Wall Street Journal*, a newspaper concerned primarily with business and financial matters. How does Shughart appeal to the interests and concerns of his original audience?

The college football career of 2006's Heisman Trophy winner, Ohio State University 1 quarterback Troy Smith, nearly was cut short at the end of his sophomore year following allegations that he had accepted $500 from a Buckeye booster. He was barred from playing in the 2005 Alamo Bowl and the next season's opener against Miami (Ohio). Quarterback Rhett Bomar was dismissed from the University of Oklahoma's football team after it was disclosed that he had earned substantially more than justified by the number of hours worked during the summer of 2006 at a job arranged for him by a patron of OU athletics. As a result of charges that, from 1993 to 1998, Coach Clem Haskins paid to have more than 400 term papers ghost-written for 18 of his players, the post-season tournament victories credited to the University of Minnesota's basketball team were erased from the NCAA's record books and the program was placed on a four-year probation from which it has not yet recovered. In recent years, gambling and point-shaving scandals have rocked the basketball programs at Arizona State, Northwestern, and Florida; player suspensions and other penalties have been handed out for illegal betting on games by members of the Boston University, Florida State, and University of Maryland football teams.

Each of these events, which are only the latest revelations in a long series of NCAA 2 rule violations, has generated the usual hand-wringing about the apparent loss of amateurism in college sports. Nostalgia for supposedly simpler times when love of the game and not money was the driving force in intercollegiate athletics has led to all sorts of reform proposals. The NCAA's decision in the late 1980s to require its member institutions to make public athletes' graduation rates is perhaps the least controversial example. Proposition 48's mandate that freshman athletes must meet more stringent test score and grade point requirements to participate in NCAA-sanctioned contests than is demanded of entering non-student-athletes has been criticized as a naked attempt to discriminate against disadvantaged (and mostly minority) high-school graduates who see college sports as a way out of poverty.

But whether or not one supports any particular reform proposal, there seems to be 3 a general consensus that something must be done. If so, why stop at half-measures? I hereby offer three suggestions for solving the crisis in college athletics.

1. *Create four-year degree programs in football and basketball.* Many colleges and 4 universities grant bachelor's degrees in vocational subjects. Art, drama, and music are a few examples, but there are others. Undergraduates who major in these areas typically are required to spend only about one of their four years in introductory English, math, history and science courses; the remainder of their time is spent in the studio, the theater or the practice hall honing the creative talents they will later sell as professionals.

Although a college education is no more necessary for success in the art world 5 than it is in the world of sports, no similar option is available for students whose talents lie on the athletic field or in the gym. Majoring in physical education is a possibility, of course, but while PE is hardly a rigorous, demanding discipline, undergraduates pursuing a degree in that major normally must spend many more hours in the classroom than their counterparts who are preparing for careers on the stage. While the music major is receiving academic credit for practice sessions and recitals, the PE major is studying and taking exams in kinesiology, exercise physiology and nutrition. Why should academic credit be given for practicing the violin, but not for practicing a three-point shot?

2. *Extend the time limit on athletic scholarships by two years.* In addition to practic- 6 ing and playing during the regular football or basketball season, college athletes must continue to work to improve their skills and keep in shape during the off-season. For football players, these off-season activities include several weeks of organized spring practice as well as year-round exercise programs in the weight room and on the running track. Basketball players participate in summer leagues and practice with their teams during the fall. In effect, college athletes are required to work at their sports for as much as 10 months a year.

These time-consuming extracurricular activities make it extremely difficult for col- 7 lege athletes to devote more than minimal effort to the studies required for maintaining their academic eligibility. They miss lectures and exams when their teams travel, and the extra tutoring they receive at athletic department expense often fails to make up the difference.

If the NCAA and its member schools are truly concerned about the academic side 8 of the college athletic experience, let them put their money where their collective mouth is. The period of an athlete's eligibility to participate in intercollegiate sports would remain at four years, but the two additional years of scholarship support could be exercised at any time during the athlete's lifetime. Athletes who use up their college eligibility and do not choose careers in professional sports would be guaranteed financial backing to remain in school and finish their undergraduate degrees. Athletes who have the talent to turn pro could complete their degrees when their playing days are over.

3. *Allow a competitive marketplace to determine the compensation of college ath-*   9
letes. Football and basketball players at the top NCAA institutions produce millions of dollars in benefits for their respective schools. Successful college athletic programs draw more fans to the football stadium and to the basketball arena. They generate revenues for the school from regular season television appearances and from invitations to participate in postseason play. There is evidence that schools attract greater financial support from public and private sources—both for their athletic and academic programs—if their teams achieve national ranking. There even is evidence that the quality of students who apply for admission to institutions of higher learning improves following a successful football or basketball season.

Despite the considerable contributions made to the wealth and welfare of his or her   10
school, however, the compensation payable to a college athlete is limited by the NCAA to a scholarship that includes tuition, books, room and board, and a nominal expense allowance. Any payment above and beyond this amount subjects the offending athletic program to NCAA sanctions. In-kind payments to players and recruits in the form of free tickets to athletic contests, T-shirts, transportation and accommodations likewise are limited. These restrictions apply to alumni and fans as well as to the institutions themselves. The NCAA also limits the amount of money athletes can earn outside of school by curtailing the use of summer jobs as a means by which coaches and boosters can pay athletes more than authorized.

The illegal financial inducements reported to be widespread in collegiate football   11
and basketball supply conclusive evidence that many college athletes are now underpaid. The relevant question is whether the current system of compensation ought to remain in place. Allowing it to do so will preserve the illusion of amateurism in college sports and permit coaches, athletic departments and college administrators to continue to benefit financially at the expense of the players. On the other hand, shifting to a market-based system of compensation would transfer some of the wealth created by big-time athletic programs to the individuals whose talents are key ingredients in the success of those programs.

It would also cause a sea change in the distribution of power among the top NCAA   12
institutions. Under the present NCAA rules, some of the major college athletic programs, such as Southern Cal, LSU and Florida in football, and Duke, North Carolina and Florida in basketball, have developed such strong winning traditions over the years that they can maintain their dominant positions without cheating.

These schools are able to attract superior high-school athletes season after season by   13
offering packages of non-monetary benefits (well-equipped training facilities, quality coaching staffs, talented teammates, national exposure and so on) that increases the present value of an amateur athlete's future professional income relative to the value

added by historically weaker athletic programs. Given this factor, along with NCAA rules that mandate uniform compensation across the board, the top institutions have a built-in competitive advantage in recruiting the best and brightest athletes.

It follows that under the current system, the weaker programs are virtually com- 14 pelled to offer illegal financial inducements to players and recruits if they wish to compete successfully with the traditional powers. It also follows that shifting to a market-based system of compensation would remove some of the built-in advantages now enjoyed by the top college athletic programs. It is surely this effect, along with the reductions in the incomes of coaches and the "fat" in athletic department budgets to be expected once a competitive marketplace is permitted to work, that is the cause of the objection to paying student-athletes a market-determined wage, not the rhetoric about the repugnance of professionalism.

It is a fight over the distribution of the college sports revenue pie that lies at the bot- 15 tom of the debate about reforming NCAA rules. And notwithstanding the high moral principles and concern for players usually expressed by debaters on all sides of the issue, the interests of the athlete are in fact often the last to be considered.

READING FOR MEANING

1. **Read to Summarize.** Write a sentence or two summarizing Shughart's proposed solution.

   For help with summarizing, see Chapter 2, pp. 24–25.

2. **Read to Respond.** Write a paragraph analyzing anything that resonates or seems surprising, such as the rules violations that Shughart lists in the first paragraph, perhaps adding other, more recent violations with which you are familiar; or Shughart's observation that playing and practicing sports "make it extremely difficult for college athletes to devote more than minimal effort" to their studies (par. 7), perhaps in relation to your own experience as an athlete in college or high school.

3. **Read to Analyze Assumptions.** Write a paragraph or two analyzing an assumption you find intriguing in Shughart's essay. For example:

   Assumptions about the benefits of amateurism. NCAA rules require that to play college sports, athletes must retain amateur status, meaning that they cannot be paid by recruiters or sponsors and that their scholarships can cover only such things as tuition and housing. Shughart argues, however, that amateurism in college sports is an "illusion" (par. 11).

   - Who, according to Shughart, benefits from keeping college athletes amateurs, and who would benefit if they were allowed to become professionals?

     You may also try looking for patterns of opposition; see Chapter 2, pp. 35–36.

   - If the NCAA assumes that amateur status protects college athletes and perhaps also college sports, what is it supposed to protect them from, and how effective has this protection been?

Assumptions about the purpose of college. Although he concedes that the physical education major is "hardly a rigorous, demanding discipline" (par. 5), Shughart proposes that football be a major in its own right. His argument hinges on the comparison of football to music and other performance arts in which students receive "academic credit for practice sessions and recitals" (par. 5). He calls them "vocational subjects" (par. 4) because their purpose is job training.

You may also try reflecting on challenges to your beliefs and values; see Chapter 2, pp. 36–37.

- In conceding that the physical education major is "hardly a rigorous, demanding discipline" (par. 5), Shughart appears to think his readers are likely to assume disciplines or subjects studied in college should be rigorous and demanding. Do you share this assumption? Why or why not?

- By calling football a "vocational subject" and proposing that there be a major in football, Shughart seems to assume the primary purpose of a college education should be job training. What other reasons, if any, might people choose to go to college?

READING LIKE A WRITER

SHOWING HOW THE PROPOSED SOLUTION WOULD HELP SOLVE THE PROBLEM AND IS FEASIBLE

"Why Not a Football Degree?" dismisses as "half-measures" previous efforts by the National Collegiate Athletic Association (NCAA) to solve what Shughart calls "the crisis in college athletics" (par. 3). He identifies an array of problems in college sports, including evidence that some athletes are being paid although they are supposed to be amateurs, not professionals; others are getting college credit they have not earned, for example for plagiarized papers; and still others are illegally betting on games. To address problems like these, Shughart makes a three-pronged proposal designed to help student athletes succeed in their academic studies as well as in their collegiate sports careers, and also eliminate "illegal financial inducements" (par. 11) while removing the "built-in advantages" (par. 14) of the most successful college sports programs.

Analyze & Write

Write a paragraph or two analyzing Shughart's argument in support of his proposed solution:

1. First, choose one of Shughart's "three suggestions" (par. 3) to analyze, and evaluate Shughart's argument. What kinds of support does the author provide? What are the strengths and weaknesses of this part of his argument?

2. Then consider how well the three parts of the proposal work together to offer a comprehensive solution to the problem as Shughart has defined it.

Kelly D. Brownell and Thomas R. Frieden

Ounces of Prevention—
The Public Policy Case for Taxes
on Sugared Beverages

Kelly D. Brownell (b. 1951) is a professor of psychology and neuroscience as well as the dean of the Sanford School of Public Policy at Duke University. An international expert who has published numerous articles and books, including *Food Fight: The Inside Story of the Food Industry, America's Obesity Crisis, and What We Can Do About It* (2003), Brownell received the 2012 American Psychological Association Award for Outstanding Lifetime Contributions to Psychology. He was also featured in the Academy Award–nominated film *Super Size Me*. Thomas R. Frieden (b. 1960), a physician specializing in public health, is the director of the U.S. Centers for Disease Control and Prevention (CDC) and served for several years as the health commissioner for the City of New York.

Their proposal "Ounces of Prevention—The Public Policy Case for Taxes on Sugared Beverages" was originally published in 2009 in the highly respected *New England Journal of Medicine*, which calls itself "the most widely read, cited, and influential general medical periodical in the world."

- **Before you read,** think about how the reputation of the publication in which this proposal first appeared, together with Brownell and Frieden's credentials, might have influenced the original audience as well as how it may affect college students reading the proposal today.

- **As you read,** notice that Brownell and Frieden include graphs and cite their sources. How do you think these features of their proposal might influence readers?

Sugar, rum, and tobacco are commodities which are nowhere necessaries of life, which are become objects of almost universal consumption, and which are therefore extremely proper subjects of taxation.
—ADAM SMITH, *THE WEALTH OF NATIONS*, 1776

The obesity epidemic has inspired calls for public health measures to prevent diet-related diseases. One controversial idea is now the subject of public debate: food taxes. Forty states already have small taxes on sugared beverages and snack foods, but in the past year, Maine and New York have proposed large taxes on sugared beverages, and similar discussions have begun in other states. The size of the taxes, their potential for generating revenue and reducing consumption, and vigorous opposition by the beverage industry have resulted in substantial controversy. Because excess consumption of unhealthful foods underlies many leading causes of death, food taxes 1 at local, state, and national levels are likely to remain part of political and public health discourse.

Sugar-sweetened beverages (soda sweetened with sugar, corn syrup, or other caloric 2 sweeteners and other carbonated and uncarbonated drinks, such as sports and energy drinks) may be the single largest driver of the obesity epidemic. A recent meta-analysis found that the intake of sugared beverages is associated with increased body weight, poor nutrition, and displacement of more healthful beverages; increasing consumption increases risk for obesity and diabetes; the strongest effects are seen in studies with the best methods (e.g., longitudinal and interventional vs. correlational studies);* and interventional studies show that reduced intake of soft drinks improves health.[1] Studies that do not support a relationship between consumption of sugared beverages and health outcomes tend to be conducted by authors supported by the beverage industry.[2] Sugared beverages are marketed extensively to children and adolescents, and in the mid-1990s, children's intake of sugared beverages surpassed that of milk. In the past decade, per capita intake of calories from sugar-sweetened beverages has increased by nearly 30 percent (see bar graph Daily Caloric Intake from Sugar-Sweetened Drinks in the United States);[3] beverages now account for 10 to 15 percent of the calories consumed by children and adolescents. For each extra can or glass of sugared beverage consumed per day, the likelihood of a child's becoming obese increases by 60 percent.[4]

DAILY CALORIC INTAKE FROM SUGAR-SWEETENED DRINKS IN THE UNITED STATES.   Data are from Nielsen and Popkin.[3]

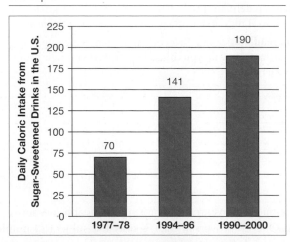

Reprinted from *American Journal of Preventative Medicine*, 2004; 27: 205–210. Nielsen SJ, Popkin BM. Changes in beverage intake between 1977 and 2001 with permission from Elsevier.

*In a *longitudinal* study, researchers observe changes taking place over a long period of time; in an *interventional* study, investigators give research subjects a measured amount of whatever is being studied and note its effects; and in a *correlational* study, researchers examine statistics to see if two or more variables have a mathematically significant similarity. [Editor's note]

Taxes on tobacco products have been highly effective in reducing consumption, and ₃ data indicate that higher prices also reduce soda consumption. A review conducted by Yale University's Rudd Center for Food Policy and Obesity suggested that for every 10 percent increase in price, consumption decreases by 7.8 percent. An industry trade publication reported even larger reductions: as prices of carbonated soft drinks increased by 6.8 percent, sales dropped by 7.8 percent, and as Coca-Cola prices increased by 12 percent, sales dropped by 14.6 percent.[5] Such studies—and the economic principles that support their findings—suggest that a tax on sugared beverages would encourage consumers to switch to more healthful beverages, which would lead to reduced caloric intake and less weight gain.

The increasing affordability of soda—and the decreasing affordability of fresh ₄ fruits and vegetables (see line graph)—probably contributes to the rise in obesity in the United States. In 2008, a group of child and health care advocates in New York proposed a one-penny-per-ounce excise tax on sugared beverages, which would be expected to reduce consumption by 13 percent—about two servings per week per person. Even if one quarter of the calories consumed from sugared beverages are replaced by other food, the decrease in consumption would lead to an estimated reduction of 8,000 calories per person per year—slightly more than 2 pounds each year for the average person. Such a reduction in calorie consumption would be expected to substantially reduce the risk of obesity and diabetes and may also reduce the risk of heart disease and other conditions.

Some argue that government should not interfere in the market and that products ₅ and prices will change as consumers demand more healthful food, but several

RELATIVE PRICE CHANGES FOR FRESH FRUITS AND VEGETABLES, SUGAR AND SWEETS, AND CARBONATED DRINKS, 1978–2009. Data are from the Bureau of Labor Statistics and represent the U.S. city averages for all urban consumers in January of each year.

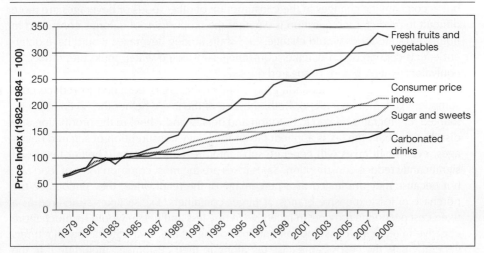

U.S. Bureau of Labor Statistics

considerations support government action. The first is externality—costs to parties not directly involved in a transaction. The contribution of unhealthful diets to health care costs is already high and is increasing—an estimated $79 billion is spent annually for overweight and obesity alone—and approximately half of these costs are paid by Medicare and Medicaid, at taxpayers' expense. Diet-related diseases also cost society in terms of decreased work productivity, increased absenteeism, poorer school performance, and reduced fitness on the part of military recruits, among other negative effects. The second consideration is information asymmetry between the parties to a transaction. In the case of sugared beverages, marketers commonly make health claims (e.g., that such beverages provide energy or vitamins) and use techniques that exploit the cognitive vulnerabilities of young children, who often cannot distinguish a television program from an advertisement. A third consideration is revenue generation, which can further increase the societal benefits of a tax on soft drinks. A penny-per-ounce excise tax would raise an estimated $1.2 billion in New York State alone. In times of economic hardship, taxes that both generate this much revenue and promote health are better options than revenue initiatives that may have adverse effects.

Objections have certainly been raised: that such a tax would be regressive, that 6 food taxes are not comparable to tobacco or alcohol taxes because people must eat to survive, that it is unfair to single out one type of food for taxation, and that the tax will not solve the obesity problem. But the poor are disproportionately affected by diet-related diseases and would derive the greatest benefit from reduced consumption; sugared beverages are not necessary for survival; Americans consume about 250 to 300 more calories daily today than they did several decades ago, and nearly half this increase is accounted for by consumption of sugared beverages; and though no single intervention will solve the obesity problem, that is hardly a reason to take no action.

The full impact of public policies becomes apparent only after they take effect. We 7 can estimate changes in sugared-drink consumption that would be prompted by a tax, but accompanying changes in the consumption of other foods or beverages are more difficult to predict. One question is whether the proportions of calories consumed in liquid and solid foods would change. And shifts among beverages would have different effects depending on whether consumers substituted water, milk, diet drinks, or equivalent generic brands of sugared drinks.

Effects will also vary depending on whether the tax is designed to reduce consumption, generate revenue, or both; the size of the tax; whether the revenue is earmarked for programs related to nutrition and health; and where in the production and distribution chain the tax is applied. Given the heavy consumption of sugared beverages, even small taxes will generate substantial revenue, but only heftier taxes will significantly reduce consumption. Sales taxes are the most common form of food tax, but because they are levied as a percentage of the retail price, they encourage the purchase of less-expensive brands or larger containers. Excise taxes structured as a fixed cost per ounce provide an incentive to buy less and hence would be much more effective in reducing consumption and improving health. In addition, manufacturers generally pass the cost of an excise tax along to their customers, including it in the price consumers see when they are making their selection, whereas sales taxes are seen only at the cash register.

Although a tax on sugared beverages would have health benefits regardless of how the revenue was used, the popularity of such a proposal increases greatly if revenues are used for programs to prevent childhood obesity, such as media campaigns, facilities and programs for physical activity, and healthier food in schools. Poll results show that support of a tax on sugared beverages ranges from 37 to 72 percent; a poll of New York residents found that 52 percent supported a "soda tax," but the number rose to 72 percent when respondents were told that the revenue would be used for obesity prevention. Perhaps the most defensible approach is to use revenue to subsidize the purchase of healthful foods. The public would then see a relationship between tax and benefit, and any regressive effects would be counteracted by the reduced costs of healthful food. 9

A penny-per-ounce excise tax could reduce consumption of sugared beverages by more than 10 percent. It is difficult to imagine producing behavior change of this magnitude through education alone, even if government devoted massive resources to the task. In contrast, a sales tax on sugared drinks would generate considerable revenue, and as with the tax on tobacco, it could become a key tool in efforts to improve health. 10

References

1. Vartanian LR, Schwartz MB, Brownell KD. Effects of soft drink consumption on nutrition and health: a systematic review and meta-analysis. Am J Public Health 2007;97:667–675.
2. Forshee RA, Anderson PA, Storey ML. Sugar-sweetened beverages and body mass index in children and adolescents: a meta-analysis. Am J Clin Nutr 2008;87:1662–71.
3. Nielsen SJ, Popkin BM. Changes in beverage intake between 1977 and 2001. Am J Prev Med 2004;27:205–210.
4. Ludwig DS, Peterson KE, Gortmaker SL. Relation between consumption of sugar-sweetened drinks and childhood obesity: a prospective, observational analysis. Lancet 2001;357:505–508.
5. Elasticity: big price increases cause Coke volume to plummet. Beverage Digest. November 21, 2008:3–4.

READING FOR MEANING

1. **Read to Summarize.** Write a sentence or two briefly summarizing Brownell and Frieden's proposed solution.

2. **Read to Respond.** Write a paragraph analyzing anything that seems surprising, such as: the idea that sports and energy beverages that are sugar-sweetened may not be good for you, perhaps in relation to your own consumption of such drinks; or the assertion that taxes on tobacco products "have been highly effective in reducing consumption" (par. 3), considering how many of your peers have chosen to be smokers or nonsmokers.

For help with summarizing, see Chapter 2, pp. 24–25.

You may also try reflecting on challenges to your beliefs and values; see Chapter 2, pp. 36–37.

For help analyzing assumptions, see Chapter 2, pp. 28–29.

3. **Read to Analyze Assumptions.** Write a paragraph or two analyzing an assumption you find intriguing in Brownell and Frieden's proposal. For example:

Assumptions about the government's role in solving health problems. Brownell and Frieden explicitly argue in favor of federal and/or state government actions to address public health problems such as those related to obesity and tobacco use.

- Why do Brownell and Frieden assume that government should have a role in influencing people's decisions about their own health? In other words, why is the so-called "obesity epidemic" a public policy problem?

- Imposing taxes is one thing government can do. What other actions could or should the government do to solve public health problems?

Assumptions about research studies. Brownell and Frieden cite a number of research studies, including a "meta-analysis," a study of previous studies.

- Brownell and Frieden explain that the meta-analysis on which they are relying examined studies that took three different approaches — longitudinal, inter-ventional, and correlational — to determine whether there is a cause-effect relationship between consuming sugar-sweetened beverages and obesity (par. 2). Why do Brownell and Frieden assume it is important to take a variety of approaches to a question like this? Do you agree or disagree?

- Brownell and Frieden also call into question studies that arrived at a different "outcome," arguing that these studies "tend to be conducted by authors supported by the beverage industry" (par. 2). Why do Brownell and Frieden assume it matters who funded the research? Should it matter?

READING LIKE A WRITER

RESPONDING TO OBJECTIONS AND ALTERNATIVE SOLUTIONS

Proposal writers usually try to respond to readers' likely objections and questions by conceding or refuting them. How writers handle objections and questions affects their credibility with readers, who usually expect writers to be respectful of other points of view and to take criticism seriously, while still arguing assertively for their solution. Brownell and Frieden respond to five possible objections. Notice that even though they devote more space to the first objection, they present all of the objections and their refutations using the same basic sentence pattern:

Transitions signaling an opposing point

Some argue that . . . , but . . . (par. 5)

Objections have certainly been raised: that . . . , that . . . , that . . . , and that. . . . But . . . , . . . , and . . . (par. 6)

| Analyze & Write |

Write a paragraph or two analyzing and evaluating how Brownell and Frieden respond to possible objections:

1. Reread paragraph 5. First, summarize the objection and Brownell and Frieden's reasons for refuting it. What cues do they provide to signal that an objection is coming and to highlight their reasons? Why do you think they call their reasons "considerations"? How convincing do you think these particular considerations were likely to be for their original *New England Journal of Medicine* audience?

2. Reread paragraph 6, in which the authors respond to four other objections. What cues do they provide to help you follow their argument? What reasons do Brownell and Frieden give to refute these objections? Which refutations, if any, do you think need further elaboration or support?

3. Given their purpose and audience, why do you think Brownell and Frieden focus so much attention on the first objection, but choose to group the other four objections together in a single paragraph?

Patrick O'Malley

More Testing, More Learning

Patrick O'Malley wrote the following proposal when he was a first-year college student. To research the problem, he interviewed two professors, talked with several students, and read published research on testing. He cited these sources using APA style, as his instructor had requested. Because of his unusual rhetorical situation — a student advising teachers on how to plan their courses — O'Malley decided to make his essay an open letter to professors on his campus, a letter that might appear in the campus newspaper.

- **Before you read,** think about your own experience with what O'Malley calls "major, infrequent, high-stakes exams" (par. 2). Do you think this kind of testing is a problem, and if so, why?

- **As you read,** consider O'Malley's decision to try to publish his proposal as an open letter in the campus newspaper. How well do you think he addresses the concerns of his readers, students as well as professors?

It's late at night. The final's tomorrow. You got a C on the midterm, so this one will 1
make or break you. Will it be like the midterm? Did you study enough? Did you study the right things? It's too late to drop the course. So what happens if you fail? No time to worry about that now — you've got a ton of notes to go over.

Although this last-minute anxiety about midterm and final exams is only too famil- 2
iar to most college students, many professors may not realize how such major, infrequent, high-stakes exams work against the best interests of students both psychologically and cognitively. They cause unnecessary amounts of stress, placing too much importance on one or two days in the students' entire term, judging ability on a single or dual performance. Reporting on recent research at Cornell University Medical School, Sian Beilock, a psychology professor at the University of Chicago, points out that "stressing about doing well on an important exam can backfire, leading students to 'choke under pressure' or to score less well than they might otherwise score if the stakes weren't so high." Moreover, Cornell's research using fMRI brain scans shows that "the pressures of a big test can reach beyond the exam itself — stunting the cognitive systems that support the attention and memory skills every day" (Beilock, 2010). So, not only do high-stakes exams discourage frequent study and undermine students' performance, they also do long-term damage to students' cognitive development. If professors gave brief exams at frequent intervals, students would be spurred to learn more and worry less. They would study more regularly, perform better on tests, and enhance their cognitive functioning.

Ideally, a professor would give an in-class test or quiz after each unit, chapter, or 3
focus of study, depending on the type of class and course material. A physics class might require a test on concepts after every chapter covered, while a history class could necessitate quizzes covering certain time periods or major events. These exams

should be given weekly or at least twice monthly. Whenever possible, they should consist of two or three essay questions rather than many multiple-choice or short-answer questions. To preserve class time for lecture and discussion, exams should take no more than 15 or 20 minutes.

The main reason professors should give frequent exams is that when they do and when they provide feedback to students on how well they are doing, students learn more in the course and perform better on major exams, projects, and papers. It makes sense that in a challenging course containing a great deal of material, students will learn more of it and put it to better use if they have to apply or "practice" it frequently on exams, which also helps them find out how much they are learning and what they need to go over again. A 2006 study reported in the journal *Psychological Science* concluded that "taking repeated tests on material leads to better long-term retention than repeated studying," according to the study's coauthors, Henry L. Roediger and Jeffrey Karpicke (ScienceWatch.com, 2008). When asked what the impact of this breakthrough research would be, they responded: "We hope that this research may be picked up in educational circles as a way to improve educational practices, both for students in the classroom and as a study strategy outside of class." The new field of mind, brain, and education research advocates the use of "retrieval testing." For example, research by Karpicke and Blunt (2011) published in *Science* found that testing was more effective than other, more traditional methods of studying both for comprehension and for analysis. Why retrieval testing works is not known. UCLA psychologist Robert Bjork speculates that it may be effective because "when we use our memories by retrieving things, we change our access" to that information. "What we recall," therefore, "becomes more recallable in the future" (qtd. in Belluck, 2011).

Many students already recognize the value of frequent testing, but their reason is that they need the professor's feedback. A Harvard study notes students' "strong preference for frequent evaluation in a course." Harvard students feel they learn least in courses that have "only a midterm and a final exam, with no other personal evaluation." Students believe they learn most in courses with "many opportunities to see how they are doing" (Light, 1990, p. 32). In a review of a number of studies of student learning, Frederiksen (1984) reports that students who take weekly quizzes achieve higher scores on final exams than students who take only a midterm exam and that testing increases retention of material tested.

Another, closely related argument in favor of multiple exams is that they encourage students to improve their study habits. Greater frequency in test taking means greater frequency in studying for tests. Students prone to cramming will be required—or at least strongly motivated—to open their textbooks and notebooks more often, making them less likely to resort to long, kamikaze nights of studying for major exams. Since there is so much to be learned in the typical course, it makes sense that frequent, careful study and review are highly beneficial. But students need motivation to study regularly, and nothing works like an exam. If students had frequent exams in all their courses, they would have to schedule study time each week and would gradually develop a habit of frequent study. It might be argued that students are adults who have to learn how to manage their own lives, but learning history or physics is more complicated than learning to drive a car or balance a checkbook. Students need coaching and practice in learning. The right way to learn new material needs to become a habit, and I believe that frequent exams are key to developing good habits of study and learning. The Harvard study concludes that "tying regular evaluation to good course organization enables students to plan their work more than a few days in advance. If quizzes and homework are scheduled on specific days, students plan their work to capitalize on them" (Light, 1990, p. 33).

By encouraging regular study habits, frequent exams would also decrease anxiety 　7 by reducing the procrastination that produces anxiety. Students would benefit psychologically if they were not subjected to the emotional ups and downs caused by major exams, when after being virtually worry-free for weeks they are suddenly ready to check into the psychiatric ward. Researchers at the University of Vermont found a strong relationship among procrastination, anxiety, and achievement. Students who regularly put off studying for exams had continuing high anxiety and lower grades than students who procrastinated less. The researchers found that even "low" procrastinators did not study regularly and recommended that professors give frequent assignments and exams to reduce procrastination and increase achievement (Rothblum, Solomon, & Murakami, 1986, pp. 393–394).

Research supports my proposed solution to the problem I have described. Com- 　8 mon sense as well as my experience and that of many of my friends support it. Why, then, do so few professors give frequent brief exams?

Some believe that such exams take up too much of the limited class time available to 　9 cover the material in the course. Most courses meet 150 minutes a week—three times a week for 50 minutes each time. A 20-minute weekly exam might take 30 minutes to administer, and that is one-fifth of each week's class time. From the student's perspective, however, this time is well spent. Better learning and greater confidence about the course seem a good trade-off for another 30 minutes of lecture. Moreover, time lost to lecturing or discussion could easily be made up in students' learning on their own through careful regular study for the weekly exams. If weekly exams still seem too time-consuming to some professors, their frequency could be reduced to every other week or their length to 5 or 10 minutes. In courses where multiple-choice exams are appropriate, several questions could be designed to take only a few minutes to answer.

Moreover, professors object to frequent exams because they take too much time to 　10 read and grade. In a 20-minute essay exam, a well-prepared student can easily write two pages. A relatively small class of 30 students might then produce 60 pages, no small amount of material to read each week. A large class of 100 or more students would produce an insurmountable pile of material. There are a number of responses to this objection. Again, professors could give exams every other week or make them very short. Instead of reading them closely, they could skim them quickly to see whether students understand an idea or can apply it to an unfamiliar problem; and instead of numerical or letter grades, they could give a plus, check, or minus. Exams could be collected and responded to only every third or fourth week. Professors who have readers or teaching assistants could rely on them to grade or check exams. And the Scantron machine is always available for instant grading of multiple-choice exams. Finally, frequent exams could be given *in place of* a midterm exam or out-of-class essay assignment.

Since frequent exams seem to some professors to create too many problems, how- 11 ever, it is reasonable to consider alternative ways to achieve the same goals. One alternative solution is to implement a program that would improve study skills. While such a program might teach students how to study for exams, it cannot prevent procrastination or reduce "large test anxiety" by a substantial amount. One research team studying anxiety and test performance found that study skills training was not effective in reducing anxiety or improving performance (Dendato & Diener, 1986, p. 134). This team, which also reviewed other research that reached the same conclusion, did find that a combination of "cognitive/relaxation therapy" and study skills training was effective. This possible solution seems complicated, however, not to mention time-consuming and expensive. It seems much easier and more effective to change the cause of the bad habit rather than treat the habit itself. That is, it would make more sense to solve the problem at its root: the method of learning and evaluation.

Still another solution might be to provide frequent study questions for students to 12 answer. These would no doubt be helpful in focusing students' time studying, but students would probably not actually write out the answers unless they were required to. To get students to complete the questions in a timely way, professors would have to collect and check the answers. In that case, however, they might as well devote the time to grading an exam. Even if it asks the same questions, a scheduled exam is preferable to a set of study questions because it takes far less time to write in class, compared to the time students would devote to responding to questions at home. In-class exams also ensure that each student produces his or her own work.

Furthermore, professors could help students prepare for midterm and final exams 13 by providing sets of questions from which the exam questions will be selected or announcing possible exam topics at the beginning of the course. This solution would have the advantage of reducing students' anxiety about learning every fact in the textbook, and it would clarify the course goals, but it would not motivate students to study carefully each new unit, concept, or text chapter in the course. I see this as a way of complementing frequent exams, not as substituting for them.

From the evidence and from my talks with professors and students, I see frequent, 14 brief in-class exams as the only way to improve students' study habits and learning, reduce their anxiety and procrastination, and increase their satisfaction with college. These exams are not a panacea, but only more parking spaces and a winning football team would do as much to improve college life. Professors can't do much about parking or football, but they can give more frequent exams. Campus administrators should get behind this effort, and professors should get together to consider giving exams more frequently. It would make a difference.

References

Beilock, S. (2010, September 3). Stressing about a high-stakes exam carries consequences beyond the test [Web log post]. Retrieved from http://www.psychologytoday.com/blog /choke/201009/stressing-about-high-stakes-exam-carries-consequences-beyond-the-test

Belluck, P. (2011, January 20). To really learn, quit studying and take a test. *The New York Times*. Retrieved from http://www.nytimes.com

Dendato, K. M., & Diener, D. (1986). Effectiveness of cognitive/relaxation therapy and study skills training in reducing self-reported anxiety and improving the academic performance of test-anxious students. *The Journal of Counseling Psychology, 33,* 131–135.

Frederiksen, N. (1984). The real test bias: Influences of testing on teaching and learning. *American Psychologist, 39,* 193–202.

Karpicke, J. D., & Blunt, J. R. (2011, January 30). Retrieval practice produces more learning than elaborative studying with concept mapping. *Science Online* doi:10.1126 /science.1199327

Light, R. J. (1990). *Explorations with students and faculty about teaching, learning, and student life.* Cambridge, MA: Harvard University Graduate School of Education and Kennedy School of Government.

Rothblum, E. D., Solomon, L., & Murakami, J. (1986). Affective, cognitive, and behavioral differences between high and low procrastinators. *Journal of Counseling Psychology, 33,* 387–394.

ScienceWatch.com (2008, February). Henry L. Roediger and Jeff Karpicke talk with ScienceWatch.com and answer a few questions about this month's fast breaking paper in the field of psychiatry/psychology [Interview]. Retrieved from http://sciencewatch.com /dr/fbp/2008/08febfbp/08febfbpRoedigerETAL

READING FOR MEANING

For help with summarizing, see Chapter 2, pp. 24–25.

1. **Read to Summarize.** Write a sentence or two summarizing O'Malley's proposed solution.

2. **Read to Respond.** Write a paragraph analyzing anything that resonates with your experience, such as whether O'Malley's solution, if it were adopted by professors, would make a difference in your own study habits or address any problems that you have with studying; or which kinds of classes, in your experience, are and are not suited to frequent brief exams.

You may also try judging the writer's credibility; see Chapter 2, pp. 45–46.

3. **Read to Analyze Assumptions.** Write a paragraph or two analyzing an assumption you find intriguing in O'Malley's essay. For example:

   Assumptions about the relationship between motivation and procrastination. O'Malley argues that college students would be "strongly motivated — to open their textbooks and notebooks more often" (par. 6) if they had to take exams frequently. He explains that the assumption underlying this argument is that "students need motivation to study regularly." In the next paragraph, however, he reviews research on procrastination that "found that even 'low' procrastinators did not study regularly" (par. 7).

- What seems to be the relationship, if any, between motivation and procrastination? If even students categorized as "low" procrastinators "did not study regularly," does it make sense to assume, as O'Malley does, that frequent tests would motivate most students to study?

- Given your own experiences and observations of other students, what would be likely to motivate most students and overcome their tendency to procrastinate?

Assumptions about the "right way to learn." O'Malley claims, "Students need coaching and practice in learning. The right way to learn new material needs to become a habit" (par. 6). He seems to assume that studying regularly is the "right way to learn" and that cramming the night before an exam is the wrong way.

- Why does O'Malley assume that cramming is inferior to studying regularly? In your experience and observations of other students, to what extent, if any, does cramming result in poorer performance on exams?

- Do you think there is a single "right way" — or at least, a best way — for students to study? If so, what is it?

You may also try reflecting on challenges to your beliefs and values; see Chapter 2, pp. 36–37.

READING LIKE A WRITER

ORGANIZING THE PROPOSAL IN A WAY THAT IS CLEAR, LOGICAL, AND CONVINCING

Topic sentences — particularly when they repeat key terms (or synonyms) from the thesis and forecasting statement — can be especially helpful cues for readers. Notice how O'Malley uses this strategy in two paragraphs from his essay:

Thesis/key terms *Forecasting statement*	If professors gave brief exams at frequent intervals, students would be spurred to learn more and worry less. *They would study more regularly, perform better on tests, and enhance their cognitive functioning.* (par. 2)
Cue	The main reason professors should give frequent exams is that when they do and when they provide feedback to students on how well they are doing, students learn more in the course and perform better on major exams, projects, and papers. (par. 4)

Repetition of key terms along with transitions that identify the topic (such as *main reasons*) and indicate the logical relationships among sentences and paragraphs (such as *however, for example,* and *since*) are both helpful. They tie together the parts of an argument and help to make a proposal well organized, readable, and logical.

Analyze & Write

Write a paragraph analyzing and evaluating O'Malley's use of cues to help readers follow the logic of his proposal:

1. First, reread paragraph 6 and paragraphs 8–12, and highlight the cues O'Malley provides.

2. Then identify two or three examples of cueing that help make this part of his argument logical.

3. Finally, evaluate how well O'Malley's use of cueing in this section and throughout the proposal helps you as a reader. Point out any places where cues are needed or could be improved.'

Writing to Learn Proposal

Write a brief essay analyzing one of the readings in this chapter (or another selection, perhaps one by a classmate). Explain how (and, perhaps, how well) the selection works as a proposal to solve a problem. Consider, for example, how it

- identifies an existing problem and demonstrates its seriousness;

- proposes a solution and shows that it would help solve the problem and is feasible — not too costly or time-consuming;

- anticipates and responds to likely objections to the proposed solution as well as any alternative solutions readers might prefer

- is organized clearly and logically, making it easy for readers to follow the argument.

Your essay could also reflect on how you applied one or more of the academic habits of mind as you read the selection:

- **Curiosity** — what questions or ideas did you have as you read the selection?

- **Critical Analysis** — what assumptions does the author make about why the problem is important and how it should be addressed?

- **Rhetorical Sensitivity** — how effective or ineffective do you think the selection is in achieving its purpose for the intended audience, given the constraints of the medium and the proposal genre?

A GUIDE TO WRITING PROPOSALS

You have probably done a good deal of analytical writing about your reading. Your instructor may also assign a capstone project to write a brief proposal of your own. This Guide to Writing offers detailed suggestions and resources to help you meet the special challenges this kind of writing presents.

THE WRITING ASSIGNMENT

Write an essay proposing a solution to a problem.

- Choose a problem affecting a community or group to which you belong.
- Research the problem and possible solutions.
- Decide how to present the problem so that readers see it exists and is serious.
- Find a solution that would help solve the problem and could be implemented without being too costly or time-consuming.
- Address likely objections to your proposed solution as well as any alternative solutions readers might prefer.
- Organize the proposal in a way that is clear, logical, and convincing.

WRITING YOUR DRAFT

Choosing a Problem

Rather than limiting yourself to the first subject that comes to mind, take a few minutes to consider your options and list as many problems as you can. When choosing a subject, keep in mind that the problem must be

- important to you and of concern to others;
- solvable, at least in part;
- one that you know a good deal about or can research in the time you have.

Choosing a problem affecting a group to which you belong (for example, as a classmate, teammate, participant in an online game site, or garage band member) or a place you have worked (a coffee shop, community pool, or radio station) gives you an advantage: You can write as an expert. You know the history of the problem, you know who to interview, and perhaps you have already thought about possible solutions. Moreover, you know who to address and how to persuade that audience to take action on your proposed solution.

If you already have a problem and possible solution(s) in mind, skip this activity. If you need to find a problem, making a chart like the one below can help you get started exploring creative solutions to real-life problems related to your school, community, or workplace.

	Problems	**Possible Solutions**
School	Can't get into required courses	• Make them large lecture courses. • Make them online or hybrid courses. • Give priority to majors.
Community	No safe place for children to play	• Use school yards for after-school sports. • Get high-school students or senior citizens to tutor kids. • Make pocket parks for neighborhood play. • Offer programs for kids at branch libraries.
Work	Inadequate training for new staff	• Make a training video or website. • Assign experienced workers to mentor trainees (for bonus pay).

Developing Your Proposal

The writing and research activities that follow will enable you to test your problem and develop an argument supporting your proposed solution.

Analyzing the Problem

Spend a few minutes thinking about what you and your readers know about the problem and how you can convince your readers that the problem you have identified is real and needs to be solved:

Brainstorm a List. Spend ten minutes listing everything you know about the problem. Write quickly, leaving judgment aside for the moment. After the ten minutes are up, you can review your list and highlight or star the most promising information.

Use Cubing. Probe the problem from a variety of perspectives:

- Describe the problem.

- Compare the problem to other, similar problems, or contrast it with other, related problems.

- Identify causes of the problem. (Consider immediate and deeper causes.)

- Consider the consequences of the problem. (Think about both short-term and long-term consequences.)

- Connect the problem to other problems in your experience.

- Analyze the problem to identify those most affected by it or any who benefit from it.

- Apply the problem to a real-life situation.

Prove the Problem's Existence and Seriousness. Use the sentence strategies below as a jumping-off point for demonstrating the existence and seriousness of the problem.

Give an example to make the problem specific

- Recently, ... has been [in the news/in movies/a political issue] because of .... [name event].

- *Example*: The film *Blackfish* compellingly describes many of the reasons why keeping orcas in captivity is—and always has been—a bad idea. (Rose, par. 1)

Use a scenario or anecdote to dramatize the problem

- The night before the final exam, ... [student's name] started to panic. Her roommate came to her rescue by insisting they .... [quit studying/gorge on ice cream/help each other review the material].

- *Example*: It's late at night. The final's tomorrow. You got a C on the midterm, so this one will make or break you. (O'Malley, par. 1)

Cite statistics to show the severity of the problem

- It has recently been reported that .... percent of .... [name group] are .... [specify problem].

- *Example*: As economists Robert Gordon and Ian Dew-Becker have established, the gains in workers' productivity for the past three decades have gone entirely to the wealthiest 10 percent. (Meyerson, par. 1)

Describe the problem's negative consequences

- According to .... [name expert/study], ... [state problem] is affecting .... [name affected group]: .... [insert quote from expert].

- *Example*: Sian Beilock, a psychology professor at the University of Chicago, points out that "stressing about doing well on an important exam can backfire, leading students to 'choke under pressure' or to score less well than they might otherwise score if the stakes weren't so high." (O'Malley, par. 2)

Show why readers should care about solving the problem

- We're all in this together. .... is not a win-lose proposition. If .... [name group] loses, we all lose.
- If we don't try to solve ...., no one else will.
- Doing nothing will only make .... worse.
- We have a moral responsibility to do something about ....

Considering Your Readers

With your understanding of the problem in mind, write for a few minutes to bring your intended readers into focus. Will you be writing to all members of your group or to only some of them (a committee that might supervise or evaluate the group, an individual in a position of authority)? Briefly justify your choice of readers.

Now gauge the impact of the problem on your readers and the attitudes they hold. How might these attitudes inform the solutions they are likely to prefer?

Freewriting.   Write without stopping for five or ten minutes about the problem's direct or indirect impact on your readers. Don't stop to reflect or consider; if you hit a roadblock, just keep coming back to the topic or raise questions you could research later. At the end of the specified time, review your writing and highlight or underline promising ideas.

Considering Values.   Comment on the values and attitudes of your readers and how they have responded to similar problems in the past. Use these sentence strategies as a jumping-off point:

- Some of my readers think .... is .... [someone else's responsibility/ not that big a problem].
- Others see .... as a matter of .... [fairness/human decency].
- Many complain about .... but do nothing because solving it seems [too hard/too costly].

Finding a Tentative Solution

List at least three possible solutions to the problem. You may want to consider using the following approaches to start:

Adapt a solution that has been tried or proposed for a similar problem

- *Example:* Rose compares her orca proposal to "wildlife sanctuaries" that already exist for "big cats, elephants and chimpanzees" (par. 5).

Focus on eliminating a cause or minimizing an effect of the problem

▸ *Example:* O'Malley's solution to stressful high-stakes exams is to eliminate the cause of the stress by inducing instructors to give more frequent low-stakes exams.

See the problem as part of a larger system, and explore solutions to the system

▸ *Example:* Meyerson argues that because the problem stems from "the redistribution of income from labor to capital," any solution must help redress the imbalance (par. 3).

Focus on solving a small part of the problem

▸ *Example:* Brownell and Frieden's solution to obesity is to reduce the consumption of sugared beverages through taxation.

Look at the problem from different points of view

▸ *Example:* Consider what students, teachers, parents, or administrators might think could be done to help solve the problem.

Think of a specific example of the problem, and consider how you could solve it

▸ *Example:* O'Malley could have focused on solving the problem of high-stakes exams in one particular course.

Researching Your Proposal

In exploring the problem and considering possible solutions, you may have identified questions you need to research. Doing research with your questions and notes in mind will help you work efficiently. But recognize that you might also find contradictory evidence that leads you to rethink your ideas.

If you are proposing a solution to a problem about which others have written, use the research strategies below to help you find out what solutions others have proposed or tried. You may also use these strategies to find out how others have defined the problem and demonstrated its seriousness.

- Enter keywords or phrases related to your solution (or problem) into the search box of an all-purpose database such as *Academic One File* (Gale) or *Academic Search Complete* (EBSCOHost) to find relevant articles in magazines and journals; a database like *LexisNexis* to find articles in newspapers; or library catalogs to find books and other resources. (Database names may change, and what is available will differ from school to school. Some libraries may even combine all three into one search link on the library's home page. Ask a librarian if you need help.) Patrick O'Malley could have tried a combination of keywords, such as *learning* and *test anxiety*, or variations on his terms (*frequent testing, improve retention*) to find relevant articles.

- *Bookmark* or keep a record of the URLs of promising sites, and download or copy information you could use in your essay. When available, download PDF files rather than HTML files because PDFs are likely to include visuals such as graphs and charts. If you copy and paste relevant information from sources into your notes, be careful to distinguish carefully between all material from sources and your own ideas. Remember to record source information with care and to cite and document any sources you use, including visuals and interviews.

To learn more about finding information, avoiding plagiarism, or documenting sources, see the Appendix, pp. 466–536.

Supporting Your Solution

Write down plausible reasons why your solution should be heard or tried. Then review your list and highlight the strongest reasons, the ones most likely to persuade your readers. Write for a few minutes about the single most convincing reason. The sentence strategies below can help you explain how your solution could help solve the problem:

It would eliminate a cause of the problem

▸ Research by .... shows it would reduce ....

It has worked elsewhere

▸ It works in ...., ..., and ...., as studies evaluating it by .... and .... show.

It would change people's behavior

▸ .... would [discourage/encourage] people to ....

Anticipating Readers' Objections

Write a few sentences defending your solution against each of the following predictable objections:

- It won't really solve the problem.
- I'm comfortable with things as they are.
- We can't afford it.
- It will take too long.
- People won't do it.
- Too few people will benefit.
- It's already been tried, with unsatisfactory results.
- You're making this proposal because it will benefit you personally.

For your proposal to succeed, readers must be convinced to take the solution seriously. Try to imagine how your prospective readers will respond.

Responding to Alternative Solutions

Identify two or three other solutions that your readers may prefer. Choose the one that poses the most serious challenge to your proposed solution. Then write a few sentences comparing your solution with the alternative one, weighing the strengths and weaknesses of each. Explain how you might demonstrate to readers that your solution has more advantages and fewer disadvantages than the alternative. (You may need to conduct additional research to respond to alternative solutions.)

Formulating a Working Thesis

A working thesis will keep you focused as you draft and revise your essay. The thesis statement in a proposal should offer the solution and may also identify the problem. Although they are not required to do so, thesis statements may also forecast the main reasons in favor of the solution. (Forecasts can help guide readers.)

Solution   If professors gave brief exams at frequent intervals, students would be
Forecast   spurred to *learn more and worry less. They would study more regularly,*
           perform better on tests, and enhance their cognitive functioning. (O'Malley,
           par. 2)

As you draft your own thesis statement, pay attention to the language you use. It should be clear and unambiguous, emphatic but appropriately qualified. Although you will probably refine your thesis statement as you draft and revise your essay, trying now to articulate it will help give your planning and drafting direction and impetus.

Working with Sources

Citing Statistics to Establish the Problem's Existence and Seriousness

Statistics can be helpful in establishing that a problem exists and is serious. Patrick O'Malley, Kelly Brownell and Thomas Frieden, and Naomi Rose use statistics for this purpose. Note that Brownell and Frieden present some of their statistics in the form of graphs. To define the problem, writers often use

(continued)

statistics in the form of percentages (underlined in the first example) or numbers (boldface in the second example).

> . . . the largest orca tank in the world is less than <u>one ten-thousandth of one percent (0.0001%)</u> the size of the smallest home range of wild orcas. (Rose, par. 2)

Percentages can seem quite impressive, but sometimes, without the raw numbers, readers may not appreciate just how remarkable the percentages really are. In the following example, readers can see at a glance that the number Rose cites is truly significant:

> Very few captive orcas make it to midlife . . . and <u>not one out of more than 200</u> held in captivity has ever come close to old age . . . ("Killer Whale"). (par. 3)

For statistics to be persuasive, they must be from sources that readers consider reliable. Researchers' trustworthiness, in turn, depends on their credentials as experts in the field they are investigating and also on the degree to which they are disinterested, or free from bias. Rose relies on her own authority as a marine scientist and also cites statistics from an authoritative online source to which she provides a hyperlink.

To find statistics relating to the problem (or possible solution) you are writing about, explore the state, local, or tribal sections of www.usa.gov, the U.S. government's official Web portal, or visit the Library of Congress page State Government Information and follow the links. In particular, visit the U.S. Census Bureau's website, which offers reliable statistics on a wide variety of issues.

Including Visuals and Other Media

Think about whether visuals — drawings, photographs, tables, or graphs — would strengthen your proposal. Notice the photographs in Bornstein's and Rose's proposals (pp. 417 and 430). Also notice the two graphs Brownell and Frieden included in their proposal (pp. 440–41). Each graph has a heading and a caption that indicates where the data comes from. Brownell and Frieden apparently created the graphs themselves.

Consider constructing your own visuals, scanning materials from books and magazines, or downloading them from the Internet. If you submit your essay electronically to other students and your instructor or if you post it on a website, you might consider including video and audio clips as well as still images. Be sure to obtain permission, as we did, if your proposal will be read outside your classroom.

For help with proper citation for visuals, see the Appendix, pp. 466–536.

Organizing Your Proposal Effectively for Your Readers

The basic parts of a proposal argument are quite simple:

1. the problem

2. the solution

3. the reasons in support of the solution

4. a response to objections or alternative solutions readers might propose

This simple plan is nearly always complicated by other factors, however. In outlining your material, you must take into consideration many other details, such as whether readers already recognize the problem, how much agreement exists on the need to solve the problem, how much attention should be given to alternative solutions, and how many objections and questions by readers should be expected. If you are writing primarily for readers who acknowledge that the problem exists and are open to your solution, you might begin with a brief introduction that ends with your thesis statement and conclude by urging your readers to action. If you are writing primarily for readers who do not recognize the problem or are likely to prefer alternative solutions, however, you may need to begin by establishing common ground and acknowledging alternative ways readers may see the problem, and then concede the strengths of alternative solutions before launching fully into your own proposal; you may want to conclude by reiterating the values you share with your readers.

Drafting Your Proposal

By this point, you have done a lot of writing

- to focus and define a problem, and develop a solution to it;

- to support your solution with reasons and evidence your readers will find persuasive;

- to refute or concede objections and alternative solutions;

- to organize your ideas to make them clear, logical, and effective for readers.

Now stitch that material together to create a draft. The next two parts of this Guide to Writing will help you evaluate and improve it.

REVIEWING AND IMPROVING THE DRAFT

This section includes two guides for Peer Review and Troubleshooting Your Draft. Your instructor may arrange a peer review in class or online where you can exchange drafts with a classmate. The Peer Review Guide will help you give each other constructive feedback regarding the basic features and strategies typical of proposal writing. (If you want to make specific suggestions for improving the draft, see Troubleshooting Your Draft on p. 463.) Also, be sure to respond to any specific concerns the writer has raised about the draft. The Troubleshooting Your Draft guide that follows will help you reread your own draft with a critical eye, sort through any feedback you've received, and consider a variety of ways to improve your draft.

A PEER REVIEW GUIDE

How effective is the presentation of the problem?

What's Working Well: Let the writer know where the problem is especially well presented—for example, where statistics, examples, or other details help readers grasp the seriousness of the problem, or where visuals such as graphs or photographs impress upon readers the need to solve the problem.

What Needs Improvement: Indicate one passage where the presentation of the problem could be improved—for example, where the effects of the problem could be made vivid, where the problem's urgency could be better emphasized, or where the problem's future impact could be shown.

How convincing is the argument supporting the proposed solution?

What's Working Well: Indicate a passage where the argument is well done—for example, where a similar solution has been shown to work effectively, where steps for implementing the solution are set out clearly, or where the costs are shown to be reasonable.

What Needs Improvement: Identify a passage where the argument could be improved—for example, where additional examples, facts, statistics, or research studies could be used to demonstrate that the solution is feasible, cost-effective, and would indeed help to solve the problem.

How effective is the writer's response to objections and alternative solutions?

What's Working Well: Identify a passage where the writer responds effectively —for example, refuting an objection to the proposed solution with concrete evidence or recognized authorities, showing that an alternative solution would have negative side effects, or comparing the feasibility of the proposed solution to an alternative that readers may favor.

> **What Needs Improvement:** Tell the writer where a response is needed or could be more effective—for example, where a valid objection to the proposed solution could be conceded or an invalid objection refuted, or where an alternative solution could be shown to take more time and be more costly than the proposed solution.

How clear and logical is the organization?

> **What's Working Well:** Mark any parts of the essay that seem notably well organized—for example, where the thesis statement clearly identifies the proposed solution, where topic sentences identify the main points, or where logical transitions make the argument easy to follow.

> **What Needs Improvement:** Identify any aspect of the organization that needs improvement—for example, where the thesis could be introduced earlier, where topic sentences could be clearer, or where logical transitions could be added.

Revising Your Draft

Revising means reenvisioning your draft—seeing it in a new way, given your purpose audience, as well as the feedback from the peer review. Don't hesitate to cut unconvincing material, add new material, and move passages around. The following chart may help you strengthen your proposal.

TROUBLESHOOTING YOUR DRAFT

To Introduce the Problem More Effectively	
If readers doubt that the problem exists or that it is very serious,	• Discuss the problem's history or describe its effects on real people. • Add information—statistics, examples, studies, and so on—that your audience is likely to find persuasive or that they can relate to. • Consider adding visuals, such as graphs, tables, or charts, if these would help clarify the problem for your audience.

(continued)

To Strengthen the Support for the Proposed Solution	
If the solution being proposed is not clear,	• Describe the solution in more detail. • Outline the steps of its implementation. • Add a visual illustrating the solution.
If readers are not convinced that the proposed solution would solve the problem,	• Explain how the solution addresses specific aspects of the problem. • Point out where else a similar solution has worked. • Cite experts or research studies.
To Improve the Response to Objections and Alternative Solutions	
If objections to the solution have not been adequately addressed,	• Acknowledge valid objections and modify your solution to concede them. • Refute invalid objections by presenting reasons and supporting evidence.
If alternative solutions preferred by readers have not been adequately addressed,	• Address alternative solutions directly, acknowledging their strengths as well as their weaknesses. • Try to show why your solution is preferable—for example, it is easier to implement, costs less, takes less time, has fewer negative side effects, and would garner more support.
To Make the Organizational Plan More Effective	
If the essay is hard to follow,	• Mark each part of the proposal more clearly with explicit topic sentences and transitions or headings. • Add a forecasting statement.

Editing and Proofreading Your Draft

Check for errors in usage, punctuation, and mechanics, and consider matters of style. If you keep a list of errors you typically make, begin by checking your draft against this list. Ask someone else to proofread your essay before you submit it to your instructor.

From our research on student writing, we know that proposal writers tend to refer to the problem or solution by using the pronoun *this* or *that* ambiguously. Edit carefully any sentences with *this* or *that* to ensure that a noun immediately follows the pronoun to make the reference clear. Check a writer's handbook for help with this potential problem.

Reflecting on Proposal

In this chapter, you have read critically several proposals and have written one of your own. To better remember what you have learned, pause now to reflect on the reading and writing activities you completed in this chapter.

1. Write a page or so reflecting on what you have learned. Begin by describing what you are most pleased with in your essay. Then explain what you think contributed to your achievement.

   - If it was something you learned from the readings, indicate which readings and specifically what you learned from them.

   - If you got good advice from a critical reader, explain exactly how the person helped you — perhaps by helping you understand a problem in your draft or by helping you add a new dimension to your writing.

2. Reflect more generally on proposals, a genre of writing that plays an important role in our society. Consider some of the following questions:

   - How confident do you feel about making a proposal that might lead to improvements in the functioning of a group or community? Does your proposal attempt to bring about fundamental or minor change in the group?

   - Whose interest would be served by the solution you propose? Who else might be affected? In what ways does your proposal challenge the status quo in the group?

   - What contribution might essays proposing solutions to problems make to our society that other genres of writing cannot make?

Strategies for Research and Documentation

As many of the essays in *Reading Critically, Writing Well* show, writers often rely on research to expand and test their own ideas about a topic. This chapter offers advice on conducting research, evaluating potential sources, integrating source material you decide to use with your own writing, and documenting this material in an acceptable way.

PLANNING A RESEARCH PROJECT

To research and write about a topic effectively at the college level requires a plan. A clear sense of your rhetorical situation, as well as the practical needs of your research task (such as the due date and the level of detail required), will help you create one. The table below lists common elements that you will need to consider not only as you plan your research project, but also as you continue to find and evaluate sources and draft your project.

OVERVIEW OF A RESEARCH PROJECT

Define your research task and set a schedule.

Analyze your rhetorical situation.

- Determine your purpose.
- Analyze your audience to understand the interest and background your readers bring to the project, and analyze your attitude to determine how you want your readers to think of you.
- Determine the genre, or type, of research project you are creating, such as a proposal or laboratory report, and the expectations for research, writing, and design associated with this genre.

Understand the assignment.

- Check your syllabus or consult your instructor about the requirements of the project (such as the number and types of resources required, the length of the project, and so forth).
- Determine the final due date, and assign interim due dates to keep your project on track.

Establish a research log.

- Create a list of keywords.
- Create a working bibliography (list of sources), and annotate entries.
- Take notes on your sources.

Choose a topic, get an overview, and narrow your topic.

Choose a topic that answers an interesting question relevant to the assignment and of interest to you and your readers.

- Consult with your instructor.
- Review textbooks and other course materials.
- Explore newspapers, magazines, and Internet sites.

Get an overview, and narrow your topic (if necessary).

- Consult subject guides or a librarian to determine the availability of sources on your topic.
- Get necessary background by consulting encyclopedias and other general reference sources.
- Start a working bibliography to keep track of the bibliographic information of potential sources. (See pp. 471–72.)
- Draft questions to guide your research.

Search for in-depth information on your topic.

Conduct a search for sources, using carefully selected search terms.

- Check the library's resources (such as the catalog, databases, or home page) for books, articles, and multimedia.
- If acceptable to your instructor, search the Internet for relevant websites, blogs, and groups.
- Keep a list of search terms in a research log, and annotate your working bibliography to keep track of sources.
- Add relevant sources to your working bibliography, and annotate each entry to record the genre (or type) of source, the source's main points, and how you would use the source.
- Refine your research questions, and draft a thesis.

(continued)

Refine your search.

Ask yourself questions like these about the sources you have found:

- Is this what I expected to find?
- Am I finding enough information?
- Am I finding too much?
- Do I need to modify my keywords?
- Do I need to recheck background sources?
- Do I need to revise my research questions?
- Do I need to modify my thesis statement?

Continue searching for relevant and reliable sources in response to your answers.

Evaluate your sources.

Determine the relevance of potential sources.

- Does the source explain terms or concepts or provide background?
- Does the source provide evidence to support your claims?
- Does the source offer alternative viewpoints or lend authority?

Determine the reliability of potential sources.

- Who wrote it?
- When was it published?
- Who published it and what is the reputation of the publisher?
- Is the source scholarly or popular (or something else)?
- Is the source printed or online?
- What does the source say?

Continue to evaluate and refine your search strategy based on your research results.

Use your research to support your ideas.

Use evidence from sources to support your ideas.

- Synthesize ideas from multiple sources.
- Support your ideas with summaries, paraphrases, and quotations as appropriate.
- Include your own analysis to demonstrate how source information supports your ideas.

Avoid plagiarism.

- Paraphrase carefully and quote accurately to avoid plagiarism.
- Carefully integrate source material into your text.
- Cite sources using an appropriate citation style.

ANALYZING YOUR RHETORICAL SITUATION AND SETTING A SCHEDULE

Making your research manageable begins with defining the scope and goals of your research project. Begin by analyzing your *rhetorical situation*:

- What is your *purpose?* Is it to explain a concept, argue for a position, or analyze the causes of an event or a behavior?

- Who is your *audience* and what will their interests, attitudes, and expectations for the project be? How many and what kinds of resources does your audience expect you to consult? (For college research projects, your audience will likely be your instructor.)

- What *genre* (or *type*) is the research project, and how will that affect the kinds of sources you use? An observational report in the social sciences may demand mainly *primary sources*, such as observations, interviews, and surveys, whereas an argument essay for a history course may require a variety of primary and *secondary sources* (from published historians).

Also be sure you consider the following practical issues before you begin your research project:

- How long should the research project be?

- When is it due?

- Are any interim assignments required (such as an outline or an annotated bibliography)?

Finally, set a schedule. Be sure to take into consideration the projects you have due for other classes as well as other responsibilities (to work or family, for example) or activities.

Some library websites may offer an online scheduler to help you with this process. Look for a link on your library's website, or try out an assignment calculator.

CHOOSING A TOPIC AND GETTING AN OVERVIEW

Often students will be assigned a topic for a research project. If you are free to choose your own topic, consult course materials such as textbooks and handouts to get ideas, and consult your instructor to make sure your topic is appropriate. Once you've chosen an appropriate topic, an overview can help you determine the kind of issues you should consider.

Sometimes conducting an Internet search may give you an idea for a topic. Wikipedia offers a wealth of information, and it is often the first stop for students who are accustomed to consulting the Internet first for information. Be aware, though, that Wikipedia is user-generated rather than traditionally published, and for this reason, the quality of information found there can be inconsistent. Many instructors do not consider Wikipedia a reliable source, so you should ask your teacher for advice on consulting it at this stage.

Your library will likely subscribe to databases, such as *Gale Virtual Reference Library* or *Oxford Reference Online*, that you can search to find information from general encyclopedias and dictionaries as well as specialized, or subject-specific encyclopedias and dictionaries.

General dictionaries, like *Britannica Online*, provide basic information about many topics. **Specialized encyclopedias** provide a comprehensive introduction to your topic, including the key terms you will need to find relevant material in catalogs and databases, and they present subtopics, enabling you to see many possibilities for focusing your research.

Frequently, libraries prepare **research guides** — lists of reliable sources on popular topics. A guide can offer very useful suggested resources for research, so check your library to find out if such a guide is available. You may also find resources that provide good overviews of topics, such as *CQ Researcher*. A reference librarian can help point you in the right direction.

FOCUSING YOUR TOPIC AND DRAFTING RESEARCH QUESTIONS

After you have gotten a sense of the kinds of sources available on your topic, you may be ready to narrow it. Focus on a topic that you can explore thoroughly in the number of pages assigned and the length of time available. Finding your own take on a subject can help you narrow it as well.

You may also want to write questions about your topic and then focus on one or two that can be answered through research. These will become the research questions that will guide your search for information. You may need to add or revise these questions as you conduct your search. The answers you devise can form the basis for your thesis statement.

ESTABLISHING A RESEARCH LOG

One of the best ways to keep track of your research is to keep all your notes in one place, in a **research log.** Your log may be digital — a folder on your computer with files for notes, lists of keywords, and your working bibliography — or analog — a notebook with pockets for copies of sources.

Finding useful sources depends on determining the right **keywords** — words or phrases that describe your topic — to use while searching catalogs, databases, and the Internet. Start your list of keywords by noting the main words from your research question or thesis statement. Look for useful terms in your search results, and use these to expand your list. Then add synonyms (or words with a similar meaning) to expand your list.

For example, a student might start with a term like *home schooling* and then add *home education* or *home study*. After reading an article about her subject, she might also add *student-paced education* or *autonomous learning* to expand her scope.

Keep in mind that different databases use different terms, and terms that work well for one subject might not be successful in another. For example, databases covering education and psychology might index sources on some of the same subjects, but they might not use the same keywords. After consulting the thesaurus in *ERIC*, a database focusing on education, the student might add *parents as teachers*; after consulting the thesaurus in the database *PSYCArticles*, she might add *nontraditional education*.

CREATING A WORKING BIBLIOGRAPHY

A **working bibliography** is an ongoing record of the sources you discover as you research your subject. In your final project, you will probably not end up citing all the sources you list in your working bibliography, but *accurately* recording the information you will need to cite a source *as you identify it* will save you time later.

Your working bibliography should include the following for each source:

- **Author(s) name(s)**

- **Title and subtitle**

- **Publication information:** A book's version or edition number (for example, *revised edition, 3rd ed.*), the name of the source's publisher (except for sources whose authors are their publishers and online sources whose titles are similar to their publishers' names), the date of publication (or copyright year), and the page numbers of the section you consulted; a periodical's name, volume and issue number, date, and the article's page numbers

- **Location information:** The call number of a book; the name of the database through which you accessed the source; the **DOI** (digital object identifier — a permanent identifying code that won't change over time or from database to database) for an article, or if one is unavailable, the full URL (ideally a perma-link, if the site provides one); the date you last accessed the source (for a Web page or website), though you will rarely need to include an access date in your paper's works-cited entry; see pp. 509–36 for more information.

You can store your working bibliography in a computer file, in specialized bibliography software, or even on note cards. Each method has its advantages:

- A **computer file** allows you to move citations into order and incorporate the bibliography into your research project easily using standard software (such as Word or Excel).

- A **citation manager** (such as RefWorks, Zotero, EndNote, or the Bedford Bibliographer) designed for creating bibliographies helps you create the citation in the specific citation style (such as MLA or APA) required by your discipline. These software programs are not perfect, however; you still need to double-check your citations against the models in the style manual you are using or in the MLA and APA citation sections of this Appendix (pp. 509–26 and 527–36).

- A **notebook** allows you to keep everything — working bibliography, annotations, notes, copies of chapters or articles — all in one place.

This Appendix presents two common documentation styles — one created by the Modern Language Association (MLA) and widely used in the humanities, and the other advocated by the American Psychological Association (APA) and used in the social sciences. Other disciplines have their own preferred styles of documentation. Confirm with your instructor which documentation style is required for your assignment so that you can follow that style for all the sources you put in your working bibliography.

ANNOTATING YOUR WORKING BIBLIOGRAPHY

An **annotated bibliography** provides an overview of sources that you have considered for your research project. Researchers frequently create annotated bibliographies to keep a record of sources and their thoughts about them. Researchers sometimes also publish annotated bibliographies to provide others with a useful tool for beginning research projects of their own.

What an annotated bibliography includes depends on the researcher's writing situation. But most answer these questions about each source:

- What kind of source is this?

- What is the main point of the source?

- How might I use the source?

- How might my sources be related?

- What information will I need to cite the source?

Some annotated bibliographies also include an introduction that explains the subject, purpose, and scope of the annotated bibliography and may describe how and why the researcher selected those sources. For instance, an annotated bibliography featuring works about computer animation might have the following introduction:

> Early animations of virtual people in computer games tended to be oblivious to their surroundings, reacting only when hit by moving objects, and then in ways that were not always appropriate — that is, a small object might generate a large

effect. In the past few years, however, computer animators have turned their attention to designing virtual people who react appropriately to events around them. The sources below represent the last two years' worth of publications on the subject from the *IEEE Xplore* database.

TAKING NOTES ON YOUR SOURCES

The summaries that you include in a working bibliography or the annotations that you make on a printed or digital copy of a source are useful reminders, but you should also make notes that analyze the text, that synthesize what you are learning with ideas you have gleaned elsewhere or with your own ideas, and that evaluate the quality of the source.

For more on annotating sources or synthesizing, see Chapter 2, pp. 17 or 27.

You will mine your notes for language to use in your draft, so be careful to

- summarize accurately, using your own words and sentence structures

- paraphrase without borrowing the language or sentence structure of the source

- quote exactly and place all language from the source in quotation marks.

You can take notes on a photocopy of a printed text or use comments or highlighting to annotate a digital text. Whenever possible, download, print, photocopy, or scan useful sources, so that you can read and make notes at your leisure and so that you can double-check your summaries, paraphrases, and quotations of sources against the original. These strategies, along with those discussed later in this chapter in the section Using Sources to Support Your Ideas (pp. 497–508), will keep you from plagiarizing inadvertently.

FINDING SOURCES

Students today are surrounded by a wealth of information — in print, online, in videos and podcasts, even face-to-face. This wealth can make finding the information you need to support your ideas exciting, but it also means you will have to develop a research strategy and sift through possible sources carefully. What you are writing about, who will read your writing project, and the type of writing you are doing will help you decide what types of sources will be most appropriate.

Does your writing project require you to depend mainly on **secondary sources**, such as books and articles that analyze and summarize a subject, or develop **primary sources,** such as interviews with experts, surveys, or observational studies you conduct yourself and laboratory reports, historical documents, diaries, letters, or works of literature written by others? Whatever sources you decide will best help you support your claims, this chapter will help you find or develop the resources you need.

SEARCHING LIBRARY CATALOGS AND DATABASES

For most college research projects, finding appropriate sources starts with your library's home page, where you can

- find (and sometimes access) books, reference sources (such as encyclopedias and dictionaries), reports, documents, multimedia resources (such as films and audio recordings), and much more;

- use your library's databases to find (and sometimes access) articles in newspapers, magazines, and scholarly journals, as well as in reference sources;

- find **research guides,** lists of reliable sources on topics frequently studied by students.

Many libraries now offer unified search, which allows patrons to search for books and articles in magazines, newspapers, and scholarly journals simultaneously, from the home page. If you aren't sure whether you will need to search for books and articles using separate catalogs and databases, consult a librarian. Your library's home page is also the place to find information about the brick-and-mortar library — its floor plan, its hours of operation, and the journals it has available in print. You might even be able to find links to what you need in other libraries or get online help from a librarian.

Using Appropriate Search Terms

Just as with a search engine like Google, you can search a library catalog or database by typing your search terms — an author's name, the title of a work, a subject term or keyword, even a call number — into the search box. To search successfully, put yourself in the position of the people writing about your topic to figure out what words they might have used. If your topic is "ecology," for example, you may find information under the keywords *ecosystem, environment, pollution,* and *endangered species,* as well as a number of other related keywords, depending on the focus of the research and your area of study.

Broaden or Narrow Your Results

When conducting a search, you may get too few hits and have to broaden your topic. To broaden your search, try the following:

Replace a specific term with a more general term	Replace *sister* or *brother* with *sibling*
Substitute a synonym for one of your keywords	Replace *home study* with *home schooling* or *student-paced education*
Combine terms with *or* to get results with either or both terms	Search *home study or home schooling* to get results that include both *home study* and *home schooling*
Add a wildcard character, usually an asterisk (*) or question mark (?) (Check the search tips to find out which wildcard character is in use.)	Search *home school** or *home school?* to retrieve results for *home school, home schooling,* and *home-schooler*

Most often, you'll get too many hits. To narrow a search, try the following:

Add a specific term	Search not just *home schooling* but *home schooling statistics*
Combine search terms into phrases or word strings	Search *Home schooling in California*

In many cases, using phrases or word strings will limit your results to items that include *all* the words you have specified. You may need to insert quotation marks around the terms or insert the word *and* between them to create a search phrase or word string. Check the search tips for the database, catalog, or search engine you are using.

Finding Books (and Other Sources)

Books housed in academic library collections offer two distinct advantages to the student researcher:

1. They provide in-depth coverage of topics.
2. They are more likely to be published by reputable presses that strive for accuracy and reliability.

You can generally search for books (as well as reference works and multimedia resources) by author's name, title, keyword, or subject heading, and narrow your search by using advanced search options.

Though you can search by keywords, most college libraries use special subject headings devised by the Library of Congress (the national library of the United States). Finding and using the subject headings most relevant to your search will make your research more productive. You can locate the subject headings your library uses by pulling up the record of a relevant book you have already found and looking for the list of words under the heading "Subject" or "Subject headings." Including these terms in your search may help you find additional relevant resources. Ask a librarian for help if you cannot identify the headings.

FIGURE A.1 **A Book's Catalog Record** An item's record provides a lot more information than just the author, title, and call number. You can also find the subject headings by which it was cataloged, the item's status (whether it has been checked out), and its location. Some libraries may allow you to place a hold on a book or find similar items. Some libraries, such as the one whose catalog is depicted here, even allow you to capture the book's record with your smartphone or have the information texted or e-mailed to you.

Finding Articles in Periodicals

Much of the information you will use to write your research project will come from articles in **periodicals,** publications such as newspapers, newsletters, magazines, or scholarly journals that are published at regular intervals. To locate relevant articles on your topic, start your search with one of your library's databases. Why not just start with a Google search? There are two very good reasons:

1. Google will pull up articles from any publication it indexes, from freely available personal websites to scholarly journals. Results rise to the top of the list based on a number of factors but not necessarily the reliability of the source. A Google search will turn up helpful sources, but you will need to spend a good deal of time sifting through the numerous hits you get to find sources that are both relevant and reliable. (Google Scholar may help you locate more reliable sources than those you might find through a typical Google search.)

2. Sources you find through Google may ask you to pay for access to articles, or they may require a subscription. Your library probably already subscribes to these sources on your behalf. Also adding databases to your search strategy will diversify your search and provide you with access to resources not available through a search engine such as Google.

Most college libraries subscribe at least to **general databases** and **subject-specific databases** as well as databases that index newspapers. General databases (such as *Academic OneFile, Academic Search Premier* or *Elite* or *Complete,* and *ProQuest Central*) index articles from both scholarly journals and popular magazines.[1] Subject-specific databases (such as *ERIC — Education Resources Information Center, MLA International Bibliography, PsycINFO,* and *General Science Full Text*) index articles only in their discipline. Newspaper databases (such as *Alt-Press Watch, LexisNexis Academic, National Newspaper Index,* and *ProQuest Newspapers*) index newspaper articles. For college-level research projects, you may use all three types of databases to find appropriate articles. (Note that many libraries also offer ways to search multiple databases at once.)

If your database search returns too many unhelpful results, use the search strategies discussed on p. 475 or use the database's advanced search options to refine your search. Many databases allow users to restrict results to articles published in academic journals, for example, or to articles that were published after a certain date (see fig. A.2 on p. 478). Use the Help option or ask a librarian for assistance.

Increasingly, databases provide access to full-text articles, either in HTML or PDF format. When you have the option, choose the PDF format, as this will provide you with photographs, graphs, and charts in context, and you will be able to

---

[1]The names of databases change over time and vary from library to library, so ask your instructor or a reference librarian if you need help.

Database

Options for narrowing search results

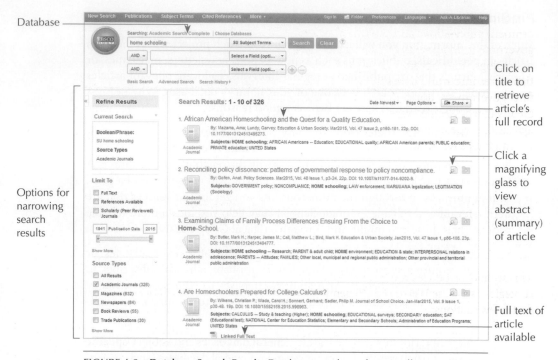

Click on title to retrieve article's full record

Click a magnifying glass to view abstract (summary) of article

Full text of article available

FIGURE A.2   **Database Search Results** Database search results may allow you to access an article directly or provide the information you need to locate (and cite) it, including the title, the author(s), and the article's publication information. The database may also provide options for narrowing a search by publication date, source type (academic journal versus newspaper, for example), and so on.

include the page numbers in your citation. If you find a citation to an article that is not accessible through a database, however, do not ignore it. Check with a librarian to find out how you can get a copy of the article.

SEARCHING FOR GOVERNMENT DOCUMENTS AND STATISTICAL INFORMATION

Federal, state, and local governments make many of their documents available directly through the Web. For example, you can access statistical data about the United States through the U.S. Census Bureau's website, and you can learn a great deal about other countries through the websites of the U.S. State Department and the CIA.

The Library of Congress provides a useful portal for finding government documents (federal, state, local, and international) through its website, and the U.S. Government Printing Office provides free electronic access to documents produced by the federal government through its FDsys Web page.

Some libraries have collections of government publications and provide access to government documents through databases or catalogs. Your library may also offer statistical resources and data sets. You can also find government documents online using an advanced Google search and specifying *.gov* as the type of site or **domain** you want to search (see fig A.3).

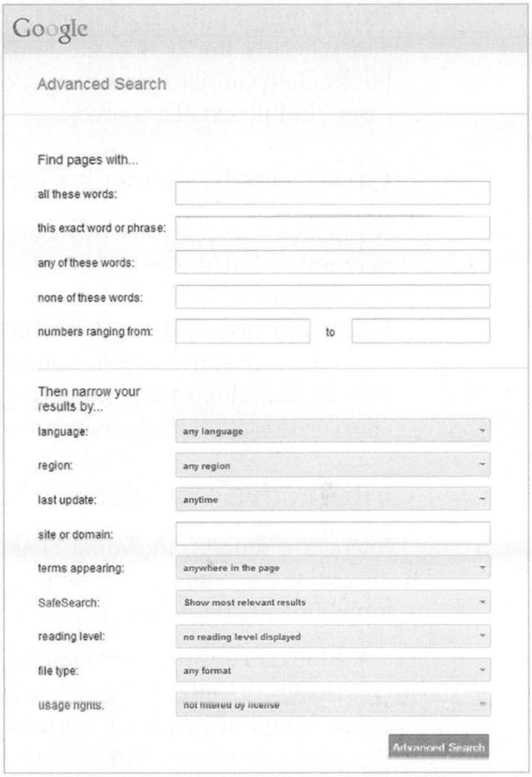

SEARCHING FOR WEBSITES AND INTERACTIVE SOURCES

This section introduces you to some tools and strategies to use the Web more efficiently. But first, a few cautions:

- *Your research project will be only as credible as the sources you use.* Because search engines index Web sources without evaluating them, not all the results a search engine generates will be reliable and relevant to your purposes.

FIGURE A.3 An Advanced Google Search
Use Google's advanced search to narrow results.

- *Web sources may not be stable.* A website that existed last week may no longer be available today, or its content may have changed. Be sure to record the information you need to cite a source when you first find it, as well as the date you find it.

- *Web sources must be documented.* No matter what your source — a library book, a scholarly article, or a website or Web page — you will need to cite and document your source in your list of works cited or references. If you are publishing your report online, check also to determine whether you will need permission to reproduce an image or any other elements.

Using Google Scholar and Google Book Search

Although you may use search engines like Google with great rapidity and out of habit, as a college researcher you are likely to find it worthwhile to familiarize yourself with other parts of the Google search site. Of particular interest to the academic writer are Google Scholar and Google Book Search. Google Scholar retrieves articles from a number of scholarly databases and a wide range of general-interest and scholarly books. Google Book Search searches both popular and scholarly books. Both Google Scholar and Google Book Search offer overviews and, in some cases, the full text of a source.

Other Useful Search Options

No matter how precisely you search the Web with a standard search engine, you may not hit on the best available resources. Starting your search from a subject guide, such as those provided by the *Internet Public Library* or the librarians at your school, can direct you to relevant and reliable sources of online information.

Whatever search engine you use, always click on the link called *Help*, *Hints*, or *Tips* on the search tool's home page to find out more about the commands and advanced-search techniques it offers to narrow (or expand) your search.

Interactive Sources

Interactive sources, including blogs, wikis, RSS feeds, social networking sites and discussion lists, can also be useful sources of information, especially if your research project focuses on a current event or late-breaking news.

- **Blogs** are websites that are updated regularly, often many times a day. They are usually organized chronologically, with the newest posts at the top, and may contain links or news stories but generally focus on the opinions of the blog host and visitors. Blogs by experts in the field are likely to be more informative than blogs by amateurs or fans.

- **Wikis** — of which Wikipedia is the best-known example — offer content contributed and modified collaboratively by a community of users. Wikis can be very useful for gleaning background information, but because (in most cases) anyone can write or revise wiki entries, many instructors will not accept them as reliable sources for college-level research projects. Use wikis cautiously.

- **RSS (Really Simple Syndication) feeds** aggregate frequently updated sites, such as news sites and blogs, into links in a single Web page or e-mail. Most search engines provide this service, as do sites such as NewzCrawler and FeedDemon. RSS feeds can be useful if you are researching news stories or political campaigns.

- **Social networking sites,** like Facebook and Twitter, allow users to create groups or pages on topics of interest or to follow the thoughts and activities of newsmakers.

- **Discussion lists** are electronic mailing lists that allow members to post comments and get feedback from others interested in the same topic. The most reliable discussion lists are moderated and attract experts on the topic. Many online communities provide some kind of indexing or search mechanism so that you can look for "threads" (conversations) related to your topic.

Although you need to evaluate carefully the information you find in all sources, you must be especially careful with information from social networking sites and discussion lists. However, such sources can provide up-to-the-minute information. Also be aware that whereas most online communities welcome guests and newcomers, others may perceive your questions as intrusive or naive. It may be useful to "lurk" (that is, just to read posts) before making a contribution.

CONDUCTING FIELD RESEARCH

In universities, government agencies, and the business world, **field research** can be as important as library research. In some majors, like education or sociology, as well as in service-learning courses, primary research projects are common. Even in the writing projects covered in Chapters 3–10, observations, interviews, and surveys may be useful or even necessary. As you consider how you might use field research in your writing projects, ask your instructor whether your institution requires you to obtain approval, and check the documentation sections that appear later in this chapter to learn about citing interviews you conduct yourself.

CONDUCTING OBSERVATIONAL STUDIES

Observational studies are commonly assigned in college writing, psychology, and sociology courses. To conduct an observational study effectively, follow these guidelines:

Planning an Observational Study

To ensure that your observational visits are productive, plan them carefully:

- **Arrange access if necessary.** Visits to a private location (such as a day-care center or school) require special permission, so be sure to arrange your visit in advance. When making your request, state your intentions and goals for your study directly and fully. You may be surprised at how receptive people can be to a college student on assignment. But have a fallback plan in case your request is refused or the business or institution places constraints on you that hamper your research.

- **Develop a hypothesis.** In advance, write down a tentative assumption about what you expect to learn from your study — your **hypothesis.** This will guide your observations and notes, and you can adjust your expectations in response to what you observe if necessary. Consider, too, how your presence will affect those whom you are observing, so you can minimize your impact or take the effect of your presence into consideration.

- **Consider how best to conduct the observation.** Decide where to place yourself to make your observations most effectively. Should you move around to observe from multiple vantage points, or will a single perspective be more productive?

Making Observations

Strategies for conducting your observation include the following:

- **Description:** Describe in detail the setting and the people you are observing. Note the physical arrangement and functions of the space, and the number, activities, and appearance of the people. Record as many details as possible, draw diagrams or sketches if helpful, and take photographs or videos if allowed (and if those you are observing do not object).

- **Narration:** Narrate the activities going on around you. Try initially to be an innocent observer: Pretend that you have never seen anything like this activity or place before, and explain what you are seeing step by step, even if what you are writing seems obvious. Include interactions among people, and capture snippets of conversations (in quotation marks) if possible.

- **Analysis and classification:** Break the scene down into its component parts, identify common threads, and organize the details into categories.

Take careful notes during your visit if you can do so unobtrusively, or immediately afterward if you can't. You can use a notebook and pencil, a laptop or tablet, or a smartphone to record your notes. Choose whatever is least disruptive to those around you. You may need to use abbreviations and symbols to capture your observations on-site, but be sure to convert such shorthand into words and phrases as soon as possible after the visit so that you don't forget its significance.

Writing Your Observational Study

Immediately after your visit, fill in any gaps in your notes, and review your notes to look for meaningful patterns. You might find mapping strategies, such as *clustering* or *outlining*, useful for discovering patterns in your notes. Take some time to reflect on what you saw. Asking yourself questions like these might help:

For more on outlining, see Chapter 2, pp. 23 24.

- How did what I observed fit my own or my readers' likely preconceptions of the place or activity? Did my observations upset any of my preconceptions? What, if anything, seemed contradictory or out of place?

- What interested me most about the activity or place? What are my readers likely to find interesting about it?

- What did I learn?

Your purpose in writing about your visit is to share your insights into the meaning and significance of your observations. Assume that your readers have never been to the place, and provide enough detail for it to come alive for them. Decide on the perspective you want to convey, and choose the details necessary to convey your insights.

CONDUCTING INTERVIEWS

A successful interview involves careful planning before the interview, but it also requires keen listening skills and the ability to ask appropriate follow-up questions while conducting the interview. Courtesy and consideration for your subject are crucial at all stages of the process.

Planning the Interview

Planning an interview involves the following:

- **Choosing an interview subject.** For a profile of an individual, your interview will primarily be with one person; for a profile of an organization, you might interview several people, all with different roles or points of view. Prepare a list of interview candidates, as busy people might turn you down.

- **Arranging the interview.** Give your prospective subject a brief description of your project, and show some sincere enthusiasm for your project. Keep in mind that the person you want to interview will be donating valuable time to you, so call ahead to arrange the interview, allow your subject to specify the amount of time she or he can spare, and come prepared.

Preparing for the Interview

In preparation for the interview, consider your objectives:

- Do you want details or a general orientation (the "big picture") from this interview?

- Do you want this interview to lead you to interviews with other key people?

- Do you want mainly facts or opinions?

- Do you need to clarify something you have observed or read? If so, what?

Making an observational visit and doing some background reading beforehand can be helpful. Find out as much as you can about the organization or company (size, location, purpose, etc.), as well as the key people.

Good questions are essential to a successful interview. You will likely want to ask a few **closed questions** (questions that request specific information) and a number of **open questions** (questions that give the respondent range and flexibility and encourage him or her to share anecdotes, personal revelations, and expressions of attitudes):

Open Questions	*Closed Questions*
• What do you think about ....?	• How do you do ....?
• Describe your reaction when .... happened.	• What does .... mean?
	• How was .... developed?
• Tell me about a time you were	

The best questions encourage the subject to talk freely but stick to the point. You may need to ask a follow-up question to refocus the discussion or to clarify a point, so be prepared. If you are unsure about a subject's answer, follow up by rephrasing that answer, prefacing it by saying something like "Let me see if I have this right" or "Am I correct in saying that you feel ....?" Avoid *forced-choice* questions ("Which do you think is the better approach: .... or ....?") and *leading* questions ("How well do you think .... is doing?").

During the Interview

Another key to good interviewing is flexibility. Ask the questions you have prepared, but also be ready to shift gears to take full advantage of what your subject can offer.

- **Take notes.** Take notes during the interview, even if you are recording your discussion. You might find it useful to divide several pages of a notebook into two columns or to set up a word processing file in two columns. Use the left-hand column to note details about the scene and your subject or about your impressions overall; in the right-hand column, write several questions and record the answers. Remember that how something is said is as important as what is said. Look for material that will give texture to your writing — gesture, verbal inflection, facial expression, body language, physical appearance (dress, hair), or anything else that makes the person an individual.

- **Listen carefully.** Avoid interrupting your subject or talking about yourself; rather, listen carefully and guide the discussion by asking follow-up questions and probing politely for more information.

- **Be considerate.** Do not stay longer than the time you were allotted unless your subject agrees to continue the discussion, and show your appreciation for the time you have been given by thanking your subject and offering her or him a copy of your finished project.

Following the Interview

After the interview, do the following:

- **Reflect on the interview.** As soon as you finish the interview, find a quiet place to reflect on it and to review and amplify your notes. Asking yourself questions like these might help: What did I learn? What seemed contradictory or surprising about the interview? How did what was said fit my own or my readers' likely expectations about the person, activity, or place? How can I summarize my impressions?

  Also make a list of any questions that arise. You may want to follow up with your subject for more information, but limit yourself to one e-mail or phone call to avoid becoming a bother.

- **Thank your subject.** Send your interview subject a thank-you note or e-mail within twenty-four hours of the interview. Try to reference something specific from the interview, something you thought was surprising or thought-provoking. And send your subject a copy of your finished project with a note of appreciation.

CONDUCTING SURVEYS

Surveys let you gauge the opinions and knowledge of large numbers of people. You might conduct a survey to gauge opinion in a political science course or to assess familiarity with a television show for a media studies course. You might also conduct a survey to assess the seriousness of a problem for a service-learning class or in response to an assignment to propose a solution to a problem (Chapter 10). You can choose to administer the survey either in person or on a survey creation and distribution site such as SurveyMonkey, SurveyGizmo, or even Facebook. This section briefly outlines procedures you can follow to carry out an informal survey, and it highlights areas where caution is needed. Colleges and universities have restrictions about the use and distribution of questionnaires, so check your institution's policy or obtain permission before beginning the survey.

Designing Your Survey

Use the following tips to design an effective survey:

- **Conduct background research.** You may need to conduct background research on your topic. For example, to create a survey on scheduling appointments at the student health center, you may first need to contact the health center to determine its scheduling practices, and you may want to interview health center personnel.

- **Focus your study.** Before starting out, decide what you expect to learn (your hypothesis). Make sure your focus is limited — focus on one or two important issues — so you can craft a brief questionnaire that respondents can complete quickly and easily and so that you can organize and report on your results more easily.

- **Write questions.** Plan to use a number of **closed questions** (questions that request specific information), such as *two-way questions, multiple-choice questions, ranking scale questions,* and *checklist questions* (see fig. A.4 on the following page). You will also likely want to include a few **open questions** (questions that give respondents the opportunity to write their answers in their own words). Closed questions are easier to tally, but open questions are likely to provide you with deeper insight and a fuller sense of respondents' opinions. Whatever questions you develop, be sure that you provide all the answer options your respondents are likely to want, and make sure your questions are clear and unambiguous.

- **Identify the population you are trying to reach.** Even for an informal study, you should try to get a reasonably representative group. For example, to study satisfaction with appointment scheduling at the student health center, you would need to include a representative sample of all the students at the school — not only those who have visited the health center. Determine the demographic makeup of your school, and arrange to reach out to a representative sample.

This is a survey about scheduling appointments at the student health center. Your participation will help determine how long students have to wait to use the clinic's services and how these services might be more conveniently scheduled. The survey should take only 3 to 4 minutes to complete. All responses are confidential.

1. Have you ever made an appointment at the clinic?   Two-way question

   ❑ Yes   ❑ No

If you answered "No" to question 1, skip to question 5.   Filter

2. How frequently have you had to wait more than 10 minutes at the clinic for a scheduled appointment?

    ❑ Always   ❑ Usually   ❑ Occasionally   ❑ Never   Multiple-choice questions

3. Have you ever had to wait more than 30 minutes at the clinic for a scheduled appointment?

    ❑ Yes   ❑ No   ❑ Uncertain

4. Based on your experience with the clinic, how would you rate its system for scheduling appointments?

    ❑ 1 (poor)   ❑ 2 (adequate)   ❑ 3 (good)   ❑ 4 (excellent)

5. Given your present work and class schedule, which times during the day (Monday through Friday) would be the most and least convenient for you to schedule appointments at the clinic? (Rank your choices from 1 for most convenient time to 4 for least convenient time.)   Ranking questions

	1	2	3	4
	(most convenient)	(more convenient)	(less convenient)	(least convenient)
morning (7 a.m.–noon)	❑	❑	❑	❑
afternoon (noon–5 p.m.)	❑	❑	❑	❑
dinnertime (5–7 p.m.)	❑	❑	❑	❑
evening (7–10 p.m.)	❑	❑	❑	❑

6. If you have had an appointment at the student health center within the last six months, please evaluate your experience.

7. If you have had an appointment at the student health center within the last six months, please indicate what you believe would most improve scheduling of appointments at the clinic.   Open questions

8. If you have *never* had an appointment at the student health center, please indicate why you have not made use of this service.

Thank you for your participation.

FIGURE A.4   **Sample Questionnaire: Scheduling at the Student Health Center**

- **Design the questionnaire.** Begin your questionnaire with a brief, clear introduction stating the purpose of your survey and explaining how you intend to use the results. Give advice on answering the questions, estimate the amount of time needed to complete the questionnaire, and — unless you are administering the survey in person — indicate the date by which completed surveys must be returned. Organize your questions from least to most complicated or in any order that seems logical, and format your questionnaire so that it is easy to read and complete.

- **Test the questionnaire.** Ask at least three readers to complete your questionnaire before you distribute it. Time them as they respond, or ask them to keep track of how long they take to complete it (some of the online services will do this for you automatically). Discuss with them any confusion or problems they experience. Review their responses with them to be certain that each question is eliciting the information you want it to elicit. From what you learn, revise your questions and adjust the format of the questionnaire.

Administering the Survey

The more respondents you have, the better, but constraints of time and expense will almost certainly limit the number. As few as twenty-five could be adequate for an informal study, but to get twenty-five responses, you may need to solicit fifty or more participants.

You can conduct the survey in person or over the telephone; use an online service such as SurveyMonkey or Zoomerang; e-mail the questionnaires; or conduct the survey using a social media site such as Facebook. You may also distribute surveys to groups of people in class or around campus and wait to collect their responses.

Each method has its advantages and disadvantages. For example, face-to-face surveys allow you to get more in-depth responses, but participants may be unwilling to answer personal questions face-to-face. Though fewer than half the surveys you solicit using survey software are likely to be completed (your invitations may wind up in a spam folder), online software will tabulate responses automatically.

Writing the Report

When writing your report, include a summary of the results, as well as an interpretation of what the results mean.

- **Summarize the results.** Once you have the completed questionnaires, tally the results from the closed questions. (If you conducted the survey online, this will have already been done for you.) You can give the results from the closed questions as percentages, either within the text of your report or in one or more tables or graphs. Next, read all respondents' answers to each open question and summarize the responses by classifying the answers. You might classify them as positive, negative, or neutral or by grouping them into more specific categories. Finally, identify quotations that express a range of responses succinctly and engagingly to use in your report.

- **Interpret the results.** Once you have tallied the responses and read answers to open questions, think about what the results mean. Does the information you gathered support your hypothesis? If so, how? If the results do not support your hypothesis, where did you go wrong? Was there a problem with the way you worded your questions or with the sample of the population you contacted? Or was your hypothesis in need of adjustment?

- **Write the report.** Research reports in the social sciences use a standard format, with headings introducing the following categories of information:

  - **Abstract:** A brief summary of the report, usually including one sentence summarizing each section

  - **Introduction:** Includes context for the study (other similar studies, if any, and their results), the question or questions the researcher wanted to answer and why this question (or these questions) is important, and the limits of what the researcher expected the survey to reveal

  - **Methods:** Includes the questionnaire, identifies the number and type of participants, and describes the methods used for administering the questionnaire and recording data

  - **Results:** Includes the data from the survey, with limited commentary or interpretation

  - **Discussion:** Includes the researcher's interpretation of results, an explanation of how the data support the hypothesis (or not), and the conclusions the researcher has drawn from the research

EVALUATING SOURCES

As soon as you start your search for sources, you should begin evaluating what you find not only to decide whether they are relevant to your research project but also to determine how *credible*, or reliable, they are.

CHOOSING RELEVANT SOURCES

Sources are **relevant** when they help you achieve your aims with your readers. Relevant sources may

- explain terms or concepts;

- provide background information;

- provide evidence in support of your claims;

- provide alternative viewpoints or interpretations;

- lend authority to your point of view.

A search for sources may reveal more books and articles than any researcher could ever actually consult. A search on the term *home schooling* in one database, for example, got 1,172 hits. Obviously, a glance at all the hits to determine which are most relevant would take far too much time. To speed up the process, resources, such as library catalogs, databases, and search engines, provide tools to narrow the results. For example, in one popular all-purpose database, you can limit results by publication date, language, and publication or source type, among other options. (Check the Help screen to learn how to use these tools.)

For more on focusing search results and selecting search terms, see pp. 474–81 earlier in this Appendix.

In the database used in Figure A.5 (p. 491), limiting the *home schooling* results to articles published in scholarly journals in English over the last ten years reduced the number of hits to 56, a far more reasonable number to review. Remember that if you have too few results or your results are not targeted correctly, you can expand your search by changing your search terms or removing limits selectively.

After you have identified a reasonable number of relevant sources, examine the sources themselves:

- Read the preface, introduction, or conclusion of books, or the first or last few paragraphs of articles, to determine which aspect of the topic is addressed or which approach to the topic is taken. To obtain a clear picture of a topic, researchers need to consider sources that address different aspects of the topic or take different approaches.

- Look at the headings or references in articles, or the table of contents and index in books, to see how much of the content relates specifically to your topic.

- Consider the way the source is written: Sources written for general readers may be accessible but may not analyze the subject in depth. Extremely specialized

Publication: What do you know about the periodical? Is it well respected?

Date: Is the article recent enough for your area of study, or is it a classic? (Some older, "classic" sources may offer authoritative perspectives, but for current controversies or recent developments, use recent sources.)

Abstract: Does the article address your topic? What angle does it take?

Authors: Are they experts in the field? Do they have relevant background?

Title: Does the article address your topic?

Length: Does the length suggest the topic is treated in depth?

Subject terms: Are any of your keywords listed? Should any of these terms be added to your keywords list?

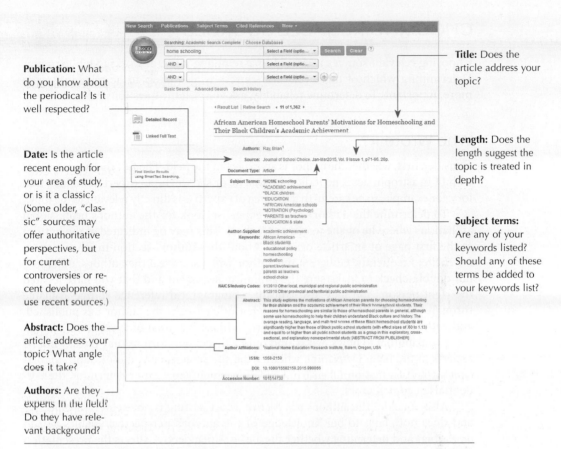

FIGURE A.5 **Analyzing the Detailed Record of an Article from a Periodicals Database** Analyze the detailed record of an article to determine whether the article itself is worth reading by asking yourself the following questions: Does the title suggest that the article addresses your topic? Are the authors experts in the field? Was the article published in a periodical that is likely to be reliable, was it published recently, and is it lengthy enough to indicate that the topic is treated in depth? Does the abstract (or summary) suggest that the article addresses your topic? If so, what angle does it take?

works may be too technical. Poorly written sources may be unreliable. (See Choosing Reliable Sources, below, for more on scholarly versus popular sources and for a discussion of why researchers should avoid sources that are poorly written or riddled with errors.)

If close scrutiny leaves you with too few sources — or too many sources from too few perspectives — conduct a search using additional or alternative keywords, or explore links to related articles, look at the references in a particularly useful article, or look for other sources by an author whose work you find useful.

CHOOSING RELIABLE SOURCES

Choosing relevant sources is crucial to assembling a useful working bibliography. Determining which of those relevant sources is also likely to be reliable is even more important. To determine reliability, ask yourself the questions below.

Who Wrote It?

Consider, first, whether the author is an expert in the field. The fact that someone has a Ph.D. in astrophysics is no indication that he or she will be an expert in military history, for example, so be careful that the area of expertise is directly relevant to the topic.

To determine the author's area of expertise, look for the author's professional affiliation (where he or she works or teaches). This may be indicated at the bottom of the first page of an article or in an "About the Author" section in a book or on a website. Frequently, Googling the author will also reveal the author's affiliation, but double-check to make sure the affiliation is current and that you have located the right person. You may also consult a biographical reference source available through your library. Looking to see what other works the author has published, and with whom, can also help you ascertain his or her areas of expertise.

Contributors to blogs, wikis, and online discussion forums may or may not be experts in the field. Determine whether the site screens contributors, and double-check any information taken from sites for which you cannot determine the credentials of contributors.

Also consider the author's *perspective*. Most writing is not neutral or objective and does not claim to be. Knowledge of the author's perspective enables you to assess bias and determine whether the author's perspective affects the presentation of his or her argument. To determine the author's perspective, look for the main point and ask yourself questions like these:

For more details on strategies for evaluating the logic of an argument, see Chapter 2, pp. 40–41.

- What evidence does the author provide to support this point? Is it from authoritative sources? Is it persuasive?

- Does the author make concessions to or refute opposing arguments?

- Does the author avoid fallacies, confrontational phrasing, and loaded words?

How Recently Was It Published?

In general, especially when you are writing about science or technology, current events, or emerging trends, you should consult the most up-to-date sources available on your subject. The date of publication for articles you locate should be indicated in your search results. For a print book, look for the copyright date on the copyright page (usually on the back of the title page); for an e-book, look for the copyright date at the beginning or end of the electronic file. If your source is a website, consider when it, and the content within it, was last updated (often indi-cated at the bottom of the Web page or home page).

You may also need older, "classic" sources that establish the principles, theo-ries, and data on which later work is based and may provide a useful perspective for evaluating other works. To determine which sources are classics, note the ones that are cited most often in encyclopedia articles, lists of works cited or references, and recent works on the subject. You may also want to consult your instructor or a librarian to help you determine which works are classics in your field.

Is the Source Scholarly, Popular, or for a Trade Group?

Scholarly sources (whether books or articles) are written by and for experts in a field of study, frequently professors or academic researchers. They can be challeng-ing to read and understand because they use the language of the field and terminol-ogy that may be unfamiliar to those outside the discipline, but they are considered reliable because the contents are written by specialists and **peer-reviewed** (reviewed by specialists) before publication. Scholarly sources also tend to delve deeply into a subject, often a narrowly defined subject. Scholarly sources may be published by a university press, a scholarly organization, or a commercial publisher (such as Klu-wer Academic or Blackwell). Though scholarly sources may provide an overview of the subject, they generally focus on a specific issue or argument and generally con-tain a great deal of original research.

In contrast, **popular sources** are written to entertain and educate the gen-eral public. For the most part, they are written by journalists who have conducted research and interviewed experts. They may include original research, especially on current events or emerging trends. Mainly, though, they report on and summarize original research and are written for interested, nonspecialist readers.

Of course, popular sources range widely along the reliability spectrum. Highly respected newspapers and magazines, such as the *New York Times*, the *Guardian*, the *Economist*, and *Harper's Magazine*, publish original research on news and cul-ture. These newspapers and magazines check facts carefully and are often consid-ered appropriate sources for research projects in entry-level courses (although you should check with your instructor to find out her or his expectations). Magazines that focus on celebrity gossip, such as *People* and *Us Weekly*, are unlikely to be con-sidered appropriate sources for a college-level research project. Table A.1 (p. 494) summarizes some of the important differences between scholarly journals and pop-ular magazines.

Trade publications — periodicals that report on news and technical advances in a specific industry — are written for those employed in the industry and include such titles as *Advertising Age*, *World Cement*, and *American Machinist*. Some trade publications may be appropriate for college research projects, especially in the sciences, but keep in mind that these publications are intended for a specialist audi-ence and may focus on marketing products to professionals in the field.

TABLE A.1   Scholarly Journals versus Popular Magazines and Trade Publications

Scholarly Journals	Popular Magazines	Trade Publications
Journals are usually published four to six times per year.	Magazines are usually published weekly or monthly.	Trade publications may be published daily, weekly, monthly, or quarterly, depending on the industry covered.
Articles are usually written by scholars (with *Ph.D.* or other academic affiliations after their names).	Authors of articles are journalists but may quote experts.	Articles may be written by professionals or by journalists with quotes from experts.
Many articles have more than one author.	Most articles have a single author.	Authors of articles may or may not be named.
In print journals, the title page often appears on the cover, and the covers frequently lack artwork.	Photographs, usually in color, appear on the covers of most print magazines.	Photographs, usually in color, appear on the covers of most print trade publications and on their websites.
Articles may include charts, tables, figures, and quotations from other scholarly sources.	Articles frequently include color pictures and sidebars.	Articles frequently include color pictures and sidebars.
An abstract (summary) of the article may appear on the first page.	A headline or engaging description may precede the article.	Headlines often include names or terms familiar only to industry insiders.
Most articles are fairly long—five to twenty pages.	Most articles are fairly short—one to five pages.	Most articles are fairly short—one to five pages.
Articles cite sources and provide a bibliography (a list of works cited or references).	Articles rarely include a list of works cited or references but may mention or quote experts.	Articles rarely include a list of works cited or references but may mention or quote experts.

Who Published It?

Determining who published or sponsored a source you are considering can help you gauge its reliability and ascertain the publication's slant (or point of view). Look to see whether the source was published by a commercial publisher (such as St. Martin's or Random House); a university press (such as the University of Nebraska Press); a corporation, an organization, or an interest group (such as the RAND Corporation, the World Wildlife Fund, or the National Restaurant

Association); a government agency (such as the Internal Revenue Service or the U.S. Census Bureau); or the author on his or her own. Determining the publisher or sponsor is particularly important for material published on the Web.

If your source is a Web page, look at the URL (uniform resource locator) to find its top-level domain, which is indicated by a suffix. Some of the most useful ones are listed here:

.gov U.S. federal government and some state or local government institutions

.org nonprofit organizations

.edu educational institutions

.com businesses and commercial enterprises

.net usually businesses or organizations associated with networks

.mil the U.S. military

For the most part, *.gov* and *.edu* are the most likely to offer reliable sources of information for a college research project. However, sources with any of these domains may vary in reliability. For example, a file with a *.com* suffix may offer a highly reliable history of a corporation and be an appropriate source for someone writing a history of corporate America, whereas a file with an *.edu* suffix may have been posted by a student or by a faculty member outside his or her area of expertise.

It is essential to look at websites carefully. Determine who sponsors the site: Is it a business, a professional group, a private organization, an educational institution, a government agency, or an individual? Look for a link, usually at the top or the bottom of the home page, called something like "Who We Are" or "About Us." If you cannot determine who sponsors a site, carefully double-check any information you find there.

Consider, too, checking how often the website has been linked to and the types of links provided by the website. That a site has been linked to repeatedly does not guarantee reliability, but the information may be helpful in conjunction with other recommendations in this chapter. To determine the number of times a Web page has been linked to, type *link:* plus the URL into a Google search box. To check the links provided, click on them and apply the criteria in this chapter.

If the source was published by a commercial publisher, check out the publisher's website, and ask yourself questions like these:

- Does the publisher offer works from a single perspective or from multiple perspectives?

- Do the works it publishes cover a wide variety of topics or focus on a particular topic?

- Does the publisher's website host links to a particular type of site?

The websites of book publishers may offer a link to a catalog. If so, look at the works it lists. Does the publisher seem to publish works on a particular topic or from a particular point of view? Does the publisher generally offer popular, academic, or professional works?

If your source is a periodical, consider whether it focuses on a particular topic or offers a single point of view. In addition to looking at the article you are considering, visit the publisher's website, which may help you determine this.

How Well Is the Source Written?

Most works that are published professionally (including popular newspapers and magazines, as well as scholarly journals and trade magazines) will have been edited carefully. These sources will generally avoid errors of grammar, punctuation, and spelling. Websites sponsored by professional organizations, too, will generally avoid these kinds of errors. Personal websites, however, are unlikely to have been professionally edited and fact-checked. If a website is riddled with errors, be very careful to double-check any information you take from that site.

What Does the Source Say?

Finally, and perhaps most important, consider the source itself. Answering the following questions can help you determine whether the source is worth consideration:

For more details on strategies for evaluating the logic of an argument, see Chapter 2, pp. 40–41.

- What is the intended audience of the source? Does the source address an audience of experts, or is it intended for a general audience?

- What is the purpose of the source? Does it review a number of different positions, or does it argue for a position of its own? If it makes its own argument, analyze the argument closely.

- What is the tone of the source? Is the tone reasonable? Does the source respond to alternative viewpoints, and are those responses logical and reasonable?

- What evidence is offered to support the argument? Is the evidence relevant and reliable? What kinds of citations or links does the source supply?

USING SOURCES TO SUPPORT YOUR IDEAS

Writing a college research project requires you to

- analyze sources to understand the arguments those sources are making, the information they are using to support their claims, and the ways those arguments and the supporting evidence they use relate to your topic;

- synthesize information from sources to support, extend, and challenge your own ideas;

- integrate information from sources with your own ideas to contribute something new to the "conversation" on your topic;

- document your sources using an appropriate documentation style.

SYNTHESIZING SOURCES

Synthesizing means making connections among ideas from texts and from your own experience. Once you have analyzed a number of sources on your topic, consider questions like the following to help you synthesize ideas and information:

- Do any of the sources you read use similar approaches or come to similar conclusions? What common themes do they explore? Do any of them use the same evidence (facts, statistics, research studies, examples) to support their claims?

- What differentiates the sources' various positions? Where do the writers disagree, and why? Does one writer seem to be responding to or challenging one or more of the others?

- Do you agree with some sources and disagree with others? What makes one source more convincing than the others? Do any of the sources you have read offer support for your claims? Do any of them challenge your conclusions? If so, can you *refute* the challenge or do you need to *concede* a point?

Sentence strategies like the following can help you clarify where you differ from or agree with the sources you have read:

- ▶ A study by X supports my position by demonstrating that ....
- ▶ X and Y think this issue is about .... But what is really at stake here is ....
- ▶ On this issue, X and Y say .... Although I understand and to some degree sympathize with their point of view, I agree with Z that this is ultimately a question of ....

The paragraph from Patrick O'Malley's paper on p. 500 shows how ideas and information from sources can be synthesized to support the writer's claim.

To learn more about synthesizing, see Chapter 2, p. 27.

ACKNOWLEDGING SOURCES AND AVOIDING PLAGIARISM

In your college writing, you will be expected to use and acknowledge **secondary sources** — books, articles, published or recorded interviews, websites, computer bulletin boards, lectures, and other print and nonprint materials — in addition to your own ideas, insights, and field research. The following information will help you decide what does and does not need to be acknowledged and will enable you to avoid *plagiarizing* inadvertently.

Determining What Does (and Does Not) Need to Be Acknowledged

For more on citing sources in MLA style, see pp. 509–26; for APA style, see pp. 528–36.

For the most part, any ideas, information, or language you borrow from a source — whether the source is in print or online — must be acknowledged by including an in-text citation and an entry in your list of works cited (MLA style) or references (APA style). The only types of information that do not require acknowledgment are common knowledge (for example, John F. Kennedy was assassinated in Dallas), facts widely available in many sources (U.S. presidents used to be inaugurated on March 4 rather than January 20), well-known quotations ("To be or not to be / That is the question"), and material you created or gathered yourself, such as photographs that you took or data from surveys that you conducted.

Remember that you need to acknowledge the source of any **visual** (photograph, table, chart, graph, diagram, drawing, map, screen shot) that you did not create yourself as well as the source of any information that you used to create your own visual. (You should also request permission from the source of a visual if your essay is going to be posted online without password protection.) When in doubt about whether you need to acknowledge a source, do so.

The documentation guidelines later in this chapter present two styles for citing sources: MLA and APA. Whichever style you use, the most important thing is that your readers be able to tell where words or ideas that are not your own begin and end. You can accomplish this most readily by taking and transcribing notes carefully, by placing parenthetical source citations correctly, and by separating your words from those of the source with **signal phrases** such as "According to Smith," "Peters claims," and "As Olmos asserts." (When you cite a source for the first time in a signal phrase, use the author's full name; after that, use just the last name.)

Avoiding Plagiarism

When you use material from another source, you need to acknowledge the source, usually by citing the author and page or publication date in your text and including a list of works cited or references at the end of your essay. Failure to acknowledge sources — even by accident — constitutes **plagiarism,** a serious transgression. By citing sources correctly, you give appropriate credit to the originator of the words and ideas you are using, offer your readers the information they need to consult those sources directly, and build your own credibility.

Writers — students and professionals alike — occasionally fail to acknowledge sources properly. Students sometimes mistakenly assume that plagiarizing occurs only when another writer's exact words are used without acknowledgment. In fact, plagiarism can also apply to paraphrases as well as to such diverse forms of expression as musical compositions, visual images, ideas, and statistics. Therefore, keep in mind that you must indicate the source of any borrowed information, idea, language, or visual or audio material you use in your essay, whether you have *paraphrased, summarized,* or *quoted* directly from the source or have reproduced it or referred to it in some other way.

Remember especially the need to document electronic sources fully and accurately. Perhaps because it is so easy to access and distribute text and visuals online and to copy material from one electronic document and paste it into another, some students do not realize, or may forget, that information, ideas, and images from electronic sources require acknowledgment in even more detail than those from print sources. At the same time, the improper (unacknowledged) use of online sources is often very easy for readers to detect.

Some people plagiarize simply because they do not know the conventions for using and acknowledging sources. Others plagiarize because they keep sloppy notes and thus fail to distinguish between their own and their sources' ideas. If you keep a working bibliography and careful notes, you will not make this serious mistake. Another reason some people plagiarize is that they feel intimidated by the writing task or the deadline. If you experience this anxiety about your work, speak to your instructor. Do not run the risk of failing a course or being expelled from your college because of plagiarism.

If you are confused about what is and what is not plagiarism, be sure to ask your instructor.

USING INFORMATION FROM SOURCES TO SUPPORT YOUR CLAIMS

When writing a research project, remember that the goal is to use the ideas and information you find in sources to support your own ideas. Make sure that each of your supporting paragraphs does three things:

1. States a claim that supports your thesis;

2. Provides evidence that supports your claim;

3. Explains to readers how the evidence supports your claim.

Consider this paragraph from Patrick O'Malley's proposal in Chapter 10, "More Testing, More Learning" (pp. 446–50):

States claim	The main reason professors should give frequent exams is that when they do and when they provide feedback to students on how well they are doing, students learn more in the course and perform better on major exams, projects, and papers. It makes sense that in
Explains how evidence supports claim	a challenging course containing a great deal of material, students will learn more of it and put it to better use if they have to apply or "practice" it frequently on exams, which also helps them find out how much they are learning and what they need to go over again.
Provides evidence	A 2006 study reported in *Psychological Science* journal concluded that "taking repeated tests on material leads to better long-term retention than repeated studying," according to the study's coauthors, Henry L. Roediger and Jeffrey Karpicke (ScienceWatch .com, 2008). When asked what the impact of this breakthrough research would be, they responded: "We hope that this research may be picked up in educational circles as a way to improve educational practices, both for students in the classroom and as a study strategy outside of class." The new field of mind, brain, and education research advocates the use of "retrieval testing." For example, research by Karpicke and Blunt (2011) published in *Science* found that testing was more effective than other, more traditional methods of studying both for comprehension and for analysis. Why retrieval testing works is not known. A UCLA psychologist, Robert Bjork, speculates that it may be effective because "when we use our memories by retrieving things, we change our access" to that information. "What we recall," therefore, "becomes more recallable in the future" (qtd. in Belluck, 2011).

O'Malley connects this body paragraph to his thesis by beginning with the transition *The main reason* and by repeating the phrase *perform better* from his forecasting statement. He synthesizes information from a variety of sources. For example, he uses quotations from some sources and a summary of another to provide evidence. And he doesn't merely stitch quotations and summary together; rather, he explains how the evidence supports his claim by stating that it "makes sense" that students "apply or 'practice'" what they learn on frequent exams.

Deciding Whether to Quote, Paraphrase, or Summarize

As illustrated in O'Malley's paragraph above, writers integrate supporting evidence by quoting, paraphrasing, or summarizing information or ideas from sources. This section provides guidelines for deciding when to use each of these three methods and how to quote, paraphrase, and summarize effectively. Note that all examples in this section (with the exception of O'Malley's paragraph) follow MLA style for in-text citations, which is explained in detail later in this chapter.

As a rule, quote only in these situations:

- When the wording of the source is particularly memorable or vivid or expresses a point so well that you cannot improve it;

- When the words of reliable and respected authorities would lend support to your position;

- When you wish to cite an author whose opinions challenge or vary greatly from those of other experts;

- When you are going to discuss the source's choice of words.

Paraphrase passages whose details you wish to use but whose language is not particularly striking. Summarize any long passages whose main points you wish to record as support for a point you are making.

Altering Quotations Using Italics, Ellipses, and Brackets

Quotations should duplicate the source exactly, even if they contain spelling errors. Add the notation *sic* (Latin for "thus") in brackets immediately after any such error to indicate that it is not your error but your source's. As long as you signal them appropriately, you may make changes to

- emphasize particular words;

- omit irrelevant information;

- insert information necessary for clarity;

- make the quotation conform grammatically to your sentence.

Using Italics for Emphasis.   You may italicize any words in the quotation that you want to emphasize; add a semicolon and the words *emphasis added* (in regular type, not italicized or underlined) to the parenthetical citation:

> In her 2001 exposé of the struggles of the working class, Ehrenreich writes, "The wages Winn-Dixie is offering—*$6 and a couple of dimes to start with*—are not enough, I decide, to compensate for this indignity" (14; emphasis added).

Using Ellipsis Marks for Omissions.   You may decide to omit words from a quotation because they are not relevant to the point you are making. When you omit words from within a quotation, use **ellipses**—three spaced periods (. . .)—in place of the missing words. When the omission occurs within a sentence, include a space before the first ellipsis mark and after the last mark:

> Hermione Roddice is described in Lawrence's *Women in Love* as a "woman of the new school, full of intellectuality and . . . nerve-worn with consciousness" (17).

When the omission falls at the end of a sentence, place a period *directly after* the final word of the sentence, followed by a space and three spaced ellipsis marks:

> But Grimaldi's commentary contends that for Aristotle rhetoric, like dialectic, had "no limited and unique subject matter upon which it must be exercised. . . . Instead, rhetoric as an art transcends all specific disciplines and may be brought into play in them" (6).

A period plus ellipses can indicate the omission not just of the rest of a sentence but also of whole sentences, paragraphs, or even pages.

When a parenthetical reference follows the ellipses at the end of a sentence, place the three spaced periods after the quotation, and place the sentence period after the final parenthesis:

> But Grimaldi's commentary contends that for Aristotle rhetoric, like dialectic, had "no limited and unique subject matter upon which it must be exercised. . . . Instead, rhetoric as an art transcends all specific disciplines . . ." (6).

When you quote only single words or phrases, you do not need to use ellipses because it will be obvious that you have left out some of the original:

> More specifically, Wharton's imagery of suffusing brightness transforms Undine before her glass into "some fabled creature whose home was in a beam of light" (21).

For the same reason, you need not use ellipses if you omit the beginning of a quoted sentence unless the rest of the sentence begins with a capitalized word and still appears to be a complete sentence.

Using Brackets for Insertions or Changes.   Use brackets around an insertion or a change needed to make a quotation conform grammatically to your sentence, such as a change in the form of a verb or pronoun or in the capitalization of the first word of the quotation. In this example from an essay on James Joyce's short story "Araby," the writer adapts Joyce's phrases "we played till our bodies glowed" and "shook music from the buckled harness" to fit the grammar of her sentences:

> In the dark, cold streets during the "short days of winter," the boys must generate their own heat by "play[ing] till [their] bodies glowed." Music is "[shaken] from the buckled harness" as if it were unnatural, and the singers in the market chant nasally of "the troubles in our native land" (30).

You may also use brackets to add or substitute explanatory material in a quotation:

> Guterson notes that among Native Americans in Florida, "education was in the home; learning by doing was reinforced by the myths and legends which repeated the basic value system of their [the Seminoles'] way of life" (159).

Some changes that make a quotation conform grammatically to another sentence may be made without any signal to readers:

- A period at the end of a quotation may be changed to a comma if you are using the quotation within your own sentence.

- Double quotation marks enclosing a quotation may be changed to single quotation marks when the quotation is enclosed within a longer quotation.

Adjusting the Punctuation within Quotations. Although punctuation within a quotation should reproduce the original, some adaptations may be necessary. Use single quotation marks for quotations within the quotation:

Original from David Guterson's *Family Matters (pp. 16–17)*	*Quoted version*
E. D. Hirsch also recognizes the connection between family and learning, suggesting in his discussion of family background and academic achievement "that the significant part of our children's education has been going on outside rather than inside the schools."	Guterson claims that E. D. Hirsch "also recognizes the connection between family and learning, suggesting in his discussion of family background and academic achievement 'that the significant part of our children's education has been going on outside rather than inside the schools'" (16–17).

If the quotation ends with a question mark or an exclamation point, retain the original punctuation:

"Did you think I loved you?" Edith later asks Dombey (566).

If a quotation ending with a question mark or an exclamation point concludes your sentence, retain the question mark or exclamation point, and put the parenthetical reference and sentence period outside the quotation marks:

Edith later asks Dombey, "Did you think I loved you?" (566).

Avoiding Grammatical Tangles. When you incorporate quotations into your writing, and especially when you omit words from quotations, you run the risk of creating ungrammatical sentences. Avoid these three common errors:

- verb incompatibility

- ungrammatical omissions

- sentence fragments

Verb incompatibility occurs when the verb form in the introductory statement is grammatically incompatible with the verb form in the quotation. When your quotation has a verb form that does not fit in with your text, it is usually possible to use just part of the quotation, thus avoiding verb incompatibility:

> The narrator suggests his bitter disappointment when ~~"I saw myself~~ as a creature
>
> driven and derided by vanity" (35).

(edit: he describes seeing himself " inserted above, replacing "I saw myself")*

As this sentence illustrates, use the present tense when you refer to events in a literary work.

Ungrammatical omissions may occur when you delete text from a quotation. To avoid this problem, try adapting the quotation (with brackets) so that its parts fit together grammatically, or use only one part of the quotation:

Option 1	*Option 2*
From the moment of the boy's arrival in Araby, the bazaar is presented as a commercial enterprise: "I could not find any sixpenny entrance and . . . hand[ed] ~~handing~~ a shilling to a weary-looking man" (34).	From the moment of the boy's arrival in Araby, the bazaar is presented as a commercial enterprise: "He "~~I~~ could not find any sixpenny entrance ~~and~~ so had to pay a shilling to get in ~~. . . handing a shilling to a weary-looking man"~~ (34).

Sentence fragments sometimes result when writers forget to include a verb in the sentence introducing a quotation, especially when the quotation itself is a complete sentence. Make sure you introduce a quotation with a complete sentence:

> The girl's interest in the bazaar ~~leading~~ leads the narrator to make what amounts to a
>
> sacred oath: "If I go . . . I will bring you something" (32).

Using In-Text or Block Quotations

Depending on its length, you may incorporate a quotation into your text by enclosing it in quotation marks or by setting it off from your text in a block without quotation marks. In either case, be sure to integrate the quotation into your essay using the strategies described here:

In-Text Quotations.   Incorporate brief quotations (no more than four typed lines of prose or three lines of poetry) into your text. You may place a quotation virtually anywhere in your sentence:

At the Beginning

> "To live a life is not to cross a field," Sutherland, quoting Pasternak, writes at the beginning of her narrative (11).

In the Middle

> Woolf begins and ends by speaking of the need of the woman writer to have "money and a room of her own" (4)—an idea that certainly spoke to Plath's condition.

At the End

> In *The Second Sex*, Simone de Beauvoir describes such an experience as one in which the girl "becomes an object, and she sees herself as object" (378).

Divided by Your Own Words

> "Science usually prefers the literal to the nonliteral term," Kinneavy writes, "—that is, figures of speech are often out of place in science" (177).

When you quote poetry within your text, use a slash (/) with spaces before and after to signal the end of each line of verse:

> Alluding to St. Augustine's distinction between the City of God and the Earthly City, Lowell writes that "much against my will / I left the City of God where [faith] belongs" (4–5).

Block Quotations. In MLA style, use the **block form** for prose quotations of five or more typed lines and for poetry quotations of four or more lines. Indent the quotation half an inch from the left margin, as shown in the following example:

> In "A Literary Legacy from Dunbar to Baraka," Margaret Walker says of Paul Lawrence Dunbar's dialect poems:
>
> > He realized that the white world in the United States tolerated his literary genius only because of his "jingles in a broken tongue," and they found the old "darky" tales and speech amusing and within the vein of folklore into which they wished to classify all Negro life. This troubled Dunbar because he realized that white America was denigrating him as a writer and as a man. (70)

In APA style, use block form for quotations of forty words or more. Indent the block quotation half an inch.

In a block quotation, double-space between lines just as you do in your text. Do not enclose the passage within quotation marks. Use a colon to introduce a block quotation unless the context calls for another punctuation mark or none at all. When quoting a single paragraph or part of one in MLA style, do not indent the first line of the quotation more than the rest. In quoting two or more paragraphs, indent the first line of each paragraph an extra quarter inch. Note that in MLA style the parenthetical page reference follows the period in block quotations. If you are using APA style, indent the first line of subsequent paragraphs in the block quotation an additional half inch from the indentation of the block quotation.

Using Punctuation to Integrate Quotations

Statements that introduce in-text quotations take a range of punctuation marks and lead-in words. Here are some examples of ways writers typically introduce quotations:

Introducing a Quotation Using a Colon.   A colon usually follows an independent clause placed before the quotation:

> As George Williams notes, protection of white privilege is critical to patterns of discrimination: "Whenever a number of persons within a society have enjoyed for a considerable period of time certain opportunities for getting wealth, for exercising power and authority, and for successfully claiming prestige and social deference, there is a strong tendency for these people to feel that these benefits are theirs 'by right'" (727).

Introducing a Quotation Using a Comma.   A comma usually follows an introduction that incorporates the quotation in its sentence structure:

> Similarly, Duncan Turner asserts, "As matters now stand, it is unwise to talk about communication without some understanding of Burke" (259).

Introducing a Quotation Using *That*.   No punctuation is generally needed with *that*, and no capital letter is used to begin the quotation:

> Noting this failure, Alice Miller asserts that "the reason for her despair was not her suffering but the impossibility of communicating her suffering to another person" (255).

Paraphrasing Sources Carefully

In a **paraphrase,** the writer restates in his or her own words the relevant information from a passage, without any additional comments or any suggestion of agreement or disagreement with the source's ideas. A paraphrase is useful for recording details of the passage when the source's exact wording is not important. Because all the details of the passage are included, a paraphrase is often about the same length as the original passage. It is better to paraphrase than to quote ordinary material in which the author's way of expressing things is not worth special attention.

Here is a passage from a book on home schooling and an example of an acceptable paraphrase of it:

Original source	*Acceptable paraphrase*
Bruner and the discovery theorists have also illuminated conditions that apparently pave the way for learning. It is significant that these conditions are unique to each learner, so unique, in fact, that in many cases classrooms can't provide them. Bruner also contends that the more one discovers information in a great variety of circumstances, the more likely one is to develop the inner categories required to organize that information. Yet life at school, which is for the most part generic and predictable, daily keeps many children from the great variety of circumstances they need to learn well.	According to Guterson, the "discovery theorists," particularly Bruner, have found that there seem to be certain conditions that help learning to take place. Because individuals require different conditions, many children are not able to learn in the classroom. According to Bruner, when people can explore information in many different situations, they learn to classify and order what they discover. The general routine of the school day, however, does not provide children with the diverse activities and situations that would allow them to learn these skills (172).

— DAVID GUTERSON, *Family Matters:
Why Homeschooling Makes Sense*, p. 172

The highlighting shows that some words in the paraphrase were taken from the source. Indeed, it would be nearly impossible for paraphrasers to avoid using any key terms from the source, and it would be counterproductive to try to do so because the original and the paraphrase necessarily share the same information and concepts. Notice, though, that of the total of eighty-five words in the paraphrase, the paraphraser uses only a name (*Bruner*) and a few other key nouns and verbs for which it would be awkward to substitute other words or phrases. If the paraphraser had wanted to use other, more distinctive language from the source — for example, the description of life at school as "generic and predictable" — these adjectives would need to be enclosed in quotation marks. In fact, the paraphraser puts quotation marks around only one of the terms from the source: "discovery theorists" — a technical term likely to be unfamiliar to readers.

Paraphrasers must, however, avoid borrowing too many words and repeating the sentence structures from a source. Here is an unacceptable paraphrase of the first sentence in the Guterson passage:

Unacceptable Paraphrase: Too Many Borrowed Words and Phrases

Repeated sentence structure	Apparently, some conditions, which have been illuminated by
Repeated words	Bruner and other discovery theorists, pave the way for people to learn.

Here, the paraphrase borrows almost all of its key language from the source sentence, including the entire phrase *pave the way for*. Even if you cite the source, this heavy borrowing would be considered plagiarism.

Here is another unacceptable paraphrase of the same sentence:

Unacceptable Paraphrase: Sentence Structure Repeated Too Closely

Repeated words
Synonyms
Repeated sentence
structure

Bruner and other *researchers* have also *identified circumstances* that *seem to ease the path* to learning.

If you compare the source's first sentence and this paraphrase of it, you will see that the paraphraser has borrowed the phrases and clauses of the source and arranged them in an almost identical sequence, simply substituting synonyms for most of the key terms. This paraphrase would also be considered plagiarism.

Summarizing to Present the Source's Main Ideas in a Balanced and Readable Way

For more on summarizing as a reading and writing strategy, see Chapter 2, pp. 24–25.

Unlike a paraphrase, a **summary** presents only the main ideas of a source, leaving out examples and details.

Here is one student's summary of five pages from David Guterson's book *Family Matters*. You can see at a glance how drastically summaries can condense information, in this case from five pages to five sentences. Depending on the summarizer's purpose, the five pages could be summarized in one sentence, the five sentences here, or three dozen sentences.

> In looking at different theories of learning that discuss individual-based programs (such as home schooling) versus the public school system, Guterson describes the disagreements among "cognitivist" theorists. One group, the "discovery theorists," believes that individual children learn by creating their own ways of sorting the information they take in from their experiences. Schools should help students develop better ways of organizing new material, not just present them with material that is already categorized, as traditional schools do. "Assimilationist theorists," by contrast, believe that children learn by linking what they don't know to information they already know. These theorists claim that traditional schools help students learn when they present information in ways that allow children to fit the new material into categories they have already developed (171–75).

Summaries like this one are more than a dry list of main ideas from a source. They are instead a coherent, readable new text composed of the source's main ideas. Summaries provide balanced coverage of a source, following the same sequence of ideas and avoiding any hint of agreement or disagreement with them.

CITING AND DOCUMENTING SOURCES IN MLA STYLE

The following guidelines are sufficient for most college research assignments in English and other humanities courses that call for MLA-style documentation. For additional information, see the *MLA Handbook for Writers of Research Papers*, Eighth Edition (2016), or check the MLA website.

USING IN-TEXT CITATIONS

The MLA system requires parenthetical in-text citations that are keyed to a list of works cited in the paper. **In-text citations** tell your readers where the ideas or words you have borrowed come from, and the entries in the **Works Cited** list allow readers to locate your sources so that they can read more about your topic.

In most cases, include the author's last name and the page number on which the borrowed material appears in the text of your research project. You can incorporate this information in two ways:

- By naming the author in the text of your research project with a signal phrase (*Simon described*) and including the page reference (in parentheses) at the end of the borrowed passage:

author's last name   appropriate verb

SIGNAL PHRASE   Simon, a well-known figure in New York literary society, described the impression Dr. James made on her as a child in the Bronx: He was a "not-too-skeletal Ichabod Crane" (68).

page number

- By including the author's name and the page number together in parentheses at the end of the borrowed passage:

PARENTHETICAL   Dr. James is described as a "not-too-skeletal Ichabod Crane"
CITATION   (Simon 68).

    author's last name + page number

WORKS-CITED   Simon, Kate. "Birthing." *Bronx Primitive: Portraits in a Childhood,*
ENTRY   Viking Books, 1982, pp. 68-77.

In most cases, you will want to use a signal phrase because doing so lets you put your source in context. The signal-phrase-plus-page-reference combination also allows you to make crystal clear where the source information begins and ends. Use a parenthetical citation alone when you have already identified the author or when citing the source of an uncontroversial fact.

The in-text citation should include as much information as is needed to lead readers to the source in your list of works cited and allow them to find the passage you are citing in that source. In most cases, that means the author's last name and the page number on which the borrowed material appears. In some cases, you may need to include other information in your in-text citation (such as a brief version of the title if the author is unnamed or if you cite more than one work by this author). In a few cases, you may not be able to include a page reference, as, for example, when you cite a website. In such cases, you may include other identifying information if the source uses explicit numbering or naming techniques, such as a paragraph number or section heading.

Directory to In-Text-Citation Models

One author 510

More than one author 511

Unknown author 511

Two or more works by the same
author 511

Two or more authors with the same
last name 511

Corporation, organization, or
government agency as author 512

Literary work (novel, play,
poem) 512

Work in an anthology 512

Religious work 513

Multivolume work (one volume,
more than one volume) 513

Indirect citation (quotation from a
secondary source) 513

Entire work 513

Work without page numbers or a
one-page work (with / without
other section numbers) 513

Work in a time-based medium 514

Two or more works cited in the same
parentheses 514

One author   When citing most works with a single author, include the author's name (usually the last name is enough)* and the page number on which the cited material appears.

author's last name + appropriate verb   page number

SIGNAL PHRASE   Simon describes Dr. James as a "not-too-skeletal Ichabod Crane" (68).

PARENTHETICAL   Dr. James is described as a "not-too-skeletal Ichabod Crane"
CITATION   (Simon 68).

author's last name + page number

*But see entries for "Two or More Works by the Same Author" and "Two or More Authors with the Same Last Name" on p. 511 and for "Work without Page Numbers or a One-Page Work" on p. 513.

author's name

BLOCK QUOTATION   In Kate Simon's story "Birthing," the description of Dr. James captures both his physical appearance and his role in the community:

> He looked so much like a story character—the gentled Scrooge of a St. Nicholas Magazine Christmas issue, a not-too-skeletal Ichabod Crane. . . . Dr. James was, even when I knew him as a child, quite an old man, retired from a prestigious and lucrative practice in Boston. . . . His was a prosperous intellectual family, the famous New England Jameses that produced William and Henry, but to the older Bronx doctors, *the* James was the magnificent old driven scarecrow. (68)

page number

(A works-cited entry for "Birthing" appears on p. 509.)

More than one author   To cite a source by two authors, include both of the authors' last names. To cite a source with three or more authors, provide just the first author's name followed by *et al.* ("and others" in Latin, not italicized).

SIGNAL PHRASE   Bernays and Painter maintain that a writer can begin a story without knowing how it will end (7).

PARENTHETICAL CITATION   A writer should "resist the temptation to give the reader too lengthy an explanation" (Bernays and Painter 7).

The Authority Rebel "tends to see himself as superior to other students in the class" (Dyal et al. 4).

Unknown author   If the author's name is unknown, use a shortened version of the title, beginning with the word by which the title is alphabetized in the works-cited list. Use the first noun and any modifiers. (In this example, the full title is "Plastic Is Found in the Sargasso Sea; Pieces of Apparent Refuse Cover Wide Atlantic Region.")

An international pollution treaty still to be ratified would prohibit ships from dumping plastic at sea ("Plastic" 68).

Two or more works by the same author   If you cite more than one work by the same author, include a shortened version of the title.

When old paint becomes transparent, it sometimes shows the artist's original plans: "a tree will show through a woman's dress" (Hellman, *Pentimento* 1).

Two or more authors with the same last name   When citing works by authors with the same last name, include each author's first initial in the citation. If the first initials are also the same, spell out the authors' first names.

Chaplin's *Modern Times* provides a good example of montage used to make an editorial statement (E. Roberts 246).

Corporation, organization, or government agency as author   In a signal phrase, use the full name of the corporation, organization, or government agency. In a parenthetical citation, use the full name if it is brief or a shortened version if it is long.

SIGNAL PHRASE   The Washington State Board for Community and Technical Colleges will raise tuition to offset budget deficits from Initiative 601 (4).

PARENTHETICAL CITATION   A tuition increase has been proposed for community and technical colleges to offset budget deficits from Initiative 601 (Washington State Board 4).

Literary work (novel, play, poem)   Provide information that will help readers find the passage you are citing no matter what edition of the novel, play, or poem they are using. For a novel or other prose work, provide the part or chapter number as well as the page numbers from the edition you used.

NOVEL OR OTHER PROSE WORK   In *Hard Times*, Tom reveals his utter narcissism by blaming Louisa for his own failure: "'You have regularly given me up. You never cared for me'" (Dickens 262; bk. 3, ch. 9).

For a play in verse, use act, scene, and line numbers instead of page numbers.

PLAY (IN VERSE)   At the beginning, Regan's fawning rhetoric hides her true attitude toward Lear: "I profess / myself an enemy to all other joys . . . / And find that I am alone felicitate / In your dear highness' love" (*King Lear* 1.1.74-75, 77-78).

For a poem, indicate the line numbers and stanzas or sections (if they are numbered) instead of page numbers.

POEM   In "Song of Myself," Whitman finds poetic details in busy urban settings, as when he describes "the blab of the pave, tires of carts . . . the driver with his interrogating thumb" (8.153-54).

If the source gives only line numbers, use the term *lines* in your first citation and use only the numbers in subsequent citations.

In "Before you thought of spring," Dickinson at first identifies the spirit of spring with a bird, possibly a robin—"A fellow in the skies / Inspiriting habiliments / Of indigo and brown" (lines 4, 7-8)—but by the end of the poem, she has linked it with poetry and perhaps even the poet herself, as the bird, like Dickinson "shouts for joy to nobody / But his seraphic self!" (15-16)

Work in an anthology   Use the name of the author of the work, not the editor of the anthology, in your in-text citation.

SIGNAL PHRASE   In "Six Days: Some Rememberings," Grace Paley recalls that when she was in jail for protesting the Vietnam War, her pen and paper were taken away and she felt "a terrible pain in the area of my heart—a nausea" (191).

PARENTHETICAL CITATION   Writers may have a visceral reaction—"a nausea" (Paley 191)—to being deprived of access to writing implements.

Religious work   In your first citation, include the element that begins your entry in the works-cited list, such as the edition name of the religious work you are citing, and include the book or section name (using standard abbreviations in parenthetical citations) and any chapter or verse numbers.

> She ignored the admonition "Pride goes before destruction, and a haughty spirit before a fall" (*New Oxford Annotated Bible*, Prov. 16.18).

Multivolume work (one volume, more than one volume)   If you cite only one volume of a multivolume work, treat the in-text citation as you would any other work, but include the volume number in the works-cited entry (see p. 518).

ONE VOLUME   Forster argued that modernist writers valued experimentation and gradually sought to blur the line between poetry and prose (150).

When you use two or more volumes of a multivolume work, include the volume number and the page number(s) in your in-text citation.

MORE THAN
ONE VOLUME   Modernist writers valued experimentation and gradually sought to blur the line between poetry and prose (Forster 3: 150).

Indirect citation (quotation from a secondary source)   If possible, locate the original source and cite that. If not possible, name the original source but also include the secondary source in which you found the material you are citing, plus the abbreviation *qtd. in.* Include the secondary source in your list of works cited.

> E. M. Forster says that "the collapse of all civilization, so realistic for us, sounded in Matthew Arnold's ears like a distant and harmonious cataract" (qtd. in Trilling 11).

Entire work   Include the reference in the text without any page numbers or parentheses.

> In *The Structure of Scientific Revolutions*, Thomas Kuhn discusses how scientists change their thinking.

Work without page numbers or a one-page work (with/without other section numbers)   If a work (such as a Web page) has no page numbers or is only one page long, omit the page number. If it uses screen numbers or paragraph numbers, insert a comma after the author's name, an identifying term (such as *screen*) or abbreviation (*par.* or *pars.*), and the number.

WITHOUT PAGE
OR OTHER
NUMBERS   The average speed on Montana's interstate highways, for example, has risen by only 2 miles per hour since the repeal of the federal speed limit, with most drivers topping out at 75 (Schmid).

WITH OTHER
SECTION
NUMBERS   Whitman considered African American speech "a source of a native grand opera" (Ellison, par. 13).

Work in a time-based medium   To cite a specific portion of a video or audio recording, include a time or range of times, as provided by your media player. Cite hours, minutes, and seconds, placing colons between them.

> Barack Obama joked that he and Dick Cheney agreed on one thing—*Hamilton* is phenomenal ("Hamilton Cast" 00:02:34-36).

Two or more works cited in the same parentheses   If you cite two or more sources for a piece of information, include them in the same parentheses, separated by semicolons.

> A few studies have considered differences between oral and written discourse production (Gould; Scardamali et al.).

CREATING A LIST OF WORKS CITED

In your MLA-style research paper, every source you cite must have a corresponding entry in the list of works cited, and every entry in your list of works cited must correspond to at least one citation in your research project.

Follow these rules when formatting your list of works cited in MLA style:

- On a new page, type "Works Cited" (centered), and double-space the whole works-cited list.

- Alphabetize entries by the first word in the citation (usually the first author's last name, or the title if the author is unknown, ignoring *A, An,* or *The*).

- Use a "hanging indent" for all entries: Do not indent the first line, but indent second and subsequent lines of the entry by half an inch (or five spaces).

- Abbreviate the names of university presses, shortening the words *University* and *Press* to *U* and *P.* For all other types of publishers, spell out words like *Publishers.*

Nowadays, many print sources are also available in an electronic format, either online or through a database your school's library subscribes to. For most online versions of a source, follow the form of the corresponding print version. For example, if you are citing an article from an online periodical, put the article title in quotation marks and italicize the name of the periodical.

For sources accessed through a database, include the following:

- Title of the database (in italics)

- Location where you accessed the source. Ideally this is a DOI, but when one is not available, provide a URL (if provided, use a permalink).

For other online sources, include the following:

- Title of the website (in italics)

- Version or edition used (if any)

- Publisher of the site, but only if distinct from its title

- Date of publication or last update; if not available, provide the date you last accessed the source at the end of the entry

Some content on the Web frequently changes or disappears, and because the same information that traditionally published books and periodicals provide is not always included for Web sources, giving your reader a complete citation is not always possible. Always keep your goal in mind: to provide enough information so that your reader can track down the source. If you cannot find all of the information listed here, include what you can.

Directory to Works-Cited-List Models

(continued)

AUTHOR LISTINGS

One author   List the author last name first (followed by a comma), and insert a period at the end of the name.

   Isaacson, Walter.

Two authors   List the first author last name first (followed by a comma). List the second author in the usual first-name / last-name order. Insert the word *and* before the second author's name, and follow the name with a period.

   Bernays, Anne, and Pamela Painter.

Three or more authors   List the first author last name first (followed by a comma). Then insert *et al.* (which means *and others* in Latin) in regular type (not italics).

   Hunt, Lynn, et al.

Unknown author

   Primary Colors: A Novel of Politics.

   "Out of Sight."

Corporation, organization, or government agency as author   Use the name of the corporation, organization, or government agency as the author.

   RAND Corporation.

   United States, National Commission on Terrorist Attacks.

Two or more works by the same author   Replace the author's name in subsequent entries with three hyphens, and alphabetize the works by the first important word in the title:

   Eugenides, Jeffrey. *The Marriage Plot.*

   ---. *Middlesex.*

   ---. "Walkabout."

BOOKS (PRINT, ELECTRONIC, DATABASE)

Basic format

Author, last name first | Title (and subtitle, if any), italicized | Publication info

PRINT Eugenides, Jeffrey. *The Marriage Plot.* Farrar, Straus and Giroux, 2011.

Publisher | Publication date

E-BOOK Eugenides, Jeffrey. *The Marriage Plot.* Kindle ed., Farrar, Straus and Giroux, 2011.

Publisher | Publication date

Original publication date | Online publication date

DATABASE Whitman, Walt. *Leaves of Grass.* 1900. *Bartleby.com,* 1999, www.bartleby.com/142/.

Location (URL)

Anthology or edited collection   If you are referring to the anthology as a whole, put the editor's name first.

Masri, Heather, editor. *Science Fiction: Stories and Contexts.* Bedford/St. Martin's, 2009.

Work in an anthology or edited collection   If you're referring to a selection in an anthology, begin the entry with the name of the selection's author. Include specific page references, and preface them with *p.* or *pp.*

Hopkinson, Nalo. "Something to Hitch Meat To." *Science Fiction: Stories and Contexts,* Bedford/St. Martin's, 2009, pp. 838-50.

If you cite more than one selection from an anthology or collection, you may create an entry for the collection as a whole (see the model above) and then cross-reference individual selections to that entry.

Selection author | Selection title | Anthology editor

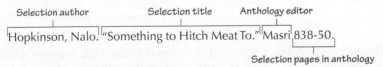
Hopkinson, Nalo. "Something to Hitch Meat To." Masri 838-50.

Selection pages in anthology

Introduction, preface, foreword, or afterword

Murfin, Ross C. Introduction. *Heart of Darkness,* by Joseph Conrad, 3rd ed., Bedford/St. Martin's, 2011, pp. 3-16.

Translation

Tolstoy, Leo. *War and Peace.* Translated by Richard Pevear and Larissa Volokhonsky, Vintage Books, 2009.

Graphic narrative   If the graphic narrative was a collaboration between a writer and an illustrator, begin your entry with the name of the person on whose work your research project focuses. If the author also created the illustrations, then follow the basic model for a book with one author (p. 517).

> Pekar, Harvey, and Joyce Brabner. *Our Cancer Year*. Illustrations by Frank Stack, Four Walls Eight Windows, 1994.

Religious work   Give the title of the edition, the editor's and translator's names as available, publisher, and date.

> *The Qu'ran: English Translation and Parallel Arabic Text*. Translated by M. A. S. Abdel Haleem, Oxford UP, 2010.

Multivolume work   If you use only one volume from a multivolume work, indicate the volume number after the title, using the abbreviation *vol*. If you use more than one volume, indicate the total number of volumes at the end of the entry.

One volume cited

> Sandburg, Carl. *Abraham Lincoln*. Vol. 2, Charles Scribner's Sons, 1926.

More than one volume cited

> Sandburg, Carl. *Abraham Lincoln*. Charles Scribner's Sons, 1926–39. 6 vols.

Later edition of a book

> Rottenberg, Annette T., and Donna Haisty Winchell. *The Structure of Argument*. 6th ed., Bedford/St. Martin's, 2009.

Republished book   Provide the original year of publication after the title of the book, followed by publication information for the edition you are using.

Original publication date

> Alcott, Louisa May. *An Old-Fashioned Girl*. 1870. Puffin Books, 1995.

Republication information

Title within a title   When a title that is normally italicized appears within a book title, do not italicize it. If the title within the title would normally be enclosed in quotation marks, include the quotation marks and also set the title in italics.

> Hertenstein, Mike. *The Double Vision of* Star Trek*: Half-Humans, Evil Twins, and Science Fiction*. Cornerstone Books, 1998.

> Miller, Edwin Haviland. *Walt Whitman's "Song of Myself": A Mosaic of Interpretation*. U of Iowa P, 1989.

Book in a series   Include the series title (without italics) and number (if any) at the end of the entry, after a period (never a comma). (Series information will appear on the title page or on the page facing the title page.)

> Zigova, Tanya, et al. *Neural Stem Cells: Methods and Protocols*. Humana Press, 2002. Methods in Molecular Biology 198.

Dictionary entry or article in another reference book

PRINT
> Trenear-Harvey, Glenmore S. "Farm Hall." *Historical Dictionary of Atomic Espionage*, Scarecrow Press, 2011.

ONLINE

Website
(same name as publisher)

Most recent update

> "Homeopathy." *Merriam-Webster.com*, 2011.

DATABASE
> Powell, Jason L. "Power Elite." *Blackwell Encyclopedia of Sociology*, edited by George Ritzer, Wiley, 2007. *Blackwell Reference Online*, doi:10.1111/b.9781405124331.2007.x.

Location (DOI)

Database (italics)

Government document

PRINT

Authors

Issuing government

> Newes-Adeyi, Gabriella, et al. *Trends in Underage Drinking in the United States, 1991-2007*. United States, Department of Health and Human Services, 2009.

Issuing department

ONLINE

Issuing agency

> United States, Department of Health and Human Services, Centers for Disease Control. "Youth Risk Behavior Surveillance— United States, 2009." *Morbidity and Mortality Weekly Report*, vol. 59, no. SS5, 4 June 2010.

Publication date

Published proceedings of a conference

Conference name included in title

> Duffett, John, editor. *Against the Crime of Silence: Proceedings of the International War Crimes Tribunal*. Nov. 1967, Stockholm, Simon and Schuster, 1970.

Pamphlet or brochure

> American Canoe Association. *Cold Water Survival*, Sport Fish Restoration and Boating Trust Fund, U.S. Coast Guard, 2001.

Doctoral dissertation

Title in italics

PUBLISHED   Jones, Anna Maria. *Problem Novels / Perverse Readers: Late-Victorian Fiction and the Perilous Pleasures of Identification.* Dissertation, U of Notre Dame, 2001.

Dissertation information

Title in quotation marks

UNPUBLISHED   Bullock, Barbara. "Basic Needs Fulfillment among Less Developed Countries: Social Progress over Two Decades of Growth." Dissertation, Vanderbilt U, 1986.

Dissertation information

ARTICLES (PRINT, ONLINE, DATABASE)

From a scholarly journal

For help distinguishing between scholarly journals and magazines, see pp. 520–21 earlier in this chapter.

Author, last name first   Title of article (in quotation marks)

PRINT   Garas-York, Keli. "Overlapping Student Environments: An Examination of the Homeschool Connection and Its Impact on Achievement." *Journal of College Admission,* vol. 42, no. 4, May 2010, pp. 430-49.

Publication date   Pages   Title of journal (italics)   Volume   Issue

ONLINE   Saho, Bala S. K. "The Appropriation of Islam in a Gambian Village: Life and Times of Shaykh Mass Kay, 1827-1936." *African Studies Quarterly*, vol. 12, no. 4, Fall 2011, asq.africa.ufl.edu/files/Saho-Vol12Is4.pdf.

Location (URL)

DATABASE   Haas, Heather A. "The Wisdom of Wizards—and Muggles and Squibs: Proverb Use in the World of *Harry Potter*." *Journal of American Folklore*, vol. 124, no. 492, April 2011, pp. 29-54. *Academic Search Complete,* go.galegroup.com/.

Database (italics)   Database location (URL)

If a journal does not use volume numbers, provide the issue number only.

Markel, J. D. "Religious Allegory and Cultural Discomfort in Mike Leigh's *Happy-Go-Lucky*: And Why *Larry Crowne* Is One of the Best Films of 2011." *Bright Lights Film Journal,* no. 74, Oct. 2011, brightlightsfilm.com/religious-allegory-and-cultural-discomfort-in-mike-leighs-happy-go-luckyand-why-larry-crowne-is-one-of-the-best-films-of-2011/.

Issue number only

URL

Online journals may not include page numbers; if paragraph or other section numbers are provided, use them instead. If the article is not on a continuous sequence of pages, give the first page number followed by a plus sign. (See entry below for a print version of a newspaper for an example.)

From a newspaper

PRINT

Weisman, Jonathan, and Jennifer Steinhauer. "Patriot Act Faces Revisions Backed by Both Parties." *The New York Times,* 1 May 2015, pp. A1+.

⎣ Noncontinuous pages

ONLINE

Weisman, Jonathan, and Jennifer Steinhauer. "Patriot Act Faces Revisions Backed by Both Parties." *The New York Times,* 30 Apr. 2015.

⎣ Website (italics)

⎣ Publication date

DATABASE

Weisman, Jonathan, and Jennifer Steinhauer. "Patriot Act Faces Revisions Backed by Both Parties." *The New York Times,* 1 May 2015, pp. A1+. *LexisNexis Academic.*

⎣ Noncontinuous pages

⎣ Database (italics)

From a magazine

PRINT

Stillman, Sarah. "Where Are the Children?" *The New Yorker,* 27 Apr. 2015, pp. 40-41.

⎣ Publication date (weekly)

⎣ Publication date (monthly)

Bennet, James. "To Stay or to Go." *The Atlantic,* Apr. 2015, p. 8.

⎣ Website (italics)

ONLINE

Bennet, James. "Editor's Note: To Stay or to Go." *The Atlantic,* Apr. 2015, www.theatlantic.com/magazine/archive/2015/04 /editors-note/386285/.

DATABASE

Sharp, Kathleen. "The Rescue Mission." *Smithsonian,* Nov. 2015, pp. 40-49. *OmniFile Full Text Select,* web.b.ebscohost.com .ezproxy.bpl.org/.

⎣ Database (italics)

Editorial or letter to the editor

"City's Blight Fight Making Difference." Editorial. *The Columbus Dispatch,* 17 Nov. 2015, www.dispatch.com/content/stories/editorials/2015/11/17/1-citys-blight -fight-making-difference.html.

Fahey, John A. "Recalling the Cuban Missile Crisis." Letter. *The Washington Post,* 28 Oct. 2012, p. A16. *LexisNexis Library Express,* www.lexisnexis.com /hottopics/Inpubliclibraryexpress/.

Review   If the review does not include an author's name, start the entry with the title of the review; then add *Review of* and the title of the work being reviewed. If the review is untitled, include the *Review of* description immediately after the author's name. For a review in an online newspaper or magazine, add the URL, ideally a permalink. For a review accessed through a database, add the database title (in italics) and the DOI or URL.

Deparle, Jason. "Immigration Nation." Review of *Exodus: How Migration Is Changing Our World,* by Paul Collier. *The Atlantic,* Nov. 2013, pp. 44-46.

MULTIMEDIA SOURCES (LIVE, PRINT, ELECTRONIC, DATABASE)

Lecture or public address

Title of lecture

Stephenson, Brittany. "Wading Out of Web Stew: Reader-Centric Course Design." Conference on College Composition and Communication, 20 Mar. 2015,

Conference title   *Date of lecture*

Marriott Waterside, Tampa.

Location of conference

Letter   If the letter has been published, treat it like a work in an anthology (p. 517), but add the recipient, the date, and any identifying number after the author's name. If the letter is unpublished, note the recipient.

Sender   *Recipient*   *Date*

DuHamel, Grace. Letter to the author. 22 Mar. 2008.

Map or chart

PRINT   *Map of Afghanistan and Surrounding Territory,* 2001.

ONLINE   "Vote on Secession, 1861." *Perry-Castañeda Library Map Collection,* U of Texas at Austin, 1976, www.lib.utexas.edu/maps/atlas _texas/texas_vote_secession_1861.jpg.

Cartoon or comic strip

Wheeler, Shannon. *The New Yorker,* 11 May 2015, p. 50. Cartoon.

Advertisement

PRINT Hospital for Special Surgery. Advertisement. *The New York Times,*
   13 Apr. 2009, p. A7.

BROADCAST Norwegian Cruise Line. Advertisement. *WNET,* PBS, 29 Apr. 2012.

ONLINE Volkswagen Passat. Advertisement. *Slate,* www.slate.com/.
   ⌐Accessed 1 Dec. 2011.⌐
         |
   Access date (*no pub date available*)

Work of art

                                                                    Location
                                                                       |
MUSEUM Palmer Payne, Elsie. *Sheep Dipping Time.* c. 1930s. Nevada Museum
   of Art, Reno.

PRINT Chihuly, Dale. *Carmine and White Flower Set.* 1987. Tacoma Art
   Museum. ⌐Abrams Press, 2011, p. 109.⌐
                        |
              Print publication information

ONLINE Sekaer, Peter. *A Sign Business Shop, New York.* 1935.
   ⌐*International Center of Photography*⌐⌐www.icp.org/exhibitions
            | |
         Website   Location (URL)
   /signs-of-life-photographs-by-peter-sekaer.⌐

Musical composition

Beethoven, Ludwig van. *Violin Concerto in D Major, Op. 61.* 1809. IMSLP Music
   Library, imslp.org/wiki/Violin_Concerto_in_D_major,_Op.61_(Beethoven,
   _Ludwig_van).

Gershwin, George. *Porgy and Bess.* 1935. Alfred A. Knopf, 1999.

Performance

The Draft. Directed by Diego Arciniegas, 10 Sept. 2015, Hibernian Hall, Boston.

Piano Concerto no. 3. By Ludwig van Beethoven, conducted by Andris Nelsons,
   performance by Paul Lewis and Boston Symphony Orchestra, Symphony Hall,
   Boston, 9 Oct. 2015.

Television or radio program, or podcast   Include the network and broadcast date.
If you streamed the program, treat it like an article you accessed through a database:
at the end of your entry, include information about the streaming service (its name
and a URL). Separate program information from database information with a
period. If you streamed or downloaded the program through an app like an iPhone's
Podcasts, list the app as you would a streaming service or database (see Downloaded

entry below). Treat a podcast that you listened to or watched online as you would an online television or radio program (see Streamed entry below).

                        Episode   *Program*   *Key contributors*

BROADCAST   "Being Mortal." *Frontline.* Written by Atul Gawande and Tom Jennings, directed by Tom Jennings and Nisha Pahuja, PBS, 22 Nov. 2011.

                                                               Network

                        Broadcast date

STREAMED   "The Choice." *The Borgias,* directed by Kari Skogland, season 2, episode 5, Showtime, 6 May 2012. *Netflix,* www.netflix.com /watch/70261634.

DOWNLOADED   "Patient Zero." *Radio Lab,* hosted by Jad Abumrad and Robert
(OR VIA APP)   Krulwich, season 10, episode 4, National Public Radio, 14 Nov. 2011. *Podcasts,* iTunes.

Film

THEATER   *Space Station.* Produced and directed by Toni Myers, narrated by Tom Cruise, IMAX, 2002.

DVD   *Casablanca.* Directed by Michael Curtiz, performances by Humphrey Bogart, Ingrid Bergman, and Paul Henreid, 1942. Warner Home Video, 2003.

Online video

Film School. "Sunny Day." *YouTube,* www.youtube.com/watch?v=8oTJFUCbsfl.

Music recording

Beethoven, Ludwig van. *Violin Concerto in D Major, Op. 61.* Performed by David Oistrakh and the U.S.S.R. State Orchestra, conducted by Alexander Gauk. Allegro Music, 1980.

Adele. "Hello." *25,* XL Recordings/Columbia, 2015.

Interview   If a personal interview takes place through e-mail, change "Personal interview" to "E-mail interview."

PRINT   Ashrawi, Hanan. "Tanks vs. Olive Branches." Interview by Rose Marie Berger, *Sojourners,* Feb. 2005, pp. 22-26.

BROADCAST   Baldwin, Alec. "Two Angry Men." Interview by Bob Garfield, *On the Media*, National Public Radio, 4 Nov. 2015. www.wnyc .org/story/two-angry-men/.

PERSONAL   Ellis, Trey. Personal interview. 3 Sept. 2015.

OTHER ELECTRONIC SOURCES

Web page or other document on a website

Editor (no author), last name first   Document title (in quotation marks)

McGann, Jerome J., editor. "Introduction to the Final Installment of the Rossetti

Title of site (italicized)

Archive." *The Complete Writings and Pictures of Dante Gabriel Rossetti:*

Publisher

A Hypermedia Archive, Institute for Advanced Technology in the Humanities,

Publication date / last update

U of Virginia, 2008, www.rossettiarchive.org/about/index.html.

Entire website or online scholarly project   For an untitled personal site, put a description such as *Home page* where the website's title would normally appear (but with no quotation marks or italics).

> Gardner, James Alan. *A Seminar on Writing Prose.* 2001, www.thinkage.ca/~jim /prose/prose.htm.

> *The Complete Writings and Pictures of Dante Gabriel Rossetti: A Hypermedia Archive.* Edited by Jerome J. McGann, Institute for Advanced Technology in the Humanities, U of Virginia, 2008, www.rossettiarchive.org/index.html.

Book or a short work in an online scholarly project   Set the title in italics if the work is a book and in quotation marks if it is an article, essay, poem, or other short work, and include the print publication information relevant to your particular use following the title.

> Heims, Marjorie. "The Strange Case of Sarah Jones." *The Free Expression Policy Project,* FEPP, www.fepproject.org/commentaries/sarahjones.html.

Original publication date

> Corelli, Marie. *The Treasure of Heaven.* 1906. *Victorian Women Writer's Project,* edited by Percy Willett, Indiana U, 10 July 1999, webapp1.dlib.indiana.edu /vwwp/view?docId=VAB7176.

Blog   Cite an entire blog as you would an entire website (see above). If the author of the blog post uses a pseudonym, use this, followed by the author's real name if you know it.

Blog title

> *Talking Points Memo.* Edited by Josh Marshall, 1 Dec. 2011, talkingpointsmemo .com/.

Pseudonym

Negative Camber. *Formula 1 Blog*, 2014, www.formula1blog.com/.

Post author   Post title

Marshall, Josh. "Coke and Grass at Amish Raid." *Talking Points Memo*, 1 Dec. 2011, talkingpointsmemo.com/edblog/coke-grass-at-amish-raid.

Wiki article   Since wikis are written and edited collectively, start your entry with the title of the article you are citing.

"John Lydon." *Wikipedia*, 14 Nov. 2011, en.wikipedia.org/wiki/John_Lydon.

Discussion group or newsgroup posting

Post author   Subject line   Group name

Yen, Jessica. "Quotations within Parentheses (Study Measures)." *Copyediting-L*, 18 Mar. 2016, list.indiana.edu/sympa/arc/copyediting-l/2016-03/msg00492.html.

Post date

E-mail message

Sender   Subject line   Recipient

Olson, Kate. "Update on State Legislative Grants." Received by Alissa Brown, 5 Nov. 2015.

Date sent

CITING AND DOCUMENTING SOURCES IN APA STYLE

When using the APA system of documentation, include both an in-text citation and a list of references at the end of the research project. **In-text citations** tell your readers where the ideas or words you have borrowed come from, and the entries in the **list of references** allow readers to locate your sources so that they can read more about your topic.

The most common types of in-text citations follow. For other, less common citation types, consult the *Publication Manual of the American Psychological Association*, Sixth Edition (2010). Most libraries will own a copy.

USING IN-TEXT CITATIONS

When citing ideas, information, or words borrowed from a source, include the author's last name and the date of publication in the text of your research project. In most cases, you will want to use a *signal phrase* to introduce the works you are citing, since doing so gives you the opportunity to put the work and its author in context. A signal phrase includes the author's last name, the date of publication, and a verb that describes the author's attitude or stance:

Smith (2011) complains that . . .

Jones (2012) defends her position by . . .

Use a parenthetical citation — *(Jones, 2015)* — when you have already introduced the author or the work or when citing the source of an uncontroversial fact. When quoting from a source, also include the page number: *Smith (2015) complains that he "never gets a break" (p. 123)*. When you are paraphrasing or summarizing, you may omit the page reference, although including it is not wrong.

Directory to In-Text-Citation Models

One author   528
More than one author   528
Unknown author   528
Two or more works by the same
   author in the same year   528
Two or more authors with the same
   last name   529

Corporation, organization, or
   government agency as author   529
Indirect citation (quotation from a
   secondary source)   529
Two or more works cited in the same
   parentheses   529

One author

SIGNAL PHRASE   Upton Sinclair (2005), a crusading journalist, wrote that workers sometimes "fell into the vats; and when they were fished out, there was never enough of them left to be worth exhibiting" (p. 134).

PARENTHETICAL CITATION   *The Jungle*, a naturalistic novel inspired by the French writer Zola, described in lurid detail the working conditions of the time, including what became of unlucky workers who fell into the vats while making sausage (Sinclair, 2005, p. 134).

author's last name + date + page

REFERENCE-LIST ENTRY   Sinclair, U. (2005). *The Jungle*. New York, NY: Oxford University Press. (Original work published 1906)

More than one author   In a signal phrase, use the word *and* between the authors' names; in a parenthetical citation, use an ampersand (&). When citing a work by three to seven authors, list all the authors in your first reference; in subsequent references, just list the first and use *et al.* (Latin for *and others*).

SIGNAL PHRASE   As Jamison and Tyree (2001) have found, racial bias does not diminish merely through exposure to individuals of other races.

PARENTHETICAL CITATION   Racial bias does not diminish through exposure (Jamison & Tyree, 2001).

FIRST CITATION   Rosenzweig, Breedlove, and Watson (2005) wrote that biological psychology is an interdisciplinary field that includes scientists from "quite different backgrounds" (p. 3).

LATER CITATIONS   Biological psychology is "the field that relates behavior to bodily processes, especially the workings of the brain" (Rosenzweig et al., 2005, p. 3).

For a first reference to a work with more than seven authors, list the first six, an ellipsis (. . .), and the last author.

Unknown author

An international pollution treaty still to be ratified would prohibit all plastic garbage from being dumped at sea ("Plastic Is Found," 1972).

The full title of the article is "Plastic Is Found in the Sargasso Sea; Pieces of Apparent Refuse Cover Wide Atlantic Region."

Two or more works by the same author in the same year   Alphabetize the works by title in your list of references, and add a lowercase letter after the date (2005a, 2005b).

Middle-class unemployed workers are better off than their lower-class counterparts because "the white collar unemployed are likely to have some assets to invest in their job search" (Ehrenreich, 2005b, p. 16).

Two or more authors with the same last name

F. Johnson (2010) conducted an intriguing study on teen smoking.

Corporation, organization, or government agency as author   Spell out the name of the organization the first time you use it, but abbreviate it in subsequent citations.

(National Institutes of Health, 2015)

(NIH, 2015)

Indirect citation (quotation from a secondary source)   Cite the secondary source in the reference list, and in your essay acknowledge the original source.

E. M. Forster said that "the collapse of all civilization, so realistic for us, sounded in Matthew Arnold's ears like a distant and harmonious cataract" (as cited in Trilling, 1955, p. 11).

Two or more works cited in the same parentheses   List sources in alphabetical order separated by semicolons.

(Johnson, 2010; NIH, 2012)

CREATING A LIST OF REFERENCES

The APA documentation system requires a list of references providing bibliographic information for every in-text citation in the text (except personal communications and entire websites). Double-space the reference list, and use a hanging indent (with the first line flush left and subsequent lines indented half an inch). Alphabetize entries by the first main word in the citation.

Directory to Reference-List Models

(continued)

One author

> Schneier, B. (2015). *Data and Goliath: The hidden battles to collect your data and control your world*. New York, NY: Norton.

More than one author

> Hunt, L., Po-Chia Hsia, R., Martin, T. R., Rosenwein, B. H., Rosenwein, H., & Smith, B. G. (2001). *The making of the West: Peoples and cultures*. Boston, MA: Bedford.

If there are more than seven authors, list only the first six, insert an ellipsis (. . .), and add the last author's name.

Unknown author   If an author is designated as "Anonymous," include the word *Anonymous* in place of the author, and alphabetize it as "Anonymous" in the reference list.

> Anonymous. (2006). *Primary colors*. New York, NY: Random House.

> Communities blowing whistle on street basketball. (2003). *USA Today*, p. 20A.

Corporation, organization, or government agency as author

> American Medical Association. (2004). *Family medical guide*. Hoboken, NJ: Wiley.

Two or more works by the same author

When you cite two or more works by the same author, arrange them in chronological (time) order.

> Pinker, S. (2005). So how does the mind work? *Mind and Language, 20*(1): 1-24. doi:10.1111/j.0268-1064.2005.00274.x
>
> Pinker, S. (2011). *The better angels of our nature: Why violence has declined.* New York, NY: Viking.

When you cite two works by the same author in the same year, alphabetize entries by title and then add a lowercase letter following each year.

> Pinker, S. (2005a). *Hotheads.* New York, NY: Pocket Penguins.
>
> Pinker, S. (2005b). So how does the mind work? *Mind and Language, 20*(1), 1-24. doi:10.1111/j.0268-1064.2005.00274.x

BOOKS (PRINT, ELECTRONIC)

When citing a book, capitalize only the first word of the title and subtitle and any proper nouns (*Dallas, Darwin*). Book titles are italicized.

Basic format for a book

PRINT

Author   Year   Title

Pinker, S. (2011). *The better angels of our nature: Why violence has declined.* New York, NY; Viking.

City, State (abbr.)   Publisher

E-BOOK

Pinker, S. (2011). *The better angels of our nature: Why violence has declined.* New York, NY: Viking. [Nook Version].

E-publication information

DATABASE

Darwin, C. (2001). *The origin of species.* Retrieved from http://bartleby.com (Original work published 1909-14)

Database information

If an e-book has been assigned a **digital object identifier** (or *doi*) — a combination of numbers and letters assigned by the publisher to identify the work — add that information at the end of the citation.

Author and editor

> Arnold, M. (1994). *Culture and anarchy* (S. Lipman, Ed.). New Haven, CT: Yale University Press. (Original work published 1869)

Edited collection

Waldman, D., & Walker, J. (Eds.). (1999). *Feminism and documentary.* Minneapolis, MN: University of Minnesota Press.

Work in an anthology or edited collection

Fairbairn-Dunlop, P. (1993). Women and agriculture in western Samoa. In J. H. Momsen & V. Kinnaird (Eds.), *Different places, different voices* (pp. 211-226). London, England: Routledge.

Translation

Tolstoy, L. (2002). *War and peace* (C. Garnett, Trans.). New York, NY: Modern Library. (Original work published 1869)

Dictionary entry or article in another reference book

Rowland, R. P. (2001). Myasthenia gravis. In *Encyclopedia Americana* (Vol. 19, p. 683). Danbury, CT: Grolier.

Introduction, preface, foreword, or afterword

Graff, G., & Phelan, J. Preface (2004). In M. Twain, *Adventures of Huckleberry Finn* (pp. iii-vii). Boston, MA: Bedford.

Later edition of a book

Axelrod, R., & Cooper, C. (2016). *The St. Martin's guide to writing* (11th ed.). Boston, MA: Bedford.

Government document

U.S. Department of Health and Human Services. (2009). *Trends in underage drinking in the United States, 1991-2007.* Washington, DC: Government Printing Office.

Note: When the author and publisher are the same, use the word *Author* (not italicized) as the name of the publisher.

Unpublished doctoral dissertation

Bullock, B. (1986). *Basic needs fulfillment among less developed countries: Social progress over two decades of growth* (Unpublished doctoral dissertation). Vanderbilt University, Nashville, TN.

ARTICLES (PRINT, ELECTRONIC)

For articles, capitalize only the first word of the title, proper nouns (*Barclay, Berlin*), and the first word following a colon (if any). Omit quotation marks around the titles of articles, but capitalize all the important words of journal, newspaper, and magazine titles, and set them in italics. If you are accessing an article through a database, follow the model for a comparable source.

From a scholarly journal

PRINT

              Author   Year   Article title

Kardefelt-Winther, D. (2015). A critical account of DSM-5 criteria for Internet gaming disorder. *Addiction Research and Theory, 23*(2), 93-98.

               Volume (issue) Pages   Journal title

Goodboy, A. K., & Martin, M. M. (2015). The personality profile of a cyberbully: Examining the dark triad. *Computers in Human Behavior, 49,* 1-4.

                Volume only Pages

Include the digital object identifier (or *doi*) when available. When a doi has not been assigned, include the journal's URL.

ELECTRONIC

Goodboy, A. K., & Martin, M. M. (2015). The personality profile of a cyberbully: Examining the dark triad. *Computers in Human Behavior, 49,* 1-4. doi:10.1016/j.chb.2015.02.052

                                       DOI

Houston, R. G., & Toma, F. (2003). Home schooling: An alternative school choice. *Southern Economic Journal, 69*(4), 920-936. Retrieved from http://www.southerneconomic.org

                                       URL

From a newspaper   Year Month Day

PRINT

Peterson, A. (2003, May 20). Finding a cure for old age. *The Wall Street Journal,* pp. D1, D5.

ELECTRONIC

Zimmer, C. (2015, May 6). Under the sea, a missing link in the evolution of complex cells. *The New York Times*. Retrieved from http://www.nytimes.com/

From a magazine If a magazine is published weekly or biweekly (every other week), include the full date following the author's name. If it is published monthly or bimonthly, include just the year and month (or months).

                        Weekly or biweekly

PRINT

Gladwell, M. (9 September 2013). Man and superman. *The New Yorker, 89*(27), 76-80.

Monthly or bimonthly

Freeland, C. (2015, May). Globalization bites back. *Atlantic, 315*(4), 82–86.

ELECTRONIC　　Freeland, C. (2015, May). Globalization bites back. *Atlantic*. Retrieved from http://theatlantic.com/

Editorial or letter to the editor

Kosinski, T. (2012, May 15). Who cares what she thinks? [Letter to the editor]. *The Chicago Sun-Times*. Retrieved from http:// www.suntimes.com/opinions /letters/12522890-474/who-cares-what-she-thinks.html

Review

"Review of" + item type + title of item reviewed

Nussbaum, E. (2015, January 26). House of chords [Review of the television series *Empire* and *Mozart in the Jungle.*] *The New Yorker, 90*(45), 70-72.

If the review is untitled, use the bracketed information as the title, retaining the brackets.

MULTIMEDIA SOURCES (PRINT, ELECTRONIC)

Television program

Label

O'Connell, C. (Writer and director). (2015, Jan. 6). Ripley: Believe it or not. [Television series episode]. In H. Hampton and S. Fitzmeyer (Creators), *American Experience*. Boston, MA: WGBH.

Film, video, or DVD

Label

Nolan, C. (Writer and director). (2010). *Inception* [Motion picture]. Los Angeles, CA: Warner Bros.

Sound recording

PODCAST　　Dubner, S. (2012, May 17). Retirement kills [Audio podcast]. *Freakonomics Radio*. Retrieved from http://www .freakonomics.com

Label

RECORDING　　Adele. (2015). Hello. On *25* [CD]. London, UK: XY Recordings/ Columbia.

Interview　Do not list personal interviews in your reference list. Instead, cite the interviewee in your text (last name and initials), and in parentheses give the notation *personal communication* (in regular type, not italicized) followed by a comma and the date of the interview. For published interviews, use the appropriate format for an article.

OTHER ELECTRONIC SOURCES

A rule of thumb for citing electronic sources not covered in one of the preceding sections is to include enough information to allow readers to access and retrieve the source. For most online sources, provide as much of the following as you can:

- name of author
- date of publication or most recent update (in parentheses; if unavailable, use the abbreviation *n.d.*)
- title of document (such as a Web page)
- title of website
- any special retrieval information, such as a URL; include the date you last accessed the source only when the content is likely to change or be updated (as on a wiki, for example)

Website The APA does not require an entry in the list of references for entire websites. Instead, give the name of the site in your text with its Web address in parentheses.

Web page or document on a website

American Cancer Society. (2011, Oct. 10). *Child and teen tobacco use*. Retrieved
    from http://www.cancer.org/Cancer/CancerCauses/TobaccoCancer
    /ChildandTeenTobaccoUse/child-and-teen-tobacco-use-what-to-do

Heins, M. (2014, September 4). Untangling the Steven Salaita Case. In *The Free
    Expression Policy Project*. Retrieved from http://www.fepproject.org
    /commentaries/Salaita.html

Discussion list and newsgroup postings Include online postings in your list of references only if you can provide data that would allow others to retrieve the source.

Label

Paikeday, T. (2005, October 10). "Esquivalience" is out [Electronic mailing
    list message]. Retrieved from http://listserv.linguistlist.org/cgi-bin
    /wa?A15ind0510b&L5ads-1#1

Label

Ditmire, S. (2005, February 10). NJ tea party [Newsgroup message]. Retrieved from
    http://groups.google.com/group/TeaParty

Blog post   Label

> Mestel, R. (2012, May 17). Fructose makes rats dumber [Blog post]. Retrieved from
>   http://www.latimes.com/health/boostershots/la-fructose-makes-rats-stupid
>   -brain-20120517,0,2305241.story?track5rss

Wiki entry   Start with the article title and include the post date, since wikis may
be updated frequently (use *n.d.* if there is no date), as well as the retrieval date.

> Sleep. (2011, November 26). Retrieved December 18, 2015, from Wiki of Science:
>   http://wikiofscience.wikidot.com/science:sleep

E-mail message   Personal correspondence, including e-mail, should not be
included in your reference list. Instead, cite the person's name in your text, and in
parentheses give the notation *personal communication* (in regular type, not italicized) and the date.

Computer software   If an individual has proprietary rights to the software, cite
that person's name as you would for a print text. Otherwise, cite as you would for an
anonymous print text.

                                       Label

> How Computers Work [Software]. (1998). Available from Que: http://www
>   .howcomputers work.net/

ACKNOWLEDGEMENTS

Bornstein, David. "Fighting Bullying with Babies" from *The New York Times*, November 8, 2010. Copyright © 2010 The New York Times. All rights reserved. Used by permission and protected by the Copyright Laws of the United States. The printing, copying, redistribution, or retransmission of this Content without express written permission is prohibited. www.nytimes.com.

Brownwell, Kelly D. and Thomas R. Frieden. "Ounces of Prevention — The Public Policy Case for Taxes on Sugared Beverages" from *The New England Journal of Medicine*, 360:1805-8, April 30, 2009. Copyright © 2009 Massachusetts Medical Society. Reprinted with permission from Massachusetts Medical Society.

Cain, Susan. "Shyness: Evolutionary Tactic?" from *The New York Times Sunday Review*; The Opinion Pages, June 25, 2011. Copyright © 2011 The New York Times. All rights reserved. Used by permission and protected by the Copyright Laws of the United States. The printing, copying, redistribution, or retransmission of this Content without express written permission is prohibited. www.nytimes.com.

Carr, Nicholas. "Is Google Making Us Stupid?" from *Atlantic Monthly* (Ideas Issue), Summer 2008. Copyright © 2008 Nicholas Carr. Reprinted by permission of the author.

Coyne, Amanda. "The Long Good-Bye: Mother's Day in Federal Prison." Copyright © 1997 Harper's Magazine. All Rights reserved. Reproduced from the May issue by special permission.

Desmond-Harris, Jenée. "Tupac and My Non-Thug Life" from *The Root*, September 13, 2011. Reprinted by permission of the author.

Dillard, Annie. Excerpt from *An American Childhood* (pp. 45–49) by Annie Dillard. Copyright © 1987 by Annie Dillard. Reprinted with permission of HarperCollins Publishers and Russell & Volkening as agents for the author.

Edge, John T. "I'm Not Leaving Until I Eat This Thing," originally published in *Oxford American* (September/October 1999). Copyright © 1999 by John T. Edge. Reprinted by permission of the author.

Etzioni, Amitai. "Working at McDonald's," originally published in *The Miami Herald*, August 24, 1986. Copyright © 1986 by Amitai Etzioni. Author of *The Spirit of Community*; Director, George Washington University Center for Communication Policy Studies. Reprinted by permission of the author.

Gladwell, Malcolm. "The Order of Things: What College Rankings Really Tell Us" by Malcolm Gladwell. Copyright © 2005 by Malcolm Gladwell. Originally published in *The New Yorker*. Reprinted by permission of the author.

Greene, Brian. "Put a Little Science in Your Life" from *The New York Times*, June 1, 2008. Copyright © 2008 The New York Times. All rights reserved. Used by permission and protected by the Copyright Laws of the United States. The printing, copying, redistribution, or retransmission of this Content without express written permission is prohibited. www.nytimes.com.

Hambrick, David Z. and Christopher Chabris. "Yes, IQ Really Matters" from *Slate*, April 13, 2014. Copyright © 2013 The Slate Group. All rights reserved. Used by permission and protected by the Copyright Laws of the United States. The printing, copying, redistribution, or retransmission of this Content without express written permission is prohibited. www.slate.com.

Jamison, Leslie. "The Immortal Horizon" from *The Empathy Exams: Essays*. Copyright © 2014 by Leslie Jamison. Reprinted with the permission of The Permissions Company, Inc., on behalf of Graywolf Press. www.graywolfpress.org.

Jennings, Dana. "Our Scars Tell the Stories of Our Lives" from *The New York Times*, July 21, 2009. Copyright © 2009 The New York Times. All rights reserved. Used by permission and protected by the Copyright Laws of the United States. The printing, copying, redistribution, or retransmission of this Content without express written permission is prohibited. www.nytimes.com.

Keegan, Marina. "Stability in Motion." Reprinted with the permission of Scribner, a Division of Simon & Schuster, Inc., from *The Opposite of Loneliness* by Marina Keegan (pp. 143–49). Copyright © 2014 by Tracy and Kevin Keegan. All rights reserved.

Index to Methods
of Development

Comparison and Contrast

Definition

Description

Process

Index of Authors, Titles, and Terms